- How much of this information do you have readily at hand, what information do you need that you don't have, and what will you need to do to get the additional information?
- Which propositions, conclusions, values, assumptions, principles, and information will your readers readily accept? Which do they already accept? Which will they be likely to resist? And which might they reject out of hand? Why?
- What level of emotion is embedded in the issues here? Do you want to emphasize and heighten the emotional dimensions of your arguments, or do you want to flatten and mute them? Why?

Conventions

- What conventions, customs, protocols, or habits of business practice are normally evoked in this kind of situation within your own organization, within your readers' organization, and within your respective legal, ethical, and cultural frameworks?
- To what extent can you confidently rely on these conventions as a guide for your actions and your writing in this situation? How can you resolve conflicting conventions? At what points and to what extent might it be useful for you to bend, break, or abandon some conventions?
- What medium is the most appropriate given the situation at hand, your goals, and your readers? A paper document? An e-mail? A phone call or face-to-face conversation? An oral presentation? Why?
- If a print or electronic document is the most appropriate medium, what kind of document does this situation typically call for (e.g., letter, memo, detailed report, etc.)? What length and format should you use? What level of formality would be appropriate given the situation and your relationship with your readers?
- Does the complexity of the situation (e.g., complex information, complex interorganizational relationships, complex project timelines) call for you to use multiple media and modes of communication? For example, do written reports need to be introduced by oral presentations? Do oral presentations need to be supplemented by written reports? Do the words of both oral and written reports need to be explained by charts, tables, pictures, and other graphics?
- Does your organization have guidelines that should determine the format and style of this document? Or do your readers follow guidelines for format and style they expect to see in documents they receive? If so, what specifics do you want to be sure to follow from these guidelines?
- What are the specific mechanical conventions for a standard business document for this situation? How rigorously should you follow the conventions of grammar, spelling, punctuation, and word usage?

Expression

- Is credibility an important issue here? In other words, do your readers already assume that you and your organization are competent, trustworthy, and well informed, or will they be skeptical? How can you build their trust and overcome any skepticism?
- To what extent should your document make explicit your own—and your organization's—underlying values, assumptions, ethical principles, cultural frameworks, and organizational practices?
- To what extent should your document embody and express your own individual voice and personality and the voice and personality of the organization you represent?
- Given your readers, the situation, and your goals, what kind of image do you want your readers to have of you and your organization? What tone of voice should readers hear in the document? What kind of relationship should this tone suggest between you and your readers?

The Writing of Business

Robert P. Inkster
St. Cloud State University

Judith M. Kilborn
St. Cloud State University

Allyn and Bacon
Boston ▸ London ▸ Toronto ▸ Sydney ▸ Tokyo ▸ Singapore

Vice President: Eben W. Ludlow
Series Editorial Assistant: Linda M. D'Angelo
Senior Marketing Manager: Lisa Kimball
Editorial-Production Administrator: Donna Simons
Editorial-Production Service: Susan Freese, Communicáto, Ltd.
Composition Buyer: Linda Cox
Manufacturing Buyer: Suzanne Lareau
Cover Administrator: Linda Knowles
Cover Designer: Studio Nine
Interior Design: Denise Hoffman, Glenview Studios
Electronic Composition: Omegatype Typography, Inc.

A Viacom Company
160 Gould Street
Needham Heights, MA 02494

Internet: www.abacon.com

Between the time website information is gathered and published, it is not unusual for some sites to have closed. Also, the transcription of URLs can result in unintended typographical errors. The publisher would appreciate being notified of any problems with URLs so that they may be corrected in subsequent editions.

Library of Congress Cataloging-in-Publication Data
Inkster, Robert P.
The writing of business / Robert P. Inkster, Judith M. Kilborn.
p. cm.
Includes bibliographical references and index.
ISBN 0-205-19868-6 (alk. paper)
1. Business writing. 2. English language—Business English.
I. Kilborn, Judith M. II. Title.
HF5718.3.I55 1998
808'.06665—dc21 98-40496
CIP

Printed in the United States of America

10 9 8 7 6 5 4 3 2 1 RRDV 03 02 01 00 99 98

Contents

Preface

The Writing of Business is predicated on the belief that writing is a way of strategically managing an increasingly complex organizational world. Writing itself is seen as social action, serving and negotiating the goals of the writers, readers, and organizations involved. It is a generative, creative part of doing business, not only an after-the-fact documenting of business that's already been done. The text assumes a reader who has complex personal and organizational agendas as well as an increasingly diverse workplace, an increasingly competitive global environment, and more technically complex workspaces.

The Writing of Business begins with managing from the center—locating the writer in his or her organizational environment—and moves increasingly outward to more distanced and diverse readers. It progresses from writing to manage daily work and enhance group productivity and accountability to writing for the global marketplace. Along the way, this text considers such genres as memos; policy and procedures manuals; letters, including job correspondence; and proposals and other formal reports. The discussion also includes genres not often covered: e-mail, minutes, agendas, business plans, and mission and vision statements as well as job descriptions and performance reviews.

Consideration of these genres is unified by the simple acronym GRACE, which stands for the five benchmarks writers need to understand when they write: Goals, Readers, Arguments, Conventions, and Expression. The GRACE heuristic, recurring in each chapter, integrates all of the strategic elements in a writing situation, rather than fragmenting them over several chapters, so that you can literally begin anywhere in the text. Also, the A in GRACE is reflective of the need for argument in business writing—to convince readers of the writer's credibility, facts, conclusions, and recommendations as well as to enable the writer to determine whether the emotional elements of issues should be heightened or muted. The GRACE acronym, both highly portable and powerful, will enable our readers to write more confidently, efficiently, and effectively.

Interwoven in the discussion are numerous examples of writing that is appropriate for the workplace—reflective of small businesses, retail and service industries, and volunteer organizations as well as large businesses. These samples suggest the diversity of contexts within business writing genres and illustrate a variety of strategies that particular writers have used in their workplaces.

Our aim throughout this text is to challenge our readers to reflect on the contexts for their writing and consider how they affect the act of writing. These contexts include writing for multiple readers with complex and perhaps conflicting goals, writing as a collaborative as well as a solitary activity, and writing as a way of managing complex situations and minimizing risk. In addition, the impact of new technologies is addressed throughout the text, including the impact of word processing, desktop publishing, electronic mail (e-mail), and the World Wide Web. For example, research via the Internet is introduced as a tool for enhancing job searches in Chapter 9 on employment correspondence, and its use is discussed further in Chapter 11, the research chapter. E-mail is discussed in the section on memos, including assumptions about the technology's perceived ephemerality and privacy. In addition, differences in print and electronic media are considered—differences in speed and its effects in the workplace, differences in the "page" and its impact on writers and readers, and differences in levels of formality.

Organization

The Writing of Business is divided into six parts. Part I focuses on writing as a way of strategically managing the complexity of the workplace. It considers writing as a tool for managing individual and group work and schedules as well as a tool for managing complexity and risk. Chapter 1 introduces the five general benchmarks—Goals, Readers, Arguments, Conventions, and Expression—that writers need to understand when they write. Chapter 2 briefly explores assumptions about writing, arguing that the assumptions people bring to their writing have a dramatic effect on how they manage writing projects. This chapter also considers strategies, tactics, and technologies for managing writing, asserting that better management of writing is better management of work.

Part II considers writing as a way of building unity and sustaining an organizational culture. In particular, Chapter 3 considers writing as a means of managing daily work and enhancing group productivity and accountability. The chapter discusses the genres of memos, agendas, and minutes in both paper and electronic media. It introduces collaboration and teamwork in organizations—in particular, working, communicating, and writing in teams and using writing to enhance the effectiveness of meetings. Chapter 4 considers writing as a means of negotiating and expressing organizational goals and practices. It explores group goal setting and problem solving, and it discusses vision and mission statements, business plans, policies and procedures statements, job descriptions, and performance reviews.

Part III extends writing across organizational boundaries as it introduces communication with customers, clients, vendors, and others. Chapter 5 investigates the contexts and conventions of letter writing. Chapter 6 considers writing letters in difficult situations—those fraught with conflict, disagreement, anger, fear, or other unpleasantness. And Chapters 7, 8, and 9 talk about courting a prospective employer or client in the employment search.

Part IV treats more complex situations where writing a letter or memo is not enough. Chapter 10 reviews contexts and conventions for the design of longer documents, such as proposals, feasibility studies, reports, and business plans. Chapter 11 identifies information sources and suggests some effective research strategies in the contemporary organization. Chapters 12 and 13 then focus in depth on proposals and formal reports, respectively, and Chapter 14 focuses on oral reports.

Part V speculates about the special risks and challenges of writing for the global marketplace and explores opportunities and risks in cross-cultural communication. Chapter 15 introduces cultural signposts underlying cross-cultural communication and discusses elements of culture and language that affect oral presentations and written documents designed for people from other cultures. It also includes specific strategies for effective cross-cultural communication.

Part VI, The Business Writer's Quick Reference, includes general strategies for revising, editing, and proofreading as well as guidelines for editing to avoid wordiness and exclusionary language. This reference also provides resources on conventions of punctuation, grammar, and style.

Features

The Writing of Business offers a number of special features:

- Writing is presented as social action, defining, serving, and negotiating the goals of the writers, readers, and organizations involved.
- The text has a strongly strategic orientation to writing in a professional, organizational context, which, at the same time, preserves the visibility of genre as a crucial aspect of strategy.
- GRACE (Goals, Readers, Arguments, Conventions, Expression) provides a powerful and portable heuristic approach to writing strategies, with each type of situation evoking the GRACE heuristic in a form modified to serve that situation.
- GRACE integrates all the strategic elements in a writing situation. It is invoked in each chapter to address a new writing situation or genre.
- A part of this integration is a discussion of issues that contemporary research and business practice have shown to be vitally important: multicultural communication; use of graphics both for *presenting* and for *generating* ideas, arguments, and information; group processes in problem definition and solution and in managing writing projects; and contemporary technology and its implications for business communication.
- A variety of writers' resources are discussed, providing students with timely, relevant material on print and electronic resources, strategies for taking advantage of the effects of computers on writing, and systematic, strategic approaches for finding and correcting sentence-level errors in their writing.
- Each chapter contains a variety of examples of real business correspondence, given primarily as whole texts.
- Summary checklists, which appear near the ends of chapters, summarize key points for quick reference.
- Suggestions for discussion, small-group work, and writing conclude each chapter except for Chapter 7, where these activities are built into the text.

Acknowledgments

Throughout the book, we have tried to minimize discussion that focuses explicitly on rhetorical theory. Some of our bibliographical references cite rhetorical works, but most of the references in the text are to works that are primarily concerned with effective management, leadership, and communication in professional organizations. Nevertheless, the theoretical roots of *The Writing of Business* are deeply embedded in our backgrounds in rhetoric, and our intellectual debts are scattered across the rhetorical landscape. There are a small handful that we want to acknowledge, in particular.

First, we have been surprised, frankly, by the extent to which tagmemic theory has permeated this text, informing the strategies for effective situational analyses and the inventional strategies, in general. The situational analysis in Chapter 2 is a particularly striking example of tagmemic analysis. The ability to shift perspective, to have a systematic process for seeing a situation as others may see it, to begin to account for conditions that caused it and for events that may flow from it, and to see the complexity of its elements and its context has struck us as precisely the kind of strategic tool that is needed for effective communication in a business and professional environment that is increasingly international and increasingly problematic and complex culturally, financially, organizationally, and rhetorically.

This complexity and diversity led us to place *argument* at the center of our thinking and particularly at the center of GRACE. And Stephen Toulmin and his interpreters have been especially useful in helping us talk about effective argument—both the making of argument and the reading of argument—in a complex rhetorical ecology where underlying assumptions and values are unlikely to be shared and where any kind of effective discourse requires tools for unpacking and understanding these deeper layers of arguments. Yet despite our heavy reliance on these two modern strains of rhetorical scholarship, we have written the book almost entirely without reference to either.

Our other debt that will be apparent to rhetoricians is to classical—in particular, Aristotelian—rhetoric. Aristotle's rhetoric is, after all, a set of strategies for the appropriate and effective negotiating of agreements in an environment characterized by complexity and indeterminacy. We have felt its presence most powerfully in *pathos* and *ethos* as the grounding for the R and the E in GRACE, as we have asserted that all professional discourse has emotional and ethical dimensions that must not be ignored.

We are grateful to be working in the tradition of some fine pedagogical texts, as well, most immediately *Business Writing Strategies and Samples,* a book that Dr. Kilborn co-authored and that we have both used and appreciated for a number of years now. We see both *The Writing of Business* and *Business Writing Strategies and Samples* in an audience-sensitive, strategic tradition that emanates from Mathes and Stevenson and continues in the work of people like Paul Anderson and Linda Flower and John Ackerman.

We would also like to acknowledge those individuals who reviewed the manuscript for Allyn and Bacon and provided useful suggestions: Deborah S. Bosley, University of North Carolina at Charlotte; Stuart C. Brown, New Mexico State University; John B. Cooper, University of Kentucky; Judi Gaitens, North Carolina State University; Mary Sue Garay, Louisiana State University; Ed Klonoski, Charter Oak State College; Nancy M. O'Rourke, Utah State University; and Philip Vassallo, Middlesex County College. And special thanks to Phil Keith, Kathy Cahill, Sue Freese, and Rex Veeder for their help in bringing this project to fruition.

Part I

Writing as Strategic Management of a Complex Organizational World

Managing Complexity and Risk with GRACE

- Managing from the Center: Locating Yourself in Your Organizational Environment
- Writing to Manage Yourself and Your Work
  - Writing and Short-Term Memory
  - Writing and Long-Term Memory
  - Writing, Creativity, and Motivation
- Writing and Risk
- Identifying What You Know and What You Need to Know
  - Goals
  - Readers
  - Arguments
  - Conventions
  - Expression
  - GRACE in Action

Whether it be the penning of a poem or the winning of a verbal joust, the precise choice of words proves important, if not all important. But in most societies, for most of the time, and most strikingly in a complex society such as ours, language is as often as not a tool—a means of accomplishing one's business—rather than the central focus of attention.

—Howard Gardner

One view of writing in an organizational environment is that decisions get made, policies get planned, products get manufactured, sales get closed, and then, after the *real* business is done, somebody writes a memo, a letter, a set of instructions, or some other document, essentially as an afterthought. As our organizational worlds have gotten more complex, though, this simple view of organizational writing has made less sense, both to people who study organizational processes and to people who study writing. More and more, writing is seen as an integral, essential part of identifying, defining, and solving complex technical and organizational problems.

We've come a long way from the kind of world in which Mr. Farmer gave Mr. Baker a sack of wheat and got back a portion of it as bread. Today, Mr. Farmer may be Con-Agra and Mr. Baker may be General Mills, and both may be so vastly integrated—both vertically and horizontally, on a global scale—that it's no longer possible to distinguish farmer from baker. We still talk of being breadwinners, but most of what we do for a living in professional environments has little to do with tangible products. Most of our work has to do with numbers, words, documents, and people—both our colleagues and people we may never even see, who may live and work on the other side of the globe. Robert Reich (1991) argues in *The Work of Nations* that these "global webs" have resulted in an economy where the most significant category of work is what he calls "symbolic-analytic services." Symbolic analysts are skilled at doing three different things:

1. They find their way efficiently through the huge stream of information that now washes around us.
2. They locate, identify, and understand the information that's relevant and useful.
3. They analyze and communicate that information in a form that's meaningful and useful to others.

Developments in information technology over the past few decades have contributed largely to these changes in the nature of our work and the ways in which we communicate with each other. These developments include more powerful computer workstations; programs that display complicated data in easily understood, attractive graphics; and networks that enable users to access information from online databases at distant locations and to communicate in real time with people across the world. In *Liberation Management: Necessary Disorganization for the Nanosecond Nineties*, Tom Peters (1992) describes how Boeing and its Japanese partners have designed aircraft, collaborating in real time from across the globe using e-mail and linking team members, suppliers, distributors, customers, and special information resources at universities and think tanks. Such partnerships are made possible by these new information technologies, and they are also just one result of stiff competition in the global marketplace.

Struggling for competitive advantage has also led to increased emphasis on quality and responsiveness to customer needs, and it has often brought about downsizing, decentralization, and replacing the corporate hierarchy with other conceptual models based on patterns of how people actually communicate with one another. The early work of Herbert A. Simon (1957)* and of W. Edwards Deming (1943)** foreshadowed the current models of organization around "quality circles" and other forms of decentralized collaborative problem-solving and performance-assessing teams. Writing in *Workplace 2000: The Revolution Reshaping American Business*, Joseph H. Boyette and Henry P. Conn (1992) predict that the "corporate pyramid" will eventually give way to a "solar system"—downsized companies concentrating on core businesses and forging partnerships with suppliers and other related businesses.

Employees at all levels collaborate to establish and refine departments' or project teams' missions and goals; assess customer needs; isolate problems in products, processes, or services; and suggest improvements. In fact, many have argued that the changes currently underway in the workplace will have as far reaching an impact as those that characterized the Industrial Revolution. In short, the workplace of the coming century will emerge with a radically different look, very different values, and strikingly different priorities.

Changing demographics are a significant part of this revolution. For example, David Jamison and Julie O'Mara (1991) point out in *Managing Workforce 2000: Gaining the Diversity Advantage* that the age, gender, and ethnic background of the workforce are changing rapidly. The workforce is "middle aging," such that the average worker's age will change from 36 in 1985 to 39 in 2000. Almost two-thirds of those entering the workforce in 2000 will be women. And Jamison and O'Mara predict that minorities, who represented 17 percent of the American workforce in 1990, will comprise 25 percent in 2000.

With these changes in the global environment and in the ways businesses organize themselves to accomplish their work, writing has become an increasingly important tool for managing work. Throughout the globe, the written word, in both paper and electronic forms, is seen less as strictly a way of archiving the business already

*Simon's *Administrative Behavior: A Study of Decision-Making Processes in Administrative Organizations* (1957) was a pioneering study of the effectiveness of informal structures and patterns of communication in organizations. He eventually received the Nobel Prize in economics for this work.

**W. Edwards Deming's early applications of rigorous statistical methods to practical issues of quality control in the 1940s provided the theoretical basis of the postwar Japanese economic revolution and have since been widely applied in the United States. For an example of Deming's early work, see *Statistical Adjustment of Data* (1943). For a later, more general discussion of his theory and its practical applications, see *Quality, Productivity, and Competitive Position* (1982).

completed and more as a vital, creative means of problem solving, collaborating, and actually doing business. The ways in which we use writing to solve complex technical and organizational problems and to locate and define ourselves in our environment becomes, in a very real sense, the writing of business.

Managing from the Center: Locating Yourself in Your Organizational Environment

We've already mentioned Boyette and Conn's argument that in thinking about organizational structure, the metaphor of a solar system is becoming more appropriate than one of a pyramid. We'd like to extend that metaphor and suggest that you imagine yourself at the center of a solar system—that you design, as it were, a kind of *egocentric solar system** whenever you find yourself in a writing situation. When you write, look around this system. Look especially for where your reader is. Is your reader in the immediate circle of people you work closely with all the time—a friend, a co-worker, your immediate supervisor, a teacher, a family member? In terms of the metaphor, is your reader in an orbit right next to you?

Look around your solar system again. Who else nearby has some interest, experience, or information related to this situation? Should people in related work groups in your organization also be readers? Should you be thinking of them as resources for helping you write what you need to write? Should they even be co-writers? Are there people in more distant orbits who should be readers or should be otherwise drawn into your process of writing this document? Perhaps your customers, clients, or vendors? Are local, regional, or national stakeholders in your company concerned about the issue you're addressing? If your primary reader, the one you first identified, isn't in your immediate circle, how can you reach out to him or her? Can you identify intervening orbits—common interests, values, and assumptions—that will help you connect with this reader?

As our discussion will show, the GRACE strategy for professional writing maps out the many potential readers who may be involved when you write for a work-related situation—even when you write what seems to be a routine letter for a class assignment. In fact, your egocentric solar system can help you visualize your practical, political, economic, rhetorical, and ethical relationships to your colleagues, your supervisors, your supervisees, your organization as a whole, and, ultimately, your relationships to the people, institutions, and cultures beyond the walls of your organization. Furthermore, recognizing your own egocentric solar system will help you remember that all those people and institutions in all those rings out there have their own egocentric solar systems—with their own relationships, alliances, obligations, and views on the universe from their own centers—and they are all different from yours.

*J. C. Mathes and Dwight Stevenson propose a similar scheme in *Designing Technical Reports: Writing for Audiences in Organizations* (1976).

FIGURE 1.1 The Egocentric Solar System

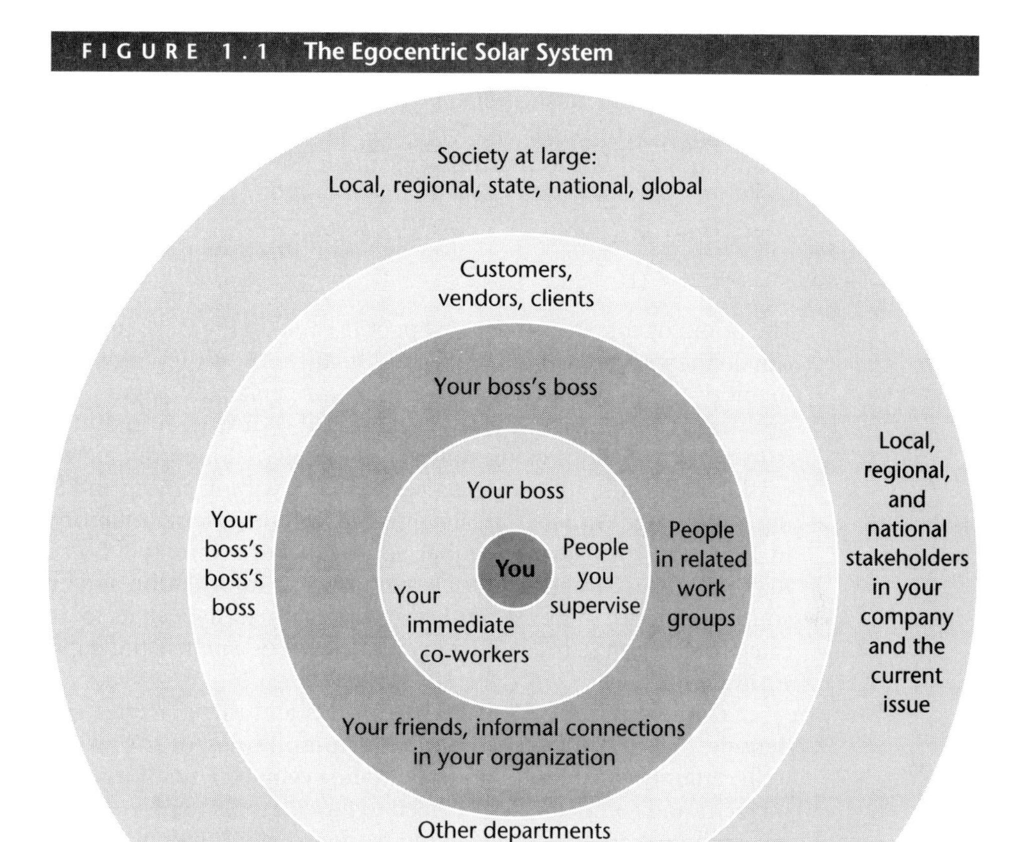

Writing to Manage Yourself and Your Work

Writing is a powerful tool for managing yourself and your individual workload. You can use writing

- To aid your short- and long-term memory
- To motivate yourself and others you work with
- To facilitate creative approaches to organizational problems, risks, and opportunities

Writing and Short-Term Memory

Here's an experiment suggested by Richard Young and Patricia Sullivan (1984) in an article titled "Why Write?" It comprises four multiplication problems. Try to do them all in your head, without using a calculator or writing anything down.

6	68	96	6,723
× 7	× 7	× 87	× 376

The point, of course, is that most people can't do the third problem, and fewer still can do the fourth problem, without difficulty unless they use some kind of external memory aid, like a calculator, computer, or pencil and paper. The more complex a problem is—whether it involves numerical or textual information—the harder it is to process without using some kind of external memory aid to make the information stand still, in a sense, so we can work with it. Young and Sullivan are drawing on George Miller's classic research on short-term memory, first published in 1956 as "The Magical Number Seven, Plus or Minus Two," which demonstrates that most of us can hold about seven pieces of information at a time, give or take a couple of pieces, in our short-term, working memory. Ask us to do a more complicated problem than that, and you'd better give us a pencil and paper or an electronic equivalent.

Think about this limit on our minds and the strategies we can use to compensate for it. Think, too, about the complexities of the working environment we'll certainly encounter in the twenty-first century. Finally, think about the kinds of literacies and competencies we need to have as tools to process the intellectual challenges thrown at us every day in our working environments. If we're not writing, and writing a lot—whether we're using paper and pencil; word-processing, database, or spreadsheet software; electronic mail; or some other external information-processing device—we're either not doing very interesting work or we're not getting the job done.

Writing and Long-Term Memory

Almost 2,500 years ago, Plato raised the concern that writing would make people mentally lazy, causing them to lose the ability to remember things by letting them rely on external written aids to memory. Just imagine Plato's reaction to the array of external aids to memory found in the typical modern office:

- Sticky notes and other "tickler" files
- Day-planning calendars
- GANTT charts and other project-management timelines
- Alarm wristwatches
- Day-planning software on both desktop and laptop computers
- Electronic pocket notebooks
- Voice mail

With all these aids and more, Plato's argument seems to be moot. Writing, whether in paper or electronic media, is a universal tool for planning, organizing, and remembering the details of our lives.

Writing, Creativity, and Motivation

The role of writing in creativity probably is closely related to the role of writing as an aid to short-term memory. Writing lets us capture information and hold it still for a while so we can look at several ideas at the same time. This, in turn, lets us see connections that we probably won't see otherwise. Writing also has something to do with enhancing communication between the two hemispheres of our brains, helping the more orderly, linear processing of the left hemisphere and the more random, creative processing of the right hemisphere complement, rather than fight, one another. Perhaps this is one reason that writers—working in groups or by themselves—can trigger such powerful insights about problems and possibilities in their workplaces. And success in creating innovative solutions to problems in your professional work has an emotional payoff, too. The satisfaction and excitement of even a small creative breakthrough fires us up, focuses our energy, and motivates us to seek further success. Writing, then, as a means of activating creative insight can be a powerful motivational tool.

Writing is explicitly used as a motivational tool by many people in business, especially in sales. Motivational workshops, speakers, tapes, and the like all stress the importance of writing down goals in order to make and keep them visible on a daily basis. Similarly, organizations in both the public and private sectors often spend months negotiating, debating, refining, and publishing mission statements that express their goals and make them continually visible—not only to themselves but to their constituents, customers, members, vendors, clients, and other publics, as well. (We will talk about these collaboratively written statements in Chapter 4.)

Writing and Risk

Have you ever had a writing task that you faced with some uncertainty and anxiety—a writing situation in which you were distinctly aware that you were taking a risk but were perhaps unsure how serious that risk was? If your answer is "no, never," you may be the first person in literate culture not to have experienced this anxiety. We contend that *every* writing task entails risk. In fact, this phenomenon can be expressed in the following maxim:

MAXIM

***Every* document—no matter how well written, no matter how thoughtfully planned, no matter how carefully edited—will confuse, mislead, or offend *somebody*.**

You can respond to this maxim in two ways: One is to give up in despair. The other is to see the maxim as permission to go ahead and attack a complex and risky writing task, freed from the paralyzing perfectionism that would otherwise block you from writing. We see the maxim as good news: There is no such thing as a perfect document, so you can stop looking for it. Rather than present the perfect arguments, the perfect evidence, and the perfect image of yourself, you only need to make the arguments that will persuade these particular readers and present these arguments in a way that will lead these people to see you as you want them to. Having laid aside the unattainable goal of perfection, you can proceed to ask yourself what your more modest, focused, realistic goals are. And thinking about these goals will lead you to fruitful questions about your readers and the arguments and conventions of presenting those arguments that will persuade your readers to see the situation as you do and to see you as you want them to.

In the following discussion, we will introduce the GRACE acronym, which generates five clusters of questions for analyzing your situation and planning your writing in light of the risks and opportunities inherent in a particular situation.

Identifying What You Know and What You Need to Know

GRACE is an acronym for *Goals, Readers, Arguments, Conventions,* and *Expression*—the five concepts for generating and organizing questions that will help you identify both your risks and your resources when you write. And having a more confident understanding of your risks and resources will help you write more confidently, efficiently, and effectively.

Goals

You're likely to find that you really can't think effectively about goals without also thinking about readers. You're always writing to somebody, and your goals reflect what effect you want your writing to have on them. In fact, a goal stated in terms of your readers is more useful than one expressed only in terms of your written text. You'll see the difference in these two examples:

> **Text-based goal:** I want to write a thank-you letter to Rich Murray, the Director of Career Services, for speaking at our meeting.
>
> **Reader-based goal:** As a result of reading my thank-you letter, I want Rich Murray to remember me and the question I asked him during our meeting so he can help me with my job search.

The reader-based goal statement goes beyond simply describing what your task is. It clarifies why you want to do the task and often generates a richer, more accurate picture of the task itself. In this example of the letter to the Career Services director, your task is actually more interesting than just writing a routine thank-you letter because it entails goals you want to achieve. Even in a routine letter, you probably have goals for your reader:

- To learn something
- To believe something
- To feel something
- To do something—or perhaps to refrain from doing something

Formulating a reader-based goal also helps you to determine better how much effort and thought you should invest in this writing task.

Readers

Writers often ask themselves sophisticated and useful questions about the reader they address directly in a letter or memo:

- What are my reader's attitudes toward the topic and toward the writer?
- What prior information does my reader have about the topic?
- How will my reader need and want to use the document, in general?

Then writers often overlook the most important question about their reader because the answer seems obvious:

- Who will read this document?

In fact, the answer may *not* be obvious. Maybe the reader is not a single reader but multiple readers spread across time, space, and organization charts. One of the greatest hazards in writing in today's complex and interconnected world is forgetting to ask who else might read a document in addition to the person addressed. Quickly sketching a customized egocentric solar system for the particular situation will help generate questions that can reduce your risk of overlooking important potential readers:

- Will the addressee pass on the document to someone else in the organization?
- Might it even go to someone outside the organization?
- Will that person understand the context of your writing, or should you anticipate the need to supply an explanation of context within the document itself?
- Will the document become part of another file? If so, will its relationship to the rest of the file be clear?
- Will the document have a long shelf life so that someone might refer to it months or even years from now in another context?

- Will all your readers understand the specific details, technical terms, and abbreviations in your document?
- Will different readers have different uses for your document? And given their respective needs, will they use it or parts of it in different ways than I intended?

Starting with the question of who will read your document helps you enrich the information you generate with the other questions you ask about your readers. If you can identify these multiple readers, then you will get a better analysis of their knowledge and attitudes. And this analysis, in turn, will help you more accurately anticipate how your readers will respond to different strategies you decide to employ when you design your document.

Think about that routine thank-you letter to Rich Murray, the campus Director of Career Services, who spoke at your meeting. What's the possibility that someone besides Murray might read the letter? Consider the following:

- Might Murray put your letter in his own personnel file if it does an especially effective job of documenting his good work as a motivational speaker?
- Who else—say, the university president, a vice-president, an alumni board member—might see that file?
- Of those people who see Murray on a regular basis, who might have an interest in your letter: recruiters from corporations, government agencies, and the nonprofit sector who visit the campus regularly?
- Might it be useful for you if Murray thought of you when he was talking with any of them?

Finally, if you're writing this letter in response to an assignment given in a class, there's one more reader who obviously should be important to you: your instructor. What goals do you hope to achieve with this document relative to your instructor?

- To increase your instructor's confidence in you as a competent, thoughtful, hard-working student?
- To get an A?

Furthermore, the presence of your instructor as another reader in this picture raises still more questions about goals. Your instructor probably has teacher-based goals that mirror your own student-based goals. Presumably, your instructor plans to read your letter with a judgmental eye, evaluating your thinking and writing in this situation. But your instructor most likely has additional goals that relate to the other readers we've just been imagining—especially Rich Murray. For example, your instructor may have told you that Murray often volunteers his own time to speak to groups like yours and that he does so with no compensation. Given this background, it may be reasonable to conclude that your instructor is interested in giving Murray some positive, useful feedback as a kind of emotional compensation and an incentive to present at a meeting like yours again.

So, now, what at first glance appeared to be a simple one-to-one communication between you and Rich Murray turns out to involve a rich, interesting, complicated web of readers whose needs and goals in approaching your letter may differ considerably. As we turn now to look directly and specifically at Rich Murray, we see him as a reader who is at the center of a web of readers or potential readers. Our view of him now probably is different and more realistic than it would have been if we had thought only of him in isolation. And the following questions, looking specifically at Murray, resonate with questions about the web of other readers:

- What arguments did he make during your class?
- What kinds of ideas and people did he seem to value?
- What are his goals?
- What conventions of relating to people and communicating with people does he follow?
- How is his own character expressed through his arguments and especially through his style of relating to people?

As you consider these questions, you likely will realize that in probing for goals for your own letter, you have already been responding to your tacit sense of Rich Murray's goals, arguments, and character. Your reader-based goal of getting Murray to remember you and your question so he can help you is based on your perception of him as someone who actually enjoys helping people search for the next step on their career ladder. Your goal to be remembered is further based on your perception of Murray as someone who's at the center of a web of people you'd like to know better: alumni, employers, recruiters, and other interesting people. You realize that you're also responding to Murray's informality, energy, and enthusiasm and his supportive, though realistic, way of advising people who are job seekers. And the arguments you're beginning to shape will speak to the goals, arguments, and character of Rich Murray as well as those of the other readers and potential readers who you now sense are present—who are, in a way, friendly eavesdroppers on this conversation between you and Murray.

Arguments

As you clarify your goals and what you know about your readers, you will, at least tacitly, be starting to form and test arguments. Consider these questions:

- What key propositions or conclusions do you want your readers to accept?
- What do they need to know and believe in order to be persuaded to take the action you want them to?
- Which arguments will your readers readily accept? Which do they already accept? Which will they be likely to resist? And which might they likely reject out of hand?
- What counter-arguments are your readers likely to make?
- What kinds of information will they need? What information will they find credible and persuasive?

- How much of this information do you have readily at hand? What information do you need that you don't have? And what will you need to do to get the additional information?
- What level of emotion is embedded in the issues here? Do you want to emphasize and heighten the emotional dimensions of your arguments, or do you want to flatten and mute the emotional dimensions?
- Is your own credibility or that of the organization you represent an important issue here? Do your readers already assume that you're competent, trustworthy, and well informed, or will they be skeptical?

Any matter in an organization that's important enough to justify a written document—even just a half-page memo—is likely to require you to think at least briefly about these questions. Even when a report is strictly factual, those facts are embedded in emotions, both your own and those of your readers, so it, too, requires trust and trustworthiness.

Think for a minute about all the different advice people have given you over the years about making a good argument. We're guessing you've heard all the following pieces of advice in one form or another, sometimes in suggesting ways to build an argument and sometimes in describing effective writing in general:

"First, you make your point, and then you support it."

"Be specific."

"Show, don't tell."

All three pieces of advice are helpful most of the time, especially if you're making an argument to somebody in the United States or other Western cultures where people tend to give special weight to empirical evidence. If someone makes a claim, one of our most common responses is "Really? Can you show me how that's so?" And when we ask this (or some less polite question, like "Oh, yeah?"), we usually mean we'd like to see some credible evidence to support the claim. These two elements, a *claim* and *supporting evidence*, are, in fact, two of the essential elements of an argument. The advice that tells you to make a claim and then support it is based on recognizing these two elements.

It's fairly rare to see an effective argument (that is, one that generates agreement) that's just a claim without any supporting evidence. Usually, when this does happen, it's a situation—often, an oral dialogue—in which both parties are looking at or listening to the same evidence and understand the evidence the same way. Here's an example: Curly and Shorty are riding their ponies along the bottom of the canyon in a rainstorm, and suddenly there's the roar of a flash flood coming down the canyon.

Shorty: We better git outta here. *(Claim)*

Curly: Yep. *(Assent)*

It's much more common to see an argument that's been truncated by dropping the explicit claim and just citing the facts of the situation as evidence. In this kind of abbreviated argument, the writer (or speaker) is relying on the reader (or audience) to infer the claim. As we'll discuss in more detail when we talk about Expression, the E of GRACE, this kind of argument is especially common in professional discourse when people are talking or writing about their own character. Often, you can lay out the facts of the matter in such a way that they speak for themselves, making a compelling case for your unstated claim.

Remember that in talking about truncated arguments, where the claim (and sometimes the evidence) is often left unsaid, we're thinking primarily about arguments in routine situations, such as writing a thank-you letter to a speaker. But you'll have to think much more deeply and systematically about the structure of your arguments in more conflicted or complex situations:

- When a situation becomes conflicted because people with different stakes are bringing different assumptions to their understanding of the situation
- When parties to the situation have high ego investments and deep emotions associated with the issues
- When the issues themselves become complex

Rather than truncating, you'll probably have to amplify your arguments. That will likely involve analyzing your own arguments and the opposing arguments, peeling through the layers of evidence and claims and uncovering the underlying assumptions and values in your own and your opponents' belief systems. In addition, you'll have to think carefully about the limits of the validity of your own arguments, possibly standing ready to concede to your opponents that in some areas, your claims don't hold. In fact, you may even make such a concession before you're asked to.

When writing situations like this become complex and conflicted, the risks rise quickly. You can sometimes even feel your pulse pounding in your ears. But these higher stakes can also make the writing challenge extremely interesting. And successfully negotiating this kind of challenge and conflict to a win/win resolution can be immensely satisfying. (In later chapters, we'll continue to unpack the layers of argument, especially in Chapter 6, where we'll discuss writing in situations that are in conflict, and in Chapters 10–13, where we'll discuss longer, more complex documents that deal with more complex situations and develop more complex arguments.)

But no matter how routine or how complex and conflicted your writing situation and the arguments involved in it, the one argumentative element you will almost always need to make explicit is the *evidence:* concrete, specific, credible facts (unless you're Shorty and Curly and the evidence is roaring down the canyon on top of you). Even in the most routine follow-up memo or thank-you letter, you need to cite enough specific detail about the event to show that you know what you're thanking the person for. In the letter to Rich Murray, for example, you need to give enough specific detail to demonstrate that you were actually at the meeting and that you were awake and listening to him speak. Especially in American culture, where we value empirical data so highly, this expectation to give specific, concrete evidence is so strong that "Show, don't tell" is almost a compulsory convention. In fact, we'll discuss this expectation again in the section Conventions.

So, let's look again at that routine thank-you letter to Rich Murray. Suppose you sensed from Murray's response to you during the meeting that he thought you had asked an intelligent and engaging question. You also sensed that he might be especially interested in helping people who are willing to take some initiative in their career planning. Given this situation in which you're asked to write a routine thank-you letter, what arguments seem likely to help achieve your goals with this reader? Let's make a tentative list:

1. Rich, your speaking at our meeting was helpful to me.
2. I am the kind of self-starting, thoughtful person who is worth the time and effort to help further.

The letter you write should probably be relatively short, so let's go with just these two arguments. We'll see if you can put the conventions of the situation to good use so your letter expresses a sense of who you are and convinces Murray that you're someone worth helping further. Again, it may be worth considering briefly the particular complexity brought to this writing situation by the fact that it may be written in a classroom situation. It may be useful to ask yourself whether these arguments support what we've concluded are the goals your instructor has set for your writing this letter. You should test the arguments, then, to see if they give Murray positive and useful feedback.

Figure 1.2 presents a letter written by a student for exactly the situation we've imagined. The student, Mike Kim, did, in fact, ask Rich Murray a question during class and wants Murray to remember him and his question. Read the letter closely to see if it serves this goal as well as that of giving Murray positive and useful feedback. Look especially at the arguments. Does the letter actually make the two arguments we've just listed? If your answer is "yes," then look again at the letter and ask yourself how Mike makes these arguments.

To begin, let's look at Mike's first argument: *Your speaking at our meeting was helpful to me.* Does he make this argument explicitly at any point in the letter? In fact, he doesn't. He does say he's been tinkering with his resume since hearing Murray's advice, and he strengthens the implication that the advice is helpful by reporting that he's made an appointment to come in for further advice. Mike also reports that he's followed Murray's explicit suggestion about registering with Career Services.

Now let's look at Mike's second argument: *I am the kind of self-starting, thoughtful person who is worth the time and effort to help further.* Again, Mike doesn't make the claim explicitly; rather, he *shows* his initiative by describing what he's done. He's already tinkered with his resume. He's found a specific prospective employer who's his target audience, and he's drafted a letter. He's already made an appointment for a follow-up meeting, and he's also registered at Career Services. His simple narrative of his actions, in fact, makes a much more compelling argument that he's a self-starting, thoughtful person than would the bald assertion of that explicit claim. And it's in-

FIGURE 1.2 Sample Thank-You Letter

720 4th Avenue South
St. Cloud, MN 56301
October 22, 1997

Rich Murray, Director
Career Services
101 Administrative Services Building
St. Cloud State University
St. Cloud, MN 56301

Dear Rich:

Thanks for speaking to us in Judy Kilborn's class last Thursday evening. Your generosity in giving up part of your evening to help us think about our careers represents the SCSU spirit at its best!

Thanks also for offering to speak with us individually if we had more questions. I've already come in to the office and made an appointment for next Tuesday morning. You may remember I asked the other night about the advisability of listing a job on my resume that indicated political or religious affiliations. I've been tinkering with my resume since then, and I'm also working on a letter to a prospective employer I'm really excited about. I'd like to see what you think about how I've handled the political and religious affiliation issue in this situation, and I'd especially like to get your take on how I've introduced it in the letter.

By the way, I took your advice and registered with Career Services when I came in to make the appointment. See you next Tuesday!

Sincerely,

Mike Kim

Mike Kim

teresting to note, looking at the preceding paragraph about Mike's first argument, that the same narrative actually carries both arguments at the same time. Interestingly enough, the same narrative appears likely to achieve the instructor's goals as well as Mike's. The concrete evidence of the effectiveness of Murray's presentation is convincingly documented in the narrative, so that we may expect Murray will be gratified and the instructor will be pleased.

For two other examples of thank-you letters written to Rich Murray in response to this same kind of session, see the letters by Joan Theisen and Heather Eckes in Figures 1.3 and 1.4, respectively. Note that Joan and Heather's letters have slightly different goals from Mike's; for example, neither Joan nor Heather is asking for a follow-up meeting. Yet the basic arguments are the same in all three letters: (1) *your speaking was helpful,* and (2) *I am a self-starting, thoughtful person.*

FIGURE 1.3 Sample Thank-You Letter Using Modified-Block Style

1524 South 18th Street
St. Cloud, MN 56303
September 20, 1996

Mr. Rich Murray
Director, Career Services
St. Cloud State University
720 4th Avenue South
St. Cloud, MN 56301

Dear Mr. Murray:

Thank you for taking the time on September 19 to meet with our English 339 class to discuss the many ways that Career Services can assist me as I begin my career search. I was unaware of the scope of services provided by your office and the competitive edge that I will have by using those services. I received helpful information about networking, informational interviews, Career Day, and Job Fair. As a non-traditional student, I appreciate your willingness to adjust your schedule and work with students who are not on campus during the day.

Your enthusiasm, encouragement, and commitment to students make me eager to begin my career search. I am receiving an excellent liberal arts education at St. Cloud State University, but I was unsure how to take the next step and market myself to future employers. I now see that this is an exciting process, not a daunting task. I'm looking forward to registering with Career Services as the first step in letting people know what I know.

Sincerely,

Joan M. Theisen

Joan M. Theisen

FIGURE 1.4 Sample Thank-You Letter Using Full-Block Style

418 5th Ave. S. #13
St. Cloud, MN 56301
September 24, 1996

Mr. Rich Murray
Director of Career Services
St. Cloud State University
Administrative Services 101
720 4th Avenue South
St. Cloud, MN 56301

Dear Rich:

Thank you for speaking to our (Judy Kilborn's) English 339 class last Thursday. Your time, information, and energy were greatly appreciated. The presentation was upbeat, informative, specialized, and interesting. You have given presentations in two of my previous classes, encouraging students to register with Career Services, and as I noted on Thursday, I did attend an orientation seminar in response to your presentations, but have opted to wait until I am a junior and more prepared to enter the job market to actually register. It was for just that reason that your presentation was so beneficial to me.

I am finally just at that point where I need to do some in-depth assessment and research in light of my future career. Your overhead titled the "Know Yourself Inventory" is great! It opened a whole new perspective for me. After working through that inventory, I realized I was short-changing and limiting myself both personally and in regard to my future career. Also helpful in your presentation was the information about the diversity of the job market. Finding out there are so many more options than I thought existed really expanded my outlook on my career search. I will definitely be pursuing further information and would appreciate any direction, assistance, or information you could share with me.

In closing, I would like to thank you again for taking the time to give such a specialized presentation to our class. The focus on subjects complementary to our classroom study was a useful reinforcer and also provided new knowledge and perspectives to blend into that study. Thanks!

Sincerely,

Heather Eckes

Heather Eckes

Conventions

Sometimes, you can find yourself almost paralyzed by the huge range of possibilities when you begin to make some decisions about the conventions of format, length, tone of expression, and so on. You can begin to narrow the range of choices by reviewing once again your goals, readers, and arguments—as well as the history and context of your writing situation:

- Given your goals, your readers, and the issues involved, what conventions or customs govern the kind of document you want to generate? For example, is your relationship to your readers such that an informal memo would be appropriate, or should you write a formal business letter?
- Are the issues and facts complex enough that a still more lengthy document is required?
- Does this situation typically call for a particular kind of document, such as a proposal, progress report, instruction manual, letter of reprimand, memo, or evaluation report?
- Does either your employer or your reader's employer have guidelines that should determine the format and style of the document?
- If you're faced with a novel situation and are unsure of the conventions, where can you get some guidance? Does someone in your organization have experience writing in this kind of situation? Can you consult a corporate or departmental style manual? Do your readers have guidelines for the format and style they expect to see in, for example, proposals they receive?

In addition, you may ask what kind of medium is conventionally appropriate here. For instance, this may be a situation when a handwritten note would be most appropriate. But perhaps a paper document is not the best medium of communication; maybe an e-mail memo would be the most appropriate response. In fact, maybe a print or electronic document is not the best conventional response in this situation. Is it possible that this is a situation where you should simply go talk to your reader face to face—say, a highly charged emotional situation where you know that a direct conversation, though uncomfortable, would be more effective and more honest than a written document? Or is this a situation—maybe a routine exchange of information with a close colleague—where just a quick phone call would be more efficient and more appropriate than a written text?

Let's explore your letter-writing assignment to Rich Murray some more. The large-scale decision about convention has been made for you: Your assignment is to write a routine letter following a conventional business letter format. Keeping in mind your goals, readers, and arguments, what other kinds of conventions does the situation seem to call for? For a start, there's one more we've already suggested: The letter probably should be short (a one-page maximum) because Murray seems like a busy person and you know your letter will be just one of many items of incoming correspondence calling for his attention. As for content, the situation calls strongly for an expression of thanks. And some form of thanks, couched in a respectful tone, would certainly be consistent with your two arguments and with the complex goals of both you and your instructor.

As you attempt to develop the second argument further, however, social and cultural conventions may present a problem because there are widespread and fairly strong conventions against too aggressive or assertive self-promotion. So you may need to make your second argument somewhat indirectly, although the specific conventions of the employment search allow (even require) you to do a certain amount of bragging.

Now, within the context of these larger conventional issues, you also have to make some decisions about the specific, fine-grained details of mechanical conventions: grammar, spelling, punctuation, and word usage. The following set of questions can get you started:

- First, do these conventions of correctness seem important in this particular writing situation?
- Would conforming consistently to the conventional rules of spelling, grammar, and the like enhance your argument that you're a competent and conscientious person? Would doing so let you make that argument at least somewhat indirectly, by using the conventions to help your readers infer that you're competent and conscientious without your saying so directly?
- Would a letter that doesn't follow standard conventions of spelling, grammar, punctuation, and usage likely convince Rich Murray that you're competent and conscientious? Probably not. Rather, the letter should be strictly conventional—in other words, correct—in its grammar, spelling, punctuation, and usage.

Expression

In its most basic form, the touchstone of expression asks how you want readers to visualize your face when they read your document. To what extent should your document embody and express your own individual voice and personality as well as the voice and personality of the organization you represent? These questions about face, voice, and personality build on the questions in the Arguments section that point to your need to persuade your readers that you're competent, trustworthy, and well informed. This kind of ethical persuasion usually can't be done directly with very good effect. For example, "Trust me—I'm not a crook!" usually doesn't generate a lot of trust. We most often draw inferences about people's character based on what we see by their actions, rather than what they say directly about themselves. And often, the text you generate is the only action readers have as a demonstration of your character.

So, given your goals, your readers, and the conventions of this situation, consider the following questions:

- How visible do you want to make your own character?
- To what extent is there a risk that your readers will find you ostentatious and overbearing if you assert your presence too strongly?

- To what extent is there a risk that your readers will find you evasive and sneaky if you mute the sense of your presence?
- What kinds of strategies will either reduce or enhance your visibility?
- What kind of presence or character do you want to assert?
- What aspects of your character will best serve your goals in writing this document?
- When your readers imagine you in their mind's eye, what do you want them to see? Do you want them to imagine you in a posture that's assertive, bold, and authoritative? Thoughtful, reflective, and speculative? Sympathetic or apologetic? Angry? What kind of expression should they imagine on your face?
- What kind of tone of voice should your readers hear? A flat, businesslike, matter-of-fact tone? An energetic, enthusiastic tone? How about a whispered, confidential tone? A loud, aggressive tone? Maybe a smooth, sophisticated tone? Or an ironic or teasing tone?
- What kind of relationship between you and your readers do you want these signals of tone and image to suggest and promote?

A matter-of-fact tone accurately describes many business documents. This tone also suggests the kind of image you might often want to project and the kind of relationship you might want to encourage: formal, impersonal, and professional. In fact, it would be fair to say that a matter-of-fact tone is one of the strong conventions in business and professional documents. However, because this tone de-emphasizes presence and personality, people sometimes assume that tone and other signals of the writer's presence are either bad or unimportant—that the only professional style is characterized by the lack of any traits expressing the writer's presence behind the words. As a result, people often don't even ask themselves about what kind of writerly presence they want their document to express. They either follow the convention without thought, or sometimes, they break the convention without thought. Doing either creates the risk of making missteps similar to the missteps writers can make when they forget to ask who their readers really are. In fact, there is no single appropriate expression of writerly personality for all occasions, any more than there is a single reader for all occasions.

The way you emphasize the various features of your character or that of the organization you represent can change along several different dimensions. For example, your attitude might range from angry to apologetic; your level of energy might range from highly assertive and energetic to passive; your directness might range from blunt to subtle; and the overall image of your personality or your organization's personality might range from vivid and colorful to muted and understated. And all the various shifts of expression along all these dimensions can be appropriate, depending on your goals; the attitudes, knowledge, and needs of your readers; the kinds of arguments you want to make; and the conventions you reasonably have at your disposal for writing any particular document in any given situation.

Our discussion of the letter-writing assignment to Rich Murray has already suggested that expression may be especially important in this letter because your arguments, supporting your reader-based goal, are ethical arguments about your character. First, how do you *show,* not just *tell,* Murray that his presentation was helpful to you? How about describing—expressing in brief, vivid, convincing detail—a change in what you're thinking and doing about your career preparation because of what he said? Would this be a more convincing expression of gratitude than just saying thanks without demonstrating your change of heart and mind? Flip back once again to Mike Kim's letter (Figure 1.2), and see how much specific action it narrates. Look also at the letters by Joan Theisen and Heather Eckes (Figures 1.3 and 1.4). To what extent do all three letters express the sincerity of the writers' thanks by *showing* each individual in some kind of specific action (either literal, physical action or verbal action) that resulted from Murray's presentation?

Would highly formal, academic language be best for expressing your sense of enthusiasm and gratitude, or would more informal stylistic conventions better express your state of mind? On the other hand, would language that's too informal and too breezy imply ignorance or a kind of rebellious disregard for conventions of professional communication? We've already said that the level of risk rises quickly the further a writer deviates from conventions, especially the sentence-level conventions of discourse that are so well established that straying from them is generally called an error.

Look now at the second argument—that you're the kind of self-starting and thoughtful person who's worth helping further. Would the same expressive narrative that supports your first argument (that Murray's coming to class helped you) also help support your second? This kind of self-expression, focusing on yourself and your own behavior, has an excellent chance of success in this situation. At first glance, the strategy may appear to violate one of the most popular maxims of writing in professional situations:

◣ MAXIM

Keep a *you* orientation, focusing on your reader and his or her needs when you write.

But upon a closer look, our strategy turns out simply to be a special application of the maxim. Murray's interest here is in you and your response to his presentation. His professional life is motivated by his service to people like you, and a good deal of his satisfaction with his work lies in knowing he has changed the way people think about their careers and themselves.

Finally, here's one specific illustration of taking advantage of the range of individual choices among the stylistic conventions of letter writing to express your own personality and your relationship to your reader: Look at the salutations of the three letters to Murray. Two of the writers (Mike and Heather) address Murray as "Dear Rich," but Joan chooses to address him as "Dear Mr. Murray." Does this mean that "Dear Rich" is correct because it's preferred by two-thirds of our samples? No, it means that Mike and Heather felt comfortable addressing Murray as "Dear Rich." Both felt their interaction with Murray—especially the relatively informal mode of expression Murray himself demonstrated—made the more informal first-name salutation an appropriate choice. On the other hand, Joan's decision to open with "Dear Mr. Murray" simply means that in spite of his relative informality in their meeting, she still felt more comfortable demonstrating her respect by addressing him—saluting him—with the more formal salutation. Both salutations are correct, in terms of the technical conventions of the genre of a business letter and the social conventions of the situation and relationships. But the difference in salutations creates a real, though subtle, difference in the writers' expressions of themselves and their relationships to Murray.

GRACE in Action

Using GRACE as a heuristic probe, we've unpacked a simple, routine letter-writing class assignment and found some rich opportunities that have implications for your life and career goals. We've discovered several potential readers who were not visible at first glance. We've identified two arguments that seem to have a good chance of helping you achieve both your immediate goals for the assignment and your broader personal goals. And we've done some risk management by considering what cultural, social, generic, stylistic, and grammatical conventions seem appropriate for this situation and by calculating the risks and rewards of expressing your goals and arguments either within or outside these conventional frameworks. If we've done all these things well, we've composed a letter that's an authentic, appropriate persuasive self-portrait—one that achieves your goals.

In this first chapter, we've also demonstrated how you can use GRACE to help you discover what you know and need to know as you write in the workplace—even in a routine letter-writing situation. And because Argument, the A of GRACE, is at the center of virtually all professional discourse, we've suggested that even routine writing situations require the bare-bone elements of argument: a claim and some supporting evidence. Subsequent chapters will show how you can apply GRACE and the five general benchmarks it represents to manage complexity, control your risks, and identify opportunities in the writing of business.

ACTIVITIES AND PROJECTS

1. To hone your analysis skills, begin a file of memos, e-mail, letters, and reports you receive at work or at home. The documents in this file should be copies, rather than originals, and all identifying information (names, addresses, and confidential data) should be masked over or crossed out. Select only those documents that you particularly like or dislike, and label them accordingly. You'll use these documents for later assignments.

2. Write a memo or e-mail to your instructor for this class, following the guidelines established in the memo from the authors shown in Figure 1.5.

FIGURE 1.5 Memo to Your Teacher

To: Our Readers

From: Bob Inkster and Judy Kilborn

Date: July 15, 1998

Subject: **Memo to Your Instructor**

Write a memo to your instructor that summarizes, processes, and evaluates your experience in this course so far. As you write, pay particular attention to your needs and course goals and also respond to the issue of readers and risk. Unless your instructor asks for a different format, use this memo as a template.

Your Needs and Course Goals

Your main goal in this memo is to give your instructor a clearer sense of your own needs and goals for the course and a sense of where you are now with relation to the course. What do you know and understand? What do you understand/not understand, like/not like in the book, the syllabus, the class discussion, and your class colleagues so far? (If you do the journal exercise, you'll have generated a lot of ideas and questions that could go into this memo—in fact, you'll probably have too much to fit into the memo, so you'll have to identify the most relevant, most urgent responses, problems, and questions you have at this point.)

Readers and Risk

What about the issue of readers and risk? How well do you know your instructor? How candid do you feel you can safely be if you have a problem or a criticism at this point? One obvious thing you should consider doing is simply asking your reader—your instructor—about this risk. Most likely, your instructor will appreciate your candor, especially this early in the course, when it's easy to explain what the plan is or to modify the plan (either the plan for the course or your own plan) before you all have a lot of time and energy invested in the course.

Your memo will allow your instructor to respond to you individually, if that's appropriate, or to use your memo and other people's memos to set part of the agenda for the discussion at the next class meeting.

3. Begin writing an academic journal that records your responses to class readings, discussions, and collaborative activities and makes connections between the classroom and your experience, knowledge, needs, and values. Keep the journal in a spiral or loose-leaf notebook or in a computer file that you can print out, submit on disk, or send to your instructor via e-mail. To prepare for class discussion, you'll probably want to write an entry responding to each class

reading—recording your thoughts, ideas, and relevant experiences from the workplace or your personal networks. Each entry should be at least one page of printed text if you plan to record what you're thinking in enough detail to enable your readers—your teacher or class colleagues—to get inside your head.

Journal entries can be on assigned topics or open assignments (meaning that you can focus on any aspect of your assigned reading or classroom discussions or activities). Use the entries to explore concepts; to connect or contrast your ideas, experiences, knowledge, and background with those of the authors'; or to react to or analyze samples in the textbook. In other words, your journal should show your interaction with the text you're reading as well as your response to classroom activities and discussion. Although summarizing may be helpful in recording the day-to-day business of the classroom and in absorbing the more difficult concepts, your entries should concentrate on recording your reactions—getting your thoughts down on paper where you can capture them, look at them, remember them, and use them as prompts for classroom discussion and small-group work or as a depository of ideas that can be developed for formal, written assignments.

Since a journal is an informal mode of writing, don't worry about mechanical correctness (spelling, punctuation, grammar, etc.). Simply let your ideas take you where they will.

Here's an idea for an initial journal entry: Write about your goals and expectations for reading this book and, if you're reading this book for a class, your goals for the class:

- What do you hope or need to learn in order to function the way you'd like to in the workplace?
- What personal goals do you hope to achieve?
- In what particular ways can your instructor, mentor, or colleagues (in a class or at work) help you achieve them?
- What other resources are available on your campus or at work to help you fulfill these professional and personal goals?
- What specific things can you do to learn what you'd like to in the course of your work with this book?

4. Generate a list of questions about job market research, employment interviews, resumes, or cover letters that you'd like to ask someone from your campus's career services office. Schedule an appointment with one of the career counselors in this office, start making plans to have him or her give a talk to a campus organization you belong to, or ask your instructor to arrange a talk on career planning for your class.

5. Spend a little time thinking about the environment in your workplace—in a part-time, seasonal, or full-time job—or in a campus or community organization you belong to. Consider your specific relationships with people you know in this context:

   - Who are the people in your own group—the people you work and interact with most often? List them and their roles or specific areas of responsibility.

- Who are the people in close proximity to your group that you interact with fairly regularly? List them and their roles or specific areas of responsibility.
- Who are the distant members of the organization whom you know very little and interact with only intermittently? List them and their roles or specific areas of responsibility.
- Finally, what important or relevant people outside this organization can you identify? List them and their roles or specific areas of responsibility.

Contextualizing the nature of your organization in this way—and mapping out relationships among yourself and others—will not only identify potential readers for assignments you might write for this class, but it will also enable you to reflect upon organizational problems, risks, and opportunities.

6. Interview a professional in your field or the field you plan to enter about the kinds and amount of writing that he or she does on the job. Be sure to ask this person to describe common goals for writing, typical readers, the sorts of information normally communicated, and the expression he or she commonly strives to achieve. Also ask about special conventions that need to be followed in his or her workplace. Finally, ask about the types of writing that are done collaboratively (including how frequently they're performed) as well as the technology that's used for writing.

7. Discuss your experience (or lack of experience) with the technology described in this chapter: computer hardware (whether laptops, desktops, or workstations networked with other computers) and software (programs for word processing, graphics, spreadsheets, databases, desktop publishing, day planning, etc.) as well as e-mail, electronic bulletin boards, listservs, newsgroups, voice mail, and so forth. How would you characterize your attitudes toward this technology? What risks and opportunities do you see in using this technology, both for yourself and your workplace?

8. Discuss your experience (or lack of experience) with the current models of organization described in this chapter—the decentralized "solar systems" that Boyette and Conn believe will replace the "corporate pyramid." Have you ever worked on a project team? Have you witnessed the increased emphasis on quality and responsiveness to customer needs? Have you studied these models in other classes? What sorts of questions and concerns do you have about the sort of environment that's been projected for "Workplace 2000"?

REFERENCES

Boyette, J. H., & Conn, H. P. (1992). *Workplace 2000: The revolution reshaping American business.* New York: Plume.

Deming, W. E. (1943). *Statistical adjustment of data.* New York: Wiley.

Deming, W. E. (1982). *Quality, productivity, and competitive position.* Cambridge, MA: MIT Press.

Jamison, D., & O'Mara, J. (1991). *Managing workforce 2000: Gaining the diversity advantage.* San Francisco: Jossey Bass.

Mathes, J. C., & Stevenson, D. (1976). *Designing technical reports: Writing for audiences in organizations.* Indianapolis: Bobbs-Merrill.

Miller, G. A. (1956). The magical number seven, plus or minus two: Some limits on our capacity for processing information. *Psychological Review, 63,* 81–97.

Peters, T. (1992). *Liberation management: Necessary disorganization for the nanosecond nineties.* New York: Fawcett Columbine.

Reich, R. (1991). *The work of nations: Preparing ourselves for 21st century capitalism.* New York: Knopf.

Simon, H. A. (1957). *Administrative behavior: A study of decision-making processes in administrative organizations.* New York: Macmillan.

Young, R., & Sullivan, P. (1984). Why write? A reconsideration. In R. J. Connors, L. S. Ede, & A. Lunsford (Eds.), *Essays on classical rhetoric and modern discourse.* Carbondale: Southern Illinois University Press.

Chapter 2

Managing Your Writing Is Managing Your Work

"Ready–fire–aim–fire–aim–fire–aim!"

—Henry Mintzberg

We argued in Chapter 1 that the *writing* of business is, in fact, the *doing* of business because we've seen people in organizations use writing as a powerful management tool—actually, a set of tools—to process all kinds of complex information, create plans, and build and express organizational visions. With writing as a tool, people negotiate not only professional transactions but even the meanings of those transactions. And like any powerful tool—the latest spreadsheet software, for example—the tool of writing will be increasingly powerful as we think more about what it is and how to manage it. So, we want to talk briefly about assumptions, strategies, tactics, and technologies for managing your writing.

The assumptions you bring to your writing will have a dramatic effect on how you manage your writing process. Most of the time, people who are dissatisfied with their writing have made some assumptions that are causing them to manage their writing ineffectively and to impose requirements on themselves that are interfering with their productivity. Very often, you can increase your productivity and your satisfaction with your writing just by experimenting with some alternative assumptions about your writing in general or about the immediate writing task at hand.

In this chapter, we will first discuss four assumptions about writing in general that we think will most likely help you manage your writing, whether you are working alone or as part of a writing team. Next, we will talk about writing as a set of distinct but closely related skilled activities, and we will suggest a vocabulary for talking about these activities so that you have a convenient language for describing and managing your writing process. Then, using GRACE as a framework, we will suggest strategies for analyzing your assumptions about writing situations and for testing alternative assumptions to see if they would help you write more productively and comfortably in response to a particular situation. Along the way, we will note some of the problems computer technology raises for writing processes and suggest strategies for using this technology to improve your writing and project management.

Useful Assumptions about Writing

ASSUMPTION 1: **Writing is an action—a doing, a process—as well as a document.**

If the writing of business is the doing of business, then writing is doing. People who do research on writing actually watch many different writers and see consistent patterns in what effective writers do. In fact, writing researchers have named different actions they see writers doing. Typically, the different actions in the writing process are given names like *planning, generating, revising, editing,* and *proofreading.* Some researchers like a simpler breakdown: *prewriting, writing,* and *rewriting.* Others believe that it's artificial and misleading to describe the writing process in terms of different kinds of actions; they argue that writing is actually one single activity—thinking—and that writers are just thinking about different things at different points in the process.

ASSUMPTION 2: **Writing isn't a single action or act but a whole range of different actions, strategies, and processes.**

We don't need all the strategies in our writing tool kit all the time. It's not efficient or effective management of our time and work to do careful planning, generating, revising, editing, and proofreading when we are faced with a familiar, routine situation that really only calls for a 12-word memo. So, in addition to the planning/generating/revising/editing/proofreading tool kit, we need another, smaller diagnostic tool kit that will help us analyze a situation and its context, get our bearings, and make some initial strategic decisions. That tool kit grows out of these assumptions.

ASSUMPTION 3: **Monitoring your own writing process and naming what you are doing at any given point in the process gives you powerfully increased control over your writing.**

We need a vocabulary that enables us to troubleshoot our own process when we get stuck. We need language that lets us ask ourselves where we are in the process, what we're thinking about, and whether we should be thinking about something else. Real writing processes rarely fit the straight-line, stepwise, efficient-looking pattern of an algorithm or formula. The application of any strategy—including GRACE—for moving toward a functional piece of writing is almost always a complex, crooked path.

Although it may feel inefficient to take a winding course, where we repeatedly reconsider the elements of our writing situation, our goals, and our writing itself, this kind of iterative, recursive process usually turns out to be an efficient way of producing a successful document. Because the writing we do is an integral part of the thinking and problem solving we do, we may even discover late in the revision process that we have written ourselves into a new, more appropriate understanding of our goals or our readers. So, while we need to remember and honor our production deadlines for generating a piece of writing, we also need to stay alert to new insights, connections, and possibilities throughout the writing process. And we also need to stay alert to what the process itself may be telling us when we feel it pulling us in a direction away from a straight line to the finish. Often, these pulls that first seem to be off task can be the source of important insights, problems, or solutions that can move us toward completing a successful document in surprising leaps.

ASSUMPTION 4: **The writing of business—both the process and the document—takes place in a rich context of other processes and documents.**

When you're writing in an organization, you don't have exclusive ownership of this task or the language you're writing. This fact has wide ramifications. The most immediate one is that you have to let go of a great deal of your individual pride of ownership in the project and the text. You have to be willing to listen to the goals, anxieties, and advice of other people who have a stake in this writing, and you have to be skilled at interpreting what people mean when they respond to your text or give you suggestions for drafting or revising it.

As writing continues to become an increasingly collaborative process, your teamwork skills will increase in importance along with your writing skills. There are almost always points at which writing is a solitary activity, but more and more writing projects are produced by teams, and the goals of the writing project are shared—often by the wider organization as well as the immediate members of the team. So, what is already a complex process when the writing and its goals belong to just one person becomes a still more complex process of project management when the goals and project are shared by a team. Questions like the following become just as important for the success of a collaborative project as do the questions generated by a GRACE analysis:

- How should the team negotiate who does what and when?
- What individual skills, interests, and information do people on the team have, and how can the team be organized so these individual resources complement each other in the most productive ways?
- What competing responsibilities do team members have?
- Who has time to do what, and how should project responsibilities be distributed so that the project goes forward efficiently and the workload is shared equitably?
- What parts of the project depend on other parts and in what ways?
- What intermediate deadlines on what parts of the project—for example, tables or graphs of financial, statistical, or other technical information—need to be set so the ultimate deadline can be met with a document that achieves the team's goals?
- Other than team members, who else has a stake in this project and should be consulted?
- Who else has resources that could contribute to the success of the project?

The written product that you generate is just one in a long series of events and documents in the life of the organization. All kinds of written and spoken transactions—last year's annual report, the organizational mission statement, an existing contract with this reader, a series of letters and memos, perhaps a similar document to a similar reader in the past, conversations, e-mail messages—have preceded and will follow this particular document.

In addition, successful management of all these people, resources, and problems in a complex writing project probably will entail still more writing that supports the larger project in the same way scaffolding supports the construction of a building. This writing may include meeting agendas and minutes for your project team and memos to the team and others who have a stake in the project. We'll talk about these uses of writing as a management tool in Chapter 3.

The fact that the written document currently in progress exists as part of a flow of documents has several important implications. For one thing, this flow takes some of the pressure off you as you generate the document because you know it doesn't have to carry the whole weight of the relationship between you and your readers. A relationship probably already exists and will continue to exist. On the other hand, ignoring other elements of the relationship with your readers and ignoring the context within your own organization is risky. You have to be sensitive to all the other written and spoken information that exists in the context of your writing project, and you need to be ready to take advantage of this context.

Analyzing Your Writing Situation, Conditions and Constraints, and Assumptions

We need strategies for giving ourselves effective writing assignments when we are engaged in particular writing situations and faced with particular writing tasks. Probably the biggest single barrier that keeps us from moving forward on any particular writing project is uncertainty. Especially on a big, complex writing project, but often even with a brief memo, there's so much we don't know, and our uncertainty causes anxiety. Our natural reaction to the anxiety is to try to avoid even thinking about the project. And when we do think about the project, we may have a tendency to think fretfully, rather than productively.

More often than we'd like, we find ourselves called upon to write in situations where we're not really even familiar with the context or the history. We may not know just who's involved in the situation or what their various stakes are in the issues. We may not know the issues—or even the facts—with much confidence. And given all this uncertainty, we surely won't have a clear sense of what our own stance is or should be or what we hope to achieve. We need to consider a series of questions that will help us map out and name the territory of this situation so we can locate what we know, where we need more information and help, and how we can get the information and help we need. And in addition to strategies for finding out what we need to know, we also need strategies for giving ourselves permission to go ahead and work productively on the writing, in spite of our uncertainty and the anxiety it causes.

The goal of this section is twofold: (1) to help you develop useful strategies for identifying and naming areas where you have a confident understanding of your writing situation and of the process and document it evokes and, just as important, (2) to provide strategies for identifying and naming areas of uncertainty in your writing situation and process so you can begin to take control of them. In fact, GRACE is one powerful strategy for doing exactly this; much of what follows will again be framed around GRACE.

The Primary Question: What Is My Writing Task?

This really is the master question. It's almost always the first question you should ask. It will lead directly to your getting started writing or to your asking additional questions that will help unpack and analyze the important details of more complex writing situations and the more complicated writing projects and documents they usually evoke. (We'll look at some additional questions in the next section.)

You may actually find that this is the only question you'll need to ask in many routine situations at work because your writing task may be quickly obvious: hand-write a reply to a memo or letter and return it to the sender; initial your approval of a purchasing decision; quickly modify the boilerplate language of a memo in your computer files, adapting it for a slightly new but generically routine service issue. You may even find that your writing task doesn't call for writing at all but rather a telephone discussion or face-to-face conversation.

You may often move so quickly from your initial analysis of a situation to your writing that you won't even be conscious of asking *What is my writing task?* Sometimes, though, you will be uncomfortably conscious of the question because you will have asked it, either tacitly or explicitly, and not known the answer. Other times, you may be able to name the task easily enough but still need to do some careful thinking and question asking. For example, you may know that your task is to draft, for your boss's signature, a letter of complaint to a vendor about delays in receiving a crucial component in your manufactured product. However, there may still be large and problematic areas of uncertainty in this task. You may not know exactly what your organization's relationship with this vendor has been in the past and what relationship your boss hopes to have in the future. And you may not know with enough confidence your boss's voice, style, or mode of expression when dealing with vendors in general or with this vendor in particular.

When asking this initial question doesn't lead you directly toward drafting a document or some other action appropriate to your situation (a phone call, a conversation across the table, etc.) but leads instead to a kind of stalemate or sense of uncertainty that leaves you unable to move forward, then you can call upon two sets of questions: The first helps you unpack the complexity and mystery of the *situation*, and the second helps you unpack the complexity of the *task* itself. In combination, these questions can help you work smarter, especially when you're stuck or feel that you're wasting a lot of effort. The second set of questions, especially, puts into action Assumption 3, stated earlier, helping you monitor your writing process by identifying and naming where you are in the process and what you are doing. The questions then help you identify alternative strategies and processes that might be more productive at that stage of the project. We'll look first at questions for unpacking the situation and then at questions for unpacking the "black box" of the writing process.

Unpacking and Demystifying the Situation

QUESTION 1: **Is this writing situation like others I've known, and if so, can I take advantage of what's familiar about it?**

If this situation is like others you've encountered before, your degree of uncertainty will decrease radically. In the extreme case, your current writing situation may be totally routine, one for which you already have an existing document that you can recycle, using it as boilerplate for a new document. Even if you don't have boilerplate, you can probably dispose of your writing task fairly quickly and confidently in a familiar situation. If you don't use the same language you've used before, you likely can use similar strategies and follow a comfortable, familiar process that's been effective before. Most of your GRACE questions about your goals, readers, arguments, conventions, and expression have probably been answered already, and the answers are probably sitting in the back of your mind. As the situation moves from the familiar to the novel, however, your level of uncertainty will increase. Likewise, the need for you to make thoughtful, inventive use of your strategic tool kit and other resources—people, information, technology, time, money, and the like—will increase, as well.

QUESTION 2: **Even if this writing situation seems familiar or routine, are there undiscovered features that are significant variations on the situations I've encountered before?**

We've talked about how risk in writing is ubiquitous. You will never have a writing situation that's risk free. Using Question 2 is a smart way of controlling risk when you're in a situation that seems utterly familiar and routine because it prompts you to ask yourself whether this situation and its context may be some novel variation on what you've encountered before. Question 2 also enables you to ask whether this situation and its context call for some thoughtful, creative variation on your routine written response.

QUESTION 3: **How complex is this writing situation, and what are its complexities?**

Like Questions 1 and 2, this question helps you get a quick picture of how demanding and difficult your task is going to be. If the situation isn't complex, your writing task may be reasonably easy and straightforward, even if the situation is novel. Perhaps you can begin drafting immediately, doing a quick, informal GRACE analysis on the fly as you write and revise. And if the situation is complex, asking these questions will help you move toward completing the task by breaking down the situation/problem—as well as your writing project itself—into manageable chunks. For example, you can discover quickly whether you can forge ahead to the finish of this document by yourself or need to consult with colleagues or others for information or advice or even for drafting parts of the document.

QUESTION 4: **What is the history of this writing situation, and what is its likely future?**

This question can help you identify both resources and risks. "This situation has a history!" is usually a coded warning to watch out for hidden agendas, conflicting interests, and personal feuds. Nonetheless, being aware of these issues can help you identify crucial points that you might otherwise miss: The history leading to this situation is dynamic. Something or someone has changed. These changes have created problems and opportunities. Asking about this dynamic historical process can help you figure out what you need to do and write in order to handle the situation successfully. There may also be established precedents, shared but unspoken expectations, and even written text that will help you reduce your uncertainty and risk as you write.

Shifting your perspective to the future of the issue gives you some immediate insights into how to manage your writing task. For one thing, this is the question you will use to set your deadline. You know the situation is dynamic. At some point, sooner or later, the opportunity presented here will be lost or the impending problem or loss to be avoided will be unavoidable. Sometimes, you will know the deadline exactly—for example, "Proposals must be received in our office by 5:00 P.M. on July 15." Other times, you will have to negotiate the deadline or set a reasonable deadline for yourself, given the constraints of the situation and other demands on your time and resources. So, *What is the history of this writing situation, and what is its likely future?* is a crucial question for your planning and management; you'll see its implications again in this chapter.

In particular, you may be able to see a trajectory of future developments that's suggested by past events, and that vision may help you formulate important arguments: Who and what caused this situation? Who and what will likely be affected by it? The answers to these kinds of questions can tell you a great deal about both your primary readers and possible secondary readers. And when used to forecast how this situation will continue to unfold, these answers can suggest the sorts of arguments you will need to make—and will be able to make—by suggesting the kinds of evidence your readers will find persuasive and the kinds of values and interests they will use to test your arguments.

QUESTION 5: **Who else and what else does this writing situation touch?**

This question, especially in combination with the others, is the ultimate probe for reconnoitering the whole contextual landscape for risks, resources, arguments, and opportunities. In Chapter 1, when we talked about locating yourself at the center of a solar system and visualizing various audiences in rings around you, we were applying a variation of this question.

The most immediate application of Question 5 is to check who the immediate stakeholders in this situation are. Question 4 already pointed to people who may be part of the history of the situation. If these people are still on the scene, they may be resources for information, arguments, and strategies. You may find allies, who are willing to support you, or opponents, who will erect barriers to the goals you need to achieve.

Other significant stakeholders may not be part of the immediate scene:

- Will other people in your organization be affected by this situation or what you write about it?
- Will people in your network of customers, clients, and vendors be affected?

- What about people in other organizations, especially governmental regulatory, legislative, or enforcement agencies?
- How much further should you look? Are there broad social, economic, environmental, and ethical ramifications to this situation? Will what you write here affect the community at large, even on a global scale?

Even a relatively small, self-contained situation can have ramifications that touch different people in ways that generate conflicting interests and goals. If you can see that your situation clearly has broad ramifications, you will probably quickly encounter competing goals—often, all of them worthwhile and desirable in their own right—along with constituencies who will argue on their behalf. At that point, you will have an interesting situation—one that is indeed complex, perhaps even more than your initial survey with Question 3 had suggested to you. You will surely find resources that will help you engage these rhetorical, political, and ethical complications. You will find people, principles, precedents, and a wealth of information that will serve as evidence for the arguments you will need to make—and those you will need to counter.

Unpacking and Demystifying Your Writing Process

If, instead of writing, you find yourself asking *What do I do now?* it's probably because *both* your task and the situation evoking it are complex enough to warrant some systematic analysis. Consider that you have choices to make in the way you give yourself assignments, whether to compose, research, test and revise, rewrite, edit, or proofread. These choices aren't absolutely dictated to you by the circumstances of your writing situation, although obviously you need to read the situation carefully and manage your process and your text appropriately in light of these circumstances. Perhaps the most obvious example of considering your circumstances is setting your deadline. You can't give yourself a three-week deadline if the document needs to speak to an issue that your readers are going to decide in a week. Managing your process and your text, then, involves a variety of subtasks, which we will discuss next.

Subtask 1: Planning

Planning, of course, is what you're doing when you ask about the complexity of your task. Two different kinds of planning are going on when you're engaged in a writing project; and it's important to do both kinds and to know which kind you're doing at any given moment. Remember that we talked earlier about the fact that writing is not only a document but also the process that produces that document.

Planning Your Document: GRACE in Action. Each time we talk about GRACE, we really are talking about the process of planning your document for a particular situation. You identify your goals, think about them in terms of who you think your readers will be, and identify and develop arguments that are appropriate for the conventions of the situation, its context, your readers, and your goals. Finally, you plan how to manipulate the conventions of design to generate a document that expresses your personality and values effectively. If your analysis calls for a brief, straightforward document, your planning and writing may be almost instantaneous. But if the appropriate written response appears to be a substantial and complex document, now you're also looking at a complex process. That process itself—if it's going to extend beyond, say, an hour or so—is going to require planning and managing.

Planning Your Process: Project Management. This type of planning involves being constructively self-conscious about what you're doing when you write, asking what you need in order to manage your writing process successfully. The whole inquiry really boils down to two questions that you ask side by side: What resources do I need to do this writing task, and what resources, including people, do I have readily at hand?

The really essential resources you need are information and time to process that information. The other resource you're likely to need is the collaborative help of other people, whether from inside or outside your own organization. The questions in Figure 2.1 constitute a project-planning checklist, a process that Linda Flower (1989) calls *planning to do*, which is different from *planning to write.**

Asking these kinds of questions helps you begin to develop an effective plan for managing the project, which is distinct from but parallel to your planning of the text itself. And the answers you discover to these questions can lead you to make strategic decisions early on that can help you avoid some project disasters. For example, what if you don't see any way to get information that seems essential to successfully completing the project? In this case, you'd better know who is in a position to renegotiate the project, either redefining the project so you won't need the information after all or helping you get the information. What if key people in your organization are adamantly opposed to the success of this project? You need to know this early on. Otherwise, you'll be confused and frustrated by odd, inexplicable barriers that will appear in your way. Knowing about this opposition may enable you to change these people's minds. And even if you can't, you'll be able to discuss this constraint on the project with the people who assigned it to you in the first place so that you and they better understand how well you are actually doing, given the circumstances of this opposition.

This latter possibility points to an important truth: Some projects simply aren't feasible, at least not as they are initially presented. An essential benefit of strategic planning is that it helps identify what your limits are on a given project. If there are things you can't do, you will figure this out early and not waste time worrying about them. This kind of planning lets you work on what you *can* do, not what you *can't*. It also enables you to decide what to do about the things you can't do. Can you *satisfice*, or sacrifice some of the quality of the project and still achieve a satisfactory result? Can you recruit additional collaborators or negotiate for more time, equipment, or information? If you can't get crucial resources and you can't compromise quality

*Flower develops this idea at length in Chapter 5 of her book.

FIGURE 2.1 Project-Planning Checklist

How much time do you have, and how much do you need?

- What's the deadline for completion? Who says this is the deadline? Is it absolute, or is it negotiable? What would happen if you missed the deadline?
- What other demands are there on your time? What other projects will be in progress along with this one, and how will their timelines affect the progress here?
- Are critical intermediate deadlines embedded in this project—subtasks that will need to be completed before others can be done? Can these be managed in stages that will let you complete the overall project? Is critical information or equipment (computers, databases, technical monitoring equipment, etc.) available for only certain periods of time? If so, what are they? Will these resources be available in a timely manner?

What information do you have, and what do you need?

- What do you already know? What do you have readily available in your own paper files or in an electronic format? What information is readily accessible in other files?
- After you inventory what information you already have and what's readily available, what else do you need? Can you get it? If so, where? What if you can't get it? Can somebody else? What if they can't get it, either?
- What if you're not sure about what you need to know? Try talking with other stakeholders in the situation, key people in your organization or others allied with yours in this situation. If the relationship and the situation allow it, even consider talking with your prospective readers. Find out what they know and what they need to know. Another alternative is to try the "Ready, fire, aim!" strategy, described later in this chapter.

What people are likely to be resources and barriers for this project?

- Who else has a stake in the successful outcome of this project? Is their interest essentially the same as yours or opposed to yours?
- What should you know about the historical, organizational, personal, and political context of this project? What does this context tell you about possible allies, collaborators, and land mines as you go forward? Can you discover this information by talking with people or by reading related documents?
- Who has information and skills that complement your own and are important for this project's success? Can you recruit them as collaborators?

by satisficing, then this may be a no-win writing project and you should re-evaluate the feasibility of doing it at all.

We have just spoken of collaboration. In Chapter 3, we will talk at greater length about writing as a member of a team and suggest ways of using written documents to build teams.

Subtask 2: Generating

Obviously, when you're writing a document, you're generating text. But in that process of drafting and composing—and often before the composing process—you're also generating information. It's usually not so obvious which should come first: research or drafting. Traditional assumptions about the writing process suggest that you should do your research first and then write about what you've found out. In practice, though, the process seems to go in reverse at least as often. People often use their drafting to work out the essential ideas and arguments they want to make and then study this frame they've created to look for holes or information gaps. These holes or gaps then become the focus of their research. This is a version of the *Ready, fire, aim!* strategy we'll discuss.

Generating Information through Research. There are two likely problems about information: You may not have enough, or you may have too much. Increasingly in our information-saturated culture, the latter is the problem—finding and selecting what you need in a sea of irrelevant information. This situation is a good argument for the strategy of composing or drafting first, before you research. If you write until you get stuck at points where you lack information, then you will have a pretty good idea of what you need to look for.

In any case, before you invest a lot of time and energy in research, you should have a clear sense of your essential goal, your important arguments, and the information your readers will find persuasive as evidence to support those arguments. Having this focus, at least in outline, will save you a lot of wasted motion in your research. Remember that in the writing of business, your goal usually is not to cover a subject in complete, exhaustive detail and display your mastery of a wide range of information; instead, your goal is to cover the limited ground that's relevant to the issue at hand and to understand its context. This can be summarized as a maxim:

MAXIM

Limit and focus your research before you begin.

We will talk in more detail about research strategies and resources in Chapter 11. For now, the following will serve as a quick reference to several of the resources you should consider, including brief evaluations of them.

- **People.** We mention people first because they are, in fact, implicated in all the other resources as well as being key resources themselves. Most of the time, people will be absolutely your best information resource, and sometimes they will be your only resource. Access to them may be limited by all kinds of constraints, however, not the least of which is time—theirs and yours.

While people are often your most lively, current, interesting, and perhaps even most reliable sources of information, they are also the most difficult in many ways, exactly because they are lively—and alive. You can make a mistake with a book, use it stupidly or thoughtlessly, even get the information wrong, and come back to it the next day and set everything right. But if you talk stupidly or thoughtlessly with a person who is an information source, you may damage your credibility so that you cut yourself off from an important source. If this person is also a prospective reader of your developing document, your problem will be compounded.

So, your approach to a person who is an information resource has some of the same features as a writing situation. You have a goal—to get the information you need—and you have an audience, or reader. You may not have a particular argument, other than that you're a reliable person who deserves to be helped, but you certainly have conventional constraints. People who are being asked for information generally expect their questioners to know something about what they're investigating. They expect you to ask informed questions, not flail around on a random fishing expedition.

So, before you seek information from people, do your homework. Think systematically about what your goals and arguments are, about what information you already have, and about what more information you still need and why. Then, do as much preliminary research using other sources as you can afford to do, being sure you look in any places that would seem obvious to the person you're going to question. Again, this advice is important enough to be condensed into a maxim:

MAXIM

When you're going to ask people something, do your homework first so you don't ask stupid questions.

In Chapter 11, we'll discuss several specific ways of querying people for information: interviews, focus groups, and surveys.

Keep in mind, too, that a wide range of people may serve as knowledgeable sources:

- Your readers may be a crucial source of information. They may have exactly the technical or financial data you need to analyze in order to write the document you're working on. If this is a document they want and need, they will likely be eager to assist you by providing the information. But if this is an unsolicited document or even a controversial document, they may be reluctant to provide the information.
- Your supervisor, colleagues, or other people in your own organization may have key information.

- A wide range of other people—including clients, vendors, competitors, fellow members of professional or other organizations, and others who are networked with you, your organization, or your readers—can be sources of vital information if they are not proscribed by restrictions protecting intellectual property or other proprietary issues.

- **Traditional paper resources.** These may be in a local public library, an academic library, or an inhouse library in your organization or department. In any of these libraries, large or small, the librarians are likely to be extremely useful research partners and resources.

- **Electronic resources.** The variety and rate of growth of electronic resources is simply staggering. Online information services like the vast Dialogue database service—a comprehensive system that includes databases covering virtually every kind of professional issue—are available through commercial services like America Online and at most academic libraries. Most academic libraries, and sometimes surprisingly small local libraries, also have a variety of CD-ROM databases onsite. The information available through these electronic media is vast, generally more current than information available through paper media, and surprisingly accessible. In addition, these databases generally offer you the ability to employ sophisticated strategies for limiting, defining, and selecting the information you receive so that you can easily filter out the huge volume of information that is not relevant to your situation.

  Recently, these kinds of database text services have been joined on the Internet by World Wide Web (WWW) sites offering not only textual information but also often spectacular, sophisticated graphic displays. Increasingly, organizations and even individuals are designing and posting their own homepages on the World Wide Web. Your readers or your readers' organization may, in fact, have such a homepage that contains specific organizational information you need or that is linked to this information. Furthermore, electronic sources of information are becoming increasingly interactive. For example, listservs—electronic mailing lists or discussion groups, where people share information and talk about special interests—have been formed by the thousands around every kind of topic and interest. You can even broadcast a query to an appropriate listserv and expect to receive a range of interesting, useful, and informed responses.

  Another handy feature of this electronically mediated information is that often it can be downloaded directly to your own computer and incorporated into your developing document without rekeying. We will discuss this process later in this chapter. In addition, we will discuss electronic resources, along with other information resources, in greater detail in Chapter 11.

Generating Text. Generating text is the most visible, tangible, measurable act in the whole writing process. And for almost everybody, it is, at one time or another, the greatest source of frustration and even despair. In the next section of this chapter, we'll talk about using GRACE as a way of identifying specific questions, assumptions, or problems that may be hampering your efficient progress in producing an effective document. Here, though, we want to talk about more generic problems that can interfere with productive generating of text.

Probably the single most useful thing writers do to increase their productivity in generating is to monitor their own processes and keep reminding themselves, when it's time to generate text, that they should quit doing the other activities that are part of producing a written document. Because writing, the actual generation of text, really does tend to be difficult (and even embarrassing and painful), writers often find it too easy to do other things—often good, productive things, like researching and generating new ideas and information—instead of putting pen to paper or fingers to keyboard. Have you heard yourself or others say, in all good faith, "I'll start writing when I get the information about ____________"? When you hear yourself or a project colleague saying this, you should probably ask critically and carefully if you really need more information or if it's time to sit down and do some serious drafting. In sum:

◣ MAXIM

When it's time to generate text, don't do the other kinds of things that are a part of developing a document. Just draft the text.

One reason drafting (composing or generating text) is often painful for writers is that they prematurely jump forward to an editing or proofreading process in the middle of drafting. We all have a self-conscious internal editor, who worries about what others will think if we make a grammatical or spelling mistake. Obviously, the time will come in the life of this document and in the cycle of this writing project when this worry will be timely and appropriate. But the drafting stage is not the time. Constantly and compulsively stopping to worry about minute sentence- and word-level corrections will radically break up your concentration on the powerful generative ideas you need to keep in focus in order to generate your text: the overall goals you have for your readers, your arguments and the information you need to recite as evidence, and the social and stylistic conventions of form and expression. These are the issues you need to concentrate on as you draft your text. If, while you are trying to generate text, you find yourself worrying about what readers will think if you misspell a word, remind yourself that you'll have time later to fix these concerns. Also keep in mind that you need to start early enough on your drafting so you can, in fact, budget the time necessary for good proofreading.

Incidentally, you shouldn't feel that you're violating this advice if, during drafting, you read back over the text you've generated and even clean up sentence- and word-level glitches. Most writers, including us, read back over our text as we draft, reminding ourselves of the direction we've developed in an argument, the tone or attitude we've been developing, or the way we've been framing a sequence of events or ideas. This is actually a way of sustaining the momentum of drafting. And often, we tinker with sentences and paragraphs in the process of playing with this overall tone or direction. But we don't (or at least, we try not to) interrupt ourselves in the middle of drafting to worry about getting fine-grained detail just perfect when we know that the larger details of how to frame arguments—or even whether to make a particular argument—are still very much in doubt. We try not to spend a lot of time worrying about what potential readers will think about these specific details. These questions are the essence of the testing and revising process, not the drafting, generating, composing process.

So now:

MAXIM

Ready, fire, aim!

This maxim has become popular among writers about business strategy. It signifies a willingness to experiment and a readiness to adjust plans and processes based on what your experiment shows. Peters and Waterman's *In Search of Excellence*—a 1982 best-seller that describes case studies of eight different companies that achieved immense success through this kind of willingness to experiment and take thoughtful risks—was a key factor in popularizing this concept as an antidote to "the paralysis of analysis" in organizational management. This advice is helpful when you're stuck in your writing. If you're unsure what to write or how to write it, or even if you're unsure what information you need, try going ahead and writing as if you know exactly what you're doing. Get a tangible product out there that you and other people in your organization—maybe even people outside your organization—can begin to study, test, and evaluate. But realize that following this "Ready, fire, aim!" strategy requires practicing some moral virtues, too. First, it requires the courage to take risks by producing and sharing text that you know is flawed. And, just as important, it requires colleagues and supervisors who have the courage and faith in you to tolerate your producing text that is flawed and to work with you and your text in a spirit of confident experimentation.

Subtask 3: Testing and Revising

People often don't recognize that testing and revising is just as creative a process as the initial composing, generating, and drafting. As you begin to generate written language, composing it on a page or computer screen, you are drafting, or drawing out a vision that you're creating. To some extent, you are almost constantly testing this emerging vision even as you create it, checking to see if it holds together as a consistent, coherent picture and makes sense as a representation of your view of reality. But at some point, and often at several points, you are likely to shift to a mode where you are more systematically and consciously testing and taking a critical second or third or fourth look, maybe with the eyes of colleagues who also have a stake in this situation and this document. Your looking again in this critical and creative way is literally a re-vision. And this re-vision, when it is effective and productive, is often just as creative as the original vision. In fact, it often is the most creative phase of your writing because you now have text in your draft you didn't have when you started: ideas, arguments, and information; a sense of goals, readers, and context; and the most effective expression of your organization.

The processes of generating, testing, revising, editing, and proofreading text are complementary and dependent on each other. It's easier to generate text when you know you don't have to get it just right on the first draft. When you know that you—or maybe supportive colleagues—will come back later to find and fix flaws, you can give yourself permission to move ahead quickly in generating text. And if your initial drafting and generation of text is productive, then your later work with that text, especially in the testing and revising process, will become easier. If you invest too much time and effort in the initial draft, however, you're going to be much more resistant to changing it, based simply on your investment in it, not necessarily on its substantive merits.

Subtasks 4 and 5: Editing and Proofreading

Both the initial generating of text and the testing/revising that follow (which, as we've seen, also generates text) scan across all the elements of GRACE: considering goals, readers, arguments, the context and its conventions, and issues of how to express your personal and organizational values, personality, and attitudes. In the process of editing and even more in the process of proofreading, your focus narrows progressively toward more and more specific questions about conventions. In editing, the range of focus tends to be primarily at the level of sentences and paragraphs, though it can extend to larger elements or focus on specific words. Typically, in editing, you're asking yourself questions like the following:

- As I look at the overall structure of this document, does it consistently follow the conventions of organization for this kind of document? If it breaks those conventions, does it do so effectively, gaining greater readability or greater credibility for its arguments or greater expressive impact?
- As I look at paragraphs, do individual ones make sense as units of text? Do clusters of paragraphs also make sense as larger units of text? Are there clear transitional signals between paragraphs and between larger units of text?
- Do individual sentences conform to grammatical conventions? Are there inadvertent sentence fragments, run-on sentences, or other problems with structure? Even if the sentences are grammatical, can any be recast for greater clarity and more efficient comprehension?
- Are my key words the best words I can use—correct, vivid, and persuasive—especially in crucial sentences that provide major conceptual maps to my argument?

Finally, in proofreading, you're asking yourself questions like this:

- Is everything here correct according to conventions—both specific for this kind of document and general conventions for spelling, grammar, usage, and punctuation?

In Part VI, we will provide specific strategies for revising, editing, and proofreading, including techniques for finding and correcting particular sentence-level errors.

Using Metathinking and Metawriting to Manage Your Writing

We've taken the time to describe the major features in the dynamic of the writing process at some length because we're convinced that this kind of thinking about your thinking—*metathinking*—can help you manage your work and writing in a more productive, more satisfying way. Here are the most important implications we see in thinking about your writing process:

1. The mental and physical acts entailed in creating a written document tend to occur in a sequence that comprises mostly planning, at first, and moves through stages that culminate with proofreading, eventually. However, there's a lot of overlap among these different acts, and the sequence doesn't necessarily run in a straight line from planning to proofreading. For example, testing and revision naturally and necessarily take you back to more generating; editing may, as well. At the same time, you may find it comfortable or convenient to jump ahead in the process. So, give yourself permission to break the sequence at any point and do the things that seem most useful and productive.
2. But remember that jumps ahead, in particular, can dramatically reduce your productivity and satisfaction. In the later phases of the process, especially proofreading, your attention is directed to local, specific points in the text, while in the earlier phases, especially generating and revising, your attention is directed to global scans that take in the whole range of GRACE. If your anxiety about fine-grained correctness compels you to do premature editing and proofreading, you will run two major risks: First, your attention to the local issues will divert you from the global issues that should be your focus. At the very least, this will slow down your drafting and revising. Worse yet, it could even cause you to miss an important global issue or key argument. Second, there's a good chance that you'll invest a significant effort in getting one or more chunks of text just right only to find later, when you do one of your revisions, that this chunk of text shouldn't even be in the document.
3. On the other hand, it's probably not productive to be dogmatic about avoiding premature editing, either. For example, if a question about the spelling of a key word is nagging at and distracting you while you're trying to generate new

text around that word, you should give yourself permission to take time out and look up the word, rather than feel uncomfortable while you're trying to draft.

We believe the key to greater productivity and satisfaction with your writing lies in being aware of your process and having a vocabulary that lets you talk to yourself and your colleagues about your process. This way, you can identify what you're doing at any given point, especially if you sense that you're not being productive at that point, and you can ask yourself if you would be more productive if you focused on some other aspect of the process.

Using GRACE to Examine Your Assumptions about Your Writing Situation

"Aaaaargh! I understand the organizational context and history, I have the resources I need, I have a deadline that's reasonable, but I still can't write this!" All of us who write have encountered this experience much more often than we would like. Fortunately, there are some things we can do, beginning with asking ourselves some questions about the assumptions we bring to this particular writing project.

Assumptions about Your Goals

Suppose you're involved in a fairly complex writing project. Often, the ultimate goal of the finished writing project can look pretty forbidding at your first approach. In fact, the blank computer screen or clean sheet of paper can be a major source of despair early in the project. At this point, you need to remind yourself that you don't have to rip a final, completed written document out of your head all at once. You need to recognize that you are responsible for two different goals. While your ultimate goal is for the document to have a desirable effect on some readers, your immediate goal is one of production and project management.

All you need to do at that moment is get started—or if you're already started, keep moving. So, you need to give yourself a writing, researching, or editing assignment that you can feel confident doing and that will definitely move the project ahead. What part of the document do you feel most prepared to work on now? Can you work on this part right now? You don't have to start with the front of the document, such as the introduction or table of contents (though you certainly could, if this is where you felt most confident and productive). You could start with what will become the middle of the document or even the end. A professional proposal writer we know calls this the "Swiss cheese strategy": You break the big document down into manageable subsections, and then you just nibble away at the document in little chunks you can handle comfortably.

Or suppose your purpose is to persuade someone to take what will be a controversial action, and you're not yet confident about how to frame your crucial argument—or perhaps what that argument will be. Don't start with trying to frame just the perfect argument in just the perfect key sentence. Start instead by narrating the relevant facts as you understand them or by framing variations on your crucial argument or other possible arguments.

Until the document is finished, your goal as its producer is simply to keep moving ahead on the text at any point where you can. If you can't make progress working on a particular point in the document, then see if you can move to some other point where the resistance isn't so strong. What is the goal for this particular part of the document? Whatever the goal, it is likely to be more easily achievable than the overall goal of the entire document.

Assumptions about Your Readers

Depending on the situation and your own sense of your relationship with your readers, you may find thinking about them encouraging and productive or intimidating and unproductive. If you can imagine your readers being grateful to you for helping them—say, answering their questions and relieving their concerns—then you will almost certainly find this visualization productive. But if you have a hard time imagining your readers and their needs, questions, and assumptions, then it may be important for you to find out more about them, perhaps from other people in your organization who have dealt with them or perhaps even from your readers themselves.

In the worst case you may find it intimidating to think about your readers at all. Then, you may well want to visualize different readers for the time being or try to ignore readers altogether temporarily if this will enable you to move forward, focusing on complicated technical or other problems, finding and organizing arguments and evidence, and generating substantial chunks of writing. After you have text generated, you can revise it for the real readers. If your readers are still too intimidating, get help from colleagues, other people who know the readers, or the readers themselves—or from documents your readers have written. You can use this information in visualizing your readers with more confidence and in shaping and reshaping your text for them.

This manipulation of your image of your readers really is a variation on the "Ready, fire, aim!" strategy. First, you "fire away," generating text as fast and efficiently as you can while concentrating on your substantive issues and arguments and evidence. Then, having gained an increased confidence in your own understanding of these issues and your ability to articulate them effectively, you reread and revise the text you've generated, aiming it specifically at the readers you now understand more clearly and confidently.

In short, you don't have to use your readers as a focus for generating your text. If it's productive to think about them when you're composing, then you should. But if thinking about them intimidates you and blocks your production, then don't think about them until you have to in revising your document.

Assumptions about Your Arguments

We talked earlier about the fact that you don't have to frame the perfect argument before you start drafting your text. You can write your way into your argument, exploring the evidence to identify any holes you need to fill and to find and make explicit the arguments that may be implicit in that evidence. Or you may find that your arguments are tightly defined and laid out for you by the conventions and context of the situation, by opposing arguments, or by your own goals.

Assumptions about the Conventions of Your Document and Situation

Thinking about conventions while trying to compose your document is a lot like thinking about your readers. If you're feeling completely at sea, wishing you had some sense of form or structure as an anchor, you should think about some of the formal conventions and use them as a frame to start hanging your ideas and arguments on. If nothing else, this kind of thinking about the writing project helps you see ways to break the overall document into subparts that may be easier to get your hands around—smaller projects, such as writing a beginning section, a definition section, or a recommendations section. And thinking about these formal conventions can help you manage the task better by highlighting areas where you need additional information or help from colleagues. And if the writing situation is one that recurs frequently in your business and calls for a routine, generic response, the conventions may essentially write the entire document for you. For example, you may have memo or letter templates on your hard drive that are so complete all you need to do is fill in the appropriate names, addresses, and dates along with a few relevant facts.

On the other hand, if editorial voices in the back of your head are nagging you about conventional forms or styles and keeping you from writing productively, you should ignore the voices and conventions and write. Then, when you begin to revise, you'll have ideas articulated, arguments framed and elaborated, and language, in general, that you can start to shape along the appropriate conventional framework.

Although we almost all resist formal conventions some of the time, most experienced writers working in professional organizations usually want to think about and use conventions when they are developing documents in their work. You can use formal conventions in several ways to help, rather than obstruct, your generating text. If you have confidence in a conventional framework or superstructure, it can serve as a powerful project-planning and management tool.

In fact, people who work on large, complex writing projects often start with a dummy of the final document in a three-ring binder. The dummy typically has a table of contents and section dividers that are keyed to it. After you've laid out a skeleton of the contents, the next thing you want to do with a dummy is look for any boilerplate you can use—chunks of written text that are standard descriptions of your organization's mission, services, personnel, products, capabilities, programs, or clients. Often, the best source for both the content and format of your dummy is a similar document the organization has developed for a similar situation. Then, you can use the dummy to identify parts of the document that need to be created or modified. If you're working on the writing project as a team, you can also use the dummy to make assignments to team members and monitor each person's progress. A dummy can be a powerful project-management tool, helping you identify which parts of the document depend on completing other parts and anticipate potential bottlenecks to the timely completion of the document. As more pieces of the project move to completion, they are added to the dummy until it finally becomes the completed project.

Assumptions about Expression

Sometimes, people get squirmy and uncomfortable when they think about the ethos they feel they need to express in their text. Although they may prefer to write in a fairly personal voice, using lively, vivid, active words, they may feel obligated to write in a stiff, formal, distant convention, where their personal voice is muted and all people—including the reader—tend to disappear. Or maybe the opposite is the case, and their text lacks the appropriate formality. Or maybe there's some other dissonance between what their sense of duty says they should do and what they feel comfortable doing.

If you find your writing stalled by this kind of discomfort, probably the first thing you should do is ask whether your assumptions about the required kind of expression are actually correct. It may well be that your intuitive uneasiness is actually hinting at an important insight about your writing situation that you are sensing dimly and need to look at directly. Resolving doubts about expression is always a judgment call. There is always a risk here, no matter what you decide. If you're not feeling confident about making the call, consult with people whose experience and judgment you trust—including your supervisors and even your readers, if appropriate.

If you're convinced the conventions of the situation call for a particular kind of expression and you're still not comfortable composing in that voice, you can do several things. One option, if possible, is to bail out of this part of the project and have it reassigned to someone who feels comfortable writing in this kind of voice. Another alternative is to write the text yourself but in a voice that is more comfortable for you. This helps you generate text that embodies the essential arguments and evidence with reasonable speed and efficiency; you now have material that you or your colleagues can revise. This is still another variation of the "Ready, fire, aim!" strategy. Yet another alternative is simply to discipline yourself to generate text in the kind of voice that you believe is appropriate, even if it feels uncomfortable to you. In some ways, this may be the least satisfactory alternative, as well as the slowest and least efficient at the moment. Even so, it may be a learning process that you will need to go through if you will be doing more projects that require you to write in this kind of voice and personality. And you can still remind yourself that if you become absolutely stopped, you can try alternatives to get started again.

Using Computers to Generate, Revise, and Edit Your Writing

The technology we use when we write, whether alone or as a member of a team, can substantially affect the way we write and the results of that process. For most people, the technology of writing has come to mean computers although we may still use pen and paper for short, informal notes or memory joggers. Yet if we're going to make the best use of computers when we write, we need to think of them as more than fancy typewriters since they can be powerful tools for gathering and sharing information, generating new text, modifying boilerplate documents, and revising and polishing text.

Using Computers to Gather, Share, and Generate Information

Gathering and Sharing Information

As we've already suggested, much of the information gathering done nowadays involves electronic research. If you have an Internet connection, you might gather information by exploring the World Wide Web or by searching and retrieving documents from distant databases. You might also gather information from professionals participating in listservs—electronic discussion groups conducted via e-mail. Keep in mind, though, that if you gather information electronically, it's very tempting to simply download to your own computer anything that's remotely relevant to what you're writing about. Since this contributes to the information overload that can be a source of writer's block, you'll probably want to read and select only the specific information that is pertinent to your goals, your readers, and the arguments you want to make. Of course, as you save this information as a file on a disk or hard drive or print a hard copy, you'll want to be sure to key in the complete bibliographic details so that you don't have to search for them later when you use this material in your text.

You might also find that the information you need is available in company-maintained databases or spreadsheets. And you might be able to locate or develop essential data—about trends, means, standard deviations, and such—using statistical packages. Finally, you can map out this data visually using graphic design software. One of the advantages of using a computer to write, then, is that you can develop or find material employing a variety of software programs and simply import it into your word-processing document.

If you're writing as a member of a team, using a computer can also simplify the process of collaborating. Team members can write sections of the text on their own computers and e-mail them to the chief writer/editor of the document. This person can then download the text and incorporate it into the document. Or team members can save their text to a disk, which the project chief can import into the main document and then edit, ensuring that document design and expression remain consistent. In addition to sharing text, data, and graphic files, members of a team can also write together, using groupware developed for collaboration. Such groupware enables people to generate, revise, and edit text together, working on the same document at the same time using networked computers. In these ways, computers can be used for finding and exchanging information and producing and refining text as individuals share files or produce them collaboratively. And since computers enable writers to import text or copy and paste text into other files, they also prevent typographical errors from being introduced because new material doesn't need to be rekeyed.

Generating New Text and Modifying Boilerplate

Computers make generating new text and modifying boilerplate documents simpler than when such work was done with pen and paper or typewriter. For instance, we talked earlier in this chapter about two strategies that can help sustain your writing momentum as you generate text: the "Ready, fire, aim!" strategy and the "Swiss cheese" strategy. Generating text on a computer makes these strategies even easier to use. Writing on a computer can help you keep up with your thoughts as you "fire away," generating text as fast as you can. And if seeing the text slows down your production, you can even darken the monitor so that you literally can't see what you're writing. This may help you concentrate on your goals, your readers, and the arguments you want to make, instead of the little glitches that slip into your text in the process of keyboarding. And, of course, you can "fire away" with confidence, knowing that you can revise, edit, and proofread later. Writing on a computer also makes the "Swiss cheese" strategy easier to use. You can nibble away at chunks of text, in no particular order, knowing that you can insert your cursor anywhere and move around the text at will. You can even develop parts of a document in separate files and combine them later, moving the chunks around, integrating them, and smoothing them into a full text.

A word of warning, though, about the lures of writing on a computer is appropriate: Given the ease of making changes in text, it's tempting to tinker with the text prematurely, to edit and proofread before text is fully generated. Try to delay this process until you've generated a full draft. Also, given the ease of changing fonts, margins, headers, and the like, it's tempting to delay generation of text by tinkering with document design, as happens in the "Fox Trot" cartoon. Finally, remember that giving in to the temptation to tinker with sentences *without* looking at a printed copy can lead to a text that may be technically correct in sentence-level conventions and expression but flawed globally in terms of focus, attention to goals or readers, and arguments, simply because of the way screen size limits our window into the text.

Source: FOXTROT © 1993 Bill Amend. Reprinted with permission of UNIVERSAL PRESS SYNDICATE.

This ease of making sentence-level modifications can work to your advantage when you need to modify boilerplate documents for new readers. You'll probably have situations so recurrent in your job that you'll use or develop form documents. The letters shown in Figures 5.7, 5.8, and 5.12 are examples of such boilerplate documents. When you face such a routine situation, you can readily adapt the form document using word-processing software. You can perform a quick GRACE analysis to determine specific changes that you want to make for this situation and reader—modifications in the arguments or the details you use to support them, changes in the way you express your goals or those of the organization, and perhaps even simple changes in name, address, date, and the like.

Using Computers to Revise and Edit

Revising on Screen versus Revising on Paper

When you write on a computer, what you see—your window into the text—is quite small, even if you have a large monitor. When you're working with hard copy, your window is larger—at minimum, 8½" × 11" and possibly larger, if you lay out pages next to one another. Because the window is smaller when you're writing on a computer, re-envisioning a whole piece of writing or large chunks of it is more difficult and unproductive on screen. In fact, numerous research studies show that text revised on screen tends to be digressive, unfocused, chattier, and less concise. So, try to avoid doing a lot of global reviewing on screen.

To compensate for the small computer monitor window, always print a double-spaced copy of your draft and work from it, so you can determine the major revisions and reorganization you need to do. Also print hard copy for editing: Letters on a screen are hard to see with accuracy, and editing from print copy will increase your ability to catch omitted words, punctuation and grammar errors, and other sentence-level mistakes. Once you've reviewed your text on paper, global revision is easy. You can cut and paste chunks of text and delete phrases, sentences, paragraphs, and even sections with a few simple keystrokes. You can also easily correct sentence-level mistakes.

Using Spell-Checkers

Spell-checkers are wonderful resources if used consistently and carefully. The problem is that many people don't take time to use them, or, if they do, they use them at such random times in the writing process that it's easy to forget whether they've checked the final copy. It's important to make spell-checking a habitual part of your writing process. For example, you might want to spell-check right before you print to ensure that each document you send out has been scanned for spelling errors and repeated words. Also, make sure that spell-checking does the job you want it to by following these simple steps:

- **Look carefully at each word the spell-checker isolates.** The speed of editing with a spell-checker has a way of mesmerizing the eyes so that writers don't always clearly see all the letters of words the spell-checker locates. For instance, it's easy to overlook errors in the spellings of proper nouns and technical terms. Force yourself to slow down and look at each letter of any word highlighted by your spell-checker.

- **Check a print dictionary for the correct spelling of a word *before* you add it to your custom dictionary.** Many times, people are so sure of their spelling that they assume highlighted words simply do not appear in the computer dictionary. Before you make this assumption, check your dictionary. Adding a misspelling to the dictionary your software uses for spell-checking will ensure that the error continues to appear in your documents.
- **Make sure that your spell-check program is set up for American English, rather than British or Australian English.** As you probably know, the spellings of many English words vary among English-speaking countries—for example, *theatre* is generally considered the British spelling, whereas *theater* is the American.

Using the Search and Replace Feature

Word-processing programs typically have a search and replace function that enables you to scan your text for specific words, phrases, or punctuation marks. Once you have a complete draft, you can use this search and replace function to systematically look for misused words or phrases, punctuation errors, and wordy and redundant patterns. Saving this search and replace process for the editing phase will allow you to concentrate on your goals, your readers, and the line of your argument when you're drafting—in other words, to focus on communicating your meaning effectively.

Here are some suggestions for using the search and replace feature efficiently:

1. **To scan for commonly misused words or phrases.** Use the search and replace function to check for words and expressions that you often confuse. For example, if you know that you tend to use *effect* (a noun meaning "result") when you should use *affect* (a verb meaning "to influence"), you might want to regularly search for the two words and verify whether you've used each correctly. You might also check for typos you tend to make when you're typing quickly or focusing very hard on getting your ideas down on paper. Let's say that one of your favorite typos is writing *the* for *then* or *to* for *too.* Since spell-checking clearly won't catch such typos (since your errors are still words), you might simply search for the *the/thens* or *to/too* pairs when you're done drafting, and make sure that each occurrence of the word is correct.
2. **To scan for punctuation errors.** You can also use the search and replace function to check for your typical punctuation errors—either scanning for particular punctuation marks or for the language that goes with them. For instance, let's assume that you tend to use a semicolon when you should use a colon before a list. You might search for each semicolon in your text and check to see if it's followed by a list. If you find such an error, you can instantly replace the semicolon with a colon.

3. **To scan for wordy and redundant patterns.** Most writers tend to fall into particular patterns of wordiness and redundancy. One writer might frequently start sentences with *It is* and *There are,* while another might use a lot of *which* and *that* clauses. Once you're aware of such patterns in your own writing, you can use the search and replace feature to find and revise them. In each instance, you can decide how you'll edit the sentence.

4. **To scan for incorrectly spelled proper names and acronyms.** If you should need to change the spelling of a proper name or acronym throughout an entire draft, use the search and replace function. Change the spelling *globally*—that is, change every instance at once, rather than finding and changing them one by one.

5. **To scan for technical terms and specific data.** Once you're done writing your draft, use the search function to help you address the needs of secondary readers. Namely, locate particular technical terms that may need definition or data that may need further explanation—in the text itself, in attachments or appendices, or in a glossary of terms.

Part VI, The Business Writer's Quick Reference, provides additional strategies for revising your texts, information on editing to avoid exclusionary language and wordiness, and techniques for finding and fixing specific errors in punctuation, grammar, and style.

In this chapter, we've described four assumptions that can help you manage your writing process and thus make it more productive and comfortable. We've presented writing as an action as well as a document and have described the range of different actions, strategies, and processes that comprise this action. We've also suggested that monitoring your process will increase your control over your writing. And we've talked about the rich context in which writing occurs—a context that is increasingly collaborative. Finally, we've presented writing as one form of communication that occurs amidst the stream of communication within an organization.

In addition, we've provided strategies for analyzing your particular writing situation, your conditions and constraints, and your assumptions. We've examined the stages or subtasks of the writing process: planning your document and process, generating or creating text (including researching via people as well as print and electronic sources), testing and revising, and editing and proofreading. We've also explored ways you can use GRACE to generate and sustain your writing momentum. Finally, we've considered the common effects of using computers for writing and have suggested ways in which you can manage this technology to your advantage.

In Chapter 3, we'll introduce you to several genres of business writing; using them can help you manage your daily work and enhance group productivity and accountability. In particular, we'll talk about memos—in both print and electronic forms—and explore how memos, e-mail, agendas, and minutes can contribute to efficient collaboration and teamwork within an organization.

WRITING CHECKLIST

The following guidelines suggest ways you can use GRACE to shift your own frame of reference on any writing situation. They can help you find alternative ways of generating text more quickly by identifying the important ideas and issues you need to consider, and they can help you test the effectiveness of your text by seeing it from multiple angles. Remember that, especially in this list, different guidelines under the same category (e.g., Assumptions about Your Readers) are offered as *alternatives* to one another. So, the advice of one guideline may actually contradict the advice of the next.

For guidelines applicable to specific types of writing, see the Writing Checklists in subsequent chapters. For all of these guidelines, remember the superordinate guideline: Disregard *any* of this advice if it would cause you to do something that's inappropriate or silly for your situation.

☑ Assumptions about Your Goals

- Remember that you really have two distinctly different goals for any writing project: to create a desirable effect on your readers and to produce and manage your project.
- Break down a project into manageable pieces using the "Swiss cheese" strategy so you can nibble away at the project in chunks.
- Start a project by narrating the facts as you understand them or by framing variations of possible arguments.
- Keep moving ahead on the text until you're done with a project.

☑ Assumptions about Your Readers

- Visualize your readers if it will help you generate text that meets their needs, answers their questions, or addresses their concerns.
- Find out more about your readers from others in your organization or from the readers themselves.
- Imagine other, more receptive readers or ignore them altogether temporarily, if doing so will help you move forward.
- Begin by "firing away," generating text as quickly as you can while concentrating on your issues, arguments, and evidence; then, reread and revise the text for your readers.

☑ Assumptions about Your Argument

- You don't need to begin with the perfect argument; instead, use your writing to explore your evidence and identify the arguments implicit in it.
- Look for arguments that are laid out for you by the conventions, by the context of the situation, by arguments offered by your readers, or by your own goals.

Assumptions about the Conventions of Your Document and Situation

- Use dummies of final documents to help you generate large, complex writing projects.
- Use a similar document the organization has developed for a comparable situation to create a dummy.
- Use a dummy to make assignments to members of a project team and to measure progress on different parts of the project.

Assumptions about Expression

- If your assumptions about what is the appropriate voice for a document are inhibiting your expression, look more closely at your writing situation and perhaps consult with people you trust about conventions of expression.
- If you don't feel comfortable composing in the voice that's conventional, write the text in a voice that's more comfortable for you and then ask colleagues to revise the expression.
- Ask someone else who's comfortable with the conventional voice to write the text.
- Try to write quickly, mimicking the voice you feel is conventional, even though it feels uncomfortable.

ACTIVITIES AND PROJECTS

1. Here are some ideas you can explore in journal entries, e-mail, or a memo to a friend or instructor. You can also use your responses as a basis for small-group work or class discussion, sharing your ideas with your colleagues and comparing your responses:
   - Describe the sorts of writing you do. What types do you do most frequently? What are the goal(s) of this writing, and who are the reader(s)? What sorts of writing do you do least frequently? And what are the goal(s) and who are the reader(s) for this writing? Of the writing that you do, what type(s) of writing do you enjoy the most and why? What sorts of writing do you enjoy least and why?
   - Explore your writing background and your current writing strengths and weaknesses. What aspects of writing do you feel comfortable about and why? What aspects of writing make you uncomfortable and why? Also set up a game plan for addressing your writing weaknesses and for building on your writing strengths.
   - Explore your attitudes toward and experiences with writing. What is your current attitude, and what experiences in school, on the job, or in your personal life have contributed to it? Now, think about yourself as a writer. How would you describe yourself? Given that description, what specific goals do you have as a writer?

- Describe a time when you experienced writer's block. Explain the sort of writing you were doing at the time and explore why you blocked. What, in particular, contributed to your writer's block or made it worse? Also, if you managed to work through the block, describe how you did it.
- Write a journal entry in which you explore your experiences with research. Consider your experience (or lack thereof) with electronic resources as well as with print materials. Also talk about any background or special skills you have in generating information through interviews, correspondence, focus groups, and surveys. As you discuss this background, explore those elements of research that you find particularly satisfying and those you find extremely frustrating.

2. Complete assignment 1. Then, in a small group, share your journal entries and answer the following questions. Have someone in your group write down your answers so that they can be shared with the class.
   - Among your group members, how are your attitudes toward writing and experiences as writers similar? List five statements about your attitudes and experiences that all of your group members can agree upon.
   - What common goals can you agree upon for yourselves as writers? List at least five common goals.
   - What factors account for the differences in your attitudes toward and experiences as writers? List several factors that account for these differences.

3. Interview a professional in your field about the types of research that are typically done—both to find and generate information. What kinds of information are typically sought, and how do people usually find or generate it? Report on the results of your interview in a memo to your colleagues or teacher and in an oral presentation.

4. Interview a professional in your field about the process of writing in his or her workplace. How is writing normally done: Individually? Collaboratively? Both? If any writing is done collaboratively, what processes, benchmarks, or strategies are used to ensure quality and facilitate productivity and accountability? What technology is typically used in the writing process: Computers that are either stand alone or networked so that group writing can occur? Word-processing packages only or databases, spreadsheets, graphics programs, and so on? Report on the results of your interview in a memo to your colleagues or teacher and in an oral presentation.

REFERENCES

Flower, L. (1989). *Problem solving strategies for writing* (3rd ed., Ch. 5). San Diego: Harcourt Brace.

Peters, T. J., & Waterman, R. H., Jr. (1982). *In search of excellence: Lessons from America's best-run companies.* New York: Harper & Row.

Part II

Writing to Build Unity and Sustain an Organizational Culture

Chapter 3

Writing to Manage Daily Work and Enhance Group Productivity and Accountability

"The horror of that moment," the King went on, "I shall never, never forget!"

"You will, though," the Queen said, "if you don't make a memorandum of it."

—Lewis Carroll

We argued in Chapter 1 that writing is more important than ever before in contemporary professional and business organizations. The accelerating pace of all professional work—combined with the increased complexity of our tasks and relationships both inside and outside our organizations—places a premium on the ability to identify and capture the information we need to do our work, to make it stand still long enough to work with it, and to organize it in a way that's useful to ourselves and others. And writing is the means by which we do this. Written documents, from sticky notes to 300-page proposals, are time-binding and information-binding tools that help us get a footing in the slippery stream of data that flows around us.

In this chapter, we're going to talk about using written documents—generally, short documents—to increase the confidence and efficiency with which we manage our own personal work and help others around us manage their work with us. We'll first talk about memos, those microbursts of written text in both paper and electronic forms that seem to keep all organizations running. Then we'll look at two forms of organizational writing that are especially powerful management tools for organizing and coordinating collaborative teams: agendas and minutes.

Take a Memo!

As routine business documents, memos—both in the traditional paper medium and in the relatively new electronic medium of e-mail—are used daily to manage organizational activity. Both communication media fulfill similar functions within businesses and follow many of the same conventions; however, print memos have a long and well-established history as a communication tool, while e-mail is a more recent and less fully explored tool. Let's briefly consider these two types of documents and their divergent backgrounds.

The names of these documents provide hints about their differences. The word *memorandum*—which current usage has shortened to *memo*—has stayed in use basically unchanged from its original Latin: a memorandum is "a notation of something to be remembered," a memory note. It wouldn't be much of an exaggeration to say that modern organizations run on memos. These short documents, which fulfill a variety of functions, are almost always appropriate if you're communicating with someone in your own organization. If you're communicating with someone outside your organization, a letter is likely to be more appropriate than a memo.

Historically, memos have been print documents. Lately, though, organizations have begun to send memos electronically. Because these electronic documents, called *e-mail* (or "electronic mail"), are transmitted through networked computers, communication is instantaneous. According to a March 1995 Lou Harris and Associates survey, sponsored by Control Data Systems, e-mail is used by 88 percent of Fortune 2,000 companies and 93 percent of federal and state agencies; public and private organizations not yet linked to the Internet plan to be connected within the next few years (Moylan, 1995). Therefore, it's likely that you'll be sending both print and electronic memos in your workplace.

Since both sorts of memos fulfill similar functions, we'll begin by talking about kinds of print and electronic memo-writing situations and their memos; then we'll discuss strategies for writing memos and e-mail using GRACE. Finally, we'll explore the differences between e-mail and memos, talk about how these differences play out in the workplace, and walk you through a special version of GRACE intended to help you decide which medium is more appropriate for specific memo-writing situations. For simplicity's sake, we'll refer to electronic memos as *e-mail* and to print memos as *memos* throughout our discussion.

Print and Electronic Memo-Writing Situations

Memos and e-mail often serve as informal documents—family notes, almost, announcing a meeting time, for example. As informal documents, they help manage daily work in a variety of ways. Memos and e-mail are customarily used to announce new policies or procedures that readers need to implement or follow or to explain current policies or procedures already in effect. For instance, the operations memo shown in Figure 3.1 has this sort of informative goal; it announces the upcoming distribution of an important policy manual and describes what readers will find in it. In addition to furnishing information that readers need in their daily work, memos also routinely request information; ask for assistance in isolating, defining, or solving problems; and convince readers that business should be done in particular ways. In fulfilling these functions, memos and e-mail provide the day-to-day written communication that both establishes and reports upon the tasks that we do within our organizations.

While memos and e-mail often serve as informal documents, they can also discuss problems and issues that are complex. For example, the memo concerning reimbursement of professional dues and licensing fees (Figure 3.2) describes contradictions in the ways reimbursements have been handled and provides pertinent information gleaned from the contract, from a ruling, and from an administrative manual so that the parameters of the issue are clear. Finally, after the issue has been clearly defined, the memo asks that readers—members of an executive management team—establish a policy to deal with the issue fairly and equitably. Although this memo is short, a little over a page, it responds to a rather complex problem and, in doing so, establishes a task for the readers. And when the readers are done with

FIGURE 3.1 Informative Memo

June 12, 1997

SM-97-36
LM 97-35

To: All Schools and Lenders

From: Therese B. Bickler *T. Bickler (QLB)*
Chief, Loan Services Branch

Subject: REVISED *COMMON MANUAL* TO BE DISTRIBUTED

EDFUND, a Service of the California Student Aid Commission, is pleased to announce that the revised *Common Manual: Unified Student Loan Policy* will be distributed to all previous recipients in July. The California Student Aid Commission (the Commission) has been advised that the revised *Common Manual* will be shipped to the Commission the first week of July. The Commission will ship copies to all prior recipients immediately thereafter.

This edition includes all policy changes approved by the *Common Manual* Governing Board through April 1997, and distributed through Commission policy bulletins through May 1997. Policy changes approved through April 1997 include the new regulations published by the United States Department of Education in the Federal Register in November 1996, which become effective July 1, 1997. Included are policy changes related to the new cash management regulations, record retention, financial responsibility standards, guarantor reserves and conflict of interest, and due diligence.

If you do not receive your copy of the *Common Manual* by the end of July, or if you need additional copies, please contact EDFUND's Shipping Center by calling (916) 555-3189.

For more information please call:
Lender Services Division
(916) 555-9970
School Services Division
(916) 555-9842
P.O. Box 510
Sacramento, CA
94245-0625

State of California
Pete Wilson
Governor

FIGURE 3.2 Memo Defining an Issue

Memorandum

Date: June 13, 1997

To: Executive Management Team

From: Randolph Meyers, Chief, Internal Audits Branch

Subject: REIMBURSING PROFESSIONAL DUES OR LICENSING FEES

Recently, one of the Commission's claim schedules was submitted to the SCO for the reimbursement of a $175 professional licensing fee. The claim was rejected by SCO because the licensing fee to be paid exceeded the $100 available for reimbursement to the nonrepresented employees. The fee in question was for the payment of a two-year AICPA licensing fee. This and similar fees have been approved by Commission management and paid by SCO in the past. If a claim was questioned by SCO, a written justification by the manager would be sufficient to allow the fee to be paid.

We have researched this issue and determined the following:

1. According to the Bargaining Unit 1 agreement that ended June 30, 1996 (no new contract exists), represented employees may be reimbursed up to $50 per year in one job-related professional society or association of the employee's choice or for job-related professional license fees such as the Certified Public Accountant (CPA) license fee. Both parties agree and understand that a different amount of reimbursement, if any, may be provided to employees in the same or similar situations. It is our understanding that other bargaining unit agreements contain similar language for payment of professional dues and fees.
2. DPA memo 88-17, dated February 25, 1989, states that nonrepresented employees may be reimbursed for Professional Society Dues, up to $100, for one organization that is directly related to the employee's scientific or professional discipline. This amount is allowed on an annual basis. The memo refers to DPA Rule 599;.922.2 effective January 1, 1998. DPA stated that this position remains in effect.
3. The State Administrative Manual (SAM) is silent on this subject.

The SCO Claims Audit Branch was contacted to determine how claims for professional dues and fees were being reviewed and to discover why identical claims are not treated consistently. We were told that any similar claims paid previously may not have been audited, as the audit branch does not perform a 100% audit. We asked if a letter justifying the need and benefit for the association dues, etc. would suffice for payment of the claim. We were advised that payment of amounts greater than $100 for reimbursement of professional dues or licensing fees cannot be paid.

It appears that the focus of the amount paid for professional dues or licensing fees is on the $100 maximum for nonrepresented employees. A review of SCO claims paid for

(continued)

FIGURE 3.2 Continued

professional dues of represented employees revealed no inquiries or rejections of the requests. Many of the dues approved and paid for represented employees exceeded $50.

I am bringing these issues to your attention for the purpose of requesting that a Commission policies and procedures memo be issued on the subject of professional dues or licensing fees. This policy should set a standard for all Commission employees. It could restrict reimbursements for professional licensing fees or association dues offered to the Commission employees to the amounts allowed by DPA and the collective bargaining agreements. Another option is to agree to pay more than the restricted amounts with appropriate approval from the cognizant control agencies. Accordingly, this policy should ensure that all Commission employees are treated equally when requests are made and approval is given for reimbursement.

this task, the result will be a policy and procedure that will affect how this issue is handled in the future. (We will talk about policies and procedures documents in Chapter 4.)

Sometimes, when issues are complex, the memos themselves tend to be highly detailed, formal documents. For example, a proposal written for a reader inside the organization is likely to be written in the form of a memo, as is a review of a technical problem or a progress report on a project. If the document is long, it's likely to be a print document, rather than an e-mail, since the multiple screens required for lengthy e-mails tend to overtax readers' short-term memory. (We'll discuss the special constraints e-mail imposes later in this chapter, and we'll talk about longer, more formal documents—such as proposals, progress reports, and project reports—in Chapters 12 and 13.)

GRACE for Memos and E-Mail

Goals

So, let's assume that you've decided you need to write a memo or e-mail. What's your initial reading of the situation, and what's your goal for writing this memo? Incidentally, this is a good time to pause and double-check your decision to write at all. Is this a situation where a quick, face-to-face conversation or phone call—more direct, personal forms of communication—would be more effective than a written note? Is there a risk that your reader, especially someone whose office is right next to yours, would find a memo strangely aloof if the situation involves just a routine exchange of information? On the other hand, does the convenience of having a tangible message waiting in the reader's "in box" or incoming e-mail file make a written memo a natural and reasonable communication even in a routine, informal situation?

These questions about your reader's feeling for the situation and for you point to the two-dimensional nature of the writing of business. Every memo you write, whether paper or electronic, has both an *action* dimension and a *relationship* dimension. While the action dimension is generally apparent, the relationship dimension is more easily taken for granted. Yet, ultimately, the organizations where we work really are nothing but networks of relationships, so if we ignore the relationship dimension of a memo, we risk doing some actual damage to the organization itself. Notice how action and relationship goals intertwine and complement each other in the following questions:

- What are your specific action goals? Are you requesting information? Requesting that your reader(s) take some specific action? Requesting that they coordinate with each other or with you? Are you announcing an action you plan to take? Are you sharing information?
- What do you want your reader(s) to learn, believe, feel, do or refrain from doing as a result of reading your memo or e-mail? In particular, how do you want to affect your relationship with this reader? Do you want to create a more informal relationship? A more formal, reserved relationship? A more collegial relationship? A more hierarchical relationship? More cooperative? More adversarial (presumably not!)?
- What else do you want this text to accomplish? Are there reasons for laying out a trail here, either paper or electronic? Is this whole situation part of a wider context, and do you need to keep this context in mind, either explicitly or implicitly in this memo?

With these questions in mind, look at Figure 3.3. The reader and writer represent two different firms who are preparing to submit collaborative proposals for several different projects of considerable complexity. It's vital that both organizations have a clear written record of who's responsible for doing what.

Deciding upon the specific goals of your text is essential because these goals will influence your choices about appropriate readers and their needs, the sorts of arguments that need to be made, the particular conventions you'll follow, and the nature of the expression you'll use.

Readers

When you write a memo, you may be writing to just your supervisor or a colleague, or you may be writing to a wider audience in the organization. If your primary goal is to establish a paper trail for later reference, you may even be writing a print memo to the file. An example of a memo to the file would be what Ross Arkell Webber calls an "after action memo." In *Becoming a Courageous Manager: Overcoming Career Problems of New Managers,* Webber (1991) suggests writing a memo to the file after any major project that recurs on a regular basis—developing an annual budget, for

FIGURE 3.3 Memo Reflecting Both Action and Relationship Goals

Professional
Consultants

MEMORANDUM

To: Tucker Consultants
2150 4T Road
Gillette, WY 82718

From: CER
Thomas L. Barker TB

Date: January 29, 1997

Subject: Wyoming Water Development Commission Statements of Interest

This describes my understanding of our team on selected projects.

Project Name	Prime Firm	Subconsultant
Level I		
Douglas Master Plan	CER	Tucker Consultants
Riverton Master Plan	CER	Tucker Consultants
Level II		
Lander Water Supply Project	CER	Tucker Consultants
Newcastle Water Supply Project	Tucker Consultants	CER

I'll start updating our 254 forms this week and plan on completing the 255 forms by February 5 in draft form for your review. All of your information would be helpful next Wednesday (2/6). Later in the week new Statements of Qualifications including a technical approach and proposed team will be completed by Friday. That squeezes your review into late next week and over the weekend for the return of your comments and editing on Monday February 10. I would like to fax you one more final version before we mail it out on the 12th which could possibly slip to the 13th if materials are sent Federal Express. UPS overnight arrives after 2:00 p.m.

We anticipate typing your 255 forms on our software for the Douglas, Riverton, and Lander projects. If our workload remains punctual, Lori could probably handle the Newcastle 255 preparation also if you prefer.

Architecture - Engineering
Materials Testing - Surveying

2237 North Main Street Sheridan, Wyoming 82801 (307)555-1711 Fax: (307)555-5014 cer@wave.net Offices in Gillette and Douglas Wyoming

example. In your memo to the file, you review the project you have just completed, noting what went well and also noting problems you encountered. On the next project cycle, that memo, along with memos from previous years, becomes a checklist for project deadlines and a guide for avoiding pitfalls. You may be the only person who reads this memo to the file, or it may also serve as a guide for your collaborators on future projects or for the person who takes over the project after you move on.

Whether you're writing for others or for yourself, to a single person or to multiple readers, thinking about the needs of your readers will help ensure that your goals for this memo are met. Consider the following:

- Who is the primary reader—the person or people to whom your memo is addressed—and what specifically will this reader or readers want or need to know in order to accept and react to this memo as you would like them to?
- Will others read this memo? Sketch a quick egocentric solar system. What other people, in nearby or distant orbits, might have an interest in this situation? Will your primary reader pass on your memo to others for action or response? Should you copy this memo to someone else for their information? All these things considered, who will see the memo besides the primary reader?
- What will these readers need to understand the context of your memo? What is their prior background concerning the topic or issue the memo addresses, and what sorts of questions are they likely to have?
- How will readers use this memo, both now and in the future? And what do you need to include to make sure this memo fulfills readers' short- and long-term needs?
- What ideas, values, or feelings are readers likely to have concerning the topic of your memo or the arguments you plan to make? How can you accommodate these responses as you frame and support your arguments?

Arguments

The arguments you need to make in your memo will essentially be determined by your goals and your readers—within the bounds allowed by the conventions of the situation:

- What problem or opportunity do you see?
- Who's in a position to do something about it?
- What do you want readers to do so you or they can solve the problem or seize the opportunity?
- What arguments do you need to make that will persuade them to do this?

In Chapter 1, we talked about the two elements that are most often visible in an argument: a claim and supporting evidence—specific, concrete information that provides the grounds for the claim. We also talked about the fact that sometimes the argument is attenuated so that one of the elements is left unspoken. For example, in a routine, non-controversial situation—where the writer relies on the reader to infer the claim, rather than making the claim explicitly—the facts may speak for themselves. And we talked about the fact that it's less common, especially in professional discourse, to see an effective argument that's just a claim without any supporting data. A healthy skepticism is one common characteristic of professional discourse, whether it's in a corporate, governmental, or public service environment. Almost every idea or project has other ideas and projects competing with it for scarce resources: time, money, and people. So, the bare claim on behalf of almost any idea or project will likely be met with a request that says, in effect, "Show me!" or "Prove it!"

Even supported claims are sometimes met with skepticism. You've probably been in a situation where you laid out the evidence for your claim and somebody still wasn't persuaded. What did you do in this situation? What should you do?

Often, we think that people must not have heard or understood the data we've cited. Sometimes this is the case, and just explaining the data can help salvage a claim that's in trouble. But other times, you've probably found that opponents or skeptics of your idea were adamantly resistant to your argument and evidence, even though it was obvious to you. Arguing in this situation can be immensely frustrating. Often, one way out of this frustration is to unpack one more element of your argument, setting out the underlying values and assumptions that you believe authorize or warrant drawing the conclusions or claims you have drawn.

The fact is that, except in the most routine situations, the facts hardly ever really speak for themselves. We all look at the facts of our world and our work through a set of values and experiences that we use to focus and make sense of these data. This interpretative lens isn't usually visible to other people. Often, we're not even aware of it ourselves. We assume that the picture we see is the same one everyone else sees. If we find ourselves frustrated by other people's inability to see what's obvious to us, the underlying reason often is that they're not looking at the facts through the same set of assumptions and values that we are, so they're drawing conclusions that are at odds with our claims.

If we can show the internal architecture of our argument by opening it up and sharing our underlying assumptions, we significantly increase the chance that we can help someone else see the same connections we see between our data and claims. So, we need to remind ourselves, even in routine situations, that there are *three* essential elements to an argument: the claims, the data, and the underlying values and assumptions that shape our understanding of the facts and that connect the facts reasonably to our claims. We need to remember that a bare claim rarely gains assent, except in those situations where the facts are already apparent and persuasive to both us and our readers. We need to remember that a recitation of the facts—specific facts—is almost always an absolutely essential element of an argument. Finally, we need to remember that our readers may not share our crucial assumptions about how to interpret and value these facts.

Think about these three elements of argument as you approach your memo-writing situation. What are the essential claims you have to make? Imagine the kind of conversation these claims would generate between you and your readers. What questions or challenges are your readers likely to raise in response to your claims?

What specific information are they going to need to understand your claims? Are they going to understand the facts the same way you do, or will you need to lay out the underlying framework of values and assumptions that give the facts the meaning you see? All these questions, based on this imaginary conversation between you and your readers, are tests of how deeply you need to go into the layers of your argument. Often in memo-writing situations, especially for routine memos, the structure of your argument can stay pretty shallow. Often in these situations, your claim is non-controversial, the facts are relatively simple, and your readers share your underlying assumptions and values. If this is the situation, it would be silly (and wasteful of everybody's time) for you to present an elaborate body of data and recite all your underlying assumptions and values.

For example, look at the *Rhetoric Society Quarterly* memo that appears in Figure 3.4. The writer, Rex, spends no time whatsoever laying out underlying assumptions or data arguing that people should undertake the tasks he identifies in the memo. Rather, he assumes consent among his readers. All he includes is the basic information identifying who will do what and when. However, his first, very brief two-sentence paragraph does quickly touch not one but two of the deeper layers of his argument. The first sentence, *I thought I should let everyone know what we discussed at the meeting,* is, in effect, his appeal to an unspoken underlying value (*Information should be shared among those who need to know.*) that authorizes or warrants his writing the memo at all. And the second sentence, *What follows is what I understand to be what we decided,* is clearly an implied qualification of his following assertions about what everyone will do. He's allowing the possibility that he may be mistaken in his memory, that there may be exceptions to the plan of action he lays out in his following list. (We'll talk more, especially in Chapter 6, about these important strategies of limiting the claims you make in an argument.)

For another example, look at the memo in Figure 3.5. This memo was broadcast as e-mail to all faculty and administrators on the university's local network. Notice the deferential "thanks" at the beginning, which is repeated at the end. Also notice how deeply you have to read into this short document before you encounter anything that looks like a claim—the end of the second paragraph, where the writer, Sandy, says, at the end of a long, compound sentence, *and sometimes your project is going to have to wait in line until I can deal with it.* (Incidentally, notice also that she doesn't say the readers will have to wait; their *projects* will have to wait.) Notice the consistent pattern in the first three paragraphs, where the text is almost entirely narrative, an accumulation of data that produces her observation at the end of the second paragraph about projects having to wait. Then, at the end of the third paragraph, an underlying ethical assumption about fairness finally is implied in her statement of concern: *I am concerned that those people have had to wait—sometimes as long as eight to ten weeks for their projects—simply because offices or individuals whose projects had a higher administrative priority have come in at the last minute.* Finally, in her fourth paragraph, having implied her assumption about fairness to other members of the organization with publications projects, she makes her explicit claim, requesting that people plan their publications projects out of consideration for others who also have projects and deadlines. In the remainder of the memo, Sandy details the kinds of lead times that are

FIGURE 3.4 Minutes Assuming Readers' Consent

Rhetoric Society Quarterly

To: Sharon Cogdill, Sandy Foderick, Bob Inkster, Barb Seefeldt, and George Yoos

From: Rex

Date: June 21, 1994

Subject: Plans for *RSQ*

I thought I should let everyone know what we had discussed at the meeting. What follows is what I understand to be what we decided:

- We will get money from Michael for Sandy this summer.
- Barb and Sandy will set up the database for the membership.
- We will send out a letter of renewal in August of this year and do so thereafter every year. Those who do not renew will be purged from the membership.
- I will contact Cheryl Glenn to discuss her role as membership Chair. In the main, we want her to work on new memberships. Some of the ways she might do that would be to:
    - arrange ad exchanges with the *Central States Speech Journal, Rhetoric Review,* and *Rhetorica;*
    - write the institutions in *Rhetoric Review's* issue on rhetoric programs to see if they have a subscription;
    - contact speech departments to ask the same question.
- This summer we will put together and publish four issues: 23.2, 23.3, 23.4, and 24.1. (We may do 3 and 4 as a double issue.) George will work on 24.1.
- We will print at least 150 extra issues to cover new memberships.
- This fall and winter we will put together and publish three more issues: 24.2, 24.3 (possible double issue), and 24.4.

appropriate for different kinds of projects. It is especially interesting to note that she does not cite convenience for herself and her office as the underlying assumption that warrants her request. Rather, the whole narrative of the data and the invocation of the issues of fairness and consideration is couched in her concern for other members who have publications projects.

We have already subjected this memo to quite a bit of scrutiny, but there's still more that can be said about it. Spend a little more time reading the memo and thinking about how you would respond as a reader. What other features of the argument or the expression of the writer's presence behind the memo or of the memo in general strike you as notable? What are the strengths of the memo? Does anything strike you as problematic?

FIGURE 3.5 E-Mail Appealing for Cooperation

#28 23-MAR-1996 13:16:47.91
From: IN%"Barnhouse@TIGGER.STCLOUD.MSUS.EDU"
To: IN%"scsu-faculty@TIGGER.STCLOUD.MSUS.EDU"
CC:
Subj: Publications timelines

Return-path: <listserv@TIGGER.STCLOUD.MSUS.EDU>
Received: from [199.17.1.115] (199.17.1.115) by TIGGER.STCLOUD.MSUS.EDU
(PMDF V5.0-4 #15418) id <01I2OGO8WI40001RG4@TIGGER.STCLOUD.MSUS.EDU>
for scsu-faculty@TIGGER.STCLOUD.MSUS.EDU; Sat, 23 Mar 1996 13:11:40 -0600 (CST)
Date: Sat, 23 Mar 1996 14:11:07 -0600
From: Barnhouse@TIGGER.STCLOUD.MSUS.EDU (Sandy Barnhouse)
Subject: Publications timelines
To: scsu-faculty@TIGGER.STCLOUD.MSUS.EDU
Errors-to: listserv@TIGGER.STCLOUD.MSUS.EDU
Message-id: <v01510100ad7a00a72a05@[199.17.1.115]>
MIME-version: 1.0
Content-type: text/plain; charset="us-ascii"
Content-transfer-encoding: 7BIT

Press RETURN for more . . .

MAIL>

#28 23-MAR-1996 13:16:47.91
Thank you for opening up this message. I receive many requests for the production of publications throughout the year--nearly 250 on average, or nearly one every day. Some of these publications are large and complex, such as the bulletins, Outlook, the Viewbook for student recruitment, etc., and others are relatively simple.

It traditionally has taken a certain amount of time to produce these projects, but now that we are into desktop publishing, the process has speeded up to some degree. However, there still is the reality of not only editing, designing and proofreading publications, but printing them and delivering them on time. The process is a little faster than it was ten years ago, but there also are the logistics and priorities of the whole university to deal with, and sometimes your project is going to have to wait in line until I can deal with it.

During the past two months I have had a large number of requests from people who've wanted things to turn around almost immediately, and in most cases I have been able to accommodate these requests, but only at the expense of people who earlier came in with reasonable expectations who were willing to wait in line. I am concerned that those people have had to wait--sometimes as long as eight to ten weeks for their projects--simply because offices or individuals whose projects had a higher administrative priority have come in at the last minute.

What I'm asking is that you take a look at your expectations and, if you are one of these folks, try to plan a little further in advance before you bring your projects to me. Generally, these are the timelines preferred not only by myself, but Printing Services and most off-campus printers:
Press RETURN for more . . .

(continued)

FIGURE 3.5 Continued

MAIL>

#28 23-MAR-1996 13:16:47.91

Type of project	Number of weekdays: Preparation	Printing
	Total	Or, in weeks:
	Brochures/posters:	
Black, no photos	5	3
	16	1 (for duplicating only)
Black + one color	6-8	9-12
	15-20	3-4
2 colors + photos	13	13
	26	4-5
Poster w. cards	13	13

Press RETURN for more . . .

MAIL>

#28 23-MAR-1996 13:16:47.91

	26	4-5
Booklets:		
4-12 pages, 1 color	10	14
	24	5
16-64 with photos	22-25	15-20
	27-45	5-9
Invitations:	7-10	7-10
	14-20	3-4

If you can keep these timelines in mind, I will have a much better chance at serving everyone who makes requests in publications, not just the people with emergencies. Thanks for reading this.

Sandy Barnhouse,
SCSU Publications Editor
AS 207 SCSU

Press RETURN for more . . .
MAIL>

#28 23-MAR-1996 13:16:47.91
720 Fourth Ave. South
St. Cloud, MN 56301-4498
(612) 555-4030
BARNHOUSE@Tigger.SCSU.MSUS.edu

Conventions

Understanding and applying the conventions for memos and e-mail, including any particular conventions that are common in your organization, can help you manage your paper load. In Chapter 2, for example, we explained how busy writers often use conventional formats as templates that serve as reminders of what they need to say and as checklists for what they have said.Conventions govern what appears in the various parts of a memo or e-mail and provide guidelines for document design. We'll begin by talking about standard parts of both print and electronic memos and then move on to routine elements of format. Because these conventions were formulated when memos were always print documents and are strongly associated with the print form, we'll refer to both forms using the word *memo* for conventions that they share. We'll refer to *e-mail* when dealing with special conventions of the electronic form.

Guidelines for What Goes Where

A memo always opens with headings that include the name(s) and title(s) of reader(s), the name(s) and title(s) of the writer(s), the date, and a subject line that previews the content. In print memos, the subject line is often boldfaced so that readers can find it easily. In both print and electronic memos, the subject line should be specific so that readers can decide whether they'll read the document now or later or perhaps entrust it to someone for action or response. The specificity of the subject line is even more important for e-mail documents since all that readers see when they open their electronic mailboxes is a list of the subject lines of their incoming e-mail. Yet conciseness is important, too. Whether reading a print or electronic memo, readers should quickly get the gist of it. In addition, e-mail subject lines that are too long are clipped off by the formatting parameters of the e-mail program. So the trick is to come up with a subject line specific enough to let readers know what to expect yet short enough to be functional.

One of the standard formats for memo headings is shown in the memo on Correct Address Procedures (see Figure 3.6). Other formats for print memo headings are illustrated in the samples throughout this chapter, as are headings for e-mail. E-mail headings are, of course, controlled by the communication program used. As you enter the program, you'll be asked to provide the readers' e-mail addresses and the subject line. The program will automatically provide other information, such as the date and time and other preset routing information.

The actual memo text comprises an overview, the body of the memo, and a closing; as we'll discuss later, sometimes summaries and attachments are used, too. The overview, which can be one or more paragraphs depending upon the memo's length, consists of three parts. The first part provides readers with the context out of which the memo arose, including any communication that triggered the memo: say, a phone conversation, an e-mail or printed memo, a report, a meeting, or even a reader's request. Regardless of the specific content of this context, its intent is to quickly orient readers and lead them into the specifics of the memo. The second part of the overview narrows the context: It defines the particular problem or situation the memo addresses or clarifies the task(s) the writer performed before writing the memo. Once

FIGURE 3.6 Memo Illustrating Standard Format

Interoffice Memorandum

To: Chris Overton

From: Kelly Mayfield

Date: November 2, 1995

Subject: Correct Address Procedures

Last week we received a memo from Mark Thomas concerning the input of customer addresses into the computer system. I was not sure if we should change current procedures to keep in line with the memo, so I called the St. Cloud Post Office to find out its preference for address set-up. The following lists standard guidelines the Post Office would like to see us follow:

- Use all capital letters
- Include the direction last
  Example: 128 COOPER AVE S (not 128 S COOPER AVE)
- Use abbreviations for street or avenue designations and for directions (AVE, ST, RD, N, S, NW, etc.) rather than spelling out the words
- Omit periods after abbreviations as shown in the previous list item
- Omit "th" and "sh" after street or avenue numbers
  Example: 1283 8 AVE S (not 1283 8TH AVE S)
- Use two spaces after the house number and before the street or avenue name
  Example: 1822 25 AVE N (not 1822 25 AVE N)

Do you want us to change our procedures to follow the guidelines established by the Post Office? Simply let me know, and I'll implement the new guidelines.

the context and problem or task have been defined, the third part of the memo overview clarifies the memo's goal. And it often forecasts specific memo content (or headings) in the order in which they'll appear.

Sometimes this three-part overview results in a two- or three-sentence opening paragraph, which moves rapidly from the context of the memo to the task or problems it involves and to the memo's goal. This happens in the sample memo in Figure 3.6: The writer quickly establishes the context for the memo (another memo about customer addresses), the problem (whether the organization should change its current procedures) and the task (the writer's call to the post office), and finally, the memo's goal (to list the post office's preferences). Sometimes, though, with longer memos, orienting readers to the specific context and goal(s) of the memo may require a longer paragraph or several paragraphs.

If the memo is short, the overview paragraph is sufficient to ease the reader into the body of the memo. For longer memos, though, you'll probably want to use a summary segment, too. An optional section of one or more paragraphs—often called an *executive summary*—allows readers to decide if they'll read the whole memo or parts of it or if they should pass it on to someone for action or response. The summary itself appears after the overview and provides a somewhat longer, more detailed statement of the memo's goal; it also briefly outlines memo content, highlighting key data, conclusions, and recommendations.

The body of the memo (one or more paragraphs) presents the specific information readers need to understand the context (the situation, problem, etc.) to which your memo responds, to understand what you present (the procedure, policy, results), and to be convinced of the validity of your data, conclusions, and recommendations. Although it may seem commonsensical, the key for developing the body of a memo is to present information simply and from the readers' viewpoint, not yours. Think of readers' needs and interests, rather than your own interests and technical background, and develop the sorts of information readers need in the order and format that's useful for them. This means that you include only information the readers need to understand or know in order to respond to your memo appropriately; this also means that you omit information that focuses on unimportant details concerning your activities or technical tasks. Focusing on readers' needs also means using acronyms and technical terms *only* if readers are sure to understand them. (If you can't avoid using a term readers may not know, define it.) Finally, focusing on readers means that you organize your memos based on their needs, first answering busy readers' most common initial question: "OK, what's this about, in general?" You therefore move from general to specific.

If you follow this formal convention consistently, you will begin each section and each paragraph with an overview sentence that helps identify its gist and then fill in the details in the following sentences. This strategy will help keep your writing on task, and readers will appreciate your telling them what's coming next. You should use this convention when you include lists and graphics, too. Introduce the list or graphic with an overview statement so that readers will know the goal of the material that follows.

A second useful convention for organizing memos is to begin with what's most important to readers and move in decreasing order of importance. Such emphasis on readers' needs may mean that you begin with your key findings, conclusions, or recommendations or with background information readers need to understand this information. This emphasis also means that unless chronology is important, lists should be ordered from most to least important, based on readers' needs. Finally, instead of burying the most important information in the middle of a memo, section, paragraph, or list, where readers may miss it, present the most important information first—in your memos, your memo sections, your paragraphs, and your lists. Following these two principles—ordering from general to specific and from most to least important, based on readers' needs—will help you generate memos that make readers' jobs easier.

In a short, routine memo, you may simply stop when you've completed the body of the memo. But as a memo gets longer and more complex and as the personal, emotional, and political context becomes more problematic, convention calls for adding a chunk of text that provides appropriate closure. There are several conventional possibilities. If the information has been complex, you may want to close by summarizing the key points. If some action is to be taken—either by you or your readers—then you may want to close by summarizing the action and emphasizing its importance. If the context is emotionally or politically charged, you may want to emphasize feelings or relationships in the closing. And if the context is quite complex, it may even be useful to combine these conventions as you close.

So, the length and expressiveness of a conventional close can vary considerably. But in general, a closing of one or more paragraphs, depending on the length of the memo, can effectively restate any key data, conclusions, and recommendations that have been presented; the closing should also emphasize reader-oriented reasons for accepting your conclusions and recommendations. In addition, you can focus the closing on readers by making sure that any action or response is requested clearly, specifically, reasonably, and courteously and by offering appropriate information or assistance to facilitate that action or response. For example, you might provide phone numbers, e-mail addresses, or a meeting time/date to make sharing information easier. Also, if you plan to take subsequent action yourself, indicate how and when.

Sometimes, in addition to the memo itself, you'll want to provide detailed information that would distract readers from the line of your argument if it were part of the memo. In this case, use attachments. *Attachments* document your findings or provide detailed how-to information for readers or others they might ask to implement, check, or confirm what you include. When you use attachments, let readers know specifically what's in them or what they should do with them. Do so by introducing the attachments in the body of your memo and by listing them in an attachment notation at the end of your memo.

Guidelines for Document Design

Document design should help your readers quickly find information they need. For instance, memos typically use short, substantive internal headings to help lead readers smoothly through the text; such headings instantly show readers the content of each memo section and the overall structure of the document. Headings in the body of the text can help writers in several ways. First, you can use headings to check for the coherence of a section: If you can't write a concrete, precise heading, the information in that section probably lacks focus or purpose or is based on your needs, rather than your readers'. Revise the section until the focus and purpose are clear and an appropriate heading is obvious. Second, you can check headings to make sure your memo follows a logical progression that will make sense to readers; revise the headings for clarity, based upon what you find.

Headings should be consistent in placement and type treatment (e.g., use of bold or italic type, capitalization style, etc.) so that readers can easily find what they need. Figure 3.7 shows one common format for using headings in memos, and several other formats are illustrated in memo samples in this chapter. Notice that the heading information omits the writer's and reader's titles because they know each

FIGURE 3.7 Memo Illustrating Standard Format for Headings

St. Cloud State University
College of Fine Arts and Humanities
Dean's Office KVAC 111
(Phone) 555-3093
(Fax) 555-4716
Office Memorandum

To: Judy Kilborn

From: Sharon Cogdill *Sharon*

Date: 16 June 1998

Subject: LEO planning

I'm excited, actually, that we're planning on making some real progress with LEO. The WebTrends analysis for April/May took me by surprise. I didn't know that so many people are using our site, and the *kind* of user is different from what we planned for! Also, I didn't predict the way they're using it—they're not following the paths we set up, at least not the big numbers of people, and not in this 8-week assessment.

I think a large number of our users are not people in trouble with their writing (whom we defined as our target audience), but teachers and tutors at other institutions who work with those people. But, according to the WebTrends data, our greatest number of users come from aol.com, which means that it's not academic types who like what we've done, but people in small businesses (?) and at home. It's so interesting that our own university is not in the list of top ten users.

And the kinds of sites our real users are interested in seem different from what we expected from the local student population. Except for the number of 404s, which we can (and must!) fix very quickly and easily, I think this analysis is nothing but really good news for us, and we should use it to rejuvenate ourselves and give us renewed energy and focus.

As I see it, there are really three timelines for us to work out: immediate, short term, and long term. This memo will address the immediate and short-term plans, and we'll deal with the long term later.

Immediate

Housekeeping

Find out which files need URLs fixed, dates fixed, end-matter fixed, etc., work that doesn't require actual writing. We need to get through this work as soon as we can. It's not that hard; we just need to sit down and do it.

Find the dead links and FIX THEM! (I hate having dead links!)

Thank you for promoting the fine arts and humanities at St. Cloud State University!

(continued)

FIGURE 3.7 Continued

Kilborn, page 2

Mindful Revision
I think maybe we could work out a plan on what needs to be written next, soon, and long term. We did this before, I think, and I haven't followed through on my part very well.

Also, you have copies of files we have—like the description of the LEO project and some ideas about a page in front of the current homepage—that we could put up reasonably quickly and easily.

Short-Term Plans

Assessment
We need to decide when and where we want the server to write the WebTrends data so that we know when to go get it. Then we need to put those dates in our schedules so we go and get that data before it is overwritten.

The Graphics
The graphics need work. In some places, we should just replace them with tables. In other places, we need to get Keith to finish the work on them. We can fix the ones that need to turn into tables. The others, we need to define clearly and specifically and turn over to Keith, with some kind of plan for keeping up with him.

New Files
We would feel like we were making substantial progress if we got up any new files we could. I have some files written in the past we haven't gotten up. I'm pretty sure they haven't been through the full review process, possibly not even any of the review process. Somewhere in my old office are files written by Dean and Joe that we could begin to review.

You have some major print handouts that are already electronic that can be tagged and put up?

Conclusions

I think for this kind of long-term, ongoing project, we need to build regular interactions and worksessions into our lives. I'm looking forward to getting together on Monday and Thursday afternoons and making a little progress. See you then!

THANK YOU FOR PROMOTING THE FINE ARTS AND HUMANITIES AT ST. CLOUD STATE UNIVERSITY!

other very well and the memo is informal. In addition to consistent placement and type treatment, headings should also be parallel to one another. In other words, they should use the same grammatical form: noun with noun, adjective and noun with adjective and noun, verb phrase with verb phrase, and so on. For instance, the memo in Figure 3.8, which provides procedures for requesting software, uses the software names (adjectives and nouns) for headings. Readers interested in requesting particular software packages could simply scan down to find what they wanted.

FIGURE 3.8 Memo Illustrating Parallel Headings

Interoffice Memorandum

Date: June 12, 1997

To: All Staff

From: John Murphy

Division: Systems/Network Administration

Extension: 5998

Regarding: **Requesting Bank Standard Software**

The following procedures should be used when requesting any of the standard software currently supported by the network. We will install software within five business days of your request for all standard PC configurations. Unique PC configurations for specialized processing may take longer. Please call the Help Desk at 555-5980 if you have any questions.

Microsoft Office (Word, Excel, Access, PowerPoint)
Requests will be accepted in writing or cc:Mail to the Network Services Help Desk. Network Services Help Desk personnel will inform all users of their installation dates. Training on the use of the MS-Office applications is expected and should be arranged through the Training Division prior to installation.

Lotus cc:Mail
Network Services is installing cc:Mail for all bank personnel. Each division manager is being contacted to arrange for installation and training for all designated people. If you have not been contacted, please send your request in writing or cc:Mail to the Network Services Help Desk. Branch locations should wait to be contacted.

Lotus Organizer
The personal electronic scheduler is available for all interested parties who request it in writing or cc:Mail to Network Services Help Desk. Network Services will inform all affected users of their installation dates so the users can make the appropriate plans.

(continued)

FIGURE 3.8 Continued

Organizer is an enhanced network product that may not be applicable for all users. People should consult with their division head prior to submitting their request. Training on the use of Organizer should be arranged through the Training Division.

FaxWorks
Requests to add desktop faxing must be submitted to the Network Service Help Desk in writing. Because of the sensitive nature of faxing, divisional VP approval at a minimum is required in order to obtain this software. Users will be kept informed of installation and training dates.

Rlink (Remote dial-up to the LAN)
Follow the same procedure as indicated above for FaxWorks.

Visio
Visio is a software package ideal for creating various charts or diagrams. Requests for this software should be submitted in writing or cc:Mail to the Network Services Help Desk. We will assume that the user has some familiarity with the package and will not provide training at installation. Users should seek training advice through the Training Division.

In addition to using headings to help readers move through your memos more efficiently, you can also use paragraph breaks, lists, and graphics, when appropriate, to simplify the text and enhance readability. Use paragraph breaks to signal to readers a shift to a related major point, an extended example or detailed illustration of your point, or a transition between one major section of a memo and another. Also break up long paragraphs into shorter ones to enhance readability. Keep in mind that paragraphs in the workplace tend to be shorter than those in academic papers.

Break out lists from the text when possible, since lists are faster for readers to process than paragraphs. For instance, lists can be used effectively for detailing steps in a process or procedure or for enumerating key points you want readers to remember. Set off individual list items with bullets (•) unless you want to emphasize the number of items or the fact that the list is sequential. In that case, make the list an ordered list by using numbers to set off each item. The memo about Commercial ATM Deposit Services in Figure 3.9 uses both unordered lists with bullets and ordered lists with numbers. Notice that the sequence of items in the bulleted list isn't as significant as that in the numbered list, which delineates the steps in a process for initiating a service. Notice that all lists in this example use complete sentences and that the subjects in the numbered list are the people responsible for taking the actions specified.

In addition to using paragraph breaks and lists to enhance readability, you can also emphasize important information through the intelligent use of *white space*. For

FIGURE 3.9 Memo Using Unordered and Ordered Lists

Constancy National Bank

Interoffice Memorandum

TO: Commercial Officers and Associates

FROM: Maria Rosalo

RE: Commercial ATM Deposit Services DATE: March 8, 1997

Over the past year, we have seen an increased demand from commercial customers wanting to make deposits at ATM machines. To meet this demand, we have developed the Commercial ATM Deposit Service. Details on this service, which is available immediately, follow.

Eligibility

- This service is available to corporations, partnerships and sole proprietorships.

Service Description

- Corporate customers may use the Commercial ATM Deposit Services for deposits and balance inquiries only. Due to security issues, corporations may not use this service for withdrawals. Sole Proprietorships that sign an amendment to the ATM agreement may be eligible to make withdrawals.
- One ATM card will be issued per approved account. A maximum of three cards per account may be issued by special request.
- Customers must use a Constancy National Bank ATM or their deposit will receive decreased availability. Customers using foreign ATMs (i.e., machines not owned by CNB) may deposit no more than six checks per deposit envelope.
- There is no additional fee for this service at this time. Pricing will be reviewed during the next pricing cycle and may increase effective July 1, 1997.

Initiating Service

There are four steps to establishing Commercial ATM Deposit Service for a customer.

1. The customer must receive and sign a *Commercial ATM Deposit Service Agreement and Disclosure.* These forms are available from either Cash Management Services or Cash Station Services.
2. The officer must ensure that the customer's financial status has been evaluated. Each application must be supported by either a Summary Analysis from Credit Services or the company's financial statement. If the customer does not have a loan relationship, a Dun & Bradstreet report should be sent with the signed ATM agreement.
3. The account officer must approve the ATM agreement by signing the "accepted by" line. The completed agreement and supporting documentation should be forwarded to Cash Station Services, 3rd Floor, 5 South.
4. Upon receipt of the completed application, Cash Station Services will initiate the ATM service and forward the ATM cards.

Please call me in Product Management at 555-4449 with any questions.

instance, the date, time, and location for a workshop are highlighted in the memo in Figure 3.10 by leaving space around them. Similarly, allowing extra space around headings and between sections and even setting the margins of the document involve decisions about using white space.

FIGURE 3.10 Memo Using White Space for Emphasis

Interoffice Memorandum

Date: July 21, 1995

To: Distribution

From: Andrew Phillips

Division: Training and Development

Extension: 3440

Regarding: **Sexual Harassment Workshop**

People have a fundamental right to work in an environment that is free from harassment of any kind, including sexual harassment. Every employee has an individual responsibility for preventing sexual harassment in the workplace.

But what behaviors constitute sexual harassment? You have been scheduled to attend a workshop where you will learn what those behaviors are and acquire a framework for appropriate workplace conduct. You will also learn what to do when confronted with sexual harassment in the workplace. Ultimately, we are planning to have all management and supervisory personnel attend this course.

Date: Tuesday, September 8, 1995
Time: 9:00 a.m.–12:15 p.m.
Place: Board Room C

Please call Don Ruperts at 555-5889 by Friday, August 18th, to confirm your attendance or reschedule.

Distribution: Phil Benjamin
Ruth Danielson
Mick Evert
Robert Jamison
Andrea Kennedy
Mitch Lender
Jackson Mitchell
Randy Morton
Richard Nichols

Finally, you can simplify complex data by presenting it graphically. Having too much specific data in a memo can quickly overwhelm the text, so if you have a lot of numbers, for example, and want readers to still get the point you're making, consider using a table or graph of some sort (a pie chart, line or bar graph, or pictogram). But if you do use a graphic, don't make it do all of the work. Introduce the graphic to your readers (tell them where it is and what it shows), insert the graphic, and comment on key trends, statistics, and the like you want readers to notice. Also highlight key data in your text as well as incorporating it in the graphic so you don't run the risk of readers not seeing it: Not every reader looks at graphics. (We'll talk more about the use and design of graphics in Chapter 10.)

In summary, then, you can enhance the readability of your memos with thoughtful use of paragraph breaks, lists, white space, and graphics. Even in e-mail, where document design options are more limited, you should still consider the impact of format on your readers. You can, for example, still use lists and white space to emphasize key information and to make screen reading less cluttered, as the e-mails in Figures 3.11 and 3.12 illustrate. You can also make e-mail sentences and paragraphs

FIGURE 3.11 E-Mail Using White Space and Lists

#5 29-MAR-1995 12:57:39.18
From: SMTP%"Angelo_Gentile@STC.stcloud.msus.edu"
To: KILBORNJ
CC:
Subj: Future President Update

Date: Wed, 29 Mar 95 12:51:10 cst
From: Angelo_Gentile@STC.stcloud.msus.edu
Message-Id: <9503291751.AB00119@STC.stcloud.msus.edu>
To: SCSU-Faculty@tigger.stcloud.msus.edu
Subject: Future President Update
X-Ceo_Options: Document

CEO comments:
See attached.

CEO document contents:

Watch your e-mail Thursday afternoon, March 30, for an announcement on the naming of SCSU's future president. We are expecting a decision to be made shortly after 4 p.m. on Thursday by the State University Board in St. Paul. We will send that information to the campus community via DG and tigger as soon as it becomes available.

Press RETURN for more . . .

(continued)

FIGURE 3.11 Continued

MAIL>
#5 29-MAR-1995 12:57:39.18

A schedule of SCSU campus meetings that the future president will be attending on Friday, March 31, follows:

SCSU Presidential Visit

Friday, March 31, 1995

10:15 a.m.	Public welcome led by Vanguard students and Admissions Ambassadors with Terry Vermillion's Afro-Cuban Drumming Group outside (or in the lobby of) Administrative Services Building

Press RETURN for more . . .

MAIL>
#5 29-MAR-1995 12:57:39.18

10:30 a.m.	Arrival at President's Office Greetings by President Bess, Office Staff, Search Committee, President's Council Administrative Services Room 201
11:15-11:45 a.m.	News Conference
12:00-12:50 p.m.	Lunch with Student Government and Vice President David Sprague Garvey Commons
1:00-1:50 p.m.	Meet with leadership of campus bargaining units Administrative Services Room 201

Press RETURN for more . . .

MAIL>
#5 29-MAR-1995 12:57:39.18

2:00-2:45 p.m.	Meet with President's Council and Academic Affairs Council Administrative Services Room 201
3:00-4:00 p.m.	All Campus Reception Atwood Center Voyageurs Room
4:30-6:00 p.m.	Community Reception Radisson Suite Hotel

FIGURE 3.12 E-Mail Using Lists, White Space, and Emoticons

Date: Wed, 28 Sep 1994 09:14:15 +0600
Reply-To: mbu-l@unicorn.acs.ttu.edu
From: BMMAID@ualr.edu
To: Multiple recipients of list <mbu-l@unicorn.acs.ttu.edu>
Subject: Cyberspace Writing Center Open House Rescheduled

INVITATION

You are invited to attend the grand opening of one of several Cyberspace Writing Centers to be held on Daedalus MOO at either:

Thursday, October 6 at 8:00 p.m. to 10:00 p.m., Eastern Time or

Monday, October 10 at 11:00 a.m. to 1:00 p.m., Eastern Time

****

Free Balloon Rides and Green M&Ms
(virtual punch and cookies, too)
and yes, a view of the lake

****

The Cyberspace Writing Centers have been created for student consultations beginning this fall. Using a combination of e-mail and one-on-one discussion held online at Daedalus MOO, undergraduate students will have the opportunity to meet with graduate students across both state lines and time zones.

****

Please come and share your input on this project!

Instructions:

1. Telnet to logos.daedalus.com 7777
2. Connect as a temporary guest, using your first or last name and a password.
   Example: create mike mexico
3. Type: @linelength 80
4. Type: @wrap on
5. Type: @go VR/WCenter

(continued)

FIGURE 3.12 Continued

For those of you who may not have participated in synchronous communication before, now's your chance. It's easy, once you get the hang of it. The basic instructions are:

To talk, simply type a " followed by whatever you want to say. Example: "Hi, so this is the Writing Center? = Jackie says, "Hi, so this is the Writing Center?

To show third-person movement or emotion, such as "Jackie laughs" simply type a : followed by the action. The colon inserts your name automatically. Example:
:laughs = Jackie laughs.

****

Detailed instructions, including etiquette, paging, movement, setting a description of yourself (even for temporary guests), etc. can be downloaded by accessing the Multi-User Dimension Instructions available at: http://www2.rscc.cc.tn.us/~jordan_jj/Cyberspace/cyberproject.html

A full description of the Cyberspace Writing Consultation Project is also available at this web site.

VR/WCenters are also located at:

CollegeTown MOO at: TELNET next.cs.bvc.edu 7777 and
Diversity University MOO at: TELNET erau.db.erau.edu 8888

(but no open houses will be held at these locations)

****

Hope to see you there!

Jennifer Jordan-Henley
jordan_jj@a1.rscc.cc.tn.us

Barry M. Maid
bmmaid@ualr.edu

shorter than those of traditional memos to accommodate the small window into the text that accompanies reading on the screen.

When you think about the format of your e-mail, keep in mind that sending text electronically strips it of special style features—such as boldface, italics, and underlining—which are often used for emphasis. Because of these constraints of technology, two special formatting conventions have developed for e-mail: Use asterisks (*) on either side of a word you wish to emphasize and a single character of underlining (_) on either side of a word or phrase you wish to underline. So, for example, if you'd like to stress a word, it should look like this:

> The budget for next fiscal year *must* be approved by the deadline.

If you'd like to underline a word or phrase, perhaps the title of a book, it should look like this:

> They used Peter Senge's _The Fifth Discipline Fieldbook_ to develop training activities for building a shared vision.

Surrounding a word or phrase with asterisks or underlining can also indicate boldface and is often used to indicate headings.

We'll explore other elements, besides document design principles, that distinguish e-mail from print memos later in this chapter. However, the guidelines we've discussed to this point, summarized in Memo Conventions Simplified (see Figure 3.13), are shared by both print memos and e-mail.

FIGURE 3.13 Memo Conventions Simplified

Heading: One of several standard formats

OPTIONAL LETTERHEAD

TO: Your Reader's Name, Title in the Organization

FROM: Your Name, Title in the Organization

DATE: Month, Day, and Year (for example, September 13, 1998)

SUBJECT: **Short, Specific Memo Title Readers Can Use to Sort Mail**

C: **List of Names, Titles of those receiving copies**

Opening: One or more paragraphs, depending upon the memo's length

Step 1: Context—Provides readers with the context out of which the memo arose to quickly orient them and lead them smoothly into the memo.

Step 2: Problem and/or Writer's Task—Defines the particular problem or situation the memo addresses and/or clarifies the task(s) the writer performed before writing the memo.

Step 3: Memo's Goal and Content—Clarifies for readers the memo's goal and forecasts specific memo segments or headings in the order in which they appear.

(continued)

FIGURE 3.13 Continued

Summary: An optional segment of one or more paragraphs used *only* in long memos; often called an *Executive Summary*

- Allows readers to decide if they'll read the whole memo—or parts of it—or if they should pass it on to someone else in the organization for action or response.
- Briefly overviews memo contents, highlighting key conclusions and/or recommendations.

Body: One or more paragraphs, depending upon the memo's length

- Presents information based upon readers' needs and interests, rather than your interests and technical background.
- Provides all information readers need to understand the context—the situation, problem, and so on—to which your memo responds.
- Includes all details readers need to understand what you present—the procedure, policy, results, conclusions, recommendations—and to accept and act upon what you present.
- Organizes body segments based on readers' needs, moving from general to specific and from most important to least important.
- Includes short, substantive headings that lead readers quickly through your text.
- Formats your information based upon readers' needs—using paragraph breaks, lists, white space, and graphics when appropriate to enhance readability and emphasize important information.

Closing: One or more paragraphs, depending upon the memo's length

- Provides closure for readers and specifies action or response needed (if any).
- Highlights reader-oriented reason(s) as to why conclusions/recommendations should be accepted.
- Requests action or response clearly, specifically, reasonably, and courteously.

Attachment(s)

- Provide detailed information, when necessary, that would distract readers from the line of your argument, were the information placed in the body of your memo.
- Documents your findings or provides detailed how-to information for readers or those they might ask to implement, check, or confirm what you include.

Even given all of these conventions for memo organization and format, you'll have plenty of decisions to make about which conventions you'll follow:

- Does this situation typically call for a particular kind of memo, such as a policy or procedure document, a proposal or progress report, an issue memo, or the like?
- Does the situation call for a print or electronic text? (We'll provide specific guidelines for determining which medium is appropriate later in this chapter.)
- Do your readers follow guidelines for format and style beyond those given here that they expect to see in memos they receive?
- Given the particular context that triggered this memo or e-mail and the readers who will receive your document, do you need to attend to additional social or cultural conventions? If so, what are they?

Expression

To ensure that your memo accomplishes your goals and addresses readers' needs, you'll probably want to do some thinking about the expression that's appropriate, given the context in which you're writing:

- What image do you want readers to have of you? Why?
- In what specific ways can you create this image in readers' minds?
- Given your goals and readers, what tone do you want readers to hear? A formal, impersonal, matter-of-fact tone that de-emphasizes your presence? A more informal, personal tone that emphasizes your character or personality?
- What particular elements of style can help you develop the tone you'd like readers to hear?

The announcement in the memo appearing in Figure 3.14 comes from the supervisor of a design department that relies heavily on its computer network and frequently works under urgent deadlines with considerable pressure. The writer knows the news in the memo will cause some dislocation in people's schedules and that some people will be unhappy about it. The informality of the memo is an intentional effort to express the collegiality of the working group. The teasing suggestion that people *get a life* is intended as a sympathetic expression of appreciation for the group's hard work. The expression in this memo is certainly far different from that in Figure 3.2, concerning reimbursement of professional dues and licensing fees; in that memo, the language is formal and precise—at times, downright stuffy. The sentences are long and complicated, and the writer attempts to establish firmly the contractual elements that pertain to the issue.

As these examples show, your goals and the readers you're addressing—as well as the arguments you want to make—will affect the expression you choose. And the conventions of the medium you select will often influence your expression, too. For instance, as we'll discuss in the section Expression (pp. 95–99), one of the most

FIGURE 3.14 Memo with Informal Closing

Engineering & Design Memo

Date: November 19, 1997

To: Engineering and Design Department

Copies: Manufacturing Department, ACS, Inc.

From: Rupert Retskni

Re: **Upgrading and Rewiring Design Lab November 28**

ACS, Inc., has scheduled the server and network for upgrading and rewiring to begin on Friday, November 28. This means we will not have normal access to our design software on the network from Wednesday evening the 26th until Monday morning December 1.

As you'll recall, we've known this was coming for some time, but, as we feared, the announcement of the exact timing doesn't give us much time to adjust. If you were expecting to work through that weekend, you'll have to coordinate with ACS on either the 24th or the 25th to download anything you need. Better yet, why don't all of us get a life and plan to take Friday off?

Enjoy the holidays!

noticeable differences between memos and e-mails is that electronic discourse tends to be more informal. Yet in the example e-mail we just looked at, such informality would have been inappropriate, given the widespread readership and the official nature of the e-mail's content and goals. In other words, based on your goals and the image you want to project to readers, you may purposely override standard conventions and use, for instance, formal expression in what is normally an informal medium. This sort of adjustment isn't unusual, considering the complexity of many business writing contexts. Thinking systematically about all of the elements that comprise the writing context, though, can help you write with GRACE, whether you're writing a memo or letter or using a print or electronic medium.

Assume, now, that you have access to an e-mail system and are considering whether you should write a print or electronic document. What sorts of differences exist between e-mail and memos, and how do these differences play out in the workplace? In addition, what sorts of assumptions do people hold about each of these media—one print and one electronic—and how trustworthy are these assumptions? Considering these differences may help you decide which medium is more appropriate in a particular writing situation.

Key Differences between Memos and E-Mail

Differences between memos and e-mail include speed, the appearance of the page and its impact on writers and readers, and the extent to which writers and readers can control other people's access to the documents.

Speed and Effects in the Workplace

One of the most significant differences between memos and e-mail is the speed of communication. Memos must be routed through the organization, and even if this occurs within the same site, it may take hours or days. In contrast, e-mail communication occurs almost instantaneously from one computer workstation to another, whether the workstations are in different places within the same physical site or across the country or the world. The instantaneous nature of e-mail enables messages to cross electronic space so quickly that some users may actually find themselves e-mailing back and forth in something approaching a real-time conversation, asking one another questions, providing clarification, information, or further elaboration of ideas.

Of course, some e-mail programs encourage real-time conversations by enabling users to "phone" their readers and converse through writing. And MOOs and MUDs*—virtual spaces made for synchronous communication—are being used more and more often instead of actual meeting rooms, especially when workers are separated at distant locations. To meet in a MOO or MUD, participants using the Internet all log onto the same computer from wherever they're located. In this virtual space, they meet in "rooms" to talk about projects, assignments, or whatever is on their meeting agendas.

Given the speed of e-mail, it's no surprise that users have dubbed text sent via the U.S. Postal Service "snail mail" and have touted e-mail's ability to promote fast turnaround time for responses. Martin Moylan's (1995) enthusiasm in "E-mail Mania" is typical: He argues that e-mail is

> faster than Federal Express, cheaper than "snail mail" or faxing, and often more efficient than a phone call. And not only does it zip messages and documents around the world but it also moves anything—spread-sheets, pictures, audio and video clips—that can be converted into a digital format. It's e-mail, and it's arguably becoming the preferred means of communication. (p. 1E)

In fact, e-mail does break through barriers of both time and place. Let's say, for instance, that you have a deadline on a project and need information from another employee who is traveling overseas. It doesn't matter if she's in Asia and it's the

*A *MOO* (mud, object oriented) is an Internet-accessible, text-based environment. In a MOO, you can move from room to room and interact with others who have also logged into it, as well. A *MUD* (multiple-user dimension, multiple-user dungeon, or multiple-user dialogue) is an Internet-accessible virtual reality originally designed for gaming and usually based on role-playing adventure games. MUDS are electronic spaces where people can play games or gather to talk and make friends (Smith, 1996).

middle of the night. You can e-mail her, and the message will immediately be transmitted to her electronic mailbox. When she wakes up in the morning, she'll find the message waiting for her and be able to reply to your inquiry at once. You won't need to play telephone tag or wait for the mail to deliver an overnight package. Because e-mail breaks the cycle of telephone tag and delivers text with a speed that's impossible with print documents (and can, in fact, save the price of paper as well as the price of delays), e-mail is often used for internal communication, especially if the reader is in another location. And when readers outside the organization have Internet access, e-mail frequently replaces letters, too, blurring the boundaries between internal and external correspondence, between letters and memos.*

Page Appearance and Its Impact on Writers and Readers

Another significant difference between memos and e-mail is the size and nature of the page. With a print memo, the window into the text is actually 8½" × 11", which reveals approximately 45 to 48 lines of text. For a one-page memo, this is the whole text. With longer memos, writers and readers can always flip pages quickly or even separate the pages and lay them out side by side to see the entire text. But the page for an e-mail is actually a window: the screen of the computer's monitor. It can be as small as 12 lines or as big as 24 lines if a larger monitor is used. Writers and readers can scroll to see the whole text, but this takes more time than flipping pages. The effects of this small "page" size on readability are substantial.

Text is notoriously hard to read onscreen—for both writers who are composing messages and for readers trying to decipher them. Because the writer's window into the text is limited by screen size, it's more difficult to keep the big picture in mind; therefore, e-mail tends to be less hierarchically organized than memos. And since it's harder to see the whole text, large-scale revision is also harder; writers therefore tend to revise more superficially. This is particularly true when the editing capabilities of the e-mail program are limited, making moving around in the text difficult. In fact, the editors on many e-mail programs are so poor that a great deal of effort is needed for the writer to move back through the document and clean up typographical and grammatical errors. Also, something about the resolution and the evanescence of the letters on the screen makes mistakes more difficult to see. E-mail messages, then, often have grammatical and spelling errors, and as a result, users usually have a higher tolerance for these errors when they read e-mail text.

This bending of the conventions of paper text is tolerated because of the speed and immediacy of e-mail. Some writers revert to the informality of a telephone conversation, ignoring many of the standard English rules of punctuation and capitalization. Such errors can lead to communication problems or degrade the confidence readers have in writers—in spite of the general convention of a higher tolerance for errors.

*Keep in mind that the speed of e-mail depends upon your server. Some systems route e-mail instantaneously; others queue e-mail messages and send them in packets every few hours.

Writers who use e-mail effectively tend to accommodate the difficulties resulting from limited screen size in several ways. First, they make the text easier to read—both for themselves and their readers—by using shorter sentences and shorter paragraphs, sometimes separated with a line of white space. Second, careful writers of e-mail reread each e-mail message closely before sending it to their readers. In fact, if it's an important message, they tend to reread at least twice: once focusing on organization and content and once checking for mistakes in grammar, punctuation, and spelling. If the e-mail text is extremely important or long and complicated, careful writers often compose the message using a word-processing program, print their message to see what revisions need to be made, revise the text, and then upload or copy the text to e-mail. In fact, if the text is long—more than three or four screens—you probably ought to reconsider whether e-mail is the most effective medium for this message or if the message truly needs to be as long as it is. Given the limitations of readers' short-term memory, many writers have difficulty with e-mail that requires multiple screens.

Expression

E-mail tends to be more informal and personal than memos—often feeling more like a telephone conversation than writing, as we just noted. Perhaps because of the instantaneous nature of the medium, e-mail seems to many people more like speaking than writing. And e-mail, in fact, incorporates many of the characteristics of oral communication, including the following:

- E-mail is likely to be chattier than memos, and offtask conversation of the sort shown in Figure 3.15 is not unusual.
- Clipped or incomplete sentences, like those illustrated in Figures 3.15, 3.16, and 3.17, are common, as well.
- Informal vocabulary and speech patterns (including the clipped sentences just noted) may slip into e-mail documents so that the language used is somewhere between print and oral language. Figures 3.15 and 3.16 demonstrate such a mix of written and oral discourse.
- Pronoun forms may be as inconsistent in e-mail as they are in speaking. For instance, the language of e-mail tends to shift as naturally as spoken language from the singular *everyone* to the plural *their.*

Some of the features of e-mail tend to encourage this informality and chattiness. For instance, the reply function of many e-mail programs allows writers to insert their responses directly after statements their readers have made, thus interspersing their text with that of their readers. Interspersing the writer's and reader's texts in this way mimics the give and take of actual conversation, as Figures 3.15, 3.16, and 3.17 illustrate.

Emerging conventions, too, tend to bolster the informal nature of e-mail. For example, as Figure 3.17 shows, many users forego standard capitalization in their e-mail. *Emoticons* also tend to be a frequent feature of e-mail; the three following

FIGURE 3.15 E-Mail with Offtask Conversation

```
#50     4-APR-1996 10:37:57.63
From:   TIGGER::KILBORNJ
To:     TIGGER::BATES
CC:     KILBORNJ
Subj:   RE: Fall Non-trad Orientation

>Great. How about Wednesday, Sept. 11th at 11am in the Women's Center,
>North Colbert? I will send confirmation and call once I have exact
>numbers. Latter is not usually known until the day before.

Works for me.

>Totally unrelated, are you, by any chance, a season ticket holder at
>the Ordway? Looking to buy 4 for LaMancha in August. Open box office
>is not until June. Bill

No, I wish I were since we're interested in going to LaMancha too. Let me know if you're
successful in hooking up with a season ticket holder.

Press RETURN for more . . .

MAIL>

#50    4-APR-1996 10:37:57.63
Judy K
```

emoticons represent, respectively, a smiley face, a wink, and laughter— :), ;), :D. These and other basic graphic cues, suggesting the author's intended tone or mood, are becoming conventions of electronic discourse. So are abbreviations like *imho* ("in my humble opinion"), *btw* ("by the way"), *IOW* ("in other words"), *pls* ("please"), and *TNX* ("thanks")—many of which actually originated in print text.

These conventions are, of course, still in flux. But the organizational uses of e-mail during its relatively brief history already show that its informality, as well as its perceived privacy, can potentially help build community within an organization—especially for employees whose only contact is in ongoing electronic communication. Figures 3.15 and 3.16 show the sorts of community-building chatter that tend to slip into e-mail. This expressive, conversational quality of the medium, with its tendency to build rapport, also makes it powerfully well suited for coordinating, negotiating, and managing workload and facilitating team projects. On the other hand, e-mail's conversational informality, combined with the fact that it is more difficult to read, generally makes it unsuitable for longer, more formal documents, such as proposals.

FIGURE 3.16 E-Mail with Clipped, Incomplete Sentences

#14 16-DEC-1995 15:00:22.98
From: TIGGER::KILBORNJ
To: SMTP%"teaching@tigger.stcloud.msus.edu"
CC: KILBORNJ
Subj: LSI information

Roseanna:

Many, *many* thanks for reminding me about the Kolb test information. I was going to send this info off last Friday when the storm moved in; many questions from students and staff about whether SCSU was closing blew this important "to do" right out of my head.

>>Would like to order the Kolb instruments for the Faculty Forum as
>>soon as possible to ensure they are available in time. Please
>>forward info for ordering;

McBer and Company is the publishing firm who sends out Kolb's Learning Style Inventory. At this point I'd call directly: (617) 555-7080

Press RETURN for more . . .
MAIL>

#14 16-DEC-1995 15:00:22.98

In case you want McBer's address, here it is:

McBer and Company
137 Newbury Street
Boston, Massachusetts 02116

>>I'll order and plan for 25 participants, although if you have a
>>few extra copies (10-15?) in the office and could bring them along
>>just in case, I will reorder and supplement your office should more
>>than 25 faculty come for the Forum.

I have no more legal copies of the test. Perhaps it would be better to order 50 since faculty at the Forum might want to use them later--although I have no idea of what the cost is now for a packet and what your budget looks like. Each packet does include an explanation about how to use the test and how the results might be interpreted. Let me know what you want to do.

Press RETURN for more . . .
MAIL>

>>It is difficult to plan, especially since
>>this is the first Forum. Looking forward to this.
>>
I'm looking forward to it too.
Thanks again for the reminder about this.
Judy Kilborn

FIGURE 3.17 Conversational E-Mail Using Reply Mode

From: TIGGER::SCOGDILL "Sharon Cogdill" 1-FEB-1996 16:43:54.29
To: TIGGER::KEWING
CC: SCOGDILL
Subj: RE: leo

Keith -

>We have been working on a new color palette as well as a more efficient
> way of creating graphics for the LEO pages.

yow! thank you, thank you.

> We also would like to suggest using some
>of the more current markup (e.g., tables) for some of the pages.

good idea

> One of our
>students has also designed an entirely new and very contemporary logo
>(retaining the lion head) that uses the color palette and is quite attractive.
>We are developing a button that could be used to return to the homepage
>and would allow title headers on the pages. There are a few design issues
>we are attempting to resolve. What we are planning to do is work on the
>graphics for two pages, redo the markup and then see how they look before
>we go too far. We would like to have your input (as always) and would
>maybe like to test on a couple students before we go forward with a major
>overhaul.

sounds good to me

>There are also one
>or two graphics where we think the communication can be improved by
>subtle changes, not in the content so much as the design, but we would like
>to go over these with you and Judy before we make the changes.

We normally meet on Thursday afternoons, or at least *they* do--the last 2 weeks I've been hacking away at my colleagues with the old verbal machete knife. So far, I'm winning, and this last one was a doozy.

>Also, I've forgotten the password to LEO, which is probably just as well.

scog laughs immoderately.

FIGURE 3.17 Continued

>I think I have generated some excitement here about LEO, and have a grad
>student available to help with some of the markup.

You are an angel, and I owe you big time.

>Let me know if and when we can get together (preferably around a blazing
>bonfire).

or over a heavy, brutal red. or an insouciant sirah. or a keg even.

I'm forwarding this to judy, joe, and kelly. possible interest from another
student today.

sharon

Assumptions about the Media

The most significant differences between memos and e-mail may be people's assumptions about the control they have over the two media: In particular, people assume that e-mail memos, in contrast to print documents, are ephemeral and private—like words spoken in conversation. In fact, they're not. The following sections examine assumptions about ephemerality and privacy and explore the effects of these assumptions in the workplace.

Perceived Ephemerality

When people write memos, they generally spend some time thinking about their readers—both the readers they're addressing and others who might see the memos. But something about the act of corresponding electronically—perhaps the speed, the few keystrokes it takes to send the e-mail from computer to computer, or perhaps the evanescence of the letters on the screen—makes it easy for people to forget their readers. In *Connections: New Ways of Working in the Networked Organization,* Sproul and Kiesler (1991) talk about people's tendencies to ignore readers' needs and to transgress social boundaries in e-mail because they perceive the communication as transitory: "When people perceive communication to be ephemeral, the stakes of communication seem smaller. People feel less committed to what they say, less concerned about it, and less worried about the social reception they will get" (p. 42). Therefore, e-mail writers may spend less time considering readers' needs and addressing them than they did when they wrote with typewriters or pen and paper. E-mail writers, who are isolated from the social clues of face-to-face communication or the formality of a paper trail, also tend to be more self-revelatory and blunt. Furthermore, without the availability of facial expression, intonation of voice, and other nonverbal emotional buffers, the message can come across as quite belligerent. For example, see Figure 3.18, an e-mail where a secretary refuses a faculty member's request for assistance with a book order.

Sometimes, lack of social awareness can lead to tone problems more serious than bluntness. *Flaming,* which Victor Vitanza (1996, p. 495) defines as "a nasty, ugly, or harassing message," occurs when people forget their electronic readers and use stronger language than they would on paper. These inappropriate messages occur, in part, because of the informality and perceived privacy of the medium (discussed in the next section). Problems with tone also occur simply because people need to be more aware of the impact of the medium on readers. An example of this is typing an e-mail memo in all caps; this message will probably be read as though its writer is yelling (or at least angry), regardless of whether that is his or her intent.

Perceived Privacy

When people write memos, they know they're leaving a paper trail that readers can follow, now and in the future. Writers generally don't assume the memos are private, and if they do, they rely on the confidence of their readers to protect the privacy of the paper artifact or even to destroy it. Of course, a reader can violate this confidence and make and distribute copies of the document. Or some unauthorized person could violate the reader's security and take the document.

However, writers of e-mail sometimes forget that these messages can be printed and copied or forwarded to other readers in the organization or—if the writer is

FIGURE 3.18 Blunt E-Mail

From: TIGGER::RSCHAEFFER 3-NOV-1995 10:55:21.19
To: JANNSENK
CC:
Subj: SPRING BOOK ORDERS

Ken:

You are teaching 102, 205, and 563 Spring Semester. I don't have time to research which books you used previously for these courses. My job is to submit your book order, not to fill out your book order form. Imagine how much time it would take for me to do this for everybody!

Either fill out the book order form and give it to me to submit, or call the two bookstores with your order.

MAIL>

THATCH by Jeff Shesol

Source: By permission of Jeff Shesol and Creators Syndicate.

hooked up to the Internet—to readers anywhere in the world. A celebrated example is Scott Zobrist's personal e-mail account of the rescue of U.S. Air Force pilot Captain Scott O'Grady from Bosnia. Zobrist's e-mail to friends in the military, written hours after the rescue operation, included information about weapons systems, radio frequencies, and flight procedures—information Captain O'Grady refused to give reporters. The e-mail account of the rescue was disseminated rapidly and, without Zobrist's permission, was posted on America Online. It's clear that Zobrist wasn't thinking about AOL's three million subscribers or the visitors to numerous websites where his e-mail was posted when he wrote to his military buddies, still flushed from the success of the dramatic rescue. Zobrist assumed the e-mail was for his buddies' eyes only.

People also assume that they can control who sees e-mail. For example, people assume that when they hit delete, the e-mail no longer exists. Yet many organizations regularly store e-mail on server backup systems, where the messages can be retrieved by the employer or members of law enforcement. So, although former National Security Council staffer Oliver North deleted hundreds of e-mail messages related to the Iran-Contra scandal, the messages were preserved on backup tapes. These messages were used in court, along with e-mail from other members of the Reagan administration; in fact, hundreds of these deleted e-mail have been published electronically and in print (Blanton, 1995). Clearly, North's e-mail wasn't private.

Employees need to remember that if an e-mail system is owned by a company, the employer has the right to inspect the contents of employees' messages, and many organizations do, in fact, check employees' e-mail. Twenty-five percent of businesses contacted for a survey by *MACWORLD* admitted eavesdropping on employee computer files, e-mail, or voice mail (Bacard, 1996). Therefore, you should assume that any e-mail that you send or receive at work probably is not private. Also assume that you should never write anything in an e-mail that you wouldn't mind sharing with your colleagues or your boss. Finally, remember that the delete command doesn't make e-mail disappear; it can still be retrieved from backup systems. In other words, remember that e-mail messages, like print memos, leave a trail that can be followed.

Determining If Your Memo Should Be Print or Electronic

When you're getting ready to write, if you have access to an electronic mail system, you'll probably want to decide whether e-mail is appropriate for the message you plan to write. The following list of questions is a special iteration of GRACE, intended to help you decide whether an electronic or print memo is more appropriate for a specific writing situation:

Goals

- Is one of your goals to respond to specific reader ideas or information? If so, can you imagine the document you plan to write interspersing your response with the reader's text—almost like the give and take of an oral conversation? If you answer yes to both of these questions, you should probably use e-mail, rather than write a traditional print memo.
- Is the immediacy of e-mail an advantage—or perhaps a priority—given your goals in this writing situation?

Readers

- Assuming now that e-mail will meet the goals of your communication, does your reader have access to e-mail, and does he or she use it regularly?
- Would the reader prefer an electronic or print document in this situation?
- Does the reader need the information you plan to provide immediately, or is there time for the memo to be routed through normal channels?
- Is the reader in a different location—perhaps another city or country—and in a different time zone?
- Is the e-mail likely to be short enough for the reader's short-term memory to process it effectively? Or is the document likely to be long enough that having a hard copy would be useful?
- Is the reader likely to need to share the information with others? If so, do those people have access to the e-mail system so that the reader can simply copy the e-mail to their accounts? Or would it be easier for the reader to share this information with colleagues using a print copy?
- Does the reader need a print copy for the organization's files or for frequent consultation—perhaps in meetings?

Arguments

- Is your argument subtle enough, complicated enough, or important enough that you want to encourage the reader's reflection by sending it in print?
- Is your argument long enough that it would be easier to read—and to write and revise, too—if it were in print?
- Does your argument require such strong awareness of the reader that a print document would be helpful in maintaining your focus on reader needs?

Conventions

- Does your organization conventionally send this kind of document via print or electronically?
- Do the constraints of privacy—confidential client or customer information, for example—and the organization's guidelines for dealing with sensitive information require that this message be sent via print?
- Is this a situation that conventionally relies upon a paper trail?

Expression

- Do you want the document to take advantage of the chatty informality of e-mail? Or would you prefer that your document be more formal and impersonal?
- Are the emotional stakes invested in the document high enough that the distance print provides would be useful for you in controlling tone? In other words, are you angry, upset, or worried about the situation and in danger of flaming if you use e-mail?

Collaboration and Teamwork in Organizations

The Writing of Teamwork: Agendas and Minutes

The confusion and frustration; loss of time, energy, and money; and general grief that result from miscommunication are everywhere: in our homes and family relations, in our businesses, in government, in the schools, in volunteer organizations, and certainly in international relations. Each of us brings different assumptions, values, priorities, and needs to each situation. Each of us sees, hears, and reads each situation differently, and sometimes our interpretations are widely different, with results that are sometimes funny but too often costly and perhaps even tragic. While writing something down never guarantees that we will all read a problem, plan, work assignment, or any other agreement the same way, having a written record generally reduces the risk of misunderstanding, often substantially. When you are a member of a team working on an important and complicated task that has a critical deadline, you don't want misunderstandings about who's going to do what and when. Agendas, minutes, and project timelines help make visible your questions and decisions about tasks and deadlines and also about the relationship of interdependent tasks. The crucial process questions we listed under Assumption 4 in Chapter 2 need to inform your agendas, minutes, and written timelines.

Developing an Agenda with GRACE

Goals. The word *agenda* literally means "a list of things to do." In that sense, listing your goals is almost equivalent to making your agenda. So, this is an obviously useful way to start working on your agenda—simply listing, in the order that seems most useful or logical or appropriate to you, the questions, problems, or projects that need to be addressed in your meeting. But in addition to these "To Do's," you will have some process goals that will influence your agenda. You want this meeting to be productive; you want the people attending to stay on task and not get distracted by issues that may be interesting but don't speak to the central points you need to address in order to accomplish the main tasks of the meeting. Consider for a few minutes how the agenda from a Midwest bank, shown in Figure 3.19, establishes the ground that will be covered in the meeting and thus encourages productivity.

Readers. Like the items on your agenda, the distribution list of your agenda should be straightforward, for the most part. Is there a clearly defined membership of the group that's meeting? They are your obvious readers, and they should be included in the distribution list (or on the "TO:" line) of your agenda. If there is no predetermined membership, then you should try to identify your readers based on their relationship to your goals for the meeting. Who needs to come to this meeting? Who needs to contribute to this discussion? Who has expertise that's needed? Who has other resources that are needed? Who's affected by the action or discussion items on your agenda? Ethical and efficient process calls for you to notify people of your plan to meet if they are likely to be affected—either positively or negatively—by any decisions or actions coming out of your meeting, whether they are going to participate in the meeting or not.

In particular, if any items on your agenda will be controversial, it may be useful to ask which of your readers will have which kinds of interests in these matters and what kinds of arguments and evidence they are likely to bring to the meeting. Remember that one of your goals for the process of the meeting is for the group to stay on task and work effectively on the issues. Notice, for instance, that the agendas shown in Figures 3.20 and 3.21 indicate which people are responsible for what topics, when they will address the group, and how long they will have. This sort of detail in an agenda helps keep meetings on target, helps people plan their individual work, and keeps the group on task. And sometimes, even as you write the agenda, you can head off unfair delaying tactics, emotional "red herring" arguments, or readers' hidden agendas by specifically requesting that particular people bring to the meeting specific information or arguments or statements of specific interests. You can't always eliminate tactics that delay or subvert an effective and ethical meeting process, but you can take a big step toward maintaining appropriate control of the meeting through a thoughtfully written agenda.

Arguments. Again, the basic things you want to persuade people to do are straightforward. First, you want to persuade the appropriate people to come—the people you've identified who have the information, the expertise, and interests or stakes in the agenda that make them key, productive participants. Second, you want to persuade these people to prepare appropriately for the meeting. You want them to come prepared with the necessary written materials or other items that are the topics on the agenda or relate to them. Participants need to have done their homework so they are prepared to offer appropriate arguments, evidence, creative or critical ideas, and even good questions that will move the meeting toward accomplishing its goals.

FIGURE 3.19 Agenda Clarifying Tasks

interoffice
MEMORANDUM

to:	MEMBERS OF SERVICE NETWORK #1		
	Robin Eckerts	Chris Erickson	Muriel Hanks
	Ron Hanson	Jerry Jackson	Wei-Ching Lu
	Anne Morris	Ed Murray	Cindy O'Hara

from: Ann Marie Thomas and Rachel Cicharz

re: Third Quarter Service Network Meeting

date: August 22, 1995

copies: Dana Roe
Chris Shore

Our next meeting will be held Tuesday, August 29, 1995, at 11:30 a.m. in Training Room #3. We will be discussing Opportunities to Serve for second quarter and sharing the information we received in the Service Network Leaders meeting.

AGENDA

1.) Dana or Chris from the Investment Center will present their Referral Incentive Program that will begin in mid-September and will be available to answer any questions you have about their products and services.
2.) Service Network #12 is planning a Halloween event at the Montrose Nature Center on Saturday, October 28. We will discuss the activities planned for this event and the possibility of putting together a group of volunteers from our network.
3.) We will discuss the current plans for putting up this year's Christmas decorations.
4.) Service Network Leaders will provide information on the M.A.P.S. program kick-off.
5.) We will discuss the current system for coordinating bank tours and come up with an alternative solution.

Bring a bag lunch and join your service network! If you cannot attend but have information that you would like to share with the group, please call Ann Marie at 8359 or Rachel at 8403.

We hope to see everyone there!

Third, you want to persuade everyone to come to the meeting with an attitude of mutual trust and cooperation and a sense of optimism that any conflicts among them or with you can be resolved.

This last persuasive task may be a great challenge if the agenda includes items that are controversial and entail personal, emotional, or financial investment by your

FIGURE 3.20 Agenda Showing Tasks and Times

Credit Card Club

February 5, 1997
1:30 PM to 3:30 PM
Conference Room E

Team Members: Jeanette Bilot, TL; Rozanne Dodson; Janet Treece; Elaine Kellogg; Jeana Cederburg; Jean Maduli; John McPhee; Reg Lockard

Mission Statement: The Credit Card Club, upon recommendation from the team leader, deliberates and revises methods to improve the efficiency and effectiveness of the Commission's Cal Card Process. If warranted, the policy and procedures are modified for executive staff approval. The team leader or representative presents the recommended changes to the executive staff.

Agenda

1. Meeting Summary	Jean	1:30
2. Letter to General Services	Jeanette	1:35
3. Dollar Limit for Credit Card	Reg	1:45
4. Executive Approval for Rocky Mountain Bank	Reg	1:55
5. Purchase Criteria (Executives)	Reg	2:00
6. Review List of Prohibited Purchases	Jeanette	2:20
7. Restrictions on Tagging Equipment	Reg	3:10
8. Meeting Evaluations	Jean	3:25

Notes

Futures Files:
- Credit Card Dollar Limits and Purchase Criteria
- Quarterly Meetings in the Future
- Revise Policy Memo for CSAC

readers. Anger, fear, and distrust may tempt some people to try to subvert the meeting and the resolution of the issues altogether. Your challenge is to allay that distrust as much as possible. Usually, your best tactic for doing so is through as complete a disclosure as is possible. If your readers suspect that there is a hidden agenda behind your written one, then they will almost surely distrust it and you and try to subvert that agenda. So if there are conflicting interests, you may be wise to identify and briefly describe these conflicts in the agenda. And you may suggest and even request strategies for dealing with these conflicts.

FIGURE 3.21 Agenda Illustrating Futures Files

June 4, 1997
9:00 a.m. to 4:00 p.m.
ARB Production Room

StyleGuiders

Team Members: Kathy Simon (Leader), Donna Jo Barnes, Jan Botha, Kathy Coleman, Jean Cortez, Jorge Esquarez, Pauline Fass, Harry Gardner, Amy Gieck, Pam Mullen, Christy Martin, Benjamin Peters, Anna Saldana, Cathy Wakefield

Mission Statement: To create a style guide to serve as a foundation for all internal and external communications in EdFund and the California Student Aid Commission.

All Day Agenda

1.	Good Morning—Ground Rules—Rest Rooms	Jean	9:00
2.	Pat Davis Design Update/Number of Guide Books	Christie/Kathy	9:15
3.	Priority Lists/Draft Table of Contents (Handouts)	Kathy S.	9:40
4.	Establish Letter Specifications (Block Style)	Kathy S.	10:10
5.	Recommendation for FAX Cover Sheet	Pauline	10:30
6.		Morning Break	10:45
7.	Recommendation for Envelopes	Jan	11:00
8.	Recommendation for Memo Format	Amy	11:20
9.	Recommendation for Voice Mail and Pagers	Kathy S.	11:45
10.		Lunch Hour	12:00
11.	Policy on Use of State Seal for CSAC	Christie	1:00
12.	DAPP Process/Forms/Numbering System	Ben/Jorge	1:15
13.	Jargon/Acronyms	Harry	1:40
14.	Grammar	DJ	2:00
15.		Afternoon Break	2:30
16.	Letter to Mgmt. Recommending Manual	Kathy S.	2:45
17.	HOW 7 Provide Training and Price Break	Kathy S.	3:00
18.	Page Layout/Miscellaneous Items	Kathy S.	3:10
19.	Assignments	Pam	3:55

Notes

Futures Files:

- Establish Training Components/Kathy C.
- Determine the number of tabs and what they should be.
- Who will own and maintain Guide when completed.
- Departments in Organizations and Formal Titles/Kathy C.

Conventions. The outline for a conventional agenda for a business meeting that appears in Figure 3.22 comes from Michael Thomsett's (1989) *The Little Black Book of Business Meetings.* Notice how his detailed suggestions for describing the topics lead to a full, ethical disclosure of the agenda. Note, too, how he calls on the writer of the agenda to assert appropriate control of the meeting by specifying what is to be accomplished, both in the overall meeting and relative to each topic. Consider also how he suggests promising an ending time as well as specifying a beginning time for the meeting. Promising a definite time for quitting—and then honoring that promise—is one argument that helps counter people's reluctance to come to meetings in the first place. Your readers are more likely to give up time on other important tasks if they can see a clear agenda and purpose in your meeting as well as a definite limit on the time commitment required. If you are writing an agenda for a formal, deliberative body, your organization may have particular conventions that will guide your development of the agenda and the minutes, as well.

Expression. On the one hand, it may seem that nothing could be more matter of fact than an agenda. After all, it's just a notation of a time and place and a list of people and topics. On the other hand, there is often strong resistance to an agenda, if only because readers usually have other things they need to do. And if the agenda includes items that are controversial, then writing it can become a significant rhetorical exercise.

As the writer of the agenda, you are in a crucial position, with a special opportunity and responsibility to set an ethical tone that will enable the participants to engage you and each other in a spirit of trust and common cause and therefore proceed to have an effective, productive meeting. To the extent that your comments about the

FIGURE 3.22 Thomsett's Agenda Guidelines

1. **Title.** Give the meeting a title. This helps clarify the focus and the range of topics to be discussed. It also helps attendees identify and distinguish your meetings from other meetings they will attend, to help you expand or limit the agenda, and to give you ideas for others who should be invited.
2. **Time and location.** Include the exact time, date, and place of the meeting. If you will be using a conference room, be sure you have reserved it before announcing your location and as part of your preliminary consultation. Include both the starting and ending time of the meeting, and plan to stay within those parameters.
3. **Theme and definition.** Write a brief description of the meeting's central theme. Define the problem or range of problems you plan to deal with in the meeting.
4. **Attendees.** List the names and departments of the people you have invited. Indicate which of the people listed is the meeting leader.
5. **Topics.** Each agenda item should include three specifics: (a) a brief title for each agenda item, (b) a description of the problem(s), and (c) the goal you want to accomplish during the meeting.

Source: Thomsett, 1989, pp. 26–27.

topics and your goals for the meeting and your requests to your readers can all be made in a way that expresses your own goodwill and your intelligent concern for your readers, this expressive aspect of the agenda can be a powerful force in setting the stage for a successful meeting.

Some organizations see agendas as expressive in other ways, too. For instance, both the Credit Card Club agenda in Figure 3.20 and the StyleGuiders agenda in Figure 3.21 overtly express the overall identity and focus of their respective teams by including their mission statements as part of their agendas. This strategy goes a long way toward building a sense of community among group members, and it keeps the team on task, too.

The agenda is clearly forward looking—a list of things you're going to do in your meeting. In some instances, agendas may look even farther into the future than the next meeting. This is certainly the case in the Credit Card Club agenda (Figure 3.20), which includes notes that the team calls "Futures Files." Such indicators of future agenda items provide continuity and a sense of onward progress for teams and committees.

Developing Minutes with GRACE

While agendas are forward looking, minutes at first glance, appear to be backward looking—a record of things you did in your meeting. In practice, though, minutes can be just as forward looking as agendas. Most of the decisions that are recorded in the minutes describe actions to be taken in the future. In fact, sometimes the minutes of one meeting include an agenda for the next meeting. Let's consider how minutes can be done GRACEfully.

Goals. Your primary goal in keeping minutes is to avoid having dropped assignments and missed deadlines that are caused by communication problems. But keeping minutes is not a sure cure for communication problems in organizations or work teams. First, you have to keep *good* minutes. Second, the people who attended the meeting and those who are affected by the decisions and actions coming from it must receive and read the minutes. You must describe agreements and state assignments as clearly as possible, so that your readers have just as clear an idea about the essential features of the meeting as you do: what happened, what each person is supposed to do next, and when each person is responsible for completing each task. Consider, for instance, the minutes for the Credit Card Club shown in Figure 3.23. Decisions made on each subject follow the meeting notes on that subject and are visually emphasized by the boldfaced "RESULT." Also, "Assignments" are clearly indicated at the end of the minutes in a simple list that specifies who's to do what.

Sometimes, assignments are stated more than once in minutes. For example, the StyleGuiders minutes in Figure 3.24 indicate relevant assignments within the discussion under each "Agenda Item," but these assignments appear again in a simple list at the end of the minutes arranged by person. This redundancy enables readers either to refer to specific agenda items within the body of the minutes to see who's working on that item or to check someone's name in the list at the bottom of the minutes to see what he or she is doing. This list also provides, of course, a handy reminder for the people who are responsible for performing the tasks enumerated there.

FIGURE 3.23 Minutes Highlighting Results

Credit Card Club

January 29, 1997
1:30 PM to 3:30 PM
Conference Room E

Team Members

(x) Jeanette Bilot, TL
(x) Rozanne Dodson
(x) Janet Treece
( ) Elaine Kellogg
(x) Reg Lockard
(x) Jean Maduli
(x) Jeana Cederburg
(x) John McPhee

Mission Statement The Credit Card Club, upon recommendation from the team leader, deliberates and revises methods to improve the efficiency and effectiveness of the Commission's Cal Card Process. If warranted, the policy and procedures are modified for executive staff approval. The team leader or representative presents the recommended changes to the executive staff.

Meeting Notes

SUBJECT: Rocky Mountain Bank
Jeanette reported that since we are authorized to spend Public Funds, we can use Rocky Mountain for the Credit Card. EdFund will acquire the card under CSAC. EdFund has no credit history but CSAC does. Reg will check with Chiefs for approval and if we can keep the "State of CA" line on card.

RESULT: Stay with Rocky Mountain Bank if Chiefs approve.

SUBJECT: Prohibited Card Purchases
The team revised the list of prohibited purchases that originally came from EDS. The list (and existing list) will be sent to managers, executives and chiefs to find out what they would like to see added for business purchases. Some legal counsel might be necessary. Reg suggested we make a strong recommendation on the degree of flexibility to elicit executive response. Frustration was expressed with the lack of restrictions set by executives. Survey question: What flexibility will there be on the credit cards?

RESULT: Revisit list and finalize changes at next meeting.

Next Meeting: February 5th at 1:30

Notes

Assignments:

- Jeanette will bring copies of DGS letter to next meeting
- Reg will ask executives about dollar limits and purchase criteria
- Reg will find out restrictions on tagging equipment
- Reg will seek approval for the Rocky Mountain Bank from executives

FIGURE 3.24 Minutes Clarifying Assignments

StyleGuiders

Meeting Notes: June 4, 1997 Room 110S

Members Present: Kathy Simon (Leader), Donna Jo Barnes, Jan Botha, Kathy Coleman, Jean Cortez, Jorge Esquarez, Pauline Fass, Harry Gardner, Amy Gieck, Pam Mullen, Christy Martin, Benjamin Peters, Anna Saldana, Cathy Wakefield

Agenda Item #1 - Pat Davis Design Update
Kathy S says Tim Roberts expects the style guide team to produce approximately 12 copies of our first style guide draft, which will be distributed to upper management for review. Strategic Design has been authorized to design the cover, spine, and tabs for the style guide. Tim Roberts also offered to let Strategic Design put the text of the style guide on PageMaker, as well as prepare samples of memos, letters, etc., for the style guide. This work can be produced by July 1. Kathy S will continue to coordinate efforts with Strategic Design.

Agenda Item #2 - Priority Lists/Draft Table of Contents
Kathy S distributed a revised priority list. She also distributed a Table of Contents based on the priority list, and a draft of a Table of Contents for the final style guide. The team discussed including a format for developing manuals.

Agenda Item #3 - Establish Letter Specifications
The team discussed various elements of external letters. The team voted to recommend the following formats:

- Salutation - a salutation with a colon (Dear Borrower: or Dear Dr. Jones:)
- Body - single spaced, with one space between paragraphs, no indentation at the beginning of paragraphs
- Complimentary Close - "Sincerely" is recommended, but refer to HOW 7 for a list of other appropriate phrases.
- Notations -

  enclosure line - enclosure
  reference initials - not recommended
  copies - use a small c with a colon (for example, "c: Bill Jones")
  blind copies - small bc with a colon ("bc:")
  mailing notations - Kathy S will collect samples for the team to review
  subject line - Kathy S will collect samples for the team to review

Agenda Item #4 - Recommendation for FAX Cover Sheet
Pauline drew up several samples.

Agenda Item #5 - Recommendation for Envelopes
Jan distributed a handout of the US Postal Service published guidelines. The team agreed to Jan's recommendation that the following format items be included in the style guide's July 1 rollout:

(continued)

FIGURE 3.24 Continued

- Addressing envelopes
- Abbreviations
- Address types
- Address element sequence
- Common addressing problems
- Stationery folding
- Foreign, military, and rural route addresses
- Placement of secondary information (such as apartments or suites)

Agenda Item #6 - Recommendation for Memo Format
Virginia drew up several samples of memos. Kathy S will ask Strategic Design about the design standard of memos.

The team voted to recommend the following formats:

- Memos should include a logo (CSAC or EdFund)
- The word "memorandum" at the top of the memo
- Use "subject:" instead of "re:"
- Use "c:" (to designate people who receive copies) at the end of the memo
- Initials beside the "from" line—used at the writer's discretion

Agenda Item #7 - Recommendations for Voice Mail and Pagers
Kathy S reports that Sue Harris has not issued policy on voice mail protocol. Sue Harris furthermore recommends that the team postpone placing voice mail instructions in the new style guide, because CSAC/EdFund is likely to have a different voice mail system when we move into the new office building.

Kathy C will obtain information on voice mail protocol from Pacific Bell.

Agenda Item #8 - Policy on Use of State Seal for CSAC
Christie will find out if CSAC as a state agency is required to carry the state seal on letterhead. Pauline suggested the state seal could also appear on letters as a watermark.

Agenda Item #9 - DAPP Process/Forms/Numbering System
Ben distributed guidelines from Business Services on designing forms and publications that are to be printed by the department. Ben will bring in samples of forms and publications printed by Business Services to the next meeting.

Agenda Item #10 - Jargon/Acronyms
Harry distributed a list of financial aid acronyms and abbreviations. Team members may e-mail Harry with acronyms to add to the list. The team voted to include the following types of acronyms and abbreviations to the style guide: 1) Financial Aid, 2) CA State Departments, 3) CSAC/EdFund departments, 4) Standard English.

FIGURE 3.24 Continued

Agenda Item #11 - Signature Block
DJ distributed examples of signature blocks. The team voted to recommend the following signature block style:

Sincerely,

Name
Position or Title
Department

Agenda Item #12 - Recommendation Letter to Management
Kathy S will prepare a cover letter draft to management which will introduce the CSAC/EDFUND Style Guide and explain our recommendations.

Agenda Item #13 - HOW 7 Training, Price Break
Kathy S reported that HOW 7 has a retail price of $27.00. The publisher offers a 30% discount for large orders. The publisher also produces a training manual for the HOW 7. Kathy S will continue to try and obtain a copy of this training manual, for use with CSAC/EDFUND style guide training. Kathy S will also inquire to the publisher about the publishing date of HOW 8.

Agenda Item #14 - Page Layout/Misc. Items
Kathy S informed the team that Strategic Design is in charge of designing the visual standards for various forms used by CSAC/EDFUND, but the style guide team will determine the wording on these forms. Kathy S will find out if Strategic Design can be permitted to design the page layout of the style guide.

Assignments:

Kathy S.	1) Find out if CSAC and EDFUND ought to have separate style guides. 2) Find out if various departments are authorized to design and use their own logos. 3) Collect samples of mailing notations and subject line (for letter notations). 4) Produce an acronym/abbreviation list for Standard English. 5) Prepare a cover letter draft to management. 6) Find out if Strategic Design can be permitted to design the page layout of the style guide. 7) Produce first draft sections for letters, memos, fax cover sheets, envelopes, and symbols. 8) Ask Strategic Design about the need for separate style guides for CSAC and EDFUND. 9) Ask Strategic Design to design a floppy disk label for templates. 10) Get feedback from Strategic Design on the format of the style guide.
Kathy C.	Obtain information on voice mail protocol from Pacific Bell.
Ben P.	1) Bring samples of publications produced by Business Services. 2) Ask Valerie about a change in logo.
Christie M.	Bring information on the state seal for CSAC letterhead.
Harry G.	Continue to compile a financial aid acronym list.

Next meeting: Wednesday, June 11, 1997, ARB Building, 9–12.

Readers. This may sound ridiculously simple and obvious, but you need to be sure the minutes actually get into the hands of all the right people. This statement immediately raises two questions: First, who are the right people? Obviously, the attendees of your meeting should be on the distribution list. Beyond this immediate group, though, there are likely to be others—probably the supervisors of the attendees at the meeting, especially those attendees who were given assignments at the meeting; certainly anyone not at the meeting who was designated as the person to complete a task; and probably anyone else whose work is likely to be affected by the decisions made at the meeting. And when you plan to send minutes to people who did not attend the meeting, you should let those who did attend know your plans so no one will be taken by surprise. One important function of the minutes is that they identify misunderstandings that may not have been visible at the end of the meeting. The minutes then generate additional discussion and probably follow-up memos and e-mail that clarify misunderstandings and perhaps renegotiate key assignments. For this reason, you should prepare and distribute the minutes as soon as possible after the meeting. This will help to assure (but never absolutely guarantee) that everyone is literally on the same page.

Arguments. Insofar as they are just a record of the key actions and decisions from your meeting, the only argumentative claim the minutes make is that they are a true and accurate record of what happened. But to the extent that they recap decisions about future actions to be taken, assignments of tasks to specific people, and deadlines for the completion of these tasks, the minutes take on a clearly persuasive burden. Those who assumed responsibilities during the meeting need to be reminded of them by the minutes and clearly notified that they will be held accountable for these assignments.

Conventions. In *The Little Black Book of Business Meetings,* Michael Thomsett (1989) suggests that someone attend meetings strictly as the recorder of minutes so that no important details are missed. But he also notes that while the minutes must be a complete report of the important decisions that were made and actions that were taken, they should not be a transcript of the meeting. He offers the outline shown in Figure 3.25.

Expression. Like the agenda, the minutes are, on one level, just a matter-of-fact listing of attendees, actions, and decisions, now seen retrospectively, rather than prospectively. But, also like the agenda, the minutes can serve an important community-building function that is mediated by the sense of goodwill and occasionally even humor that you are able to express. The image of your personal ethic, as expressed in the minutes, may at times be very important, especially as you continue to seek the cooperation of those who have been assigned tasks or of key players who have substantial interests at stake in the decisions and plans that came out of the meeting. At other times, of course, the minutes really are simply a matter-of-fact narrative of what happened.

One interesting feature of both the minutes in Figure 3.4 and those in Figure 3.26 is that neither identifies itself as a set of minutes. The minutes of the edito-

FIGURE 3.25 Thomsett's Minutes Guidelines

Date and time. When did the meeting take place (date, starting time, and ending time)?

Attendees. Who was at the meeting (name and title of each person, identification of leader)?

Agenda topics discussed. Describe the topic briefly.

Definition of problems. Include one or two sentences stating the issue.

Alternatives presented. What ideas were offered and who offered them? Include brief comments or major points, and the name of the person stating them.

Solutions agreed on. What was the outcome? Explain the actual solution the meeting attendees agreed should be acted on to solve the problem.

Assignments made and accepted. What people were given the assignment? If they attended, state that they acknowledged and accepted the task and that they understood the assignment; if they did not attend, comment that a follow-up contact is required.

Deadlines. When will the work be done? Does this include a contingent deadline?

Follow-up actions. What actions must be taken after the meeting? Who is responsible? Who will monitor follow-up, and how will it be reported to the responsible person?

Source: Thomsett, 1989, p. 64.

rial group from the *Rhetoric Society Quarterly* are written in a memo format and lack several of the conventional features that Thomsett identifies: specific notation of both the time and place of the meeting as well as who was present and who was absent, for example. The minutes of the banking groups, identified specifically as the Service Network Meeting, likewise do not identify themselves as minutes but rather as a memo. However, conventional features missing in the minutes of the editorial group are found here: persons present or absent, time, place, and so on. There are several other interesting differences in the two samples. For example, the bankers seem to be chattier than the rhetoricians, judging by both the lengths and contents of the respective memos. What differences in the goals of the two memos—and the relationships of the respective writers to their readers—do you suppose might account for these differences in expression?

The Teamwork of Writing: Project Management

When you work on a writing project as part of a team, your management task, which is already complicated, becomes even more so. Now, you have message-based goals for what you want the writing to achieve, task-based goals for how to push the writing

FIGURE 3.26 Minutes Formatted as Memo

Memo

TO: Service Network #11

FROM: Laura Neufeldt

SUBJECT: **Service Network Meeting**

DATE: September 15, 1997

Present: Clare Anson, Bob Lauer, Margaret McIntire, Randi Meyers, Laura Neufeldt, Pat Summers, Chris Tatum-Richards, Mary Taylor,

Absent: Vicki Vannoys (part-time), Todd Jefferts (meeting)

Service Network 11 met on September 12, 1997, Downtown.

NEW MEMBERS: We have two new members in our network. Please welcome Clare Anson and Todd Jefferts to the bank. Clare is a teller at Midtown, and Todd is in the Credit & Loan Administration department.

INVESTMENT CENTER: Randi explained the details of the referral program that is being sponsored by the Investment Center. Chris and Randi would like to receive about 100 qualified referrals during September and October. We picked "Prime Best Passers" as our team name.

We had the following Opportunities to Serve:

ARTWORK: One of the bank customers commented on how much she liked the artwork in the lobby. The customer said the bank should buy some of the artwork and display it in the bank.

INVESTMENT SAVINGS ACCOUNTS: Some customers have requested deposit tickets for investment savings accounts. Some have been told that there is a cost associated with ordering them. Some tellers have been ordering them without charging the customer or have been just encoding some deposit tickets with the account number on the bottom. Maybe some guidelines should be set when customers make this kind of request.

project to completion, and relationship-based goals for keeping the members of the team working together productively and comfortably.

Researchers have found that the attitudes, relationships, and behaviors that are effective and productive in collaborative writing teams are exactly those that common sense would suggest. And, not surprisingly, these are also the same attitudes, rela-

FIGURE 3.26 Continued

Page 2, September 15, 1997

ANNUAL PERCENTAGE YIELD: Some of our CD customers have complained about the accuracy of the annual percentage yields on CDs for special promotions like the 15-month CD. Some of the customers are trying to calculate the yield but are not able to come up with the same yield that we state in the paper or on the CD rate board. This is because the yields are based on 24 months for the 15-month CD. Some customers feel that they are being deceived, but the bank is complying with the regulations on this issue. Maybe the bank could state what the **YIELD TO MATURITY** on a specific CD is so that the customer is well informed to make the appropriate choice when purchasing a CD.

MATCHING COMPETITORS' CD RATES: Another issue related to CDs is that some customers are asking the bank to match a CD rate from a competitor. In one case one family member was not able to receive a higher rate from one employee, but later another family member was able to negotiate a higher rate with a different employee. When a situation like this happens, either Margaret or Pat must be notified before the special rate is given to the customer. Our network thought it might be a good idea to establish when an employee can offer these special rates and under what circumstances. Also, employee(s) could be given the authority to offer a special rate within certain limits.

CLASSIFIED ADS: Clare brought up the idea of adding a classified section to the newsletter so that employees who have something they want to sell could find someone in the bank who is interested in buying the item.

Some items from the Service Network Leaders meeting follow:

READY EQUITY STATEMENTS: Some customers have not received their ready equity statements since the statements have been sent out separately from checking account statements. This situation is being monitored by Credit & Loan Administration.

MAILING ADDRESSES: Some of the mail that comes to the bank is not being properly addressed to a department or person. All staff members should try to encourage their customers to try and use the correct identifying address.

(continued)

tionships, and behaviors that contemporary literature on effective management holds up as the virtues we should strive for in our organizations. Furthermore, these virtues, including those we talked about earlier, are the same old-fashioned virtues that people talked about openly a couple of generations ago but have been hesitant to discuss more recently: courage that enables you and your colleagues to build a mutual trust

FIGURE 3.26 Continued

Page 3, September 15, 1997

DEBIT CARD PIN NUMBERS: When customers are interested in a debit card, bank employees should let the customers know that they have an opportunity to preselect their PIN number so the bank can reduce the number of cards that are being reordered.

SMART: If anyone is interested in being on the **SMART** committee, contact Alicia at ext. 6756.

The next meeting will be scheduled for November 28 DOWNTOWN at 8:15 a.m. in the Safe Deposit conference room.

At the next meeting, we will be voting on a **NEW NETWORK LEADER** for 1998.

I have attached the Opportunities to Serve to look over before our next meeting.

If anyone has something to contribute to the Network Leaders Meeting, please give me a call at ext. 3225.

Attachment: Opportunities to Serve for November meeting

for each other's ideas and language and commitment to your joint success, and a work ethic that enables you to commit to the project and to each other and to honor your individual commitment and responsibilities.

In later chapters, we will look at specific types of longer writing projects, including reports and proposals. These longer projects—like any other that require thoughtful teamwork, planning, and coordination—benefit from the same kinds of writing that support team projects generally: memos, agendas, and minutes, both formal and informal. In fact, the memo to the rhetoricians (Figure 3.4) is an example of this exact thing: a written document designed to manage the production of other, larger written documents.

WRITING CHECKLIST

You can use the following guidelines to write memos, e-mail, agendas, and minutes that will help you manage your daily work and enhance group productivity. For any of these guidelines, remember the superordinate guideline: Disregard *any* of this advice if it would cause you to do something that's inappropriate or silly for your situation.

☑ Memos

- Think about how your readers will use the information in your memo and how you want them to react.
- Determine the essential claims you want to make and imagine what evidence readers will need to accept these claims.
- Begin with an overview that provides context, defines the task or problem, and clarifies the memo's goal; if the memo is long, follow this overview with a formal summary.
- In the body of your memo, present information readers need to understand your arguments and their situational context and to be convinced that your claims are valid.
- Present your information simply and from the readers' viewpoint.
- Begin each section and each paragraph with an overview sentence that provides its gist; then fill in the details.
- Start with what's most important to readers and move to what's less important; begin with key findings, conclusions, and recommendations.
- Close by summarizing key points or asking directly for action, emphasizing how it is significant for the readers or the organization.
- Use attachments for detailed information that would distract readers from the memo's central point.
- Use short, substantive headings to help readers find things; also use paragraph breaks, lists, white space, and graphics to simplify the text and enhance readability.
- Match your expression to your goals, readers, and argument.

☑ E-Mail

- Make reading e-mail easy by using shorter sentences and paragraphs than you would in paper memos.
- If a message is more than three or four screens, consider whether e-mail is the most effective medium.
- Reread to catch mistakes.
- Remember that expression in e-mail is often more informal and personal than that in memos; e-mail also incorporates many of the features of oral communication (chattiness, clipped or incomplete sentences, informal vocabulary and speech patterns, and pronoun shifts).
- Don't put anything in an e-mail that you wouldn't put in print; e-mail can be backed up, forwarded, printed, and used as a paper trail.
- Since it's easy to be self-revelatory or blunt in e-mail, make sure that your expression is appropriate for your goals and readers.

☑ Agendas

- Use agendas to keep meetings productive and on task.
- Make arguments straightforward to persuade the appropriate people to come to the meeting, prepared and with a cooperative attitude so that things can be accomplished.
- Specify what is to be accomplished in the meeting relative to individual topics, and clarify who's responsible for what.
- Establish clear time limits for meetings, including how long will be allotted for each topic.

☑ Minutes

- Describe agreements made at the meeting.
- Clarify who's accountable for particular assignments and when they are due.
- Specify what actions must be taken and who's responsible for taking them.
- Include on the distribution list those who attended the meeting; supervisors of those given assignments and those whose work will be affected by what happened at the meeting should receive minutes, too.
- Prepare and distribute minutes as soon after the meeting as possible.

ACTIVITIES AND PROJECTS

1. In a small group, use the GRACE benchmarks to evaluate the effectiveness of the memo samples in this book and to recommend needed revisions. Ask a group member to record your responses to the memos so that you can share them with colleagues.
2. Collect several examples of e-mail, print them, and bring them into a small-group discussion. Your group should assess the organizational and stylistic features of these e-mail examples and select positive and negative examples to present to other colleagues. Your specific reasons for selecting these examples should, of course, be part of your presentation.
3. Use the GRACE benchmarks to revise a memo or e-mail you've written on the job.
4. Write a memo to your instructor, analyzing and evaluating the effectiveness of memo samples you've been collecting for your document file. The primary goals of this memo are to demonstrate that you understand the business writing principles you've been studying well enough to analyze and evaluate memos and to communicate your assessment in a conventional memo.

5. Send an e-mail to an instructor or trainer reporting on your progress in a group learning project. In your progress report, be sure to assess honestly your contributions to group discussion, your writing's strengths and weaknesses, and your plans for building upon your strengths and addressing your weaknesses. Also ask questions and raise concerns that you have about the learning activity, class, or workshop in general.

6. Extend your e-mail voice by posting something to a newsgroup or listserv. Both are electronic discussion groups; there are, however, a few key differences between the two. First, entries for a newsgroup are posted on a central computer, and anyone who has access to the computer can join the conversation. In contrast, a listserv is limited to those who subscribe and is therefore a bit more private than a newsgroup. Second, to read or post messages to the newsgroup, you'll need to follow the directions your teacher will give you to access the computer where the postings are archived. Postings to listservs are accessed differently: The listserv program actually sends every e-mail posted to the listserv to subscribers' accounts so you don't have to go to the managing computer to get the postings.

   Post at least twice a week, responding to readings and discussions—and, of course, replying to the postings of class colleagues. Electronic etiquette, or *netiquette,* requires that you remember that newsgroups and listservs are public; if you want to post a private message to one of the newgroup or listserv participants, send it to his or her private e-mail address. Netiquette also requires that you communicate courteously with the group's participants. *Flaming* or *spamming* (posting multiple messages, like chain mail, or other nuisance e-mail that has no relevance for the group) is off limits. Think about your readers' needs and interests as you write.

7. Find the name and electronic address of a listserv dealing with topics in your field or major and join that listserv. *Lurk* (read the postings without responding to them) until you have a sense of the conventions that are followed in that electronic discussion group. And when you feel as if you know the protocol listserv participants follow and have something to say that they'd be interested in reading, begin posting messages.

8. The series of e-mail in Figure 3.27 resulted from an ongoing project: Students and faculty at a middle-sized midwestern university were developing a website. The team members used this e-mail to keep themselves organized and the project moving: to "make visible . . . questions and decisions about tasks and deadlines and also about the relationships of interdependent tasks." As an aside, much of what the writers are talking about in this e-mail is the actual coding of the documents using *html,* or hypertext markup language—the coding that enables web browsers to see the format of the files so that simple text and graphic files can be seen as formatted text with glossy graphics and colorful backgrounds. Read these e-mail messages and talk about the specific ways in which they might contribute to project management and team building.

FIGURE 3.27 E-Mail Communication Series

From: TIGGER::SCOGDILL "Sharon Cogdill" 6-MAR-1995 20:43:38.31
To: KILBORNJ
CC:
Subj: copy of my note to the guys

From: TIGGER::SCOGDILL "Sharon Cogdill" 6-MAR-1995 20:41:51.67
To: JOE,KELLY
CC: SCOGDILL
Subj: hey!

Joe and Kelly -

Trying a multiple send here.

So get onto Netscape and open http://condor.stcloud.msus.edu/leo and tell me what you think.

The home page needs links, etc., but Mr. Larry Whatshisname forgot to give me write privileges though I'm owner. Great. Will fix things tomorrow.

Judy and I had a meeting. We need all the graphics to be resized (thanks, Kelly) and converted (thanks, Joe). Use 6-bit color when you index them and save them as CompuServe GIF.

Joe, aim at getting them all converted and put into the LEO folder in Keith's Photoshop folder. I'll help you put them into Leo when I get back Tues afternoon, assuming whatshisname has given me write privileges by then.

We need a list and copies of all the files we want to put up ready by early afternoon. Judy is taking this job on, but she'll need help.

We're actually much better off than I thought, thanks to Judy and Keith and you all.

I'm going to work on the links now.

See you tomorrow.
sharon
St. Cloud, Minnesota: 9 inches of snow, and me with new snow shoes.

FIGURE 3.27 Continued

From: TIGGER::SCOGDILL "Sharon Cogdill" 7-MAY-1995 14:18:10.84
To: KILBORNJ,KELLY,JOE,KEWING
CC: SCOGDILL
Subj: uploading files to leo

Judy and Kelly, in particular:
Joe and Kewing, fyi:

I have spent hours in the last 3 days working on the dir structure of leo. *Please* do not upload any more files without ascertaining which files I have been working on.

Judy--test your resume documents.

Kelly--test your apa docs.

New directories, new pathnames.

Also, there are still a number of files in the main directory that appear to me to be related to resumes and apa documentation, but which were not (I don't think, anyway) called by any of the documents I moved and worked on.

I moved only those documents needed by your "home page" document.

I have fixed the pathnames in index.html, so you all *should* be able to find your docs via the write place homepage. haha.

We should sit down and go through these directories, fixing all the little glitches so they really are finished.

How're your papers going? Me? I've been doing leo.

kewing: Where's the write place masthead??? huh? yea? well? I've left the img src in the files to link to the leo masthead still, but . . .

yrs,
who *should* be grading papers, hahahahahahaha,
sharon

(continued)

FIGURE 3.27 Continued

From: TIGGER::SCOGDILL "Sharon Cogdill" 28-MAY-1995 21:59:52.39
To: KELLY,JOE,KILBORNJ
CC: SCOGDILL
Subj: leo update

Hi. I've been working on the leo files. I have made 2 changes to all the files that I could.

I've changed the incorrect URL, and I've changed the name of wpindex.html to catalogue.html. I didn't have write access to all the documents, so I didn't change anything in these docs:

joe's document conclude.html

and kelly's documents american, contemporary, englishlit, general, medieval, minority, modern, renaissance, restoration, romantics, and search.html.

You probably already knew this. And Kelly had told me he wanted to upload files. Kelly, want to work together on how the links should be written to these documents?

fyi, I've sent a list of the following files to Larry, hoping he can figure out the formatting problem we're having.

definition.html
descriptive.html
genproofed.html
intro.html
process.html
sentpatt.html
catalogue.html

possibly new formatting difficulties were added in the last up- and downloading processes.

happy whatever-holiday-it-is day,
sharon

FIGURE 3.27 Continued

From: TIGGER::KEWING 20-SEP-1995 13:13:20.22
To: SCOGDILL,PTHORSON
CC:
Subj: LEO Web mtg

I have tentatively set 2:00 p.m. on Thursday, 28 Sept in my office (initially) to get together to talk about moving LEO to the LRS server. We will establish the mgmt rights and look at moving LEO materials from condor. This should establish a more or less permanent home for LEO documents.

Sharon--invite Judy to come along.

We should also discuss ideas surrounding the development of a local moo.

Keith

From: TIGGER::SCOGDILL "Sharon Cogdill" 21-SEP-1995 12:41:09.98
To: KILBORNJ
CC:
Subj: *i* can't make the meting next wek

From: TIGGER::SCOGDILL "Sharon Cogdill" 21-SEP-1995 12:23:12.25
To: TIGGER::KEWING
CC: SCOGDILL
Subj: RE: LEO Web mtg

Keith -
>I have tentatively set 2:00 p.m. on Thursday, 28 Sept in my office (initially)
>to get together to talk about moving LEO to the LRS server. We will
>establish the mgmt rights and look at moving LEO materials from condor.
>This should establish a more or less permanent home for LEO documents.

Oops, I forgot to tell you that I'll be in Phoenix that day. Can we make it for the following week?

>We should also discuss ideas surrounding the development of a local moo.

YEEEHAAAWW!!!

yrs,
sharon with an excedngly frutrating kyboard

(continued)

FIGURE 3.27 Continued

From: TIGGER::KEWING 21-SEP-1995 14:02:25.19
To: TIGGER::SCOGDILL
CC:
Subj: RE: LEO Web mtg

Okay, okay . . .

You get to go to Phoenix, I get to go to Cold Spring. Must have someting to do with our respective reputations.

I'll try to reschedule the time to meet with Phil. tentatively set for 5 Oct at 2:00 p.m.

Keith

REFERENCES

Bacard, A. (1996, June 1). Frequently asked questions about e-mail privacy. In *The computer privacy handbook* [Online]. Available: http://www.well.com/user/abacard/email.html (1995, February 25).

Blanton, T. (Ed.). (1995, November 22). *White House e-mail: The top secret messages the Reagan/Bush White House tried to destroy.* Washington, DC: National Security Archive.

Moylan, M. J. (1995, December 11). E-mail mania. *St. Paul Pioneer Press,* p. 1E.

Smith, J. (n.d.). Frequently asked questions: Basic information about MUDS and MUDding [Online]. Available: http://www.math.okstate.edu/~jds/mudfaq_p1.html (1996, June 30).

Sproul, L., & Kielser, S. (1991). *Connections: New ways of working in the networked organization.* Cambridge, MA: MIT Press.

Thomsett, M. C. (1989). *The little black book of business meetings.* New York: American Management Association.

Vitanza, V. (1996). *CyberReader.* Boston: Allyn and Bacon.

Webber, R. A. (1991). *Becoming a courageous manager: Overcoming career problems of new managers.* Englewood Cliffs, NH: Prentice Hall.

Chapter 4

Writing to Negotiate and Express Institutional Goals, Values, and Practices

Companies that have cultivated their individual identities by shaping values, making heroes, spelling out rites and rituals, and acknowledging the cultural network have an edge. These corporations have values and beliefs to pass along—not just products. They have stories to tell—not just profits to make. They have heroes whom managers and workers can emulate—not just faceless bureaucrats. In short, they are human institutions that provide practical meaning for people, both on and off the job.

—Terrence E. Deal and Allan A. Kennedy

Writing is probably the most powerful instrument available for the building of what Terrence Deal and Allan Kennedy (1982, p. 15) call "strong organizational culture." Writing down your goals, values, and practices forces a kind of rigorous focus that oral renderings rarely match. In any reasonably open, democratic organization, this sharpened focus, in turn, generates deliberation and negotiation of what the written texts mean. And this deliberation and negotiation, in turn, often lead to thoughtful and fruitful revisions, yielding still more fitting and widely shared written expressions of a strong organizational culture.

At their best, these written artifacts embody an institutional memory that inspires, motivates, and informs a shared vision and sense of purpose. At their worst, they are the objects of scorn and derision among cynical, alienated employees. This scorn and derision don't necessarily mean that these are bad documents, however. Rather, the problem often is that an organization's cultural artifacts—its vision and mission statements, its strategic plans, and its written policies and procedures—represent an ideal vision that is far distant from its actual practice. This hypocrisy of institutionalized mismatches between what an organization says and what it does is such an irresistible target of ridicule that it now appears regularly in newspaper cartoons like Garry Trudeau's "Doonesbury," Cathy Guisewite's "Cathy," and Scott Adams' "Dilbert." In fact, Adams, an M.B.A. graduate from the University of California at Berkeley, has created a kind of cottage industry of corporate ridicule with books like *The Dilbert Principle* (1995b), *Still Pumped from Using the Mouse* (1996), and *Bring Me the Head of Willy the Mailboy!* (1995a).

There's a cynical line of conventional wisdom that says statements of corporate values and institutional visions or missions don't really mean anything. But, in fact, both the power and the problems with these documents come from the fact that they *do* mean something. The problem develops when these expressions of institutional values and goals do not match actual practice. The problem is not the meaninglessness of the word but the incoherence between word and deed.

"Talking the Talk" and "Walking the Walk"

One of our strongest, most persistent themes in this book is the collaborative nature of writing in professional organizations and the interdependence among colleagues, clients, and even competitors in work and in the writing of work. It would be especially ironic, then, if community-building documents, like those we discuss in this chapter, were written by some executive in isolation and imposed on the members of the organization. Some management texts advise a top-down approach to these documents, whereby an executive or small group of executives write the mission statement and broad outline of the strategic plan and then require the rest of the organization to fill in the details. We suggest a more collaborative, democratic approach, allowing for a greater sharing of the initiative in drafting these documents. Text that claims to embody an institutional culture must truly be owned by the members of the institution—if it is to be effective as a rallying point for them.

It isn't enough, however, to have a widely participative process in creating these key artifacts of an organization's culture. If the organization is to achieve coherence between its "talk" and "walk," then these documents have to be lived as well as owned. And this is the real difficulty. In *Organizations*, James G. March and Herbert A. Simon (1958) proposed what they called "a Gresham's Law of Planning," giving expression to a phenomenon we have probably all experienced: "Daily routine drives out planning." In fact, daily routine can drive out just about everything else, including our long-term vision and sense of corporate mission. The powerful inertia of our routine, programmed tasks—and the comfortable sense of security and accomplishment they give us—can be a compelling force that keeps us from thinking about our mission or making plans in the first place. And the same inertia keeps drawing us back to the habitual and routine, even when it is absolutely at odds with what we asserted that we are really about when we wrote our mission statement, strategic plans, and even job descriptions.

On the other hand, Gresham's law also points to the value of these institutional expressions of ideals and purpose. It's a fact of our corporate lives, as well as our individual lives, that we almost never achieve exactly what we planned and hoped to. But the gap between the two is always interesting, and it's almost always fruitful to study the gap and learn from it. Sometimes, it turns out, our plans and sense of mission weren't realistic, and this is demonstrated in our subsequent institutional actions and their consequences. Sometimes, unanticipated change makes a plan or job description obsolete. And sometimes, we just don't perform up to par. But without having a vision of ourselves and our purpose that has been made tangible in a written artifact, it's difficult to make intelligent judgments about how well we're doing. We need the talk, embodied in these documents, to measure our walk. And we need to evaluate the talk in light of our walk—to do a reality check on our vision.

Expressing Missions and Visions

In *The Dilbert Principle,* Scott Adams (1995) defines a mission statement as "a long, awkward sentence that demonstrates management's inability to think clearly." And he adds, "If for some reason the company's Mission Statements do not cause a turnaround in profitability, you might need a Vision Statement. In stark contrast to the detailed road map provided by a Mission Statement, a Vision Statement is more of a 'high-level' guide for the company. The higher the better, because you want a vision that will last the ages" (pp. 36–37).

One of the features of mission statements and vision statements that Adams ridicules is their propensity for saying the obvious, and, in a sense, he's right. In *The Fifth Discipline Fieldbook,* Peter M. Senge and colleagues (1994) talk about the process of building a shared vision. They identify five different strategies for sharing an organizational vision, each one involving greater ownership on the part of the organization's members. As Figure 4.1 illustrates, the lowest level of ownership comes from the strategy they call *Telling,* where the leader simply tells the members what the vision will be. The second level is *Selling,* and the third, fourth, and fifth levels are, respectively, *Testing, Consulting,* and *Co-Creating.* When a good mission statement or vision statement has been born of the process of co-creation, it will likely seem obvious to all who participated—which isn't necessarily a bad thing, Adams' point notwithstanding.

Effective mission statements and vision statements express the essential values or goals of an organization in a form that makes them visible to the members of the organization and to those outside it. Because most organizational cultures are fairly complex, even in small organizations, a lot of things could be said in these statements. So, there's often a temptation to add more and more language. At the same

DILBERT

Source: DILBERT reprinted by permission of United Feature Syndicate, Inc.

FIGURE 4.1 Strategies for Sharing an Organizational Vision

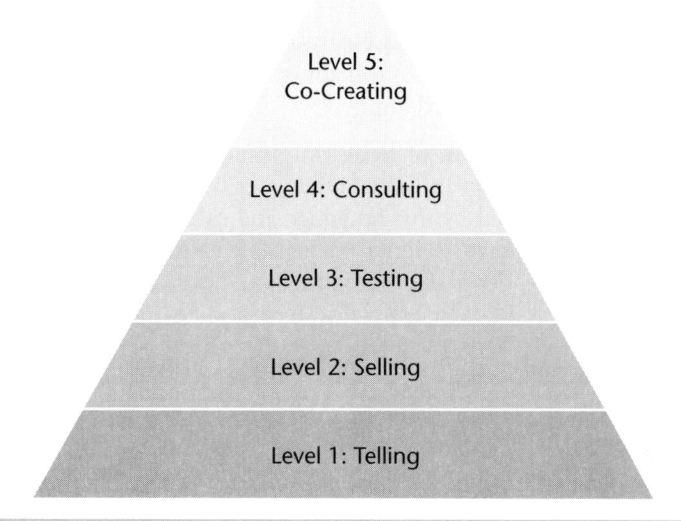

Source: Based on Senge et al., 1994.

time, though, these statements need to be portable because they provide a touchstone or benchmark for measuring and evaluating the organization's other documents and its plans, decisions, and projects. Figure 4.2 is an example of a vision statement for an exceptionally large, complex, and important institution. Yet the statement is just 52 words, short enough to be memorized by millions of schoolchildren. And it's been around for quite a while, too, showing that the concept of having a vision statement or mission statement isn't just a management fad. You may recognize this statement as the Preamble to the Constitution of the United States.

FIGURE 4.2 Preamble to the U.S. Constitution

We the People of the United States, in Order to form a more perfect Union, establish Justice, insure domestic Tranquillity, provide for the common defense, promote the general Welfare, and secure the Blessings of Liberty to ourselves and our Posterity, do ordain and establish this Constitution for the United States of America.

Essential Elements of Mission and Vision Statements

If you're asked to help write a mission or vision statement or to review existing statements, the following list of four essential elements should be a helpful guide for you:

1. **Expression of a clear sense of identity.** Look at the Preamble, for example. There's no question about whom the document claims to represent: the people of the United States.
2. **Expression of clear, tangible goals.** If we look again at the Preamble, we can see that while the language is broad, distinct kinds of policies and actions are enabled by this language and others are vitiated by it. For example, this is not language designed to facilitate formation of a dictatorship. On the other hand, a reader of the Preamble would expect the document that follows it to establish a military, a judicial system, and a structure of governance.
3. **Expression of the values that inform the goals.** Again, in the Preamble, we see the invocation of justice and liberty as warrants in support of the proposition of establishing the Constitution.
4. **Brevity, portability, and memorability of expression.** Distilled to their essence, statements of vision or mission become an overarching statement of purpose or action that may be reduced to a slogan of just a sentence or phrase: "We try harder" (Avis); "A computer on every desktop" (Microsoft); "Cover the world" (Sherwin Williams), "E Pluribus Unum" (the United States). But this portability and memorability also can work against you and your organization in the wrong circumstances, so you need to be sure a vision statement really expresses what you want. For example, consider the U-Haul slogan, "Adventures in Moving"; imagine how many times U-Haul representatives must have had that phrase thrown at them by angry customers when their trucks or trailers have broken down on the road.

The Difference between a Mission Statement and a Vision Statement

Actually, we hesitated quite a while before we worked up the courage to try to explain the distinction between a *mission statement* and a *vision statement.* People who talk about these statements tend to fall into two groups: those who try to distinguish between the two and those who make fun of the first group. We think it's helpful to think about the two kinds of statements as being the opposite sides of the same coin or, more to the point, expressions of essentially the same thing from the opposite sides of the brain.*

**Hemisphericity,* the differentiation in function of the left and right hemispheres of the brain, has become a popular and fruitful line of theory, research, and practice. For some of the seminal research and interpretation of hemisphericity, see Sperry's (1974) "Messages from the Laboratory," Orstein's (1972) *The Psychology of Consciousness,* and Bruner's (1962) *On Knowing: Essays for the Left Hand.*

The *vision statement* emanates from the right side of the brain and is therefore a left-handed statement, tending literally to be expressed in visionary, sensory terms. It focuses on the horizon, providing the organization with a clear sense of where it's going: what dreams it hopes to realize, how it intends to position itself in the industry, what reputation it plans to establish, how it wishes others to see it, and so on. The *mission statement,* on the other hand, tends to take a more businesslike, left-brained approach to the same phenomenon, speaking of what the organization is called to do—what it focuses on daily as it moves toward the fulfillment of its vision. In other words, the mission statement is a step toward operationalizing the image that is seen in the vision statement. The other documents of the organization—strategic plans (often including specific goals and statements of values), job descriptions, and the like—are further steps toward specifying and localizing the corporate vision in all the institution's various nooks and crannies.

Consider, for example, the mission statement and vision statement of a much smaller governmental unit than that of the United States: the California Student Aid Commission. Figure 4.3 shows their vision statement, which is 29 words. Figure 4.4 shows their mission statement, which immediately follows their vision statement in their own documents. Coincidentally, the mission statement is also 29 words long. Like the Preamble to the U.S. Constitution, both the vision statement and mission statement of the California Student Aid Commission explicitly express the organization's identity. And notice that while the vision statement announces that the commission "will continue to play a major role in student financial aid services and will be recognized as a leader nationwide in providing quality services," it doesn't say specifically what its role will be. In fact, it would be possible for the specific mission of the agency to change while its broad vision of itself and its purpose stayed the same. Hence, Adams' quip about vision statements lasting "for the ages."

FIGURE 4.3 Vision Statement for the California Student Aid Commission

The California Student Aid Commission will continue to play a major role in student financial aid services and will be recognized as a leader nationwide in providing quality services.

FIGURE 4.4 Mission Statement of the California Student Aid Commission

The mission of the California Student Aid Commission is to help all students achieve their educational goals by providing financial aid services of the highest quality to its customers.

Writing Strategic Plans with GRACE

Goals

Both in corporate environments and public institutions, planning documents generally serve two complementary purposes. On the one hand, they are literally what their name implies: documents that both embody and express a process of strategic thought. Good plans are characterized by the following qualities:

1. They include institutional introspection—language that answers basic questions about mission, vision, and values.
2. Their introspection includes a careful, realistic audit of the institution's resources and accomplishments to date.
3. The two levels of introspection, generic and specific, are coherent. In other words, broad institutional mission and vision should be consistent with specific institutional resources and accomplishments. For example, a company that has a vision of becoming a leader in certain technological niches should have personnel with the appropriate expertise and experience to make that vision plausible.
4. They constitute a realistic assessment of the environment where the institution hopes to realize its plan. This almost always includes an understanding of the demographics and behaviors of the people the institution hopes to serve as well as an understanding of the alternatives these people have: competing institutions or products or services that offer similar benefits.
5. They project a set of future acts that are coherent with one another and with the other elements of the plan.

So, plans first serve the purpose made obvious by their very names. They are tools that help us imagine more clearly who we are and discover more realistically where we want to go. But in addition to this strategic function, plans also serve, at some level, a persuasive purpose. This persuasive aspect is clearly present in the Executive Summary we've excerpted from the plan for the Intensive English Center (see Figure 4.5.) Notice that an essential element of the plan is to request financial support for the new intensive English program, a request clearly articulated in the summary and supported in elaborate detail in the remainder of the report. On the other hand, Research & Development Strategic Plan 1997, written by the EdFund service of the California Student Aid Commission, is written to promote internal planning and coordination. Sections of this strategic plan are excerpted in Figure 4.6. (pp. 141–147).

Even if a plan is strictly an internal document, there is persuasive energy in both its formation (e.g., "Hey, we don't have the resources to put that in the plan.") and its application (e.g., "Hey, according to the plan, we should be trying to. . . ."). And if a plan is intended as an external document—to be read by bankers, potential investors,

FIGURE 4.5 Sample Progress Report and Plan

Progress Report and Plan

Intensive English Center at St. Cloud State University

September 11, 1997

The Vision:

An innovative, entrepreneurial program structure producing an academically superior program of community service and enhanced internationalization of the student body and faculty

(continued)

FIGURE 4.5 Continued

Executive Summary

Progress Report and Plan
Intensive English Center at
St. Cloud State University

September 11, 1997

Introduction
The St. Cloud State University Intensive English Center (IEC) is a non-credit-bearing, revenue-generating program established in the Department of English, College of Fine Arts and Humanities. The IEC program began its instructional operation on September 8, 1997.

In order to extend the development of professionally based ESL/TESL programs at SCSU, it would be helpful for SCSU to guarantee cash flow for the IEC for three years and to be prepared to lose money on IEC operation in one or more of these years. Cost and revenue projections for the first three years, 1997–2000, are listed in the attached pro forma budget. If these projections become reality, the IEC would only lose money in its first year of operation and would break even in its second and third years. These projections are somewhat conservative, and we hope that we will be able to improve on them in each year.

Vision
An innovative, entrepreneurial program structure producing an academically superior program of community service and enhanced internationalization of the student body and faculty.

Goals
The primary goal of the Center is to provide high-quality, academic, intensive instruction of English as a Second Language to student populations whose primary language is other than English. The secondary goal is to expose students to American culture and to facilitate understanding of academic life in the U.S. as well as to enhance their perception of cross-cultural communication and cultural behavioral patterns.

Curriculum
The IEC curriculum is based on a six-level model for language instruction. Each level can be completed in one academic term. The 1997–98 Fall program starts with students enrolled in two levels.

Background
The design of the Intensive English Center has been based on research into the structure of the most successful intensive English programs in the United States, which have the following features:

FIGURE 4.5 Continued

Executive Summary
IEC Progress Report and Plan
September 11, 1997
Page 2

- The TESL Graduate program and the intensive English program are both affiliated with the same academic unit, and the synergies that result help internationalize the institution at large.
- The intensive English program brings students into the regular university programs who would not otherwise come to the institution.
- The intensive English program is financially self-sustaining.

The Institutional Benefits of the IEC
Benefit #1: Pipeline for recruiting international students into college programs after completion of IEC instruction.

Benefit #2: Direct, immediate recruiting of international students who respond to IEC promotional efforts and who are eligible for immediate enrollment in SCSU college programs.

Benefit #3: Community outreach serving linguistic minorities who are economically disadvantaged.

Benefit #4: Teaching experience for TESL graduate students at SCSU.

Benefit #5: Research center for TESL.

Benefit #6: An innovative program structure ensuring academic integrity while benefiting from entrepreneurial creativity and initiative.

Benefit #7: Enhanced academic reputation for SCSU nationally and internationally.

Benefit #8: A financially self-sustaining center within three years.

Institutional Strengths SCSU Brings to the IEC
The IEC is a natural extension of the good work that has preceded it both on campus and abroad. The following institutional strengths are especially notable.

Strength #1: The community of St. Cloud and SCSU are perceived as safe and friendly and can be advertised as such.

Strength #2: There is a well established ESL/TESL program in the English Department.

Strength #3: The program has experienced, expert leadership.

Strength #4: SCSU has established international connections.

Strength #5: Institutional commitment has been substantial, and the trajectory of that commitment is rising.

(continued)

FIGURE 4.5 Continued

Executive Summary
IEC Progress Report and Plan
September 11, 1997
Page 3

Threats and Constraints
Despite the program's great promise, there are distinct threats to the success of the IEC and constraints upon its ability to succeed. Foremost of these are the following.

Threat/Constraint #1: The market for intensive English instruction is populated with numerous competitors. A significant number of these competing programs are high quality. We must compete on both price and quality.

IEC's Strategic Response:
- Low cost. We have priced our instruction about 20% below the mean fees of other good intensive English programs in the United States.
- High quality and safety. We have designed the program to compete in quality with the very best programs. Close personal attention and support also give further substance to our advertising claims that we have a safe, as well as high quality, program.
- Program accreditation. We will apply for program accreditation as soon as possible: 1998–99.
- Program visibility. Within our tight budget constraints, we have already achieved significant program visibility through networking and advertising.

Threat/Constraint #2: Student enrollments in intensive English centers are unpredictable and can fluctuate significantly even during the academic year.

IEC's Strategic Response:
- Use flexible staffing.
- Use flexible scheduling.
- Increasing stability through growth.

Threat/Constraint #3: Conversion to semesters presents an additional unknown in pricing and scheduling.

IEC's Strategic Response
- Maintain current pricing despite potential price resistance.
- Explain fee structure to prospective students in terms of costs per month, which will remain constant and will be competitive with other programs.

Threat/Constraint #4: Despite the exciting promise the IEC holds for the future, present resources are insufficient for it to survive.

IEC's Strategic Response
- Rely on supplemental institutional support near term.
- Develop proposals for outside support.
- Pursue other strategies of program development and cost containment.

FIGURE 4.5 Continued

Pro Forma Financial Statement, Intensive English Center, 1997–2000 (Including English Department Staffing & Supplies Contributions)

	1997–98 Two Levels of Instruction	1998–99 Three Levels of Instruction	1999–00 Scenario #1: Four Levels of Instruction	1999-00 Scenario #2: Five Levels of Instruction
Staffing Costs				
TAs × $5,000	$25,000 (5 TAs, 4 from English)	$50,000 (10 TAs)	$70,000 (14 TAs)	$85,000 (17 TAs)
FTNP 100% at 31,600	31,600	31,600	63,200	63,200
FTNP 1 × 66.7% at 21,160	21,160	21,160		21,160
Eng. Dept. Administrative Support (5% of Chair salary)	2,500	2,500	2,500	2,500
Secretarial Support (10%, 15%, and 20% of office salaries/year)	7,200	10,800	14,400	14,400
Summer extra duty days	2,800	2,800	2,800	2,800
Subtotal	$90,260	$118,860	$152,900	$189,060
Operating Costs				
Promotion/Advertising:				
—Recruiting/Workshops/ Networking	$3,000	$4,000	$7,000	$7,000
—Membership dues (NAFSA, TESOL, AAAL)	330	360	600	600
—Accreditation		1,500		
—Brochures	1,000	2,000	2,000	2,000
—Advertising	2,900	4,000	4,000	4,000
Student Activities, Cultural Events ($200 per student/term)	6,000	10,800	14,400	18,000
Guest Lectures	300 ($100 per term)	400 ($200 per term)	400 ($200 per term)	400 ($200 per term)
Educational Materials (tapes, videos, software, printed matter)	380	960	1,500	1,500
Equipment (CD/tape recorders, video camera, OHP)	150	650	1,000	1,000

(continued)

FIGURE 4.5 Continued

IEC Pro Forma Finacial Statement 1997–2000
Page 2

Routine Office Costs				
—Postage	800	900	1,100	1,100
—Phone	300	350	400	400
—Office Supplies (including $1700/year from English Departmt.)	2,200	2,300	2,500	2,500
—Copying	50	100	120	140
Subtotal	$17,410	$27,720	$34,620	$38,640
Total Expenses	$107,670	$146,580	$187,520	$227,700
Revenues				
Carryforward from initial $10,000 allocation 1996–97*	3,000			
Tuition	60,000 (10 stud × 2000 × 3 terms	162,000 (27 stud × 3000 × 2 terms)	216,000 (36 stud × 3000 × 2 terms)	270,000 (45 stud × 3000 × 2 terms)
Application Fees	500 ($25 per student)	810 ($30 per student)	1,080 ($30 per student)	1,350 ($30 per student)
Total Revenues	$63,500	$162,810	$217,080	$271,350
Net Revenue	($44,170)	$16,230	$29,560	$43,650

***Note:** The funds carried forward were originally allocated for Dr. James Robinson's trip to Korea, which had to be cancelled.

Comments:

1. This statement was prepared for Dr. Suzanne Williams, Vice President for Academic Affairs, by Marya Teutsch-Dwyer and Bob Inkster, October 27, 1997.
2. The numbers in this projection do not reflect the inter-programmatic synergies between the IEC and the other programs within the English Department. For example, the costs of TAs support the English Department's graduate program as well as helping staff the IEC.
3. Queries we have received from prospective applicants since our earlier projections on September 11, 1997, suggest that our enrollment and revenue projections are quite conservative.

FIGURE 4.6 Sample Strategic Plan

Research & Development

STRATEGIC PLAN

1997

EdFund - a Service of the California Student Aid Commission

(continued)

FIGURE 4.6 Continued

Research & Development

EDFUND - A Service of the California Student Aid Commission

TABLE OF CONTENTS

FIGURE 4.6 Continued

Research & Development

EDFUND - A Service of the California Student Aid Commission

Annual Planning Process

I. Establish/Update Research and Development's Strategic Plan:
- Shared Values
- Vision
- Mission
- Goal
- Objectives
- Current Planned Projects
- Core Competencies

II. Identify Research and Development's internal and external customers.

III. Determine the customers' expectations, using Research and Development's automated survey process.

IV. Confirm customer expectations using the appropriate tools and techniques.

V. Prioritize the confirmed customer expectations based on improvement potential and gap, organizational-timing, and inter-relational analyses.

VI. Establish and quantify project performance measures and project list based on previous analyses.

VII. Present survey and analyses' results and proposed project list to executives to obtain needed resources and consensus to proceed.

VIII. Create and implement action plans for projects on the project list.

IX. Monitor and report projects' status and organizational performance improvements as necessary.

NOTE: Value-added changes to the project list may be made with the approval of Research and Development's staff and executive officers.

Rev. 3/24/97

1

(continued)

FIGURE 4.6 Continued

Research & Development

EDFUND - A Service of the California Student Aid Commission

Shared Values

Promoting a quality environment in the work place and using quality philosophy, techniques, and tools, Research and Development staff will strive to:

1. Be honest and trustworthy.
2. Treat others as our most valued customers.
3. Support each other and our customers.
4. Treat others with respect and diplomacy.
5. Respect each others' time.
6. Keep commitments that are made.
7. Embrace a life-long learning concept to maintain state-of-the-art knowledge and skills.
8. Encourage cooperation and discourage competition.
9. Maintain confidentiality when handling private information.
10. Openly communicate and share information with members of the Research and Development team and others as appropriate.
11. Build relationships with others based on loyalty and trust.
12. Inspire commitment and pride-of-ownership in our work.
13. Provide leadership that supports and encourages motivation.
14. Focus on what's right for EdFund rather than what's right for Research and Development.
15. Maintain a sense of humor.
16. Celebrate accomplishments and successes.
17. Achieve excellence in all that we do.

Rev. 3/24/97

2

FIGURE 4.6 Continued

Vision

Research and Development enhances EdFund's position as the leading provider of student financial aid by perpetually expanding services and improving the efficiency and effectiveness of business processes.

Mission

Research and Development expands and improves services to customers and increases revenue by:
- Enhancing quality;
- Promoting partnerships with stakeholders; and
- Streamlining processes to reduce time and costs.

Goal

Achieve cost benefit improvements by establishing the vision, mission, goal and objectives of Research and Development and surveying EdFund's internal and external customers to identify and prioritize essential improvements.

Objectives

- Focus on the customers, envision their needs, and deliver exemplary services;
- Apply quality techniques and tools to assure sound business judgments, decisions, and practices;
- Partner with stakeholders to promote commitment and mutual cooperation.

Rev. 3/24/97

3

(continued)

FIGURE 4.6 Continued

Research & Development

EDFUND - A Service of the California Student Aid Commission

Planned Projects—1997

Priority	EdFund Project Description
1	Establish/Update Research and Development's Strategic Plan: Vision Mission Goal Objectives Tasks
1	Develop a Strategic Plan for Research and Development
1	Coordinate with others to develop and distribute EdFund's Strategic Plan
1	Assist executive and senior management to improve meeting processes starting with the Chief's meeting process
	Assist Support Services to:
1	—Streamline and automate the purchasing system for EdFund
1	—Streamline and automate the distribution of publications from the shipping center
1	—Streamline and automate the FAPS distribution process
1	Assist Financial Operations to streamline EdFund's accounting processes and develop procedures manuals
1	Draft policy for permitting EdFund's employees to have an EdFund-owned PC at home
1	Improve and automate the customer survey process for EdFund
1	Coordinate the reorganization of Investigations

4

FIGURE 4.6 Continued

Research & Development

EDFUND - A Service of the California Student Aid Commission

Duty Statement

Employee Name	Classification	Working Title
Kelly Roberts	**Staff Services Analyst**	**Policy Analyst**
Division/Branch	Position Number	Date
Research and Development	**270-5157-716**	**01/01/97**

Summary of Responsibilities:
This position works closely with and reports directly to Research and Development's Leader (Leader). Incumbent is responsible for a wide range of duties relating to administrative and personnel matters.

The incumbent will:

- Focus on EdFund's vision, mission, and policies and consistently apply them;
- Insure that all tasks are completed efficiently and effectively;
- Assist the Leader by performing confidential and complex research and analyzing data on a wide range of topics;
- Serve as the Commission's and EdFund's Coordinator for Internal Policy and Procedures Memos;
- Coordinate the Commission's and EdFund's signature authorization process. Serve as the liaison to auditors and State control agencies which provide oversight;
- Serve as the Commission's Filing Officer/Official for Statements of Economic Interest;
- Delegate and oversee assignments for clerical level Student Assistants;
- Independently accomplish tasks and projects whenever possible to reduce the workload of the Leader; and
- Perform miscellaneous administrative responsibilities.

Percentage of Time	Statement of Duties / Job Elements
35%	Perform annual review and update of all existing policies for the Commission and EdFund. Assist staff with writing and researching new and existing policies involving their specific areas.

10

FIGURE 4.7 Five Essential Elements of a Business Plan

1. Broad introspection into values and mission
2. Specific introspection into resources and achievements
3. Integration of broad internal vision with specific resources and achievements
4. Assessment of external environment
5. Projections of specific actions that are coherent with each other and with the other elements of the plan

boards of directors, legislative budget committees, and the like—then it explicitly takes on the character of a proposal (as we will also discuss in Chapter 12). The five essential elements of a business plan, listed in Figure 4.7, become arguments that make claims upon the readers, asking for time, money, equipment, staff, and other resources to solve the problems or seize the opportunities that are explicated in the plan.

First, though, we talk about the processes—and the constraints—of developing and using plans to help establish and monitor the direction and speed of your institution's movement. Plans, like every other kind of document we will discuss in this chapter, get a distinctly mixed review from both practitioners and scholars. Henry Mintzberg's (1994) *The Rise and Fall of Strategic Planning* gives a good overview of both the power and the dangers of plans. He points to compelling case studies of large, smart organizations, such as Texas Instruments, that have ridden elaborately and thoughtfully constructed corporate strategic plans to the brink of catastrophe. The case studies Mintzberg cites should be sobering to anyone who is devoted to planning as a cure for whatever ails an organization. Mintzberg identifies and analyzes three fallacies that he says underlie a great deal of planning:

1. **The fallacy of predetermination** lies in the belief that if an organization can just collect enough information and analyze it rigorously enough, it will be able to forecast the future. Mintzberg argues that the environment is far too complex to forecast far into the future with any meaningful degree of confidence.

2. **The fallacy of detachment** lies in the belief that it's desirable to separate planning and implementation. The classic model of this radical separation of planning and doing is the military, with the general far in the background, plotting strategy in the abstract, while the troops attempt to implement the strategy under circumstances that are far more complex and perhaps far different from the general's abstractions.

3. **The fallacy of formalization** lies in the belief that analysis can substitute for synthesis, when, in fact, the two mental processes are opposites. Too often, Mintzberg says, plans are developed using only left-brain, analytical, formula-driven thinking. He pleads for a more balanced planning process that calls on intuitive and creative insights, as well.

Mintzberg argues that planning is a human art—certainly one that employs rigorous data collection and analysis but an art nonetheless. He quotes with approval the remark "Ready, fire, aim!" made famous by Peters and Waterman (1982), and he adds that the more apt description of strategy formation would be "Ready, fire, aim, fire, aim, fire, aim, . . ." In other words, Mintzberg argues, planning and action need to be brought closer together. He says, "People act in order to think, and they think in order to act. The two proceed in tandem, like two feet walking, eventually converging in viable patterns of behavior (that is, realized strategies)" (p. 286).

Goals and Expression

In an interesting sense, *expression* really comes first in a planning document. In fact, that's why we began our chapter discussion with mission/vision statements. In its most simple terms, a plan is a map for getting from Point A to Point B. Too often, people forget to think about where either point is and simply muddle along. Other people will invest considerable effort in determining where Point B is but will take Point A—where they are now—for granted. In fact, Point A is primary. You need to clarify and express your institutional identity *before* you can begin to think effectively about where you want to go. Ask yourself these questions:

- What values and aspirations inform your institutional culture?
- What goals do they enable?
- What goals do they preclude?

If you don't ask these kinds of questions first, you may find yourself and your organization committed to and invested in a goal that is inconsistent with your personal and organization values and aspirations. The mission/vision statement provides a benchmark for these "heart and soul" orientations for both Point A and Point B, and the strategic plan enriches the detail in this vision. We can see this in both the EdFund and Intensive English Center (IEC) sample plans. The IEC even puts its vision statement on the title page, and the EdFund plan notes vision, mission, goal, and objectives prominently in its table of contents and devotes its third page to these statements.

Readers

Even if the strategic plan is an entirely internal document, it would be a mistake to assume that you're just writing it for yourself and your immediate colleagues. Executives use strategic plans to decide institutional priorities and allocate resources. Strategic plans can determine who gets new equipment, increased salaries, more supplies, and larger space, and they can even determine who stays, gets promoted, or gets fired (downsized). So you need to think carefully about who your readers are and what their own plans may be for this strategic plan you're developing. The following questions should help you identify threats and opportunities represented by your readers for you and your planning document itself, and they may suggest further, more specific questions as you work through them:

- Who's going to read this document? (Are you sure these are the only readers?)
- Is this a routine, periodic planning exercise? (Again, are you sure?)
- What general perception do your readers have of you and the program or project that's represented by this plan?
- What's the nastiest thing somebody could do to you or your program based on this document? How can you write the document to mitigate or eliminate this threat?
- Is there a reader (or maybe more than one) who'd be willing to be surprised by an unconventional, unexpected, creative program idea?
- What kinds of information and arguments are your readers likely to see and believe? Narrative text? Financial numbers and other statistics? Are they likely to respond more strongly to hard data or to ideas, concepts, and visions?

Arguments: Using SWOT to Develop Arguments

A convention commonly called *situational analysis* and often abbreviated as *SWOT analysis* is probably the most commonly used format for organizing a strategic plan. The SWOT acronym stands for *Strengths, Weakness, Opportunities,* and *Threats.* SWOT follows essentially the process we have been suggesting: First, you do an organizational introspection, an audit of your organizational strengths and weaknesses (and, by the way, your organizational values and aspirations). Then, you turn your attention outward, to the opportunities and threats in your environment. You might find opportunities in an emerging new technology that complements your organization's strengths or your products and services. The convergence of this new technology and your organization's strengths may reveal a new market opportunity. Or you might find threats in an emerging new technology. A classic example of an entire national industry's failure to see a threat in an emerging new technology is the Swiss watch manufacturing industry's slow recognition of the ramifications of the highly accurate electronic quartz technology for timing devices. You might find opportunities or threats in new legislation—at the local, state, national, or even international level—or in emerging demographic trends at any of these levels. You might find opportunities or threats in developments among your competitors, customers, or vendors. Having taken this situational audit, looking both internally and externally, you next imagine a set of alternative scenarios for plausible strategies for your organization or your particular division of the organization, evaluating each in terms of its promise based on your SWOT situation.

You can even develop a four-celled matrix for your SWOT analysis, using the matrix in Figure 4.8 to help you visualize where strengths, weaknesses, opportunities, and threats converge. Each of the four cells then suggests an action plan. For example, Cell 1, where your strengths and opportunities converge, constitutes a list of conditions you should capitalize on.

FIGURE 4.8 SWOT Analysis Matrix

	Strengths	Weaknesses
Opportunities	**Cell 1.** Capitalize to take advantage of strengths and opportunities.	**Cell 2.** Improve on these to take better advantage of the opportunities.
Threats	**Cell 3.** Monitor these. A move toward Cell 1, for example, calls for a change of strategy to capitalizing.	**Cell 4.** Eliminate or mitigate either weakness or threat, if possible.

SWOT is a powerful analytical tactic as well as an effective organizational convention for laying out your argument as your plan unfolds. In addition, it nicely complements the more general kind of situational analysis we described in Chapter 2 for getting a confident grip on complex situations. In fact, we think your exploration of all four elements of the SWOT acronym can be enhanced when you explicitly shift perspectives so that you're sure to ask yourself how your organization's strengths and weaknesses and its opportunities and threats have developed over time. You can then ask what these past developments suggest about future trends. And you can further enhance this insight by thinking systematically about wider contexts—by asking how events and conditions widely distant from your immediate organizational environment may present significant opportunities or threats in the future.

Conventions

The conventional elements of the argument in a business plan, SWOT, generally comprise the bulk of the narrative of the document, but they aren't the whole plan or its whole set of conventions. First, the business plan is typically a longer document. A quick scan of four plans on hand at this moment shows page counts of 16, 36, 37, and 39 pages. Given this typically longer length, it's important that you help your readers make their way using these roadmapping conventions (which we will discuss further in Chapter 10): summary, table of contents, page numbers, informative headers, white space to separate and emphasize important points, and so on. For example, three of the four business plans here on the desk have tables of contents. The fourth is a 16-page plan that uses exceptionally clear document design signals instead of a table of contents: Informative headers and subheaders, bullets, white space, and other graphic and typographic signals help readers find their way in the document. And even with all these helpful traffic signals for the reader, we would still recommend adding a table of contents.

To give you an idea of the organizational conventions used in these four quite different plans, Figures 4.9 through 4.12 present the tables of contents of the three longer plans, followed by a table of contents that we've made from the headers of the fourth plan. The headers may not strike you as being very informative (contrary to

FIGURE 4.9 Table of Contents, Plan 1

Table of Contents

FIGURE 4.10 Table of Contents, Plan 2

Table of Contents

I. The Business
   A. General Description
   B. Market
   C. Location
   D. Competition
   E. Personnel
   F. Management
   G. Summary
II. Financial Statements
   A. Balance Sheet
   B. Breakdown Analysis
   C. Income Projections
   D. Working Capital Analysis
III. Appendix

our advice here and in Chapter 10 for creating headers), largely because the specific information has been distilled out of them to protect the anonymity of their respective businesses.

Because of the very nature of business plans, organizations tend to be protective, even secretive, about these documents. To take a dramatic example, imagine that you are a small company, precariously poised between solid success and potential failure in a highly competitive market. Suppose that you've just completed a strategic market analysis and discovered what you're sure is an emerging need in the marketplace that your company can fill if you can act quickly to modify your product and get it into the market in six months. If you can be into the market before your competitors see this opportunity, the future of your company is likely to be secure, but if other larger, stronger competitors also come into the market about the same time as your company, you probably won't be able to compete, and the investment you make in your product modification will threaten the viability of your company. You've done a careful SWOT analysis that demonstrates both the threat and the opportunity. So now the question is this: Do you want your competitors—or anybody else who isn't an insider or investor—to know about your plan? For most businesses, the answer is

FIGURE 4.11 Table of Contents, Plan 3. For ease of reference, the writers included all the tables and figures in the Table of Contents. (The tables and figures are distributed throughout this document, rather than in an appendix.) Each table or figure is given a title that describes its content and is identified by its chapter number and order of appearance in the chapter. For example, Figure 7–1, Cash Requirements, 1998, 1999, 2000, is the first figure in Chapter 7.0, Finance.

Table of Contents

Chapter Headings

Tables and Figures

a quick and resounding no. As a result, samples of business plans are fairly hard to obtain. One recently published collection of good business plans is Kristin Kahrs and Karin Koek's (1996) *Business Plans Handbook.* Another is David Gumpert's (1996) *Inc. Magazine Presents How to Really Create a Successful Business Plan.* Paul Tiffany and Steven Peterson's (1997) *Business Plans for Dummies* has an extended sample showing the business plan of a California winery.

One of the interesting things about the two sample plans (see Figures 4.5 and 4.6) is the contrast between them. For example, while both have some elements of

FIGURE 4.12 Table of Contents, Plan 4

Table of Contents

Executive Summary

Company Overview

- **Business Mission Statement**
- **Corporate Goals and Objectives**
- **Corporate Values Statement**
- **Corporate Vision Statement**

Business Environment

- **Market Trends**
  - **Table: Annual U.S. Consumption since 1940**
  - **Table: Projected U.S. Consumption through 2000**
- **Market Segment Growth**
  - (Four tables showing trends in different segments)
- **Buyer Behavior**
- **Competition in the Segments**
  - **Industry Leaders**
  - **Leaders in Target Market Segment 1**
  - **Leaders in Target Market Segment 2**
- **Industry Forces in the Target Market Segments**

Company Description and Strategy

- **Table: Sales and Revenues of Past Five Years**
- **Table: Profits of Past Five Years**
- **Growth Strategy**
- **Competitive Advantage**

Action Plan

Financial Review (Including pro-forma income statement)

SWOT, the SWOT analysis, with its entrepreneurial orientation, is much more prominent in the plan for the Intensive English Center than in the plan for EdFund. In a sense, it could be said that the only element of SWOT that's really apparent in the EdFund plan is an analysis of strengths in the section Core Competencies. In a strict marketing sense, opportunities and threats are simply not significant issues for EdFund because it is the private sector arm of a state agency with essentially a monopoly and a captive constituency. Nevertheless, the document takes special care to emphasize and inculcate customer service as a central organizational value. Prominently listed in the table of contents is a document called Customer Creed, a seven-point statement of service-oriented values. Point 1, for example, says, "The customer is our reason for being here."

In comparison, the Intensive English Center plan really has all four elements of a SWOT analysis, although this exact language (Strengths, Weaknesses, Opportunities, Threats) doesn't always appear in the document. For example, the document has a major section titled The Institutional Benefits of the IEC, which really is a discussion of the opportunities. Another major section is titled Threats and Constraints, and it combines a discussion of threats and weaknesses. The section called Institutional Strengths clearly correlates with the strengths element of SWOT.

Using GRACE to Improve Policies and Procedures Manuals

Of all the documents you will encounter in your professional career, either as a writer or a reader, policies and procedures manuals are possibly the most notorious source of frustration and the most consistent target of sardonic humor in cartoon strips, from "Doonesbury" to "Dilbert." There are systemic forces all around contending to make policies and procedures manuals bad documents. For one thing, people who are assigned to write them are rarely given the time to do a really good job. For another, the goals of these documents are often mixed or confused, either intentionally or unintentionally. Often, what starts out to be an informative, instructional document becomes instead a legalistic, backside-covering set of disclaimers of responsibility. Documents intended to make people's work safer and more effective instead lead readers into costly, even fatal mistakes.

Given this discouraging state of affairs, we may ask why anybody would want to write a manual at all. The answer, of course, is that manuals really do serve important functions in organizations. Like mission/vision statements and plans, they provide a tangible embodiment of the collective mind, will, and memory of the organization. While employees sometimes resist and resent having their freedom to act in the organization constrained by established policies and procedures, the fact is that policies and procedures are often liberating and enabling. Suppose, for example, that you are about to start a complex task that could be completed any number of different ways. Each of these alternatives would produce a somewhat different result, however, and your colleagues' work will be made easier or harder, depending on how it relates to yours. If there is an established policy or procedure for completing the task, then you are freed from having to decide among these alternatives and worrying about the ramifications for your colleagues. Or, if you are looking for some piece of equipment, document, or electronically stored piece of information, your search will be made immeasurably easier if an established policy has been followed for storing that equipment, document, or information. You simply consult the manual as a guide to your own search procedure and then look where the manual indicates you should.

If you are faced with the task of writing a set of policies and procedures, you can do several things to increase the chances that your document will do what it is intended to do. GRACE again provides a framework both for finding potential pitfalls and finding strategies for avoiding them.

Goals: Damage Control and Affirmative Goals

Tom Peters (1994) gives us a healthy caution flag about policies and procedures manuals. Here's what he says in *The Pursuit of WOW!*

> I'd rather read just about anything than a company policy and procedures manual. Inevitably such manuals are collections of "don'ts." And "don'ts" stop initiative, squelch innovation, stymie creativity. When I see a thick manual, I know I'm looking at a slow company, one that's struggling under a lot of "Halt, who goes there"-ism and excess baggage. (pp. 69–70)

Peters believes policies and procedures manuals should be sets of "do" manuals, rather than "don't" manuals. Even if a policy is stated in negative terms, it should have an affirmative function. For example, being able to tell a difficult customer or vendor "That's against our policy" can be a vital resource at a critical time in a difficult negotiation. This is a policy that's framed as a "don't" but empowers an employee to act with confidence in a difficult situation. And if it's taught and learned alongside policies that show the employee how to offer alternatives, then it can make life better for everyone it touches—even the customer or client who is initially affected by it negatively. But if you can't find an affirmative goal for a procedure or policy you're writing, maybe you should look again at that procedure or policy critically, asking whether it should even exist.

First, Do No Harm!

Your first goal in writing a policy or procedure is damage control. You don't want somebody blowing up expensive equipment, hurting themselves, or committing the organization to some project that's perhaps inconsistent with the corporate mission, wastes resources, damages client relationships, or is even against the law. So, first and most important, ask yourself what would be the worst possible thing that could happen if someone misread or didn't read your policy or procedure statement. Imagine someone in the situation where this policy or procedure applies:

- What must this person do?
- And what must this person not do?
- What would be the most dangerous or harmful thing someone could do—or not do—in this situation?

This is where you should direct your reader's attention first—on the most dangerous step. Never mind where them step might come in the normal procedure. Too often, writers of procedures or policies assume that people who are working through them will first read the document completely and then follow the steps as written. Relying on this assumption, writers don't say anything about this critical, dangerous step until they reach the point in the procedure where they understand the step belongs. But people who are working through these procedures generally bring their own assumptions to the task. They may not read written procedures completely. They may not even be aware that instructions exist. They may assume there's a different sequence to the procedures, and they may act on this assumption so that they come to the critical step without having seen the writers' warning. This assumption that your reader will be of like mind with you in approaching procedures is just one of several dangerous assumptions that can lead you astray as a writer and can lead users to sometimes disastrous results. We'll talk about others in a later section on readers.

PAVLOV®

Source: PAVLOV © 1997 Ted Martin. Reprinted with permission of UNIVERSAL PRESS SYNDICATE. All rights reserved.

After Damage Control, Set Affirmative Goals

Once you're confident you've headed your readers away from potential catastrophes, the next step is to decide what specific affirmative goals you need to achieve with this policy or procedure statement. So, here's the second crucial question: What specific corporate goal does the policy or procedure serve?

An important part of this exploration may be asking yourself about multiple goals and how they may interact and even conflict:

- What are your instructional goals for this policy/procedure statement?
- What are your other goals for this policy/procedure statement? For instance, is the statement intended for external readers—as a barrier to certain kinds of business relationships or a shield against certain kinds of demands or litigation?
- If there are mixed goals, how do they interact and, possibly, conflict?
- Does any particular policy or procedure statement have legal ramifications? Often, the answer here is yes, and if you suspect this might be the case, you may want to consult your legal counsel. Policies and procedures that have legal implications generally are cleared by the organization's lawyers, and these documents often cite the legal code upon which they are based. The Information Security General Policy shown in Figure 4.13 is an example of such a policy. Note that your organization may be at particular legal risk if you have a formal written policy or procedure that is systematically ignored or not followed. That is why guidelines intended to ensure compliance often include a statement that clarifies how information about the policy or procedure will be disseminated. For instance, the Information Security General Policy stipulates the following:

  > As part of the "New Employee Package" ensure that the employee has received, read, completed, and signed (as appropriate) the Information Security and Confidentiality Agreement, Section 502 of the California Penal Code, and the EdFund policy governing access to information assets.

As you think about specific goals for your policies and procedures documents, remember these broad, general goals, too:

- The policy/procedure must be available and conveniently accessible to the people who need to know it.
- The people who need to know the policy/procedure must know that it's available and applies to them.
- Because the organization is dynamic and evolving, policies and procedures will change; the physical embodiment of these policies and procedures—the manual—must be set up to accommodate change readily.

Finally, it's vital to remember that all these goals are pointing to a context around your written text. No policy or procedure and no manual of policies and procedures,

FIGURE 4.13 Sample Policy Memo

EdFund - *A Service of the California Student Aid Commission*

<table>
<tr><td colspan="2">SECURITY & RISK MGMT POLICY AND PROCEDURES MEMO</td><td>CONTROL NUMBER:
FY 96-97 S-101ef</td></tr>
<tr><td colspan="2">SUBJECT:
Information Security General Policy</td><td>EFFECTIVE DATE:
01/01/97</td></tr>
<tr><td>APPROVED BY:
Joe Rodriguez</td><td>APPROVED BY:
Connie Chang</td><td>CONTACT:
Security and Risk Mgmt Office</td></tr>
</table>

EdFund is committed to the protection of the information assets it owns or in its custody. An intricate part of this commitment is EdFund's dedication to the compliance with federal and state information security laws, regulations, generally accepted system security principles, as well as EDP audit requirements. In administration of this policy, employees will be given access to information assets only for the purpose of performing their job and with the signed approval from authorized EdFund staff.

DEFINITION OF INFORMATION ASSETS
Information Assets are defined as:

- All categories of information, automated or manually recorded, on any media, including (but not limited to) records, files, and data bases; and
- Information technology facilities, file storage equipment, computer systems, telecommunication equipment and software owned or leased.

POLICY
ALL employees, which includes students, contractors, subcontractors, and emergency hires, must have a signed Information Security and Confidentiality Agreement (Attachment A) on file in the Security and Risk Management Office before being given access to any EdFund or California Student Aid Commission's information assets.

Supervisors and Managers are responsible for determining the need for, and authorizing the access to EdFund's information assets. Supervisors and Managers are also responsible for monitoring the activities of each authorized employee to ensure compliance with EdFund policies.

Responsibilities of Supervisors and Managers
- Determine what information assets their employees shall have access to and the level of access needed for the employee to accomplish his/her job.
- As part of the "New Employee Package" ensure that the employee has received, read, completed, and signed (as appropriate) the Information Security and Confidentiality Agreement, Section 502 of the California Penal Code, and the EdFund policy governing access to information assets.

FIGURE 4.13 Continued

(EdFund New Employee Packages can be obtained from the Human Resources Office, Student and Contractor New Employee Packages must be obtained from the Contract Services Section within the Support Services Office.)

- Submit the Information Security and Confidentiality Agreement and the Internal Access Request form (Attachment B) to the Security and Risk Management Office.
- For employees who have changed job duties, submit a new Information Security and Confidentiality Agreement and Internal Access Request form to the Security and Risk Management Office when the employee no longer requires access, or requires different access, to any computerized system.
- Upon the separation of any employee, submit to the Security and Risk Management Office the Internal Access Request form deleting all system(s) access. (This step is to be performed when completing the Exit Clearance form.)

It must be understood that:

- Access authorization may be promptly revoked when willful violations of the Information Security and Confidentiality Agreement occur. Willful violations include, but are not limited to:
  - The use of the logon and password of another individual, with or without that individual's permission.
  - The providing of his or her password to someone else to use.
  - The unauthorized modification, disclosure, or destruction of confidential information.
  - The unauthorized modification, disclosure, or destruction of data.
  - The introduction of a virus or worm.
  - The downloading or loading of non-EdFund authorized software.

GENERAL

- All employees are expected to promptly report any perceived wrongdoing to the Security and Risk Management Office. (It is the policy of the Security and Risk Management Office to handle all matters with the utmost confidentiality.)
- Periodic audits will be conducted to identify actual or potential violations of information security and confidentiality requirements.
- The Security and Risk Management Office may report observations or reports of noncompliance to the police, investigators, auditors, etc., as deemed appropriate. Anyone who does not comply with applicable laws and security requirements may be subject to legal and/or disciplinary action.

Questions regarding this policy should be directed to the Security and Risk Management Office.

even the best written in the world, can jump in front of its readers and force them to read. Written policies and procedures are just one tool in a complete, coherent system of management and coordination. If employees are going to read and understand policies and procedures, they need to be given the time and opportunity to do so, and they have to be taught why these policies and procedures are important. So, these documents have to be part of a thoughtful, ongoing program of orientation, acculturation, education, and re-education. Crucial policies and procedures need to be made visible—and audible—to employees.

And if they are vital to the well-being of an employee, a customer, or the organization at large, then it may not be sufficient to have policies and procedures exist only as written paper or electronic documents. These crucial materials may need to be designed into the structure of the product or the organization itself. For example, if there is a dangerous, destructive error that an employee or customer could make in assembling or operating a piece of equipment, then the equipment should contain the directions for the correct assembly or operation. As we discuss in the following section, Dangerous Assumption 1, the ideal situation is to design the equipment so that its assembly or operation is foolproof.

Certainly, policies and procedures need to be compiled in manuals and stored systematically in cabinets, on shelves, or on computer disks so that they are preserved and available for reference. But people need to know that these policies and procedures exist, and they need to know how to access them. Further, they need to understand why and when they should access them. This knowledge about the organization's policies and procedures documents—and a sense of their value and relevance—can't come only from the documents. The goals of these documents arise from their organizational context, and that same context needs to point to the documents and the policies and procedures they embody so they can be retrieved and used in context.

Readers and Dangerous Assumptions

It's safe to say that the people reading your policies and procedures are not reading avidly for pleasure. In fact, as we've noted, readers of procedures are notorious nonreaders. In particular, you should be wary of making the following kinds of assumptions about your readers:

DANGEROUS ASSUMPTION 1: **My readers will read the complete statement or set of instructions before acting on it.**

We mentioned this assumption earlier, noting that it's not necessarily safe to assume your readers will read the policy or procedure at all. They may not even know it exists. This means you need to do several things. First, as we've already suggested, you have to supplement policies and procedures statements with orientation and training sessions that make people aware of why and where these resources exist. Second, you need to make these policies and procedures visible and accessible to the people who need them. Third, these kinds of policy and procedure concerns should be considered in the basic design of your organization's products and work environment and tools. For a simple example, consider the 3½" floppy computer disk. The signals that indicate the correct and incorrect ways to insert the disk into a computer are inherent in the design of the disk. If you try to insert it into the computer the wrong way, it won't go in. This concern for the message that a product, tool, or workspace communicates by its inherent design suggests one other thing that we think is important: People who write policies and procedures manuals (especially procedures manuals for customers), should be involved in the design, production, and testing of the product itself, and they should use GRACE—not only in creating documentation for the product but in creating the product, too. For an excellent discussion of design strategies that help make things more understandable for people who use them, see Donald A. Norman's (1990) *The Design of Everyday Things.*

DANGEROUS ASSUMPTION 2: **Readers share my interest in the history and details of these policies and procedures.**

The people reading your procedure instructions will primarily want to know how to finish their task efficiently and safely. Normally, they won't be interested in how the procedure came about, and they are likely to be impatient with historical information about the policy or procedure if they don't see how it helps them do what they need to do.

DANGEROUS ASSUMPTION 3: **Readers will approach the situation that calls forth this policy or procedure in the same way I do—with the same assumptions about cause and effect, chronological sequence of subprocedures, and importance and value of the policy or procedure.**

Assumption 3 represents the hazard you will encounter if you write with your eye only on the hazard represented by Assumption 2. Not to give essential information about the context and relevance of the policy or procedure may leave readers assuming it doesn't apply to them. So, it's important to clarify what the readers' responsibilities are and to specify when the policy or procedure is applicable. For instance, the document on Building and Personal Security (see Figure 4.14) opens by insisting that every reader's individual compliance is required to make sure that all staff members are safe; the document goes on to clarify exactly what employees are obligated to do. The document also provides information that will help readers to determine who "unauthorized persons" are, including categories of people that readers might not think of as unauthorized: someone the reader recognizes who might have been fired recently or guests or relatives of employees. In some situations, a brief narrative of how the procedure came about might persuade a resistant reader to comply: for instance, "This procedure was established in 1997 after six people injured themselves assembling the components incorrectly." Likewise, if someone is reading your policy statement, it may help him or her to understand how to apply that policy to different complex situations if the context that evoked the policy is explained. It may even help someone understand when *not* to follow this particular policy or procedure by explaining the limits of its scope of applicability.

FIGURE 4.14 Sample Policy Memo

EdFund - *A Service of the California Student Aid Commission*

SECURITY & RISK MGMT POLICY AND PROCEDURES MEMO		CONTROL NUMBER: **FY 96-97 S-103ef**
SUBJECT: **Building and Personal Security**		EFFECTIVE DATE: 01/01/97
APPROVED BY: Joe Rodriguez	APPROVED BY: Connie Chang	CONTACT: Security and Risk Mgmt Ofc.

All staff are reminded that their individual compliance with this policy is necessary to ensure the safety of all staff.

"Unauthorized persons" must not be allowed access to the work area. An "unauthorized person" is anyone, including recognized staff, that does not possess an active working security access badge. Anyone requesting access that does not possess a security access badge must be directed to the security guard located in the reception area for assistance. To ensure employee safety, there must be no exceptions to this policy.

Employees *must not:*

- Enter or leave the work area using the reception area access door. This could enable unauthorized persons to simply follow employees into the work area.
- Loan his/her badge to another employee. It you do, you will be held responsible for any unauthorized actions the borrower of the badge may take.
- Let anyone, including other recognized staff, personal visitors, or even relatives of staff, into the work areas. Even it you escort them into the office work area, you may be responsible for creating a dangerous situation. For example, a person you recognize asks that you let them into the work area because they have forgotten their security access badge. Even though you may recognize this person, this person's employment may have recently been terminated and this person may be intending some type of harm.
- Escort guests, friends, or relatives into the work area without having them register with the guard. The cafeteria or empty conference rooms should be used when visiting with relatives or personal guests.
- Give friends, relatives, strangers, or other non-authorized employees, personal information about staff. Do not tell anyone (including staff) personally or by phone anything about other staff. For example, if an inquiry is made regarding where an employee is, don't say that the employee is at home sick. Instead, say that the employee is "unavailable" and then ask if you may take a message. The employee may not want anyone to know they are at home. Another example might be that a very friendly stranger asks you to point out and identify a collection staff person in the hallway. This same friendly stranger may intend physical harm.

Understandably, it is difficult to always follow the security measures noted above. However, chronic noncompliance may result in an adverse action being taken against you.

FIGURE 4.14 Continued

It is essential that each of us do our part to the best of our abilities. Everyone should understand that adhering to this policy is the only way we can reasonably ensure the safety of all staff. Remembering this, you should not put other staff on the spot by asking if they will let you into an area. Rather than get frustrated with staff who comply with this policy, we should thank them for following this safety policy and protecting everyone.

Employees who work early or late shifts or overtime when other staff are not generally around, should be especially cautious when entering or leaving work. Practice the buddy system by coordinating with other staff or the security guards when entering or leaving the building.

If you have any questions concerning this policy, please contact the Security and Risk Management Office at 555-4843.

DANGEROUS ASSUMPTION 4: **Readers will read these policies and procedures in essentially the same kind of environment and circumstances that I'm in as I write them.**

It's absolutely vital to visualize the readers of your policy or procedure in the circumstances where they are likely to need to read it. The most obvious illustration of this need would be an emergency procedure. Imagine the range of likely scenarios where someone would need to refer to your instructions for this procedure:

- What kinds of physical constraints might be present? Limited lighting or perhaps even no lighting at all?
- What about other conditions that could affect either your reader or the physical text of your instructions? Extreme cold or extreme heat? Water, grease, wind, dust, chemicals, blood, or other factors that might degrade the legibility of your instructions or the ability of your reader to interpret them effectively and efficiently?
- What about time as a limiting factor? How much time is your reader likely to have to read, perhaps test, and put into action your instructions for this policy or procedure?
- What about adverse psychological or social conditions that might impinge on your reader? Suppose, for example, that he or she is trying to use your instructions to follow life-saving procedures or summon appropriate help in a medical emergency.

You need to visualize each situation carefully and be to sure place essential information where your reader will find it immediately. (This, of course, is also another example of the need to complement the written policy with training and instruction.)

Or, suppose readers will likely have to refer to a policy on resolving a conflict over a disputed transaction—while in the middle of a tense, difficult negotiation with an angry, aggressive customer. In order to help these readers, you will need to anticipate their questions and provide the written policy support they need to serve the interests of your own organization: for instance, "Sorry, corporate policy won't let me give you cash under these conditions." And at the same time, anticipate their need to act, perhaps in creative and entrepreneurial ways, and help them understand quickly and confidently what actions they *are* authorized to take: "But I can give you an immediate credit or exchange, or we can mail you a check within two weeks."

One of the best ways to get a realistic view of the readers of your policies and procedures (if you have the time and resources) is to interview people who actually work in the situations where these policies and procedures apply. If possible, place yourself in one of these worksites, doing the work yourself, so that you can understand, literally from inside a user's head, what your readers need. Another effective way to help ensure the effectiveness of your writing in these situations is to pilot-test drafts among users and get their feedback after actually using the documents. (Consult Chapter 11 for detailed discussion of focus-group and interview techniques if you're considering these kinds of reader research.)

What if your resources won't permit these more elaborate kinds of surveying your readers and testing your writing in actual field tests? You still need to research your readers' needs as carefully and creatively as your time and resources will allow so that you will minimize all three risky assumptions.

Arguments

Your first thought may be that arguments really don't apply when writing policies and procedures. After all, a written policy or procedure is just a straightforward, matter-of-fact exposition. But look again at the risky assumptions we've just talked about and the contexts we've described where readers may be consulting your document. Remember that most readers of policies and procedures are resistant ones whose primary interest while they're reading usually is doing something else. And their resistance to actually complying with the policy or procedure can be very high if they perceive that it's at odds with the way they would prefer to do things.

So, you may want to make several important arguments, either explicitly or implicitly, when you're designing or introducing policies and procedures documents. In some cases, you'll probably want to make these arguments in the documents. In other cases, you'll want to make the arguments in orientation sessions and on other occasions when you're teaching or referring to the policies and procedures.

Authority

It may be meaningful or relevant to your readers to know the authority for this policy or procedure, especially if they're likely to be resistant to other kinds of arguments. For example, policy statements frequently have just a brief note, either at the bottom or the top of the document, that gives the date of the formal adoption of the policy and names the governing entity that approved it. It might say something like "Approved by safety committee, Sept. 11, 1995." And if policies or procedures are based upon legal codes or other sorts of state or federal mandates, these laws or mandates are generally mentioned in the policy or procedure, as well. Consider, for instance, the appeals to authority in the Information Security General Policy (Figure 4.13), in the document concerning Compliance with the Information Practices Act of 1977 (Figure 4.15), and in policies governing the Youth Mentor Program (Figure 4.16). The policies concerning information are grounded in state legal codes, and the organizations and their employees are bound by these codes and policies to limit access to certain sorts of information. The guidelines for the Youth Mentor Program have resulted from an executive order from the state governor. Given the legal ramifications of these policies, appeals to authority are a central part of their arguments.

In fact, it's no surprise that authority figures so largely in these documents since the organizations are parts of the California state government. The state government of the most populous state in the union is perhaps the very kind of large, slow, organization Tom Peters (1994) was complaining about when we quoted him a few pages back. In bureaucracies this large—especially public, government institutions—extensive rules, regulations, statutes, and other guidelines for procedures and policies are perhaps inevitable. Look at Figure 4.17—the Table of Contents of the Guidebook for the California Student Aid Commission's Performance Evaluation Program (PEP). Notice that the entire first section is devoted to PEP Philosophy, Goals, and Objectives. And in the document itself (which we don't show here), the subsection Authorizing Regulations takes up an entire page of single-spaced text.

Utility

Readers' resistance is likely to dissolve most quickly if they are convinced that a policy or procedure is useful to them or, more broadly, to the organization. One caution, of course, is that you don't want to belabor this argument or any other because then you will be wasting your readers' valuable time, impeding their progress in reading, understanding, and applying the policy or procedure. Often, the utility of a policy or procedure will be clear to those who are applying it. If it is *not,* this may be an important red flag to you when you're writing the policy or procedure. Back up and ask yourself whether this is one of those policies or procedures that Tom Peters (1994) talks about hating in *The Pursuit of WOW!*

Delimitations

The delimitations argument complements both the authority and the utility argument. It can be useful to point out where the policy or procedure does *not* apply. Readers will have more confidence in your authority and utility arguments if you help them identify the policies and procedures that do not apply to their situation at the moment. You can even use the delimitations argument as an effective test in the design of policies and procedures. As you ponder the adoption and writing of a policy or procedure statement, ask yourself where and to whom this document really does and does not need to apply. You may find these questions serve as a filter to eliminate unnecessary policies and procedures.

FIGURE 4.15 Sample Policy Memo

EdFund - *A Service of the California Student Aid Commission*

SECURITY & RISK MGMT POLICY AND PROCEDURES MEMO		CONTROL NUMBER: **FY 96-97 S-102ef**
SUBJECT: **Compliance with the Information Practices Act of 1977**		EFFECTIVE DATE: 01/01/97
APPROVED BY: *Joe Rodriguez*	APPROVED BY: *Connie Chang*	CONTACT: Security and Risk Mgmt Ofc.

The Information Practices Act (IPA) provides guidelines to assure fair treatment of individuals who are the subjects of state agency records. The IPA places specific requirements on state agencies in the collection, use, maintenance, and dissemination of personal information about individuals. With specific exceptions, individuals may review, obtain copies, request amendments and corrections, and dispute information pertaining to them in state records.

EdFund as an auxiliary organization of the California Student Aid Commission (Commission) is required to adhere to the same laws as the Commission as it pertains to the collection, use, dissemination, retention, and disposition of personal information.

Specify policy guidelines for the proper administration of the IPA's provisions are as follows:

RULES OF CONDUCT

Employees responsible for the operation, disclosure, or maintenance of records containing personal information shall follow the rules of conduct for the proper administration of the IPA's provisions. The rules of conduct are as follows (California Civil Code, IPA, Section 1798.20):

1. All employees responsible for the collection, maintenance, use, and dissemination of personal information about individuals must comply with the provisions of the California Civil Code, IPA, Section 1798, et seq. Personal information is defined as information that identifies or describes an individual, including, but not limited to, his or her name, social security number, physical description, home address, home phone number, education, financial matters, and medical or employment history.
2. Employees must not require individuals to disclose personal information which is not necessary and relevant to the lawful State function for which the employee is responsible.
3. Employees must only disclose personal information to those individuals or government entities to whom the release of this information is authorized, as defined under the conditions of disclosure.

FIGURE 4.15 Continued

4. Employees must keep an accurate record of the disclosures of personal information authorized in #3 above, which must include the individual's and institution's names, title, date, nature and purpose the information was disclosed.
5. Employees must assist individuals who seek information on accessing records pertaining to themselves in making their inquiry clear and concise, so that the records are easily located.
6. Employees must make every reasonable effort to see that inquiries and access requests, by individuals for their personal records, are responded to within 30 days of receipt of request for active records and 60 days of receipt of request for inactive records that have been archived.
7. Employees must not disclose personal information relating to individuals for their own interest or advantage. The intentional violation of this policy shall be cause for disciplinary action, including dismissal, and possible civil action for invasion of privacy.
8. Employees responsible for maintaining records which contain personal information must take all necessary precautions to assure that proper administrative, technical, and physical safeguards are established and followed, in order to protect the confidentiality of the records.

RECORD OF SOURCES OF INFORMATION
Employees responsible for the collection of personal information must maintain the source or sources of the information. The source or sources of information must be maintained in a readily accessible form, so that the information may easily be located for inspection by the requester (California Civil Code, IPA, Sections 1798.16, 1798.34).

SAFEGUARDS FOR PERSONAL INFORMATION
Employees who are responsible for safeguarding personal information, must take all precautionary measures to ensure that all records containing personal information are kept in a secure area or in locked storage equipment and that access is restricted to only those employees who must have access in order to perform their assigned duties (California Civil Code, IPA, Section 1798.21).

CONDITIONS OF DISCLOSURE
Employees may not disclose any personal information in a manner which would link the information to the individual to whom it pertains (California Civil Code, IPA, Section 1798.3).

(continued)

FIGURE 4.15 Continued

Examples of personal information are:

1. Name
3. Social Security Number
4. Medical or employment history
5. Physical description
6. Financial information
7. Records marked (stamped, etc.) "confidential"

Employees may disclose personal information to the public under any of the following criteria (California Civil Code, IPA, Section 1798.24):

1. To the individual to whom the information pertains;
2. With the prior written, voluntary consent of the individual to whom the information pertains, but only in the time limit agreed to by the individual in the written consent;
3. To the duly appointed guardian or conservator of the individual, provided it can be proven with reasonable certainty such person is the authorized representative of the individual;
4. To those officers, employees, attorneys, agents, or volunteers of the California Student Aid Commission or EdFund, if the disclosure is relevant and necessary in the ordinary course of the performance of their official duties, and it is related to the purpose for which the information was acquired;
5. To a governmental entity when required by state or federal law;
6. Pursuant to the California Public Records Act, Chapter 3.5;
7. To a person who has provided the institution with advance, adequate, written assurance that the information will be used solely for statistical research or reporting purposes, when the information to be disclosed is in a form that will not identify any individual;
8. To any person pursuant to a subpoena court order, or other compulsory legal process, if, before the disclosure, the institution reasonably attempts to notify the individual to whom the information pertains, and if the notification is not prohibited by law:
9. To any person pursuant to a search warrant:
10. To a law enforcement or regulatory agency when required for an investigation of unlawful activity or for licensing, certification, or regulatory purposes, unless the disclosure is otherwise prohibited by law.

MAINTAINING RECORDS OF DISCLOSURES

Those employees responsible for the disclosure of personal information, must maintain a record of each disclosure. The record must contain:

1. Date of disclosure;
2. Nature and purpose of disclosure;

FIGURE 4.15 Continued

3. Name of person and institution to whom information is disclosed; and
4. Business address of the person to whom information is disclosed (California Civil Code, IPA, Section 1798.25).

RETENTION PERIOD FOR RECORDS OF DISCLOSURES
The records of disclosures must be maintained for three years or until the record containing the personal information is destroyed, whichever is shorter (California Civil Code, IPA, Section 1798.27).

COPIES OF RECORDS
Authorized individuals or institutions requesting copies of personal information will be charged a fee of ten cents per page for making copies (California Civil Code, IPA, Section 1798.33).

REQUESTS FOR INSPECTION, AMENDMENT, OR CORRECTION OF RECORDS
Written inquiries by the subject individual for access to, amendment of, or correction of his or her record must be reviewed, approved, or denied within 30 days from receipt of the request. If the request is denied, the individual must be provided in writing the reason for the denial and the procedures for the individual to request for a review/appeal of the decision (California Civil Code, IPA, Sections 1798.34–1798.36).

INVASION OF PRIVACY
Employees who intentionally disclose information, not otherwise public, which they know or should reasonably know was obtained from personal information, may be subject to a civil action for invasion of privacy by the individual to whom the information pertains (Public Law 93-579) (California Civil Code, IPA, Section 1798.53).

PRIVACY NOTICE
Subject individuals whose social security number is requested must be informed whether disclosure is mandatory or voluntary, by what statutory authority the number is solicited, and what it will be used for.

Questions regarding this policy memo should be directed to your manager or the Security and Risk Management Office.

FIGURE 4.16 Sample Policy Memo

CSAC

GENERAL INFO POLICY AND PROCEDURES MEMO

		CONTROL NUMBER: **FY 96-97 G-025**
SUBJECT: **Youth Mentor Program**		EFFECTIVE DATE: 01/02/97
APPROVED BY: Michael Neu	APPROVED BY: Connie Chang	CONTACT: Human Resources Branch

The Governor signed Executive Order W-132-96 earlier this year directing State agencies, departments, boards, and commissions to allow and encourage employees to engage in mentoring activities. Mentoring activities are defined as working with "at-risk" children and youth on a one-to-one basis through a bonafide mentoring organization. Employees who participate in this program do so on a voluntary basis.

Eligible employees may be authorized up to forty (40) hours of paid State release time per year to participate in mentoring activity, subject to departmental operational needs. In order to be eligible for the paid State release time the following conditions must be met:

- Employees must be employed in a permanent full-time position and have successfully completed the probationary period for their current position.
- Employees must request paid State release time in advance from their immediate supervisor.
- Employees must use an equal number of hours of their personal time (approved annual leave, vacation, personal leave, or personal holiday, during the work day and/or personal time after work) in order to be granted paid State release time. For example, if an employee requests eight hours of paid State release time, he or she must have used eight hours of their personal time prior to receiving approval for the paid State release time. "Mentor leave" does not have to be requested in the same week or month that the personal time was used. It does, however, have to be requested and used before the end of the calendar year.
- Employees must commit to mentor a child or youth through a bonafide mentoring organization for a minimum of twelve months.

Mentor hours will be tracked by the volunteer's immediate supervisor who will maintain a mentor track sheet for each volunteer (see Attachment) and by the unit timekeeper who will key the hours into the Human Resources Information System (HRIS). Each mentor is responsible for obtaining and providing verification of all "personal" and "mentor" hours worked and presenting this verification to their supervisor.

FIGURE 4.16 Continued

The following definitions and information provided will assist supervisors in the completion of the "Mentor Tracking Sheet."

Date: Identifies the day you used "personal paid leave" or "mentor hours," to participate in the mentor program.

Total Hours Available: is the result of "personal hours donated" and "mentor hours used."

Personal Hours Donated: is personal paid leave time used towards participation in the mentor program.

Mentor Hours Accrued: is paid leave time which will be matched by an equal number of personal hours used.

Mentor Hours Used: is for accumulated mentor leave via an approved absence request.

The required 40 hour balance is the combined total of personal and State donated hours allowed per calendar year for "mentor leave." These are the mentor hours charged to the mentor's paid leave time which will be matched by an equal number of mentor hours donated and paid by the State. As hours are used they are subtracted from the State contributed hours and discontinued once the 40 hour leave bank is depleted. However, mentors can continue to use their own paid leave or personal time through the end of the calendar year. This time should continue to be tracked for reporting purposes only.

As the supervisor receives and approves absence requests for "mentor leave," the forms will be forwarded to the timekeepers to post the "mentor leave" hours into HRIS. These totals will be reflected on the "Employee Leave Balance Summary." The "mentor leave" code for the HRIS is "MEN."

Although Workweek Group (WWG) 4C (exempt) employees are not required to maintain an hourly accounting of their time, in order to track the success of the State's mentoring efforts, WWG 4C employees must record their use of "mentor leave" even if the leave is utilized in less than eight-hour increments.

If you have additional questions contact the Youth Mentor Program Coordinator, Lori Rosa at 555-4370. If you have questions regarding the timekeeping, contact Janice Martins at 555-9776.

ATTACHMENT

FIGURE 4.17 Table of Contents for Performance Evaluation Program

Performance Evaluation Program

Table of Contents

PEP Guidebook Revision I
9/19/97

Conventions

Conventions for writing, compiling, and publishing policies and procedures vary widely, depending on their organizational contexts and the situations in which they're used. One of the early decisions you'll need to make in designing a system of policies and procedures documents has to do with how you organize the whole system. On the one hand, if records of organizational policies and procedures are to be meaningful, they need to be accessible to the relevant people at the appropriate times and places. On the other hand, effective and coherent organizational governance generally requires that you compile policies and procedures in comprehensive, coherent documents—in manuals of policies and procedures—and that these documents be stored in some central, safe place, so there's a written institutional memory of how things are done. For a small organization or division, all policies and procedures might be assembled in a single manual. But even small organizations may prefer multiple manuals, thoughtfully compiled so that each serves as a reasonably complete guide to some group within the organization without distracting its readers with a lot of information that's normally not useful to them.

These competing functions—centralization and accessibility—suggest the need for conventions of redundancy. Crucially important policies and procedures need to be published several different times in several different places so they will be visible to all who need to see them. A centralized manual or collection of manuals should provide a complete and coherent expression of organizational policies and procedures. And a system of local, ad hoc policy statements and procedure statements—strategically designed and located to give employees and customers immediate, even unavoidable, access—will help assure that those policies and procedures compiled in a central office will actually be applied in practice. Some organizations are even making all policies and procedures available electronically—in a specific location (a particular drive, for instance) on a networked computer system.

Conventions for Centralized Policies and Procedures Manuals

- Give manuals a physical design that enables you to change them as company policies, procedures, products, and services change. For example, use three-ring binders or others that let you tear out and insert sheets.
- Segment overall organizational policies and procedures into separate manuals according to who will need which kinds of information.
- Apply the same care within individual manuals, segmenting and organizing the content according to who will need which kinds of information. For instance, look at Figure 4.18, an excerpt from the *Lender Procedural Manual* for the California Student Aid Commission. This excerpt is from section 5 of the manual, Borrower Eligibility and Loan Certification. Notice that this title appears in large, sans serif, bold type at the top of every page. A busy reader who's flipping hurriedly through the manual can identify the section with a glance at the top of the page. Also notice that the designers of the manual have created a redundant system for marking off the subsections within section 5. First, they've used

FIGURE 4.18 Excerpt from Procedures Manual

5 Borrower Eligibility and Loan Certification

5.8
SCHOOL CERTIFICATION OF THE APPLICATION AND PROMISSORY NOTE

5.8.E.
Forwarding the School-Certified Application
The certified loan application may be submitted to the Commission for guarantee approval by several different processes. (See Example 5-2. Stafford Loan Application Flow Chart and Example 5-3, PLUS Loan Application Flow Chart.) The processing options available are as follows:

Manual Processing

When submitting loan applications to the Commission for manual data entry into FAPS, mail the applications to the address below. The Commission staff will review the applications to verify completion. If applications are incomplete, they will be returned to the school, lender, or borrower, as appropriate. Once the applications are complete, re-submit them to the Commission for manual data entry.

Regular Mail:
California Student Aid Commission
Application & File Services Branch
P.O. Box 5121
Sacramento, CA 94245–0621

Overnight Mail Only:
California Student Aid Commission
Application & File Services Branch
2600 14th Street, Ste 50, North Building
Sacramento, CA 95814

Electronic Processing Options

FAPS On-Line—FAPS is an integrated financial aid mainframe computer system developed by the Commission. FAPS provides external users (schools, lenders, and servicers) telecommunication access to the Commission's database by using computer on-line access or batch processing. Accessing FAPS allows schools and lenders to obtain instant FFELP loan guarantees, FFELP history, and default prevention information.

PCFAPS Personal Computer Financial Aid Processing System—PCFAPS is a personal-computer-based program that allows schools easy access to the Commission's mainframe FAPS. Through PCFAPS, a school can create loan records by data entry from a remote personal computer or by downloading data from the school's mainframe system. PCFAPS provides on-line access or batch processing and allows schools to enter FFELP applications on-line, interface with their student database, or dial in to FAPS for inquiry and/or to make updates to loan information. PCFAPS also allows access to grant and loan reports provided by the Commission.

ASAP - Automated Stafford Application Processing—ASAP is a loan application process that eliminates the need for the school to complete a paper copy application. By marking the ASAP indicator in FAPS or PCFAPS on the electronic loan application, the school can inform the Commission and the lender that the paper-

California Student Aid Commission
Lender Procedural Manual
revised: 9/6/96

FIGURE 4.18 Continued

5 Borrower Eligibility and Loan Certification

less application process is being used. At the time of guarantee, the Commission will print and mail the promissory note directly to the borrower, issue a Disclosure Statement and guarantee report to the lender, and inform the school of the guarantee status. Once the lender receives the promissory note from the borrower, the lender sends a check and Disclosure Statement to the school.

APLUS - Automated Parent Loans for Undergraduate Students—APLUS is a loan application process that eliminates the need for the school to complete a paper copy application. By marking the APLUS indicator in FAPS or PCFAPS on the electronic loan application, the school can inform the Commission and the lender that the paperless application process is being used. At the time of guarantee, the Commission will print and mail the promissory note directly to the borrower, issue a Disclosure Statement and guarantee report to the lender, and inform the school of the guarantee status. Once the lender receives the promissory note from the borrower, the lender sends a check and disclosure statement to the school.

Loan Application Data Change Form (L-25)
On occasion, the school may need to update loan data after the loan has been guaranteed. To do so, the school must send a completed Loan Application Data Change Form (L-25) to the lender for approval. (See Example 5-4.) The lender will forward the form to the Commission's Application and File Services Branch at the address below. The Commission will not approve any changes where the data may result in an erroneous guarantee or an invalid disbursement schedule on FAPS.

When the changes are approved, the Commission will send a copy of the Loan Application Data Change Form (L-25) to the lender and the school.

Regular Mail:
California Student Aid Commission
Application & File Services Branch
P.O. Box 5121
Sacramento, CA 94245–0621

Overnight Mail Only:
California Student Aid Commission
Application & File Services Branch
2600 14th Street, Ste 50, North Building
Sacramento, CA 95814

California Student Aid Commission
Lender Procedural Manual
revised: 9/6/96

a decimal system for ordering the subsections. The excerpt here is subsection 5.8, School Certification of the Application and Promissory Note, and the first discussion within subsection 5.8 is 5.8.E, Forwarding the School-Certified Application. What happened to sections 5.8.A through 5.8.D? Is the manual missing sections? No. The decimal section numbers may be subject to regulatory or legislative changes that create gaps, which may be completely beyond the control of the writers of the manual. In order for the manual to be consistent with other documents within the wider system of governance, then, the decimal numbers may not be perfectly sequential.

Given these unpredictable, yet correct, omissions within the manual, the writers have created the redundant traffic signals of numbering the pages within the section. The fact that page numbers appear at the bottoms of pages in addition to the decimal numbering of subsections helps readers stay oriented and confident about the completeness and correctness of the manual. You can see at a glance that the excerpt begins with page 5-6. This redundancy is an important double-check for readers. It's part of the design plan that allows the manual to change as policies and procedures change.

Notice that the writers also give the revision date at the bottom of each page. This again helps readers know that a section is current, and it especially helps users of the manual know which updated revisions need to replace which sections of the manual.

- Use detailed tables of contents and indexes for effective directional signals to facilitate use of the manuals as reference tools. Look again at the table of contents for the PEP program guidebook revision (Figure 4.17).

Conventions for Designing Individual Policies and Procedures

- Agree on a standard institutional format for all policy statements and procedure statements, and follow the format consistently.
- Use prominent topic and keyword headers and titles that give readers quick reference points for finding the policies or procedures they need.
- First, highlight any special risks or concerns the readers must know:
  - Give a quick, clear description of where and when the policy or procedure is applicable. If necessary, tell when it's *not* applicable, as well.
  - Give other necessary contextual information.
  - Refer to other related policies and procedures.
  - For procedures, list all the materials, tools, reference information, and other help—including the number of people needed to complete the procedure successfully.
  - For procedures, make the sequence clear.
- Prefer the active voice: Tell *who* does *what.*
- For procedures, use commands: for example, "First make sure the power supply is disconnected."

- When a policy or procedure requires the use of a particular form, make the form part of the document so that readers can see exactly what is required. For instance the Information Security General Policy (Figure 4.13) includes as attachments an Information Security and Confidentiality Agreement that new employees must sign and an Internal Access Request form that supervisors or managers must complete when requesting information.
- Revise and edit aggressively to reconcile the competing conventions of clarity, completeness, brevity, and ease of reading.

Expression

All the kinds of documents we're discussing in this chapter are, in fact, expressive documents—expressing the visions, goals, and values of your organization. How you make these statements, then, is especially important. With policies and procedures, your expression needs to match your goal of having people read, understand, and comply. And if you can write these documents so that your readers comply cheerfully, then you've probably achieved a rare success. If your document is written for customers or clients, this is especially a goal worth striving for.

Within individual policy statements or procedure statements written for in-house readers, tone of expression is less important since the individual statement stands within the context of the organization's ethos or culture. But even here, where a bossy, imperative voice laying out a series of procedural steps is entirely appropriate, the wider context of the document—its introduction, for example—and certainly the spirit in which it is introduced in a training or orientation workshop should express your corporate ethos. The excerpt from the *Credit and Collection Manual* (see Figure 4.19), for instance, does a particularly good job in communicating the organization's point of view about appropriate collection procedures. And it follows the stylistic conventions introduced in the previous list, including using the active voice and commands to clearly and understandably establish the procedure for coping with voice mail during the telephone collection process.

Job Descriptions and Performance Reviews

Job descriptions and performance reviews are the crucial documents in defining, negotiating, and reconciling the goals and activities of the organization with those of the individuals who make up that organization. In a healthy organization, all the documents we've talked about in this chapter are coherent with one another. But achieving this coherence can entail difficult processes of negotiation. Every one of these documents can quickly become either the source or the target of controversy and conflict. This is again true of job descriptions and especially of performance reviews. In fact, a strong case can be made against the whole idea of performance reviews as they are traditionally done. For example, management consultant Peter Scholte's appraisal of performance appraisal is summarized with the tart comment "It's a crock!" Chris

FIGURE 4.19 Excerpt from a Procedures Manual

Credit and Collection Manual

4.31 Telephone Collecting—Coping with Voice Mail

- Speak slowly and distinctly, leave the date and time of your call, our company name, and your name and phone number.
- If the customer does not respond to the first voice mail message, phone again within three days. If you contact voice mail the second time, remind the customer with a phrase such as "Jane, this is Betty Smith with Merrimac Corporation. I'm disappointed you didn't respond to my voice mail message of last Tuesday, so I'm calling again to —."
- If the person you are contacting does not respond to the second voice mail message within two days, contact a supervisor by phone, or contact the person or supervisor by FAX or mail (see Section 4.41). Caution: Be careful with the tone of a FAX message. Ask the addressee to investigate and contact you. Don't use "pay up or else" language in a FAX. Informing a customer that he must pay or the account will be given to a third-party collector must be done by certified mail. It may be confirmed in a phone conversation. FAXing a collection threat may violate the confidential nature of the communication.

Lee (1996), the managing editor of *Training* magazine, quotes Scholte and several other practitioners and consultants in a brief but comprehensive evaluation of performance appraisal processes. The criticisms brought to bear on the formal annual performance review and report sound very much like the criticisms Mintzberg and others have made of strategic planning: (1) The process and the documents it generates tend to be too rigid for a dynamic system operating in a changing environment, and (2) the information used in the process tends to be misleading in any case. We believe this problem with performance reviews has at least partly to do with the difficulty of reconciling conflicting goals in performance review processes and documents. So, once again, GRACE becomes a framework for thinking not only about the written document but also about the process associated with producing it.

Goals in Job Descriptions

The job description really has just a single overarching goal: to translate the institutional mission into individual action. But depending on the circumstances and the readers, it functions to achieve that goal in four different ways:

1. It's a device for selecting and hiring an appropriately qualified employee to help achieve particular institutional goals.

2. It's a map that helps an employee make rational decisions about how to organize tasks and set priorities at work.
3. It's a metric for both the employee and the institution to review and assess job performance.
4. It's a legal document that's part of the paper trail the institution establishes to verify that its major personnel actions—hiring and firing, in particular—have been taken legally and have been based on qualifications and job performance.

Goals in Performance Reviews

As we mentioned above, performance reviews tend to suffer from two sets of conflicting goals. On the one hand, the goal of the performance review is to improve the coherence between individual actions and corporate goals. In this sense, the performance review has the affirmative goal of boosting employee commitment, loyalty, performance, and, as a necessary component, morale. But on the other hand, the performance review serves the defensive goal of protecting the organization in the event of litigation. And it frequently is a crucial element in decisions about pay raises and promotions. Organizations that are concerned about protecting themselves from lawsuits for illegal discrimination in hiring, evaluating, or dismissing employees will likely want to use the kinds of formal annual performance reviews that Scholte, Lee, and others have found so problematic and that employees almost universally find demoralizing.

This conflict in goals can make the entire process of writing a performance review extremely difficult. Like the highly refined strategic long-range plan, the formal annual performance review tends to suffer from a general distancing in time and detail. This distance between the act and the word, between the "talk" and the "walk," impairs the feedback process. The long-range plan presumes to forecast events far into the future. The annual performance review presumes to evaluate and correct acts that occurred up to a year in the past—acts that may well have been forgotten by the actors and that may have taken place in situations that will not occur again.

Formal long-range strategic plans tend to be constructed by people who are distanced from the daily dirt-under-the-fingernails reality of actual operations, resources, and constraints. Likewise, formal annual performance reviews tend to be done by people who are similarly distanced from the actual events. They are done by supervisors using an abstract template of criteria for the review that may not be appropriate for the realities of the actual work situation. In both cases, the risk is an uncoupling of the "talk" and the "walk," an incoherence between word and deed that disempowers employees with discouraging nonsense, rather than empower them with evaluations that provide meaningful and helpful feedback. The solution, according to much of the literature, such as Chris Lee's (1996) article, is to move the evaluation closer to the act that is evaluated—closer in time, in physical distance, and in the persons responsible for the evaluation. This would mean conducting performance reviews much more frequently, giving the people who are being reviewed an active role in the review, and even allowing them to take the initiative for much of the performance review process

DILBERT

Source: DILBERT reprinted by permission of United Feature Syndicate, Inc.

and writing. In other words, the same kind of "Ready, fire, aim, fire, aim, fire, aim, . . ." process that Mintzberg advocates on the larger institutional scale for planning and strategy formation also seems to work well on the level of smaller organizational units and even for individual people within the organization. (For more leads on putting this kind of process into action, we recommend Lee's accessible, highly readable article, which is listed in the References at the end of this chapter.)

Whether you're the reviewer or the reviewee—or perhaps responsible for planning and designing performance reviews—you should try to clarify exactly the goals of the review. If the organization's goals and interests are best served by a review that gives maximally informative and helpful feedback to employees, then give thoughtful consideration to relocating the formal evaluation for salary, promotion, or retention to another time and place in the organization.

Readers

A prospective employee who's looking at the organizational vision and mission statements on a company's web page should be able to infer some general sense of what it's like to work for that company. Even so, the job description will probably be the most helpful document to a person who's trying to visualize what it would be like to work for your organization. And once an employee is on board and working, the job description needs to grow and flex to stay consistent with the actual goals and responsibilities of the position as they continue to evolve. So, the employee, immediate colleagues, supervisor, and perhaps even supervisees all become both readers and potential co-writers of the evolving job description. Moving out through an egocentric solar system (see Figure 4.20), we can see other more remote but still potentially extremely important readers—supervisors of supervisors, for example—and finally readers outside the organization: perhaps readers of a proposal to which the job description is attached or even lawyers and a judge if the job description were ever to become evidence in litigation.

Obviously the immediate participants in a performance review, the reviewer and the reviewee, are readers of the review. If the reviewee, the employee being evaluated, is not a reader, then the process is profoundly flawed and almost certainly illegal. Employees have a legal right to see their performance reviews and to comment on them in writing. Beyond these immediate participants, the document will almost always have at least one further reader, typically a specialist in the human resources (personnel) office, who will examine the document to see that the review process and criteria conform to organizational policies and legal guidelines. If there are other readers, it probably means that the process has become seriously conflicted and may be heading for a formal grievance or litigation. The potential readers here are the same as for the job description: lawyers, grievance officers, judges, and juries. It's the image of this kind of potential reader that makes writing a performance review—and doing the performance review at all—such an anxiety-producing exercise.

FIGURE 4.20 Potential Readers of Job Descriptions

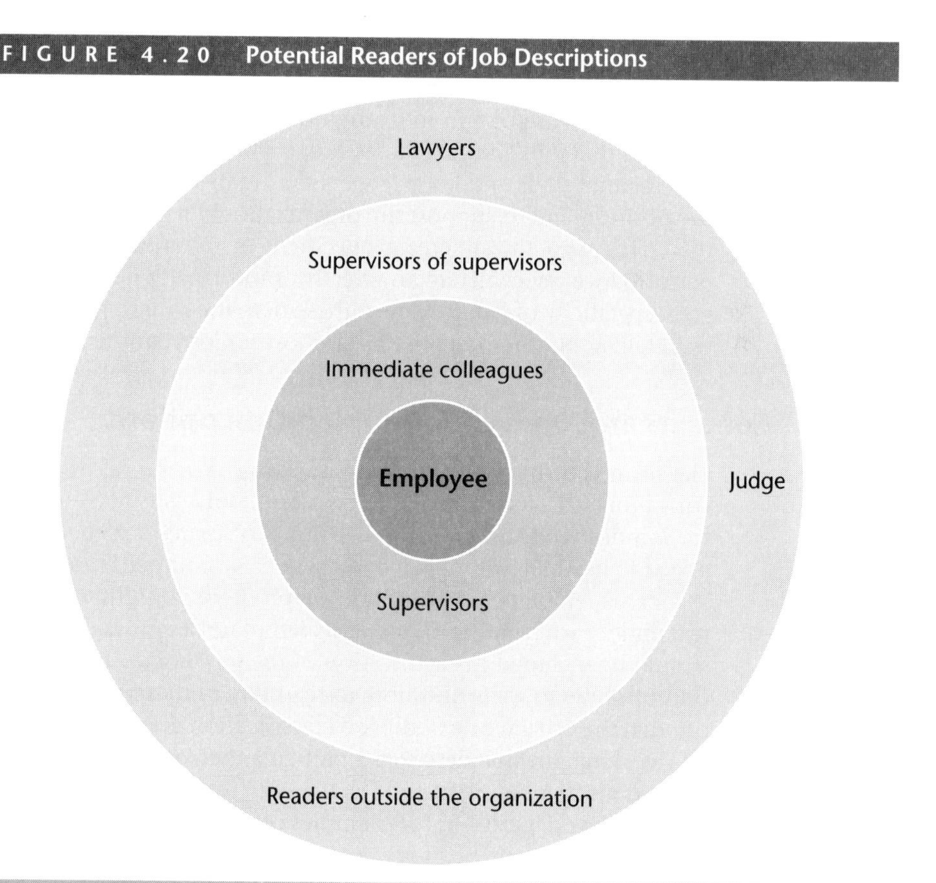

Arguments in Job Descriptions and Performance Reviews

The broad generic argument on the institutional side of both the job description and the performance review has to do with the organization's mission. For example, see the job description for an administrative assistant at Kalamazoo Valley Community College in Figure 4.21. The description says, "A primary responsibility of all persons assigned to this job title is to support the instructional mission of the college," and all job descriptions written by PMG, the consulting group that developed this description, begin with exactly this emphasis.

The arguments in both job descriptions and performance reviews walk an interesting line between generality and specificity. You'll see in the next section that job descriptions tend strongly to be more general than performance reviews. In fact, a standard disclaimer, such as that at the bottom of the job description from Kalamazoo Valley Community College, is language saying that the job description is not to be construed as describing the specific duties and responsibilities of any particular position. This kind of strategy in the generic job description that's used for hiring people into position categories allows room for a specific employee and supervisor in a specific office to tailor the employee's duties according to the needs of that particular office, the talents of the employee, and the complementary talents of fellow employees. At the same time, though, the job description needs to be specific enough to help make useful and meaningful distinctions about the qualifications of candidates for that job. The list of knowledge and skills, for example, has to identify clearly the essential skills and knowledge a candidate must have in order to be successful in the position and to support the organizational mission.

This move toward greater specificity of argument reaches its maximum with the performance review. Here an effective (and legally defensible) document demands great specificity of detail. In fact, these demands are so pervasive and unyielding that we'll talk about them in the next section as Conventions.

Contexts and Conventions of Job Descriptions

The form shown in Figure 4.22 comes from a proposal by PMG, a human resources consulting firm, submitted to Texas A & M University at Corpus Christi. It's a template for job descriptions, showing the kinds of issues, language, and format PMG proposed to use in developing a comprehensive compensation plan for the university.

This template is a good starting place for your job descriptions in general. The text under each heading on the PMG template describes the kinds of information that should be included in each section of the job description and gives helpful pointers on both how to write and how to read text in these sections. For example, it points out that the official title of the job classification does not necessarily preclude the use of a working title that describes a particular person's specific responsibilities. See Marianne Ramos' job description (Figure 4.23) and the Duty Statement for the Staff Services Analyst (Figure 4.6) for examples of working titles that are different from generic position titles.

FIGURE 4.21 Sample Job Description

KALAMAZOO VALLEY COMMUNITY COLLEGE
JOB DESCRIPTION

TITLE	Class. Code	Pay Grade	Eff. Date	OFCCP Code	FLSA
ADMINISTRATIVE ASSISTANT					

BASIC FUNCTION AND RESPONSIBILITY: A primary responsibility of all persons assigned to this job title is to support the instructional mission of the College and to promote positive student and customer relations. Provide administrative and research assistance for the designated supervisor.

CHARACTERISTIC DUTIES AND RESPONSIBILITIES: The essential functions, pursuant to the Americans with Disabilities Act, may include the characteristic duties, knowledges, skills, abilities noted herein; however, this list represents EXAMPLES ONLY, and is not a comprehensive listing of all functions and tasks performed by positions found in this job classification.

Research and analyze data pertinent to assigned department programs, goals/objectives and prepare reports explaining findings and recommendations; assist in developing or revising departmental policies and procedures; compile and analyze information used by supervisor to formulate budget proposals; monitor expenditures; process and follow-up on purchase requisitions via CIMS System; and, process financial, personnel and payroll documents.

Review and answer or prepare correspondence relating to assigned department; interpret institution policies and procedures; and, provide information, assistance and clarification to interested parties.

Provide administrative support to supervisor; attend meetings and serve as supervisor's representative; serve on committees and councils; and, assist supervisor by maintaining appointment calendar, making travel arrangements, and prioritizing incoming mail.

Recommend hires; train, supervise and evaluate assigned staff; develop work priorities/schedules; arrange for training; develop department procedures and strategies; and, through the Human Resource Services Department, develop sound and acceptable personnel practices.

CONTINUED ON REVERSE SIDE

(continued)

FIGURE 4.21 Continued

KALAMAZOO VALLEY COMMUNITY COLLEGE
JOB DESCRIPTION
CONTINUED

TITLE **ADMINISTRATIVE ASSISTANT**

REPORTS TO **DESIGNATED SUPERVISOR**

SUPERVISION EXERCISED
Administrative and functional supervision is exercised over up to two full-time and two part-time employees.

SKILLS AND KNOWLEDGE
Knowledge of basic mathematics and statistics.
Knowledge of research and analysis techniques and methods.
Knowledge of acceptable supervisory principles and practices.
Knowledge of institutional policies and procedures.
Skill in planning, organizing and directing the work of subordinates.
Skill in preparing, presenting, and reviewing oral and written information and reports.
Skill in conducting research and analyzing subject area information.
Skill in developing, recommending, interpreting and applying policies and procedures.
Skill in analyzing financial records and preparing reports.

ENTRY QUALIFICATIONS
An Associate's Degree in Business Administration, Office Technology or related field and experience equivalent to two years of office management or administrative type work.

This description is intended to indicate the kinds of tasks and levels of work difficulty required of positions given this title and shall not be construed as declaring what the specific duties and responsibilities of any particular position shall be. It is not intended to limit or any way modify the right of any supervisor to assign, direct, and control the work of employees under supervision. The use of a particular expression or illustration describing duties shall not be held to exclude other duties not mentioned that are of similar kind or level of difficulty.

FIGURE 4.22 Template for Job Decriptions

JOB DESCRIPTION FORMAT

TITLE:________________ **CLASS. CODE** **PAY GRADE** **EFF. DATE** **FLSA** **OFCCP**

TITLE
This is the title recommended for the job classification, which may or may not be the same as the current title. It is recommended as being reflective of the work performed and being consistent with other titles throughout the institution. It is not intended necessarily to preclude the use of a "working title" which lends credibility with contacts outside the institution. For example, a Clerk in the Human Resources Department given the responsibility of processing tuition waivers may wish to sign paperwork associated with the program as "Tuition Waiver Coordinator" [of course with the proper supervisory approval].

BASIC FUNCTION AND RESPONSIBILITY
This is a single statement summarizing the function of the classification which differentiates one classification from all others.

CHARACTERISTIC DUTIES AND RESPONSIBILITIES
This section is *not* intended to be a comprehensive list of tasks performed by an incumbent. Rather, it is intended to reflect the types and levels of responsibility of incumbents assigned to the classification. This factor is especially important when dealing with descriptions for multi-incumbent classifications. Not all duties will be performed by each individual incumbent, and some duties of particular incumbents may not be the same for others within the classification.

REPORTS TO
This section identifies the reporting relationship by giving the title of the supervisor.

SUPERVISION EXERCISED
This section identifies if supervision of others is required and, if so, the level of that supervision.
Administrative: decisions or recommendations regarding personnel decisions.
Functional: limited to assigning and reviewing work/acting as a group leader. Temporary supervisory responsibilities during vacations/short-term illness should not be recognized.

SKILLS AND KNOWLEDGES
This section is not intended to duplicate entry qualifications, but rather to allow for the identification of special attributes required of the classification, but not required for entry.

ENTRY QUALIFICATIONS
This section identifies the *minimum* level of knowledge necessary for an individual entering the classification. This can be stated in terms of education, experience or a combination of the two. This section must also include any required certification/licensure. Documentable skills and/or abilities such as keyboarding, shorthand, drafting, etc. may also be included in this section.

DISCLAIMER STATEMENT
This description is intended to indicate the kinds of tasks and levels of work difficulty required of positions assigned this classification title and **shall not** be construed as declaring what the specific duties and responsibilities of any particular position shall be. It is not intended to limit or any way modify the right of any supervisor to assign, direct, and control the work of employees under supervision. The use of a particular expression or illustration describing duties shall not be held to exclude other duties not mentioned that are of similar kind or level of difficulty.

FIGURE 4.23 Position Description

State of Minnesota **POSITION DESCRIPTION A**	EMPLOYEE'S NAME MARIANNE RAMOS		
AGENCY/DIVISION St. Cloud State University	ACTIVITY Department of English		
CLASSIFICATION TITLE Clerk Typist III	WORKING TITLE (if different) Secretary	POSITION CONTROL NUMBER 179590	
PREPARED BY Marianne Ramos	PREVIOUS INCUMBENT	APPRAISAL PERIOD TO	
EMPLOYEE'S SIGNATURE (this position description accurately reflects my current job) *Marianne Ramos*	DATE 8/9/98	SUPERVISOR'S SIGNATURE (this position description reflects the employee's current job) *Randall Meyers*	DATE

POSITION PURPOSE

This position exists to provide administrative support to the Chairperson and faculty of the English Department.

REPORTABILITY

Reports to:

Chair of the English Department

Supervises:

Workstudy/student help employees (approx. 7)

DIMENSIONS

Budget:

Student help budgets for: English Department, English Computer Lab, The Write Place and ESL. (Approximately $40,000)

Budgets for seven scholarship accounts.

Clientele:

32 full-time and 5–8 part-time faculty members; 26 graduate/teaching assistants; approximately 30–40 student workers; English majors and minors; and, students and visitors to the department.

FIGURE 4.23 Continued

Resp. No.	Principal Responsibilities, Tasks, Performance Indicators	Priority	% of Time	Discretion
1.	*Responsibility:* To serve as administrative assistant for the department. **Tasks:** a. To take and transcribe minutes of department meetings. To take and transcribe minutes of departmental committee meetings when called upon to do so. b. To prepare departmental correspondence from dictated notes, rough draft copy or computer disk. c. To compose departmental correspondence. d. To meet with and assist teaching assistants and new faculty on departmental and university policies. e. To determine priorities in scheduling work assignments. f. To keep accurate records of all departmental minutes and correspondence prepared. g. Design and help prepare the "Handbook for Teaching Assistants and Faculty," composing parts pertinent to my area of expertise. h. Meet with and apprise teaching assistants and new faculty of University and office procedures/policies. i. Research, develop and maintain a departmental policies manual. **Performance Indicator:** a. Work is produced accurately and on time to assure efficient support for department and chairperson. b. An accurate file of all minutes, correspondence and policies is kept.	A	15	B

(continued)

FIGURE 4.23 Continued

Resp. No.	Principal Responsibilities, Tasks, Performance Indicators	Priority	% of Time	Discretion
6.	*Responsibility:* To coordinate materials and prepare reports for departmental activities. a. English Department Scholarships (Lawrence B. and Clara S. Coard Memorial, English Department, Abigail Falk Creative Writing Prize, James A. and Muriel Grunerud, John Melton Scholarship in Literature, Drew Roser Memorial and June M. Hiemenz Spychala Memorial). 1. Design and prepare application forms. 2. To compose and distribute publicity for the department scholarship program. 3. Research and submit a report to the Scholarship Committee on the scholastic record for each applicant, the criteria set for selection of recipients for each award, and a calculation of the funds available for each award determined by figuring out interest available per set formula. 4. Design announcements of awards and compose notices of awards to the appropriate offices. 5. Complete appropriate forms for initiation of funds. b. To be responsible for publicizing, through various offices and with posters, the Thursday-At-One presentations sponsored by the department. c. Design and post notices of English 162 and 163 test-out dates and final results. d. Design and prepare "Essaying," a departmental booklet containing sample essays of English 162 students. **Performance Indicator:** a. Work is completed accurately and on time. b. Accurate files are kept of all activities. c. All due dates are met.	A	15	A

FIGURE 4.23 Continued

POSITION DESCRIPTION C	EMPLOYEE NAME Marianne Ramos	POSITION CONTROL NUMBER 179590

NATURE AND SCOPE (relationships, knowledge, skills and abilities; problem solving and creativity; and freedom to act.)

Relationship: This position serves as a focal point for the chairperson and staff in securing the performance of departmental administrative services. Activities involve contact with other university offices:

Records and Registration	Administrative Affairs
Alumni and Foundation	Printing Services
Graduate and Continuing Studies	Computer Services
Academic Affairs	Financial Aid

Planning, coordinating, and cooperating with the other office staff to optimize coverage during office hours is necessary. Communication and coordination of work schedules (across the entire range from stepping across the hall for copying, to breaks, to days off, to extended vacations) to maximize the office's ability to respond to shifting demands and workload is a must.

Knowledge, Skills, and Abilities: A high level of skill in the use of computer equipment and various types of software is required. Nearly all work is done on the computer. Word processing and graphic design skills are used extensively and continue to change. This position requires the knowledge of several computer systems and software programs. Training in new and existing technologies and procedures to optimize personal and office effectiveness is required. The incumbent is called upon to trouble-shoot when a student worker, faculty member or fellow staff member is having difficulty with a computer or printer.

The person in this position must possess knowledge of human nature and be able to exercise tact in contacts with people so that the English Department is properly represented.

Problem Solving: There are two major problem-solving activities in this position. The first deals with determining priorities in work assignments for the secretary and the student workers, and the most efficient distribution and scheduling of this work. The second has to do with the daily requests and problems posed by both students and faculty over the counter and by phone. The person in this position must be familiar enough with university policies and procedures to handle these matters and to refer to the Chairperson only those which require his/her knowledge or authority. Excellent managerial skills are required.

Freedom to Act: This position presents a great deal of freedom to act. After accepting work assignments, the person in this position is free to determine priorities, set work schedules, route the flow of work, and see that deadlines are met. Only the work prepared for his/her signature is reviewed by the Chairperson. Office staff meetings are regularly scheduled.

Contexts and Conventions of Performance Reviews

Performance reviews almost inevitably present writing situations with some level of conflict and emotion, and the conventions for writing good performance reviews, with their emphasis on specific arguments about specific behaviors, reflect the kinds of strategies we will suggest in Chapter 6. Thoughtfully designed and specifically documented arguments in performance reviews not only help resolve conflict at the moment of the evaluation; they also are essential in defending personnel decisions that end up in legal disputes. The following list presents features of performance review documents that fared well in legal cases challenging their validity.* Given their track record, these features constitute a helpful checklist:

1. The performance review document shows that the appraisal was based on a job description that, in turn, described the expectations of persons working in that position.
2. The appraisal process was behavior oriented, rather than trait oriented. That is, instead of characterizing a person's traits (e.g., lazy, energetic, committed, enthusiastic, cooperative, insubordinate, etc.), the review process and report described his or her specific behaviors (e.g., averaged 10 sales calls a day; continued to play computer games in reception area in view of customers after being directed not to on four specific dates; rearranged own work schedule and provided two days' overtime help on our crucial sales proposal; etc.).
3. Performance evaluators followed specific written instructions. Notice the State of Minnesota form shown in Figure 4.24. If you are designing performance evaluations for your organization, include written instructions that will help raters remember to use specific descriptions of specific behaviors to characterize people they are evaluating and to ground their evaluative criteria in the job description. If you are writing performance evaluations in an organization that does not provide these kinds of written instructions, write an accompanying memo that you can attach to all your evaluations, describing how you have grounded the evaluation in the job description, based it on specific behaviors, and consulted with the person being evaluated (see 4 below).
4. Evaluators discussed their performance review with the employee who was being evaluated. Notice on the Minnesota form that space is provided for the employee to respond to the evaluation and the signature of the employee being evaluated is required.

The acronym BARS, *behaviorally anchored rating scales,* describes a specific technique for helping assure that ratings on performance reviews are based on behaviors. A BARS document has a scale (say, from 1–10), but rather than simply describing the

*See especially Field and Holley (1982), "The Relationship of Performance Appraisal System Characteristics to Verdicts in Selected Employment Discrimination Cases." More generally, see Swan and Margulies (1991), *How to Do a Superior Performance Appraisal.*

FIGURE 4.24 Sample Performance Evaluation Form

State of Minnesota

Performance Review

PE 00072 03
(12 84)

In compliance with Minnesota Statutes, Chapter 13.04, Subd. 2, we are informing you that the information collected through the use of this form will be used to document your performance on an annual basis. The information may be used in decisions concerning advancement, reassignment, future training needs, performance-related salary adjustments, and as evidence in contested disciplinary actions. It is legally required. Without it, there is no objective data on which to evaluate performance; therefore, no performance-based salary increases will be granted. This information is available to you, your supervisor, personnel director, and other employees in your agency whose job assignment requires access.

EMPLOYEE'S NAME	AGENCY/DIVISION	
CLASSIFICATION TITLE	WORKING TITLE (if different)	POSITION CONTROL NUMBER
APPRAISAL PERIOD to	DATE PERFORMANCE INDICATORS ESTABLISHED	DATE REVIEWED WITH EMPLOYEE

A. **EVALUATION OF RESPONSIBILITIES** identified in the employee's position description. Rate each principal responsibility using the appropriate evaluation factors of quantity, quality and time. If a factor is not included in the employee's performance indicators or is inappropriate for measuring the employee's performance of a given responsibility, cross out that factor. Use the COMMENTS section to support and/or qualify your evaluation. Comment (justification) must be given when either "Below Standards" or "Greatly Exceeds Standards" is used.

RESP. or OBJ. No.	PRIORITY	% OF TIME	Evaluation Factors (Use only those that are appropriate)	LEVELS OF PERFORMANCE					COMMENTS
				Below Standards	Minimally Meets Standards	Fully Meets Standards	Exceeds Standards	Greatly Exceeds Standards	
			Quantity Quality Time	( ) ( ) ( )	( ) ( ) ( )	( ) ( ) ( )	( ) ( ) ( )	( ) ( ) ( )	
			Quantity Quality Time	( ) ( ) ( )	( ) ( ) ( )	( ) ( ) ( )	( ) ( ) ( )	( ) ( ) ( )	
			Quantity Quality Time	( ) ( ) ( )	( ) ( ) ( )	( ) ( ) ( )	( ) ( ) ( )	( ) ( ) ( )	
			Quantity Quality Time	( ) ( ) ( )	( ) ( ) ( )	( ) ( ) ( )	( ) ( ) ( )	( ) ( ) ( )	
			Quantity Quality Time	( ) ( ) ( )	( ) ( ) ( )	( ) ( ) ( )	( ) ( ) ( )	( ) ( ) ( )	

(continued)

FIGURE 4.24 Continued

B. **ADDITIONAL COMMENTS AND CONCERNS** to be considered in the performance review. Add anything that is relevant to the employee's performance not included in Section A.

C. **OVERALL PERFORMANCE LEVEL OF EMPLOYEE.** Check appropriate statement below. Consider all data in Sections A and B.

	Performance is outstanding. The employee's achievements and contributions consistently exceed standards, expectations and requirements.
	Performance is above expectations. The employee typically performs at a higher level than the job requires.
	Performance is satisfactory. The employee meets job requirements and expectations.
	Performance is marginal. The employee meets some, but not all job requirements and expectations. Improvement is necessary.
	Performance is unsatisfactory. The employee does not meet job requirements and expectations. Substantial improvement is needed to justify retention in the position.

D. **POSITION DESCRIPTION REVIEW** is to be completed each year. Description should be revised if the position changes (need not be rewritten each year). The position description must be entirely rewritten every three years. A copy of the employee's revised or rewritten position description should be submitted to the agency's personnel office with a copy of the review form.

The current position description is:

☐ an accurate reflection of the current responsibilities and performance standards.

☐ revised to reflect changes in the position.

☐ rewritten because it is three years old.

E. **EMPLOYEE COMMENTS AND CONCERNS** (Employee is encouraged but not required to comment on appraisal and performance.)

SIGNATURE OF RATER (I have completed the above evaluation)	Date
SIGNATURE OF EMPLOYEE (I have read the above evaluation)	Date
SIGNATURE OF RATER'S SUPERVISOR (I have reviewed and concur with the above evaluation)	Date

presence or absence of a trait (punctuality, say), the scale includes descriptions of behaviors associated with the various numbers or with sectors along the scale: for instance, 10 means "always 10–15 minutes early for all work sessions"; 9 means "always on time"; 7–8 means "late no more than four times per year and always calls ahead"; and so on down to 1, which means "late three times/week or more, despite weekly reminders." See the Minnesota state form (Figure 4.24), which represents a similar effort to incorporate specific behaviors into a scale by referring to the employee's detailed job description and then seeking a scaled response. Notice also that the form requires a detailed description if the rating deviates more than one column from the middle column on the scale, which denotes normal or satisfactory performance.

Some personnel consultants recommend a critical incident log, where specific instances of noteworthy employee behavior—either superior performance or problematic performance—are documented when they occur. These events are then incorporated into the formal performance review. As with all narratives associated with performance, critical incident reports are most useful when they emphasize behaviors, rather than traits. The Employee Performance Log illustrated in Figure 4.25 is a sample critical incident log from the manual *Performance Standards and Appraisal in California State Government.* Notice the amount of detail in the log, specifying what was and wasn't done and when as well as the date on which each incident was discussed.

Expression

Job descriptions—like mission statements, vision statements, and plans—are inherently expressive documents, setting forth the expectations and goals for someone working in a particular position. Conversely, performance reviews—especially traditional, formal, annual reviews—are explicitly descriptive and evaluative documents. Yet extensive evidence shows that evaluative feedback tends to be most readily understood, accepted, and acted on when it is offered in an expressive mode.

For example, the following formula, which was made popular by Kenneth Blanchard and Spencer Johnson's (1982) *The One-Minute Manager,* is an effective way of framing feedback to people—both when you're praising them and when you're trying to persuade them to change what they've been doing: "When you do XXX, then YYY happens, and, as a result, your colleagues and the organization have to deal with ZZZ." To make the formula concrete, here's one possible instance: "When you're the designated receptionist and you leave the office to distribute the mail, then I'm frustrated in my work because I have to cover the phone and answer customer inquiries, and the checks don't get processed in time." (In Chapter 6, we'll talk about this formula as well as other strategies for communicating effectively in difficult situations.) Notice that in addition to being an expressive statement, sometimes called an *"I" statement,* this formula also invites specific detail in describing all three of its elements: the behavior, its effect on the speaker/writer, and the consequences.

We started this chapter by talking about the power of writing as an instrument for building an institutional culture. Over the past century, corporate culture, in general, has changed profoundly. One of the most significant aspects of this change has been

FIGURE 4.25 Sample Critical Incident Log

EMPLOYEE PERFORMANCE LOG

Atkinson	Chris
Employee Last Name	**First Name**

Performance Appraisal Period From: July 1,1997 **To:** June 30, 1998

Incidents of Good Performance: Date	Incidents of Good Performance	Incidents of Poor Performance: Date	Incidents of Poor Performance	Date Disc'd
8/2	Friday 3:00 p.m.—Audit report was praised for its accuracy & speedy completion, 1 wk. before due date. Disc'd 8/2.	10/4	Monday 9:30 a.m. Absent. Said it was due to "recurring and very painful stomach problem."	10/4
9/2	Monday 9:00 a.m.—Presentation at Director's Staff Mtg. was praised for its effectiveness & relevance. Disc'd 9/2.	10/6	8:45 a.m. Tardy. 30 mins.	10/6
		10/8	9:15 a.m. Tardy. 45 mins.	10/8
		10/13	9:15 a.m. Tardy. No reason given.	10/13
5/7	Saturday 8:00 a.m.–4:00 p.m.—Volunteered to work Saturday to insure that the Budget Proposal for the Montgomery project was completed for Monday's meeting at Finance. Disc'd 5/7.	10/18	Absent all day. Failed to call in. On 10/19, said forgot to tell me of a dental appointment.	10/19
		10/25	11:00 a.m. Missed deadline for important project to be completed at time of Div. Mtg.	10/25
6/3	Volunteered to coordinate the departmental United Fund Campaign. Director commended Chris for meeting the annual goal. Disc'd 6/9.	10/27	Complaint from Budget Officer about Chris' rude phone manner @ 3:00 p.m. phone call.	10/28

the way people and institutions think about their work and their relationship to it. A century ago, organizations generally treated an employee as *homo economicus,* a creature motivated to work strictly by selfish economic gain. Organizations generally assumed that their employees were simply units of labor in the organizational machine. They assumed there was an inherent friction or resistance to work—laziness—in these units of labor and that the paycheck was the only lubricant for this friction. Our epigraph at the beginning of this chapter is from Terrence Deal and Allan Kennedy's (1982) book *Corporate Cultures: The Rites and Rituals of Corporate Life.* It's one of a long line of documents attesting to the fact that our motivation to do well as employees is much more complex than simply receiving our paycheck. As Deal and Kennedy point out, most of us make enormous emotional investments in our work and in the institutions where we work. We participate in making the corporate culture, we inform that culture with our own values and aspirations, and, in turn, our own identities and values are informed by the values and aspirations of our workplaces.

A century or so ago, when organizations were thought of primarily as machines and employees as fungible parts within the machines, expressions of corporate values, visions, and missions were rarely seen. Today, they are seen everywhere. The risk of their current popularity is that they may well be seen as a fad—and, indeed, in many organizations they may simply be a fad. But thoughtful and sophisticated organizations recognize themselves as value-laden cultures, as organic, human institutions whose very existence is constituted in the words of their corporate documents. They recognize those documents as arguments, and they recognize their corporate values and visions as warrants for those documents; therefore, they see the absolute necessity of making those warrants explicit and visible for themselves, their employees, and the other institutions and people who are part of their external environment.

WRITING CHECKLIST

The following guidelines will help you to write mission and vision statements, strategic plans, policies and procedures manuals, and job descriptions and performance reviews that negotiate and express institutional goals, values, and practices. For any of these guidelines, remember the superordinate guideline: Disregard *any* of this advice if it would cause you to do something that's inappropriate or silly for your situation.

☑ Mission and Vision Statements

- Draft community-building documents collaboratively, including mission and vision statements; those that result from true collaboration will be effective for all who participated in the process.
- Express the organization's essential values and goals so that they are visible to those inside and outside of the organization.

- Express three essential elements: (1) a clear sense of identity; (2) clear, tangible goals; and (3) the values that inform the goals.
- Strive for brevity, portability, and memorability of expression in mission and vision statements.
- Express vision statements in visionary, sensory terms; operationalize in mission statements the image put forth in the vision statement.

Strategic Plans

- Use strategic plans to make arguments for time, money, equipment, staff, or other resources.
- Include as your readers executives who determine organizational priorities and allocate resources and staff.
- Clarify and express your institutional identity before you determine your goals.
- Make sure your goals are consistent with individual and organizational values and aspirations.
- Using SWOT analysis, first look inward at your organization's strengths and weaknesses (and values and aspirations); then look outward at opportunities and threats in the environment. Finally, based on this analysis, imagine strategies for achieving your goals and mitigating your risks.
- Answer basic questions about your organization's mission, vision, and values.
- Provide a realistic audit of your organization's resources and accomplishments.
- Align your organization's mission and vision with its resources and accomplishments.
- Assess realistically the environment in which your organization hopes to realize its plan.
- Project future action coherent with other elements of the plan.

Policies and Procedures Manuals

- Remember that the first goal in writing a policy or procedure is to prevent employees from hurting themselves or others, from damaging equipment, or from committing the company to something that's harmful or contrary to the company's mission.
- Keep in mind that the second aim is to clarify the organizational goals the policy or procedure serves, the context in which these goals exist, and the means of accomplishing these goals.
- Design your policies and procedures so they free employees from deciding among alternative ways to complete tasks and from worrying about the ramifications for colleagues.

- Focus on "do" rather than on "don't."
- Write policies and procedures that empower employees to act with confidence in difficult situations.
- Present positive alternatives when teaching policies that prohibit something.
- Don't assume people know your policies and procedures exist, where to find them, and how to use them.
- Don't assume readers will read the complete statement or set of instructions before acting on it.
- Don't assume readers share your interest in the history and details of the policy or procedure.
- Don't assume readers will approach the situation that calls forth the policy or procedure the same way you do.
- Don't assume readers will read the policy or procedure in the same environment or circumstances in which you wrote it.
- Design and test policies and procedures in consultation with users during interviews, focus groups, and pilot tests.
- Include appeals to authority, utility, and delimitations when appropriate.
- Compile policies and procedures in comprehensive manuals or electronic archives in a central, safe place so there are written records of how things are done.
- Make important policies and procedures available several different times in several places so they're visible for all who need to see them.
- Use a physical design for manuals that enables employees to add and remove documents as policies and procedures change.
- Segment and organize documents according to who needs what information.
- Use redundant directional signals—page numbers, numbering within subsections, detailed tables of contents and indexes, and the like.
- Follow any agreed upon institutional format, use topic and keyword headers and titles, and place visual emphasis on risks or concerns.
- Make the sequence of steps in a procedure clear, and provide necessary contextual information.
- Use the active voice and frequently use commands.

☑ Job Descriptions and Performance Reviews

- Keep in mind the multiple goals of job descriptions: to provide the basis for hiring employees to achieve particular institutional goals; to help individual employees organize tasks and set priorities; to enable both the employee and the organization to review an individual's job performance; and to provide a legal document to verify that hiring and firing have been based on qualifications and job performance.

- Set forth the expectations and goals for someone working in a particular position in a job description; describe and evaluate the work of someone working in a particular position in a performance review.
- Keep in mind that the employees, immediate colleagues, and the supervisor should be readers and co-writers of a job description.
- Make job descriptions for hiring general enough so that the employee and supervisor have room to tailor the employee's duties to the needs of the office, the employee, and fellow employees, but make the description specific enough to make meaningful distinctions among candidates.
- Conduct performance reviews frequently, and ensure that those persons being evaluated take an active part in the process.
- Remember that the participants in a performance review should be readers of the review; if the reviewee is not a reader, the process is flawed and probably illegal.
- Write performance reviews based on job descriptions.
- Make sure that assessments are behavior oriented, rather than trait oriented.

ACTIVITIES AND PROJECTS

1. Consider the context in which your organization's mission statement was produced and the product that resulted. First, determine the historical context of your organization's current mission statement. What process was used to produce the statement, and who was involved? Describe as specifically as possible how the statement was created and participants' contributions in its development. Next, consider Bryan Smith's terms for strategies for sharing an organizational vision (see Senge et al., 1994). Which term best describes the process that was used to develop this mission statement: Telling? Selling? Testing? Consulting? Co-Creating? Why is the term you selected most appropriate?
2. Get a copy of the mission statement for an organization that you frequently interact with as a customer or client. Given your unique perspective of that organization's products or services, respond to the mission statement. First of all, decide whether you believe that the organization "walks the walk" as well as "talks the talk." Explain your perspective. Next, consider whether the mission statement includes all four essential elements: expression of a clear sense of identity; expression of clear, tangible goals; expression of the values that inform the goals; and brevity, portability, and memorability of expression. Elaborate on how the statement does or doesn't achieve all four elements.
3. Look more closely at the mission and vision statements for the California Student Aid Commission (Figures 4.3 and 4.4). How would you describe the relationship between the two? What connections do you see? What threads are

consistent in the two statements? What differences do you see, and why do you believe they occur? Next, consider the relationship between these two statements and the following statement of purpose, role, and responsibilities:

> The primary purpose of the California Student Aid Commission is to ensure the effective and efficient administration of state-authorized financial aid programs for students attending California colleges, universities, and other post-secondary institutions. This includes grant, work study, and loan programs supported by the State of California and the federal government. The Commission has a responsibility to provide leadership on financial aid issues and to make public policy recommendations concerning financial aid programs. To meet these responsibilities, the Commission collects information on student financial aid issues, evaluates the effectiveness of its programs, conducts research assessing California's financial needs, engages in long-range planning as a foundation for program improvement, and disseminates information to parents, students, and California educational institutions.

4. Reread the agendas and minutes in Chapter 3 for the StyleGuiders and the Credit Card Club (Figures 3.20, 3.21, and 3.23). Consider the content of these agendas and minutes in light of the mission statements for the respective committees.

5. Compose a mission statement you might add to an agenda or minutes that you wrote as a response to Chapter 3 or that you composed on the job. Ideally, you should co-create this mission statement with the group for which you wrote the agenda or minutes. If that isn't possible, write this mission statement yourself, making sure that it accurately reflects the "walk" of your group and incorporates the four essential elements of a mission statement.

6. Read the Strategic Plan for EdFund's Research & Development branch (Figure 4.6). Discuss the interrelationships among the parts of the plan, especially among the Shared Values; Vision, Mission, Goal, Objectives; Planned Projects; Duty Statements; and Customer Creed. In what particular ways do these parts relate to or complement each other?

7. Compare and contrast Marianne Ramos' position description (Figure 4.23) and the Duty Statement for the Staff Services Analyst (Figure 4.6). What similarities and differences do you see in the conventions and sorts of arguments represented by these descriptions? And how might these descriptions be used to help manage work and review the work that's being done?

8. Look carefully at the section of the procedures manual entitled Borrower Eligibility and Loan Certification (Figure 4.18). Evaluate the effectiveness of document design. What features enhance the functionality of this text? Why? What features appear to be conventions for the organization? How well do these conventions work? How might the format and layout of these procedures be improved?

9. The policies and procedures documents from EdFund and CSAC (Figures 4.13 through 4.16) follow format conventions established by the organizations (which are actually a public organization that has recently split into two organizations, both using the same document design conventions). Determine what these conventions are by reviewing the documents. Then talk about how these conventions would contribute to the efficiency of these organizations. Finally, suggest any ways in which the conventions might be changed to enhance document design or improve the functionality of these memos within the organizations.

10. Given Tom Peters' belief that policies and procedures manuals should be "do" manuals rather than "don't" manuals and that even policies that are stated in negative terms should have affirmative functions, review the EdFund policy memo on Building and Personal Security (Figure 4.14). Does this policy use "must nots" effectively? Support your point of view with evidence from the memo.

11. Select a task that you perform routinely on the job, and write a procedures document that could be used to train a new employee to perform it. Pilot-test your document to gain useful feedback, and revise it based upon this feedback.

12. Select an unwritten policy that is currently in force within your organization and write it down, or develop a new policy that's needed. To make sure that the currently unwritten policy is written down to reflect actual practice, use interviews or a focus group to gain the input of those people who actually work in situations where the policy applies. Or if you're writing a new policy, use interviews or a focus group to determine what the new policy should include. Be sure to pilot-test the document by gaining feedback from those who will use the policy.

13. Interview someone in an organization about how its records of policies and procedures are kept. What means are used for storing and maintaining a comprehensive collection of policies and procedures? Who is responsible for maintaining these records? What are the conventions for maintaining policies and procedures—Physical design (the particulars of the paper and/or electronic collection)? Organization and segmenting of materials? Indexes for materials? In addition, what conventions are followed in designing individual policies and procedures?

14. Collect the job descriptions of several colleagues you work with on a daily basis; with each person's help, compare what is in the job description with what he or she actually does. Is the job description an accurate reflection of the person's job duties? Could the job description be used to measure that person's job performance in a reasonable and useful way? Why or why not? After you've had the opportunity to talk with several people about their job descriptions, revise one of them (maybe even revise your own) so that it's an accurate reflection of the

position that can contribute to the efficiency and humaneness of the performance review process.

15. Interview someone who carries out performance reviews within an organization. Determine the particular goals of performance reviews within that organization and the specific processes and documents that are a part of that review. Find out, too, the criteria that are used during reviews. Finally, ask your interviewee for advice on conducting performance reviews ethically and humanely and for writing the accompanying documents. If time permits and it seems appropriate, ask your interviewee for pointers he or she would give someone undergoing a performance review.

16. Take on the role of a perspective evaluator, and write a performance review of yourself. Make sure that you use your actual job description as the basis for your review, and describe your behaviors, rather than your traits. After drafting this performance review, use the review to speculate about the specific ways in which you might do your job better. Also write about how well the job description captures what you actually do on the job.

REFERENCES

Adams, S. (1995a). *Bring me the head of Willy the mailboy!* Kansas City, MO: Andrews and McMeel.

Adams, S. (1995b). *The Dilbert principle.* New York: HarperCollins.

Adams, S. (1996). *Still pumped from using the mouse.* Kansas City, MO: Andrews and McMeel.

Blanchard, K., & Johnson, S. (1982). *The one-minute manager.* New York: Morrow.

Bruner, J. S. (1962). *On knowing: Essays for the left hand.* Cambridge, MA: Belknap Press.

Deal, T., & Kennedy, A. (1982). *Corporate cultures: The rites and rituals of corporate life.* Reading, MA: Addison-Wesley.

Field, H. S., & Holley, W. H. (1982). The relationship of performance appraisal system characteristics to verdicts in selected employment discrimination cases. *Academy of Management Journal, 25,* 392–406.

Gumpert, D. E. (1996). Inc. *Magazine presents how to really create a successful business plan: Featuring the business plans of Pizza Hut, Software Publishing Corp., Celestial Seasonings, People Express, Ben & Jerry's.* Boston: Inc.

Kahrs, K., & Koek, K. E. (Eds.). (1996). *Business plans handbook: A compilation of actual business plans developed by small businesses throughout North America.* New York: Gale Research.

Lee, C. (1996, May). Performance appraisal: Can we manage away the curse? *Training,* 47.

March, J. G., & Simon, H. A. (1958). *Organizations.* New York: Wiley.

Mintzberg, H. (1994). *The rise and fall of strategic planning: Preconceiving roles for planning, plans, planners.* New York: Macmillan.

Norman, D. A. (1990). *The design of everyday things.* New York: Doubleday.

Orstein, R. E. (1972). *The psychology of consciousness.* New York: Viking.

Peters, T. J. (1994). *The pursuit of wow!* New York: Vintage Books.

Peters, T. J., & Waterman, R. H., Jr. (1982). *In search of excellence: Lessons from America's best-run companies.* New York: Harper & Row.

Senge, P. M., Roberts, C., Ross, R. B., Smith, B. J., & Kleiner, A. (1994). *The fifth discipline fieldbook: Strategies and tools for building a learning organization.* New York: Doubleday.

Sperry, R. (1974). Messages from the laboratory. *Engineering and Science,* 29–32.

Swan, W. S., & Margulies, P. (1991). *How to do a superior performance appraisal.* New York: Wiley.

Tiffany, P., & Peterson, S. D. (1997). *Business plans for dummies.* Foster City, CA: IDG Books.

Part III

Writing to Build and Manage Relationships across Organizational Boundaries

Chapter 5

Contexts and Conventions of Business Letters

I didn't have time to write a short letter, so I wrote a long one instead.
—Mark Twain

Letters are the original mode of written business communication, and they remain a universal mode in all kinds of contexts and situations, covering the entire range of goals and readers. Along with memos (and, increasingly, e-mail), letters make up the bulk of written communication across the professions. So, to the extent that the writing of business really is the doing of business, the ability to write effective letters in your workplace is a crucial factor in your having a successful professional career.

When Should You Write a Letter?

Part of the sophistication of being a good letter writer has to do with knowing when to write a letter and, just as important, when *not* to write a letter. Remember the possibility we've been mentioning since we first introduced GRACE in Chapter 1: The particular situation where you find yourself may actually be best handled with a communication that's not even written. So, one question you'll want to ask yourself in almost every situation is whether you should even be writing. And if you decide that you should be, you may still find that a letter is not the most appropriate written document. For example, the situation and its problems and issues may be too complex to be processed with just a letter; they may require a full-dress report, proposal, or other substantial document.

Assessing the Risks of Writing and Not Writing

When you raise the question of whether you should write a letter, you'll probably move toward an answer by asking several more specifically focused questions that will help you analyze your situation. The following may be especially helpful:

QUESTION 1: **Does a letter seem too formal or legalistic or, in some other way, not quite appropriate for the situation?**

Often, in a context that has included informal, friendly, conversational dialogue, a letter may seem to suggest a sudden distancing or chilling of the relationship—or even a loss of trust. But if the situation is one that requires a paper trail, you will need to take this risk. You can mitigate this problem by anticipating it—noting conversationally ahead of time that you'll be writing a letter. And reasonable people in professional and business relationships generally understand and expect this kind of mixing of informal conversation and more formal written documentation.

QUESTION 2: Do you need a paper trail?

For political or personal or legal reasons, it may be important to have a paper trail that documents what you have done, said, agreed to do, or perhaps *not* agreed to do. In this case, you must write the letter—or a series of letters. Here's another example: Suppose you're required to renew an agreement with a vendor by a certain date in order to keep the same price schedule you've had for the current quarter. You don't want to take a chance on just making a telephone call in this situation. You want a piece of paper—a dated letter—as evidence that you've renewed the same terms.

QUESTION 3: Would a direct confrontation be unpleasant—maybe even dangerous?

Is another party in this situation likely to react to a face-to-face spoken encounter with a strong response that might include intimidating counter-arguments or emotionally taxing demands, accusations, threats, or the like? Sometimes, this kind of confrontation is necessary, and you simply have to live through it. But if it's not essential to have the confrontation and you can save yourself an unpleasant experience by writing a letter, doing so may be preferable, even if you don't need to establish a paper trail.

QUESTION 4: Is there a chance that your letter could become a weapon to be used against you?

This risk is especially high in situations characterized by conflict and high emotion (which we'll discuss at length in Chapter 6). But it's a risk that's present, to some extent, in almost every letter you write. And there's always the risk of simply stumbling and saying something you don't mean, even if you're writing in a routine situation that's not emotionally charged. So, you need to be sure the letter says what you want it to mean and that it makes only the commitments you want it to make. Be especially careful if you're writing out of a strong emotional response of your own. (In this case, you need to look carefully at Chapter 6.)

Letter-Writing Contexts and Situations—and Their Conventions

"Send this SOB the 'Dear Valued Customer' letter."

While letter-writing contexts are infinitely diverse and each situation is unique, there are a finite number of generic *types* of situations, and each tends to generate similar goals, readers, arguments, and conventions. So, it's useful to assess the specific situation and context you're in and to think about whether you recognize it as one that calls for particular goals and conventions of argument and expression. If you do recognize it as a type you've seen before, then your GRACE analysis will be much more efficient.

This is not to say that you should simply have 17 boilerplate form letters for the 17 most common situations you encounter—sending out letter 13 through an automatic mail-merge program for situation 13. The epitome of how badly this strategy can go wrong is told in the story of a disgruntled customer who had written a letter to the manufacturer of a product that had disappointed him. In reply to his letter, he received a letter expressing the company's deep concern about the quality of its products and the satisfaction of its customers. Then, he noticed that someone had inadvertently enclosed his original letter along with the reply. And attached to his letter was the following note: "Send this SOB the 'Dear Valued Customer' letter."

Analyzing and Evaluating Your Context

It's hard to know in this "SOB" situation whether the boilerplate letter itself would have been effective. It might have been—especially if it was tailored thoughtfully to this individual customer and his specific concern. Given the carelessness of the physical handling of the documents, though, we'd have to guess little thought was given to the uniqueness of the situation. While there are generic similarities among situations, each is unique and requires some level of thoughtful analysis. The amount of time and effort you invest in that analysis should depend on how far the situation at hand deviates from a familiar, generic situation, how important the issues and the people involved are to you and your organization, and how much of your time and attention are being demanded by other tasks. The following questions can help you frame a quick situational analysis. If you find yourself struggling to answer these questions because the situation is complex and novel, you may want to consult a friend or colleague who has had some experience with an analogous situation and whose judgment you trust:

- Does this situation call for a letter? Is some other response, such as a phone call or direct conversation, more appropriate?
- If some other response is equally appropriate, which would be easier?
- Does this situation call for a combination of responses—a phone call followed by a letter, for example?
- If this is a letter-writing situation, who should write it? Who should sign it? (These won't necessarily be the same person.)
- How tricky, difficult, or dangerous is this situation?
- How much effort is going to be required to do a good job?
- What's the worst thing that could happen if it goes badly?
- How much time, energy, and effort do you have to devote to this letter?
- Where can you get help if you need it?

Moving toward the Text with GRACE

Now, having done a broad contextual analysis of the situation, you can use GRACE to focus more directly on the questions you need to ask in order to generate effective text for your letter.

Goals

In Chapter 3, we noted that all memo-writing situations have two major dimensions, a relationship dimension and an action dimension, that co-exist in some kind of ratio. These two dimensions are even more dramatically present in most letter-writing situations. Sometimes, the crucial elements of the situation have to do with relationships, whether between you and your reader personally or between your organizations. Either something has already had an impact on the relationship or you are seeking to create an impact on the relationship. At the same time, there is always an action dimension, either your own or your reader's, and it is either in the past or in the future.

These multiple dimensions cause much of the difficulty people have in writing business letters, partly because the goals attached to these different dimensions can conflict with one another. For example, writing a letter to establish or maintain a relationship is a lot easier to do if you don't have to argue for some action that your reader opposes. And writing to justify some action you've taken or plan to take or that you want your reader to take is easier to do if you don't have to be concerned about the relationship between the two of you. You can actually map out these two dimensions on a grid like the one shown in Figure 5.1, and it can help you quickly visualize the kind of situation in which you're probably engaging.

If you don't read the matrix as a literal description of all the possible combinations of goals, it's a useful summary of the interplay between action and relationship goals. The matrix is especially useful in pointing out the stark difference you may have in goals. For example, in one situation, you may be able to take the relationship entirely for granted, and in another situation, the relationship may be your paramount concern. But the differences won't often be this sharp. In emphasizing the sharpness of the difference, the matrix can make subtle differences disappear. So don't assume, based on the matrix, that there's only a yes/no response to either the action orientation or the relationship orientation.

Look carefully at Tom Barker's letter to Bob Carr in Figure 5.2. It is almost entirely oriented along the action dimension. First, it reviews the facts and issues from an earlier discussion and tour of the site of a proposed municipal improvement project. In the first paragraph, it reports back the writer's understanding of the reader's deadlines and financial resources. Then, in the second paragraph, it lists the elements of the improvement project in a bulleted list. In the third paragraph, it goes on to make what is, in fact, a miniproposal, where it recites what the firm will do and gives a cost estimate expressed as a range between minimum and maximum costs. But the orientation to the action dimension is not exclusive. Even from the salutation ("Dear Bob"), a relationship dimension is present. In the first paragraph, the acute attention to the reader's needs and deadlines demonstrates the writer's personal care about them. And, of course, the final one-sentence paragraph ("We appreciate the opportunity to continue a professional relationship with Clearmont that began in 1976.") speaks specifically, albeit with a light touch, to the relationship dimension of the letter. The two institutions—the city and the engineering firm—have a 20-year relationship, and the writer obviously thinks this history is significant.

FIGURE 5.1 Action/Relationship Matrix

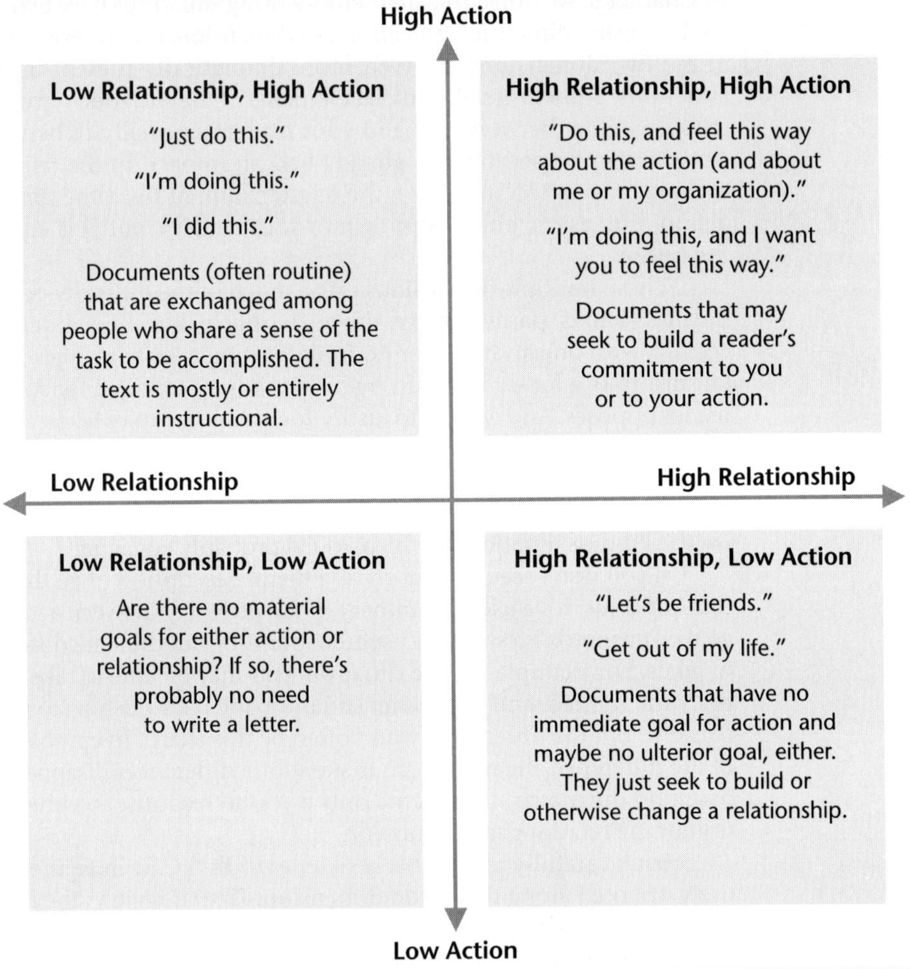

High Action

Low Relationship, High Action	High Relationship, High Action
"Just do this." "I'm doing this." "I did this." Documents (often routine) that are exchanged among people who share a sense of the task to be accomplished. The text is mostly or entirely instructional.	"Do this, and feel this way about the action (and about me or my organization)." "I'm doing this, and I want you to feel this way." Documents that may seek to build a reader's commitment to you or to your action.
Low Relationship, Low Action	**High Relationship, Low Action**
Are there no material goals for either action or relationship? If so, there's probably no need to write a letter.	"Let's be friends." "Get out of my life." Documents that have no immediate goal for action and maybe no ulterior goal, either. They just seek to build or otherwise change a relationship.

Low Relationship ← → High Relationship

Low Action

Think about an actual letter-writing situation in your own experience, or look at one of the possible letter-writing situations at the end of this chapter or in Chapter 6. Try using the matrix to answer the following questions:

- What do you hope and expect will happen as a result of your letter? List both your relationship goals and action goals in order of importance.
- What is your relationship with your reader(s)? What are your goals for the relationship? Do you want to establish a new relationship? Change an existing relationship? End your relationship?
- If you are expecting or hoping for an action by your reader or readers, what *exactly* do you want them to do—or to quit doing or avoid doing? Analyze

FIGURE 5.2 Letter Oriented along the Action Dimension

Professional
Consultants

April 18, 1997

Mr. Bob Carr, Mayor
Town of Clearmont
P.O. Box 50
Clearmont, Wyoming 82835

RE: Engineering Recommendations and Cost Estimates Infrastructure Improvements

Dear Bob:

This letter follows our discussion and tour of Clearmont and presents my understanding of your request. You and the Council plan to establish a program of specific street and other improvements by June 17, 1997, and would like cost estimates in time for your special Council meeting on April 28. If the present capital facilities tax would be extended in 1998, Clearmont would receive about $12,000 per year for an estimated 7.6 years under the $20 million scenario. Including a permanent trust fund, this would increase the total tax to $25 million and raise Clearmont's share to about $115,000 collected over 9.6 years. Actually, the total revenue collected could be much higher if sales tax revenues continue rising at their present rate. Total funds available for construction might approach $200,000 with matching grants.

You mentioned several improvements:

- Improve drainage and repair base failure on Railway Street.
- Reconstruct the concrete valley pan on Water Street.
- Pave three blocks of Railway Street between Meade and Piney Avenues to improve access to a potential industrial park area.
- Possible use of irrigation water for trees and lawn areas around town.

A memorandum containing engineering recommendations and order of magnitude cost estimates will be mailed to you by April 24, 1997. We will request compensation based on time expended for collecting the information and preparation of the memorandum. The fee for this work will probably be more than $400, but it will not exceed $700.

We appreciate the opportunity to continue a professional relationship with Clearmont that began in 1976.

Sincerely,

Tom Barker

Thomas L. Barker, PE

Architecture - Engineering
Materials Testing - Surveying

2237 North Main Street Sheridan, Wyoming 82801 (307)555-1711 Fax: (307)555-5014 cer@wave.net Offices in Gillette and Douglas Wyoming

this action and its context carefully. Now ask yourself what your readers need from you in order to do what you want them to.

- How are your action goals and relationship goals interacting? How are they conflicting with and complicating each other? How are they supporting and reinforcing each other?

Readers

Who Are Those Guys? As in all writing situations, the first question you need to ask in preparing to write a letter is who your readers are. Who should the letter be addressed to? Who should formally receive copies of it—that is, who needs to know the issues and content of your letter? Who else is likely to read the letter? Imagine an egocentric solar system for your reader. Maybe even take a few moments to sketch out a solar system around your primary reader. Who's in the important orbits around him or her? You may not know the names of specific people, but you can still ask what kinds of people or positions are likely to be in close orbit around your reader.

It's hardly possible to overestimate the importance of having good insight into the readers of your business correspondence. If you've experimented with the action/relationship matrix at all, you've probably recognized that both your action goals and relationship goals are reader based. So, even when the relationship dimension is routine and unproblematic, you still need to make the thoughtful effort of anticipating your readers' questions so they can respond appropriately and you can achieve your action goals. People often ask for things in letters that their readers would be happy to give them or do for them—but then don't tell their readers what they need to know in order to fulfill the request. For instance, people try to set up meetings and forget to specify where and when they want to meet. People ask readers to respond and forget to give them phone numbers and addresses or tell them when they are available. People ask others to contact someone or deliver or pick up something and don't say where to do these things.

What Are They Asking When They Read My Letter? You need to make the imaginative leap inside your readers' heads, reading the letter from their perspective and testing to see if it tells what they need to know to take the action that is your goal in writing the letter. One quick test is a variation of the journalist's five W's: Who? What? Why? When? Where? Imagine your readers asking these questions:

- **Who's writing to me and why?** For us, it's axiomatic that busy readers of professional correspondence are going to approach a business letter or memo with three immediate questions: Who is writing to me? What's it about? Why are they writing to me? And it's also axiomatic that these same readers are going to lose patience if you don't answer these questions quickly. Rather than let this possibility of losing your readers raise your anxiety level, use it to generate ideas for starting your letter. Simply start the letter by answering your reader's questions. If you've just had a conversation with him or her that resulted in a request for the letter, start the letter by saying so. If you're writing the letter because someone the reader knows suggested that you and the reader could both benefit from working together in some way, start the letter by saying this. Identifying whatever historical or organizational context led you to write the letter—especially the most recent transaction that triggered this letter-writing event—is probably an effective way to start.

- **What does any of this have to do with me or my organization? Why should we care?** As you've begun to think about drafting this letter, you've already reflected some on your own goals. You now need to do some goal matching, imagining your readers' goals, interests, abilities, and resources and how they match with your own. At some level, it will be useful to ask yourself a series of questions about the lens of interests, resources, and needs your readers will look through when they read your letter. What kinds of political, economic, personal, and organizational agendas and interests do they have? What kinds of experience and what kinds of assumptions and values will they likely bring to reading your letter, and how are they likely to use these experiences, assumptions, and values as warrants to test your arguments? Where are their agendas, interests, experience, assumptions, and values likely to intersect with your own, and where are they likely to conflict?
- **OK, the action this letter asks for may make sense. Where, when, and how would we do what it asks?** If your readers have reached this question in their own processing of your letter, they're close to buying the whole program. But you still have to give them the information they need in order to do what you hope they'll do. And this information needs to make sense to them. You can expand the goals question discussed earlier, telling in more specific operational detail exactly you want your readers to do:
  - When do they need to act?
  - Where do they need to go?
  - What resources do they need?
  - Where can they get what they need?
  - What people do they need to work with?
  - Why is this important for them to do?

You can continue to amplify and unpack these questions if your readers need still more information. For example, if they need to work with other people, what are the critical stages and deadlines that these other people need to meet? If your readers need other resources and information, can you include these in the letter? If you can't, then how can you let your readers know how to get these other things?

Arguments

Letters, by definition, are short documents, and short documents, by definition, can't have long arguments. This means your arguments in your letters—like those in your memos—must be efficient. If you are dealing with a large, complex, important issue that needs to be argued elaborately and supported with extensive evidence and elaboration of your underlying assumptions and values, you probably need to write a fully developed report or proposal. You'll probably still need to write a letter, even in this case, but it will be a cover letter that introduces and briefly gives the context and background of your fully elaborated document.

Is There an Argument in This Letter? Even assuming the arguments in your letters will all be relatively brief, they may still be vastly different in intensity and urgency. In a routine letter about a routine situation, the arguments may hardly be visible at all. See Figure 5.3, for example. Where is the argument in this letter? And *what* is the argument? On one level, the argument couldn't be more obvious or straightforward: The first sentence presents an arguable proposition. And the second paragraph narrates a set of facts—a series of events—that support the proposition that Terry will have the protective sleeves by 10:00 A.M. the next day.

But on another level, the opening sentence really isn't so much an argumentative proposition as a simple projection or forecast, something that is a matter of fact. Pat clearly expects Terry to believe her, not to engage in a debate about the credibility of the claim or the relevance of the data she offers or even any of the underlying assumptions (such as "Courier services can be trusted to deliver their packages when they promise."). While the narrative is an argument on one level ("You can believe me when I say the sleeves will be there because . . ."), it is also part of another argument at a deeper level.

The first sentence, of course, is important in both arguments. It is especially important to Terry because it answers the question that is probably uppermost in Terry's mind: Will I get my transducers in time? And because it is such a reader-centered beginning, the first sentence is an important part of Pat's second argument. But Pat isn't using it as the claim here. Pat is using that first sentence and the entire second para-

FIGURE 5.3 Routine Letter about Routine Situation

Dear Terry:

You'll have your 500 NoSun protective sleeves by 10 o'clock tomorrow morning.

As soon as we heard from you—about an hour ago—we assigned a special crew to expedite the quality assurance review and the packaging. DHL courier service just picked up the order, so the sleeves are on their way already.

It's a privilege to be able to help our friends!

Sincerely,

Pat Kellogg

Pat Kellogg

graph as data to support the claim that's implicit in that *last* sentence, a claim about the kind of relationship that their two organizations have and that the two people have personally: They aren't just business acquaintances; they're friends. As friends who value their relationship with Terry's company and who care about Terry's needs, Pat's company takes special pains, including assigning a special crew of people who will not only expedite Terry's order but also make sure there are no shortcuts on quality control. Furthermore, Pat says, taking these pains to help a friend solve a problem is *not* a pain; it's a privilege.

If we wanted to push this line of thought, we could go to yet another level and speculate about underlying values/assumptions and their implications. What are some of the characteristics of friendship as distinguished from those typical of a mere business relationship? For example, friends truly care about one another's well-being, and they sometimes enact this caring even against their own immediate self-interest. Friends are loyal, and this loyalty is reciprocal. Surely, if Pat's company had an emergency need and Terry's company were in a position to help, it would only be reasonable for them to do so. And if a competitor offered protective sleeves to Terry at a discounted price, surely Terry's company would want to be loyal to Pat—for *both* professional and personal reasons. Pat's concern for the quality of NoSun's product and service means more than just friendship. It means Terry's company can confidently expect to operate more effectively because of their professional, as well as their personal, relationship with Pat's company.

Are these arguments really present in Pat's letter? We think so. Are the arguments fair? Again, we think so. It's possible to read the arguments as cynically self-serving but only if one concludes that Pat is being insincere, and there's no evidence here of insincerity. In fact, the underlying actions are themselves expressions of Pat's sincerity.

Which Direction Is the Argument Running? Our first argument in the letter from Pat to Terry runs the way most arguments run in business letters. This is what's often called the *direct* pattern (see Figure 5.4). The letter begins with the claim and then amplifies the argument with evidence and perhaps even an explicit statement of an underlying set of values or assumptions on which the writer has based the claim. Pat makes the claim that the sleeves will be there tomorrow morning by 10. This claim is then followed by narrating the facts of the preparation and packaging of the sleeves and the pickup by the courier. This pattern has some real benefits. For one thing, it answers the readers' ubiquitous question: Why is he or she writing to me? Using your claim or conclusion thus serves as a good advance organizer for your reader: "Aha, this is what the letter's about."

In other situations, you might decide that the *indirect* pattern is a more effective way of laying out your argument (see Figure 5.5). Rather than foregrounding the claim by presenting it first, you mute the claim, at least initially, by first laying out the evidence that justifies it. This strategy can be useful if you know your readers are inclined to be skeptical of the claim you want to make.

A well-written narrative that tells a powerful, moving story can even shift your readers' underlying ethical assumptions and help them understand and interpret the facts from a perspective that's sympathetic with your own. If you can tell your story

FIGURE 5.4 Direct Pattern

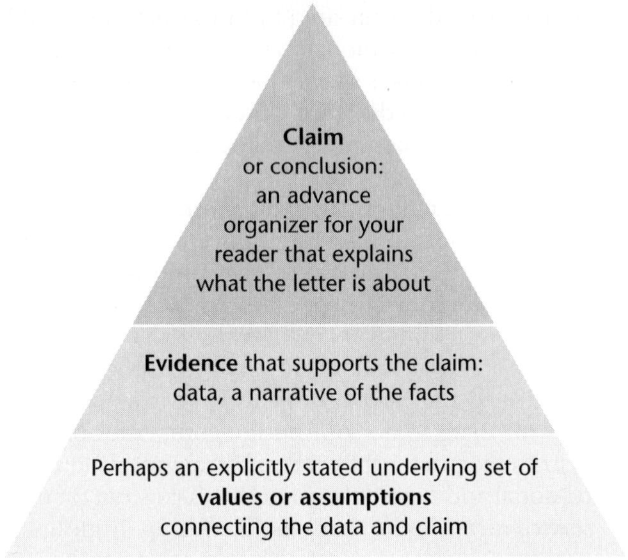

Claim
or conclusion:
an advance
organizer for your
reader that explains
what the letter is about

Evidence that supports the claim:
data, a narrative of the facts

Perhaps an explicitly stated underlying set of
values or assumptions
connecting the data and claim

FIGURE 5.5 Indirect Pattern

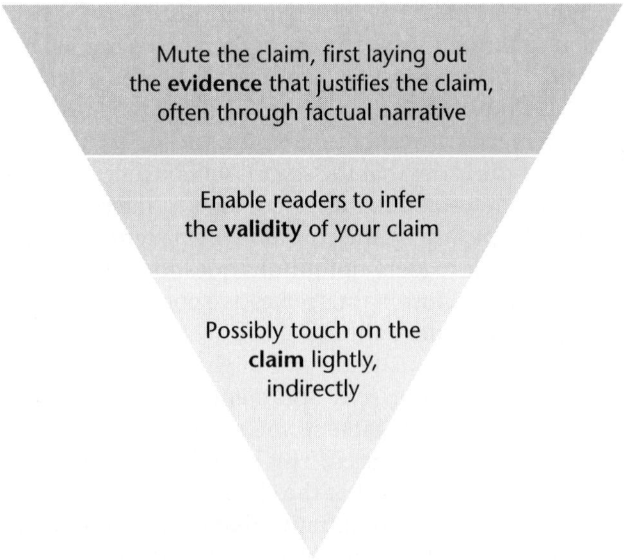

Mute the claim, first laying out
the **evidence** that justifies the claim,
often through factual narrative

Enable readers to infer
the **validity** of your claim

Possibly touch on the
claim lightly,
indirectly

in a way that successfully invites your readers to identify with your perspective, then they will be able to see how your claim is legitimately linked to the data you recite.

In its most extreme application, the indirect strategy might eliminate the claim altogether, just leaving the reader to infer the claim and underlying rationale from the data you've recited. In fact, this is almost the case with the second argument in Pat's letter to Terry. The first two paragraphs of the letter are virtually a factual narrative, although the letter begins in the future with the assertion that Terry will receive the protective sleeves. The claim of friendship is made only in the last sentence—and then only fleetingly and indirectly.

So, this little, short, matter-of-fact letter turns out to have some interestingly complex features. We find there are really two different arguments going on, as Figure 5.6 shows. And if we look at the letter through the action/relationship matrix, we find that one of the arguments is an action argument and the second is a relationship argument. It becomes even more interesting when we notice the way each argument is presented. The action argument follows the convention of a direct, assertive, action-oriented pattern, leading with the claim. The relationship argument (which can be very difficult to make without seeming heavy handed) runs right alongside the action argument but follows the much less assertive, more subtle conventional form of the indirect pattern, where the claim of friendship is made only at the end and even then with a very light touch.

Conventions

The letter from Pat to Terry is a fairly typical routine business letter, serving both to communicate some operational information (in this case, the delivery time of the

FIGURE 5.6 Two Parallel Arguments

Action Argument (direct, assertive, action oriented)	**Relationship Argument** (less assertive, more subtle, indirect)
Opening paragraph: Claim that sleeves will be there tomorrow by 10 A.M.	
Body paragraph: Narrative of the facts of preparing and packaging the sleeves and sending them via the courier.	**Body paragraph:** Narrative of the facts of preparing and packaging the sleeves and sending them via the courier.
	Closing paragraph: Claim of friendship.

sleeves) and to build or maintain goodwill between the writer and reader. The lengthy analysis we've inflicted on that simple, short letter may have left you with the impression that it was drafted with great effort and through a long, difficult process. Actually, this probably wasn't the case at all. The fact is, this letter is a conventional business letter: brief, straightforward, positive, and upbeat. Given the speed and urgency of the situation in which it must have been written, the letter was probably drafted in a matter of minutes, and the writer almost certainly wasn't thinking systematically about all the subtle implications of the second argument, the relationship argument. Even so, we can infer that Pat is an experienced business correspondent with a sensitive ear for nuances in writing situations and a well-developed mastery of the social and rhetorical conventions of business letters.

This kind of sensitivity to differences in writing situations is what enables many professionals to produce powerful, appropriately tailored letters that they adapt from boilerplate form letters. As we noted at the beginning of this chapter, you'll begin to encounter familiar types of writing situations after you have worked in a profession (or especially in a particular office) for some time. When you encounter a situation that's familiar to you or perhaps familiar to your organization in general, it seems wasteful and inefficient to reinvent a letter when there may be one in a file or on a disk that nearly speaks to the precise situation at hand. With a thoughtful analysis of the special features of your immediate situation—your goals, readers, and special arguments—you may find that you can modify an existing form letter with excellent persuasive effect.

The formal conventions of business letters are strong enough that most people recognize such documents at a glance. Yet there are no single, fixed, correct conventions for the organization, style, and format of a business letter. Many business and professional firms have standard templates and style guides for memos, letters, reports, proposals, and other documents so that all these texts will represent the organization with a consistent style and appearance. If you're writing as a representative of an organization, make sure you follow any official style guide or template that might apply to your letter.

If you're writing a letter in a situation where there are no established formal conventions, we recommend using the *full-block, modified-block,* or *AMS style,* which is a variation of the full-block style suggested by the American Management Society (AMS). Remember that these are just three of several standard stylistic conventions; your organization may prescribe a different convention. Because the full-block, modified-block, and AMS styles are simple, functional, and conservative conventions, they give you a low-risk strategy for laying out the formal structure of your letters if you're writing in a situation where no particular formal convention is called for.

Key Features of the Full-Block Style. See Figure 5.7 for an example of a business letter following the full-block style. Notice these features:

- Every line starts at the left margin.
- The body of the letter and the two address blocks are single spaced.
- The return address, of course, is your own address, which is a preprinted letterhead if you are using company stationery. The inside address is your reader's address, as it will appear on the envelope.

FIGURE 5.7 Sample of Full-Block Style

Constancy National Bank
434 W. Americus Lane
St. Louis, MO 54095
(219) 555-4039

Marcia L. Bennett
Vice President
TEL: (219) 555-4332

July 20, 1995

Mr. Michael Green
Green & Dubrowski Inc.
552 Elmtree Way
St. Louis, MO 54095

Dear Michael:

You may have learned that our parent company, Bank of North America, and ANC Banking, Inc. announced that they have signed a definitive agreement providing for a merger of equals which is expected to be completed in the first quarter of 1996. The new name of the combined companies will be Bank of North America ANC Corporation, and its headquarters will be in St. Louis. The principal subsidiary banks will be the First Bank of St. Louis, ANC Banking (Iowa) headquartered in Des Moines, ANC Bank (Kansas) headquartered in Kansas City, Constancy National Bank, and Independence National Bank. ANC Banking (St. Louis) will be merged into Constancy National Bank.

I believe that this merger of the two premier midwestern banks will mark the beginning of an exciting and mutually rewarding association. I also believe that it will enhance the ability of Constancy National to serve its customers.

Our aim at Constancy National is "business as usual." We will continue to focus our efforts and resources on St. Louis and Kansas City area businesses and take great pride in our abilities to serve our customers with sophisticated financial services, while maintaining an attentive, personalized banking relationship. As always, our commitment to superior service will remain our priority.

Please do not hesitate to call me directly with any questions or concerns. We appreciate and thank you for your business.

Best Regards,

Marcia L. Bennett

Marcia L. Bennett
Vice President

- The vertical space between the return address block or letterhead and the inside address block flexes—either stretches or contracts—depending on the length of the body of the letter so that the letter is approximately balanced between the top and bottom of the page. If the letter is long enough that it fills the page, then the space between the return address and the inside address is just a double space.
- A double space follows the inside address, the salutation, and each paragraph of the body, including the last paragraph before the complimentary close.
- To provide room for your signature, a quadruple space separates the complimentary close and your name/title.
- Additional blocks at the end of the letter (identifying initials, enclosure notation, and copy notation) are typically separated by double spaces.

Key Features of the Modified-Block Style. The key difference between the modified-block and full-block styles is that in modified-block, the return address block and the signature block start at the middle of the page, rather than the left margin (see Figure 5.8). In all other respects, modified-block style is like full-block style:

- Every line *except the return address block or letterhead, the dateline, and the signature block* starts at the left margin.
- The body of the letter and the two address blocks are single spaced.
- The return address or letterhead is your own address, and the inside address is your reader's address, as it will appear on the envelope
- The vertical space between the return address block and the inside address block flexes—either stretches or contracts—depending on the length of the body of the letter so that the letter is approximately balanced between the top and bottom of the page. If the letter is long enough that it fills the page, then the space between the return address and the inside address is just a double space.
- A double space follows the inside address, the salutation, and each paragraph of the body, including the last paragraph before the complimentary close.
- To provide room for your signature, a quadruple space separates the complimentary close and your name/title.
- Additional blocks at the end of the letter (identifying initials, enclosure notation, and copy notation) are typically separated by double spaces.

Key Features of the AMS (American Management Society) Style. See Figure 5.9 for a template of AMS style, which is like the full-block style in the following features:

- Every line starts at the left margin.
- The body and the two address blocks are single spaced.
- The vertical space between the return address block or letterhead and the inside address block flexes—either stretches or contracts—depending on the length of the body of the letter so that the letter is approximately balanced

FIGURE 5.8 Sample of Modified-Block Style

Constancy National Bank
434 W. Americus Lane
St. Louis, MO 54095
(219) 555-4039

Robert T. Marcus **TEL: (219) 555-2520**
President & Chief Executive Officer **FAX: (219) 555-7543**

April 11, 1995

Mr. Randall McKay
Lexington Healthcare
5524 W. Randolph
Kansas City, MO 54422

Dear Mr. McKay:

I was delighted to learn from Andrea Madison that you have brought your banking business to Constancy National Bank. On behalf of everyone here, it is my pleasure to extend a warm welcome to you and your company.

As we begin this new banking relationship, I have confidence that you will be pleased with the level of service we provide. We are deeply interested in learning your goals and your visions for reaching them. You have my personal commitment that we will continually strive to ensure that your requirements are always met.

Personalized attention is the foundation of our service, and it begins by taking the time to understand what companies are looking for in their bank. I hope you will not hesitate to call me and share your thoughts anytime I might be helpful to you. By knowing what is important to you, it is my expectation that we will be in a position to serve you efficiently and help your company to grow and prosper.

We appreciate this opportunity to serve you, and we look forward to establishing a strong and mutually rewarding banking relationship in the years to come.

Sincerely,

Robert T. Marcus

Robert T. Marcus

RTM/md

FIGURE 5.9 Sample of AMS Format

IJK Communication Services
3720 Fourth Avenue South • Casper, WY 82601
307-555-4542 • www.ijkservices.com

November 9, 1997

Charles Cooper, President
Environmental Consulting Services
123 North Main
Casper, WY 82601

Subject: Environmental Impact Study (EIS) for the Sourdough Creek Dam Project

Chuck, it's my pleasure to commit IJK Communication Services as a subcontractor in support of your bid to write the Environmental Impact Study (EIS) for the Sourdough Creek Dam Project.

Based on our review of the RFP and our discussions in your offices last week, IJK Communication Services is prepared to commit a total of 480 staff hours to the project at a cost of $18,000. A detailed timeline for our services, identifying the specific personnel to be assigned, their responsibilities on the project, and their rates, is enclosed. Also enclosed are our standard fee schedule, our qualifications and services brochure, and resumes of key personnel who will assist on the project.

We understand that the project, if awarded, will run on a tight ten-week schedule and that time is of the essence. If your bid is successful, we will be prepared to begin planning and designing the tabulation and interpretation of data immediately after May 1 and to complete the report by July 15.

We will be happy to discuss further details of our proposed participation in the project, either with your staff or with the proposal reviewers. Please call us any time.

Felicia Gordon

Felicia Gordon
President, IJK Communication Services

FG/bg

Encl: [1] project staff and timeline
[2] standard fee schedule
[3] qualifications & services brochure
[4] resumes for Gordon, Way, and Bumb

between the top and bottom of the page. If the letter is long enough to fill the page, then the space between the return address or letterhead and the inside address is just a double space.
- Additional blocks at the end of the letter (identifying initials, enclosure notation, and copy notation) are typically separated by double spaces.

The key differences between the full-block style and the AMS style are these:

- The AMS style omits the salutation, using a subject line instead. This convention calls for you to address the reader by name in the first sentence of the body of the letter.
- The AMS style also omits the complimentary close. To follow this convention, press the Return key four times after the last paragraph of the body before keying in your name. Doing so will leave room for your signature.

Expression

We've mentioned before that the predominant "face," or expression, in written professional discourse is neutral, objective, and impersonal. But this never has been the *only* face of business correspondence. For centuries, thoughtful professionals have made rhetorically smart decisions about the human face that they want to present in their letters as well as the ethical, emotional dimensions of character that it expresses.

Precisely because the professional face—neutral and self-effacing—is such a strong convention in business letters and in professional discourse, in general, it's important for you to be comfortable and competent writing in this way. This face may, in fact, be the default in many letter-writing situations you encounter. But deciding on the professional face should be an informed choice that's based on your relationship and action goals, your insight into your readers, the kinds of arguments you need to make in this situation, and your reading of the conventions for it.

The key issue relative to expression is what image your readers should have of you in order for your letter to have the best chance of achieving both your relationship goals and action goals. Does your analysis suggest that some more assertive expression of your character and your general state of mind would be useful? For example, would a clear, candid expression of anger and frustration—or of compassion and concern or still some other kind of emotion—serve your rhetorical purposes? The answer might well be yes. Would it be rhetorically effective to narrate your own personal experience and how it warrants the claims you make in your arguments? Might it be more effective than an impersonal, detached, objective argument? The answer may well be yes or no. Reading your situation and its context and history through the lens of GRACE will help you make smart strategic decisions when you write your letters, and it will help you test and revise your letters more effectively.

Here's just one final caution about expression in your letters: Remember that nothing in the action/relationship matrix suggests that venting your anger or frustration on your reader is an appropriate letter-writing goal. Often, in letter-writing situations, as in memo-writing situations, you are writing in anger. Expressing your anger or frustration may be entirely appropriate—both ethically and rhetorically—or it may not be, depending on the situation, the people, and the context. It is not, in itself, a good goal, and you need to monitor yourself carefully in situations where you are writing out of significant emotional stress. So, if you find you've drafted a letter that expresses vivid, strong emotions and perhaps makes vivid, harsh assertions or accusations, evaluate it through the lens of GRACE with great care. It may be that this initial draft should go into the "round file" or the shredder after it has achieved its therapeutic purpose of letting you vent your anxiety or anger. We'll look at emotionally charged, conflicted situations in some depth in Chapter 6.

WRITING CHECKLIST

The following guidelines will help you write letters that build and manage relationships across organizational boundaries. These guidelines point out the importance of attending to both relationship and action dimensions in any letter-writing situation. (For additional guidelines for handling difficult or conflicted situations, see Chapter 6.) For any of these guidelines, remember the superordinate guideline: Disregard *any* of this advice if it would cause you to do something that's inappropriate or silly for your situation.

☑ Routine Letters

- Map out the relationship and action dimensions of your letter-writing situation to visualize quickly the context you're addressing.
- List your relationship goals and action goals.
- Consider how these goals interact with each other.
- Ask what readers need in order to accomplish both relationship and action goals.
- Ask who your readers are—that is, who should be addressed in your letter, who should receive copies, and who else might read the letter.
- Anticipate readers' questions to achieve your action goals.
- Determine what questions readers will ask when they read your letter.
- Since letters are short documents and thus can't have long arguments, your arguments need to be efficient.
- In general, use the *direct* pattern in business letters: Begin with the claim, and then present supporting evidence and sometimes underlying values and assumptions.
- Consider whether you'll need to use the *indirect* pattern, which mutes the claim by first laying out the context and evidence justifying the claim.
- Using the indirect pattern, you can help readers shift to a perspective sympathetic with your own by using a well-written narrative.
- Sometimes when using the indirect strategy, you might leave out the claim altogether, leaving the reader to infer both the claim and the rationale.

- Make your business letters brief, straightforward, and positive.
- For efficiency, consider using form letters, but modify them effectively by thoughtfully analyzing the special features of your situation—your goals, your readers, and your arguments.
- Follow any standard templates and style guides for letters so they represent your company or agency with a consistent style and appearance.
- If you have no established formal conventions, use full-block, modified-block, or AMS style.
- In general, use the neutral, objective, impersonal voice that's such a strong convention in business writing.
- But deliberately base your expression on your relationship and action goals, your insight into your readers, your arguments, and the conventions of the situation.
- Monitor your expression carefully when you're writing under strong emotions since writing to express anger or frustration is not, in itself, a good goal.

ACTIVITIES AND PROJECTS

1. See Figure 5.10, which is another draft of the routine letter we examined earlier in Figure 5.3. Compare and evaluate the two drafts. They're really identical in terms of the data, and most of the words are nearly the same. What do you sense is different in the two letters? What different effects on the reader seem likely?

FIGURE 5.10 Another Version of a Routine Letter

Dear Terry:

Your emergency order for 500 NoSun protective sleeves arrived via FAX about an hour ago.

We assigned a special crew to expedite the quality assurance review and the packaging, and DHL courier service just picked up the order. You'll have the sleeves by 8 o'clock tomorrow morning.

It's a privilege to be able to help our friends!

Sincerely,

Pat Kellogg

Pat Kellogg

How significant do you think these differences might be? Which draft would you probably send? How would you send it?

2. Read the letter in Figure 5.11 and think about these questions:
   - What's the context of the letter? Can you figure it out from the letter itself? Will Mr. Lee recognize the context?
   - Do a quick GRACE analysis on the letter, focusing especially on goals and arguments. What are the action goals? What are the relationship goals? What are the related arguments?

3. Use the GRACE benchmarks to evaluate the effectiveness of the two form letters from Constancy National Bank in Figures 5.7 and 5.8. The form letter in Figure 5.7 was written by the marketing department for the signature of all bank vice presidents and was intended as a formal announcement of a merger. The form letter in Figure 5.8 was also written by the marketing department—in this

FIGURE 5.11 Letter for Analysis

Dear Mr. Lee:

Thanks for the opportunity to meet with you and Ms. Young today. It was a pleasure learning more about the product line of Pac-West Instrumentation and seeing your Los Angeles production facility.

As promised, I am enclosing the specification sheet for the NoSun, our U-V resistant sleeve that we believe would be compatible with your L22-WS transducer.

If you believe a compatibility test is called for, we can ship a set of four NoSuns via DHL courier overnight without charge. Or, if you prefer to send the transducers to us, we can do the tests at our field site in the Red Desert. If it's compatible with your transducer, we're confident the NoSun sleeve will solve the corrosion problems you have been experiencing, and we know you'll be impressed with its weather resistance.

I'll be back in Los Angeles next Wednesday, and I'll touch base again then. In the meantime, please call me or Pat Kellogg if you have any questions or if you want to proceed with a field test.

Sincerely,

Chris Novak

Chris Novak

instance, for the signature of the bank president and CEO. Employees in commercial lending could ask that the letter be sent to their new commercial clients. As you use GRACE to consider the strengths and weaknesses of these two letters, be sure to consider where you would place each letter on the action/relationship matrix: low relationship, high action; high relationship, high action; low relationship, low action; or high relationship, low action. Explain your decision.

4. The letter from Friendship Ventures in Figure 5.12 is a thank-you for a small donation the readers made. Analyze the letter and determine where you would place it on the action/relationship matrix: low relationship, high action; high relationship, high action; low relationship, low action; or high relationship, low action. Also explain why you believe this placement is accurate. Then, consider the specific goals that are apparent in this letter and the ways in which they are apparent. In addition, consider what the writer's claims are and how he is supporting them. Finally, how would you describe the writer's expression? Why?

5. The letter from Allianz in Figure 5.13 is intended to build goodwill in the face of tragic flooding in the reader's area of the country. Perform a GRACEful analysis of the letter; then decide where you would place it on the action/relationship matrix and why.

6. The letter from Susan Jacobson in Figure 5.14 is a sales letter from a veterinarian to a well-established clientele. Consider how this readership affects the ways in which the writer has framed her argument—her claim, data, and warrants—and the expression she has used. Be specific in your analysis of argument, readers, and expression.

7. Begin collecting a document file of letters that you receive at work, in campus or community organizations, and at home. Collect letters of all sorts: well-written and poorly written letters, low- and high-relationship letters, low- and high-action letters, form letters, and letters written to you personally and individually. This document file will be used for individual and small-group activities later in the class term.

8. Analyze the letter in Figure 5.15 from Thomas Barker to J. D. Pole Construction Company and TLT Services. What specifically are the actions Barker is seeking? Consider the action/relationship ratio in this letter. Does the relationship dimension seem unusually high? Why do you suppose this might be? What fees will Pole Construction and TLT Services receive for their work?

9. Review the letters in your document file (see Activity 7). Using the GRACE benchmarks, select two letters: one that is highly effective and one that is highly ineffective. Share the letters in a small group, and be prepared to explain why you believe each is effective or ineffective.

10. Review the letters in your document file (see Activity 7). Select one that you feel needs substantive revision and revise it using the GRACE benchmarks to ensure that you've worked through your revision fully and systematically.

FIGURE 5.12 Letter Thanking a Donor

Friendship Ventures
Operating Camp Friendship and Eden Wood Center

10509 10th St. NW • Annandale, Minnesota 55302
(612) 555-8376 • Fax (612) 555-3238

August 29, 1996

John & Judith Clayborn
1228 18th Ave. N.
St. Cloud, MN 56303

Dear John & Judith:
Thank your very much for your pledge of $30 to help a child or adult attend Camp Friendship or participate in one of the other services offered by Friendship Ventures.

1996 has been an exciting year! Your investments have allowed for the continuous expansion of programs and services that we offer. Examples of this expansion would include our Ventures Travel Program which will accommodate 368 persons on 64 trips throughout the United States and Canada. This program has increased tremendously in its popularity with the clients that we serve. Another magnificent example of your investment at work is our Respite Program which allows guardians to have their son or daughter with a disability stay with us for the weekend. This enables those feeling "stressed" to have a place for their child to stay that is nurturing and safe. This service will be utilized by 772 clients in 1996. Lastly, we have developed an Environmental Education Program which provides a truly inclusive experience for all children with or without disabilities. A portion of this curriculum, "Diversity in Abilities," allows students without disabilities to experience situations which simulate living with a disability.

Your support has been building better lives for children and adults and their families. Thank you for caring enough to help us promote the companionship, independence and self-esteem sought by our many clients!

Yours in friendship,

Michael F. Maile

Michael F. Maile
Director of Development

Serving children and adults with developmental disabilities since 1964

FIGURE 5.13 Goodwill Letter

Allianz Life Insurance Company
of North America

May 30, 1997

John A McLean
863 Summit Avenue
Saint Cloud MN 56303-2703

RE: Policy Number - 004629837
Insured - John A McLean

Dear Mr. McLean:

We are aware that your area recently experienced a natural disaster and sincerely hope that you personally did not suffer any losses.

If the flood affected you financially, we want you to know that Allianz Life is willing to make special payment arrangements for your insurance premiums. Whether you may need to change to a lower mode of payment or simply require an extension of time, just call our toll-free number. One of our Customer Service Representatives will be happy to assist you.

We do appreciate your business. Should you have any questions regarding your insurance coverage, please let us know.

Sincerely,

Robert S. James

Robert S. James
President
Individual Marketing

Home Office: Minneapolis, Minnesota
Administrative Office: P.O. Box 560 / Dallas, Texas 75221 / Telephone (214) 555-7000 / Call Toll Free 800-555-9030

FIGURE 5.14 Sales Letter

Peterson Veterinary Clinic

Telephone (320) 555-5050

1410 U.S. Highway 21 SW
Cokato, MN 55321

February 23, 1996

Dear Animal Owner:

Peterson Veterinary Clinic cares about your animal's health as much as you do. Since 1986, we have been providing quality health care for your animals. As new technology in the veterinary field develops, we want to use those advances to keep your animals healthy. We are proud to introduce a system which does that: The Vet Test.

The Vet Test is a remarkable system that enables us to check your animal's health from the inside. By measuring the levels of enzymes and minerals in the bloodstream, The Vet Test can accurately diagnose infections and diseases that affect the internal organs, such as kidney infections and diabetes. This capability assures us and you that your animal is healthy internally.

Also, The Vet Test is quick; we can get test results to you within an hour of administering the test. We will no longer have to wait for test results from a laboratory, which can take up to two weeks. Instead, we can make a diagnosis and begin treatment immediately, making your animal healthy again in a shorter amount of time.

The Vet Test enables Peterson Veterinary Clinic to maintain our level of quality animal health care. We care about your animal's health, and The Vet Test will let us continue to provide the personal service our customers have come to expect from Peterson Veterinary Clinic.

Sincerely,

Susan Jacobson

Susan Jacobson
Office Assistant

FIGURE 5.15 Letter for Analysis

Professional Consultants

December 15, 1997

J. D. Pole Construction Company
PO Box 207
Sheridan, WY 82801
ATTN: Mr. Bill MacArthur, General Manager

TLT Services
PO Box 67
Buffalo, WY 82834
ATTN: Mike Klinger, Partner

RE: Multi-Purpose Wellness Complex, Phase I

Dear Bill and Mike:

The Sheridan Stadium Foundation Board, during their meeting on December 11, 1996, requested that CER summarize the status of the sprinkler system at the High School. Our perspective is that the sprinkler system served by the turbine pump has been in a start up phase since late 1995. Each zone was operated for a few minutes at that time, and $3,000 was retained anticipating a spring 1996 inspection. The retainage was paid without the inspection, and the system was subsequently damaged by seeding activities on the discus area and concrete work east of the track. There have also been leak repairs on the pipes and modifications to a flushing hydrant at the northeast corner of the soccer field. We still have no product literature on the sprinkler heads installed in the discus area. Last fall Mike Kinzer agreed to perform some miscellaneous repairs to the system that have not yet occurred.

As you know, School District personnel apparently tampered with the sprinkler heads including the removal of some screens. Now that they have assumed responsibility for operation and maintenance of the system, periodic inspection of the screen in the diversion manhole should prevent any sand from entering the pump in the future.

The Stadium Board and the School District have successfully relied on the integrity of J. D. Pole Construction Company and TLT Services in the past, and once again are requesting that the miscellaneous sprinkler system work discussed last fall be completed

Architecture - Engineering
Materials Testing - Surveying

2237 North Main Street Sheridan, Wyoming 82801 (307)555-1711 Fax: (307)555-5014 cer@wave.net Offices in Gillette and Douglas Wyoming

(continued)

FIGURE 5.15 Continued

by April 1, 1997, to avoid potential malfunction during the irrigation season. We would also request that your time and materials expended on this system in 1997 be documented for proper donor recognition.

Terry Burgess reported that coaches from other Wyoming communities have stated that the football field has the finest playing surface in the state. My bet is that soccer coaches will say the same this spring. Two of the major reasons that Sheridan County School District No. 2 has the finest athletic facility in Wyoming are J. D. Pole Construction Company and TLT Services. It was a team effort of which we should all be proud.

Sincerely,

Tom Barker

Thomas Barker

Architecture - Engineering
Materials Testing - Surveying

2237 North Main Street Sheridan, Wyoming 82801 (307)555-1711 Fax: (307)555-5014 cer@wave.net Offices in Gillette and Douglas Wyoming

11. Write a high-relationship, low-action letter that you can actually use for work or as a representative of a campus or community organization. Use the GRACE benchmarks to help you plan, write, and revise your document. Ask your peers for feedback once you have a fairly polished draft.
12. Pick a situation at work or in a campus or community organization that calls for a high-relationship, high-action letter. Analyze the situation using GRACE. Then write a letter in response to this situation, convincing a particular reader or readers to take a specific course of action.
13. Write a routine letter for work or for a community or campus organization. In spite of the fact that this letter is routine, use the GRACE benchmarks to ensure that the letter achieves your goals and is well adapted to reader needs.

Chapter 6

Writing with GRACE in Difficult Situations: Conflict, Disagreement, and Emotion

- Three Generic Conflict Situations and Their Goals
  - Complaints
  - Bad News
  - Negotiations
- Four Principles for Successfully Negotiating Conflicts and Handling Difficult People
- Engaging the Conflict with GRACE
  - Goals
  - Readers
  - Arguments
  - Conventions
  - Expression

In business we try to hide emotions, especially in male-dominated operations. We downplay the care and feeding of relationships; we lament the time consumed in attending to feelings. Not even the most close-to-the-vest honcho, however, can deny the steamroller of feeling that overtakes us in times of crisis. We'd do well to remember that emotions are at work all the time—and always *cry out for explicit recognition.*

—Tom Peters

Writing in professional environments would be a lot easier—and a lot less interesting—if it weren't complicated by the presence of people and all their conflicting interests, interpretations, and emotions. In this chapter, we'll begin by talking about three typical conflict situations, their complications, and some strategies for finding your way toward successful resolutions, assuming that letter writing is generally going to be part of those resolutions. Then, we'll look at some principles for successfully negotiating conflicts and handling difficult people in general. And finally, we'll study some proven strategies for managing conflict in ethical, professionally responsible ways allowing the possibility of constructive problem solving aimed at achieving mutually satisfactory outcomes.

Three Generic Conflict Situations and Their Goals

Complaints

As you read through these pages discussing the letter of complaint, think about yourself in this situation: You have driven to a university campus in the next state to visit a good friend or a relative—a brother or sister, a child, or even a spouse. You've brought along some large, bulky items for this person—a small dormitory refrigerator, some golf clubs, and a large fan, among other things—and on Saturday morning, you pull up in the dorm parking lot to unload them and take them into the dorm. You think about parking next to the door, but the curb there is painted yellow. You look around, reading all the signs you see, and decide you should just park in the dorm parking lot, where there are plenty of open spots. You find a spot, not as convenient as the curbside parking, and you haul your freight into the dorm. About 15 minutes later, you've gotten everything set up in the dorm, and you all decide to go out for a ride to enjoy the seasonal sights around the campus and the community. When you return to your vehicle, you find a parking ticket: $20 fine for parking in the dorm parking lot without a permit. This seems unfair. What do you do? You have some time to think about it because the ticket says the fine is payable in two weeks.

As you read through the rest of this section on complaint letters, think about how the discussion might apply to your problem with this ticket.

Maybe the most important thing we can say about letters of complaint is that they almost never are *just* letters of complaint. A simple, unadulterated complaint is pure expression—something like "Ouch! That hurt!" Think about the situation we've just imagined, your unfair parking ticket. If you decide to write a letter in which all you do is grumble at someone, you'll probably feel better just for having vented your displeasure. But if you receive an apology and a voiding of the ticket, you'll probably feel quite a bit better. This is actually what happened, and the complaint letter that triggered the apology and voided ticket appears in Figure 6.1. The letter of apology appears in Figure 6.2, and a short newsletter article follows the writers' suggestion that the parking policy be explained (Figure 6.3).

FIGURE 6.1 Letter of Complaint

1716 Tenth Avenue South
St. Cloud, MN 56301
April 10, 1997

Donna Eddleman
Director, First-Year Experience
Michigan Technological University
Houghton, MI 49931

Dear Ms. Eddleman:

Last weekend we made the 720-mile round trip from St. Cloud, MN to Houghton to visit our son Ben, a freshman at MTU. This is our fourth trip—about a year ago when Ben was selecting colleges, in September to deliver him, in October for Homecoming weekend, and now again in April.

We had a delightful weekend. It was especially exciting to talk with Ben about his classes, his instructors, his course assignments, and the ideas that are impacting and challenging him. We visited the Humanities computer lab and got a taste of Ben's work-study job responsibilities. We examined the mineral display outside the Seaman mineral collection. At the bookstore our purchases included an MTU decal for our car. Ben did some research for his econ paper at the library. We saw the auditorium where Clifford Stoll recently spoke to MTU students. Ben hadn't been in a car since he arrived back from spring break, so we enjoyed driving around the Houghton-Hancock area. We were awed by the power of Lake Superior when we stood on the eroding banks of the state park that's out past Hancock.

(continued)

FIGURE 6.1 Continued

Donna Eddleman, page 2

We also brought a load of things for Ben—a small refrigerator, groceries, a set of golf clubs, and other miscellaneous items. His room is on the third floor on the south of Wadsworth Hall, not too far from the door. We decided not to park on the yellow curb in front of the door (there's no "loading zone" sign) and instead found a spot in the lot close by, where there were many open spaces. The three of us made a few trips into the dorm to carry the heavy, bulky items and then visited in his room, rearranging things to accommodate the refrigerator, looking over his CAD projects, and going over his course selection and schedule plans for next fall.

When we came out, we found the enclosed parking ticket under our windshield wiper. We looked around to see where we should have parked, but spaces along the south of the building are reserved and curbs are painted yellow, a universal sign for no parking. We realize that campus parking spots on any campus are limited, and when we read all the signs in the parking lot, we did learn that the lot was restricted. But we still could not find a visitor parking slot anywhere on the south side of the dorm. So what are parents supposed to do when they bring things that need to be taken into the dorm or when they want to visit their son/daughter in the dorms? Parking by the union is not very realistic. Maybe there's a place on campus where we could have picked up a temporary permit on a Saturday morning. Because Ben doesn't have a car on campus, he wasn't aware of parking restrictions or how quickly parking tickets are given.

Perhaps *The Millennium Bunch* newsletter to parents could include a visitor parking permit that we could write the date on. Or perhaps the newsletter should include a warning that there's no convenient place to park by the dorms and that parking tickets cost $20. Maybe the dorm desks could have temporary parking permits for visiting parents. If these are already available, a sign by the door or in the parking lot could alert visitors to that fact.

We had a good trip, with just one exception. The parking ticket still seems unfair.

Sincerely,

Chris Inkster

Bob Inkster

Chris and Bob Inkster
1716 10th Avenue South
St. Cloud, MN 56301

FIGURE 6.2 Letter of Apology

Michigan Technological University
1701 Townsend Drive
Houghton, Michigan 49931-1196

Residential Services
Office of the Director
(906) 555-2682
Fax: (906) 555-3560

April 25, 1997

Mr. & Mrs Bob Inkster
1716 10th Avenue South
St. Cloud, MN 56301

Dear Chris & Bob,

I wish all our student customers had responsible and cordial parents like you! Yes, we provide "Guest Passes" for family and friends at our reception desks, but you are correct in that we do not have visible signs displaying this information. Our Residential Services department will definitely improve on the communication to our residents and guests.

On behalf of Michigan Tech Residential Services, we hope that your decision to return to our "Copper Country" in the future isn't tainted by this incident. A $20.00 check for refund payment of the citation ticket should reach you shortly in the mail.

Sincerely & please return to MTU,

Andre A. Bonen

Andre A. Bonen
Manager of Facilities
Residential Services

AB/pm

cc: John Rovano
John Ahola
Mary Yeo

Michigan Technological University is an equal opportunity institution/equal opportunity employer.
Printed on Recycled Paper

FIGURE 6.3 Newsletter Article

Parking at MTU
Donna M. Eddleman

Recently I received a letter from a parent who had visited the Michigan Tech campus. She spoke of the delightful weekend her family had with their son . . . all except for the parking ticket they found on their car after parking in the lot closest to the residence hall. They had parked in that particular lot because of the need to unpack some heavy and bulky items they had purchased for their son's room.

Parking on the Michigan Tech campus, as is the case on many campuses, is a challenge. Prime parking space is often replaced by buildings and more likely than not, the few parking lots that do exist and are closest to the buildings are either pay lots, or have restricted use. Even I have fallen prey to the parking demons on occasion.

At the urging of the parent mentioned above, I would like to make you aware of the following:

- Visitor parking passes are available in the Admissions Office, located in the Administration Building, Monday through Friday between the hours of 8:00 am and 5:00 pm.
- These same passes are available 24 hours a day, seven days a week in the Public Safety Office located in Wadsworth Hall.
- Visitor parking passes are also available at residence hall reception desks.

It appears that we have been remiss in making this information available to parents, and I apologize for that oversight (we are always learning!). If you have questions about a ticket which is/has been issued, please contact the Public Safety Office at 906/555-2216.

So, if you're thinking you need to write a letter (or a memo) in a situation where someone has done something that seems wrong to you and that has injured or inconvenienced you, stop a moment and ask yourself what your real goal is: blowing off steam or getting the problem fixed? If you have a practical, problem-solving goal in writing your complaint, you're really writing a persuasive letter, hoping to induce your readers to take an action that you want taken. Most letters of complaint, then, are actually persuasive letters. And because they often generate a counter-proposal that initiates a process of negotiation, many letters of complaint are also a subspecies of letters of negotiation, which we'll talk about in more general terms later in this chapter after we talk about bad news letters. GRACE helps us identify the following general tasks in developing an effective letter of complaint.

TASK 1: **Determine the central core of your letter.**

Your first task is to decide, *thoughtfully,* what your problem really is and what needs to happen for you to be satisfied. Write down this information, and you have the core of your letter.

Exactly what is the problem, anyway? This question probably seems utterly obvious and even trivial. But it's crucial, and your answers, if you really think about this question, may surprise you. You need to think carefully about what's really bothering you. Too often, people fail to complain about what's really bothering them. We're all guilty of doing this. And then we may find ourselves even more frustrated than before because our audience, our readers, may, in fact, help us solve a problem that's not really the heart of our concern.

TASK 2: **Narrate and amplify what happened and why it's problematic.**

Now you need to amplify—in as simple and specific detail as you can—exactly what happened, what was the result, and why that result is problematic for you. In recent decades, a strong convention has emerged for framing and arranging arguments in complaints, both when they are made orally and when they are written in a letter or a memo. We see this convention, traveling under different names, widely dispersed through the literature of management, organizational communication, education, and even family relations. While this convention appears formulaic, it is grounded in sophisticated insights about how we communicate emotionally that come from modern psychology and psychotherapy. Later in this chapter, we'll take a deeper look at Rogerian rhetoric, in particular, a set of communication strategies coming from the work of psychologist Carl Rogers. For the moment, though, we're just talking about a conventional format for framing your complaint. The template shown in Figure 6.4 is adapted from Blanchard and Johnson's (1982) *The One-Minute Manager.* The same format is used for both what they call the "one-minute praising" and the "one-minute reprimand."

FIGURE 6.4 Template for Framing a Complaint

When you . . . [Narrate here the specific behavior in literal, concrete, nonjudgmental detail] . . . , then . . . [Narrate here the specific results in literal, concrete detail] . . . , and this means [Explain here why the results are problematic if the narration of the results doesn't already make the problem obvious].

Source: Based on Blanchard & Johnson, 1982.

TASK 3: **Explain a satisfactory resolution.**

Next, you need to explain—again, in specific detail—exactly what you think would be a satisfactory resolution of this problematic situation. Ask yourself these questions:

- Who needs to do what? To work toward an answer to this question, try bringing back the solar system metaphor. Scan the area around the problem. Who shows up on your radar? Can you clearly identify who's causing the problem? Can you tell whether they're acting on their own authority or on orders from somebody else?
- Who's in a position to fix the problem? Do they have an interest in fixing the problem? In *not* fixing the problem?
- Who else is affected by the problem? Are there potential allies here? Would the public at large, or public interest groups or professional credentialing associations or governmental agencies, be interested in the problem?

You may know exactly who these people are. It may be obvious who your reader is and who else should get copies of your complaint letter. Or you may need to ponder these questions and do a little research. The person who's the cause of the problem may or may not be who you want to write. That person's boss, or someone even further up the organizational chart, may be your best reader. In fact, the president or chief executive officer of the organization may be a good target reader. But here's an important caveat: Think twice about going over someone's head and breaking the chain of command. People will be understandably resentful if you get them in trouble with the boss over something that you haven't even told them was a problem and that they may have been happy to change.

TASK 4: **Test your argument.**

Next, you'll need to test the elements of your argument:

- Have you made a plausible claim that embodies your needs and your goal?
- Have you cited the necessary data to support that claim?
- Have you taken into account the legal and ethical principles and assumptions that warrant your making this claim?

If you've laid out a description of the problem, as described earlier, you've begun to build your argument. The basic claim in the complaint letter is that there's a disjunction between *what is* and *what ought to be.* The effective complaint letter makes that claim succinctly and provides specific, meaningful data to document the claim and explain how this situation is problematic. Typically, but not always, the letter also makes specific, claims about how the problem can be corrected. And if you believe important legal or ethical principles are at stake, you may or may not want to state them explicitly. You may also find it useful to address the important relationship dimension of the situation—affirming your confidence in your reader's knowledge, ability, and good intentions, in general, and indicating your expectation that the reader will understand the problem and its consequences, in particular. And you may want to express explicitly your own goodwill toward the reader and the reader's organization.

So, as you look for places to find arguments, keep these issues in mind:

- The gap between what is and what ought to be
- Specific injury, loss, or inconvenience the gap causes
- How the gap can be closed
- Legal, ethical principles at stake
- Your reader's goodwill and ability to solve the problem
- Your reader's stake in solving the problem
- Your own expertise and goodwill in complaining
- Your own stake in solving the problem—your "Ouch!"

Emotion and Strategy

One of the satisfying things about writing a letter or memo of complaint can be the emotional catharsis it gives you. You blow off steam and feel better. But if you find that blowing off steam is your *primary* goal, you need to think carefully about new problems that may be generated by your venting. One safety valve that careful professionals sometimes use is to write an initial draft—in which they vent all their frustration, anger, contempt, and suspicion, which is usually directed at their reader—and then set it aside and go on to write their real letter. We call this the written version of primal scream therapy. In effect, you step outside, where nobody can hear you, and you yell, using the specific details of your aggravating situation, "I'm mad as hell, and I'm not going to take it anymore!" Then you step back and say, "OK, I feel better now. I'm ready to think about this strategically and rhetorically."

At the same time, it's important to remember that the expression of your emotion can be a powerful part of your argument. Communicating that emotion appropriately is often the crucial factor in helping your reader understand the seriousness of the problem and its implications, and it can be a powerful motivator, providing energy on all sides to search for a solution. Using strategies like the "When you . . . " convention for framing a complaint (see Figure 6.4) can help you harness the energy of the emotional dimension of a problematic situation while also reducing the risk that the emotional element will fly out of control.

Bad News

In a bad news situation, there's obviously some kind of history between you and your reader: He or she has applied for a job, made a complaint or request, placed an order to buy your products or services, offered to sell you a product or service, or otherwise engaged you in some kind of negotiation or at least attempted to. In the bad news letter (or, if your reader is within your own organizational orbit, it might be a memo), you have to tell your reader that you can't solve the problem, fulfill the request, or buy the product or service. You have to say *no.*

At the same time, though, there's always the relationship dimension to your communication. Denial and rejection are usually uncomfortable experiences, so you're likely causing your reader some discomfort. And if you're rejecting a bid to buy or sell a product or service, you may be exposing your reader to financial risk or practical inconvenience, as well. A significant goal in the bad news document, then, is finding ways to mitigate the reader's discomfort, risk, or inconvenience. This means that the bad news letter very often is, in fact, a subspecies of the letter of negotiation, just like the complaint letter. Sometimes, your goal in a bad news letter is to shut off negotiations or forestall them entirely. Just as often, though, your goal is to keep the channels of communication open—to try to find alternative ways of helping achieve your reader's goals.

TASK 1: Decide whether to end or continue negotiations.

When you have to say no to a request, offer, or complaint, your first task is to decide whether your goal in responding is to try to end negotiations or keep them open. The following questions can help you decide:

- Is your relationship with this reader/organization one that you want to maintain or nurture? If your answer is a definite, confident no, then this should be an easy letter to write.
- What exactly is the request or offer? It's crucial that you know what's being asked of you. You don't want to turn down an offer or request that you could say yes to. If you're not sure what the request or offer means, then your initial response probably should be a request for more information.
- What exactly are the reader's underlying goals in making the request/offer? Again, your best initial response might be to request more information. You may be able to discover that you can still meet your reader's underlying goals even though you can't meet this *specific* request.
- Exactly what constraints are keeping you from meeting the request/offer? Are there legal or ethical constraints? Practical constraints—time, personnel, products, money? Given these constraints, can your response to the request/offer help meet the reader's underlying goals at least in part?

TASK 2: Make sure your reader knows that you've understood.

Your second task probably is to make sure your reader knows that you understood her or his request/offer. Sometimes, it will be obvious that you did understand. For example, if you've been conducting a hiring campaign for employees with certain qualifications and your reader has replied with letters, resumes, and other information (perhaps even interviews), then it's obvious that he or she is seeking a job with your organization. It would be ludicrous to start a rejection letter to this person by saying something like "I understand you were seeking to work for us." Beginning the letter by saying something like "Thank you for allowing us to review your credentials in our search for . . ." would be reasonable.

On the other hand, imagine a situation in which you receive a FAX requesting a shipment of 100,000 thingamajigs by Monday. You only have 25,000 in stock, and given the demand from your other customers, it would take you two months to stockpile an additional 75,000. An order for 100,000 is ridiculously large. The largest order anyone has made before is 10,000 units.

In Scenario 1, you reply with a FAX, saying, simply,

> "We are unable to fill your order."

Your customer replies with another FAX, saying,

> "Thanks anyhow. We'll try Ace Thingamajig Inc. [your competitor]."

In Scenario 2, you reply, saying,

> "We have received your order for 100,000 thingamijigs to be delivered by Monday. This is an exceptionally large order. Could you please confirm that this is the quantity you are requesting? We can ship 25,000 units to you by Monday and complete the order in additional lots of 5,000 units at a time over the next two months."

Here, your customer replies with a FAX, saying,

> "Oh, did we say 100,000? We meant 10,000 units. Sorry about the typo. Yes, please ship 10,000, not 100,000, units so that we have them Monday. It's good to know that you could handle the larger order with the additional lead time."

If the unit profit on a thingamajig is $10, your Scenario 1 reply cost your company $100,000—and may have lost a customer to your competitor.

But the action dimension isn't the only dimension where it's important for the reader to know you've understood. The relationship dimension is also vitally important. Research ranging from psychotherapeutic studies on individual patients to focus group research to mass-marketing research confirms that people need to know they've been heard and understood, even if the reply they receive isn't the exact solution they were hoping for. A large part of the rest of this chapter is grounded in some of the most important of this research and its practical applications in written and oral communication.

TASK 3: Consider using the balanced organizational convention for bad news letters.

The conventional format for organizing a bad news letter is the *balanced* format, in which your main point—the bad news—is sandwiched in the middle of the letter. Often, this format is explained as a strategy of "sugarcoating": The "bitter pill" of the bad news is wrapped in mollifying language that talks about how much you value your relationship with your reader and that offers, if possible, some alternative way(s) of meeting your reader's needs. You don't emphasize the bad news; rather, you bury it in the middle of the letter and state it only once. As soon as you have announced the bad news, you immediately move to offer alternatives, if possible, and give assurances of your goodwill toward your reader.

We think this sugarcoating explanation of the balanced format does it a disservice, making it appear a cynical, almost deceptive formula in which you essentially try to sneak the bad news into your reader's psyche. A better explanation is that the balanced format is an intuitive use of exactly the kinds of strategies and questions we listed earlier. As Figure 6.5 shows, first, you are making sure your reader knows you understand and empathize with his or her concerns. Then, you discuss the legal, ethical, and practical constraints on your ability to meet those needs. This analysis demonstrates the reasonableness of your conclusion, which you set forth next: the bad news that you can't meet your reader's offer or request. Finally, you try to find alternative ways of meeting your reader's needs.

FIGURE 6.5 The Balanced Format

Buffering Opening Paragraph

- Makes sure readers know you understand and empathize with their concerns

↓

Body Paragraphs

- Clarify the legal, ethical, and/or practical constraints on your ability to meet readers' needs—the analysis and facts that lead to your conclusion
- Bury your conclusion—the bad news—in the middle of the letter and state it only once
- Provide alternatives, when possible
- Assure readers of your goodwill

↓

Buffering Closing Paragraph

- Affirms a friendly, professional relationship
- Looks forward to future collaboration
- Invites alternative proposals or projects—or attempts to end the association humanely

Tom Barker's memo to Joy Sand & Gravel (Figure 6.6) is an interesting example of a bad news document. Barker immediately establishes the context for the memo—first through identifying the project in his subject line and then by acknowledging receipt of a FAX copy of an analysis of limestone. He next takes the affirmative step of agreeing to accept the analysis for purposes of determining the quantity of limestone delivered. But then he lays out the bad news: He rejects the analysis as a measure of actual lime, or calcium carbonate. And he closes the first paragraph by expressing the underlying principle that is the rationale for his rejection. He says a current analysis, not one that's six years old, should be used to determine the actual content of lime. The second paragraph is almost entirely technical data and processing of the data through a formula. The formula constitutes another assumption that Barker uses to justify his concluding sentence of the paragraph, which now takes the affirmative step of specifying the minimum quantity his firm, CER, will accept (though there is still the firm, unequivocal language of "no less than"). His last paragraph moves a further step onto the ground of an affirmative rhetoric of cooperation by restating how payment will be determined—in language that is now devoid of negatives. So, we see here a rhythm that, in fact, follows the typical bad news convention: First, Barker acknowledges the reader's correspondence and offers as much good news as he can. Then, comes the rejection and a systematic rationale for it. And finally, Barker makes an affirmative statement of a satisfactory solution.

TASK 4: Choose your format thoughtfully.

Don't just use the balanced format automatically and thoughtlessly. People who are receiving bad news letters often know your reply is going to be yes or no. And there are many situations where if the answer is no, your negotiations will be over. In these situations, the balanced format may be less appropriate than a direct format, where you lead with the bad news. Writing a prefatory paragraph—in which you recite your appreciation for the reader, analyze your rationale for your decision, and narrate the decision-making process, all before telling your reader the bad news—may operate less as a buffer for the bad news than as an unintentionally cruel teasing. So, ask yourself thoughtfully whether this particular bad news situation is one where your letter should break the balanced convention of starting with a buffering first paragraph. Rejection letters to job applicants are an interesting case in point. Most of them follow the balanced format, buffering the bad news. At the same time, though, the buffering material at the front of the letter is boilerplate text, which goes out in exactly the same words to all the unsuccessful applicants. To the extent that it claims to express a particular empathic relationship with the reader, it is obviously insincere. And at the same time, it stands as a barrier to the reader's learning, directly and concisely, what he or she most wants to know: Am I still in the running for this position?

Even in situations where you may decide to eliminate the opening buffer, a closing buffer following the bad news is generally an appropriate rhetorical move. At the very least, you're offering your reader a kindness when you close with language that affirms a friendly and productive professional relationship, looks forward to future

FIGURE 6.6 Sample Bad News Letter

Professional
Consultants

MEMORANDUM

To Joy Sand & Gravel
27 Main Street
LaBarge, WY 83123

From: CER
Thomas L. Barker *TB*

Date: May 6, 1997

Subject: AML 16F-2 - Lime Application

On April 30, 1997, Tim Townsend FAXed an analysis of lime products loaded at the Holly Sugar Corporation factory near Worland, Wyoming. We are accepting the analysis dated April 5, 1991, for purposes of determining the number of bulk tons delivered to the site. But, we are rejecting this analysis for purposes of payment because it was conducted six years ago and we believe an analysis conducted in 1997 would be appropriate for determining the actual quantity of lime for payment purposes.

The specifications require that the quantity of lime applied to the soil be determined by multiplying its purity, moisture content, and the proportion passing the #100 sieve. The reported average values are 83% calcium carbonate, 15.92% moisture, and 83.79% passing the #100 sieve. The specified computation is (0.8300)(1 – .1592)(0.8379) = 0.5847. 150 tons ÷ 0.5847 = 256.5 tons. Therefore CER will accept no less than 250 tons of bulk lime delivered to the project to accomplish the design objective.

The actual payment quantity will be determined on the basis of an up-to-date analysis with parameters multiplied by the actual number of bulk tons delivered to Project 16F-2.

xc: Tim Townsend
Barry Shelly

Architecture - Engineering
Materials Testing - Surveying

2237 North Main Street Sheridan, Wyoming 82801 (307)555-1711 Fax: (307)555-5014 cer@link.net Offices in Gillette and Douglas Wyoming collaboration, invites alternative proposals or projects, or otherwise either invites an ongoing association or attempts to end one in a humane way. In the latter case, however, where you need to bring the association to a close, be very careful in your buffering material that you do not raise false hopes or carelessly make statements that can be construed as commitments to an ongoing association. In an extreme situation—for example, one where litigation appears likely—even a buffer that follows the bad news may not be advisable.

Negotiations

We've already pointed out that many letters that are characterized as complaint letters or bad news letters are, in fact, negotiation letters. Suppose you have purchased several new computers that are all malfunctioning. You are in an intolerable situation. Productivity is almost at zero. Because of the new computers, customers are getting incorrect billings, shipping is getting erroneous orders, and your whole operation is in disarray. You send a letter, via FAX, to the vendor who sold you the computers, in which you explain the situation and ask him or her to replace the computers immediately. The vendor replies right away with a FAX, explaining that the computers can't be replaced now and offering to begin right away to find other solutions to your problem. You immediately get on the one computer that seems to be working properly and send an e-mail to the vendor, saying that the alternatives suggested won't be effective because of the timing of commitments you've made to your sales representatives. You must have at least some relief by the end of the week.

What we've described here, of course, is a complaint letter followed by a bad news letter followed by another complaint letter. But all, in fact, are negotiations. Very often, when you write a persuasive letter, asking your reader to take some specific action, he or she can't or won't comply in exactly the way you ask. Maybe the situation turns out to be somehow more complex than you thought or represented in your initial letter. Likewise, the situation may include conditions that the bad news reply doesn't take into account. It would be a mistake for either party to conclude that the situation should necessarily be resolved on exactly the terms proposed in his or her letter. Professional relationships and transactions are too complex for this optimistic assumption to hold true all the time. Whether you're renegotiating a union contract, involving hundreds of pages and affecting thousands of people, or simply trying to get a pencil sharpener fixed, there are likely layers of claims and counter-claims, complexities of information that aren't apparent on the surface, and conflicting assumptions, interests, values, priorities, and principles of making judgments that lead to complex layers of argument and counter-argument.

Professional work is a thicket of such complexities and conflicts, and the writing of business is, in large part, the negotiating of these conflicts. Two of the best sets of advice we've seen dealing specifically with negotiations are books written by members of the Program on Negotiation at Harvard Law School: *Getting to Yes: Negotiating Agreement without Giving In,* by Roger Fisher and William Ury (1992), and *Getting Past No: Negotiating with Difficult People,* by William Ury (1991). Fisher and Ury part company with many people who write about strategy in negotiations in proposing what they call "principled negotiation." Whereas many of the conventional tactics in negotiations include a variety of feints and deceptions, Fisher and Ury argue that the most effective negotiators engage primarily in careful, truthful disclosure of their own needs and in thoughtful, even empathic efforts to understand the other party's needs. Rather than staking out a position that demands more than you actually want, need, or expect and then gradually making concessions toward a reasonable position, Fisher and Ury advise starting with a firm position based on a careful, principled analysis of your real needs. In his book on negotiating with difficult people, Ury proposes tactics for "breakthrough negotiation," including ways of controlling your own emotions and ego involvement, finding and communicating an empathic understanding of your opponent, helping your opponent move from a turf-protecting to a problem-solving frame of mind, helping your opponent find satisfactory alternatives to the original oppositional position, and helping your opponent see the risks of not negotiating together in good faith.

A particularly interesting concept in Ury's book (1991) is the *BATNA:* the *best alternative to a negotiated agreement.* Ury concedes that negotiating with difficult people will not always result in a successful, mutually beneficial agreement. Given this fact, he argues that it's important to decide thoughtfully ahead of time what is your BATNA—what is the best thing you can do in case you simply cannot find a way to make the negotiations work. Ury argues that in order to be an effective negotiator with difficult people, you have to have figured out ahead to time what your strategy will be if the negotiations fail, and you have to have decided under what circumstances you will embrace that alternative. Then, he says, you can negotiate both firmly and in good faith, knowing what you cannot concede in the negotiation.

The crucial goal in any negotiation is to keep it moving forward. Both you and your opponent need to understand the mutual benefits of collaborating to understand and solve the problem that affects both of you. Failure to sustain the negotiating process means loss to all parties. Because this process is so vitally important and so difficult, the rest of this chapter is devoted to it.

Four Principles for Successfully Negotiating Conflicts and Handling Difficult People

PRINCIPLE 1: Don't be surprised by disagreement, conflict, and emotion.

Reliable evidence, objective facts and numbers, and systematic, rational problem solving are hallmarks of effective management and effective discourse in business and the professions. But this data collection and analysis and this problem solving are grounded in human interests, guided by personal commitments to ethical principles, and motivated by human passions. All our perceptions are, in this sense, *interested*—that is, framed by our own interests, which often are not exactly congruent with those of our readers or even our colleagues. So, it's important to expect that disagreement, conflict, and emotion will often be important elements when you write.

To some extent, everything we do and write arises out of a history of prior transactions that have some level of emotional energy. Even a routine memo carries some of this contextual emotional energy and speaks to people who have their own emotional, ethical, or economic stake in the communication—generally, one that is somehow different from our own. All writing, then, carries this risk of accidentally "pushing someone's buttons." And when the situation is already emotionally charged, the risks of an accidental miscommunication are even higher.

If you remember that these risks are present all the time, you will be less likely to be thrown completely off stride if a situation does suddenly erupt with a highly emotional conflict. You can remind yourself—and others, too—that this emotional dimension is a natural part of the discourse of business and of life, and you can begin to devise ways to cope with the emotion and conflict and even to use them productively. In fact, if you are heading into a situation where this kind of conflict seems likely, you can even rehearse some strategies, such as Rogerian argument, which we'll discuss in detail later.

PRINCIPLE 2: When disagreement, conflict, and anger occur, resolve to use them productively.

The good thing about disagreement, conflict, and emotional involvement is that they raise the energy level and interest of everyone involved. In this sense, they offer an opportunity for constructive deliberation, both written and spoken, where you and your readers can clarify your goals, your values and ethical assumptions, your mutual interests, and even your perceptions of the facts, leading to greater understanding, commitment, trust, cooperation, effectiveness, success, and satisfaction all around. At the same time, the risk in this kind of situation is that the energy generated can lead in the opposite direction—to greater misunderstanding, distrust, and so on.

In these difficult situations, it's almost always useful to take the time and effort to analyze the situation for disagreement, conflict, and anger. How does each contribute to the difficulty? How does each element—disagreement over facts, conflict over goals and assumptions, and the emotions that give them energy—contribute to the others? What strategies may be available for mitigating the potential difficulty suggested by each element, and what strategies may be available for using each element productively?

PRINCIPLE 3: Decide whether this situation constitutes a fight, a game, or a debate.

In his classic book *Fights, Games, and Debates,* Anatol Rapoport (1960) distinguishes among these types of conflict according to their goals. In the most basic and simplified terms, he says, the goal in a *fight* is to harm your opponent. In a *game,* the goal is to outwit or otherwise outmaneuver your opponent. And in a *debate,* the goal is to persuade your opponent to see things as you do. Of course, all three situations are usually more complex than this. For example, in a chapter titled What If the Opponent Is Both Friend and Foe? Rapoport describes many kinds of situations where your own interests and those of your opponent are joined in complicated ways while they are opposed in others.

And in a later chapter, Ways of Persuasion, which we will use extensively here, Rapoport points out that sometimes your opponent in a debate isn't actually the person you need to persuade. Sometimes, it's another person or group. In these situations, a debate takes on some of the features of a game. Think back to the situation where you're negotiating with the vendor who sold you the computers that are giving you grief. Suppose this negotiation really doesn't seem to be leading toward a reasonable agreement, and you're thinking about what William Ury calls your BATNA: your best alternative to a negotiated agreement. Suppose there's a mechanism for filing a grievance with an arbitrator who has the authority to make rulings in these kinds of disputes. With this alternative in mind, your letters, e-mails, and FAXes will take on the additional goal of convincing this third party that you have acted reasonably and appropriately in this conflict and that your opponent, your vendor, has not. So, you need to think carefully about who *all* your readers are.

PRINCIPLE 4: **Irrespective of this conflict's present status, resolve not to define it as a game or a fight; move the conflict in the direction of a debate or, preferably, a negotiation.**

Here's an interesting paradox: Before people can have an argument, they first have to agree, at least tacitly, that they have a disagreement. They must have a mutual sense that there is a conflict. Perhaps they have conflicting data. Perhaps they're using conflicting principles to interpret and evaluate the data. Perhaps they have conflicting interests that inform their understandings of the data and principles. In any case, they have a shared sense of conflict. And if they are to have an argument, they must both sense that the conflict is significant enough to warrant having an argument. So, if you find yourself in a situation where you're arguing with somebody about a conflict between you, stop and remember that you already share some significant common ground. Likewise, before people can have a fight, both must agree to fight. The same goes for a game or a debate.

By refusing to be either the aggressor or the victim in a conflict though and by insisting on a principled negotiation, you can often (not always) bring your opponent to engage you in principles, fair deliberation, and negotiation.

If you're in a two-way conflict—either between two individuals or two groups of people—there are basically four ways of dealing with it, based on satisfying each of the two parties. We can actually set up a matrix of four generic strategies, as Figure 6.7 illustrates. Obviously, the most desirable quadrant is the *problem-solving* quadrant, where the mutual goal is win/win. The first challenge, though, is getting a mutual commitment to work in that quadrant. And the first barrier may be your own resistance. Your own competitive energy—your emotional investment in your position—may push you toward the *bullying*, or win/lose, quadrant. Or your reluctance to confront an assertive reader/opponent may push you toward a strategy of *avoiding* or *conceding*. And if these impulses are pushing you away from the productive problem-solving mode of the win/win quadrant, they may be pushing your reader toward other

FIGURE 6.7 Four Different Ways of Dealing with Conflict

Bullying: Win/Lose	Problem Solving: Win/Win
In bullying, your concern is for your own satisfaction with the resolution of the conflict, with no regard for achieving your opponents' (your readers') goals. The mindset here is simply to win a fight.	Problem solving requires a shared commitment to satisfying both your own and your readers' goals. It requires trust and mutual respect and an effort to understand each other's goals.
Avoiding: Lose/Lose	**Conceding: Lose/Win**
If avoiding is strategic at all, it is a negative strategy. Some counterproductive, gamelike tactics like sniping may find their way into written text, but no productive writing or other action that engages the issue occurs. Neither you nor the other party achieves your goal.	Conceding is a strategy of capitulating to your opponents' goals, aimed at agreement without negotiation on behalf of your own goals. You clearly lose and your opponent clearly wins, but the resolution has not been tested in a debate and may not be the best solution for *either* party.

quadrants, too. As you begin to analyze your situation with GRACE, you may discover an additional layer of goals. At the same time that you're thinking about the goals you'd like to achieve through this written discourse, you may have to think about goals that will allow you to engage in the discourse in the first place—strategies for getting both yourself and your readers into the problem-solving, win/win quadrant.

Engaging the Conflict with GRACE

Goals

In Chapter 5, we talked at some length about the fact that you always have two dimensions to your goals in writing a letter: the action dimension and the relationship dimension. In situations of conflict, disagreement, and emotion, the stakes are raised in both dimensions. When the situation is conflicted and the emotional stakes are high, process and procedure take on greater importance and urgency. Your substantive arguments and how you make them are always important, but now, in a conflicted situation, you may have to do considerable groundwork before you can even begin to make these arguments. A procedural misstep can throw you from a productive debate into an unproductive fight. Principles 1 through 4 combine to add the following procedural goal to your substantive goals: You must first persuade both yourself and your opponent to engage in a debate in the problem-solving quadrant. If your own goal is to have a fight—to harm your reader—we don't have much advice for you, other than to reconsider carefully before investing your intelligence and energy in such an unproductive way. If you think your reader's goal is to have a fight—to harm you—there are some things you can do—basically, some gaming strategies—to try to persuade your opponent to redefine the situation as either a game or, ultimately, as a debate.

One of the most useful sources of help here is another classic book, *Coping with Difficult People,* by Robert M. Bramson (1988). Many of the modes of difficult behavior Bramson discusses occur in contexts that are usually spoken, so you will likely want to be prepared to use the strategies for engaging behaviors productively in dynamic, spoken exchanges. But the strategies adapt to written situations, as well. In fact, Bramson specifically suggests writing as an alternative to face-to-face confrontation with the difficult person he characterizes as a "Sherman Tank," if you're feeling too intimidated to stage the initial confrontation directly.

Bramson classifies seven types of difficult people: Hostile-Aggressives, Complainers, Silent Unresponsives, Super-Agreeables, Negativists, Know-It-All Experts (colorfully divided into Bulldozers, who really are extremely competent, and Balloons, who are just faking—full of hot air), and Indecisives. These seven categories, with all their variety, are actually all habits of behavior for avoiding the problem-solving quadrant.

Just based on Bramson's names for these people, you can speculate about which cell of the winning/losing matrix each will most likely be in. And thinking about where each will tend to be should help you select useful strategies for moving him or her into the problem-solving, win/win cell. As you look at where we've assumed each is most likely to be (see Figure 6.8), think about whether you agree with us. We think the Hostile-Aggressives and probably the Know-It-All Experts tend toward the bullying quadrant, seeking to avoid substantive deliberation by simply forcing agreement to their position. Complainers and Negativists may be in that quadrant, too, but their passivity would more likely put them in the avoiding quadrant with the Silent Unresponsives and the Indecisives. The Super-Agreeables would be in the conceding quadrant, and so might the Indecisives. At first glance, the Super-Agreeables might seem, well, both super and agreeable. But as Bramson points out, the problem with them is that they don't really engage the substantive concerns that you and they need to address. They "talk the talk" but don't "walk the walk" of agreement. They're not really persuaded to take the course of action you believe should be taken, even though they say they agree.

The strategies for getting these different kinds of difficult people to engage in productive dialogue are widely different. Because the Hostile-Aggressives can be the

FIGURE 6.8 The Winning/Losing Matrix and Difficult People

Bullying: Win/Lose	Problem Solving: Win/Win
■ Hostile-Aggressives (three types): 1. Sherman Tanks 2. Snipers 3. Exploders ■ Know-It-All Experts (two types): 1. Bulldozers 2. Balloons ■ Complainers (sometimes) ■ Negativists (sometimes)	
Avoiding: Lose/Lose	**Conceding: Lose/Win**
■ Silent Unresponsives ■ Indecisives ■ Complainers ■ Negativists	■ Super-Agreeables ■ Indecisives

most painful of the difficult people and because writing may sometimes be a productive approach with them, we'll talk here about coping strategies Bramson identifies for each of the three types: Sherman Tanks, Snipers, and Exploders. There's something very important you should notice about all three of these coping strategies—and, for that matter, about all the other coping strategies we talk about: These are not strategies for conflict avoidance but strategies for conflict management and resolution.

Here are descriptions of Bramson's three types of people and recommendations for dealing with them:

1. **Sherman Tanks** attack and attempt to run over or through you. They interrupt and dismiss you, reject your ideas, and then keep on rolling, as if you're not

there. Bramson's advice for dealing with Sherman Tanks can be summarized as follows:

- You have to stand up for yourself with an aggressive person, not roll over and lie down, or you won't make the genuine, solid contact you need to make with the person. If you're being pushed aside, don't let overpoliteness keep you from asserting your stand. For example, if you are interrupted, try to cut back in, saying something like "You interrupted me." Assert your own position in opposition to the Sherman Tank's without saying that his or her position is wrong. You can use language like "That hasn't been my experience with that product," "I'm really not comfortable with that interpretation," "I can see your reasoning here, but when I consider the fact that . . . ," or other language that stakes out your own position in a nonhostile but assertive way.
- Be assertive, but don't fight. Get the person's attention, but do it carefully. Address him or her by name, as you would normally. In a face-to-face confrontation, if the person is highly emotional—yelling, gesticulating, and the like—give the person time to run down. If you're writing, you can do the same thing by acknowledging his or her anger. (We'll talk more about this in the Arguments section.) If you lose a fight, then you obviously lose. But if you win a fight, you may still lose. Your Sherman Tank may turn into a Sniper or lie in wait to sabotage you in some other way. Be prepared to be friendly afterward. Remember, the strongly assertive person isn't necessarily hostile to you. And even the genuinely hostile Sherman Tank tends to respect the integrity of a nonhostile but assertive opponent with the courage of her or his convictions.

2. **Snipers** attack indirectly from under the cover of social and situational conventions, rather than launch direct, frontal attacks. Often, their remarks aren't even addressed to you but are whispered as asides, delivered as clever and sarcastic jokes, or posed as questions, delivered with a smile and other nonverbal signals that belie the hostile intent. The Sniper is relying on you to observe social conventions of avoiding confrontation and to ignore the dig or laugh off the sarcastic joke. So, your first step has to be to surface the attack with a question such as "Does your comment mean you disapprove of my idea?" The possible responses range from denial to further ridicule. If the response is further ridicule, then you have to continue to smoke out the Sniper with further probing questions. One of Bramson's suggestions is "Sounds like you're ridiculing me. Are you?" It's important that you draw out the Sniper with questions, rather than accusations, because you want to provide some alternatives to raw confrontation. The Sniper may tell you what the problem is. If this complaint is vague, ask him or her to be more specific. And if you surface a specific complaint, seek confirmation or denial from others. If the complaint is legitimate, you can offer to deal with it—at an appropriate time if the present moment isn't appropriate.

3. **Exploders** are Hostile-Aggressives who suddenly become enraged, often without warning. Your main goal with an Exploder is to help him or her reduce the

rage and get over the tantrum. Simply giving this person a brief time and space may be sufficient. This may be easier in a writing situation than in a face-to-face meeting, perhaps involving several people. Bramson suggests getting the person's attention with some neutral words, such as "Yes! Yes!" or "Wait a minute!" or "Stop! Stop!" You certainly do not want to argue or scold. Rather, you want to acknowledge the Exploder's anger and make clear that you take it and the issue seriously. Bramson recommends using language that explicitly makes this acknowledgment and this assurance—something like "I can see you're really upset about this, and I want to talk about it too. Let's . . . [take a 10-minute break and talk about it in my office] . . . [make a firm appointment to talk about it after the meeting]" . . . or the like.

You can see that one of the key ingredients in maneuvering a Hostile-Aggressive person into the problem-solving quadrant is direct, forthright engagement. As we noted earlier, these are not strategies for the faint of heart. Notice that in each, the goal is to clarify, define, and bring the conflict into sharper focus, rather than avoid the conflict. A second key element is treating both yourself and your opponent with respect and seriousness. Note that in discussing all three types, the strategy acknowledges the hostility—and, in fact, makes it an explicit part of the discussion—rather than pretend it doesn't exist or doesn't have any bearing on how the issues are being addressed.

In these difficult situations, you need to think systematically about relationship goals and process goals as well as your substantive action goals. In fact, you may need to have the extra patience to deal extensively with process goals—getting readers to engage you in the conflict productively in the problem-solving quadrant—before you can begin to work on your action goals.

Readers

From the time we introduced GRACE, we've said that understanding your readers and their perspective on the issues you're writing about is crucial to the successful writing of your business. We have urged you to do creative, imaginative visualizing of your readers—imagining the scenario where they will read your letter, memo, or other document and what they will think and feel in starting to read it. Even if you never meet your readers, this process of imagining a human face can help you anticipate what needs, questions, assumptions, and arguments they will bring to your document and how to design your own arguments effectively.

At the same time, it's crucial to remember that you can never know for sure what's going on in your readers' minds. In an article titled "The Writer's Audience Is Always a Fiction," Walter Ong (1975) argues convincingly that whenever we compose a letter, proposal, poem, speech, or any other text, we have in mind some image of our readers or our listeners. Even when we're speaking off the cuff, he says, we are anticipating what our immediate listeners will hear, do, and say in response to us. In other words, we are always inventing or imagining our readers or listeners when we are assembling words to present to them. Like any other imaginative creation, these readers we envision are never quite perfect facsimiles of the real people they represent. Usually, if we're thoughtful, imaginative, and careful, we come up with reasonably good likenesses of the real thing, and our communication is reasonably successful.

Nonetheless, the risk of error—of creating a fiction that's not representative of our real readers—is always present. And as emotions rise, both our own and our readers', it becomes even more difficult to interpret and construe our readers' needs, goals, motives, and arguments. The emotional investment in our own perception of the situation and of our needs, our righteous ethical commitment to the justice of our cause, our competitive instincts in the heat of conflict, and our anxiety about what our readers may be thinking all create a powerful filter through which we process the information coming to us from our opposition. This is the most serious risk facing us in a situation that's tense with conflict and charged with emotion: the risk of creating fictions about our readers that will serve both us and them badly—for instance, demonizing our readers, imagining them as unreasonable, self-serving, ill-willed, stupid, deceptive cheaters who wouldn't understand a reasonable argument and simply deserve to be brushed aside, defeated, or dismissed. This kind of perception is contagious. It tends to make us suspicious and wary, and when we start acting like this, our readers start to wonder what's the matter with *us*—perhaps we're unreasonable, self-

GOFF
"As a special service to keep the phone costs of our angry customers low, I'm going to hang up now."

Source: Reprinted with permission of Ted Goff.

serving, ill-willed, stupid, deceptive cheaters. And the next thing you know, we've all convinced each other that there's no point in trying to communicate.

But what if we and our readers need each other? What if, in reflecting on our goals, we realize these readers are a crucial element in the solution of our problem, and what if we're a crucial element in the solution of the readers' problem? We've just assured mutual frustration—and probably further conflict and distrust.

The problem here results from a natural and fundamentally useful human tendency to categorize. If we didn't classify and categorize, our experience would be meaningless. We would have no way of discriminating one experience from another. We are making essential classifications of our experiences, including the people we know, all the time. Just look back at Bramson (1988) and his taxonomy of difficult people. Classifying a reader—especially one who is an antagonist who has frustrated and intimidated you—can be a crucial step in devising a strategy for engaging that person productively. Doing so involves making some intelligent guesses about how this reader will respond to different arguments and to different ways you might present or express yourself. And you have to make these guesses based on whatever information you have at hand: perhaps the reader's official title or position, his or her career path within the organization and elsewhere, a taxonomy of his or her communication style, leadership style, or learning style (such as we'll talk about in Chapter 7). Perhaps a taxonomy such as Bramson's will help you predict the kind of difficult behavior you're likely to encounter and to rehearse strategies for countering it. But these are only guesses, only rough approximations of the real reader. Any classification you make, no matter how sophisticated and careful, will be a grossly oversimplified reduction of the actual person.

Arguments

We've talked about arguments as claims that you justify through data and through underlying principles for giving meaning and value to the data.* Your readers might resist your claims for several kinds of reasons:

- They may not understand the data.
- They may not understand your claim.
- They may not understand or agree with your underlying principles, and so they may not see the reasonable link between the data and your claim.

*Anyone who is familiar with the work of Stephen Toulmin will immediately recognize our debt to his *The Uses of Argument* (1958) in this chapter—indeed, throughout this book. And as we have already noted, our discussion is also deeply informed by the work of psychotherapist Carl Rogers, especially as it was adapted in Anatol Rapoport's *Fights, Games, and Debates* (1960) and in Young, Becker, and Pike's *Rhetoric: Discovery and Change* (1970). We are also indebted to Richard Fulkerson's *Teaching the Argument in Writing* (1996) as well as to several textbook applications of Toulmin, especially those by Ross Winterowd (1989) and by Timothy Crusius and Carolyn Channell (1997).

- They may understand your argument completely and still reject your claim because they hold an allegiance to other, conflicting principles.
- They may understand your argument completely and may even agree with it, in principle, but they may still reject it because it threatens some personal interest they hold.

We need to say up front that allegiances to conflicting principles and interests are huge, often insurmountable barriers to successful arguments—especially if we define successful arguments as those that we win. We need to think of argument as something more than a sparring match to be won or lost. We need to think of it as a cooperative exercise in exploring the data, the competing claims, and the underlying principles and interests. Ultimately, we need to think of argument as a tool for learning and sharing alternative world views and for negotiating the ramifications of these views.

Anatole Rapoport (1960) describes three strategies that are commonly used to try to bring about a conversion in someone's world view, based on three different views of persuasion. The first is, essentially, *brainwashing*—creating circumstances that make it intolerable for the person not to accept your view. Totalitarian regimes have used this strategy extensively, pummeling their constituents with document after document reiterating their assumptions and their version of the data. Rapoport cites the coercion in Orwell's *1984*, where the main character is finally convinced that 2 + 2 = 5, as an example of this coercive kind of persuasion. Obviously, we don't recommend this strategy.

The second strategy is what Rapoport calls "explaining the image away," or *debunking* the image. An example of this would be debunking a reader's image by explaining to her that she felt that way because she was a woman, because she was a Republican, or because she had a friend who was affected by the issue at hand. It's interesting that Rapoport, writing in 1960, noted that this strategy was widely popular in current political and popular discourse. In the almost four decades since, this kind of argument—which was once routinely condemned as illegitimate *ad hominem* argument because it attacked the person, rather than the issue—has continued to gain in popularity. In some ways, it looks superficially like the strategies of argument we're about to recommend as an adaptation of Rapoport's third strategy; we'll explain how the strategies are different.

The third strategy Rapoport identifies for changing a person's image of the world is that of *reducing the threat* that such a change represents. Drawing on Carl Rogers, Rapoport identifies three perceptions that, when conveyed to your opponent/reader, will reduce this threat:

1. Confirming that he or she has been understood
2. Affirming the area of validity of the opponent's position
3. Inducing the assumption of similarity

The tactics you employ to gain an empathic understanding of your reader's position and to induce a similarly empathic understanding of your own are the foundation of *Rogerian argument.* We will talk about three tactics, in particular.

If argument were a routine process of citing data, interpreting and explaining the data based on a set of principles, and producing unproblematic, logical conclusions, then there certainly would be no need for this chapter. But disagreements persist for generations, even centuries, and people hold directly opposing claims with all the moral and intellectual energy of their beings. Does this mean there's no hope for persuasion? At times, the answer surely seems yes. Is there no hope for reconciliation or cooperation? Here, we think there is always cause for optimism. If you cannot always persuade your readers on all your substantive claims, you can still manage your arguments in a way that enables you to work with these people in productive, ethical relationships and in terms of mutual respect.

Figure 6.9 spells out the arguments for two opposing sets of interests in a contemporary workplace conflict: e-mail privacy. In effect, the chart is a cross-section of one point in the conflict, showing all the levels of two opposing arguments. Perhaps the most striking thing about this chart is that *six* elements of the argument are identified, not just the basic three elements we've been talking about. Let's look at some of the nomenclature for a minute. The first new word we encounter is *warrant,* used to describe the underlying principle or value. The only thing really new here is the word, but you may find it useful to think of the underlying principle, assumption, or value as operating much the same way a search warrant operates: giving a law officer authority to make a particular search. In the same way, a warrant in an argument gives you the authority to make your claim based on the data.

Like search warrants, warrants in arguments can be challenged. A reader might say that the principle you're relying on to make your claim isn't valid—or that it's valid but doesn't apply to this situation. This constitutes the fourth element in the argument, and it illustrates how it's possible for arguments to go on endlessly. The challenge or backing is really a whole new claim, which opens up the possibility of a complete new set of elements, including data and additional underlying principles and assumptions.

DILBERT

Source: DILBERT reprinted by permission of United Feature Syndicate, Inc.

FIGURE 6.9 Charting the Levels of Opposing Arguments—E-Mail Privacy

The Employer's Interest	The Employees' Interest
Claim Employers should have access to employees' e-mail messages at work.	***Claim*** Employers should not have access to employees' e-mail messages at work.
Data The employer owns the computers and network equipment and is paying for the network service as well as the employees' time.	***Data*** All employees have communications at work that are not directly task related.
Principle/Assumption Giving Meaning and Value to the Data and Serving as a Warrant for the Claim Employers are entitled to the intellectual property that is created by their employees while at work and while using their resources.	***Principle/Assumption Giving Meaning and Value to the Data and Serving as a Warrant for the Claim*** The right to privacy is a fundamental human right.
Backing for the Principle/Assumption and/or Challenge to an Opposing Principle/Assumption Employees' rights to privacy must be limited by their responsibilities to the group, or the organization will disintegrate to chaos.	***Backing for the Principle/Assumption and/or Challenge to an Opposing Principle/Assumption*** Employers' rights to the fruits of their employees' work on the job do not justify intruding on private employee communications while they are at work.
Reservation . . . unless we are prepared, as a society, to say that people who invest their capital in business ventures are not entitled to the fruits of their investment.	***Reservation*** . . . unless we are prepared, as a society, to say that people must give up their right to privacy in order to have a paycheck.
Qualification . . . unless the messages are of a purely private nature and employees have not been given notice that their e-mail is subject to monitoring.	***Qualification*** . . . unless the e-mail is directly work related and employees are given prior notice of the monitoring.

While the backing/challenge points out the potentially infinite complexity of the argument—showing how argument can be layered on argument indefinitely—it's not the most interesting new element in the structure of argument. We find the *reservations* and the *qualifications* the most interesting new elements because they both open the possibility of creative thinking and problem solving.

Let's look at the reservations first. Those articulated on both sides of the e-mail-privacy conflict chart are, in a sense, ways of thinking the unthinkable. In a conflict, where the underlying moral and ethical principles are strongly held, reservations that abandon the key underlying principle probably are unacceptable. But in a disagreement where the underlying assumptions and principles are not held so closely, reservations—a changing of underlying principles or assumptions—may be a promising way of resolving an impasse. For example, in Figure 6.6, Joy Sand and Gravel was obviously operating with the unspoken assumption that an analysis of limestone from their quarry, if done competently, would be good indefinitely. Tom Barker's memo calls for them to abandon that assumption and embrace his principle that the analysis should be a current one of the actual materials delivered to his jobsite. And presumably they accepted Barker's principle because doing so wouldn't threaten their core sense of who they are and what they believe.

When you look at both sides of Figure 6.9, notice how the qualifications feel different from the reservations, even though they look very much alike in their structure. If you accept our assumption that argument is more than just a fight, more than a game, and, ultimately, even more than a debate, then the qualification is perhaps the most interesting of the new elements. Our contention is that argument, when it is most effective, functions as a process of cooperative exploration—of differing interpretations of the world and of a specific conflict, in particular. Argument also serves as a process for discovering common ground that can be occupied by both interpretations. Unlike the reservation, the qualification does not require you to abandon your underlying principle in order to find common ground.

Try this experiment: On each side of the chart, read first the claim and then the reservation. Here we are, first on the left-hand side of the chart:

> Employers should have access to employees' e-mail messages at work . . . unless we are prepared, as a society, to say that people who invest their capital in business ventures are not entitled to the fruits of their investment.

Now try the right-hand side:

> Employers should not have access to employees' e-mail messages at work . . . unless we are prepared, as a society, to say that people must give up their right to privacy in order to have a paycheck.

Do you feel a jolting sensation? You probably do, irrespective of which side you read. The jolt comes with the sudden reversal of underlying principle.

Now try the same exercise, this time reading first the claim and then the qualification. Here is the left-hand side:

> Employers should have access to employees' e-mail messages at work . . . unless the messages are of a purely private nature and employees have not been given notice that their e-mail is subject to monitoring.

And now here's the right-hand side:

> Employers should not have access to employees' e-mail messages at work . . . unless the e-mail is directly work related and employees are given prior notice of the monitoring.

Do you feel the jolt on either side here? Be careful. Take a moment before you answer. We're not asking if you *agree* with the statements. It's entirely possible that you may not agree with either one. We're asking if you feel a jolt between the early part of the sentence and the latter part that begins with *unless.* We think your answer is probably going to be no. The jolt isn't there because the qualification doesn't constitute an abandonment of the underlying principle. If you qualify your claim, you identify territory where you're able to see that another principle—different from the one that undergirds your initial claim—operates validly and qualifies or even complements your original principle.

Now we'd like you to look at the qualified claims side by side. On the one hand, we have the assertion that employers should have access to employees' e-mail messages at work unless the messages are of a purely private nature and employees have not been given notice that their e-mail is subject to monitoring. On the other hand, we have the assertion that employers should not have access to employees' e-mail messages at work unless the e-mail is directly work related and employees are given prior notice of the monitoring. The remarkable thing about these two assertions is that despite having begun from diametrically opposed claims, based on opposing principles, they now claim almost the same area of validity.

Does this mean we just solved the privacy conflict? Of course not. All you have to do is move back up the chart two steps to the backings and challenges, and you'll see that we haven't. The arguments are far too complex and the principles too devoutly held by the many different sides of the debate to be reduced to an easy solution like this. But this exercise does show how two particular parties to the conflict might move toward common ground if they can listen carefully and empathically to the opposing claims, the data, and especially to the underlying principles that warrant those claims. And the chart also shows that it's possible, under the right circumstances, to find this common ground without abandoning principles on either side. The following four tactics should help you find this ground.

TACTIC 1: Use the structure of argument to clarify and deepen your understanding of your own principles, interests, and perceptions of this conflict.

First, you need to understand as clearly as possible what your own stake in this conflict is. You can start by testing your claims, your data, and your underlying principles and assumptions:

- Test your claims: What are they? Are you claiming too much? Are you claiming enough?
- Are your claims really consistent with the facts?
- Are your claims really consistent with your assumptions and your principles?
- Are your claims consistent with both your immediate and your long-range goals and interests?
- Test the limits of each claim for points where you might be able to qualify it without compromising your underlying principles or assumptions.

- Test your underlying assumptions for points where you may, in fact, be willing to compromise or modify your assumptions or principles. In other words, test for possible reservations.
- Test your emotional commitment to your claims and to your underlying principles/values/assumptions. When you consider possible reservations and qualifications, which ones bother you? For example, do the reservations in the chart of a privacy debate (i.e., to say that people who invest their capital in business ventures are not entitled to the fruits of their investment or to say that people must give up their right to privacy in order to have a paycheck) bother you? Do you feel a "slippery slope" that might pull you toward an unacceptable abandonment of your principles or goals if you qualify your claim in particular ways? Try to articulate this fear—and any others you discover—as well as you can.

TACTIC 2: **Use the structure of argument to clarify and deepen your understanding of your readers' principles, interests, and perceptions of this conflict.**

Try to lay aside your own assumptions and your own image of this situation for the time being and "put on your readers' spectacles." Rogerian argument begins with this attempt to achieve an empathic understanding of your opponents'—in this case, your readers'—argument. A key Rogerian rule is that once your opponent has spoken in an oral argument, you can make your own affirmative case only after having "first restated the ideas and feelings of the previous speaker accurately, and to that speaker's satisfaction" (Rogers, 1952, p. 85).

The key to this tactic probably lies in the requirement that you characterize your opponents'/readers' position to their satisfaction. This requirement helps keep you from straying into a debunking strategy, where you say about your readers (and maybe *to* your readers, also) that their assumptions are faulty because of distortions caused by their narrow parochial experience (e.g., "You're just saying that because you're from . . .") or their self-interest (e.g., "You're just saying that because then you wouldn't have to . . ."). Certainly, your readers' personal, political, social, and economic interests are part of the picture here. And certainly, they are part of the data, part of the reality that you need to factor into your analysis and your argument. But they are not the *principles* on which your readers' arguments are grounded. For this tactic of characterizing your readers' position to be effective, you have to find the principles on which the claims and the interests or goals are based, and you have to try to characterize their interests and claims and goals as principled—to the extent that you can.

Look again at Tom Barker's letter to Joy Sand & Gravel (Figure 6.6). Notice that Barker affirms at the outset that the argument in Joy's FAX is a principled one. He even partially accepts their analysis—for the limited purpose of determining the weight of the materials delivered. Having acknowledged his readers' good faith, he goes on to make his own principled argument that an alternative analysis is required for purposes of determining actual lime content.

This taking of your readers' perspective—especially if you are immersed in the emotion of the conflict—can be immensely hard. It requires that you treat your readers' opposing argument and underlying assumptions and interests as if they have validity—at a time when your every impulse is to reject the entire argument out of hand. Rogers (1952) acknowledges this difficulty when he describes how hard it is for a psychological counselor to engage in what he calls "client-centered therapy," which is where this idea of reader-centered, Rogerian argument comes from. Rogers comments on how frightening it is for a counselor who is working with a severely disturbed, perhaps psychotic, patient. If the other person's perspective seems pathological, bizarre, or dangerous, you may have good reason to be fearful of trying to get inside that view. But what if trying on this other view, really achieving this empathic understanding, changes your own view? What if you can't get back to the reality that you now see from your current, comfortable perspective?

This uneasiness about an opposing world view is part of what tempts us to debunk it by explaining it away, rather than really trying to immerse ourselves in it so we can see the claims, facts, and principles as our readers see them. But having the vocabulary from the chart (Figure 6.9) can help us stay on the task of understanding, rather than explaining away, a perspective that we are resisting. It can help us treat that vision—and the readers who hold it—with the kind of empathic understanding and respect that we want in return. Consider these questions:

- Test your readers' claims: What are they? Are they claiming too much? Are they claiming enough?
- Are their claims really consistent with the facts?
- Are their claims really consistent with their assumptions and their principles? Are their claims consistent with your own assumptions and principles?
- Are their claims consistent with both their immediate and their long-range goals and interests? Are they consistent with your own goals and interests?
- Test the limits of each of their claims for points where they might be able to qualify the claim without compromising their underlying principles or assumptions.
- Test their underlying principles for points where it appears they might be willing to compromise or modify assumptions or principles. Test their underlying assumptions and principles for areas of validity that you can accept.
- Try to understand your readers' emotional commitment to their claims and to their underlying principles/values/assumptions. When you consider possible reservations and qualifications to your readers' principles and assumptions, which ones seem likely to be comfortable to your readers? Which seem most likely to be painful or difficult? For example, do the reservations in the chart of the e-mail privacy debate (i.e., to say that people who invest their capital in business ventures are not entitled to the fruits of their investment or to say that people must give up their right to privacy in order to have a paycheck) seem likely to bother your readers? Are they likely to feel a "slippery slope"? Try to get your readers to articulate this fear, if possible, and try to find points where you can qualify your own claims to accommodate your readers' fears.

If your readers' underlying assumptions and principles are radically different from your own, then your struggle to find large areas of common ground may be almost impossible. You may be trying to negotiate a shift in each other's world view that is so profound that it's equivalent to a total conversion. Most of the time, though, you can find substantial common ground, where you can acknowledge areas of validity of your readers' claims and applicability of their principles.

TACTIC 3: **Point out where you see the validity of your readers' claims and the applicability of the underlying warrants.**

The traditional treatment of an opponent's argument, dating back at least 2,500 years to Aristotle, is to point out where it is not valid. Rogers (1952) recommends doing just the opposite: pointing out where your opponent's argument *is* valid. After all, he says, you're drawing the same boundary in either case. You're delineating the areas where your reader's argument is and is not valid. You're just standing on the other side of the boundary as you lay it out. It's interesting that when two religious denominations a few years back decided to talk about their respective articles of faith and practices of worship, they began by clarifying the points where they were in substantial agreement. They noted that their disagreements had already been documented for several centuries, and they believed that affirmations of their mutually held beliefs would be more productive.

This tactic—actually taking the time and effort to demonstrate to your readers that you see the principles underlying their claims as well as the areas of applicability of those principles and the areas of validity of those claims—is immensely powerful in reducing readers' sense of threat and inducing an assumption of similarity. If you can, by this initiative, help your readers see that you are sincerely engaged in trying to understand their opposing point of view and recognize its areas of validity, then you will make a powerful ethical argument. Namely, you are a person of good faith who can be trusted as an opponent and with whom one can collaborate in the problem-solving, win/win quadrant in this disagreement. You will also lay the groundwork for Tactic 4.

TACTIC 4: **Help your readers unpack and understand your own argument in a way that reciprocates your empathic unpacking of their argument.**

Think about the elements of your argument, as you have unpacked them for yourself based on the chart of the e-mail privacy conflict (Figure 6.9). Look especially at the underlying principles you're relying on. Are they consistent with the ones your readers are relying on? If so, disclosing those principles will help induce the assumption of similarity. If not, acknowledging incompatibilities will help confirm that you have understood them. Either way, you're helping create a vision for your readers that will lead toward greater understanding and trust. Now look at your backing for your principles and your challenge to the opposing principles. Are your challenges to the opposing principles based on your concerns/fears about their implications? Are there "slippery slopes" here that appear as though they could carry you away to implications that would be unacceptable? Try to talk about your concerns frankly and directly. You might even use a variation of the "When XXX, then YYY, so ZZZ" formula that we talked about earlier in the chapter, saying something like this: "I'm worried about the possibility that [the readers' claim or the principle they're relying on] could be used to justify [here you state your fear]." If you can explain this concern after you've acknowledged areas of validity of your readers' claims or principles, you're still helping create a vision for your readers that will lead toward greater understanding and trust.

Now, look at your reservations and qualifications. Can you talk about your qualifications, laying out territory beyond which you don't want to make your claims? In the same way that you've delineated the areas of validity of your readers' claims, you can delineate the areas of validity of your own claim, drawing lines of demarcation that limit the region of validity of your claims. And remember that these lines denote territory on both sides of the line. When you concede that the territory on one side is the area beyond which your claims hold true, you are, by implication, embracing the territory on the other side as the area of validity of the claims—just as you are implying the limits of your readers' claims when you follow Rogers' advice and point out the area of its validity. Likewise, can you identify principles that are not important to your vision but that may be important barriers to your readers' accepting it? If you can dismiss these as reservations, then you will certainly reduce your readers' anxiety about your remaining principles and the claims you're making because of them.

Some Risks and Limitations of the Tactics and of Rogerian Argument in General

The Risk of Agreement. This seems an odd risk at first glance. Isn't agreement what we're aiming for here? But what if you end up agreeing with an opposing position? What if, in the process of trying to achieve an empathic understanding of your readers' position, by viewing the world through their spectacles, you suddenly see—*really* see—the validity and applicability of the principles on which that position is based? What if, instead of converting your reader, you find that you have converted yourself? Dealing in good faith by being willing to move into the problem-solving quadrant in a conflict always entails the risk of learning something that will alter your entire view of the matter, and maybe even your view of the world beyond the immediate conflict.

The Risk of Bad Faith—Your Own and Your Readers'. It's possible to engage in these tactics cynically and deceptively, to seem to be working in the win/win, problem-solving quadrant when you're really working in the win/lose, bullying quadrant, where the argument takes on a form of coercive manipulation that wears the garment of empathic understanding. It's even possible for this kind of deception to be successful over that short term. But this is a success purchased at a high cost: loss of faith and respect. You need to be on guard against this kind of cynicism, both in yourself and in your opponent.

The Limitation of Time. Remember that we're talking about conflicted situations where people have often made major investments of ego and emotion (and often time and money) in their positions. Resolution of a conflict is likely to take a long time where competing claims are grounded in principle so deeply and strongly held that they constitute the core of people's identities. In fact, some of the conflict will probably never be resolved. One of William Ury's (1991) maxims in *Getting Past No* is "Go slow in order to go fast." His point, of course, is that you can't rush prematurely to an agreement and then expect it to hold together. The conflicting interests, egos, and principles need to find real, legitimate reasons to work in the problem-solving quadrant. Moreover, they need to participate in the ownership of any agreement, or they will ultimately reject it.

Conventions

In one sense, almost all the ideas we've talked about in this chapter have constituted a set of conventions something like the Geneva Conventions—a set of rules, tactics, and strategies for how to wage a fair and effective engagement in a conflicted, emotional, and perhaps dangerous rhetorical situation. We've examined conventional ways of writing complaint letters, bad news letters, and negotiation letters. We've adapted rules and tactics from several of the best theorists and practitioners on how to manage conflict effectively and ethically. What remain are only a few general rules, some of which will, in fact, be review:

1. Be very careful what and when you write in a conflicted situation, especially if you are in an angry, attacking frame of mind. As we said earlier, this anger may be entirely appropriate, and expressing it vividly may be absolutely your best argumentative strategy. Then again, it may not be. You need to judge the situation carefully. If you see just a single reader and he or she is nearby and accessible, is it possible that you should be talking, instead of writing? Even the most carefully drafted document can be misread, especially at the affective, or emotional, level. Your reader may radically misconstrue your attitude, despite your best attempts to express it appropriately. If you talk, rather than write, to this person, you are present to watch and listen for immediate cues that he or she is misunderstanding you, and you can respond immediately with clarifications and corrections. However, the risk of being misunderstood at the logical or factual level of argument also increases in conflicted situations. A written document stands as a record at least of the words that you used, even if both your meaning and your attitude behind those words may still be subject to further interpretation and argument. So, it's useful to ask yourself whether you need to create a paper trail (or e-mail trail) for future evidence. Or maybe you should do both—write *and* talk.

2. In a conflict, try to avoid the temptation to humiliate or beat up your reader. Another one of Ury's (1991) maxims is "Try to bring them to their senses, not to

their knees." Avoid pulling rank, bullying, or invoking allies who will bully or humiliate. Resist the temptation to broadcast letters or e-mail your opponent has sent you in order to humiliate him or her.

3. At the same time, try to avoid giving your reader any opportunity to embarrass or humiliate you in these ways.

4. Specifically, be sure you don't commit some embarrassing *faux pas* by carelessly breaking some formal convention—a misspelling, a grammatical error, a formatting fumble in a letter or memo, or some similar mistake.

Expression

Even more than conventions, expression has been at the heart of most of what we've been talking about in this chapter. When conflicts of values and ethical assumptions and basic goals occur, they need to be identified and clarified before they can be effectively addressed. Likewise, when conflict and disagreement generate heightened emotions, those emotions also need to be identified, named, and acknowledged. Not to express the emotional dimensions of a serious conflict too often lets those emotions run uncontrolled beneath the surface of the dialogue—only to pop out in unexpected, usually unproductive ways. Not to express the underlying values, assumptions, aspirations, and goals that serve as the warrants for your arguments heightens the risk that your readers will misunderstand your arguments and their moral force. And if you don't, in turn, understand the underlying warrants of your readers' arguments, then you will likely make the same mistake about their arguments. The whole thrust of Rogerian argument is to express these vital elements of all sides of an issue, to set them forth so that all who are engaged in the conflict can gain a full understanding—logical, empathic, and ethical—of each other's positions. Moreover, people will begin to see each other as people of goodwill and competence, even though they are in conflict, and work together in the problem-solving quadrant of the matrix of conflict resolution.

Expression is always important in the writing of business. Even in drafting routine documents, you're wise to pause and ask yourself if the image of you—the facial expression, the tone of voice, the personality and value system implied by your language—is right for this occasion. And when a situation becomes conflicted or has the potential to, then effective, appropriate expression—by all parties to the conflict—becomes the mode by which understanding and mutual trust are made possible. These, in turn, make possible the further task of trying to achieve a mutually satisfactory resolution. At the same time, expression that is ineffective—whether bullying or humiliating or condescending or disrespectful—is likewise a powerful element in a conflicted situation, creating an energy that pushes the participants toward the other three quadrants of bullying, avoiding, or conceding. This chapter has been about creating and expressing an ethos of integrity, mutual respect, and trust that captures the energy and emotion of conflict and creates the impetus for working in the problem-solving quadrant.

WRITING CHECKLIST

The following guidelines will help you write letters responding to difficult situations—those characterized by conflict, disagreement, or emotion. For more general guidelines relevant to any letter-writing situation, see the Chapter 5 Writing Checklist. For any of these guidelines, remember the superordinate guideline: Disregard *any* of this advice if it would cause you to do something that's inappropriate or silly for your situation.

☑ Complaint Letters

- Decide exactly what your problem is and what needs to happen to satisfy you.
- Narrate and amplify, as simply and specifically as you can, what happened and why it was problematic for you.
- Explain what you would find a satisfactory resolution of this problem and who specifically needs to be involved in this resolution.
- Test your argument to be sure that you've made a plausible claim embodying your needs and goals, that you've cited necessary supporting data, and that you've taken into account the legal and ethical principles and assumptions warranting your claim.
- Step back from your emotion and think about the problem strategically and rhetorically; the primary goal of your letter should *not* be emotional catharsis.
- To harness your emotion effectively, frame your complaint using the "When you . . ." convention.

☑ Bad News Letters

- Since bad news letters tell your reader no—that you can't solve a problem, fulfill a request, or buy a product or service—you need to find ways to mitigate his or her discomfort, risk, or inconvenience.
- Decide if you want to end negotiations or keep them open.
- Make sure your reader knows you've understood; people need to know that they've been heard and understood, even if the reply they receive isn't the one they were hoping for.
- Consider using the balanced organizational convention, in which your main point, the bad news, is sandwiched in the middle of the letter and stated only once.
- Provide alternative solutions to the reader's problem, if possible, and assure him or her of your goodwill.
- Choose your format carefully, deciding whether the balanced format is most appropriate for your goals and reader.
- If possible, close with a buffer that affirms a friendly, professional relationship and looks forward to future collaboration.
- When you need to bring an association to a close, don't raise false hopes or make statements that could be construed as commitments to ongoing association.

☑ Negotiation Letters

- Start with a firm position based on a careful, principled analysis of your real needs.
- Determine ahead of time your BATNA: your best alternative to a negotiated agreement. Then, you can negotiate firmly and in good faith.
- Remember that the primary goal is to keep negotiations moving forward.
- Don't be surprised by disagreement, conflict, and emotion, and when they occur, use them productively.
- Decide whether this situation, at this moment, constitutes a fight, a game, or a debate.
- Move the conflict in the direction of a debate or, preferably, a mutual problem-solving negotiation.

ACTIVITIES AND PROJECTS

1. Review the letters in your document file (see Activity 7, Chapter 5). Select one involving a complaint, bad news, or negotiation. Since you received this letter and have personal knowledge of how it made you feel, describe your reaction specifically. What emotions or conflicts were inherent in this letter-writing situation—both for you and for the writer? From your perspective, did the letter dampen the emotions and conflict? Heighten them? Not affect them at all? Why did the letter have this effect on you?
2. Review the letters in your document file. Select one involving a complaint, bad news, or negotiation that you feel needs substantive revision. (This letter might, in fact, be the same one you selected for Activity 1.) Revise the letter, using the GRACE benchmarks to ensure that you've worked through your revision fully and systematically. Since you were the person who received this letter, this assignment will give you the opportunity to write the letter that you wish you'd received, instead of the one you actually got.
3. The series of letters in Figures 6.10 through 6.12 between Beth Murphy and Rosemary Williams demonstrate the ways in which arguments—claims, warrants, and data—and the ways in which they are expressed can heighten, rather than ameliorate, that conflict. Do a GRACEful analysis of these letters and the situations that triggered them. Then describe the problems you see in these letters and how the letters might be reframed to deal with the conflict more successfully.
4. Assume that you have received the complaint letter in Figure 6.13. Using the principles of GRACE, write a response to resolve the conflict, rather than heighten the emotion and make things worse.

FIGURE 6.10 Complaint Letter Series—Letter 1

208 Hawthorn Lane
Akron, OH
April 26, 1997

Ms. Rosemary Williams
Store Manager, Bridal Bows Unlimited
1009 Grand Avenue
Cleveland, OH

Dear Ms. Williams:

Wouldn't you agree that both attractive merchandise and fair, efficient service are necessary to keep customers coming into a bridal store like Bridal Bows Unlimited?

When I put down an initial deposit of $100 for my bridal gown at Bridal Bows Unlimited, I felt that your merchandise was both well-made and unusual in design. However, the quality of service I have received since then has made me question the desirability of patronizing your salon. I began to feel apprehensive when I was measured for my dress. Although the sample dress, a size 10, almost fit me, I was told that I needed a size 15 dress. Knowing that Bridal Bows Unlimited charges an additional fee for alterations of more than one size made me a bit nervous about the additional money I would need to pay beyond the $1800 for the dress itself.

The day I was fitted for the bridal gown, Melissa instructed me to put an additional $250 down on the bridal gown within the next week and said that a total of $900 would be required before the dress would actually be ordered. I decided to pay the additional deposit—despite the fact that I was now having second thoughts about Bridal Bows Unlimited's fair treatment. Thus I scheduled an appointment with Melissa.

Because I could not bring in my check during the agreed upon time, I called Melissa to reschedule my appointment. She seemed surprised when I called, even though she had emphasized the importance of my coming in and seeing her. At that time, we reset the appointment for Tuesday at 7. When I came in on Tuesday with my $250 check, I asked to see Melissa, and the clerk said it was unnecessary. I wondered why I had received conflicting information from the two people.

In addition, because your set-up requires a different consultant for each aspect of wedding apparel, I was spending a lot of time talking to different people to find out procedures for ordering bridesmaids dresses and other necessary items. I felt that if I was providing Bridal Bows Unlimited with several thousand dollars worth of business, I should not be the one to go out of my way to find simple answers to simple questions.

At that point, my wedding plans changed; my fiancé and I postponed the wedding indefinitely. I knew that my dress had not yet been ordered and that I technically deserved a refund. Your

(continued)

FIGURE 6.10 Continued

Williams, page 2

pamphlet, "A Guide to Special Orders," specifically states that "A one-half deposit of your total sale is required to order your gown." In addition, it says, "No refunds or exchanges will be made on any in stock merchandise purchased at Bridal Bows Unlimited. Special orders cannot be canceled once they have been accepted by the manufacturer." Therefore, because my dress was a special order rather than "in stock merchandise" and because I had only paid $350 of the $900 required to actually order the dress, I decided to ask for a refund.

My mother called Jessica about a refund, and she said there would be no problem, that I simply needed to talk to you. When you asked me why I wanted a refund and I told you my wedding had been indefinitely postponed, you said that if my fiancé had been killed or if we were not getting married, that those reasons would be acceptable. You also suggested that buying the dress now would be a good investment. Perhaps if I had received acceptable service from Bridal Bows Unlimited, I might have gone ahead and gotten the dress or accepted a credit slip for Bridal Bows Unlimited merchandise. After all, I did like the quality of the dresses I had seen. However, paying almost $2000 for a dress I wasn't sure I would be able to wear was a risky investment. Moreover, I doubt that anyone would purchase merchandise, however good its quality, when they had received poor service before the order was even placed.

When I got home, my mother again called you. You asked her if I had found the same dress somewhere else for a cheaper price, and my mother again explained that the wedding had been indefinitely postponed. You then said that we would need to put the refund request in writing. I sent this written request on March 24.

Well-run bridal salons realize that high quality merchandise must be accompanied by good service and fair treatment to insure customer good will and thus a good reputation. I have made a reasonable request: that you refund the $350 deposit due me according to your own printed policy. Although I requested this refund in a letter sent exactly one month ago, you have not responded either by mail or phone. Therefore, if I do not receive a $350 check by Monday, May 9th, I will refer this problem to the Consumer Fraud Division of the State's Attorney's Office.

Sincerely,

Beth Murphy

Beth Murphy

FIGURE 6.11 Complaint Letter Series—Letter 2

Bridal Bows Unlimited
1009 Grand Avenue
Cleveland, OH

216-555-8997

April 26, 1997

Beth Murphy
208 Hawthorn Lane
Akron, OH

Dear Miss Murphy:

After receiving your letter regarding the refund on your bridal order, your account has been approved for refund by our corporation. Your refund check will be mailed in approximately six to eight weeks.

Yours Truly,

Bridal Bows Unlimited

Rosemary Williams

Rosemary Williams
Store Manager

FIGURE 6.12 Complaint Letter Series—Letter 3

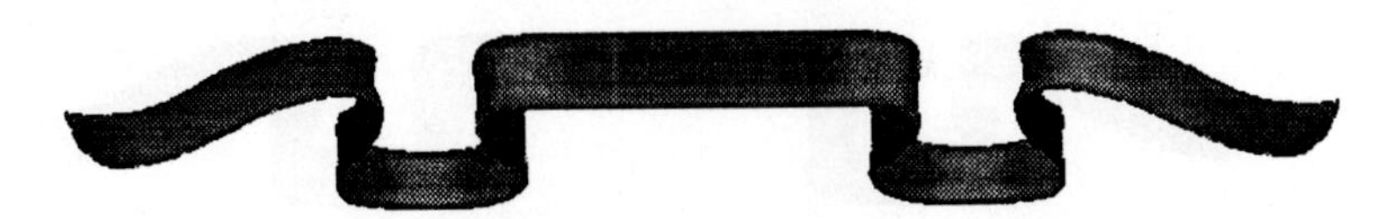

Bridal Bows Unlimited
1009 Grand Avenue
Cleveland, OH

216-555-8997

April 28, 1997

Beth Murphy
208 Hawthorn Lane
Akron, OH

Dear Miss Murphy:

In regards to your letter dated April 26, both of our responses were mailed the same day.

After trying very hard for a long time, I finally received good results from our corp., all in your favor and to your benifit. (see letter mailed 4-26-97).

I am sending your letter back, as it probably will be of more use to you in the future than to me.

I am also taking this opportunity to thank you for mailing it to me, but your threats are meaningless.

Signing legal business contracts, commits an individual to the terms, rules and policies of such.

After signing a contract, any changes or postponements made outside of that contract is out of our hands.

We try very hard to assist an unsatisfied customer, such as yourself, when in return, rudeness and untruthfulness are the results, then I wonder, was it worth it????

Your refund check will be issued according to our store policy, which consists of 4 to 6 weeks.

I am sorry if our good services were not acceptable to your standards, Miss Murphy.

Good luck to you in the future and to all the people you will be dealing with.

Sincerely,

Mrs. Williams

Mrs. Williams
Store Manager

FIGURE 6.13 Complaint Letter

September 11, 1997

Murchison's Studio
384 Market Street
Cheyenne, WY 82001

Dear Murchison's:

I am writing to explain why I am not paying the additional $60 overtime fee. I would have been happy to pay for the additional time if certain things had not happened on my wedding day. My husband and I have paid one thousand dollars for Murchison's services. We had requested Ann, and three days before our wedding day, we were told that her father would be taking over the duties. Under the circumstances, we understood completely. At the wedding, however, my entire wedding party and relatives who were photographed got barked at. I understand that the photographer was dealing with a very excited crew, but everyone was cooperating fully. For some odd reason, the photographer was under the impression that everyone had done this before and acted rudely when we did not understand exactly what he wanted us to do. When we tried to pose the proper way, rude comments were said and smart remarks were given. Some of my friends and family came hundreds, and even thousands, of miles to celebrate with us on this joyous occasion, and we did not need to be treated in such an unprofessional manner. My family and relatives were appalled at the manner in which we were treated. After the wedding, many comments were said to me about the photographer that were very unkind; and to us, that was extremely embarrassing.

I was flabbergasted to hear that the photographer solicited business at my wedding reception to numerous people. These people were my guests and relatives, not your clients. I paid you one thousand dollars to take pictures, not to hound my family. That was rude and extremely inconsiderate of you to do at my wedding. Was our business not enough? You get a thousand dollars, and then you proceed to scrape up extra business from my loved ones at my expense. That was very unprofessional and uncouth.

While I was looking at the proofs after the wedding, I immediately noticed that there was not a picture taken of me dancing with my father. As a professional wedding photographer, that should have been done. My husband and I told you at our pre-wedding meeting that the reception dancing pictures were very important. I have never danced with my father nor have I ever seen my father dance. This was an extreme oversight on your part, and it is horrible that you did not make that a priority.

I also noticed that some pictures that had been taken at the church were missing. I called your studio and was told that they did not exist. Everyone in these pictures remembers them being taken. The pictures were taken of my husband's immediate family and one of

(continued)

FIGURE 6.13 Continued

my husband's family including me. I was told by your studio that the photographer probably just forgot that he had run out of film and did not add a new roll. I hope that our photographer, being a so-called professional, would know when the proper film was in the camera at such a moment that could never be recaptured. You should have been aware of your film situation at all times. Your only job at the wedding was to take pictures. Now my family is left without pictures that my mother-in-law had wanted to put on Christmas cards.

Finally, I am enclosing a picture of the reception taken by my uncle. I was shocked and in total disbelief that this occurred. When I looked at the picture, I was puzzled as to who this man was posing with my family as if he was such. It finally occurred to me that this man was our photographer, smiling with a glass and plate in hand next to my family as if he was supposed to be there. Unfortunately, this was probably the time when I was dancing with my father.

All of these things described above were just too much. I couldn't keep quiet. There were, however, some very lovely pictures taken that day. I will be ordering pictures from your business, not that I have any other choice. I expect that the rest of my business with Murchison's will be more professional. I expect that my Art Leather Album and photograph order will be taken care of in a more professional manner. I refuse to pay the additional $60 fee due to what has happened. Because of my future orders and the past circumstances you should, as a professional, understand. Just as your motto says, "Your wedding is as important to us as it is to you," I know that you will stand behind your product and take care of my business. Cheyenne is a small town that my family has lived in for ten years. In attendance at our wedding were quite a few people who also live in Cheyenne and Laramie. Unfortunately, small towns can be bad for a reputation. Handling weddings poorly can make a good reputation sour quickly. I hope that the future handling of my business will improve quickly and dramatically and that you correct this conduct for future weddings. In closing, many young couples soon to be wed were at our wedding that now know what they do not want, and that "extra" business you wanted is now lost.

Robin McKenzie

Robin McKenzie
1231 Rodeo Avenue
Cheyenne, Wyoming 82001

5. In a letter to the editor of his local paper (see Figure 6.14), Richard Osgood, arguing for increased funding to local schools and complaining about current legislative practice, asks his readers to contact the governor or state legislators and to share their concerns. Do a GRACEful analysis of the letter. Include a description of the possible emotional dimensions of the context underlying the letter. Consider also the claims, data, and warrants that Richard is making and how he is structuring his argument. Then determine where you would place the letter on the matrix of conflict resolution strategies: bullying (win/lose), problem solving (win/win), avoiding (lose/lose), or conceding (lose/win). Explain your decision.

6. The letter from Pat Alexander in Figure 6.15 is a request for an investigation of a medical situation with obvious emotional, ethical, and legal dimensions. First, consider who is likely to read this letter and why. Also assess what specific risks are involved for both Pat and her readers. Then, look closely at how Pat develops the argument. What claims, data, and warrants are present in the letter? Look particularly at any warrants in the letter: What underlying values, assumptions, aspirations, or goals might help readers understand and accept the argument and its moral force? Are these likely to be accepted by the readers? Why or why not? Is Pat's request valid, warranted, and appropriate? Why or why not?

7. This chapter is about writing in situations of conflict, disagreement, or misunderstanding. Yet Tom Barker's letter to Floyd Flamingo in Figure 6.16 makes no reference to a conflict or misunderstanding. No explicit claim is made, nor is any underlying principle or assumption articulated. Rather, the letter is a simple, straightforward narration of the activities during a particular two-hour period. Can you infer what probably has prompted the letter? Under what kinds of circumstances would this likely be an effective letter? What kinds of circumstances might call for a different strategy? What kind of advice do you suppose Tom Barker might give Mrs. Williams of Bridal Bows Unlimited (see Activity 3)?

8. Suppose you're Maria of the King Star Computer Company, and you've just received Brad Rossiter's letter (see Figure 6.17) on behalf of Kendeco Industrial Supply. What does Brad want? What will you write back to Brad? Why?

9. In Larry Thompson's letter to TCI cable (see Figure 6.18), there are four different points at which he either asks a question or makes a request. Find and mark each of these points. What do these locations suggest about the direction Larry's arguments are running? (Think about the discussion of direction of arguments in Chapter 5.) Suppose you're the customer service manager at TCI. You expect you may receive additional letters about some of the issues Larry raises. Lay out at least three different strategies for responding to these issues, and give a short rationale, based on GRACE, for each strategy.

FIGURE 6.14 Letter to the Editor

283 Ridley Drive
Spring Valley, MN 56320
May 15, 1997

Letter to the Editor, *The St. Cloud Times*
2700 Seventh Street North
St. Cloud, MN 56301

Dear St. Cloud Times Readers:

In his 1994 bid for re-election, Governor Carlson claimed that he would be an "education governor." However, schools in outstate Minnesota are still waiting for his support. Governor Carlson needs to shift his focus toward education issues, especially school funding.

This past year, Governor Carlson supported a freeze in funding for most outstate schools, including Spring Valley High School. After years of cuts and freezes, Spring Valley students will really feel the pinch this year as expenses rise and funding falls behind. To make up for the $400,000 cut in money left after building costs, etc., activities face cuts *again,* teachers' salaries will be frozen *again,* and class sizes will increase. In spite of the cuts and freezes, Carlson has increased demands on the schools with laws raising graduation standards, requiring schools to buy more computers, etc. More kids than ever will slip through the cracks as important services schools provide are neglected, like books, small classes, counselors, and activities.

The money the state does spend on schools is not always fairly distributed. Under the current system, students in wealthy communities with large tax bases receive *additional* state funding. Schools in poor and middle-class rural areas receive *less* state support. This is due to a policy that is meant to encourage local school funding. For Spring Valley, raising $100,000 through referendums, etc., would earn an additional $200,000 in state funding. Unfortunately, some communities cannot raise money as easily as the suburban metro schools this policy helps. The result: some schools in suburbs of the Twin Cities have twice as much per-pupil money as many schools in our area. This disparity is both unfair and unreasonable. It suggests our state's lawmakers, including Carlson, consider our students less worthy of the state's support than metro students.

Governor Carlson needs to address these problems, rather than ignore them. He clearly cares more about the Twins' new stadium than the schools. Every day on television and radio, Governor Carlson asks for Minnesotans to support the stadium deals. What the Twins need, he claims, is public funding. If the next generation of Minnesota students fails to compete economically, it will not be because the Twins don't have an outdoor stadium. It will be because Governor Carlson failed to give schools appropriate funding and support.

If you share my concerns about the schools and want Governor Carlson to make education a higher priority, contact him or your state senator or representative.

Sincerely,

Richard Osgood

Richard Osgood

FIGURE 6.15 Letter Requesting Investigation

872 Anderson Court
Montgomery, IL 60543
August 15, 1998

Mr. Roger Mortinson
Administrative Services
Montgomery Clinic
8876 Illinois Way
Montgomery, IL 60543

Dear Mr. Mortinson:

As a member of the health services community, I am sure that your number one priority is to provide efficient and competent professionals for the clients that you serve. HMO plans such as Partners in Health and Medical Care, Inc. use your facilities because they also believe in your ability and commitment to provide the best possible care for individuals and their families. This is the reason that I am writing to you.

On April 18, 1997, I made an appointment with Montgomery Clinic for lower right-side abdominal pain. My regular physician, Dr. Suzanne Imholte, was out of the office at the time, and I scheduled an appointment with Dr. Mark Headly instead.

At the time of my consultation with Dr. Headly, I was still feeling lower abdominal pain. Dr. Headly looked at my file and did a pressure exam on my abdomen. Dr. Headly did not perform a gynecological or rectal exam, nor did he order a blood test to measure my white blood cell count. At that point, he prescribed Ortho-Cyclen to alleviate the symptoms which he believed to be caused by an ovarian cyst. I had been diagnosed with this cyst earlier that month by Dr. Imholte.

Four days later, on April 22, 1997, I was admitted to Montgomery Hospital for an emergency appendectomy. At the time of my arrival at the hospital, my white cell count was 12,999, the normal count of a healthy person being between 5,000 and 8,000. After my surgery, I was informed by my surgeon, Dr. Prentiss Horton, that my appendix had ruptured and the resulting infection had spread into my blood stream and throughout my body. Due to the amount of infection, he estimated that my appendix had been ruptured for at least three to four days.

(continued)

FIGURE 6.15 Continued

Mr. Roger Mortinson, Administrative Services, page 2

As a result of my hospital stay of seven days, and Dr. Horton's orders not to return to classes for another seven days, I was absent from two weeks of my college classes. I was not able to finish my classes for the semester, nor was I able to reclaim the money that I had lost for these incomplete classes. Further, I was forced because of this absence to delay my graduation from the end of spring to the end of summer semester.

As health care professionals, I am sure you realize that thorough and competent doctors are essential in maintaining an atmosphere and reputation of quality and efficient health care within a community and its surrounding areas. That is why I am requesting that Dr. Mark Headly's role in my hospitalization be investigated and reviewed by the clinic administration.

Sincerely,

Pat Alexander

Pat Alexander

FIGURE 6.16 Persuasive Reply to Complaint

Professional
Consultants

March 31, 1997

Mr. Floyd Flamingo
PO Box 4100
Sheridan, WY 82801

Dear Floyd:

I asked Bill Pugh to describe his activity on the afternoon that you closed the transaction on your house. The title company called and FAXed a legal description that Bill determined was 60 acres and not 10. Bill found the 10 acre legal description that was prepared in conjunction with your survey certificate for the bank and made a sketch for the title company to illustrate how the 10 acres was located within the 60 acre tract.

Bill interrupted his current project that day because the transaction was to close immediately. Two hours had elapsed between the title company's initial phone call and when they were satisfied by the 10 acre legal description and the sketch of the two parcels.

Best personal regards,

Tom Barker

Tom Barker

TB/lm

Architecture - Engineering
Materials Testing - Surveying

2237 North Main Street Sheridan, Wyoming 82801 (307)555-1711 Fax: (307)555-5014 cer@link.net Offices in Gillette and Douglas Wyoming

FIGURE 6.17 Complaint Letter

Kendeco Industrial Supply • 6619 Sunridge Drive, St. Cloud, MN 56304 • (320) 555-9872

Kendeco Industrial Supply

February 18, 1998

King Star Computer
9465 Technology Drive
Sunnyvale, CA 55555

Attention: Maria

On January 8, I ordered ten 16 megabyte 72 pin EDO memory modules from King Star Computer. I specifically requested that each SIMM be tested before they were shipped. You promised each SIMM would be tested and shipped by January 9. I received all ten memory modules on January 11, shipped January 8. Eight of the ten SIMMs were DOA. Because the original sealed packaging on all the SIMMs was intact, this tells me the memory was NOT tested as promised.

Although we have since received our full order of working memory modules, our company depends on receiving memory in working order and cannot afford delays associated with reshipping. You are usually very thorough, but this is the second time in the last six months that I have received parts that were DOA. Please take appropriate action to ensure that parts are thoroughly tested and in working order.

I appreciate your concern in this matter.

Sincerely,

Brad Rossiter

Brad Rossiter
System Administrator Assistant

FIGURE 6.18 Complaint Letter

Larry Thompson
2706 6th Avenue S. #106
St. Cloud, MN 56301
January 12, 1997

TCI of Central Minnesota
P. O. Box 118
St. Cloud, MN 56302-1188

Attention: Billing/Service Department

I am a local customer of TCI and subscribe to expanded basic cable. I would like to comment on two recent changes in your local service, as well as to request additional information on these changes. I received my monthly cable bill on January 8, 1997, which contained an increase in my monthly rate from $28.42 to $30.09. You did not provide an explanation for this rate increase in my monthly statement. I would appreciate an explanation as to why this rate increase is necessary.

In addition to the increase in your monthly cable rates, you recently have made changes to your cable channel offerings, changes that took effect on December 30, 1996. You removed several channels from your expanded cable line-up and have replaced them with new offerings. I did receive an advance announcement of these changes on my monthly statement. However, as with the rate increase, you did not provide an explanation for these changes. Two of the channels removed from your expanded basic service are favorites of mine—WGN and E! I would like to know your criteria for making such changes to your cable line-up. Also, why aren't your customers given the chance to participate in this process?

I find your service to be generally quite good. But perhaps your local monopoly on cable television services has lessened the importance you give to customer input. I would appreciate a written response to my concerns.

Thank You,

Larry Thompson

Larry Thompson

FIGURE 6.19 Persuasive Request

18392 Metcalf Road
Sauk Rapid, MN 56379
February 23, 1996

Senator Rod Grams
U.S. Capitol
Washington, D.C. 20503

Dear Senator Grams:

Congratulations on your fine representation in the U.S. Senate. I am writing to you as one of the many who voted for you. You and I also have a common career starting point, as I am also in the broadcast industry. Like you, I have goals in other areas, and I am a full-time, non-traditional college student at St. Cloud State University. Recent budget discussions about funding for student loans is obviously of great concern for students like me, and I hope you share that concern as one who cares about the future of this great country.

I work a full-time, forty-four hour schedule as a talk radio host six days a week, and I carry sixteen credits as a student each quarter. It isn't an easy project, but it is necessary in order to accomplish my goals. In spite of my commitment, it would be impossible without low-interest student loan money available to assist in meeting the spiraling costs of tuition and supplies. My goals as an education major are to be able to make a positive difference in the lives of young people as they lead us into the new century. As a U.S. senator, you are in a position to accomplish that same goal.

Students need an advocate in Washington. These are voting members of the Minnesota population with voting parents. They are trying to better themselves and American society. Today, they need the qualifications and credentials of a college education in order to succeed. Advancing technology and a demanding job market require skilled and talented people, but today's college students face a harsh environment. Financial concerns are a big factor, and more students are having to work longer hours than ever before outside of school in order to meet expenses. Most students simply could not complete their education without the continuation of low-interest Guaranteed Student Loans at a level to keep up with the expenses of higher education. I'm sure you agree that educational opportunities must exist in order for the United States to succeed in an increasingly competitive world market.

Senator Grams, it is vital for the positive future of America that you vote for a continuation of student loan funding, and it is important that you convince your colleagues to do the same. It is the responsibility of today's generation to help ensure the success of tomorrow's. Thank you.

Sincerely,

Tom M. Lucas

Tom M. Lucas

10. Evaluate the letter to Senator Grams in Figure 6.19. First, look at the elements of Tom's argument. What are his claims? His data? His underlying assumptions and principles? And what probable reader reservations is he anticipating? Next, look at the way he frames his argument—in particular, the structure and strategies he uses to attempt to persuade his reader to vote yes on a continuation of student loan funding. Finally, consider how you might respond to Tom's argument were you to write a follow-up letter.
11. Write a complaint, bad news, or negotiations letter that you can actually use for work or as a representative of a campus or community organization. Use the GRACE benchmarks to help you plan, write, and revise your document, and ask your peers for feedback, once you have a fairly polished draft.
12. Pick an emotional or conflicted situation—at work or in a campus or community organization—that calls for a carefully crafted letter in which Rogerian argument is appropriate. Remember that such argument attempts to demonstrate an empathic understanding of the reader's position and to induce a similarly empathic understanding of the writer's position. As you prepare to write, review the discussion of argument, including the tactics for employing Rogerian argument. Think carefully, too, about your goals and readers as well as the specific nature of the argument you want to make. Then, craft a GRACEful letter in response to the emotional, conflicted situation you've selected, convincing a particular reader or readers to take a specific course of action or adopt a certain belief. Once the letter is drafted, review it carefully, being particularly attentive to the effectiveness of your expression. Is the image created the right one for the occasion? Finally, ask your peers to analyze the effectiveness of your letter and to make specific suggestions for improvement.

REFERENCES

Blanchard, K., & Johnson, S. (1982). *The one-minute manager.* New York: Morrow.

Bramson, R. M. (1988). *Coping with difficult people.* New York: Dell.

Crusius, T., & Channell, C. (1997). *The aims of argument: A rhetoric and reader* (2nd ed.). Mountain View, CA: Mayfield.

Fisher, R., & Ury, W. (1992). *Getting to yes: Negotiating agreement without giving in.* New York: Viking.

Fulkerson, R. (1996). *Teaching the argument in writing.* Urbana: National Council of Teachers of English.

Ong, W. J. (1975, January). The writer's audience is always a fiction. *The Publication of the Modern Language Association, 90,* 9–21.

Rapoport, A. (1960). *Fights, games, and debates.* Ann Arbor: University of Michigan Press.

Rogers, C. (1952). Communication: Its blocking and its facilitation. *ETC., A Review of General Semantics, 9,* 83–88.

Toulmin, S. (1958). *The uses of argument.* New York: Cambridge University Press.

Ury, W. (1991). *Getting past no: Negotiating with difficult people.* New York: Bantam.

Winterowd, R. (1989). *The contemporary writer: A practical rhetoric.* (3rd ed.). San Diego: Harcourt Brace.

Young, R. E., Becker, A. L., & Pike, K. L. (1970). *Rhetoric: Discovery and change.* Fort Worth, TX: Harcourt Brace.

Chapter 7

Managing Your Career Search

Huge life-decisions are often made in the whim of a moment. This is, indeed, the way most career choices (and career-changes) are made. No wonder surveys of worker dissatisfaction find that up to 80%, or four out of every five workers, are dissatisfied with some important aspect of their jobs or career. It's not a pretty picture.

The alternative to whim and impulse *is* planning, *and* hard thinking *and* work. *For the lazy, this is not good news. But as we grow older, and hopefully wiser, most of us begin to see the merit of this kind of homework.*

Choices made intelligently, based on the sure knowledge of who we are, almost always turn out to be far superior to choices made by a roll of the dice.

That is why it is so important for you to do your homework, identifying your favorite and strongest skills, and your favorite fields of knowledge, before you choose a career, change a career, or go out to pound the pavement.

—Richard Nelson Bolles

You don't need us to tell you in this book that the writing of your career or job search is some of the most important writing you can do. You already know that, in this situation, you are writing as if your life depended on it—because, in fact, your quality of life and career *do* depend on the writing and managing of your career search. The problem with this knowledge is that it can lead you to some disabling assumptions.

Think back to what we said in Chapter 2 about analyzing any writing situation. Every writing situation has a context. Sending a letter and resume to a prospective employer is an important benchmark event, and the documents are important components in your life and career. But they are only a part of your life and career, one little package in the whole flow of information and events that make up your life. Prospective employers are not going to hire your resume and letter. They're going to hire *you.* And they're going to hire you based on the whole picture and the whole context they can know about you. Prospective employers are interested in how you interact with people, and your letter and resume only hint at this information. Their hiring decision will be based on their direct contact with you and on the testimonials of other witnesses—your references and other people in your network. Prospective employers are interested in the quality of your work and the energy of your commitment to it—again, qualities your resume and letter can only hint at. An employer's hiring decision will be based on more substantial information—most likely testimonials from people in your network; evidence from a portfolio of your work, if you have one; and maybe even direct observation of you at work if you've worked for the employer as an intern or temporary employee.

We've just used the word *network* a couple of times. It's gotten to be a popular word in recent years. In fact, it's even been turned into a verb. You not only *have* a network—comprising people you know, respect, and support and who know, respect, and support you—but you also *build* a network by *networking*. Some people tend to look at this process with a cynical eye, feeling that it's an embodiment of the maxim that "It's not what you know; it's who you know." We think a more appropriate interpretation of networking is the one offered by our friend Rich Murray: "It's not so much what you know *or* who you know; it's who knows what you know!"

We think this is a more realistic perspective on networking and on the career search, in general. Networking is simply what we all do all the time—relate to other people in what we hope are mutually supportive, productive, and meaningful ways. Rather than being a sharp break from what we do normally, then, the career search is simply a more specifically intentional and focused extension of our normal relations. The implications of this fact go in two directions: First, it lets you see the career search as something that is not a radical break from your normal life, to recognize it as simply people relating to people. Second, it underscores the fact that, in some sense, we are always engaged in the career search. With each significant course, with each significant project or professional assignment we complete successfully, we are potentially writing another entry on our resumes and building another link in our personal and professional network. But with each blown assignment, with each thoughtless or unethical act, we can build quite a different network and create a very different unwritten resume, which can follow us and cast an unwanted shadow on our efforts when we do shift into an active, formal job search.

We hope that what we've said up to this point will help reduce the alienation, discomfort, and self-consciousness that almost always come with doing a career search, especially your first one. But we probably cannot eliminate this discomfort altogether. Although Americans are often thought of as brash, the fact is that most of us are really fairly shy and self-conscious. We tend to think our voice sounds funny—even wrong, bad—the first time we hear it recorded. We often don't like pictures of ourselves. And when we listen to the voice in our employment correspondence and picture ourselves represented there and when we listen to ourselves talk during an employment interview, we sometimes almost don't even recognize the person we hear and see, especially if we're not accustomed to reading, writing, and listening to employment rhetoric. All this makes it difficult to judge whether our own resume, employment correspondence, and interviewing are effective representations of ourselves. And this uncertainty adds more stress to an already stressful situation.

The best way we know of reducing this stress is by reducing these areas of uncertainty—both about your own talents and inclinations and about prospective employers and their needs, interests, and characteristics. So, most of this chapter is a series of exercises in writing, exploring, and clarifying your own interests, values, and talents; in researching potential employers; in developing, clarifying, and using your own personal and professional network; and in interviewing a prospective employer.

As you embark on your career search, you'll want to investigate the sorts of positions that are appropriate, given your background and training, and you'll want to explore the types of environments where people in these positions work. You'll probably also find it useful to imagine yourself at work in such environments. And you'll want to find out names and details about the particular companies that offer the sorts of positions in which you see yourself so that you can determine if your background, skills, and values match the needs of the company and the position. This kind of exploration—systematically looking both inward and outward—produces a certain amount of anxiety, especially given the time in which we live.

We live in a time of unprecedented and accelerating change. The technology of the workplace, especially the technology of communication, is changing right before our eyes. Jobs are changing. Organizations—and the ways they relate to their employees, owners, customers, and each other—are changing. We hear a whole new vocabulary describing changed organizational practices: *outsourcing, TQM (total quality management), just-in-time management, downsizing, quality circles, rightsizing,* and so forth. Some of this language—that of quality circles, for example—describes tendencies toward change that is humane and empowering for employees. Some of the other language, though, has a distinctly sinister side—the euphemism *rightsizing,* for example, can mean you and a thousand of your fellow employees just got fired. The language and thought of current management theory and practice very often embody the view that people, or *human resources,* are interchangeable resources, just like computer chips or corn or coal, rather than members of a community or culture that is the organization. In this view, employees are like any other commodity—something to be purchased as cheaply as possible, to have on hand just in time, to be used with maximum efficiency and productivity, and to be removed from inventory as soon as the immediate need has been satisfied. Hence, just-in-time management is coming to mean not only waiting until the last minute to have the nuts and bolts and other subassembly parts on hand, but also waiting until the last minute to have the people who work with them on hand, too. It means getting people off the payroll as soon as their project is completed, through downsizing, rightsizing, or other strategies such as *outsourcing,* where the organization hires contract labor for all kinds of services that were formerly done inhouse, from sweeping the floor to doing public relations.

All these things mean that people's career paths are now much less stable and much less predictable than they were in the past. And these conditions mean that from now on, throughout your career, you will continually need to audit your strengths, values, goals, interests, and career opportunities and keep a finger on the pulse of your organization, industry, profession, and workplace (including government agencies) as a whole.

We are changing, too, and would be even if we weren't being impacted by all these other changes. In other words, life is like any other project we're working on and documenting in some written form: Life's a draft! We are constantly writing, rewriting, and revising. And each time we do, GRACE is a useful framework for measuring the effectiveness of the arguments we are able to make for ourselves. We will begin our discussion of the career search, then, with GRACE and the writing of your career. Next, we will ask you to work through several exercises that can help you assess where you are now and determine your strengths, weaknesses, and interests; consider yourself and your organizational environment; and research careers and organizations using paper and electronic sources as well as informational interviews. Finally, we will consider six things you can do that will help you write all of your employment correspondence.

You may find this chapter difficult going, simply because it raises complex questions about who you are and who you want to become. Keep in mind, though, that we don't expect hurried answers. In fact, you'll probably want to use this chapter as an ongoing resource throughout your career search—maybe even throughout your career. For example, you may want to spend some time doing preliminary work on an exercise, then go off for a while to do a bit of research or think about the concepts the exercise raises, and later come back to do additional work on the exercise. Or you may at a later date want to refer to resources listed in the chapter or reread sections of the text when you're actively involved in a particular employment search task, like an informational interview. Use this chapter, then, like the GRACE benchmarks: as a long-term resource to help manage your career search.

GRACE and the Writing of Your Career

GRACE is iterative: You can recycle her usefully over and over again, and you will see new ways of thinking about and designing not only your writing but your career, as well. Your goals this year may not be your goals a year from now, and this will affect who should be the readers of your life story as presented in your resume and related documents. It will certainly affect the arguments you want to make, and the experience you gain, even in a year, will change the arguments you will be able to make. The changing nature of work and of organizations will radically alter the kinds of warrants by which employers will measure the evidence of people's qualifications and will change the conventions that govern how people work and communicate with each other. Finally, in the middle of all this flux, we will all be shoved and pushed from all kinds of directions. These forces of change will challenge our core values and our sense of who we are, and if we are to maintain our integrity as human beings, we will need to continue to express, for ourselves as well as for others, those essential values that we will not compromise. So, as you move into a career search, it's useful to consider the following questions about your goals in the career search, the readers of your employment correspondence, the arguments they might find convincing, and your personal conventions and expression.

Goals

What are your goals, and are they really right for you? Are you aiming at the right kind of career or job now, given the kind of person you are—your interests, skills, and experience, your personality (including your preferred modes of learning and communicating with others), and your ethical values? If you're just beginning this process of self-examination, you may not be able to answer these questions yet. In fact, rather than think immediately about your goals, you may be more comfortable starting with the questions under Conventions and Expression—questions that ask what kind of person you are and what kind of personal expression you want to make in your career and life. You may also want to work through Exercise 1, Self-Assessment, and Exercise 2, You and the Organizational Environment. Then, you may find it easier to home in on your career goals. At some point, though, you should be able to answer the following questions, preferably in writing so that you make your goals tangible and visible:

- At the end of your career, what would you like to be able to look back at and see that you accomplished for yourself? Your family? The organization(s) where you worked? Your profession? Your community?
- What would you like to be doing five years from now? Ten years from now? Twenty years?
- What would you like to do in your next job? How would this job be a stepping stone toward what you want to achieve five, ten, and twenty years from now?

Readers

Who reads you? To whom do you feel responsible and accountable, both professionally and personally? Who do you want to be your readers, both in your career as a whole and in your immediate job search? Answering these questions and the questions that follow will help you decide where you should be searching for your job. As was true of the questions about your goals, you probably can't answer a lot of these questions immediately. But they're good questions to ask, whether you're asking them of yourself, people who know you, or people you interview for career information:

- What kinds of readers do your goals seem to invite? In other words, what kinds of prospective employers might be interested in someone like you?
- Do you admire people like this? Are you like them? Do you want to become like them?
- Now, as you think about what you'd like to do in your next job, who's in a position to hire you for that job?
- What organizations or kinds of organizations and what people or kinds of people within those organizations hire people like you to do the things you like to do?
- Do you know what they do and how they work? If not, how might you find out?

As you consider potential readers for your employment documents, you might find it useful to map out these readers on an egocentric solar system. We've provided one for you later in this chapter in our discussion of the career network (p. 321).

Arguments

Three broad arguments are always relevant to any career search situation:

1. **I can do.** The first argument, "I can do," aims to convince a prospective employer that you're competent to do the job. This competence has two dimen-

sions: technical competence and interpersonal competence. *Technical competence,* the ability to do technical work or learn to do the work, is just as important as ever, but in most organizations, it's not enough by itself. In the contemporary professional environment, *interpersonal competence,* the ability to work cooperatively and effectively in a team environment, is becoming as vital a qualification as technical competence.

2. **I want to do.** The second argument, "I want to do," aims to convince a prospective employer that you not only want to work but that you want to do the specific kind of work this employer would have you do. In order to make this argument, you need to know with a good deal of specificity what people do when they work for this employer; you also need to know with some real confidence that this is work that you would really enjoy doing. Knowing both things requires some study, research, and thought. And that's what most of this chapter is about.

3. **I will do.** The third argument, "I will do," aims to convince a prospective employer that you are a person of good character—that you can be trusted to deal in good faith with your employer, your colleagues, your customers and clients, and the public at large.

Imagining the Career Search as a Dialogue: The Layers of Argument

At this stage of your career search, it's useful to spend some time thinking about all the levels of your arguments—even though you won't make all of them explicit in the documents you draft or the interviews and other conversations you have as part of your career search. And it's also useful to begin thinking about which layers of your arguments you *will* make explicit in these various situations and documents.

If you think of the career search as a dialogue, you want your readers, your prospective employers, ultimately to say to you, "You're hired!" But in the meantime, throughout the process, you want them to say to themselves, "I believe this person [you] can do the job, wants to do the job, and will do the job." And you need to figure out what you can say and write to them that will make them start saying this to themselves.

The conventions of argument in career search dialogues tend to constrain fairly tightly the way you can construct your arguments. We'll talk about this in considerably more detail in Chapters 8 and 9, when we talk about resumes and letters, but we want you to start to think about these constraints and conventional expectations now. Even making the three basic claims can be problematic, if only for the reason we mentioned at the beginning of this chapter: It's not easy to brag about ourselves, even if it's true.

Aside from modesty, making the claims effectively can still be a challenge. Certainly, making a bare claim without supporting data won't be effective. Prospective employers are justifiably skeptical. They expect to see data—evidence that you can do, want to do, and will do. In fact, people frequently decide *not* to make all three claims explicitly—unless someone asks them point-blank questions: "Do you think you're really qualified to do this job? Are you really interested in this organization and this job? Why? Are you really willing to make the commitments and sacrifices, and will you work as hard as it takes to do a good job in this position?"

While you may decide not to make some of the claims explicitly, you need to remember that your goal throughout the process is to have your readers saying to themselves, "This person can do, wants to do, will do." For example, people often choose not to make any of the three claims explicit in their resumes. But they organize their data—the summary of their education and experience—so that it constructs a picture of a person who can do, wants to do, and will do.

Clearly, the safest element of your argument, and certainly the most important, is the data. Here, again, we see the importance of the exercises we offer in this chapter. It's absolutely vital that you have a clear sense of your own qualifications, goals, values, and interests—and as clear a sense as possible of your readers' goals and values, too.

What about your warrants? In a sense, we've just answered this question. We've just said it's vital to have a clear sense of your own values and your readers' values. But making warrants explicit in the rhetoric of the career search can be risky. For example, it seems condescending, even a bit ludicrous, to begin a job search letter by explaining to prospective employers that they should hire somebody who's honest, competent, and hard working—as if they'd be surprised by this information. So, most of the time, you're probably not going to want to make your warrants explicit in your written employment documents. However, it's pretty common for prospective employers to ask you to talk explicitly about your warrants in an interview situation. For example, questions like these are commonly asked in interviews: "Why do you think this position would be a good career step for you? Why do you think you're a good candidate for this job?" With questions like these, prospective employers are probing to see if your underlying values and aspirations are congruent with the layers of argument that you're making explicit in your employment documents.

Thinking through your potential arguments in this systematic way helps you find gaps that can guide you in your career search and preparation. Do you find that you really can't muster the kind of specific evidence you need to make a convincing case for a "can do" argument? Then you've discovered some useful information. You can set about the process of getting the kind of experience, coursework, or certification you need. Do you find that you have a lot of good experience that serves as evidence of your qualifications but that your reader still isn't impressed, even though you're well contented with your qualifications yourself? Maybe you need to look for other readers. Looking for other readers in this case means looking at alternative career paths, where the kinds of evidence you can offer for your qualifications will be valued and seen as warranting your claim that you are well qualified.

Conventions

How would you characterize your own personal conventions—your own day-to-day habits of thinking and acting? The following three sets of questions will give you a skeletal framework for beginning to analyze your normal, conventional modes of operating and processing the world and other people. And Exercises 2, 3, and 4 will take you into considerably greater depth in this investigation. Ask yourself if these questions:

- What do your conventional and habitual ways of acting and thinking suggest to you about the kinds of environments—physical, emotional, interpersonal, and so on—you would be most comfortable working in?
- What do they suggest about how you could match or perhaps adjust your own conventional ways of thinking and doing to accommodate your work environment if there seems to be a mismatch?
- Who is a good source of advice about identifying your personal conventions, analyzing potential work environments, projecting potential levels of matching or mismatching, and developing strategies for identifying more compatible environments or developing accommodation strategies? Career counselors? Other counselors? Could you schedule an informational interview with someone who does what you think you'd like to do?

Expression

Remember that expression is that part of GRACE that draws your focus inward, to the core ethical values and personality traits that are the essential you. In many communication situations, there are good reasons why you don't want to put these elements on display—maybe they're not relevant for a particular occasion, or maybe it's useful for you to highlight particular aspects of your character and to mute others. But for almost all occasions, it's useful to take at least a glance inward. And for this occasion, a long, thoughtful gaze will be appropriate. Something approaching a kind of Zen meditation wouldn't be out of line here. After all, you're in the process of clarifying what you should do with most of the waking hours of your life for the next several decades. Later in this chapter, Exercise 2 and, to some extent Exercises 1 and 3, will suggest effective means of doing this introspection. The following questions provide a broad framework for getting started:

- Who are you, who are you becoming, and who do you want to become?
- What are your most important, core values?
- Knowing that every career choice demands some compromise and that no career choice gives you everything with no trade-off required, what are you willing to trade (time, family, money, security, emotional and ethical satisfaction, stimulation and novelty and excitement, prestige and social standing, power, etc.), and what do you believe is essential in your career choice? You can explore these issues further by completing Exercise 2.
- Given the short time—however long it is—that you have on this planet, what kind of statement do you want your life to make?
- How can your career choice enable you to make this statement that you feel called to make, either directly through your work or indirectly by enabling you to make it outside your work?

Source: PAVLOV © 1997 Ted Martin. Reprinted with permission of UNIVERSAL PRESS SYNDICATE. All rights reserved.

Career Search Exercises

If you've taken the time to jot down preliminary answers to the GRACE questions posed earlier, you've already begun to assess where you are now and to tentatively map out your career and organizational research. The exercises that follow will enable you to begin exploring yourself and your career options in more detail. But remember, as you work through these exercises, that we don't expect you to finish them in one sitting.

Exercise 1: Self-Assessment

The more time you can spend on the two parts of this self-assessment exercise, the better. In fact, we think you should try to develop the habit of continually monitoring and auditing what you do and assessing what transferable skills this represents. For an initial cut, you might even take just half an hour in class to begin the process using the Strengths, Weaknesses, and Interests Worksheet (Figure 7.1) that follows in Part A; then give yourself several days during which you just remember to be more conscious than usual about what you're doing in your work and to think about what technical abilities or interpersonal skills are represented by what you're doing. Once you've taken a few days to process this information, make an initial pass through

Part B, where we ask you to interpret your experiences in terms of marketable skills. Finally, take the time to reflect on what you've done in your work in the past and to analyze how it fits into the three broad employment arguments we've described under the A in GRACE.

Part A: Experience, Strengths, and Weaknesses Worksheet

Notice that we've set up columns in the worksheet (Figure 7.1) for you to describe things you do now or have done before and to identify and think about both strengths and weaknesses. Thinking about your weaknesses at the same time you're thinking about your strengths has several advantages. First, it's easier to think about your weaknesses in the context of your strengths. You're less likely to panic in thinking about a weakness when you're looking at one or more strengths at the same time. This context also helps you see that many of our weaknesses are actually the flip side of our strengths. For example, if you're an especially bold, outspoken, assertive person, you may not be as good a listener as you'd like to be. On the other hand, if you're a really good listener, there may be times when you'd like to be less reserved and more assertive. If you see a weakness that seems really glaring, analyze it along two different dimensions: (1) Is it relevant to what you want to do? and (2) Is it important to you? And if you think it is both relevant and important, you can begin to analyze how you can strengthen your performance or compensate for this weakness. In fact, this kind of ongoing self-assessment is an important job skill even after you've gotten the job you seek because it's the first step in a lifelong process of learning, growth, and professional development. Finally, this whole process of identifying, assessing, and articulating how you feel about your weaknesses and what you plan to do about them is a good rehearsal for one of the most often asked questions in employment interviews: "Tell us about your strengths and weaknesses."

Part B: Interpreting Your Experiences in Terms of Marketable Skills

The list of skills that appears in Figure 7.2 is derived from a widely used list developed by Paul Breen in 1982 titled "76 Career-Related Liberal Arts Skills." While it was developed specifically for liberal arts students, we have worked with hundreds of people with many different backgrounds and interests who have found it useful in analyzing the kinds of learning or experience they've had. We've sorted the skills into the following eight categories:

1. Communication skills
2. Personal character skills
3. Human relations and interpersonal skills
4. Management and administrative skills
5. Information management skills
6. Critical-thinking skills
7. Creative-thinking skills
8. Career development skills

FIGURE 7.1 Strengths, Weaknesses, and Interests Worksheet

"Can do," "Want to do," "Will do"	Analysis/Interpretation	Ratings		
Things I do now or have done before	**Type of technical skill, relationship skill, ethic, etc.**	**Strength (1–10)**	**Interest (1–10)**	**Relevance (1–10)**
On the Job ■ Specific technical, physical, or financial operations (in detail) ■ Specific interpersonal relations, communications, and responsibilities (in detail) ■ Professional and technical certifications ■ Awards, recognition, and promotions				
In School: Academic and extracurricular activities ■ Specific technical, physical, or financial operations (in detail) ■ Specific interpersonal relations, communications, and responsibilities (in detail) ■ Degrees, majors, and certifications ■ Awards and honors ■ Offices				

In the Community: Volunteer, service, social, political activities ■ Specific technical, physical, or financial operations (in detail) ■ Specific interpersonal relations, communications, and responsibilities (in detail) ■ Awards and honors ■ Offices		
In the Home: Parenting, caretaking, and managing ■ Specific technical, physical, or financial operations (in detail) ■ Specific interpersonal relations, communications, and responsibilities (in detail)		
On My Own: Personal growth, arts, travel, hobbies, and so on ■ Specific technical, physical, or financial operations (in detail) ■ Specific interpersonal relations, communications, and responsibilities (in detail) ■ Awards, honors, and certifications		

FIGURE 7.2 Eight Kinds of Career-Related Skills

1. **Communication Skills**
   - Listen, paraphrase, and respond accurately, fairly, and empathically.
   - Read texts, people, and situations accurately and respond accurately and appropriately, both orally and in writing.
   - Write effectively in different formats and media.
   - Speak effectively to individuals and groups.
   - Express your needs, wants, opinions, feelings, and values without violating the rights of others.
   - Convey a positive self-image to others.

2. **Personal Character Skills**
   - Assess a course of action in terms of the long-range effects on general human welfare.
   - Make decisions that will maximize both individual and collective good.
   - Generate trust and confidence in others.
   - Take appropriate risks.
   - Follow through with a plan or decision.
   - Persist with a project when faced with the possibility of failure.
   - Recognize when a project cannot be carried out or is not worth the time or effort required to complete it.
   - Analyze, critique, and learn from experience, including criticism by others.
   - Accept the consequences of your actions.

3. **Human Relations and Interpersonal Skills**
   - Interact effectively with peers, superiors, and subordinates under different circumstances, including stressful conditions of time and other pressures.
   - Understand the feelings and needs of others.
   - Make and keep appropriate commitments to others.
   - Maintain group cooperation and support.
   - Persuade others to cooperate in a common cause or task.
   - Keep a group on task and moving toward achievement of a common goal.
   - Teach a skill, concept, or principle to others.
   - Reflect upon and understand the behaviors of yourself and others in group situations.

4. **Management and Administrative Skills**
   - Analyze problems and opportunities, assess needs, and identify realistic goals and tasks associated with them.

FIGURE 7.2 Continued

- Identify alternative courses of action and set priorities.
- Identify resources and people who can contribute to the completion of a task.
- Organize people and resources to achieve specific goals.
- Delegate responsibility for completion of a task.
- Motivate and lead people.
- Manage time, money, and other resources effectively, including accommodating multiple demands.

5. Information Management Skills

- Formulate questions that help clarify a particular problem, topic, or issue.
- Identify information sources appropriate to special needs or problems.
- Use a variety of information technologies, media, and sources of information.
- Compile, organize, and synthesize information, using appropriate concepts and principles.
- Evaluate information using appropriate standards of validity, ethicality, relevance, usefulness, effectiveness, and the like.
- Apply information creatively to specific problems or tasks.

6. Critical-Thinking Skills

- Identify quickly and accurately the critical issues when making a decision or solving a problem.
- Reason from specific experiences or data to a general unifying principle that applies to the different cases.
- Identify and define the key parts of a problem.
- Recognize the historical, social, political, and other contexts of a problem.
- Design an experiment, plan, or model that systematically defines a problem.
- Identify and apply reasonable criteria for assessing the value or appropriateness of an action or strategy.
- Reason from general principles, applying them to specific situations appropriately.
- Take given premises and reason to their conclusion.
- Analyze the interrelationships of events and ideas from several perspectives.

7. Creative-Thinking Skills

- Create innovative solutions to complex problems.
- Adapt your concepts and behavior to changing conventions and norms.
- Predict future trends and patterns.
- Appreciate the contributions of art, literature, science, and technology to your personal and professional lives and to society.

(continued)

FIGURE 7.2 Continued

8. Career Development Skills

- Identify, describe, and assess the relative importance of your needs, values, interests, strengths, and weaknesses and develop these into personal growth goals.
- Assess your own characteristics and abilities and relate them to information about job or career opportunities.
- Identify and translate the skills developed in one environment (e.g., school) to the requirements of another environment (e.g., work).
- Build a network of friends, mentors, and others who provide career-building support, advice, and contacts.
- Market yourself to prospective employers.

Source: Based on Breen, 1982.

Using this list, go back through your Strengths, Weaknesses, and Interests Worksheet and identify five key skills that are your significant strengths and that are important to you. List these in the first column on the Key Skills Worksheet, Figure 7.3. In the second column, describe where and how you've best used, developed, and demonstrated each skill. Then, in the third column, specify exactly how it seems to you each skill is relevant to the sort of position you're seeking.

Exercise 2: You and the Organizational Environment

Once you've had a chance to assess yourself—your strengths, weaknesses, and interests as well as your skills—it's time to begin thinking about how your character and conventional ways of acting might fit into particular sorts of working environments. This exercise, which has four parts, is intended to help you find matches between you and specific types of organizational settings. Parts A and B focus primarily on the foundational character elements we have in mind when we're talking about Expression, the E in GRACE. Part C focuses primarily on your habitual styles of learning and communicating, your conventional ways of acting—the C in GRACE. Finally, Part D offers a framework for visualizing the kinds of organizational environments where you could thrive, personally and professionally.

Of course, the different parts of this exercise overlap because there's a lot of common ground between a person's foundational character and style or habitual mode of acting. But we believe you can increase the adaptability of your style without compromising your core principles and values. We also believe that basic survival skills in professional organizations of the twenty-first century will include the ability to adapt your style of learning and communicating to different situations and different people—colleagues, clients, supervisors, and others.

FIGURE 7.3 Key Skills Worksheet

My Key Skills	Where and How I've Demonstrated These Skills	How These Skills Are Relevant to a Position
Key Skill 1:	______________	______________
	______________	______________
	______________	______________
Key Skill 2:	______________	______________
	______________	______________
	______________	______________
Key Skill 3:	______________	______________
	______________	______________
	______________	______________
Key Skill 4:	______________	______________
	______________	______________
	______________	______________
Key Skill 5:	______________	______________
	______________	______________
	______________	______________

So, a major goal of this exercise is to help increase your sense of control and flexibility in the ways you learn and communicate. We aim to do this by increasing your awareness of both your own and other people's styles of learning and communicating. And we also hope the exercise will help you sort out your core values, which cannot be compromised, and distinguish them from other values and, especially, from habits of learning and communicating that really can and should be flexible and responsive to different situations and people.

Just as we suggested with Exercise 1, you may find it helpful to take an initial quick run at Exercise 2 while in the company of others who are also approaching it for the first time. But, again, we recommend that you give yourself some time—several days, at least—for introspection and reflection before you review the exercise again.

Part A: Things I Value Most

Figure 7.4 includes a list of 15 things of value that people probably hope to derive from their work. You would probably agree that everything on this list is good. But we're asking you to rank them from 1–15 according to how significant each is to you, where 1 is the most important and 15, the least important. You probably won't be entirely comfortable putting some good things at the bottom of the list, but remember that you're not saying these things are unimportant—just that they're not as urgent for you at this time as some of the other things on the list.

FIGURE 7.4 Things I Value Most

Thing of Value	Your Ranking (1–15)
Time of my own	________
Money	________
Job security	________
Physical safety	________
Family	________
Location	________
Prestige	________
Spiritual satisfaction	________
Political power	________
Creative expression	________
Novelty, excitement	________
Intellectual challenge	________
Emotional satisfaction	________
Interpersonal solidarity	________
Physical challenge	________

Part B: Qualities I Possess Most Strongly

Figure 7.5 includes a list of 13 personal qualities. Rank them in order from 1 to 13, where 1 is the personal quality that describes you *most* accurately and 13, the quality that describes you *least* accurately. You'll probably have a bit easier time ranking the items in this list than those in the list in Part A.

Part C: Styles of Learning and Communicating

Many, but not all, of the following questions come in pairs that highlight opposing styles of learning and communicating. After the questions, we'll offer a framework for thinking about and interpreting them. Remember that you'll notice some overlap between the aim of these questions and those in Parts A and B. Ask yourself the following:

- Do you prefer working in situations where the primary focus is on the task to be achieved and there's little politicking or concern about people's feelings? Or do you enjoy working with people-based problems, where the decision-making process and people's feelings about it are important?

FIGURE 7.5 Personal Qualities I Possess

Personal Qualities	Your Ranking (1–13)
Consistently on task	________
Creative, imaginative	________
Punctual	________
Thorough	________
Principled, ethical	________
Deliberate, careful	________
Loyal	________
Objective	________
Honest, trustworthy	________
Quick, insightful	________
Clear, logical	________
Bright, intuitive	________
Thoughtful, considerate	________

- Do you enjoy working on or thinking about a lot of different problems or aspects of a problem at once, or do you prefer to work through one problem or one aspect of it at a time, finishing it before you go on?
- Do you like working on problems that call for a stepwise, systematic, logical problem-solving process? Or do you prefer working on problems that call for solutions requiring intuitive, creative leaps of insight?
- Do you enjoy working on problems that require hands-on, digging-in kinds of actions and processes, or do you prefer working on conceptual problems that require thinking in abstract ideas or images?
- If you're trying to figure something out, would you rather read some instructions, listen to an audiotape of instructions, look at an explanatory diagram or other visual picture, or have somebody work through the problem, allowing you to observe?
- Do you like to be able to take as much time as possible to reflect on the whole range of perspectives on a problem or issue? Or do you prefer to cut as quickly as possible to the essential elements of the problem and resolve it efficiently and decisively?

This next set of questions asks you to think about both how you take in and communicate information and ideas. They ask whether you are a words person, a numbers person, an images person, or a people person, and they explore these four orientations in several different dimensions. Ask yourself the following:

- Are you comfortable speaking in most one-on-one situations?
- Do you enjoy the give and take of discussions and meetings?
- Do you enjoy dealing with conflict, helping people resolve differences?
- Do you enjoy persuading others to see your point of view?
- Are you comfortable and confident processing and interpreting financial data, statistical data, engineering data, or other quantitative data?
- Do you enjoy explaining quantitative data to others?
- Are you comfortable and confident using and interpreting visual images, aural (sound) images, or other kinds of images?
- Do you enjoy using images to explain concepts to others?
- Are you comfortable and confident writing in most situations?

In framing these questions, especially for Parts B and C, we've had primarily in mind four popular instruments or tests for measuring people's personality types and learning and communicating styles:

1. **The Learning Styles Inventory (LSI),** based on the research of David Kolb (1984), measures people's learning preferences, determining whether they prefer to encounter their environment by *feeling* the world through concrete experience or by *thinking* about the world through abstract conceptualization. The LSI also determines if people feel more comfortable taking their time to reflect carefully and thoroughly on their observations or if they have a penchant for acting, learning best by experimentation.

2. **The Myers-Briggs Type Indicator (MBTI;** Myers, 1976) measures four different dimensions: *introversion* vs. *extroversion, intuitive* vs. *systematic reasoning, thinking* vs. *feeling,* and *judging* vs. *perceiving.* Scores on the MBTI are reported as a series of four letters that represent a person's preference along each of the four dimensions. For example, someone who scores an INTJ has indicated a tendency toward introversion (I), intuitive thinking (N), a preference for thinking over feeling (T), and a tendency to move quickly to a decision, to make a judgment, rather than continuing to observe or perceive (J).

3. **The "Comm-Style" questionnaire,** designed by Robert Truell (1976) and Associates, tracks people's preferred styles of communicating in situations involving different levels of stress, classifying a person as an *affiliator, analyzer, conceptualizer,* or *activator* in preferred communication style.

4. **Hersey and Blanchard's (1969) questionnaire on leadership styles** measures four different possible orientations to leadership based on orientation to the task at hand (*task orientation*) and orientation to the people with whom one works (*relationship orientation*).

Important warning! Whether you just work through our informal questions in this exercise or take one or more of the formal tests, be careful not to cut off career possibilities by placing yourself in a rigid pigeonhole. (Be careful not to let others pigeonhole you, either.) Occasionally, disturbing reports surface about organizations basing their hiring decisions on prospective employees' scores on one or another of these instruments—in particular, the MBTI. You should know that you are not obligated to tell a prospective employer your MBTI score if you happened to take the Myers-Briggs. In fact, career advisors we know recommend that you ask why you're being asked the question and that you be prepared to discuss how any of several MBTI types, including yours, could be appropriate for the kind of position you're seeking.

The makers of all these test instruments emphasize that they are only measuring preferences, not marking off absolute categories. For example, if the Comm-Styles instrument identifies your preferred communication style as that of an *affiliator,* this doesn't mean you're incapable of thinking analytically (*analyzer*), taking decisive action (*activator*), or thinking abstractly about long-term planning (*conceptualizer*). It just means that you tend to be sensitive to people's feelings when you communicate with them. At the same time, if you score as an *activator* on the Comm-Styles instrument, this doesn't mean you're incapable of thinking or feeling. It just means you have a penchant for taking action, for moving as quickly as possible toward closure on an issue. So these classifications are soft in the sense that no category excludes the possibility of capacities, even strong capacities, in the others. Furthermore, they are only estimates, based on your subjective responses to questions asked on the instruments, and they are therefore subject to error. And while your responses to these questions will tend to be stable (if you score as an *activator* this year, you probably will next year, too), most people who take one of these tests at different times find that their scores do tend to shift somewhat with the changing circumstances of their lives and their work.

If these categories are soft anyway and if there's some risk of this information being misused, why bother even thinking about these issues? While these dimensions of your personal styles of learning, communicating, and interacting with people may be soft, they are nonetheless real, and they are sometimes decisive factors in how well people succeed in their careers. And to a certain extent, your scores on these instruments can give you some early warnings and other useful information in deciding about the kind of career you should pursue. For example, if you score strongly as an ENFP (extroverted/intuitive/feeling/perceiving) on the Myers-Briggs and you're contemplating a career that would require you to work in isolation, analyzing large volumes of detailed numerical data and making judgments based on your analysis, you should know that you're going to be working very much against your personality type. But does this mean you should absolutely exclude this as a career possibility if you had your heart set on it? No. Remember the warning about pigeonholes.

The scores on these instruments can also be helpful once you're on the job, collaborating informally with others or working as a member of a project team. When you're working in a situation that conflicts with your most comfortable style of learn-

Source: © Tribune Media Services, Inc. All Rights Reserved. Reprinted with permission.

ing or relating to others, having done this kind of exercise gives you a vocabulary for thinking about your situation, analyzing the conflict, and developing strategies for compensating. And if you take one of these tests with colleagues, you will have the vocabulary for understanding conflicting styles and for appreciating each other's complementary strengths.

For both your career search and your work on the job, then, we recommend that, if it's convenient, you arrange with a counselor, advisor, or instructor to take one of the tests that have been developed for helping people identify their preferred styles of learning, communicating, and relating to others. In particular, we have found Kolb's Learning Styles Inventory (LSI), the Myers-Briggs Type Indicator (MBTI), the Truell and Associates' Comm-Style instrument, and the Hersey and Blanchard leadership instrument to be helpful. There are others, as well, such as the DISC personality-type instrument, which is popular in many business organizations.

Part D: Visualizing the Work Environment

The final part of Exercise 2 is a process of translating your self-audit into language that describes working environments, professional tasks, and career paths. We invite you now to imagine the kind of working environment, the kind of work, the kind of organization, and the kinds of rewards that you would find satisfying, given your skills, experience, interests, and styles of learning, communicating, and relating to other people and to your work. The following questions should help you start this process, and you'll certainly think of other questions as well as variations on our questions:

- Do you want and expect to be paid a regular salary—"a day's wages for a day's work"—or do you prefer being paid on an incentive system, such as sales commissions, where your compensation is tied to your performance?
- If you have a vision of where you'd like to be and what you'd like to be doing five years from now, ten years from now, and maybe even beyond, what immediate career steps would give you the best opportunity for getting there?
- What kinds of jobs would let you do the things you are really good at and really love doing? You may want to do some informational interviewing (see Exercise 4) to help you answer this and the previous question.
- How important is geographic location for you? Career counselors advise being as flexible as you possibly can on geographic location.
- Visualize the actual physical environment that would be the ideal working environment for you. What would it look like? What would it sound like? What would it smell like and feel like? Is it big, small, quiet, noisy, busy, calm, private, public, light, dark, open, enclosed? What kinds of equipment are you using? Is it high tech or low tech?
- Visualize yourself working in this environment. What kinds of things are you doing? What kinds of people are you working with? What are they doing? How

do you relate to each other? Teammates? Superiors? Subordinates? Complementary departments or functions? and so on.

- Imagine the ideal emotional environment of your work. Are relationships among people an important part of the environment? Do you feel strong friendships, trust, interdependence, or community spirit? Or is the atmosphere one where you just do your job in a good, professional way and relationships are strictly business? Are you and other people emotionally involved in the success or the excellence of the work itself?
- Because no environment is going to be perfect, imagine deviations from these ideal features. How much variation can you live with along each of these dimensions? Which features can you compromise most readily, and which are more important?
- Given your analysis to this point—skills, talents, experience, values, personal styles and preferences, and goals—what kinds of immediate job alternatives would be acceptable? List as many as you can think of.
- Of the immediate job alternatives you've identified, which seem most desirable—most likely to help achieve the intermediate range goals you've identified? Give these alternatives a desirability ranking, beginning with the alternative that seems the most desirable or promising to you.
- Which of these immediate job alternatives seems to be the most feasible, given the apparent match between your qualifications and those required? Again, rank the items in your list.

Now, you have two different lists of priorities that you can use to guide your employment campaign. And with some reasonable luck, some of the most desirable alternatives will also be some of the most feasible alternatives. Make some lists and draft some descriptions of the most important features of a workplace where you would be successful, and describe why you think these features would be important to your success. Describe also how you would adapt to environments that don't meet your ideal. Share these descriptions with some people you trust and respect. Consider sharing them with someone during an information interview, which we will describe in Exercise 4.

Exercise 3: Career Research and Organizational Reconnaissance

Either individually or with a class or other group, make an appointment with a reference librarian at your college library or large public library. Ask to be introduced to the following kinds of reference materials on career-related topics:

- Encyclopedias that describe various professional careers, their employment outlooks, qualifications required, work environments, typical salaries, and so on

- Books and other materials that offer career and job search advice
- Encyclopedic business references—such as *Standard & Poors, Value Line,* and *A. M. Best*—that provide extensive general information about large, publicly owned corporations
- Business references that specialize in information about smaller, publicly owned corporations and even, perhaps, private companies—with a national, regional, or local focus
- Newspaper indexes and indexes of business journals (to identify articles about specific organizations you're interested in)
- Electronic indexes of newspapers, business journals, and other journals—available either online or on CD-ROM
- Business journals
- Vertical files of corporate annual reports, governmental reports, and the like
- Electronic databases of corporate information, such as *Disclosure*
- Indexes of professional, governmental, business, and trade associations and organizations and their publications, membership directories, and so on
- Web databases of job openings such as E-Span (http://www.espan.com) and the Online Career Center (http://www.occ.com), which enable you to search by job title, geographical location, and salary, or services like CareerPath (http://www.careerpath.com), which link to job openings listed in a number of major metropolitan newspapers, including the *Los Angeles Times, New York Times,* and *Washington Post*
- Other career resources on the web, including publications like *Career Magazine* (http://www.careermag.com), *Internet Business Network's* web guide to the job search, and *1st Steps in the Hunt* (http://www.interbiznet.com/hunt), which provide articles about various facets of the job search; services like *Career Planning Process* (http://www.bgsu.edu/offices/careers/process/), which offer resources for self-assessment; or more general employment sites like *CareerNet* (http://www.careers.org/), which include useful links to employers and job hunt resources
- Directories and guides to graduate and professional schools as well as catalogs of specific schools, if this is a career alternative you're considering
- Directories of governmental agencies—federal, state, and local
- Directories of public service organizations and other nonprofit agencies
- Telephone directories, including World Wide Web and microfiche directories nationwide

- The library's own computerized catalog and ancillary search devices, especially its features that allow sophisticated keyword searches, limiting and expanding searches via Boolean logic, capturing abstracts or whole text, and so on
- Web browsers and other search engines that enable you to find organizations' websites and other information archived on the Internet

For your own peace of mind, you need to know as much as possible about an organization's goals and work so that you're confident in making a mental match and imagining yourself in the organization. And this confidence will also help you make your "want to do" argument. Remember that the "want to do" argument is powerful when you can show that you know in some detail what your reader's organization does—what kinds of projects, professional skills, and organizational culture are represented—and when you can then explain how your own professional skills, experience, interests, and personal character match with those of the organization. There are certainly organizations where you *won't* want to work when you know more about them. It's better to find this out now, in the library, than six months from now, after you and the organization have made major financial and emotional investments in each other.

Exercise 4: Informational Interviews

In this exercise, we invite you to identify at least one person who does the kind of work you believe you'd like to do and arrange an interview. This interviewing process is becoming an increasingly important part of the process of career exploration. Probably the best book on informational interviews—and one of the best books on career planning and job searching, in general—is Richard Bolles' (1998) *What Color Is Your Parachute?** Bolles sees the informational interview as the key element in a job search campaign, and he gives extensive advice about identifying interviewees, planning the interview, following up, and making sure that each informational interview creates productive leads for subsequent interviews.

If you're not extensively experienced in your prospective career area, you need to talk with someone who can give you a real-time, up-to-the-minute perspective on career requirements, trends, prospects, and especially risks and opportunities that may be on the horizon in the kind of work you're investigating. It's important to be able to test your impressions of a career choice against the reality of someone's current experience in it. And as the time approaches for you to focus your resume, write application letters, and go on job interviews, your credibility as a job candidate will be hugely enhanced by the specific, current professional insights you can gain from having done several informational interviews. Furthermore, the more informational interviews you do, the more people you have working in your prospective profession who know you and are able speak about you to others.

*Bolles has published new annual editions of this book for years. We recommend consulting a recent edition.

Thinking about a Good Person to Interview

Start here by thinking about your egocentric solar system and the process we described in Chapter 1. Is there someone in your immediate circle of friends, relatives, colleagues, professors, or clients, who does what you're interested in doing? This kind of direct connection, if you have it, is best. Next best is an indirect connection: a friend of a friend, a parent of a friend (POF), or a friend of a parent (FOP). Having some kind of personal contact, some person in common, is a powerful element in a person's agreeing to give an informational interview. If you don't have a personal link, maybe you can use an institutional link—memberships in the same professional organization or connections to the same university, for instance. In fact, the career services offices on some campuses keep files of alumni who have agreed to give informational interviews to students from their alma mater.

If you don't have either a personal or institutional link, then you'll have to make a cold call. But even here, you can improve your chances of getting an interview and having a productive interview by doing your homework. Here is where the kind of research we describe in Exercise 3 will come in handy. You may even need to supplement your paper- and computer-based research with a judicious telephone call or two to make sure you're connecting to the right person.

Following Etiquette in Scheduling and Holding Interviews

Be sure that you follow the conventions in scheduling and holding your informational interviews:

- When you make the request to meet, we recommend avoiding use of the words *information interview* or *informational interview.* Rather, describe specifically the kinds of information you're seeking and the kinds of questions you'll be asking. Along with this description, tell enough about yourself to make clear that you have bona fide reasons for asking for the interview—your relevant education and experience, for example. This is also a point where you should mention any link you have to this person—the person you know in common, for example.
- When people agree to give interviews like this, they're taking a risk. One risk is that you'll waste their time by turning out not to be really interested or qualified for what they do. Another risk is that you'll use the request for an informational interview as a smokescreen to get in the door and then campaign for a job offer. In your requests, you need to assure your prospective interviewees that you won't subject them to this risk. Do this by asking each person for a specific, limited amount of time (15 minutes is reasonable) and, again, by demonstrating your specific interests, qualifications, and intentions for the interview.
- When you get to the interview, make sure you honor the promises you made or implied in your request. In particular, don't turn the interview into a request for a job and observe the time carefully so that you don't overstay the time you indicated—unless your interviewee specifically invites you to stay longer after you have offered to leave.

- Certainly, you'll want to follow the normal conventions of courtesy, including the strong convention that people should be well prepared with relevant questions when they ask someone to share their time and expertise in an interview.

Thinking about What You Want to Find Out

Your preparation for an informational interview includes the sort of research we've already asked you to do in the previous exercises. In fact, after completing your self-assessment, your matching analysis, and your career research and organizational reconnaissance, you'll probably have a good sense of what you want to find out about the kind of work your interview subject does. But remember that this informational interview is your opportunity to tap into the perspective of someone who's already doing the sort of work you might want to do, so maximize the time you spend together by laying the groundwork for your discussion. If you haven't investigated the company at which your interviewee works or found out anything about his or her type of position as part of Exercise 3, do some preliminary background work. You'll be able to ask better questions, get better information, and make a more enthusiastic ally if you're already knowledgeable about some of your interviewee's work or the company's work.

You'll also want to prepare a list of questions to ask during the interview. You'll probably want to find out details about the interviewee's present job, the background and qualifications needed in the position, and career prospects in that field. And you'll want to glean any advice the interviewee has about useful contacts and career preparation. The following sorts of questions are typical in informational interviews, but you should modify this list according to your own circumstances, background, and interests and based on your research and self-assessment. Don't plan to ask *all* these questions, and don't use them as a mechanical checklist.

Details about the Interviewee's Present Job

- How would you describe a typical day or week in your job?
- What skills are essential in this position?
- What are the most important duties or functions of the job?
- What are the most difficult or challenging aspects of the job?
- What are the most rewarding elements of the job?
- What demands, if any, does your work place on you outside the ordinary work week?
- How much flexibility do you have in terms of dress, work schedule, vacation, and location on your job?

Background and Qualifications Needed in the Position

Think about using some of your analysis from Exercise 2 as the basis for specially tailored questions here. For example, suppose you've concluded (based on Exercise 2) that you're a reflective person who likes to take the time to consider all sides to an issue. You might ask, "How comfortable would the pace of your work be for someone who tends to try to figure out the different aspects of the picture before making a decision?" Other more generic questions people often ask about the background and qualifications needed in the position include these:

- What credential, degrees, or licenses, are required?
- What kind of past experience is expected, and how does one go about getting this experience?
- If you were to hire someone for this position, what factors would be the most important—academic preparation, work experience, personality, specific skills, or knowledge of your organization—and why?
- How would you describe the people who usually do well in this career field?

Career Contacts and Prospects in the Field

- Who actually hires people for this kind of job, and where are these companies located?
- How do people generally find out about these jobs—through advertising, professional journals, professional associations, and the like?
- What's a typical salary range for someone with my background, and how much do salaries vary by employer, region, and industry?
- What kinds of nonsalary benefits are typical of this kind of work—job security, health benefits, sick leave, vacation, retirement plans, work abroad, or day care?
- How would you describe the career prospects in this field? How far can a person go in this career field, and what does the career track look like?
- How does one advance in this field?
- How rapidly is the career field growing and in what areas or industries?
- Where will the jobs be in five to ten years?
- If your work here were suddenly eliminated, could you pursue good career-related opportunities elsewhere?

Advice about Useful Contacts and Career Preparation

- How well suited is my background for this kind of work?
- What do I need to do to become more marketable in this career field? If you were in my situation, what would you do?
- Who else do you think I should talk to, and may I have your permission to tell them how I got their name?

Again, remember what we said about honoring your promise to limit the time of the interview. You'll need to watch the clock and select your questions carefully to make sure you stay within the time you've promised. Of all these questions, this last set is perhaps the most important, so be sure you don't get caught without the chance to ask them. Actually, they are also nice questions to bring the interview to a sense of closure, too, so they are useful in two ways.

Six Things You Can Do to Manage Your Career Search

The GRACEful management of your career search really consists of remembering and doing just six things. We offer them here as a summary.

FIRST: **Don't demand too much of your resume and other employment documents. Remember that they don't get you hired by themselves.**

We've said that the *writing* of your career search is the *doing* of your career search. Our maxim tends to work in reverse, too: The *doing* of your life and career are the *writing* of your life and career. With each course you take and with each significant job assignment you complete, you are writing your resume. People will read you and decide whether to hire you based only in part on the dossier you give them. They will be looking for confirmation of the inferences they draw from your dossier, and they will use a variety of ways to validate and amplify their initial impression. They will be using the network of people they know and trust and who know you and can give them recommendations about you. If people in their own network don't know you, they will try people in your network that you tell them about. And they will be using their direct contact with you—interviews, internships, previous employment with them, for example.

The crucial point to remember here is that your employment dossier almost certainly will not and cannot, by itself, get you a job. This takes some of the pressure off you when you are drafting your resumes, application letters, and any other career-related documents. However, it also means that you should give continual attention to how you write your career in fact—to building a record of achievement and a network of credible witnesses to that achievement.

SECOND: **Develop and use your network of friends, colleagues, advisors, and others to help you evaluate your career and career-related documents and identify and evaluate prospective readers of these documents.**

Most of the job search literature affirms the importance of developing and using a network to find and land a job. The importance of networking in the career search cannot, we believe, be overstated: You can network to gather information about career options, available positions, and specific organizations, and you can network for feedback on your career options and employment materials.

Start thinking about your own network using the egocentric solar system we talked about in Chapter 1. We've reproduced a copy of this solar system in Figure 7.6, which you can use to map out your network as it exists now and as it grows and develops throughout your job search. Start now by jotting down names of people on the concentric circles of the solar system. Ask yourself these questions:

- Who among your family, friends, classmates, and co-workers might be particularly good sources of information or feedback—about you, about possible careers or jobs, about businesses?

FIGURE 7.6 Using the Egocentric Solar System to Map Out Your Career Network

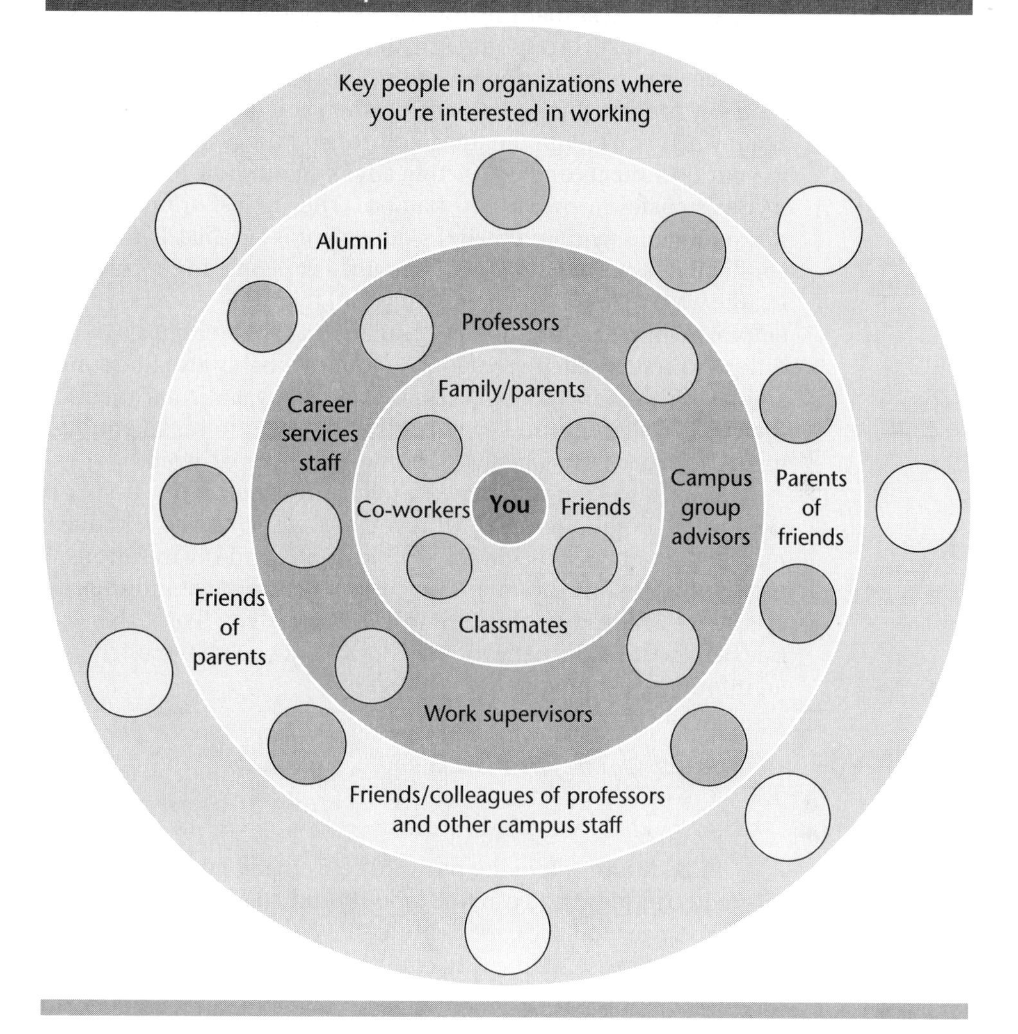

- Whom among work supervisors, career services staff, advisors of campus groups, or professors should you talk to?
- Which parents of friends, friends of parents, colleagues of professors, and other campus staff might be good resources?
- Do you know or can you find the names of alumni of your university who would be willing to provide information or feedback?
- What organizations or sorts of organizations might you be interested in considering as potential employers? And what key people in these organizations might you contact?

As you progress through your job search, you should continue to add to this career network.

You'll want as many reality checks as possible on your resumes, letters of application, and other correspondence; in other words, you'll want feedback on whether the image you're projecting in your job correspondence is appropriate and effective. Probably the first thing you'll notice when you talk to the second person—and then again when you talk to the third, fourth, and the rest—will be conflicting responses to your documents and conflicting advice about how to write them. Don't let these inconsistencies throw you off balance. They're just another demonstration of our maxim that no writing strategy or document is risk free. Rather than be distressed by conflicting responses, analyze them and ask people to explain why they're responding the ways they are. You'll probably find that people are assuming slightly different employment scenarios, different readers, and different goals in their reading. In addition to these conflicting responses, you'll probably also find some common themes among the responses of your various readers. Pay particular attention to these because they will likely point to key strengths and weaknesses in your employment documents and to key strategies you should either use or avoid.

You'll also want your network to help you identify the best career choices for you right now—both in terms of who you are and what you're trained to do—and find information about specific sorts of positions and organizations. You can certainly gather much of this information and response through informal conversation; however, as we've already mentioned in this chapter, you'll probably want to select at least one person from this network who does what you're interested in doing and arrange an informational interview.

THIRD: Do a systematic self-audit to reduce the uncertainty about your own strengths, values, and goals.

In addition to looking outward to as many good sources of information, advice, and critique as you can find, you should do some careful, systematic looking inward. You need to have confidence in the core of who you are and who you want to become. Otherwise, all the rich, conflicting advice and opportunities will simply confuse you, pulling you in several directions at once. Much of this chapter, including the overview of GRACE as a tool for career exploration, provides a series of exercises for doing this kind of audit—beginning with the process of looking inward. Exercise 1 invited you to identify and analyze your strengths and weaknesses, and Exercise 2 offered a series of tasks for exploring your core values and personal styles and matching them with work environments and professional actions. Again, we recommend that you supplement GRACE and these exercises with some good career counseling, perhaps taking one of the tests to explore your preferred learning style, communication style, or personality type. We also encourage you to keep firmly in mind what you know about yourself as you gather information through print and electronic resources as well as informational interviews because your sense of who you are should help determine where you look and what you look for.

FOURTH: **Make the important investment in researching your readers' organizations so that you can be confident that the company and position are compatible with who you are and what you value.**

Exercise 3 is designed to help you become more familiar with the resources available—paper and electronic—for doing effective reconnaissance on prospective employers, and Exercise 4 takes you through an informational interview process. Both processes require a real commitment of time and effort, but it's a wise investment. You'll feel better—more confident, more knowledgeable—in communicating with prospective employers. You'll ask better questions, and you'll anticipate their questions better. And both you and they will be able to make better informed decisions about how good a match you'd be for each other.

FIFTH: **Use what you know about yourself, the organization, and the position to tailor your job correspondence and your job search strategy, in general.**

Writing one letter and one resume that you send to all potential employers is risky business. If you use a generic resume and application letter, you will run the risk of boring your readers, who are all too familiar with canned presentations. You will also miss the opportunity to speak to the specific needs of your individual readers' organizations. On the other hand, you can minimize your risks and maximize your job opportunities if you use what you know about yourself, the organization to which you're applying, and the specific position you seek to tailor all of your job application materials. When you customize each cover letter and resume for the particular reader, you can show that your background, skills, and values match the needs of the company and the position. And when you customize other job correspondence—even thank-yous for informational or job interviews—you show readers that you've truly listened and responded to what they've said. (We will talk more about adapting employment rhetoric to specific readers when we discuss resumes in Chapter 8 and cover letters and other employment correspondence in Chapter 9.)

SIXTH: **Keep the faith.**

Remember that the career search, like any other project, is a draft. If you've done the five steps we've just summarized and haven't gotten the job you wanted, don't give up on the process—or yourself. Review what you've done, what you've said, and what you've written. Review what other people have said and written to you. Analyze the process. Think about what you've done well. Think about what you'd like to improve or learn more about. Consult with a career counselor if you feel you need help assessing what's happened up to this point. Think about doing more informational interviews—to help you further assess your strengths, interests, and values; to get more reality checks on assumptions you're making about the match between you and potential employers; and to get more leads on where to look next. Then, start working on the second draft of this project—and preparing for the opportunity to work on the third draft and beyond.

Finally, remember your network: not just your professional career-related network but your network of family and friends, too. Remember that your career search and your career are just one part of the web of your life. Keeping this perspective is an important part of the GRACEful management of your career search—and your career. Don't forget to nurture all these relationships and to let them nurture you, too, especially if you find yourself struggling in your career search.

WRITING CHECKLIST

The following guidelines will help you to manage your career search. Doing so involves self-assessment and career and organizational research. (For guidelines relevant to the writing of your career—resumes and employment letters—see the Writing Checklists for Chapters 8 and 9.) For any of these guidelines, remember the superordinate guideline: Disregard *any* of this advice if it would cause you to do something that's inappropriate or silly for your situation.

Self-Assessment

- Reduce the uncertainty and stress of the career search through systematic research into your own interests and values.
- Since prospective employers expect to see evidence that you "can do," "want to do," and "will do," think about your potential arguments systematically to help find gaps in your career search and preparation.
- Audit your strengths, weaknesses, and interests.
- Figure out what technical abilities and interpersonal skills you're using in your work.
- Interpret your experiences in terms of marketable skills.
- Rehearse for interviews by considering your weaknesses and articulating what you plan to do about them.
- Identify your key skills and why they're important to you, record when and how you've demonstrated each, and clarify how each is relevant to the sort of position you're seeking.
- Begin to find matches between you—your character and conventional ways of acting—and specific types of work settings.
- Take into account what you value, the qualities you possess most strongly, and your styles of learning and communicating.
- Take advantage of instruments for measuring learning and communication styles to gain useful information for making career decisions.
- Determine the working environment, the kind of work and organization, and the particular rewards you'd find satisfying.

☑ Career and Organizational Research

- Reduce the uncertainty and stress of the career search through systematic research into the needs, interests, and characteristics of prospective employers.
- Find out as much as possible about the organization's goals and work so that you can discover and then explain how your skills, experience, interests, and character match those of the organization.
- Explore paper and electronic resources on careers and organizations.
- Interview people who do the sort of work you'd like to do; someone already in the job can inform you about career requirements, trends, and prospects and enable you to test your impressions of a position with the day-to-day reality.
- Be clear about why you're asking for an interview, what link you have to this person, and how long you plan to meet.
- When you meet for the interview, keep your promises not to turn the interview into a request for a job and not to overstay the time you requested.
- Complete your self-assessment, career search, and organizational reconnaissance before the interview so you have a good sense of what you want to find out about the job.
- Prepare a list of questions for the interview concerning the person's job, background and qualifications needed, career prospects, useful contacts, and career preparation.
- Follow etiquette in scheduling and holding informational interviews, including thank-you letters as follow-ups to the meetings.

REFERENCES

Bolles, R. N. (1998). *The 1998 what color is your parachute? A practical manual for job-hunters & career-changers.* Berkeley, CA: Ten Speed Press.

Breen, P. (1982). *76 career-related liberal arts skills.* San Francisco: The Learning Center.

Hersey, P., & Blanchard, K. H. (1969). *Management of organizational behavior: Utilizing human resources.* Englewood Cliffs, NJ: Prentice-Hall.

Kolb, D. A. (1984). *Experiential learning: Experience as the source of learning and development.* Englewood Cliffs, NJ: Prentice-Hall.

Myers, I. B. (1976). *Myers-Briggs type indicator.* Palo Alto, CA: Consulting Psychologists Press.

Truell, R. (1976). *Comm-style.* Williamsville, NY: George Truell Associates.

Chapter 8

The Resume: Making the Most of Your Life

The resume is an argument, not a chronicle.

—Robert P. Inkster and Judith M. Kilborn

Resumes—and the ways people read, write, and use them—have changed a lot in the recent past. Most people who are now middle aged can remember when, as they were entering their careers, the standard resume was simply a chronological listing of jobs they had held plus a summary of personal information about them: height, weight, age, health, marital status, gender, and the like. This kind of resume is still common in many parts of the world, but in the United States, an employer's reaction to this kind of resume would probably be powerfully negative, no matter how impressive the credentials it documented.

Most people who are now, like us, in middle age probably also remember sending out two or three dozen resumes—maybe even two or three hundred—in the shotgun-style job search that was common practice when we were seeking entry-level positions. Standard practice was that we made one generic resume—the kind of chronicle we have just described—and we sent it to the personnel office of every organization that looked like even a remotely plausible employment prospect. And with that resume, we sent a generic letter that argued we could do what we thought we could do for a generic employer. For young job seekers who had clearly specialized talents and educations—say, someone finishing a degree in mechanical engineering or accounting—this generic letter and resume had a kind of automatic, natural vocational focus; there was also a kind of automatically defined audience that the resume and letter addressed. But the typical liberal arts major, or even someone receiving a degree like an M.B.A., might send out literally hundreds of resumes.

By and large, this shotgun practice has stopped although computer technology has brought it back, to some extent, in the form of the electronic resume, which can be broadcast over the Internet via electronic resume services. Career counselors are now virtually unanimous in advising job seekers to limit the number of resumes they send out and to focus the presentation of their credentials in a way that highlights specific skills and interests along with specific types of positions and responsibilities that they desire and for which they are specifically qualified. Today, most job seekers identify a specific type of job in a particular organization or small number of organizations. They then evaluate all the information they can discover about the culture of each organization: the economic and political environment in which it operates and the personal and organizational networks that link it to people and organizations they know. Next, based on this knowledge and thoughtful evaluation, they launch a strategic campaign aimed at the target. In this job search strategy, the resume is now recognized as a rhetorical document with a persuasive goal that is aimed at a particular audience or set of readers. The economic, legal, and cultural contexts have changed, and as a result, the strategies of the job search have changed. As a part of that change, the rhetoric of the job search—the resume and other texts, both written and oral—has also changed. For the resume, this change can be summarized in the following maxim:

The resume is an argument, not a chronicle.

As we cross from the twentieth to the twenty-first century in American culture, we have to recognize that the resume is not simply an objective, statistical, chronological summary. Rather, it asserts a set of values: *your* values. It puts forth certain arguments about you. And, in fact, resumes have always and everywhere served this value-laden, persuasive function although it has often been muted. Your challenge, at this point, is defining this persuasive function, clarifying the values you want to assert, and identifying the people you want to assert them to. We propose that you do this with GRACE.

Developing Your Resume with GRACE

Goals

Our focus in this chapter is on using your resume in your job search, but you may have uses for your resume in a wide variety of situations and contexts. For example, if your resume is being used as part of an appendix to the personnel section of a project proposal, your goal will be narrowly defined and subordinated to the larger goal of the proposal it is attached to. (We'll talk about such other uses of resumes in Chapter 12.)

An interesting thing often happens when people think about their goals for writing a resume in the context of a job search: They often go too far and set too ambitious a goal for their resume. When we first introduced GRACE, we noted that writers in organizational contexts often don't go far enough when they think about their goals. They express their goal only as a text-based goal, saying something like "I need to write a thank-you letter to Rich Murray"; then they stop without considering whether they have reader-based and action-based goals. What do they want Rich Murray to do, think, or feel as a result of receiving their thank-you letter? What action or decision do they want to occur? With resumes, though, people often set their sights too high. Ask yourself why you want to write a resume. Did you answer "To get a job"? Most people will say so, and that response can cause you real trouble as you go about writing the resume. In fact, it can raise your anxiety so high that you can't even get the resume written. So, this is not a good goal. Instead, you need to identify a goal or set of goals that will help you write an effective resume.

The goal of the job search resume is *not* to get you a job. It's to get you on the "short list." You want the reader of the resume to flag you as an interesting person whose name should be put on the short list of folks who will be invited for an interview or asked to provide further information about themselves and their qualifications and experience. Furthermore, your resume doesn't have to get you on every interview list. You only need it to get you on one or more of the interview lists you're really interested in. And don't forget your overall goal in the job search itself: It's not to get a job; it's to get the right job—a job you will love and do well and find fulfilling. In all your communication with a prospective employer, the process of assessing and evaluating should go both ways. Both you and the employer need to be convinced this is the right connection.

So, the goal of the resume really isn't to get you a job. It's to open a conversation with an organization that's interesting to you by convincing them you're a person they should be interested in. And the goal of that conversation is to reach a point where both parties—you and the prospective employer—are convinced you're good for each other. Rarely have people been hired into permanent, entry-level positions based only on their resumes. So, that little one-page resume doesn't have to make the whole case as to why you should be hired. In fact, if you try to force it to make that case, you may strain it to the breaking point and do yourself a disservice in the process.

Readers

There is a fairly vigorous debate over where job candidates should send their resumes. Generally, personnel or human resources officers tend to advise sending resumes to their offices. Most career counselors we know, though, advise sending your resume to someone in the organization who is in charge of the kinds of projects you would like to work on. Based on our own experience and research and our use of GRACE, we tend to agree with the career counselors. Here's why.

Imagine that you are responsible for processing new employment queries in the human resources office in a Fortune 500 company. How many letters and resumes do you get in a day? Reports indicate that you may receive well over 100 letters and resumes daily during peak periods. In other words, you are processing about 1,000 resumes every week. Now imagine what kinds of questions you probably ask yourself as you start to read a stack of resumes. Are you reading with the goal of finding a good candidate to invite for an interview, or are you reading with the goal of eliminating as many as possible of these 1,000 or so resumes? Probably, you're looking for any reasonable excuse to stop reading the resume you're looking at and put it in the "reject" pile.

On the other hand, imagine that you are responsible for some particular part of the company's operations and receive a resume and letter addressed to you. How many employment queries like this do you receive in a week? Probably far fewer than 1,000. Are you are just as busy and hurried as the person in the human resources office? Yes, you probably are, but you're probably asking yourself a different set of questions as you read. You're probably looking for anything in the resume that suggests this person can help you solve the problems and complete the projects you're working on. So, you're likely to be reading this resume in a way that's radically different from the way the person in human resources would read it.

In fact, we know someone—a recent graduate of a mid-sized midwestern university—who sent two employment queries to a Fortune 100 company: one to the human resources office and one, based on careful research, to a project manager in the technical area where she believed she was qualified. She got two replies from the company on the same day. One was a letter from the human resources office, advising her that nothing was available at that time. The other was a telephone call from the project manager, asking her to come for an interview. She interviewed, accepted a job offer, and is still happily employed there.

Does all this mean you shouldn't send a resume to the personnel or human resources office? Not at all. In the first place, there is no fixed rule for who your readers should be. They will change with the situation, the organization, and your employment goals. And no matter who you decide your primary reader is, the personnel office can still be a secondary reader.

In summary, then, remember two crucial points when you begin to think about your readers:

1. You have some control over who your readers are—not just the organizations you write to but the people within the organizations. Exercise this control thoughtfully to your advantage, identifying readers who will understand and appreciate the arguments you make in your resume.
2. You need to visualize your readers realistically, which probably means visualizing people who are busy, distracted, and perhaps skeptical and even resistant in approaching your resume. This readerly orientation will help you develop more effective arguments and make smart decisions about how you will manipulate the conventions of resume writing.

Arguments

Prospective employers are making a major commitment and risking a lot if they hire you as a new employee. They will invest extensive time, money, and educational resources in you, especially in the early part of your employment. They will trust you with expensive equipment, perhaps large sums of money, perhaps delicate customer and client relationships, and other employees' and clients' well-being. If you are careless with equipment, money, or information, they risk losing valuable assets. If you are careless in your personal management of tasks and time, they risk missing crucial deadlines and alienating or even injuring clients and other employees. If you are an obnoxious or thoughtless co-worker, the morale and effectiveness of their other employees will suffer. Given all this, it's not likely that the bare-bones claims that summarize the basic career search argument will be sufficient to convince prospective employers you're a person they should be interested in. They are going to be looking with great interest—and a critical eye—for convincing evidence that you "can do," "want to do," and "will do."

Remember, from Chapter 7, that these are the three basic arguments in the rhetoric of the career search. The first argument, "can do," is based on your technical ability and interpersonal competence. Here, you argue, "I am qualified to do the job (or have the background and ability to learn to do the job), and I have the social skills and personality to work effectively and cooperatively as a member of the organization and smaller teams within it."

People who hire employees, engage consultants or vendors, select candidates for graduate schools, or do any other kind of high-stakes selecting of people know that the most reliable predictor of what you will do in the future is what you have done in a similar situation in the past. So, while the resume is an argument and not just a chronicle, some of the most powerful resume arguments take the shape of chronicles. Rather than emphasize the claim "I can do," they emphasize the data: "I did."

Figure 8.1 shows an excerpt from Jill Sicora's resume. As a double major in computer science and mathematics with a high grade-point average, Jill knew she had a strong "can do" argument for her technical ability that was clearly visible in her description of her education and her experience. But she was concerned that the same evidence that documented her technical abilities also might be read as evidence that she lacked interpersonal skills. With this in mind, Jill took special care to emphasize her "soft skills": communication skills, teamwork skills, and dependability under pressure of deadlines. In her descriptions of her three significant employment experiences, she first described the technical side of her work. Then she closed her descriptions with the following phrases:

> Gained confidence in my technical abilities and excelled in a team environment. *(Summer job as a software engineer)*
>
> Worked as a dependable team member in a deadline-oriented atmosphere. *(Summer job as a secretary in a management consulting group)*
>
> Improved phone communication skills through frequent telephone contact with brokerage clients. *(Job as a stockbroker's assistant)*

The second argument, "want to do," is based on your interest and commitment to doing this particular job. Here, you argue, "I have a thoughtful, informed, sincere interest in the kind of work your organization does and, especially, the specific kinds of things you would need me to do." You can make the "want to do" argument most directly and generally most effectively in your letter, where you can talk specifically about the organization you're writing to, but you have some chances to make the argument in the resume, too. For example, if your work history shows a progressive development in skills and experience, moving you consistently toward the kind of position you're now seeking, that pattern is a strong argument that you've been committed to this goal for some time—as long as the pattern goes back.

The career objective is the one place in the resume where you can make the "want to do" argument directly. Look at Mary Vigil's objective, for example:

> An LPN position in a health care setting with challenging opportunities as I continue with my education toward a B.S. degree in nursing at the University of Colorado

FIGURE 8.1 Sample Resume Using "Can Do" Argument

JILL R. SICORA

12741 Florida Avenue S.
St. Louis Park, MN 55426
(320) 555-1755

CAREER OBJECTIVE

Entry-level position in computer science which utilizes my skills in computer programming and my interest in working with people

EDUCATION

St. Cloud State University St. Cloud, MN
B.S. Computer Science (nationally accredited) and B. A. Mathematics, May 1998
Grade Point Average: 3.75 (on a 4.0 scale)

Computer Languages: C, Pascal, LISP, VAX-11 Assembly
Computer Operating Systems: UNIX, VMS
Computer Hardware: Sun workstations, Macintosh, VAX

Foreign Languages: 3 years Spanish

WORK EXPERIENCE

May 1997– Sept. 1997
3-M St. Paul, MN
Title: Software Engineer
Job Summary: Worked in the Software and Electronics Resource Center. Developed software involving image processing and graphics on the Macintosh II. Gained confidence in my technical abilities and excelled in a team environment.

Mar. 1996– Sept. 1996
Touche Ross & Co. Minneapolis, MN
Title: Secretary
Job Summary: Worked in Management Consulting division. Used Macintosh extensively to prepare graphics and text in client reports and presentations for Touche Ross executives. Worked as a dependable team member in a deadline-oriented atmosphere.

Sept. 1995– Mar. 1996
Hayne, Miller, and Swearingen, Inc. Minneapolis, MN
Title: Stockbroker's Assistant
Job Summary: Used Macintosh to create and maintain client/stock spreadsheets, corporate stock reports, and business letters. Improved phone communication skills through frequent telephone contact with brokerage clients.

AWARDS AND INTERESTS

- Publicity officer of Association for Computing Machinery
- Recipient of St. Cloud State University Math and Computer Science Scholarship
- Flautist in St. Cloud Municipal Band
- Valedictorian of 1992 Milaca High School graduating class

REFERENCES

Furnished on request

And if you can complement this kind of career objective statement with an employment history that traces a clearly focused pattern consistent with the objective, then the resonance between the two makes a powerful "want to do" argument. In fact, Mary's resume in Figure 8.2 is an example of this resonance.

The third argument, "will do," is based on your character. Here, you argue, "I have the ethical character to work honestly, cooperatively, and effectively as a team member in your organization. I will deal in good faith with people both inside and outside your organization."

Of all the arguments, the character argument is the most difficult to make. In fact, it is almost impossible to make the argument about your character directly because of the strong American cultural convention about immodest boasting. You can present evidence of character, to some extent. For example, you may be able to point out that you have been hired back repeatedly for summer employment by the same organization after each schoolyear. Or you may be able to point out that you have been repeatedly asked back as a consultant by several clients. You may be able to point to service awards, citizenship awards, elected positions of trust in various organizations, and other indicators that people find you reliable and trustworthy. For example, in Figure 8.3, Margaret Ann Minton is able to show a progression of increasingly responsible positions over the several years of her employment at Fingerhut Corporation. More subtle aspects of character, however, must be demonstrated through the way you present yourself in the resume. This makes the expression of your character—through both the content of your arguments and the ways you employ the conventions of the resume—a crucial element of your resume development.

As you look over the sample resumes, try to imagine the personalities and characters of the various people standing behind them. An especially distinctive resume, we believe, is that of Dan Thompson, shown in Figure 8.4. Note, in particular, his extensive, repeated use of specific numbers in describing his past performance. Notice also his objective: "Management responsibility involving product research, development, and marketing." Does Dan's apparent habit of thinking and communicating in rich, specific, quantitative detail seem a useful characteristic for someone interested in marketing and sales management?

Many career service professionals advise that the most effective resume is what is often called the *analytical resume.* In terms of format, it can follow any of the conventions we'll talk about in the next section. The analytical resume has a unique purpose, however, in that it's based on your careful, thorough analysis of a specific target company. It's a product of the kind of matching process we encouraged you to start with the exercises in Chapter 7. First, you analyze the needs of your prospective employer and the job qualifications required. You might ask all the following questions as a start:

- What are the required tasks?
- What specific technical skills are required?
- What initial training and education are required?
- What are the organizational or managerial responsibilities?
- What is the nature of working relationships?

FIGURE 8.2 Sample Resume Using "Want to Do" Argument

MARY VIGIL
801 7th Street South, Apt. 304
Trinidad, CO 81082
(303) 555-8260

PROFESSIONAL OBJECTIVE

An LPN position in a health care setting with challenging opportunities as I continue with my education toward a B.S. degree in nursing at the University of Colorado

WORK EXPERIENCE

LPN; St. Luke's Hospital, Trinidad, CO; December 1994–present

- Hold position in Home Care Department
- Care for pediatric clients with various disorders
- Have cared for respirator-dependent child with a tracheostomy and gastrostomy
- Perform physical therapy, teaching, and sensory stimulation programs with the clients

LPN; Southern Colorado Homecare, Walsenburg, CO; November 1993–October 1994

- Performed in-home care for elderly man with Parkinson's disease
- Provided care for tracheostomy, gastrostomy, and urinary catheter
- Administered IV medications
- Performed physical therapy with client

LPN; Reservist for 114th Combat Support Hospital; October 1991–present

- Awarded Expert Field Medical Badge in Summer 1995
- Promoted to Sergeant in June 1994
- Worked in various Army medical facilities
- Obtained training in IV insertions and blood drawing

EDUCATION

University of Southern Colorado

Core courses for the University of Colorado's Nursing Program
Liberal Arts Electives
Overall GPA 3.9/4.0

Laramie County Community College

Practical Nursing Program
Graduated in June 1993 with GPA of 3.2/4.0
Licensed in October 1993

REFERENCES AVAILABLE UPON REQUEST

FIGURE 8.3 Sample Resume Using "Will Do" Argument

MARGARET ANN MINTON
1236 9th Street North
Sartell, MN 56377
(320) 555-8495

OBJECTIVE

An internship in researching, developing, and administering social policies and programs within an urban setting

EDUCATION

Bachelor of Arts—Local and Urban Affairs with minor in Speech Communication
St. Cloud State University, St. Cloud, MN—May 1998

EXPERIENCE

Fingerhut Corporation, St. Cloud, MN (1990–present)

Training Supervisor

- developed training program for 200 employees for Data Entry Department
- worked with large groups and one-to-one
- efficiently prioritized workload
- delegated tasks and responsibilities

Assistant Supervisor

- gave direct feedback to 35 employees; worked closely with 65 others
- monitored work flow of department
- handled confidential information
- performed well under the pressure of constant deadlines

Data Entry Trainer

- coached employees individually to meet department standards
- presented new work positively to the department
- assisted supervisory staff with employee evaluations

Data Entry Operator

- met quality and production standards
- adapted to changing work volumes and hours

BACKGROUND

- financed college education 100% by working 25–40 hours/week while attending classes
- serve as area solicitor for Fingerhut's United Way campaign
- enjoy the outdoors and sports activities; spending time with children and youth

REFERENCES AVAILABLE UPON REQUEST

FIGURE 8.4 Sample Resume Using Quantitative Detail

DANIEL THOMPSON
445 Slater Road
Eagan, MN 55122
(612) 555-0723

OBJECTIVE

Management responsibility involving product research, development, and marketing

EXPERIENCE

Salesman—Tenneco Automotive, Inc. (NAPA Mufflers & Shocks Division), Lincolnshire, IL, January 1989 to present

- Perform technical sales to over 75 NAPA jobbers in Minnesota, North Dakota, South Dakota, and Wisconsin territory with 40% travel
- Coordinate sales programs and product information from Tenneco Automotive to NAPA Distribution Center to NAPA jobbers to retail and wholesale customers
- Accomplished 35% sales increase in a declining market (exhaust)
- Developed marketing program that resulted in 15% sales increase in truck market (shocks)
- Earned top warehouse sales (dollars and percent increase) in Midwest Division

Salesman—Echlin, Inc. (NAPA United Brake Parts Division), McHenry, IL, August 1982 to December 1988

- Performed technical sales to over 125 NAPA jobbers in Minnesota, North Dakota, and Montana territory with 75% travel
- Worked with inside jobbers and outside salespeople regarding product knowledge, new products, market trends, national sales programs, and sales skills training
- Held technical seminars on technological changes for professional technicians
- Earned Rookie of the Year (1983), Ring of Recognition (1986), and Factory Rep of the Year (1988)

Recruiter—Career Centers, Inc., Minneapolis, MN, January 1981 to July 1982

- Located positions for salespeople seeking employment changes and recruited candidates for companies to fit specific job openings
- Averaged 50 telemarketing sales calls/day and interviewed 3–4 candidates/day
- Became second leading producer of seven in company

Salesman/Installer—B & K Auto Trim, Inc., St. Paul, MN, March 1977 to January 1981

- Established sales route entirely from cold calls and sold and serviced these accounts weekly
- Averaged 10 sales calls/day
- Traveled 60,000 miles/year
- Increased sales volume in territory from $0 to over $100,000 annually

Assistant Manager—Perkins Cake & Steak, Inc., Minneapolis, MN, August 1976 to March 1977

- Scheduled employees and provided menu and food preparation knowledge
- Interviewed, hired, and trained new employees
- Supervised 74 employees

Salesman—W. O. W. Life Insurance Society, Omaha, NE, July 1975 to July 1976

- Made cold calls, prospected, kept records, and performed service work
- Developed new territory for company

EDUCATION

B.S.—English Literature with Writing Minor, 1990, St. Cloud State University, St. Cloud, MN

REFERENCES available upon request

These questions clearly suggest the kind of research project we proposed in Chapter 7. You may well want to return to the exercises and suggested resources there for assistance in analyzing your prospective employer's needs and the requirements of the position. Next, having analyzed the features your prospective employer requires, analyze again your own features—your experience, education, and personal qualifications. And state your own experience and qualifications in terms of your specific reader's needs. We will talk more about ways of doing this later, when we consider conventions for organizing work experience.

Conventions

Overall Content and Organization

When prospective employers read resumes, they expect to see certain sorts of information. First, they expect to see standard identifying data: your name, address(es), and phone number(s) so they know whose credentials they're reviewing. Next, many prospective employers anticipate a statement about the position being sought—the career or employment objective—which we'll talk about in more detail later. Then, after being oriented in this way, readers are ready to survey the particulars about your education and work history as well as details about campus and community activities in which you've participated—in other words, the evidence that you *can do* what you say you *want to do* in your statement of objective.

For those who will soon graduate or have just graduated from college, this information conventionally follows this order:

1. Education
2. Work experience
3. Activities and honors

The reason for this conventional order is no mystery. Since readers review resumes very quickly, the most important information should be presented first and the less important information later. For soon-to-be or recent college graduates, the most compelling evidence is ordinarily educational background. Yet if your work experience or activities and honors are unusually strong and will set you off from other soon-to-be or recent college graduates, you can change this conventional order so that you lead with your strongest credentials. For example, Thomas Fong's resume (see Figure 8.5) reverses the conventional organization for the resume of a graduating college student. Looking at Thomas' resume, what would you say are the risks and benefits of breaking the convention as he does?

As you move farther away from your formal education and develop a longer and stronger work history, the work experience section of your resume will move closer to the top and the education section will move closer to the bottom. This tendency is illustrated by the pair of resumes by Andrew McKenzie in Figures 8.6 and 8.7—one written when he was looking for his first position in computer programming and another written eight years later as he was seeking a project leader position.

FIGURE 8.5 Sample Resume with Unconventional Organization

Thomas Fong

Employment Objective

To obtain an internship in the computer science field

Professional Experience

May 1996–present, ***Kendeco Industrial Supply,*** *St. Cloud, MN*
System Administrator Assistant

- Assist and back up the System Administrator with all day-to-day network and server operations. Our servers run UNIX SVR4 2.4, Ntrigue 3.0, and Linux.
- Program database and CGI applications in C and Java.

May–August 1994 and 1995, ***WinApps,*** *Edina, MN*
Computer Programmer

- 1995: Worked independently to create small interfaces for larger database programs. Visual Basic 3.0 was used exclusively for all projects.
- 1994: Worked in a team to design and implement a telecommunications project using Paradox 5.0's Object Pal language.

January 1995–July 1995, ***North Hennepin Community College,*** *Brooklyn Park, MN*
Computer Services Technician

- Assisted the network administrator in various projects for different departments.
- Introduced the idea of installing a Linux WWW server for the college and installed the CERN WWW server software on a Slackware Linux server.

December 1992–December 1995, ***North Hennepin Community College,*** *Brooklyn Park, MN*
Computer Services Technician

- Assisted students with projects using Dbase, Paradox, Access, Lotus 1-2-3, Word, WordPerfect, Minitab, Intel Assembly Language, Turbo Pascal, Turbo C, and Web browsing and searching.

Education

1995–1997, ***St. Cloud State University,*** *St. Cloud MN*

- Accepted into the CSAB Accredited Computer Science program.
- Completed courses in C, Pascal, Ada, Data Structures, File Processing, Computer Architecture, Systems Programming, and advanced mathematics and physics.
- Will graduate Spring 1998.

1992–1995, ***North Hennepin Community College,*** *Brooklyn Park, MN*

- Associate in Arts Degree, June 1995

fong@eeyore.stcloudstate.edu 619 Michigan Ave. S. E. #306 St. Cloud, MN 56304 (320) 555-1333

FIGURE 8.6 Sample Resume Seeking First Position

Andrew McKenzie
747 Crystal Lane #702
Mount Prospect, Illinois 60056
(312) 555-6276

OBJECTIVE

To secure a position as an Applications Programmer

EDUCATIONAL BACKGROUND

DePaul University; Chicago, Illinois
Computer Career Program (CCP), April 1989

CCP is an accelerated postgraduate program designed for individuals seeking to make a career change into the computer field, or those wishing to enhance their current job skills through an intensive computer education. The program emphasizes structured coding techniques, structured analysis and design, editing and validating data and full documentation procedures.

Curriculum:

- Advanced COBOL
- JCL
- OS/MVS
- VSAM/ISAM
- Easytrieve
- Command level CICS
- IBM Utilities
- TSO/ISPF
- System Design and Analysis

Hardware:
IBM 4381, VAX 11/780, and IBM PC

Group System Project:

- Acted as Project Leader for a team of five people
- Analyzed, designed and implemented an on-line and batch payroll system
- Created structured specifications, documentation and user manuals

University of Illinois; Chicago, Illinois
Bachelor of Arts, Psychology and Criminal Justice, 1985

FIGURE 8.6 Continued

Andrew McKenzie
page 2

ADDITIONAL COMPUTER-RELATED SKILLS

Micro-computer Experience

- Lotus 1-2-3
- WordPerfect 5.0
- Appleworks
- MS-DOS
- dBase III Plus
- ProComm
- KERMIT file transfer
- Prodos

EMPLOYMENT HISTORY

Cavity Masters, Inc.
Franklin Park, Illinois
June, 1976 to Present

Assistant Shop Manager for this tool and die company. Responsibilities included the following: Schedule and coordinate job production; supervise and train personnel; determine job quotations for inquiries; and provide support and assistance in defining customer needs. Promoted from **Machinist** to this position in 1986.

Terri-Laine Enterprises
Bensenville, Illinois
Spring and Fall Semesters, 1984

Responsibilities at this part-time position included the following: Mounted and matted artwork, assembled custom frames, and manufactured custom frame moldings.

Budget Rent-A-Car
Elmhurst, Illinois
Fall Semester 1983

Responsibilities at this part-time position included the following: Prepared and serviced automobiles for rental, delivered cars to customers and transported customers from hotels and airports to company locations.

* * * * * * *

REFERENCES AVAILABLE UPON REQUEST

FIGURE 8.7 Sample Resume Seeking Midcareer Position

Andrew McKenzie
11284 Park Plain
Des Plaines, IL 60175
(847) 555-8998

Technical Skills:

COBOL	COBOL2	CICS	IMS DB
VSAM	DB2	JCL	OS/MVS
TSO/ISPF	Easytrieve	TELON	Intertest
Expediter	File-Aid	Smartest	Panvalet
Librarian	OS/400 CL	Visual Basic	

Experience:

March, 1996–Present—***Project Leader*** for Transamerica Commercial Finance Corporation.

- Analyzed and designed a distributed Client/Server application (Pyramid On-Line) to provide TCFC dealer customers access to their account data through a Windows based PC application.
- Evaluated Client/Server development tools to be used in the Pyramid On-Line project.
- Designed application and system architecture for the Pyramid On-Line project.

June, 1995–March, 1996—***Project Manager*** for United Stationers Supply Co.

- Associated Stationers merged with United Stationers in March 1995. The ACS/ASI application development team was acquired from ACS in order to support the ASI systems during the merger.
- Transferred to the Order Entry and Inventory Management area as Project Manager. Responsible for all development and support activities.
- Managed the design and implementation of enhancements to the ASI system to support the USSCO product code format on the ASI system by October 1, 1995.
- Supervised merger activities for application data conversions, and location conversions/shutdowns.

June, 1994–June, 1995—***Project Manager*** for Affiliated Computer Services (ACS).

- Managed the Financial systems area, as well as all mainframe Purchasing and AS/400 based Inventory Management systems.
- Conducted interviews for new hires and contractors.
- Arranged technical training for application development staff.
- Prepared and conducted employee performance reviews.
- Managed multiple projects outside of the Financial area, including numerous Order Entry and Inventory Management projects.
- Managed the implementation of an AS/400 EDI system and an automated PC FAX system for outbound purchase orders.
- Analyzed and eliminated unreliable and functionally obsolete assembler CICS navigation components.

October, 1993–June, 1994—***Project Leader*** for Affiliated Computer Services (ACS).

- Transferred to the Inventory Management team as a Project Leader.
- Established operational and disaster recovery procedures for the AS/400.
- Researched and evaluated third party software products to enable "lights out" operation of the AS/400.
- Eliminated mainframe Purchasing system, and redesigned and implemented major changes to the mainframe Inventory Management system.

FIGURE 8.7 Continued

August, 1992–October, 1993—***Senior Programmer Analyst*** for Affiliated Computer Services (ACS).
- Joined this Dallas based outsourcer as part of the ASI/ACS outsourcing contract.
- Supervised the Financial systems area on all development and support activities.
- Conducted technical and general interviews for new hire candidates.
- Supervised the startup of 2 new locations, and the conversion of inventory related data from Lynn-Edwards, a company acquired by ASI.
- Implemented E3TRIM system, an AS/400 based Inventory Management and Purchasing package.
- Designed and implemented custom interfaces between the mainframe inventory and item systems and the AS/400 E3TRIM system.
- Coordinated network requirements for AS/400 terminal traffic and data transmissions.

January, 1992–August, 1992—***Senior Programmer Analyst*** for Boise Cascade Office Products.
- Boise Cascade sold the wholesale side of their business, which became Associated Stationers (ASI) in January of 1992.
- Supervised the design and implementation of a project to run both companies on one system, with separate financial statements, customer statements, customer rebate payments and vendor payments.
- Managed the migration of the ASI Financial applications to ACS, a Dallas based outsourcer.
- Coordinated all technical problems between the Chicago application development team and the Dallas technical support team throughout the migration.

August, 1990–January, 1992—***Programmer Specialist*** for Boise Cascade Office Products.
- Designed and implemented enhancements to custom A/R system.
- Designed a custom on-line system to interface with D&B Accounts Payable package, including extended invoice history inquiry and on-line check reconciliation systems.
- Prepared materials for user training on A/R and A/P systems, and conducted user training sessions.
- Provided ongoing support of Financial systems.

June, 1989–August, 1990—***Programmer Analyst*** for Boise Cascade Office Products.
- Implemented an IMS/CICS based Accounts Receivable and Credit Collections system as part of a major system wide re-engineering project.
- Coded and tested on-line cash application screens and automated batch cash application processes.
- Planned and executed system test plans for 50 on-line screens and 150 batch job cycles.
- Created both technical and user documentation for the A/R and Credit systems.

Education:

DePaul University; Chicago, Illinois
Computer Career Program (CCP); April, 1989

University of Illinois; Chicago, Illinois
Bachelor of Arts, Psychology and Criminal Justice, 1985

Additional Computer Experience:

MS-DOS	MS-Windows	MS-Excel
MS-Word	MS-Access	MS-Project
Delphi	BASIC	Pascal

References available upon request

The following sections describe conventions for each category of information normally included in a resume, following the most frequently used order for recent college graduates. Keep in mind, though, that you should break any of these conventions if doing so is appropriate, given your employment goals and readers.

Presenting Identification Information

An identification section is normally the first part of a resume. It should include your name, address(es), and phone number(s). Your name should be visually emphasized in some way so readers can find it easily. For example, people often highlight their names with larger or bolder type, solid capital letters, or underlining. And typically, the name is set off by vertical and horizontal white space. If you're living at your permanent home and going to school, your name, address, and phone number will probably be set up as one block of information. However, if your hometown is in one place and you're working temporarily or going to school in another, include both addresses and phone numbers in two separate blocks of information.

Although this is the only identification information readers require, recently people have started to add other information to this section of their resumes. For instance, if you have an e-mail account, you might want to include your e-mail address so readers can contact you via the Internet. Or if you have your own homepage and it provides additional information or demonstrates skills that support the sorts of arguments you're making about yourself, include the URL (the uniform resource locator, or web address) so that your readers can visit your website. If you have a FAX number, you should include it, too.

Career or Employment Objectives

A career or employment objective often comes second in the resume, after the identification section. Should you state your career or employment objective? The convention here will vary, depending on your situation. If you are actively seeking a job, then most career counselors advise having an objective statement; most recruiters and human resources people report that they expect to see an objective statement, as well. Again, expectations can vary among fields, and the convention in some career areas (broadcast journalism, for instance) is to omit a statement of objective in the resume. So, if you're unsure of the current convention for the field in which you're seeking a position, check with professionals in that field.

One nice thing about the convention of including a career or employment objective in your resume is that it forces you to think about what you want: the particular type of position or positions you'll seek, the skills or functions you wish to perform, and the size or location of companies to which you'll apply. You'll also find that a natural part of refining your career objective is thinking about your strengths—the skills and abilities you have and the functions you've performed in jobs or activities—and where and how you'd like to put them to work. And once you've developed your objective, it will help you focus the rest of your resume information.

Other benefits of the convention of stating an objective are that it explicitly invites a direct claim under the "want to do" argument and also permits you to make a "can do" argument in summarizing your qualifications as they relate to your career objective. And the way you state the objective can even make an indirect assertion about your character by implying altruistic or other idealistic motives. The following example may be a bit inflated, for purposes of this illustration, but it shows what we mean:

> **Objective:** Entry-level occupational counseling position with a health services organization requiring excellent writing skills and the ability to relate empathetically with senior clients

As you develop your career or employment objective, keep in mind the following conventions:

- Career or employment objectives should be clear, concise statements that focus on prospective employer's needs. Including "I"-centered or obvious statements—such as "where I can learn" or "which will enable me to advance"—simply emphasizes what's already evident since prospective employers naturally assume that you'll want to learn and advance on the job. Thoughtlessly pointing out the obvious in this way, then, not only pads your objective; it also starts off your resume with a "gimme" attitude and emphasizes not what you can offer but what you expect to gain. Consider, for example, the difference between the following two objectives:

  Professional Objective
  A summer internship in the public relations field that could develop into a full-time position as a public relations specialist beginning this fall

  Professional Objective
  A summer internship in the public relations field using my background in desktop publishing and experience designing documents for the World Wide Web

  The first objective is clearly "I"-centered, and the second focuses on the prospective employer's needs.

- Career or employment objectives should be partial, rather than complete, sentences: complete sentences, inevitably starting with "I" since you're the actor, would simply sound "I"-centered.

- Your career or employment objective should be as concrete as you can make it. Specify the position you'd like and perhaps the general atmosphere or geographical location you'd prefer, as the following example illustrates:

  Employment Objective
  A position as Economic Development Specialist with the Akron Area Economic Development Partnership

- Once you've decided on the format you'll use to present your experience (which we will describe later in this chapter), you might want to coordinate your objective with that format. For example, if you're using a functional format to present your background, you'll probably want to emphasize in your objective functions you'd like to perform in the position you're seeking. The following is an example of a functional objective:

  Professional Objective
  A position in production supervision or in the support areas of manufacturing with emphasis on materials or quality control

  Or if you're using a skills format to present your experience, you might want to introduce in your objective key skills you can bring to the position. The following objective introduces key skills:

  Employment Objective
  A field engineering position with a construction company that requires skills in cost controlling, planning, scheduling, and estimating

  If you're seeking a part-time or summer job or looking for an internship, your objective should mention this so readers don't assume you're looking for a full-time, permanent position. For instance, the following objective appeared in the resume of an applicant for a summer internship:

  Job Objective
  A summer internship in financial accounting with a large public accounting firm

  What if you are currently employed—especially if you're happily employed—and not currently seeking other employment? Then, it doesn't make sense to have a statement about your career objective in your resume. But you can still make a direct "can do" argument through a brief summary of your qualifications and experience. In fact, you can use a statement of qualifications and experience in addition to your statement of career objective if you feel it's appropriate. Here's an example:

  Summary of Qualifications: Six years' experience in project management with increasing scope of financial and technical responsibility. Eight years' experience in metallurgical process design and modeling. Overseas experience in Chile, Australia, and Turkey. Fluent in Spanish.

  Including a summary of qualifications and experience makes a lot of sense if your resume is part of a formal proposal or if you're simply updating your resume. Such summaries provide a nice way of assessing where you are in your career.

Presenting Your Education

If you're just finishing your degree, the education section of your resume will be crucial—especially if you're making the argument that based on your experience, you are qualified to do the job or have the education and ability to learn to do the job. At minimum, most recruiters and human resource people expect to find in this section the degree(s) you received, your major(s) and minor(s), the month(s) and year(s) you graduated, and the location(s) and name(s) of the school(s) you attended. If you attended more than one school after you graduated from high school, most readers will expect you to include all of them in reverse chronological order, as the following examples illustrate:

EDUCATION

Northwestern University, Evanston, IL, Bachelor of Science, May 1998
Major: Marketing Minor: Economics GPA: 3.2 (4.00)

Marketing Coursework
Marketing Channels, Consumer Behavior, Marketing Management, Marketing Research, International Marketing, and Transportation Management

Parkland Community College, Decatur, IL, Associates Degree, June 1996

Education

Master of Science in Educational Administration, May 1998
Washington State University, Pullman, WA
GPA: 3.95/4.00
Master's Thesis: "Designing Multicultural Curricula for Secondary Classrooms"

Bachelor of Science in Social Work, June 1996
Colorado State University, Fort Collins, CO

Yet if you're going to convince prospective employers that you've got the educational background they're looking for, the education section of your resume should include much more:

- If you've earned a second major, include that, too. Having completed double majors shows that you're organized and industrious enough to fulfill the requirements for two different programs and that you've thought carefully about the skills needed for particular positions. The student whose educational background is presented below, for instance, knew the high premium placed on writing skills in the very competitive journalism job market and chose her double major accordingly:

Education

Bachelor of Science in Mass Communications
News Editorial Sequence, May 1998
Sacramento State University, Sacramento, CA

(continued)

Significant Coursework: Advanced news writing and reporting, advanced editing and makeup, visual communication, photojournalism, mass media law and print job production workshop

Bachelor of Arts in English
Writing Emphasis, May 1998
Sacramento State University, Sacramento, CA

Significant Coursework: Theories of persuasion and rhetoric in writing, business writing, advanced expository writing and numerous literature and poetry courses

Having double majors can also show long-term interest in a particular type of position combining both backgrounds.

- Should you mention your grade-point average (GPA)? Part of the answer to this question has to do with where you are in your career. If you are currently in school or have recently graduated and are just beginning your career, then your GPA is relevant. But if you are five years past earning your degree and have established a solid basis for a professional career, your GPA is far less relevant as evidence of your qualifications.

  Another part of the answer to this question lies in the sort of position you're applying for and the expectations of your readers. For instance, if your readers expect applicants to demonstrate accuracy and attention to detail, having a high GPA may be essential, especially if the competition is heavy—as in major accounting firms, for example. On the other hand, if you're applying for a nontechnical sales position where interpersonal communication is the primary skill being sought, your readers might even wonder about a high GPA.

  A final point to remember is that you're not required to volunteer information on the resume that might be viewed as negative. One rule of thumb is that a GPA of 3.0 or above is usually worth mentioning on the resume.

- If you've earned special certifications relevant to the position you're seeking, include them in the education section of your resume as the following examples illustrate:

EDUCATION

University of Illinois, Champaign, IL
B.A. in English and B.S. Minor in Information Media
School Librarian/Audiovisual Coordinator Licensure
Summa Cum Laude, May 1998
GPA: Major and Minor 4.0; Overall 3.97

EDUCATION

University of Wisconsin, Madison, WI
B.S. in Marketing, May 1998
Management Minor

University of Minnesota Extension, Minneapolis, MN
Certificate of Forestry Management, July 1996

Minneapolis Technical Institute, Minneapolis, MN
Diploma in Word Processing, June 1995

- If you've taken classes that will set you off from other applicants with the same degree(s), list them. But be sure to include only advanced coursework, listing it from most to least important (given the job you're seeking) and grouping class titles from the same areas. Here's an example:

Education

University of West Virginia, Morgantown, VA
Bachelor of Science in Supervision Technology, August 1998

Supervision Courses:
Supervisory Management, Personnel Management, Motion and Time Studies, Occupational Safety and Health, Worker Motivation, Employee Training and Development, Managerial Development, Organizational Communication

You can even make this list easier for readers to process by categorizing and naming groups of courses, as this sample shows:

Education
St. Cloud State University, St. Cloud, MN—AACSB Accredited
Degree: Bachelor of Science in Marketing, May 1998

Marketing Courses:
Marketing Channels, Consumer Behavior, Marketing Management, Marketing Research, International Marketing, and Transportation Management

Economics Courses:
Microeconomics, Macroeconomics, Business Cycles and Forecasting, Money and Banking, and History of Economic Thought

- If you've taken seminars or workshops or completed special projects that correspond closely with your employment objective, you might want to include them. Remember that hands-on experience, whether in the classroom or the workplace, demonstrates that you understand class concepts well enough to apply them. The following examples show this:

EDUCATION

Purdue University, West Lafayette, Indiana
Major: Building Construction and Contracting
Bachelor of Science, May 1998

Significant Courses
Plans and Specifications, Bidding, Field Operations, Surveying, Occupational Safety and Health, Scheduling, Structural Systems, Temporary Structures, Mechanical and Electrical Systems, Soils and Foundations, Construction Supervision

(continued)

Relevant Projects
- Analyzed field operations of earthwork at construction site of Caterpillar Manufacturing Plant in Lafayette, Indiana
- Performed field ratings on the construction site of the Purdue Athletic Facility in West Lafayette, Indiana

TEACHER PREPARATION

Partners in Alternative Teacher Education (PATE): A pilot program in District 742, emphasizing experimental learning and involving area teachers, university faculty, and education majors

Phase I: Nine weeks of classroom observations and seminars
Phase II: Ten weeks of student teaching
Phase III: Debriefing

Pre-Student Teaching Experience: One week of workshops on Effective Elements of Instruction and Madeline Hunter Lesson Design at Kimball High School, Kimball, MN, prior to 1997–1998 schoolyear

Independent Study: Tutoring Practicum, Writing Center Materials and Research

Significant Major and Minor Courses: Research Writing, Creative Writing, Advanced Expository Writing, Business Writing, References and Bibliography, Selection and Evaluation of Media, Microcomputers, Photography

- Finally, given the highly technical and global nature of today's workplace, consider including computer skills, any foreign languages you speak, and long-term overseas experiences, such as study abroad programs. Here are several examples:

Facility with Software Word for Windows
MSWord
WordPerfect
DBase
Filemaker Pro
QuarkXPress

Foreign Language Ability
Bilingual in English and Spanish; Fluent in French

Overseas Experience
Study Abroad Program, Costa Rica, Fall and Winter, 1998
Study Abroad Program, Toulouse, France, Summer 1997
Extensive travel in France, Spain, and Italy

Remember that the information you provide in the education section of your resume depends upon the specific argument you're making as well as where you are in your career. Much of the information we've just presented assumes that you are just finishing your degree and are making the argument that, based on your education, you are qualified to do the job or have the education and ability to learn to do the job. But keep in mind that as you move further and further away from your formal education, the education section of your resume will be less and less important and therefore will be presented with decreasing amounts of detail.

Organizing Work Experience

What general resume style should you use: chronological, functional, skills, or some creative variation?

Chronological Resumes. The chronological resume, most frequently used in the past, is the most conservative style. In general, it organizes work experience according to time, beginning with the most recent job and working backward to the least recent job. For instance, one section of a chronological resume might look like this:

Professional Experience

Engineering Co-op, Bell Helicopter Textron, Fort Worth, Texas

Summer 1998, **Rotor Dynamics Group**
- Used flight dynamics simulation computer programs such as DNAWO6 (Myklestad), C81, and DNAWO1/O2
- Evaluated rotors, rotor-fuselage combinations, and test stands using data from simulation programs

Summer 1997, **Research Design Group**
- Drafted rotor parts for research and flight test programs
- Designed simple parts, such as tail rotor balance fixtures

Summer 1996, **Materials and Methods Lab**
- Tested composite specimens to verify materials specifications
- Fabricated composite structures for research programs

Chronological resumes tend to be overused, though. We've already said that the resume is an argument, not a chronicle, and it's often hard to marshal an argument if you're tied to a chronological organization; it's also very easy to get carried away with chronicling your job experience and include irrelevant detail. Nevertheless, a chronological resume is especially appropriate under the following conditions:

- You're applying for a position with a conservative firm or a government agency.
- Your work history isn't spotty, with embarrassing holes you need to explain. (A chronological organization will emphasize any gaps in your work history.)
- Your most recent job or jobs are similar to the position you're applying for.
- You have a strong, continuing work history—with progressively more responsible positions—related directly to the career direction you're pursuing.

In fact, the sort of argument that seems most natural for a chronological resume is the "want to do" argument since you can design a chronological resume to demonstrate long-term interest and commitment to a field through increasingly more responsible positions related directly to the position you seek. Making the "will do" character argument might be natural, too, if you've been rehired by the same company summer after summer and have received more responsibility each year.

If you decide to use a chronological resume, think about how to use formatting effectively. Since dates tend to dominate chronological resumes, an original layout that downplays dates and highlights significant aspects of your work history is sometimes difficult to design. Remember that dates won't sell your skills; you need the visual elements of your resume to support the argument you're making. See Jill Sicora's resume in Figure 8.1, Andrew McKenzie's resumes in Figures 8.6 and 8.7, and Gregory B. Kittilson's resume in Figure 8.8 for full examples of chronological presentations.

Functional Resumes. The functional resume organizes work experience—and sometimes campus or community activities—according to position titles or functions (e.g., Systems Analyst, Special Events Coordinator, Probation Officer). Arrange your titles in descending order of importance, based on your career goal, providing details about your responsibilities, duties, and results after each title. One section of a functional resume might look like this:

EXPERIENCE

Finance Manager, Grand Mesa Girl Scout Council, Grand Junction, CO
September 1994–present

- Oversee all expenditures and revenues in $900,000 budget
- Prepare all financial reports and audit materials
- Implement a computerized accounting system
- Manage all personnel records, payroll, and tax reports
- Reconcile balances in six funds and bank statements

Accounting Supervisor, Western Waterbeds, Inc., Loveland, CO
September 1990–August 1994

- Supervised seven employees
- Managed personnel records, payroll, and tax reports
- Prepared financial reports
- Projected cashflow for investment decisions
- Reconciled bank statements
- Coordinated advertising and pricing promotions

Administrative Assistant, Skilled Jobs for Women, Loveland, CO
June 1990–August 1990

- Coordinated fiscal operations with services
- Wrote monthly reimbursement claims to State of Colorado

In general, the functional resume is appropriate under the following conditions:

- You want to emphasize your accomplishments and the positions you've held, rather than your skills or the length of time you've worked at various jobs.
- Your background fits one of these categories:
  - You've had impressive job titles and duties.
  - You can't list work experience in chronological order without revealing gaps.
  - You've performed functions directly related to your career goal, even through you've held jobs or completed assignments not directly related to your career.

FIGURE 8.8 Sample Chronological Resume

GREGORY B. KITTILSON
3205 Midway Boulevard, Apartment 5
Sartell, MN 56377
(320) 555-3341

EDUCATION:

1989–Present **St. Cloud State University,** St. Cloud, MN—GPA: 3.67 on a 4.00 scale
Bachelor of Science in ABET accredited Electrical Engineering Program, May 1992
- Coursework included digital compensator/filter design, cache development, expert systems, control systems, and C programming language
- Designed and built a temperature sensor using an analog-to-digital conversion interface PC slot card and hardware interrupt

1987–1989 **North Hennepin Community College,** Brooklyn Park, MN—GPA: 3.54 on a 4.00 scale
Associate of Arts with honors, March 1989

1983–1986 **United States Army Intelligence School,** Ft. Devens, MA
Coursework included Instrumentation Signal External Analysis, Space Collection Operations, and Electronic Non-Communications/Signal Intelligence Interceptor and Analyst

EXPERIENCE:

1991–1992 **Senior Design Team Project,** SCSU
- The project involves development and construction of a Robot Motion Controller using a TMS320C25 Digital Signal Processor to control six DC motors with the ability to change compensator design

1991 **Summer Intern,** Manufacturing Technology Services of Central Minnesota and SCSU
- The project involved automation of a lens grinder using three stepper motors
- The control system used a Z80 processor in STD bus configuration
- Intense mathematical equations enabled automated lens cuts of less than three diopters, including plano cuts
- Firmware was developed in FORTH
- Two students with one professor comprised the design team

1990–1992 **Student Assistant and Grader,** SCSU
- Created graphical user interface for PC controller card utilizing Microsoft Quick C and implemented digital controller examples, including motor control using the PC card and software package
- Student grader for various classes at professors' request

1988–1989 **Computer Lab Assistant,** North Hennepin Community College
- Assisted students and faculty with hardware and software problems
- Utilized many DOS/MS Windows applications, including Lotus 123, WordPerfect, and Ventura Publisher

1983–1987 **Electronic Warfare Non-Communications Analyst,** US Army
- Processed and analyzed PCM, PPM/PAM, and PSK instrumentation signals by means of spectrum analyzers, oscilloscopes, demodulators, filters, visicorders, and on-site computer database
- Served as technical advisor and consultant for mission operation
- Honorably discharged at the rank of Sergeant

(continued)

FIGURE 8.8 Continued

ACHIEVEMENTS:

- 1991–1992 IEEE SCSU Branch Student President
- 1991–1992 Eta Kappa Nu Iota Omicron Chapter Vice President
- 1991 Inductee Eta Kappa Nu Electrical Engineering Honor Fraternity
- 1990–1991 IEEE SCSU Branch Newsletter Editor
- SCSU Certificates of Scholastic Achievement
- Service Award from North Hennepin Community College
- 1989 Inductee Phi Theta Kappa National Junior College Honor Society
- 1988–1989 Organizing Editor for North Hennepin Community College's Student Newspaper
- Army Commendation Medal for technical abilities, Army Achievement and Good Conduct Medal

SECURITY CLEARANCE: Possessed Top Secret Clearance with Special Background Investigation while in military.

REFERENCES: References are available upon request.

Because this resume style depends upon actual job titles for its effectiveness, it's more difficult to make an effective "can do" argument with a functional resume if you've had limited paid or volunteer experience. See Margaret Ann Minton's resume in Figure 8.3 and Melissa Wellington's resume in Figure 8.9 for full examples of functional presentation.

Skills Resumes. The skills resume, which has been very popular recently, stresses the abilities you've demonstrated through paid work experience and volunteer activities. Because a skills resume is structured based on your areas of expertise, it can be an effective vehicle for making the argument that you "can do" based on your technical ability and interpersonal competence, especially if you have had mostly volunteer work and no particularly eye-catching job titles.

Prospective employers find this resume style very useful for applicants just starting their careers for several reasons:

1. Skills resumes require applicants to select three or four of their strongest skills (relevant to the job sought, of course) and present work experience under these skills categories. To select and support these skills, applicants must know themselves and the company's requirements pretty well. In other words, skills resumes demonstrate applicants' analytical abilities as well as job skills.

FIGURE 8.9 Sample Functional Resume

MELISSA WELLINGTON

2501 33rd Avenue N
St. Cloud, MN 56304
(320) 259-8829

CAREER OBJECTIVE

A summer internship that will utilize my experience and education in biology

EDUCATION

St. Cloud State University; St. Cloud, Minnesota
Bachelor of Elective Studies in Biology with an Emphasis in Wildlife Management
G.P.A. 3.93/4.0; Graduation: Spring 1997

Course Emphasis
Biology (70 hours, including 12 hours wildlife management, ornithology)
Botany (16 hours, including 8 hours taxonomy)
Chemistry (17 hours)

EXPERIENCE

Naturalist; Heritage Nature Center, St. Cloud, MN; March 1997–Present
- Conduct programs and tours for public and school groups
- Oversee native pond display management
- Create informative displays on selected topics
- Lead Ranger Rick nature activities for 6–9 year olds

Undergraduate Research Assistant; U.S. Fish and Wildlife Service, St. Paul, MN; September 1991–August 1996
- Created a computer management program for wolf and deer studies data
- Prepared and oversaw mailing list correspondence
- Aided office staff with various clerical duties
- Expanded personal computer knowledge to include Lotus, WordPerfect 5.1, and programming in DBase III Plus

Manager; Noah's Ark Pet Center, Arlington Heights, IL; August 1987–March 1993
- Hired, trained, and supervised staff of sixteen
- Created all livestock and merchandise displays
- Implemented animal maintenance plan for livestock, including exotic mammals, birds, and reptiles
- Maintained financial records of store
- Earned Achievement Awards: Manager of the Year, Store of the Year, Store of the Month

Docent; Como Zoo, St. Paul, MN; June 1993–June 1994
- Conducted on-site educational programs, including handling of various live animals for children and other groups
- Researched natural history of selected animals in zoo collection for new docent training manual
- Observed new arrivals (Puffin Watch) for signs of illness or stress
- Observed gorillas (Gorilla Watch) for behavioral cues of female's ovulation

ACTIVITIES

African Studies Club, President
Creative Writing Club, Member
Audubon Society, Member

HONORS

First Place Fiction Writing Contest, *Harvest Magazine,* St. Cloud State University, 1997
Nominated One of St. Cloud State University's Outstanding Students, 1997

References Available Upon Request

2. Because skills resumes emphasize job applicants' abilities, regardless of where they were acquired, this format enables applicants to provide a lot of detail about their participation in campus and community activities—information employers want to know about recent college graduates.
3. Skills resumes enable prospective employers to readily determine what the applicants' strengths are.

Here's a section of a skills resume:

Communication
- Designed and presented a three-hour workshop on editing strategies for 34 writers on staff at the *Chronicle,* the student newspaper
- Wrote a feature article on SCSU students' views of the State University System merger for the *Times*
- Created a 20-minute educational video on careers in journalism, which will be used as a marketing tool for high school juniors and seniors by the mass communications department
- Trained 32 undergraduate mass communications majors to use QuarkXPress during three four-hour workshops

Coordination
- Oversaw the planning and production of *The Communications Club Newsletter*
- Organized and coordinated the development and production of the *Performing Arts Club (PLA) Newsletter*
- Coordinated the writing, editing, and production of an informational brochure for the Learning Skills Center
- Coordinated Shoemaker Hall's 1998 spring formal for 200 people, including entertainment, food and beverages, location, transportation, decorations, and advertising
- Planned drama night, a swimnastics show, and aerobic dance classes for the Whispering Hills Girl Scout Camp

Leadership
- Introduced and implemented on- and off-campus group activities, ranging from social functions (hall dances, field trips, sports tournaments, and dinners) to educational activities (speakers from health and career services)
- Initiated and promoted Speech Communications Club public relations ideas, such as *The Communications Club Newsletter*
- Motivated individuals toward a healthy lifestyle while teaching aerobic dance classes through the Learning Exchange

You should consider using a skills resume under these circumstances:

- Your skills are more impressive than your job titles or length of experience.
- You've successfully applied skills relevant to the job you're seeking in campus or community organizations as well as in the workplace.

- You have little paid work experience but lots of volunteer experience.
- You've recently changed career paths. In fact, when career goals change, a skills resume may be the most persuasive format for presenting your background.

As we've already suggested, a skills resume is probably the easiest way of making the argument that you "can do" a job, based on either your technical or interpersonal competence. And if you're a soon-to-be college graduate with relatively little relevant job experience but extensive involvement in campus or community organizations, you can readily incorporate details about the skills you've used in your volunteer experience right along with those demonstrated in your paid jobs. Keep in mind, though, that skills resumes are often perceived as appropriate for recent college graduates but not for those applicants who are in midcareer: Some employers are suspicious when more experienced job candidates use this approach because they feel the skills format makes it easier to cover embarrassing gaps in employment.

So, it may be that you'll select a skills format to apply for your first position and a functional or chronological resume to apply for jobs later in your career when you can include impressive job titles or demonstrate progressively more responsible and relevant experience. And if you do elect to use a skills resume, be sure that you clearly and immediately document the skills you claim. Perhaps the greatest hazard of the skills resume is raising a reader's skepticism by claiming a skill in large, prominent, boldfaced print but locating the documentation at the bottom of the resume.

You'll find that the process for developing a skills resume is fairly straightforward. First, choose three or four of your strongest skills; these skills should, of course, be fundamental for the kind of position you're seeking. Then, pick details from your work experience and activities that demonstrate how and when you have successfully demonstrated these skills. Finally, order the skills and the details under them from most to least important. See Karen Meehan's resume in Figure 8.10 for a complete example of a skills presentation.

Creative Resumes. Creative variations of these conventional resume formats are sometimes used for applicants seeking creative or artistic positions. A creative resume is appropriate if your artistic skills—used to enhance the visual design of your resume—market your creativity in an appropriate way, given your prospective employer and your career goals. Generally, such resumes highlight qualifications in an effective yet unusual way to catch prospective employers' attention. For instance, a job applicant seeking a position responsible for the visual designs of newsletters might prepare a creative resume that demonstrates her eye for layout.

It's important to keep in mind, however, that creative resumes are not so much a convention as they are a rejection of convention, and as is always the case, breaking convention is not without risk. Ironically, one risk with creative resumes is that of becoming cliched. For example, designing a resume as an advertisement when seeking an advertising position probably has been done often enough that the approach has become hackneyed. Another risk is misjudging the appropriateness of the creative

FIGURE 8.10 Sample Skills Resume

Karen M. Meehan

Permanent Address:
364 Kachemak Bay Circle
Anchorage, Alaska 99502
(907) 555-6231
e-mail: meehan@alnet.net

University Address:
1737 Fortieth Avenue North
St. Cloud, MN 56303
(320) 555-5406
e-mail: meehak01@eeyore.stcloud.msus.edu

OBJECTIVE
To obtain a position in Anchorage that utilizes the skills of communication, research, and leadership obtained through prior work experience

EDUCATION
St. Cloud State University; St. Cloud, Minnesota: Bachelor of Arts Degree, November 1996
Double major: English with writing emphasis and French; GPA: 3.8/4.0

SKILLS
Communication
- Wrote a twelve-year history of projects and expenditures carried out through a federally funded housing and community development grant program overseen by the Municipality of Anchorage
- Wrote 49 policies and procedure documents as well as completed a managerially approved 36 page policy and procedures manual for a day care assistance office implemented by the Municipality of Anchorage
- Updated and reformatted 34 intraoffice letters and forms
- Addressed audiences ranging from 10–500 on educational issues
- Responded to questions and added commentary on a statewide Ratnet call-in program
- Lived and studied in Toulouse, France, for five months

Research
- Researched twenty years of project and financial information for a HUD sponsored grant office
- Generated statistical graphs of three grant programs based on case characteristics for a period of three fiscal years
- Completed filing of a backlog of memos, correspondence and meeting minutes
- Researched and rectified cases of possible fraud through telephone contact and completion of documentation

Leadership
- Represented students of the State of Alaska from May of 1992 to May of 1993 as State Board of Education Student Advisory Member
- Lobbied for students and Department of Education in Juneau, Alaska, on educational issues

WORK EXPERIENCE
Day Care Assistance Office, Municipality of Anchorage; Anchorage, Alaska
- Senior Office Assistant; summers and breaks 1993–present
- Through Kelly Temporary Services in 1994 and Winter 1994/1995

Community Development Block Grant Division, Municipality of Anchorage; Anchorage, Alaska
- Summer intern; summer 1996
- Through Olsten Staffing Services

AWARDS and ACTIVITIES
Phi Kappa Phi Honor Society and SCSU Scholastic Achievement awards
Habitat for Humanity International, Campus Chapter
Volunteer Notetaker for Student Disability Services
International Studies Program (Toulouse, France)
French Tutor, St. Cloud State University Department of Foreign Languages and Literature

References Available Upon Request

Source: © 1995, Washington Post Writers Group. Reprinted with permission.

approach for the readers and their organization. The further you deviate from convention, the greater the risk. On the other hand, this kind of creative risk taking may be exactly what some readers value. Keeping in mind your goals, your readers, and the arguments you want to make should enable you to present your background in an appropriate format—conventional or not.

Activities and Honors

You may want to include a section covering college and community activities and honors. As you construct it, think about how prospective employers may use this information. For instance, many readers use this section to verify long-term interest in the field you're seeking work in. Therefore, it makes sense to include any professional organizations you belong to. For instance, the following honors and activities section documents the applicant's active interest in his career goal, management of wildlife resources:

ACTIVITIES AND HONORS

Member
- The Wildlife Society
- North American Crane Working Group
- Iowa Prairie Chicken Society
- National Wildlife Federation

Recipient
- Mayer Scholarship in Wildlife Biology, 1998
- Dean's List, 1996–1998

Many readers also use the honors and activities section of a resume to confirm that the writer's personality and preferences match those needed for the position. For example, if a position requires frequent collaboration, readers might check for evidence that you're a team player, rather than a loner, looking for activities you've done as a member of a group and discounting solitary hobbies. And readers might look for additional evidence that you have the skills being sought. As an illustration, the following resume section documents the leadership skills and initiative needed to run marketing campaigns, which is what the candidate wants to do:

Organizations

American Advertising Federation (AAF), Member 1995–present

Texas Press, Member 1996–present

Student Advertising Association (SAA), Member 1992–present
- President, May 1997–present
- Membership Director, September 1997–May 1998
- SAA Representative, AAF National Conference in Washington, D.C., June 1997
- SAA Representative, 1997 Advertising Women of New York Annual College Career Conference, November 1997
- SAA Scholarship Recipient, May 1997

Readers sometimes use the activities and honors section of a resume to answer questions they can't ask. For instance, although a recruiter can't ask if you're healthy, he or she might check to see if you provide evidence of health by listing involvement in sports. Finally, occasionally readers use the activities and honors section of a resume to provide them with an ice-breaker to put the applicant at ease during an interview. If an applicant indicates during an oncampus interview that she plays tennis, for example, and the recruiter does, too, the recruiter might ask her for suggestions of where he might play while he is in town.

No matter what the readers' intent when they review resumes, remember that you can influence the sorts of impressions they form of you through careful selection of detail—the sorts of evidence you use to support your argument.

References

Although not all prospective employers will want to check applicants' references, the last section of the resume should handle references in some way. Most job applicants indicate their willingness to provide references in the last line of their resume by stating "References available upon request." Then, if prospective employers request references, the applicant can supply information—names, addresses, and phone numbers—for the specific number and type of references requested. Many applicants specify that their references are available through the career services unit at their school, where they already have a file of recommendation letters for prospective employers who request them. And if a particular reader requests references in the job notice, job applicants should include their references right on their resumes. If you're unsure whether you should list references on your resume, look carefully at the job listing or ask a professional in your field for advice since conventions for handling references are sometimes field specific.

There are some fairly strong conventions you should follow as you begin putting together your list of references:

1. Remember that when people serve as references, they're making a substantial commitment of time. It takes time to write specific, persuasive letters of recommendation; even answering phone inquiries about a person takes time away from daily work, adding to and interrupting busy schedules. So, it's essential that you follow the social conventions and ask people ahead of time for permission to list them as references. Don't assume that someone is willing to provide favorable references or that they have the time to write letters of recommendation or answer phone inquiries. Such assumptions can cause you great embarrassment. If you list people without their permission, they may be angry, unresponsive to inquiries about you, or brutally honest about your failure to request their permission or their lack of confidence in you as a job applicant. And even if they are willing to serve as references, if you haven't asked for their permission, people might not be prepared to talk about you if prospective employers call, asking for information. Your references might need to check their files for dates of employment or think about your specific contributions to the workplace. Or they might simply need time to think about you in a different context from the one they're used to.
2. To help your references think through what they'll say about you in a letter or on the phone, convention also encourages you to let them know the specific position or positions you're seeking and the types or specific names of companies you're applying to. It's also a good idea to provide your references each with a current copy of your resume so they can get a sense of how their experience with you fits into your entire employment or educational background.
3. It's important to think about how your references will complement one another. Conventionally, a references list includes people from both academic and employment settings. But in addition to achieving a balance in school and work references, think about how people will complement one another in what they say about your technical and interpersonal skills, your knowledge, your contributions to the classroom or workplace, and your aptitudes, attitudes, and character. Remember that references can provide to prospective employers their views of who you are and what you're capable of as well as what you've already accomplished. In other words, they can help you make the sorts of arguments you wish to make.
4. When you put together your list of references, be sure to include their professional designations (e.g., *Dr.*, *Ms.*) and titles (e.g., *Marketing Director, Operations Manager*) as well as their work addresses and phone numbers.

Coverage

Questions job applicants generally have about coverage include how far back they should go in recounting educational background or work history and whether personal information, interests, and hobbies should be included.

Scope of Work History. Should you include information from high school? From college? A helpful guideline to use here is that information that's prior to the last two major mileposts in your career should probably come off the resume, unless there is a strong, specific reason to keep it there. For example, if you're approaching college graduation, perhaps everything explicitly having to do with high school, even your graduation, should come off your resume. Anyone who has graduated from college may be presumed to have graduated from high school, and a college graduate's resume that still talks about high school achievement may invite the question whether he or she has done anything meaningful since high school.

Personal Information. What about personal information—height, weight, health, age, religion, race, political affiliation, and so on? Should you include a picture of yourself? According to current American business practice, codified in both federal and state regulations and statutes, personal information like this is—well—*personal.* It is illegal to discriminate among prospective employees using characteristics that do not relate to a person's ability to do the job. If some characteristic is vitally job related, an employer may ask you about it. For example, if a job requires a certain level of strength or dexterity, an employer may explain its relevance and ask you about it. For jobs entailing physical labor, it's common for an employer to say something like "This job requires frequent lifting of heavy packages. Can you comfortably lift 45 pounds from the floor to a height of 48 inches?"

However, it is illegal to ask questions about your race, religion, gender, marital status, parental status, age, political or other affiliation, or any physical characteristic (such as height, weight, and health), except when a personal characteristic is clearly and directly relevant to the ability to perform that job competently—such as the lifting example just mentioned, for instance. You are not required to volunteer any information about these characteristics. So typically, you won't include this kind of personal information on your resume.

But suppose some of your most challenging and rewarding work has been as an employee, a volunteer, or intern with, say, a Republican senator, Catholic Charities, the NAACP, or some other organization strongly identified with a particular group or cause. If you include this work on your resume, will your reader readily infer that you are a member of that group or support that cause? People who have had jobs or volunteer experiences like these generally are enthusiastic about the powerful learning experiences they represent but may have misgivings about listing them on their resumes because they worry that someone may discriminate against them. In fact, this is a risk. But it's one of those risks that you have to calculate. You have to judge the risk of being unfairly stereotyped against the gain of setting forth an experience and an affiliation that may have shaped who you are.

If the risk seems unacceptable to you, then you should probably leave the information off your resume. As you ponder this question, though, also consider whether you would want to work for a person who would discriminate in this way. An applicant who had been very involved in the Fellowship for Christian Athletes, for example, decided to list his membership, even though he was sure he would run into religious bias and be cut out of consideration for some positions. He decided that his religion was so much a part of who he was that he wanted to work for a company that valued and respected this part of him. Including the Fellowship of Christian Athletes on his resume, then, was his way of ensuring that the company that hired him met his standards.

Personal Interests and Hobbies. Should you tell about personal interests and hobbies? You're not required to talk about your personal interests, and a lot of people choose not to. It depends largely upon what your personal interests are and to what extent they are job and career related. A thoughtful listing of your personal interests can be an effective "want to do" or "will do" character argument. For instance, suppose that in addition to being a marketing major, you are an excellent golfer. If a company that manufactures and sells golf equipment is looking for a well-qualified marketing trainee, you will likely be an interesting candidate.

Here's one caution: Don't get too enthusiastic in listing personal interests, especially if they're not directly job related. The reader may wonder when you have time to do any work!

Document Design

Since employers receive so many resumes and process them so quickly, even the resume's superficial appearance is crucially important. Your goal here is for someone who just glances at your resume to see it as professional and inviting. Designing an attractive resume is as important as dressing appropriately for an interview: You want the initial impression your resume creates to be favorable so that the reader reads on, rather than burying your resume in a file cabinet or dumping it in the "circular file." Of course, this means that your resume should be clean and neat, but it also means that you should invest some time in developing an effective format, use a readable font, and select an appropriate paper for the sorts of businesses you'll be contacting.

Before we move into a discussion of specific document design conventions, consider briefly the visual impact of the resume in Figure 8.11 compared to that of its revision in Figure 8.4. When you look at these resumes, what strikes you? What do you remember about the candidate whose credentials are presented on these pages? What impressions do you have of him as an individual? What elements of document design contribute positively to the images you hold of him? What elements help you find key information quickly? What elements make it harder for you to find and absorb information? As you'll discover in the following discussion, problems with document design undercut readability in resumes and undermine the arguments that writers make about themselves.

In general, the document design of your resume should do three things for your readers:

1. Help them quickly spot your most important qualifications
2. Help them easily find the documentation of your qualifications
3. Make it easy for them to reach you and to follow up

FIGURE 8.11 Sample Resume with Document Design Problems

DANIEL THOMPSON

445 Slater Road
Eagan, MN 55122
(612) 555-0723

OBJECTIVE: Management responsibility involving product research, development, and marketing

EXPERIENCE:

SALESMAN—Tenneco Automotive, Inc. (NAPA Mufflers & Shocks Division), Lincolnshire, IL, January 1989 to present. Perform technical sales to over 75 NAPA jobbers in Minnesota, North Dakota, South Dakota, and Wisconsin territory with 40% travel. Coordinate sales programs and product information from Tenneco Automotive to NAPA Distribution Center to NAPA jobbers to retail and wholesale customers. ACCOMPLISHED 35% SALES INCREASE IN A DECLINING MARKET (EXHAUST). DEVELOPED MARKETING PROGRAM THAT RESULTED IN 15% SALES INCREASE IN TRUCK MARKET. EARNED TOP WAREHOUSE SALES (DOLLARS AND PERCENT INCREASE) IN MIDWEST DIVISION.

SALESMAN—Echlin, Inc. (NAPA United Brake Parts Division), McHenry, IL, August 1982 to December 1988. Performed technical sales to over 125 NAPA jobbers in Minnesota, North Dakota, and Montana territory with 75%. Worked with inside jobbers and outside salespeople regarding product knowledge, new products, market trends, national sales programs, and sales skills. Held technical seminars on technological changes for professional technicians. EARNED ROOKIE OF THE YEAR (1983), RING OF RECOGNITION (1986), AND FACTORY REP OF THE YEAR (1988).

RECRUITER—Career Centers, Inc., Minneapolis, MN, January 1981 to July 1982. Located positions for salespeople seeking employment changes and recruited candidates for companies to fit specific job opening. Averaged 50 telemarketing sales calls/day and interviewed 3–4 candidates/day. BECAME SECOND LEADING PRODUCER OF SEVEN IN COMPANY.

SALESMAN/INSTALLER—B & K Auto Trim, Inc., St. Paul, MN, March 1977 to January 1981. Established sales route entirely from cold calls and sold and serviced these accounts weekly. Averaged 10 sales calls/day. Traveled 60,000 miles/year. INCREASED SALES VOLUME IN TERRITORY FROM $0 TO OVER $100,000 ANNUALLY.

ASSISTANT MANAGER—Perkins Cake & Steak, Inc., Minneapolis, MN, August 1976 to March 1977. Scheduled employees and provided menu and food preparation knowledge. Interviewed, hired, and trained new employees. SUPERVISED 74 EMPLOYEES.

SALESMAN—W. O. W. Life Insurance Society, Omaha, NE, July 1975 to July 1976. Made cold calls, prospected, kept records, and performed service work. DEVELOPED NEW TERRITORY FOR COMPANY.

EDUCATION: B.S.—English Literature with Writing Minor, 1990, St. Cloud State University, St. Cloud, MN

REFERENCES: available upon request

The following conventions of resume design can contribute to the image of you as a professional by increasing the attractiveness and readability of your resume:

- **White space.** For the most part, use horizontal and vertical white space to emphasize important information and make your resume open, inviting, and easy to read.

- **Headings.** Side headings are generally preferred over centered headings since centered headings disrupt the normal reading line and slow readers down.

- **Lists versus paragraphs.** Organizing information in lists is generally preferred to writing it out in paragraph format. As the early draft of the Thompson resume illustrates (Figure 8.11), displaying information in block paragraphs can make readers' jobs much harder. In contrast, consistent indentation and the effective use of lists can help readers comprehend quickly what you've accomplished. For instance, notice how difficult it is to find information in the following example because of the use of full sentences and paragraphs. Notice also that full sentences encourage the repetition of "I" as the subject of sentences, which is hard to avoid since the writer of the resume has presumably done everything recorded there:

  United Way Voluntary Action Center, Rochester, NY
  I explored printing options and expense estimates for a fundraising project by making phone calls and personal visits to area print shops and lumber companies. I also wrote a weekly newspaper column for the local newspaper as well as news releases and promotional materials. I organized, promoted, and participated in a fundraising event during the annual community summer festival. I created and presented a two-hour workshop, "Persuasive Writing Strategies for Promotional Materials," to 18 volunteer coordinators.

  The next example is much easier to read, even though the information is exactly the same because it uses verb phrases, rather than full sentences, and a list, rather than paragraph, form:

  United Way Voluntary Action Center, Rochester, NY
  - Explored printing options and expense estimates for a fundraising project by making phone calls and personal visits to area print shops and lumber companies
  - Wrote a weekly newspaper column for the local newspaper
  - Prepared news releases and promotional materials for the local newspaper
  - Organized, promoted, and participated in a fundraising event during the annual community summer festival
  - Created and presented a two-hour workshop, "Persuasive Writing Strategies for Promotional Materials," to 18 volunteer coordinators

  As this example shows, presenting information in lists using verb phrases tends to speed up reading and make the writing sound more forceful.

- **Type treatments.** Use boldface, italics, solid capital letters, and underlining judiciously to help readers find information. Carefully selected, these type treatments can emphasize important details and lead readers' eyes to information you want them to notice. But be sure not to overdo it: Too much of any or all of these treatments will provide mixed messages about what's important and lessen readability, as this sample shows:

  EDUCATION

  Bachelor of Science, December 1998
  University of Tulsa, Tulsa, OK
  Majors in Finance and Economics, 3.4 GPA (on a 4-point scale)
  Cincinnati State Technical and Community College, Cincinnati, OH 1994–1996
  Courses in business, economics, and general education

  PROFESSIONAL EXPERIENCE

  Assistant Manager, A & W Drive-In, Tulsa, OK, 1996–present.
  Opened and closed restaurant. Supervised up to seven employees at one time.
  Handled customer complaints. Balanced tills and cash accounts.

  High School Soccer Coach, Wyoming High School, Cincinnati, OH, 1995. Coached Boy's Junior Varsity and assisted Varsity Teams. Supervised team members.
  Arranged transportation, equipment, and referees.

  In particular, be careful about overusing underlining or solid capitals. Text with a lot of underlining can be busy, distracting readers from the details you're using to support your argument, and text that overdoes capitalization can make readers feel as if you're yelling at them. This is part of the problem with the Thompson resume in Figure 8.11. Although the resume writer used capitals to emphasize important facts about himself, the overuse of capitals—in combination with the block paragraph format—is likely to confuse readers about what is important. You should also use italics sparingly, since the slant of italic type lessens readability.

- **Typeface.** In general, you'll want to select an easily readable typeface. Remember that prospective employers read a lot of print information, so don't make their jobs harder by making them squint. Select reasonably sized type, certainly no smaller than 10 point—the size of this text. And you'll find that *serif* fonts (which have little feet on the bottoms that help establish the reading line)—for instance, Times Roman and Palatino—are more readable than *sans serif* fonts, such as Geneva and Helvetica. You should also use the same font throughout—or at most one font for the headings and another for the body text. Remember that using multiple fonts will draw readers' attention to the type itself and away from what you're saying.

- **Paper.** Select good-quality paper—ideally, linen, parchment, or lade and a minimum of 20 pound weight. Remember that resumes get passed around quite a bit, so you'll want the paper to be high enough in quality to handle pretty rough treatment. The color should, of course, be appropriate for the image you want to create and the readers you're addressing. A bright color may be exactly what you want if you're applying for a public relations position at a progressive advertising firm, but it would surely offend readers from a more conservative firm looking for a CPA, for example. And some bright colors, especially reds, may make it difficult for readers to photocopy or FAX your resume. Ivory, off white, pale beige, and light gray are always safe choices.

- **Length.** Should you aim for a one-page resume? By and large, the answer is "yes." Most companies expect resumes to be one page, particularly those from recent college graduates. But two-page resumes are sometimes in vogue, and it makes sense to check on current practice—particularly current practice in your field. It also makes sense to use a two-page resume if you'd have to cram everything onto one page in order to make the sort of argument you want to make about your background.

Style and Correctness

Style in your resume can be a powerful way to argue your communication competence, to transmit your feeling of confidence, and to express your image as a professional. But to be effective, you must describe your experience concretely using language that presents you as you would like to be seen. In general, describe your past accomplishments and current work experience in specific terms. Clarify results with numbers wherever possible since numbers, especially large ones, impress prospective employers. Consider, for instance, the persuasiveness of the concrete details in this example:

Teaching Assistant
Mechanical Engineering Technology; Michigan Technological University, Houghton, MI, 7/97–5/98
- Trained and supervised 83 students in gas arc welding
- Provided oral and written evaluation for three major projects for each student
- Supervised 6 work study students who each worked 14 hours per week maintaining lab equipment

Residence Hall Counselor
Meredith Hall; Michigan Technological University, 8/96–7/97
- Supervised activities of 51 floor residents
- Planned, implemented, and promoted talks by 12 academic and community leaders for a special program called "Developing Leadership Skills for the 21st Century"
- Served as liaison between the residents and the administration

Using action verbs to describe what you have accomplished will help make your experience visible to readers. Action verbs convey a sense of confidence and professional accountability that builds with each item in your lists of work experience and activities—for example, *organized, coordinated, sold.* In contrast, vague lead-ins like *I was responsible for* may leave readers wondering exactly what you did or what you're hiding. Using active verbs will not only clarify for readers exactly what you've done but will also help you maintain the parallelism—a strong convention for lists—that makes resume reading smooth, fast, and easy. This partial list of active verbs may help you think of your background in concrete terms:

adapted
administered
advertised
advised
aided
analyzed
answered
applied
arranged
assessed
assigned
audited
collaborated
completed
communicated
compiled
conducted
coordinated
corrected
counseled
created
delegated
designed
determined
developed
directed
edited
employed
established
evaluated
expanded
guided
headed
hired
identified
implemented
improved
increased
initiated
introduced
led
managed
negotiated
operated
ordered
organized
originated
oversaw
planned
prepared
produced
programmed
raised
rated
recruited
regulated
researched
revised
scheduled
served
settled
sold
solved
started
supervised
systematized
taught
trained
wrote

Think for a few minutes about the work you've performed in your jobs or in community or campus organizations:

- Which of these strong verbs describes accurately the tasks you've completed?
- Which helps to create the sort of image you want to project to prospective employers?
- Which expresses the values and attitudes you'd like to communicate to readers?
- What other active verbs would help you create the image or communicate the values and attitudes that would be appropriate, given the position you're seeking?

As you choose language to describe your background, think about the position you're applying for. Will readers expect you to know and use technical vocabulary to describe what you've done? Should you name particular equipment, processes, or approaches using technical jargon or proper names? Consider, for example, the use of technical terminology in this example:

Bechtel Power Corporation
Gaithersburg, Maryland; Summer 1998
Summer Intern with Nuclear Staff Thermal-Hydraulics Group

- Calculated Three Mile Island reactor drain-down and dry steady-state simulations, which were part of the successful effort to lift the Unit 2 reactor pressure vessel head
- Completed Farley Reactor Cavity Analysis that produced force and moment histories for the revision of the Farley Final Safety Analysis Report

Bechtel Power Corporation
Gaithersburg, Maryland; Summer 1997
Summer Intern with Nuclear Staff Thermal-Hydraulics Group

- Assisted senior engineers with calculations of simulated main steamline breaks, subcompartment and containment analysis
- Assisted with hydrogen generation calculations for equipment qualifications and igniter box performance
- Prepared a post data processor for a subcompartment analysis computer code
- Fabricated a summary chart of containment and subcompartment analysis results of the Thermal-Hydraulics Group

As you consider the kind of terminology to use in your resume, remember that the language should help you achieve your goals and marshal the argument you're making for the specific readers you're addressing. The language should also be consistent with the way you want to express yourself.

Expression

There's a powerful ambivalence about expression in the resume. On the one hand, all those basic arguments in the resume are really expressive arguments. The whole purpose of the resume is to achieve an effective expression of the kind of person you are. On the other hand, we've just discussed a long list of conventions that will constrain the way you talk about yourself in the resume. All three of the basic arguments—"can do," "want to do," and "will do"—are constrained by these conventions. Furthermore, the "can do" argument and especially the "will do" argument are constrained by cultural conventions against boasting. In other discussions of GRACE, we've noted that the character argument, which we've been calling here the "will do" argument, is particularly difficult to make directly. In fact, we've noted how often people interpret a direct and persistent appeal to one's own good character as evidence of one's *bad* character!

So, we see the resume challenge as your using GRACE to find ways of expressing your character. How can you take a document that has traditionally been seen as a chronicle in the past and use it as an effective argument that expresses your character, identity, and goals in life? Some of the conventions—the career objective and summary of qualifications for example—specifically give you permission to make the three basic arguments directly at those points in your resume. The other conventions give you ways of making the arguments indirectly—and even allow you to make the "can do" argument directly. Certainly, even the constricting conventions of correctness in spelling, punctuation, and usage offer the opportunity to show that you are a person who cares about getting a job done right and paying attention to details. And while breaking some conventions certainly entails some risk, it may be a risk you want to take—depending on your situation, readers, and goals. The really essential question is what kind of picture, what kind of person, do you want to display or express in this document? What visual image of you do you want your readers to see? What tone of voice do you want them to hear? What posture, facial expression, and other nonverbal expressions of your character do you want them to imagine when they read your resume?

GRACE for Online Resumes

Given the colossal growth in the number of World Wide Web sites over the past several years, it's no surprise that *online resumes* have become one of the newest means for job seekers to market their credentials. Some job applicants develop resumes for the web and post them in their Internet accounts or those of their academic departments or career services. Prospective employers use key terms in search engines to find the credentials of those people with backgrounds relevant to positions they wish to fill. Other job seekers submit their credentials to online employment services, which maintain resume databases that can be searched—and are searched primarily by large employers or recruitment firms—for matches with as many as 20 employer-selected criteria. Credentials for such resume databases are usually submitted via the following means:

- Job seekers can upload their resumes in ASCII or text-only form.*
- Applicants can key particulars about their background into generic forms available at the website.
- Job seekers can FAX or send via "snail mail" scannable versions of their resumes to the service—generally for an additional fee.

Although online resumes are relatively new and currently the most useful to people seeking technical positions, we encourage you to supplement the print version of your resume with an electronic counterpart. Keep in mind, though, that the readers for these resumes and the ways in which they are "read" are somewhat different, and the conventions for these electronic documents are still in flux. So, if you plan to develop an online version of your resume, you'd be wise to take your resume

**ASCII (American Standard Code for Information Interchange)* and *text-only* are formats in which text files can be saved that strip out all formatting, literally leaving only the text in the file.

through a special iteration of GRACE, intended for the online context of the document. Here are some of the issues we see when we look at the online resume through GRACE.

Goals

Although online resumes certainly are intended to achieve the same sorts of goals as print resumes, simply putting a print resume online without considering the medium and its goals is a mistake, for several reasons:

1. Whether you submit your resume to a resume databank or upload it to your own Internet account, remember that your resume must produce "hits." That is, when prospective employers use a resume database or a web search engine to locate people with particular credentials, they will be looking for matches with key terms they select to describe the position. Every match produces a *"hit,"* or the selection of a resume that fits established criteria. One goal of your online resume, then, should be to produce the maximum number of hits for the sorts of jobs you're interested in. And as we'll discuss in the Conventions section, producing these hits requires that you break some of the stylistic conventions of print resumes.
2. Since your online resume uses electronic media, it should not look exactly like your print resume. Rather, it should take advantage of the hypertextuality of the medium and be designed for the screen it will be viewed on. We'll talk more about this in the sections Arguments, Conventions, and Expression.
3. Since the effectiveness of online resumes depends upon your use of computer technology, you should use an online resume to make the "can do" argument that you have technical competence in using computers and in designing attractive documents for the web environment.

Readers

As we've already suggested, the readers of online resumes are different from those of print resumes. The majority of readers of online resumes are representatives of large corporations, recruitment firms, or technical firms looking for job applicants with technical backgrounds. Regardless of their backgrounds, these readers sometimes browse through resumes collected at a particular site—such as a campus career services site, a department site displaying the credentials of all recent graduates in a given major, or a site for members of a professional organization in a specific field. But more often, they search an employment database or the web in general. When prospective employers review resumes that result from a search, keep in mind that they are not the first readers of those resumes. The first readers are literally nonhuman: computers that scan the database or the World Wide Web for resumes using particular key terms humans have programmed them to locate. If your resume isn't selected by the computer, no human eyes may ever see it.

Arguments

Given the environment and readers typical of online resumes, you'll probably want to use your online resume to make the argument that you "can do" the sorts of technical tasks that the readers will need to you to complete. In keeping with this, online resumes are perfect for showing that you can use computers, can design for the World Wide Web, have an eye for what looks good on the screen, understand the information highway, or can market (yourself as well as products your reader might want you to sell) using relatively new technologies.

Conventions

As we've already suggested, the conventions for online resumes are still in flux. However, several strong conventions are already emerging. One of the strongest is related to the fact that, whether they are a part of a resume database or simply sitting in your Internet account, these resumes are scanned for keywords. Therefore, unlike print resumes, in which action verbs and verb phrases predominate, in effective online resumes, *nouns* predominate. You should be particularly careful to include keywords or essential characteristics that employers might use when searching for the sorts of positions you're interested in. The more key nouns your resume includes that match employers' needs, the more hits your resume is likely to generate. Sometimes, these nouns will be part of the actual text of your online resume, but other times, they will be invisible to all but the search engines people might use to find your resume. For instance, note that in the html coding for Bradley Blazek's web resume (see Figure 8.12), in the head after "meta name," Bradley has actually listed keywords that will be captured by search engines yet remain invisible to the human eye when the resume is viewed through a web browser.*

Another strong convention for online resumes sent to employment service databases is that they tend to be simple in design and typeface. Since computer search mechanisms are programmed to process text and may have difficulty with complex visuals like tables, you should simplify the design of any resume that will be scanned, avoiding horizontal and vertical lines, boxes, graphics, and icons. And although we've recommended that you use a serif font in your print resume to establish a strong reading line, your online resume should use a sans serif font, which will create fewer problems during scanning. For the same reason, avoid italics, boldface, and underlining in a resume that will be scanned.

Although online resumes sent to databases tend to be simple in design, web resumes are often more complex visually than print resumes. Many web resumes use background textures and colors, font colors, and simple graphics and icons. Keep in mind, though, that web pages that are too complex or busy are likely to distract readers from their content—in this case, your credentials. Also remember that the web is really busy at times. If your reader must wait forever to download complex graphics, he or she might simply stop downloading your file and move onto another resume. And since

**Hypertext markup language (html)* is the coding added to word-proccessed text files that enables them to be viewed through web browsers.

FIGURE 8.12 HTML Coding for Brad Blazek's Web Resume

```
<HTML>
<HEAD><TITLE>Qualifications of Brad Blazek</TITLE></HEAD>
<meta name="keywords" value="resume,computers,information systems,
project management,analytical,business,management,team,teamwork,
project,project planning,planning">
<BODY BGPROPERTIES="FIXED" BODY BACKGROUND="bkgrnd.gif"
TEXT="#000000" LINK="blue" VLINK="#800000" ALINK="#22AA22">

<CENTER>
<hr width="50%">
<B><A NAME="top"><FONT SIZE=6 COLOR="000000">Bradley C.
Blazek</FONT></B>

<hr width="50%">
<I><B><FONT SIZE=5>Presentation of
Qualifications<BR></I></FONT></B>

<hr width="30%"></CENTER><BR>

<B><CENTER>To view an area of my resume in which you are interested,
please click on one of the following links:<BR></CENTER></B>

<H5><CENTER><A HREF="#overview"> Overview</A> / <A
HREF="#objectiv"> Objective</A> / <A HREF="#strength">
Strengths</A> / <A HREF="#experien"> Professional Experience</A> /
<A HREF="#educatio"> Education</A> / <A HREF="#computer">
Computer Skills</A> / <A HREF="#honors"> Activities and Honors</A>
</CENTER></H5>

<HR WIDTH=85%>
<UL><A NAME="overview"><H3>OVERVIEW</H3>
Thank you for taking the time to look over my qualifications. I am currently
a senior at St. Cloud State University in search of a summer internship in the
Information Systems field. Although I have accumulated a solid knowledge
base for my technical skills, I am seeking a project management position
where I will be able to utilize my analytical business skills and business
background. If you have any questions or comments, please contact me at: <A
HREF="mailto:blazeb01@tigger.stcloud.msus.edu">
blazeb01@tigger.stcloud.msus.edu </A>.

<P>I am looking for a position that offers an opportunity to feature my
management skills, both with people and project planning. I strongly believe
in teamwork and sharing knowledge. The process of building an effective
team is a reward unto itself. I also believe a balance should be struck between
professional and personal goals and activities. I am looking to enter an
```

(continued)

FIGURE 8.12 Continued

```
organization which not only encourages, but demands this balance
within their employees. </UL>
<CENTER><H6><A HREF="#top">Return to Top</A></H6></CENTER>

<HR WIDTH=85%>
<UL><A NAME="objectiv"><H3>OBJECTIVE</H3>
An Information Systems position within a dynamic environment in the
Minneapolis area which will utilize my business, analytical, communication,
and systems skills and knowledge. </UL>
<CENTER><H6><A HREF="#top">Return to Top</A></H6></CENTER>

<HR WIDTH=85%>

<UL><A NAME="strength"><H3>PERSONAL STRENGTHS</H3>
As a capable and motivated individual with excellent oral and written
communication skills, I seek to utilize my strong leadership abilities. I am
perceptive, flexible, and team-oriented; I take ownership of problems and
enjoy finding creative solutions to complex problems.  Anticipating a
Bachelor of Science degree in Business Computers Information Systems in
November, 1997, I have acquired a wide range of knowledge in computer
hardware and software as well as systems analysis and design. Organized and
thorough, I also have the proven ability to coordinate a wide variety of tasks
and responsibilities. Experience has granted me a solid foundation in business
processes and techniques ranging from Management theories to Accounting
procedures. </UL>
<CENTER><H6><A HREF="#top">Return to Top</A></H6></CENTER>

<HR WIDTH=85%>
<UL><A NAME="experien"><H3>PROFESSIONAL
EXPERIENCE</H3></UL>

<B><UL>June 1996--October 1996<BR>Larson, Allen, Weishair, CPA's<BR>
Minneapolis, MN<BR></B><I>Plan Administrator </I></UL>
<UL>
<IMG SRC="blu_dot1.gif" BORDER=0> Administered full service
administration for employee benefit plans.
<BR><IMG SRC="blu_dot1.gif" BORDER=0> Evaluated benefit plans
including: 401(k), profit sharing, and welfare benefit plans.
<BR><IMG SRC="blu_dot1.gif"BORDER=0> Involved in evaluation and
selection of mutual funds for LAWCO Investment Committee.
<BR><IMG SRC="blu_dot1.gif" BORDER=0> Performed personal financial
planning evaluations and consultations.</UL><BR>
<CENTER><H6><A HREF="#top">Return to Top</A></H6></CENTER>
<HR WIDTH=70%><BR>

<B><UL>December 1993 -- February 1996<BR>First Bank System<BR> Edina,
MN & Grand Forks, ND<BR></B><I>Teller</I></UL>
```

FIGURE 8.12 Continued

```
<UL>
<IMG SRC="blu_dot1.gif" BORDER=0> Held deposit, withdrawal, statement
reconciliation, customer service, and daily cash box responsibilities.
<BR><IMG SRC="blu_dot1.gif" BORDER=0> Customer service and conflict
resolution skills were vital.
<BR><IMG SRC="blu_dot1.gif" BORDER=0> Computer knowledge was
required with speed and accuracy highly stressed.</UL><BR><BR>
<CENTER><H6><A HREF="#top">Return to Top</A></H6></CENTER>
<HR WIDTH=70%><BR>

<B><UL>October 1996 - Present<BR>Gander Mountain - Maple Grove <BR>
Maple Grove, MN<BR></B><I>Customer Service Associate</I></UL>
<UL>
<IMG SRC="blu_dot1.gif" BORDER=0> Perform cashiering and merchandise
returns for customers.
<BR><IMG SRC="blu_dot1.gif" BORDER=0> Deal with problem customers
and conflict resolution daily.
<BR><IMG SRC="blu_dot1.gif" BORDER=0> Very visible, people oriented
position requiring superior interpersonal skills.</UL><BR>
<CENTER><H6><A HREF="#top">Return to Top</A></H6></CENTER>

<HR WIDTH=85%>
<UL><A NAME="educatio"><H3>EDUCATION</H3>
<P><B>Bachelor of Science Degree, <A
HREF="http://www.stcloud.msus.edu/~bcis" target = "all">Business
Computer Information Systems</A>, November 1997<BR>
<A HREF="http://www.stcloud.msus.edu" target = "all"> St. Cloud State
University</A>, St. Cloud, MN<BR></B></UL>
<UL>Currently enrolled as a senior in the Business Computers Information
Systems program in the College of Business.<BR><BR>
<IMG SRC="blu_dot1.gif" BORDER=0><B> Major Coursework:</B>
Systems Analysis & Design I & II, Application Development I & II, IS
Management, Business Statistics I & II.
<BR><IMG SRC="blu_dot1.gif" BORDER=0><B> Coursework
Remaining:</B> Data Base Development, Telecommunication Processing,
Decision Support Systems.
<BR><IMG SRC="blu_dot1.gif" BORDER=0><B> Overall GPA:</B> 3.375 /
4.0</UL>
<CENTER><H6><A HREF="#top">Return to Top</A></H6></CENTER>

<HR WIDTH=85%>
<UL><A NAME="computer"><H3>COMPUTER SKILLS</H3></UL>
<P><UL>
<IMG SRC="blu_dot1.gif" BORDER=0><B> Operating Systems:</B>
<UL>DOS, Unix, and OS/2</UL>
```

(continued)

FIGURE 8.12 Continued

```
<BR><IMG SRC="blu_dot1.gif" BORDER=0><B> Programming
Languages:</B> <UL>COBOL, Ada, C, HTML, Visual Basic</UL>
<BR><IMG SRC="blu_dot1.gif" BORDER=0><B> Software
Packages:</B><UL>Microsoft Windows 95, and Windows 3.1, Microsoft
Excel, Word, PowerPoint, and Access; Microsoft Works, Lotus, Lotus Notes,
and Wordperfect.</UL></UL>
<CENTER><H6><A HREF="#top">Return to Top</A></H6></CENTER>

<HR WIDTH=85%>
<UL><A NAME="honors"><H3>ACTIVITIES & HONORS</H3></UL>
<UL>
<IMG SRC="blu_dot1.gif" BORDER=0> Dean's List: St. Cloud State
University, Fall '96
<BR><IMG SRC="blu_dot1.gif" BORDER=0><A
HREF="http://www.stcloud.msus.edu/~bcisclub"> BCIS Club</A>, Chapter
Representative for Association of Information Technology Professionals,
Spring '97
<BR><IMG SRC="blu_dot1.gif" BORDER=0><A
HREF="http://www.stcloud.msus.edu/~bcisclub"> BCIS Club</A>, Member,
Fall '96 & Winter '97
<BR><IMG SRC="blu_dot1.gif" BORDER=0> Student Hall Government,<A
HREF="http://www.bemidji.msus.edu/"> Bemidji State University</A> Fall
'92 - Spring '93
<BR><IMG SRC="blu_dot1.gif" BORDER=0> Student Hall Government,<A
HREF="http://www.mankato.msus.edu/"> Mankato State University</A>
Fall '91 - Spring '92</UL>
<CENTER><H6><A HREF="#top">Return to
Top</A></H6></CENTER><BR><BR>

<HR WIDTH=85%><CENTER>A little fly-fishing humor!!<BR>
<IMG SRC="harvard.gif" BORDER=0></CENTER>

<CENTER><H6><A HREF="#top">Return to Top</A></H6></CENTER>

<HR WIDTH=85%>
<CENTER><H4>Your Comments Are Appreciated:</H4><A
HREF="mailto:blazeb01@tigger.stcloud.msus.edu"> <IMG SRC="mailbox.gif"
BORDER=0 ALT="Write
Me!"><BR>blazeb01@tigger.stcloud.msus.edu</A><HR
WIDTH=85%><H5>This Resume Was Created Without The Use Of Any Text
Editors, Simply A Lot Of Patience. <BR>Last Modified On April 2,
1997<BR></H5></CENTER></BODY></HTML>
```

screen text is harder to read than print text, most web resumes use more white space than print resumes and use fonts that are designed for the screen, rather than the page.

The major difference between web resumes and print resumes, though, is the way they unfold for readers, or their hypertextuality. It's not unusual, for example, for a web resume's initial screen to include the writer's name and career objective and a simple set of links to education, experience, and honors and activities. Each of these links, then, might connect with more concrete descriptions of the writer's credentials in each of these areas. And these concrete descriptions might link to additional evidence of your abilities on other web pages created by you or by others. For instance, the names of papers you've presented at conferences, poetry you've published, or the portfolio you've developed might link to the actual texts of the papers, poetry, or portfolio. Mention of study you've completed overseas might link to a description of that program located on a computer in another country. And names of organizations for whom you've worked or volunteered might be linked to their websites. You can see examples of this sort of hypertextuality in web resumes by Bradley Blazek and Sheri L. Manson in Figures 8.13 and 8.14. As you review these resumes, consider those

FIGURE 8.13 Sample Web Resume

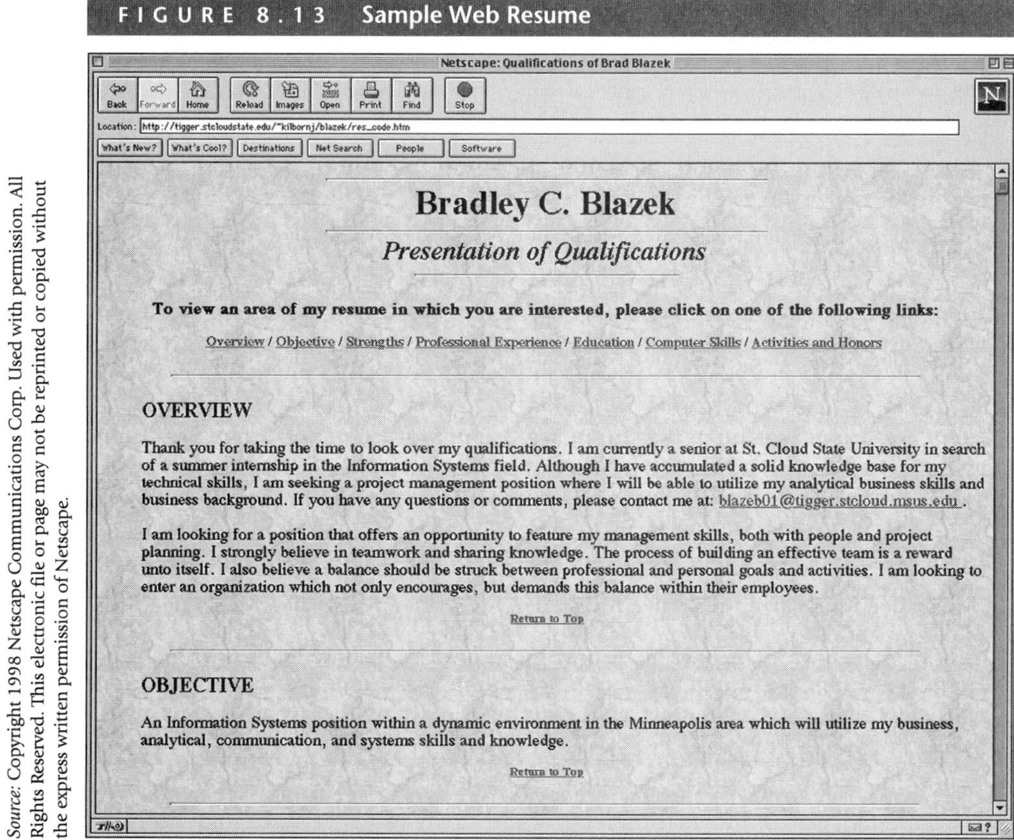

Bradley C. Blazek

Presentation of Qualifications

To view an area of my resume in which you are interested, please click on one of the following links:

Overview / Objective / Strengths / Professional Experience / Education / Computer Skills / Activities and Honors

OVERVIEW

Thank you for taking the time to look over my qualifications. I am currently a senior at St. Cloud State University in search of a summer internship in the Information Systems field. Although I have accumulated a solid knowledge base for my technical skills, I am seeking a project management position where I will be able to utilize my analytical business skills and business background. If you have any questions or comments, please contact me at: blazeb01@tigger.stcloud.msus.edu .

I am looking for a position that offers an opportunity to feature my management skills, both with people and project planning. I strongly believe in teamwork and sharing knowledge. The process of building an effective team is a reward unto itself. I also believe a balance should be struck between professional and personal goals and activities. I am looking to enter an organization which not only encourages, but demands this balance within their employees.

Return to Top

OBJECTIVE

An Information Systems position within a dynamic environment in the Minneapolis area which will utilize my business, analytical, communication, and systems skills and knowledge.

Return to Top

(continued)

FIGURE 8.13 Continued

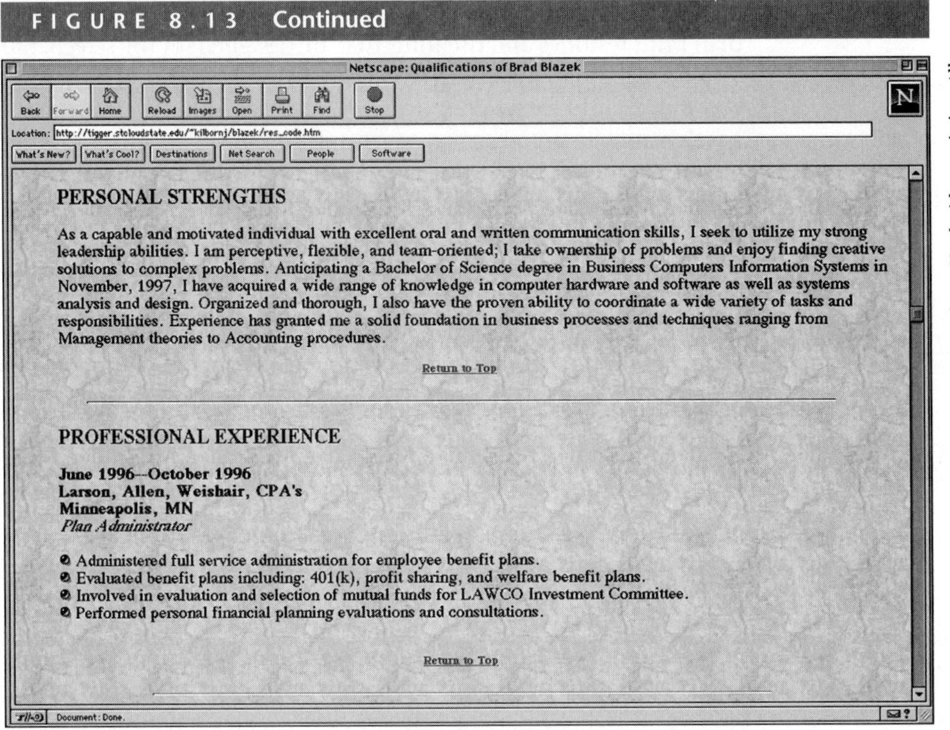
Netscape: Qualifications of Brad Blazek

Location: http://tigger.stcloudstate.edu/~kilbornj/blazek/res_code.htm

PERSONAL STRENGTHS

As a capable and motivated individual with excellent oral and written communication skills, I seek to utilize my strong leadership abilities. I am perceptive, flexible, and team-oriented; I take ownership of problems and enjoy finding creative solutions to complex problems. Anticipating a Bachelor of Science degree in Business Computers Information Systems in November, 1997, I have acquired a wide range of knowledge in computer hardware and software as well as systems analysis and design. Organized and thorough, I also have the proven ability to coordinate a wide variety of tasks and responsibilities. Experience has granted me a solid foundation in business processes and techniques ranging from Management theories to Accounting procedures.

Return to Top

PROFESSIONAL EXPERIENCE

June 1996--October 1996
Larson, Allen, Weishair, CPA's
Minneapolis, MN
Plan Administrator

- Administered full service administration for employee benefit plans.
- Evaluated benefit plans including: 401(k), profit sharing, and welfare benefit plans.
- Involved in evaluation and selection of mutual funds for LAWCO Investment Committee.
- Performed personal financial planning evaluations and consultations.

Return to Top

Document: Done.

features that make them like print documents as well as those that undercut print conventions. You also might want to compare Bradley's web resume to his print resume, which appears in Figure 8.15.

You'll notice that the hypertextuality of electronic resumes tends to work against the print convention for resume length. Since electronic resumes are viewed as screen text, the one-page limit often mentioned for print resumes becomes irrelevant. If the electronic resume is one file, the reader can scroll down seamlessly to the end of the text, no matter what its length, without the intrusion of page breaks. And the best web resumes, which are a series of interlinking documents, actually may seem shorter than the same text read in one scrolling screen or on paper because linking feels relatively effortless—as effortless, perhaps, as flipping channels on a television.

A final convention coming into usage for web resumes or resumes uploaded to employment databases is one concerning privacy. Although print resumes may include people's home addresses and phone numbers, online resumes tend to replace this information with a "mail to" line, so prospective employers can contact job seekers directly though their e-mail accounts or through a message system at a commercial employment service or university career service. Sometimes, job seekers dealing

FIGURE 8.13 Continued

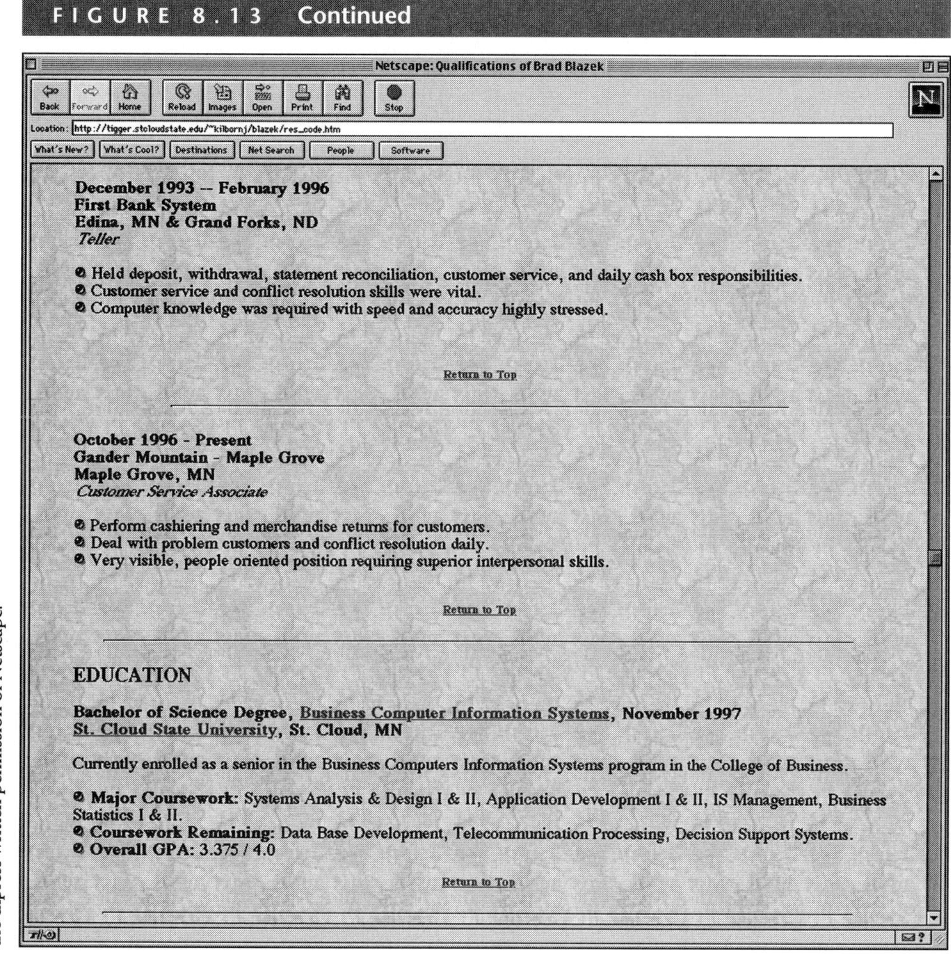

December 1993 -- February 1996
First Bank System
Edina, MN & Grand Forks, ND
Teller

- Held deposit, withdrawal, statement reconciliation, customer service, and daily cash box responsibilities.
- Customer service and conflict resolution skills were vital.
- Computer knowledge was required with speed and accuracy highly stressed.

Return to Top

October 1996 - Present
Gander Mountain - Maple Grove
Maple Grove, MN
Customer Service Associate

- Perform cashiering and merchandise returns for customers.
- Deal with problem customers and conflict resolution daily.
- Very visible, people oriented position requiring superior interpersonal skills.

Return to Top

EDUCATION

Bachelor of Science Degree, Business Computer Information Systems, November 1997
St. Cloud State University, St. Cloud, MN

Currently enrolled as a senior in the Business Computers Information Systems program in the College of Business.

- **Major Coursework:** Systems Analysis & Design I & II, Application Development I & II, IS Management, Business Statistics I & II.
- **Coursework Remaining:** Data Base Development, Telecommunication Processing, Decision Support Systems.
- **Overall GPA:** 3.375 / 4.0

Return to Top

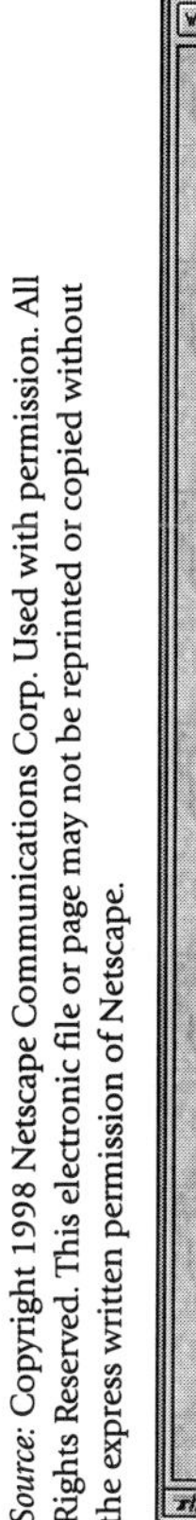

(continued)

with commercial employment services may even be given the option of keeping confidential their names and any other identifying information, including specific names and locations of employers; these job seekers would be given messages and specific contact information for interested companies so that the responsibility for follow-up and for revealing confidential information would remain in their hands. Such confidentiality is a must for job candidates who are already employed and wouldn't want their current employers to find their resumes online. But even more important, you should keep in mind your basic security and personal privacy. As you make decisions about whether to include private information on your online resume, remember that it will be accessible to literally anyone online, anywhere in the world.

FIGURE 8.13 Continued

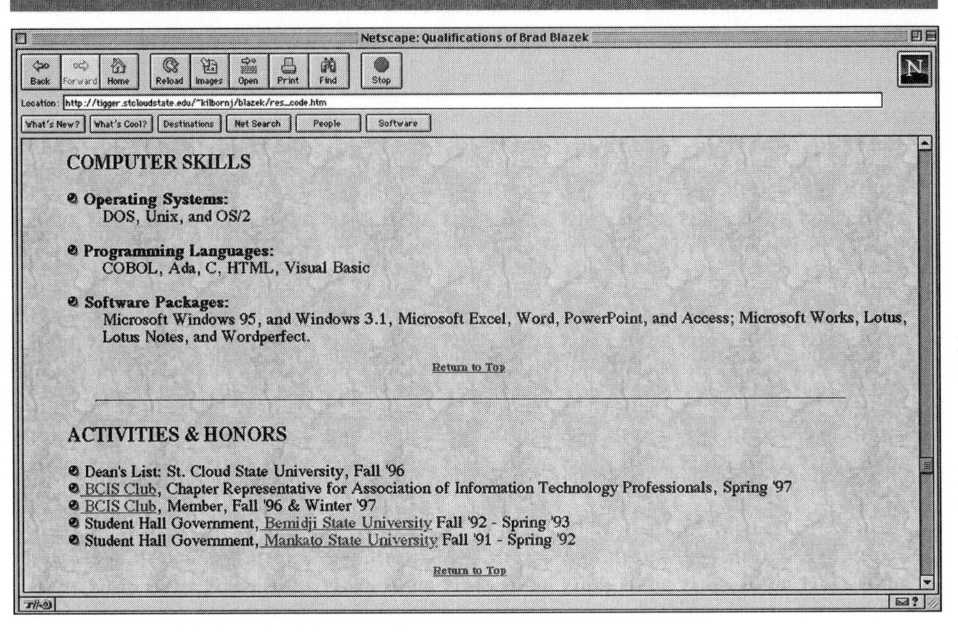

Netscape: Qualifications of Brad Blazek

Back | Forward | Home | Reload | Images | Open | Print | Find | Stop

Location: http://tigger.stcloudstate.edu/~kilbornj/blazek/res_code.htm

What's New? | What's Cool? | Destinations | Net Search | People | Software

COMPUTER SKILLS

- **Operating Systems:**
  DOS, Unix, and OS/2
- **Programming Languages:**
  COBOL, Ada, C, HTML, Visual Basic
- **Software Packages:**
  Microsoft Windows 95, and Windows 3.1, Microsoft Excel, Word, PowerPoint, and Access; Microsoft Works, Lotus, Lotus Notes, and Wordperfect.

Return to Top

ACTIVITIES & HONORS

- Dean's List: St. Cloud State University, Fall '96
- BCIS Club, Chapter Representative for Association of Information Technology Professionals, Spring '97
- BCIS Club, Member, Fall '96 & Winter '97
- Student Hall Government, Bemidji State University Fall '92 - Spring '93
- Student Hall Government, Mankato State University Fall '91 - Spring '92

Return to Top

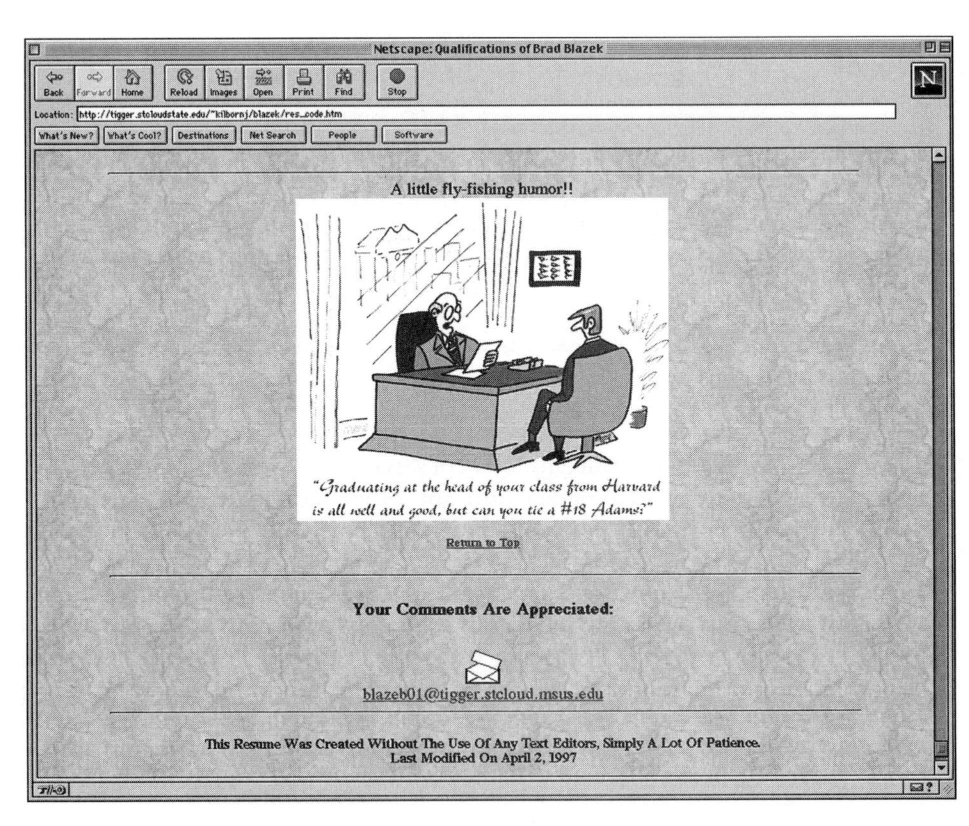

Netscape: Qualifications of Brad Blazek

Back | Forward | Home | Reload | Images | Open | Print | Find | Stop

Location: http://tigger.stcloudstate.edu/~kilbornj/blazek/res_code.htm

What's New? | What's Cool? | Destinations | Net Search | People | Software

A little fly-fishing humor!!

"Graduating at the head of your class from Harvard is all well and good, but can you tie a #18 Adams?"

Return to Top

Your Comments Are Appreciated:

blazeb01@tigger.stcloud.msus.edu

This Resume Was Created Without The Use Of Any Text Editors, Simply A Lot Of Patience.
Last Modified On April 2, 1997

FIGURE 8.14 Sample Web Resume

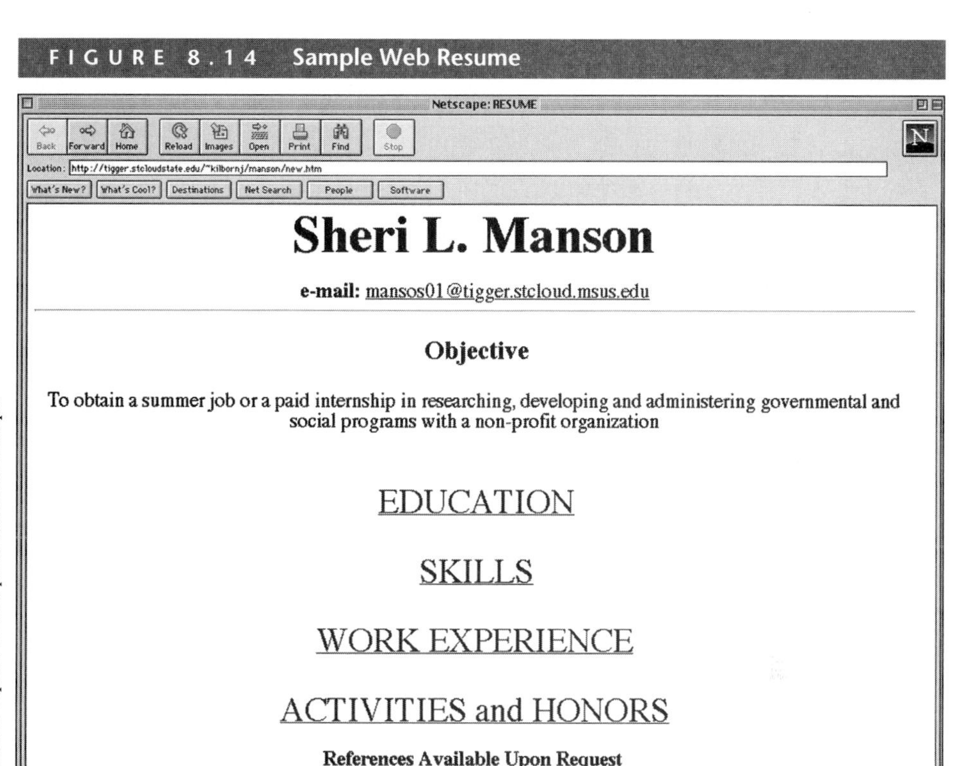
Netscape: RESUME

Back Forward Home Reload Images Open Print Find Stop

Location: http://tigger.stcloudstate.edu/~kilbornj/manson/new.htm

What's New? What's Cool? Destinations Net Search People Software

Sheri L. Manson

e-mail: mansos01@tigger.stcloud.msus.edu

Objective

To obtain a summer job or a paid internship in researching, developing and administering governmental and social programs with a non-profit organization

EDUCATION

SKILLS

WORK EXPERIENCE

ACTIVITIES and HONORS

References Available Upon Request

Document: Done.

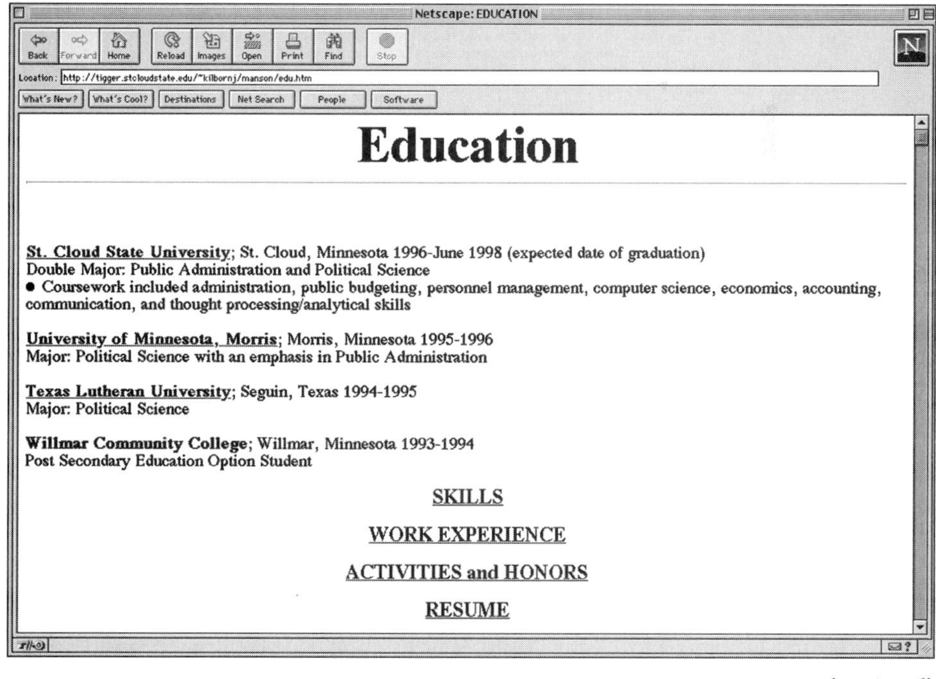
Netscape: EDUCATION

Back Forward Home Reload Images Open Print Find Stop

Location: http://tigger.stcloudstate.edu/~kilbornj/manson/edu.htm

What's New? What's Cool? Destinations Net Search People Software

Education

St. Cloud State University; St. Cloud, Minnesota 1996-June 1998 (expected date of graduation)
Double Major: Public Administration and Political Science
- Coursework included administration, public budgeting, personnel management, computer science, economics, accounting, communication, and thought processing/analytical skills

University of Minnesota, Morris; Morris, Minnesota 1995-1996
Major: Political Science with an emphasis in Public Administration

Texas Lutheran University; Seguin, Texas 1994-1995
Major: Political Science

Willmar Community College; Willmar, Minnesota 1993-1994
Post Secondary Education Option Student

SKILLS

WORK EXPERIENCE

ACTIVITIES and HONORS

RESUME

(continued)

FIGURE 8.14 Continued

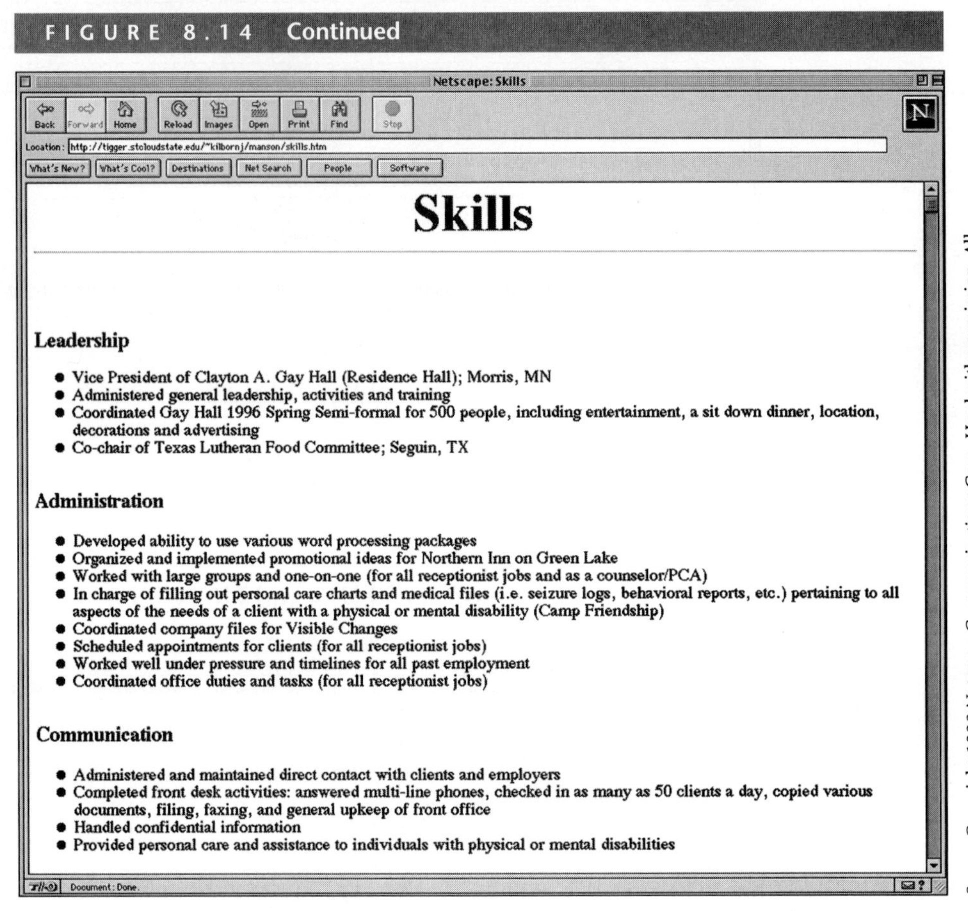

Netscape: Skills

Location: http://tigger.stcloudstate.edu/~kilbornj/manson/skills.htm

Skills

Leadership

- Vice President of Clayton A. Gay Hall (Residence Hall); Morris, MN
- Administered general leadership, activities and training
- Coordinated Gay Hall 1996 Spring Semi-formal for 500 people, including entertainment, a sit down dinner, location, decorations and advertising
- Co-chair of Texas Lutheran Food Committee; Seguin, TX

Administration

- Developed ability to use various word processing packages
- Organized and implemented promotional ideas for Northern Inn on Green Lake
- Worked with large groups and one-on-one (for all receptionist jobs and as a counselor/PCA)
- In charge of filling out personal care charts and medical files (i.e. seizure logs, behavioral reports, etc.) pertaining to all aspects of the needs of a client with a physical or mental disability (Camp Friendship)
- Coordinated company files for Visible Changes
- Scheduled appointments for clients (for all receptionist jobs)
- Worked well under pressure and timelines for all past employment
- Coordinated office duties and tasks (for all receptionist jobs)

Communication

- Administered and maintained direct contact with clients and employers
- Completed front desk activities: answered multi-line phones, checked in as many as 50 clients a day, copied various documents, filing, faxing, and general upkeep of front office
- Handled confidential information
- Provided personal care and assistance to individuals with physical or mental disabilities

Document: Done.

Expression

Needless to say, if you're designing an online resume—making decisions about the colors and graphics you'll use and other websites you'll link to—you have many opportunities for expressing your own identity but face many risks, too. Your primary concern in deciding what's appropriate should be your reader. Consider these questions:

- What sorts of organizations are you hoping to attract via your online resume, and what sorts of readers at these organizations are you hoping to impress?
- Does your online or web resume express the essential you through the keywords you've used?
- Will your online resume match you to the sorts of positions you're seeking and the kinds of employers you'd like to work for?

FIGURE 8.14 Continued

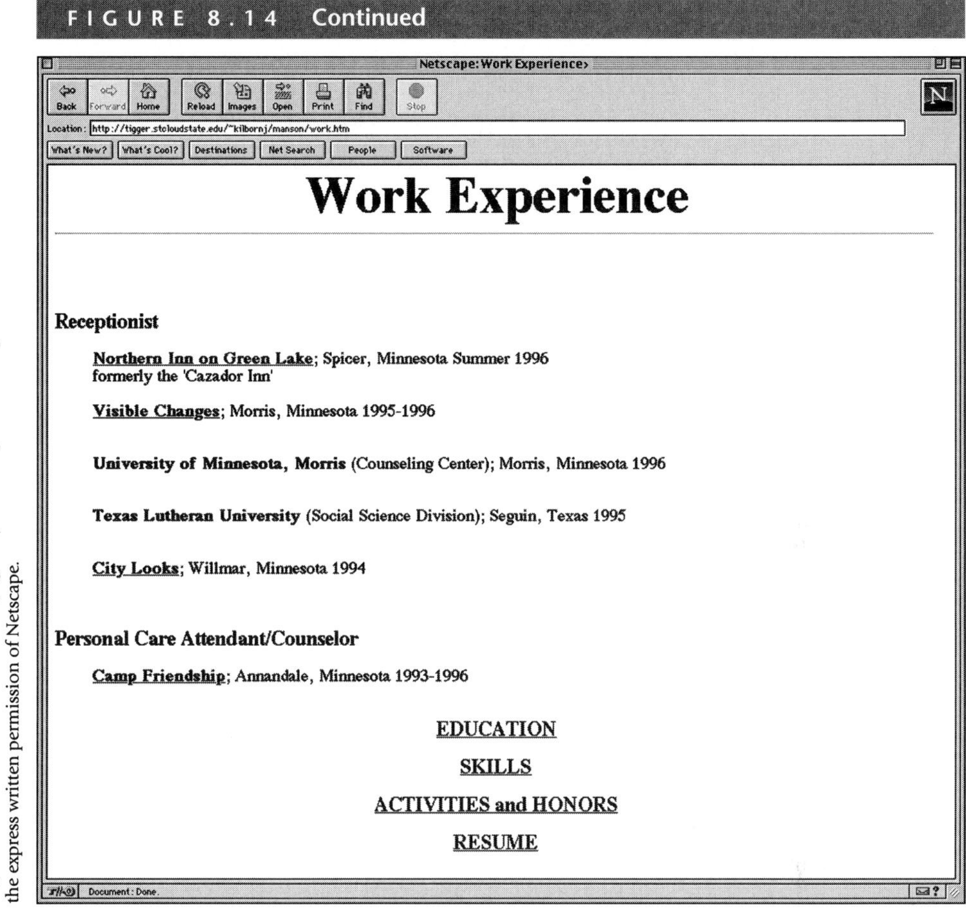

(continued)

- Does your web resume have the sort of visual impact that is appropriate for the kind of job you're seeking and the type of reader you hope to impress?
- Does it make the kind of statement you want to make about yourself?
- Does it express convincingly your technical competence in computers and visual design?

When in doubt about the appropriateness of some aspect of visual design or some new trend in web design, it's probably safest to err on the side of conservatism.

Since the conventions of online resumes will keep shifting as the technology matures, your online resume may, in fact, follow far different conventions and attract far different readers than we've suggested here. And your opportunities for expressing yourself and achieving your goals are likely to be more extensive too. Nevertheless, as we move into the twenty-first century, most job searchers are likely to prepare both print and electronic versions of their resumes.

FIGURE 8.14 Continued

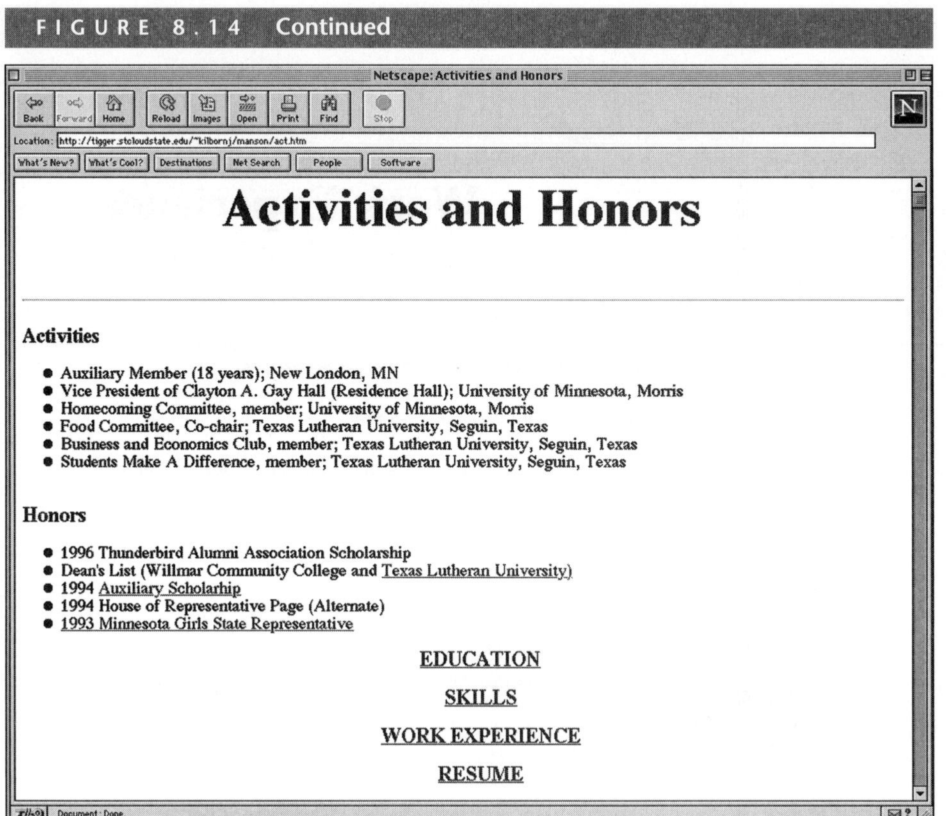

As this chapter suggests, resumes—as well as readers' expectations of them—have changed substantially from the time when a generic print resume chronologically related a job applicant's work history to a generic reader. Nowadays, effective resumes are arguments, rather than chronicles—compelling arguments that convince readers that the applicants "can do," "want to do," or "will do" what the prospective employer needs to have done. And in order to make these arguments, effective resume writers have invested considerable amounts of time—both in assessing their own backgrounds and in researching the organizations they are addressing—so they know how to adapt their resumes to individual readers with particular needs and interests. Today, many job seekers also take advantage of the World Wide Web and design online resumes that they can upload to their Internet accounts or that online employment services can upload to resume databases. Both print and online resumes are intended to begin a conversation with potential employers, a conversation that will hopefully continue for years. It's important to remember, though, that the resume is not by itself responsible for initiating and maintaining that conversation; it will be accompanied by other employment documents that will complement and extend its argument. It is to these other employment documents that we turn in Chapter 9, Building Effective Employment Letters.

FIGURE 8.15 Sample Functional Resume

BRADLEY C. BLAZEK

123 Main Street, Morristown, MN 55000 Tel. 612-555-1997
E-Mail: bblaze@tigger.stcloud.msus.edu Web Page: http://www.stcloud.msus.edu/~bblaze

OBJECTIVE

To utilize and expand my knowledge of information systems in an environment where I may contribute my business, analytical, and communication skills while being challenged to learn more

EDUCATION

ST. CLOUD STATE UNIVERSITY
Business Computer Information Systems Major, Graduation Date: November 1997
Major Coursework: Systems Analysis & Design I & II, Application Development I & II, IS Management
Coursework Remaining: Data Base Development, Telecommunications Processing, Decision Support Systems
Programming Languages: COBOL, Ada, C, HTML, and Visual Basic
GPA: 3.375/4.0

EXPERIENCE

LARSON, ALLEN, WEISHAIR & CO., CPA'S
Plan Administrator, June 1996–October 1996
- Performed full service administration of benefit plans for businesses
- Evaluated benefit plans including: 401(k), profit sharing, and welfare benefit plans
- Involved in evaluation and selection of mutual funds for investing division of LAWCO
- Performed personal financial planning with individual clients

FIRST BANK SYSTEM-GRAND FORKS, ND & EDINA, MN
Teller, December 1993–February 1996
- Held deposit, withdrawal, statement reconciliation, customer service, and daily cash box responsibilities
- Used vital customer service and conflict resolution skills
- Applied computer knowledge with speed and accuracy

GANDER MOUNTAIN-MAPLE GROVE
Customer Service Associate, October 1996–present
- Perform cashiering, merchandise returns, and cash box auditing
- Deal with problem customers and conflict resolution daily
- Very visible, people oriented position requiring superior interpersonal skills

ACTIVITIES AND HONORS

- Dean's List, St. Cloud State University, Fall 1996
- BCIS CLUB, Chapter Rep for Association of Information Technology Professionals, Spring 1997
- BCIS CLUB, Member, Fall and Winter 1997
- Student Hall Government, Mankato State University, Fall 1991 through Spring 1992
- Student Hall Government, Bemidji State University, Fall 1992 through Spring 1993

REFERENCES AVAILABLE ON REQUEST

WRITING CHECKLIST

The following guidelines will help you write print and online resumes that make the most of your life. For guidelines about managing your career search or writing your employment letters, see the Writing Checklists for Chapters 7 and 9, respectively. For any of these guidelines, remember the superordinate guideline: Disregard *any* of this advice if it would cause you to do something that's inappropriate or silly for your situation.

☑ Resumes

- Remember that the goal of a job search resume is not to get you a job but to get you on the "short list" of people who will be invited for interviews.
- Also keep in mind that your overall goal in the job search is to get you the *right* job, not just any job.
- Use your resume to begin a conversation with an organization that might lead to a match.
- Send your resume to someone in the organization in charge of the kinds of projects you'd like to do.
- Identify readers within organizations who will understand and appreciate the arguments you make in your resume.
- Remind yourself that your readers are likely to be busy, distracted, and perhaps skeptical or resistant when reading your resume.
- Provide evidence that you "can do," "want to do," and "will do."
- You can make the "will do" argument (based on character) directly through mention of service or citizenship awards, for instance, or indirectly through the way you present yourself in the resume.
- Include your name, addresses, and phone numbers and your e-mail address or the URLs for your websites.
- Make a direct claim about your qualifications or an indirect claim about your character in your career objective.
- State your objective clearly, concisely, and concretely and focus on prospective employers' needs.
- Clarify that you're looking for an internship, part-time, or summer job if you're not seeking a full-time, permanent position.
- At minimum, state your degrees, majors and minors, graduation date, and the locations and names of schools attended in the education section of your resume.
- Consider including second majors, GPAs, certifications, significant classes, seminars or workshops, special projects, computers, and foreign language skills, as long as they are relevant.
- Use a chronological resume if you can demonstrate long-term interest and commitment in a field.

- Use a functional resume if you want to stress your accomplishments and positions held.
- Use a skills resume to stress abilities you've demonstrated through work experience and volunteer activities, especially if you're making a "can do" argument based on technical and interpersonal competence.
- Use activities and honors sections to demonstrate long-term interest in a field, to confirm that your personality and preferences match those needed for the position, and to answer questions readers might have but can't ask (about health, for instance).
- Indicate willingness to provide references to prospective employers as the last item in your resume.
- Ask people ahead of time for permission to list them as references.
- Select your references carefully so they can help you make arguments about your technical and interpersonal competence as well as your character.
- Don't include information prior to the last two major mileposts in your career or information that is personal.
- Talk about personal interests or hobbies that are job related only if doing so helps you make "want to do" or "will do" character arguments.
- Your resume should be clean and neat, effectively formatted, and readable.
- Document design should help readers spot your most important qualifications and your documentation of them; design should also make it easy for readers to contact you.
- Use horizontal and vertical white space, side headings and lists, and an easily readable typeface to emphasize important information and make your resume inviting to read.
- Present your experience concretely, using action verbs.
- Select language that helps you to build your argument.
- Follow the conventions of spelling, punctuation, and usage to show that you care about getting the job done correctly and that you pay attention to details.

☑ Online Resumes

- Design your online resume to produce "hits" for the sorts of jobs you're seeking.
- Your online resume shouldn't look like your print resume; rather, it should be designed as a hypertextual screen document.
- Make the argument that you "can do" the sorts of technical tasks readers are looking for, including using computers and the World Wide Web.
- Instead of using action verbs and verb phrases in your online resume, use nouns in the text itself and in keywords visible to search engines; doing so will produce "hits."
- If you intend to send your online resume to an employment service database, keep it simple in design and typeface so that it will scan well.

- Design your web resume so it's more complex visually than your print resume, using background textures and colors, font colors, and graphics and icons.
- Avoid making graphics busy and distracting, however.
- Design your web resume so it unfolds for readers; link initial web screens to concrete evidence of credentials.
- Supplement your regular mail address and phone number with a "mail to" line, so people can contact you via e-mail.

ACTIVITIES AND PROJECTS

1. Interview a professional in your field about resumes. What does this person prefer to see in resumes? What sorts of background, preparation, and credentials does he or she look for? What, if any, particular conventions in this field govern what information is given and how it is presented?

2. Select a specific reader, organization, and position as a target for your resume. Then, analyze the needs and priorities of this reader and organization and the functions of this position and design your resume specifically for this target. Use GRACE as a series of benchmarks for generating information, shaping your argument, and deciding upon the organization and layout of your text. Once you have a complete draft of your resume, make enough copies so that each person in a group of your peers can have a copy to review and give you some thoughtful feedback. Also get as much feedback on your resume as you can from professors, career counselors, and (if possible) professionals in your field. Carefully think about and respond to their feedback as you revise.

3. Write a memo or e-mail to your instructor as part of the preparation for writing your resume. In the process of writing, be sure to answer the following questions:
   - Who will your primary readers be (both companies and individuals)?
   - What arguments do you plan to make in your resume, and how do you plan to support them?
   - What format will you use to develop your resume (chronological, functional, skills, creative), and why do you think this is a particularly good choice for you?

   In addition, be sure to raise any questions or concerns that you have about your resume.

4. Write one or more resumes to accompany the employment letters you'll write in response to Exercise 11, Chapter 9. Will all of the letters speak to similar situations, goals, and readers and make essentially similar arguments? If so, then a single resume will most likely serve for all three letters. But if the letters are seeking significantly different goals, you should massage the resume, customizing it for two or more different goals and readers.

5. Use a search engine to find World Wide Web sites offering resume services for both employers and job searchers. Check out sites that offer to scan or upload resumes to a database as well as those that give advice on writing resumes. If you can, find a site that maintains a database of resumes in your field. Read through the process the website describes for using its services and the guidelines it has for dealing with privacy issues (if any); if the database is public, browse through some resumes to find samples that are effective. Then write a description and analysis of what you have found.

6. Search the World Wide Web for sites that present online resumes. Browse through numerous resumes, noting what formats and styles do and don't work well. And write down the URLs (uniform resource locators, or addresses for websites) of examples that you think are particularly good or particularly bad. Then compare notes with colleagues in a small group: Together, look at the samples you've collected and critique them. Then come up with a list of principles for writing effective online resumes that you can share with the entire class.

7. Create an online version of your resume. The following html guidelines provide a basic introduction to html for coding your resume to prepare it as a web document. For more current and complete information about html coding, visit one of the following sites on the web, which provide online manuals for writing web documents, and download the instructions:

Advanced HTML	http://commsun.its.csiro.au/wwwinfo/htmladva.htm
Art and the Zen of Web Sites	http://www.tlcsystems.com/webtips.html
The Bare Bones Guide to HTML	http://www.werbach.com/barebones/
Creating Killer Web Sites Core Page	http://www.killersites.com/core.html
HTML Primer	http://www.ncsa.uiuc.edu/General/Internet/HTMLPrimer.html
Information Technologies Workshop: Hypertext	http://lrs.stcloud.msus.edu/cim/courses/pine/web.html
Introduction to HTML	http://www.utoronto.ca/webdocs/HTMLdocs/NewHTML/htmlindex.html
Style Guide for Hypertext	http://www.w3.org/pub/WWW/Provider/Style/Overview.html
Web Authoring Links	http://wrt.syr.edu/wrt/misc/www.html
Writing HTML: A Tutorial for Creating WWW Pages	http://hakatai.mcli.dist.maricopa.edu/tut/index.html

To prepare your online resume, follow these steps:

- Begin with the word-processed file that you created for your resume. It doesn't matter what word-processing program or computer platform you've used. You'll revise this file using your word-processing program to add html coding so that Netscape (or another web browser) can read it. Or you'll use an html editing program to add the coding to your document.
- Once you have added the coding, your electronic resume will be put on a server or you will put it on a server so that others can access it via the web.
- You'll need to decide what alterations to make in your resume as you revise it for an online version:
  - Do you want your online resume to look like your print resume? Or do you want to make alterations to take advantage of the electronic medium and the difference in the page?
  - Do you want your resume to be one document that readers can scroll through from top to bottom? If so, your resume will be one file—perhaps with internal links.
  - Would you prefer your resume to be a series of interlinking files so that readers can, for example, click on a "hot link" to call up another (perhaps more detailed) file? If so, your resume will have several files that will be linked via coding.
  - Do you want your resume to use any special lines, icons, or graphics? If so, you'll need to create those elements in a graphic program, use clip art, or download images from the Internet; the images will need to be saved in GIF or JPEG format* in order to be read by the web browser. In addition, you'll need to insert coding to call up the graphics files.
  - Do you want to revise your resume so you can submit it to a resume service, where it will be searched using key terms? If so, you'll need to think of what terms your prospective employers will use when they search resume databases. Remember that computers technically do the searching, not humans.

Viewing other online resumes might help you make these decisions. A variety of resume samples are available on the web. Use a search engine to find samples for review. If you like what you see on an online resume and want to know how a specific feature or resume was coded, you can look at the source under Options. You'll see exactly the coding that was used for that particular web document.

*A *GIF (Graphic Image File or Graphic Interchange Format)* or *JPEG (Joint Photographic Experts)* is a graphic created in an imaging program like PhotoShop. GIFs are useful for graphics, cartoons, line art, and flat illustrations, while JPEGs are useful for photographs and gray-scale files.

Here are some general html guidelines:

- All word-processed documents that you want your browser to read as web documents must be saved in text-only or ASCII format. You can select one of these formats when you save your file. Select the Save As option; then select Text Only if you're using a Macintosh and Text Only or ASCII (most likely ASCII) if you're using a PC.
- All word-processed documents that you want your browser to read as web documents must be saved with an html (Macintosh) or htm (PC) extension.
- Turn "smart quotes" off and replace any smart quotes (curly quotes) in your resume. (Smart quotes show up as weird characters when viewed through a web browser.) If you're using a Macintosh, turn off smart quotes under Tools and Preferences; if you're using Windows, they're listed under Tools and Autocorrect.
- Most html coding is relatively simple. You turn on a specific format by inserting a code before the word(s) you want to format in a particular way. Then you turn off the formatting feature by inserting another code after the word(s). Usually, the code to turn off a formatting feature is the same as the code to turn it on with the addition of a slash before the code. For instance, you would use <B>and </B> to turn boldface on and then off, as the following example shows:

```
<B>This text will be boldfaced when viewed through a web browser.</B>
```

- Some formatting codes are only turned on. For instance, <HR> is used when you would like to insert a line.
 and <P> will insert single-spaced and double-spaced carriage returns, respectively. No codes are used to turn off these formatting features. Here are some basic html formatting codes:

<HR>	Provides a separating line
 	Provides a single-spaced carriage return
<P>	Provides a double-spaced carriage return
<center>	Placed before a word or phrase, centers that text. To turn off, place </center> after the text.
<B>	Placed before a word or phrase, boldfaces that text. </B> turns off boldface.
<H1>	Placed before a word or phrase, makes that text a large heading. </H1> turns off the heading.
<H2>	Placed before a word or phrase, makes that text a smaller heading. </H2> turns off the heading.
<H3>	Placed before a word or phrase, makes that text an even smaller heading. </H3> turns off the heading.

8. Construct a list of references that you can hand to interviewers or send to employers at their request. Include on this list people's names and job titles, a brief description of the nature of their professional relationship with you, and their work addresses and phone numbers. Make sure that as you put this list together, you follow the conventions governing references (including asking permission, providing information about the position you're seeking, offering a resume, and so on).

Chapter 9

Building Effective Employment Letters

The most important thing . . . regarding your skills, is that you not merely claim you have certain skills, but prove you have them. You must set yourself apart from other job-hunters by being a Proof-giver, not merely a Claimer.

—Richard Nelson Bolles

There's a strong tendency for all of us to think about the employment letter as a single letter speaking to a single type of situation with a single message: "I'd like a job." But we all need to keep in mind that our situation, purpose, and message can vary radically when we're writing employment letters. In fact, a variety of situations and contexts during the employment search provide you with the opportunity to continue the conversation you've initiated with a prospective employer. And in writing these employment letters, you can make and reinforce the argument that you have a strong, informed interest in the prospective employer's organization.

Situations and Contexts for Employment Letters

To start with, not all employment letters are "I want a job" letters. In fact, as we argued at length in Chapter 7, almost no one expects to get a job based solely on a letter and resume. So even the "I want a job" letter is normally a request for an interview, not a job, necessarily.

But the variation ranges much more widely than this. In Chapter 7, we mentioned letters requesting information interviews, for example, and in Chapter 8, when we talked about listing references on your resume, we talked about the need to write people for permission to list them as references before listing them or otherwise giving their names to anyone. So, there are two important situational variations: requests for information or interviews and requests for letters of recommendation. In addition, there are a variety of follow-up situations that call for letters:

- A follow-up to your initial letter and resume that you send to an employer
- A follow-up letter after an interview or a visit to a prospective employer's work site, generally called a *second interview*
- A follow up to a rejection letter
- A thank-you letter to someone who has given you a reference, a career lead, or other help
- An acceptance letter replying to a job offer
- A rejection of a job offer
- A letter of negotiation, where you have received an offer that's attractive but still doesn't include everything you had hoped for

Our primary focus in this chapter will still be the application letter, which you write to someone you hope will eventually offer you a job—or at least an interview.

(This letter is sometimes called a *cover letter* since it accompanies the resume and is literally placed on top of the resume when they are sent out.) But we'll also look briefly at these employment letter contexts and their conventions:

- Letters requesting references or other help and letters of thanks for the help
- Letters to prospective employers after your initial letters
- Letters responding to actions by prospective employers: invitations to interviews, job offers, rejections, and the like

Making GRACEful Contact with Prospective Employers

Goals

Your most obvious goal in your employment search is to find a job that's the right job for you. In addition, your search also has a parallel goal that may ultimately be even more important than getting that next job: the lifelong process of building a network of friends, mentors, and advisors who will not only help you get jobs but will help you do your jobs better when you get them. As you approach the task of writing an initial letter to a prospective employer, these two large, momentous goals for the overall process of the career search can tend to draw your focus from the task at hand. So, remember that the *immediate* goal of this letter is really fairly straightforward and well defined. Employment counselors often express the goal for the letter in this maxim:

> **MAXIM**
>
> **The goal of the employment letter is to get the reader to read the resume.**

Together as a package, the letter and resume have the goal of starting a conversation with the reader. The kinds of conversations you hope to start with your letter/resume packages are not necessarily just job interviews. For example, in many of these letters, you may simply be seeking the advice and friendship of people who are working in the field where you want to work—or where you think you want to work. In this case, you may be seeking an *informational interview,* where you get a professional's insights on what a day-by-day career in your area of interest is really like; what kinds of skills, education, and experience are likely to lead to what this person does; and what this career path is like, in general. You may also be looking for advice about job prospects in several different kinds of organizations, not just in that organization. Or you may be hoping to find a mentor who would continue to give you career advice, job tips, and recommendations—perhaps even eventually an internship or job.

The important point here is that you should not think of your letter and resume as a one-shot, isolated communication. Think of that communication package as an invitation to a conversation that might conceivably go on for years. In Chapter 7, especially in the Activities and Projects, we talked at length about the kinds of ideas and questions you might want to raise in these conversations, and we discussed some of the conventions of informational interviews.

Readers

We have mentioned more than once that the resume and letter are a package—your employment package. This means that the same considerations about identifying an appropriate reader for your resume also apply to your letter. In Chapter 8, we discussed the difficult, often delicate question of whether to send your resume (and letter) to the personnel or HR (human resources) office. We concluded that the HR office is very often not your best reader; in general, HR people have far too many employment packages to read. We noted that your chances of getting a sympathetic reading of your employment package improve immensely if you can identify a particular person in the organization who is responsible for projects or functions that are the kinds of things you're interested in and do well.

So, the most desirable reader is that particular person who's been thinking, "Boy, I need the help of somebody who can ________." If you can find this reader and if you are a person who can ________, whatever ________ is, then the chances that your employment package will get a sympathetic reading will probably improve at least a hundredfold. So, it's worth doing the kind of research we talked about in Chapter 7 to try to find this reader. In reality, though, even with the best research and sleuthing, you may not find this perfect reader. So you may end up *satisficing:* writing to the best, most promising reader you can find under the circumstances.

Whoever your reader is, it's important to get as realistic a vision of this person's state of mind as possible. We think it's useful to imagine this person picking up your letter with the resume attached. What's the most likely question on this person's mind? Unless your research tells you otherwise, we think it's most likely something like "Why is this person writing to me?" Your reader is most likely busy and distracted, preoccupied with other documents, other people, and other responsibilities. This person is going to examine your letter with a skeptical, reluctant eye, looking for a reason to get rid of this uninvited chore. So, you need to answer your reader's question immediately. Why are you writing? You need to tell why—clearly and in terms that speak to this person's professional and organizational needs and responsibilities.

Doing this successfully requires two things: information and the thoughtful shaping of that information into arguments that speak effectively to your reader. The normal indexes in the library or official documents of organizations or directories in career services offices don't have categories like "People who hire people like me" or "People who do things I like to do" or "People I should talk to." You have to start by making some guesses, by scanning documents—paper or electronic—published by the organization itself or by other services. You have to think creatively about all your possible information sources, both inside or outside the organization. Do you know someone who actually works in the organization itself? Can you meet somebody who works in the organization? Do you know somebody who knows somebody who works in the organization?

This kind of personal contact can be your very best source of information—but it shouldn't be your only one. You need to do your reading homework, too. Read the corporate annual reports; articles about the organization in newspapers or magazines; evaluations, abstracts of self-study, and accreditation reports; and financial statements if they are available and relevant. You may even want to read similar documents about the organization's competitors, clients, and vendors.

All this reading and person-to-person gumshoeing will do two things for you:

1. It will generate specific names of people in the organization who are prospective readers of your letter or who could help you identify specific readers of your letter.
2. It will give you powerful data for what we think is your most important argument in the letter: that you have a strong and informed interest in this organization.

Arguments

As we discussed in Chapters 7 and 8, the conventions of argument in the rhetoric of the job search tend to limit how much you can make direct claims in all three of the basic arguments: *"can do," "want to do,"* and *"will do."* So, it's useful to think again about the layered structure of argument that we charted in Chapter 6. With each argument, you'll find it helpful to ask which layers of argument it's appropriate for you to present: *claim, data,* and *underlying assumptions.* As we'll discuss in detail, the primary layer of the argument in employment discourse is the data—the biography of your education and experience. The same broad basic arguments we talked about in Chapters 7 and 8 are still the arguments you want to make in your letter. Because the "want to do" argument tends to be the first argument in the letter, we'll talk about it first.

ARGUMENT 1: "Want to do."

As noted earlier, if this letter is your initial contact with this reader, it's almost inevitable that the first question on the reader's mind will be "Why is this person writing to me? What is this person's specific interest in me and in my organization?" The "want to do" argument answers this question.

Figure 9.1 shows a sample "want to do" argument. Notice that it is more than just an assertion that the writer wants to work for Duz-Great. It's an assertion *and* a demonstration. In the terms we used in Chapter 1, it's a *claim* and *supporting data.* It demonstrates that the writer actually understands the Duz-Great product and its benefits as well as some specific things the Duz-Great organization would need to have done in the Yukon. It also shows that the writer is interested in doing these specific kinds of marketing analyses. The level of detail and obvious energy and effort the writer has invested in knowing this detail about Duz-Great and its benefits, especially in the Yukon, constitute a compelling proof that the writer understands and is committed, in general, to the broader mission of Duz-Great.

FIGURE 9.1 Sample "Want to Do" Argument

I'd love to be a part of the Duz-Great Yukon marketing team. My family has used Duz-Great for years with great success, so I know firsthand how environmentally friendly it is. That's why, when I had a chance to do a marketing profile for my management class, I chose Duz-Great. I was especially interested to find that you have identified the Yukon as the most promising marketing opportunity for Duz-Great for the next decade because I have spent the last three summers in the Yukon, and I think Duz-Great would do wonders for the Thingamajigs up there.

In order to make claims like these effectively, you need to do the kind of organizational reconnaissance we proposed in Exercise 3 of Chapter 7, perhaps including some long-distance telephoning. You may even need to supplement that research with an informational interview, as we proposed in Exercise 4 of Chapter 7.

One of the best things about a good "want to do" argument is that it tends to incorporate the other arguments. When you begin to document your claim of interest with specific evidence of what you know about the organization, you're actually enacting the "will do" argument. You're demonstrating your work ethic by showing that you've made the effort to learn something about the company. And when you talk in specific, informed terms about why you find this specific information significant and interesting, you are demonstrating your technical competence—that you understand what the organization publishes about what it does. Finally, in talking about what the reader and the reader's organization are doing and connecting that specific information to your own interests, you are demonstrating your interpersonal competence—your ability to understand and identify with organizational projects and goals and to share a commitment to them.

But here are two important caveats:

CAVEAT 1: Don't assume that all employment letters should necessarily begin with or emphasize the "want to do" argument.

Remember, we're not talking about a formula for writing employment letters. We're talking about a smart way of reading and responding to your letter-writing situation. There will often be situations where your reader already knows you and where your interest is well established. There may be situations so exclusively and narrowly defined that the fact that you would even *inquire* about a position demonstrates your interest. You may be—now or later—so qualified in a given technical specialty that your expertise and experience essentially embody your "want to do" argument. Certainly, if you are writing a follow-up letter and responding to a request for specific information about technical qualifications, it would be bizarre to mute the discussion of technical qualifications and offer primarily a "want to do" argument.

CAVEAT 2: **Be careful about telling readers things they already know.**

First, here's an example of a layer of the argument that's probably better left unspoken: "Duz-Great Corporation needs to hire the best-qualified marketing people available for its Yukon campaign." If you've done a solid organizational analysis and identified the best reader for your employment package, this person is very likely in charge of hiring marketing people for Duz-Great. The risk here isn't that your reader will quarrel with this warrant. The risk is that your reader will find it obvious—and may find it condescending of you to point it out.

In a similar way, readers may be taken aback if you offer data they already know. Here's an example: "The Yukon is the most promising marketing opportunity for Duz-Great in the next decade." At first glance, this example may seem to contradict what we've just said above about making arguments that are grounded in specific information about the reader's organization. But a second glance shows that this example is not one of those arguments. It's just a bald statement of fact about the reader's organization. Look again at the way this same information is framed in the example above: "I was especially interested to find that you have identified the Yukon as the most promising marketing opportunity for Duz-Great for the next decade, because I have spent . . . " Here, the writer is investing the data with personal significance that documents a genuine, informed interest in the reader's organization.

ARGUMENT 2: **"Can do."**

The "can do" argument is the most obvious one in the rhetoric of the job search. It simply says you are qualified to do the job—or have the education, experience, and ability to learn to do the job with a reasonable investment of the prospective employer's time and money. As we noted in Chapters 7 and 8, it's less obvious that there are two facets to the "can do" argument:

- **Technical competence** is the ability to use the language and other tools of your particular position or your profession effectively and efficiently.
- **Interpersonal competence** is the ability to use your technical abilities in cooperation with colleagues, supervisors, and people you supervise.

Both facets of the argument are crucial because the work you do will not take place in a vacuum. You will have to depend on other people for information, equipment and other resources to do your job, and other people will depend on you in order to do their work. More and more often, your work will *be* their work, and their work will be yours. You will be working with others—side by side and mind with mind—on the same problem, at the same time. In situations like this, your technical competence will be useless if you can't draw from and contribute to other people's working and thinking.

Figure 9.2 shows an example of a "can do" argument. On one level, this is just a "what I did last summer" narrative, but it also embodies both facets of the "can do" argument. This person is claiming technical competence in document design and graphical layout as well as the two major office computer platforms used in editing and design. And the claim doesn't stop here: The brief description culminates with a

FIGURE 9.2 Sample "Can Do" Argument

> During my internship with the public relations agency last summer, I worked primarily in document design and layout. We used both Macintosh and Windows platforms because our clients were giving us material from both. I especially enjoyed the challenge of working as part of a three-member team under the pressure of meeting a client's tight deadline.

claim that the person actually enjoyed the challenge of working cooperatively under the pressure of a tight deadline, so it draws on interpersonal competence, too.

CAVEAT 3: **Be careful about pre-empting the reader's decisions.**

For example, there sometimes is significant risk in the claim "I am the best qualified person for this job." It's the *reader's* responsibility to make that claim, not yours as the job seeker. There's a certain amount of "puffing up" that's allowed and even expected from job seekers, and, in fact, it's not uncommon to see this very claim being made. But there's a line between reasonable confidence, which is a virtue, and cockiness, which is not. This claim may lie on either side of that line, depending on the circumstances. (We'll talk more about this under Expression.)

ARGUMENT 3: **"Will do."**

The "will do" argument says that you have the ethical character to deal in good faith with people both inside and outside the organization. It says you will give a full day's work for a day's pay—not only to get the job done but to get the job done well. It says you will be a faithful custodian of the financial, physical, and human resources that become your responsibility and that you can be trusted to represent your employer faithfully and honestly in your dealings with customers, clients, vendors, and others. We've noted before how the "will do" argument is especially difficult to make. Cultural conventions against making direct ethical claims for yourself are so strong that to say "I'm an honest, hard-working person" immediately arouses suspicion that you're neither honest nor hard working. So, like the other two arguments, the "will do" argument generally omits the direct claim and just offers data—a story of your trustworthiness in past actions that leaves the reader to infer that you'll act ethically in the future.

Figure 9.3 shows an example of a "will do" argument. As with the earlier two examples, this paragraph is, on one level, a basic factual description of what happened. But again, as with the other two examples, the writer has presented this data so there's a clear point—in other words, this writer doesn't leave the reader wondering "So what?" The ethical claim—the "will do claim"—is clearly implicit in this paragraph. The reader presumes that Smith Stores didn't have to hire this person back each summer and concludes that Smith Stores found the writer dependable and reliable. The information about increasing responsibility reinforces this implicit claim and, further, suggests a strong work ethic, people skills, and teachability. The fact that the writer was given supervisory responsibility in two different departments clearly suggests not only a willingness to take responsibility but a versatility of both talent and interest. Finally, the fact that the writer returned each summer will not be lost on the reader, either. Five summers of returning to the same employer suggests a strong sense of loyalty to one's employer.

Another significant feature of the "will do" argument is that it's the most portable of all the arguments in the rhetoric of the job search. Interpersonal competence tends to transfer readily from one kind of employment site to another, whereas technical competence does not transfer so readily across different kinds of environments and technical demands. Likewise, interest in a particular kind of work does not reliably predict interest in another. But honesty, loyalty, a strong work ethic, and commitment to quality all tend to be transferable from one kind of work situation to another. Hence, people with relatively little directly relevant work experience should look especially hard for opportunities to make powerful "will do" arguments. If you have extensive experience as a volunteer or a homemaker, for example, you should glean this part of your biography with special care for examples that demonstrate your general character, your work ethic, your time management skills, your people skills, and your ability to learn and adapt to new situations and to take responsibility in these situations.

CAVEAT #4: Don't assume you can never make claims directly.

Throughout this discussion of argument, we talked about the virtue of modesty in making your claims. For instance, the Smith Stores example (Figure 9.3), which we've just praised, doesn't make any direct "can do," "want to do," or "will do" claims. We like the way it makes those claims implicitly. Even so, don't feel that you can't make these claims at all. Again, we're not talking about "do" and "don't" formulas here. We're talking about smart reading of your situation and your readers and smart expression of your authentic character.

For examples of letters making these claims quite directly, see those written by Karen Meehan, Karin Lagaard, Rachel Davis, Brad Rossiter, and Melissa Wellington, which appear in Figures 9.4 through 9.8. For a letter that makes the claim much more indirectly, see Tom Lucas' letter in Figure 9.9.

FIGURE 9.3 Sample "Will Do" Argument

> Smith Stores has asked me to come back and work for them every summer for the last five years, and they have increased my responsibility each year. Last year, they assigned me to supervise the accounting and customer service departments when those managers went on vacation.

FIGURE 9.4 Sample Application Letter with Direct Claim

3737 Fourteenth Street South
St. Cloud, MN 56303
January 9, 1996

Ms. Christine Steward, Division Manager
Housing and Community Development Block Grant Division
P. O. Box 1936
Anchorage, AK 99537-6250

Dear Ms. Steward:

"Oh, we have a home, we just need a house to put it in."

This statement by a ten-year-old homeless girl sums up why I believe the combination of my background, experience, writing skills, and commitment to make a difference will be an asset to Community Development Block Grant Division. I look forward to working with other people to provide citizens with the means to live in houses where memories are made. Please consider hiring me for a three-month summer position. During this time I will be able to help close out FY '96, bring in FY '97, and begin work on various writing projects.

Anchorage is my home; I have grown up here and watched it change and grow. The experience received while working with the Anchorage Day Care Assistance Office during summers and breaks has initiated an understanding of the Municipality and introduced me to business writing and research for grant programs. My educational background will allow me to begin updating policy and procedures and editing drafts of the 1996 Consolidated Plan with a competence acquainted with today's written communication.

My extra-curricular activities, such as involvement in the Campus Chapter of Habitat for Humanity and my International Studies experience, have given me a perspective on further change and growth in our community. Travels have shown me the diverse living conditions existing throughout Europe and the United States. The drooping eyes of a young child begging on the streets of Rome are still burned into my mind, right next to the memory of a family in Florida with whom I worked side by side constructing their first home. The warmth I felt contributing to this home will be expressed in every gesture of my work with the Community Development Block Grant office: be it a word in a sentence or reviewing a loan application with a client.

In providing me a summer position, you will experience the optimism, determination, and sincerity I can bring to the Community Development Block Grant Division. I will be in Anchorage during the first week in March and am interested in speaking with you in person to answer any further questions you may have after reviewing my enclosed resume. You can reach me in Anchorage at 555-0662 or in St. Cloud at (320) 555-1339. Thank you.

Sincerely,

Karen M. Meehan

Karen M. Meehan

Enclosure: Resume

FIGURE 9.5 Sample Application Letter with Direct Claim

182 8th Avenue S. E.
St. Cloud, MN 56304
October 17, 1997

Carol Martinson
Program Manager
Central Minnesota Initiative Fund
2258-½ East Broadway
P.O. Box 59
Little Falls, MN 56345

Dear Ms. Martinson:

Through my education and experience, I have learned that the best and most effective planners are those with good peripheral vision—those who not only have mastered the technical side of planning but also understand the relationship between planning issues and the major forces in the community around them. Your advertisement in the St. Cloud Urban Affairs Office describes the type of internship I am seeking.

The experience received while working for the City of Crosslake last summer has expanded my vision of the planning process and my passion for this exciting field. I am looking for the opportunity to work with local community groups in your area. The Central Minnesota Initiative Fund interests me because it works with fourteen counties in Central Minnesota. A position with your organization will enable me to demonstrate the reality of planning practice and see what goes on under the surface of events on a broad spectrum.

My education has given me the knowledge of the intent and purpose of city planning principles, and my professional experience has provided me the tools to implement planning thought. I have successfully demonstrated my research skills in academics and as an advisory member on the Comprehensive Planning Committee of Crosslake.

As an intern, I would be a knowledgeable and determined representative voice for community development issues. Please contact me at the above address or call me at (320) 555-4938 to discuss intern opportunities. Thank you for your time and consideration.

Sincerely,

Karin L. Lagaard

Karin L. Lagaard

Enclosure: Resume

FIGURE 9.6 Sample Application Letter with Direct Claim

35 Mitchell Hall
St. Cloud, MN 56301
February 15, 1997

Ms. Carol Hruby
First American Trust Company
1208 East College Drive
Marshall, MN 56258

Dear Ms. Hruby:

Enclosed please find my application and resume for consideration in filling the Tax Coordinating position currently open at your Marshall office. I am well qualified for this position given my educational background and previous work experience.

This job interests me for a number of reasons. As Tax Coordinator at the St. Cloud office for the 1996 tax season, I have gained much valuable experience in tax work. Working with Depreciation Schedules, Tax Worksheets, Estimate Requirements, and Carry-overs, I am responsible for preparing and delivering the clean files of over 300 non-grantor trusts to the appropriate accounting firms. My knowledge and experience would be an asset to the company, and the company would be a superb outlet for my interests and skills.

I appreciate your time in reviewing my application and resume. You can reach me at (320) 555-3791 during the evening or at (320) 555-7174 during the day. I look forward to hearing from you very soon.

Sincerely,

Rachel A. Davis

Rachel A. Davis

Enclosure: resume

FIGURE 9.7 Sample Application Letter with Direct Claim

6119 Michigan Avenue, #106
St. Cloud, MN 56304
January 25, 1997

Mr. Tom Cross
System Administrator
Kendeco Industrial Supply
4151 Sunridge Drive
St. Cloud, MN 56304

Dear Mr. Cross:

While reading the news group cloudnet.chat, I saw your announcement of a position opening in your system administration department. The announcement indicated that Kendeco is searching for applicants with C and UNIX experience. I believe my extensive background and interest in C and UNIX qualify me for this position.

I am currently a student at St. Cloud State University majoring in computer science. The computer science program is accredited by CSAB and offers many challenging courses. My current GPA is 3.5, and I plan to graduate in the spring of 1998. In three years of professional experience in the computer industry, I have developed communications and technical skills. While at WinApps, I learned the basics of software development and how to work effectively within a team. Because I understand that being in the system administration department is not all software development, I believe my technical experience (as described in my enclosed resume) may be particularly useful.

I hope to meet with you in an interview to further discuss my qualifications, experience, and interest in working for Kendeco. Please e-mail me at rossiter@tigger.stcloudstate.edu or telephone me anytime at 320-555-1333 to schedule an appointment.

Sincerely,

Brad Rossiter

Brad Rossiter

Enclosure: Resume

FIGURE 9.8 Sample Application Letter with Direct Claim

251 33rd Avenue North
St. Cloud, MN 56304
March 7, 1997

Roger Holmes
Chief, Section of Wildlife
Minnesota Department of Natural Resources
Box 67, 300 Centennial Building
St. Paul, MN 55155

Dear Mr. Holmes:

With over eight years of retail experience as well as two years of naturalist interpretive work, I can bring to the Department of Natural Resources a valuable public contact background. Upon my graduation from St. Cloud State University, I will also have four years of academic excellence that has emphasized a holistic approach to wildlife management in preparation for an entry-level field biologist position.

My program in wildlife management included a strong base of plant taxonomy as well as field work that focused on avian biology. This background will enable me to participate in census and survey data collection so vital for establishing habitat protection and development plans. In addition, my previous computer experience with the U.S. Fish and Wildlife Service will help me work effectively in data interpretation.

I have viewed conservation from a number of perspectives. As a docent at Como Zoo in St. Paul, I participated in two captive animal studies. As a naturalist at Heritage Nature Center in St. Cloud, I gained interpretive experience. And finally, as a biological aid with the U.S. Fish and Wildlife Service, I learned the basic operations of conducting a long-term study. I understand these qualities are essential for effective field biologists.

I would appreciate the opportunity to speak with you at your convenience. I can be contacted at (320) 555-8829. Thank you for your consideration.

Sincerely,

Melissa Wellington

Melissa Wellington

Enclosure: Resume

FIGURE 9.9 Sample Application Letter with Indirect Claim

534 2nd Avenue North
Sauk Rapids, MN 56379
January 8, 1998

Mr. John Rabe, Host
Minnesota Public Radio
2145 East 7th Street
St. Paul, MN 55101

Dear Mr. Rabe:

I entered the competitive industry of commercial broadcasting thirteen years ago with a mission of quality. The source of my idealism was a childhood spent basking in the warmth and professionalism of news and information-based radio in '60s and '70s Chicago. It was radio based on truth, trust, and responsibility, which still are my goals as a professional broadcaster. My concern with commercial broadcasting springs from a gradually deteriorating base of responsibility standards. Fortunately, radio listeners still have Minnesota Public Radio to which professional broadcasters such as I can aspire.

During my career, I have enjoyed the opportunities that I have had to provide programming at a special higher level and to work closely with an award-winning news staff on a daily basis. My interview skills are exercised regularly as I have conversed on-air with newsmakers from all over Minnesota and the country. The tastes which form the basis of my style include popular, jazz, and classical music, as well as reading great literature and writing. My college studies focus on English with a writing emphasis and Psychology, which have further enhanced my communication skills. True and honest communication is my most important contribution.

I am very interested in learning more about a new focus on public broadcasting, where my personal and professional goals can be realized. I would like to meet you in person to discuss any opportunities that you might currently have available and to get your perspective on this challenging area of professional broadcasting. Please call me at (320) 555-3945 at a convenient time to set up a meeting. I have an answering machine. It is my hope that it will be a mutually beneficial meeting, *"All Things Considered."* Thank you.

Respectfully,

Thomas M. Lucas

Thomas M. Lucas

Enclosure: Resume

Conventions

In most career search situations, both the social and formal conventions of letter writing tend to be pretty inflexible, especially when the competition for jobs is strong and readers need filters to help them keep their "short" list short. One of the strong conventions has to do with the employment package itself. Most career services advisors we know quote it as a maxim:

> **MAXIM**
>
> **Don't send the letter without a resume, and don't send the resume without a letter.**

The resume and cover letter are complementary parts of a complete employment package. It would be a rare situation, indeed, where you'd send a letter without a resume or a resume without a letter. If you were in a conversation and someone asked you for a resume on the spot, it would be common to hand him or her a resume without a letter. But you'd almost invariably want to follow up with a letter, and you might even want to send a *second* resume at that time. You don't know what might have happened to that first resume. It might have been passed on to someone else, filed away, lost, or any number of things.

It's also appropriate to send a resume with your letter in other employment-related contexts. For example, if you're writing someone for permission to use them as a reference, it's a good idea to enclose a resume to help your referee remember details of the good things you've done. An exception to the rule may occur when you're following up after an extensive interview situation, where you know the reader has copies of your resume on file. Sending yet another resume in this situation may strike your reader as excessive. In most situations, though, it's safe to err on the side of redundancy and send a resume with a letter.

For every general rule or piece of advice, there are exceptions. Elizabeth Kuoppala's letter to the Department of Medicinal Chemistry at SUNY Buffalo (see Figure 9.10) is probably one exception to the rule to always send a resume with a letter. Notice that her situation is not the conventional job application situation, though. Her letter is certainly a cover letter, but it's accompanying an application for graduate school that probably serves the same function as a resume in providing relevant information about her. Also, her letter is a bit longer than the conventional job application letter and includes much of the information one would normally expect to find in a resume.

Ways into the Employment Letter

Immediately establishing the context in which you're writing is a strong convention in professional letters, in general, and in employment letters, it's imperative. Rarely

FIGURE 9.10 Sample Cover Letter for Graduate School Application

1050 North 23rd Avenue
St. Cloud, MN 56303
October 14, 1997

Michael Detty, Ph.D.
Director of Graduate Studies
Department of Medicinal Chemistry
39 Cooke Hall
Box 601
Buffalo, NY 14260-1200

Dear Dr. Detty:

I am applying to the Ph.D. program in Medicinal Chemistry because of my determination to give hope of therapeutic aid to the less fortunate, because of my fascination with pursuing new ideas, and because my life experiences have prepared me for the challenges of independent research.

I had the opportunity after graduating from my rural Minnesota high school in 1989 to study and work in Finland, the land of my forefathers. Upon my return home, I followed the family tradition of seeking employment in the blue-collar industry. As a locomotive engineer for US Steel, I was awed by the sheer power of the machine, but I was soon bored with the mundane nature of my work. I spent many of my off-hours visiting the rehabilitation center for alcoholics, trying to understand the desperation of those feeling choked by the stagnation of life on Minnesota's Iron Range.

Determined to break free from the rut that claimed the spirits of many of my coworkers, I began my studies at St. Cloud State University and my work as a live-in care giver for a person in the advanced stages of Parkinson's disease. My frustration with the patient's helplessness was tempered my sophomore year when I was introduced to the principles of synthetic organic chemistry and their therapeutic applications.

That summer, 1996, I went back to US Steel to work as a summer intern in the Quality Assurance Laboratory. I enjoyed writing the Laboratory Contingency Plan in consultation with the Company Industrial Hygienist and officials from Mining Safety & Health Administration and the Environmental Engineering Department. I was excited also by the instrumentation used for analyzing ores, oils, and water: Inductively coupled plasma atomic emission spectrometer, sulfur analyzer, and Fourier Transform infrared interferometer. But at the ISO-certified company, most of my work involved strictly following well-documented procedures, and I felt that the only thoughts I was permitted were the parrots of other people's thinking.

Last summer, 1997, as an undergraduate research assistant in the laboratory of Dr. Janet Morrow at the State University of New York-Buffalo, I was introduced to the challenge of carrying out novel research. I experienced both the frustration of failed synthesis and the joy of creation as we endeavored to prepare organic compounds for use as metal ligands in the transesterification of ribonucleic acid. As I explored the vast array of

(continued)

FIGURE 9.10 Continued

research being undertaken at UB, I marveled at the powerful applications of technologies such as NMR spectroscopy and Secondary Ion Mass Spectrometry. In every group I visited, I was intrigued by individuality and boundless opportunity. Nowhere did I find the monotonous drudgery of my industrial experiences.

I am applying to the University at Buffalo's Medicinal Chemistry doctoral program because its strong emphasis on synthetic organic chemistry combined with its broad interdisciplinary scope will be an excellent foundation for a career in academic research. I feel confident that my summer experiences and my work for the Department of Chemistry at St. Cloud State University, combined with my undergraduate coursework, have prepared me well for graduate work.

I thank you for considering my application.

Sincerely,

Elizabeth Kuoppala

Elizabeth Kuoppala

does the reader of your employment letter approach this reading task with a sense of leisurely interest. The insistent question "Why is this person writing to me?" needs an immediate answer because readers of employment letters and the resumes that accompany them are notoriously impatient.

If you're responding to an ad, flier, e-mail posting, or other announcement, tell your reader right away exactly how you learned about the position. Also describe the position briefly but exactly. See Brad Rossiter's letter (Figure 9.7), for example. Employers often advertise more than one position at the same time. If you heard of the position by word of mouth from someone your reader knows, then you should certainly mention that person, unless there's a specific reason not to. If your initial letter is a prospecting inquiry, you should still identify, as specifically as possible, the kind of job you're looking for and mention any connections or leads from people your reader might know.

Even if the letter is not your initial contact, your reader may still need an orientation. Maybe the reader won't immediately remember you. Or the reader may remember you and still not know why you're writing. Did your reader ask you to follow up an earlier letter or conversation with some additional information? Are you taking the initiative of following up on your own? In either case, remind your reader of any contacts you've already had, and if you haven't had any, establish immediately the context of why you're writing. As we've just noted, one of the most effective ways of giving this context is to make a brief but effectively documented "want to do" argument. In other words, say right up front that you're interested in a job with this organization and say what that job is.

If this is your initial contact, your reader is also likely to be asking "How did this person get my name?" Unless you will violate the confidentiality of a source, you should probably answer this question. Have you met this person before? Certainly, you should mention when, where, and other contextual information. Do you know someone in common? You should almost certainly mention this. And why are you writing to this particular person or this particular department in this particular company? What specific information leads you to have the interest you have? These last two questions, of course, suggest a transition into the main part of your letter, the heart of your "can do," "want to do," and "will do" arguments.

Ways of Developing Body Paragraphs

In the main part of the letter, you show why you're someone who should be invited to an interview. Here, you need to decide which claims and which evidence will be most persuasive for this reader, at this time, and under these circumstances. You don't want to make your reader work too hard. Remember, people who read job-seeking letters are impatient readers. Remember, also, that you're not trying to convince somebody to hire you, just to talk with you.

With all these factors, convention strongly favors relatively short, tightly developed paragraphs. So, as you look at each paragraph in the body of your letter, review it with a critical eye, asking yourself, "So what is the point in this paragraph? Will my reader clearly see and appreciate my point? Does my evidence support my point?" And as you look at the paragraphs, one after another, ask whether this is the best way for your self-portrait to unfold. For example, are you leading with what seems to be the most compelling argument for your qualifications? Usually, you should.

Ways Out of the Employment Letter

You've figured out an effective and GRACEful entry into your employment letter, and you've made the arguments you need to make. Now what? How do you get out? Let's cycle back to the beginning—to your goals—for a moment. Why were you writing this letter? To get an interview? To follow up after an interview in a way you hope will keep the conversation going?

Like the beginning of the letter, the final paragraph is a hook, linking the letter to the flow of events and people around it. Whereas the beginning set the context and identified your purpose in writing, the ending needs to direct the reader toward the specific action you seek. It needs to describe what you want to do and what you want your reader to do. And you need to look at it carefully to make sure you're giving your reader all the information necessary to do what you want. Here's a list of questions you may find useful in drafting and revising your closing paragraph:

- What do you want to happen next?
- Do you want the reader to call or write you with an invitation to an interview?

- Do you want to offer your e-mail address?
- How about giving your phone number here—and saying when you'll be at that number or how you can be reached if you're not there?
- Do you have an answering machine or voice mail, where your reader can leave a message?
- Is there another number where you can be reached during the day?
- Are there regular hours when you can and can't be reached?
- Do you have travel plans that would put you conveniently close to the reader for an interview at some specific time soon?
- Are there other constraints on your work schedule or calendar—major travel plans, commitments to project deadlines, graduation schedules, and the like—that your reader should know about in order to expedite further contact with you?

Here's a question that needs some especially careful thinking: What about making the offer "I'll call you"? Is it easier for you to follow up? Would you prefer to follow up with a phone call, rather than wait for the reader to call you? This can be an effective tactic. It gives you more control over the ongoing exchange. On the other hand, it has definite risks. In responding to a recent survey of midsized corporate employers in Minnesota, about one-third of the employers said they liked having a job seeker volunteer to take the initiative in following up, but nearly half strongly disliked it. Those who disliked the "I'll call you" tactic noted that they already felt overwhelmed by the volume of mail they were getting from job seekers and that follow-up calls were a distraction that added to their burden and impeded their ability to follow up. So, if you decide to announce that you'll take the initiative in following up, understand that there is some risk in doing so. You may be able to mitigate that risk if you can offer some need for taking the initiative. For example, it may be that you have a vacation scheduled to begin in three weeks or so and you will be traveling to the city where your reader is located. If your reader wants to talk with you but doesn't get back to you for 3½ weeks, then you both will be disappointed.

Formatting Employment Letters

In addition to following the conventions governing the document design of letters, in general, you'll want to follow several conventions for employment letters, in particular:

1. Many people include their phone numbers in their return addresses, right above the dateline. You might want to do this so that readers can readily get in touch with you—even if your letter and resume get separated.
2. It's conventional to indicate that an enclosure accompanies the letter; double-space below the writer's typed name in the signature block and type the word *resume* to the right of the word *Enclosure.*
3. It's conventional to mention the resume in the text of your letter, drawing the reader's attention to something specific that you want him or her to notice.

For instance, after talking about how you've developed team-building skills through community and campus activities, direct your reader's eyes to details concerning these activities provided on your resume. But a word of warning about the placement of this reference is important: Place it late in your letter—ideally, in the last or second-to-last paragraph—so that your reader can finish your letter and then move smoothly into reading your resume *without* having to decide whether to continue reading the letter.

Expression

Like the resume, the employment letter is, at its core, an expressive document. All three of the generic arguments are expressive arguments: I "can do," "want to do," and "will do." And the fact that the employment letter is explicitly addressed to a specific reader makes it all the more expressive. Yet one reason employment letters and resumes are difficult to write is that deeply ingrained cultural taboos against bragging about ourselves inhibit us from talking effectively about ourselves in positive terms. People from other cultures may think of Americans as flamboyantly self-promoting, but in fact, there is still a powerful ethic of modesty (notwithstanding the behavior of many sports, entertainment, and political celebrities). All this makes the "will do" argument especially difficult. Here, more than with any other argument, making a direct claim entails risks of undermining the claim itself: "Trust me. I care only about your best interests. I am not a crook."

Rather than make the claim directly, then, you may be on far safer ground to try to embody and enact your ethical stance in the way you express yourself in your letter as you make your other arguments. Ask yourself these questions:

- Do you disclose—in a style that is clear, vivid, and specific—how and why you are interested in the reader's organization and how that interest is grounded in your experience and expertise along with your knowledge of that organization?
- Do you express appropriate confidence in your abilities and pride in your accomplishments?
- At the same time, do you express appropriate appreciation for your teachers, supervisors, mentors, and colleagues?
- And do you express an appropriately humble eagerness to learn more about your own technical field and about the reader's organization?
- Do the brief stories you tell in support of your "can do" and "want to do" arguments allow the reader to see the ethical system that informs your behavior?
- At the sentence level, is your language forthright, clear, and professionally appropriate?
- Is your jargon appropriate, or does it serve to obscure what you've done?
- Are your sentences cast in the active voice? (Almost without exception, they should be. You want to show yourself as a doer.)

- On the other hand, are you starting every sentence with *I* so that you're sounding a bit egomaniacal?
- Are you showing a thoughtful appreciation for the situation and your reader by observing the conventions of an employment letter?
- Are you showing a certain creativity or willingness to take some risks by pushing or breaking certain conventions? (Do you want to? The answer, more often than not, may be "no.")
- If so, are you showing a savvy awareness of the conventions in any case—and demonstrating tactics for mitigating the risks (such as explaining a tight deadline if you're proposing to follow up your letter with a telephone call)?

Other Contexts, Goals, and Readers in the Employment Search

One of the best things about networking as a concept for thinking about the job search is that it helps break the spell of thinking of the job search letter and resume as having—or needing to have—some almost superhuman power to get you a job. The networking concept puts the job search back in a more realistic context, and the communication we'll talk about now is concerned at least as much with nurturing this network as it is with getting the job that's immediately in front of you.

Nurturing and Using Your Network: Requests and Thanks

We've talked before about the fact that most professional communication has two orientations: task orientation and relationship orientation. And that's certainly true of the letters of request and thanks that you write to friends, colleagues, and mentors in your network. While these situations tend, in general, to be straightforward and routine, you should still handle them thoughtfully. For an extended, general GRACE for letters, see Chapter 5. What follows is a sharply abbreviated GRACE.

Goals

If your letter is a request for a reference, you clearly have both a task and a relationship orientation. You want your reader to agree to be a witness to your qualifications, and you need to tell her or him what kind of testimony would be most helpful for you and useful for your prospective employer. In some cases, you're asking your reader to take an active role, writing a letter of support. Other times, you're asking him or her to take a passive role, just allowing you to list his or her name and phone number so a prospective employer can call. In either case, you're also invoking the relationship you've had with this reader—your employer, teacher, coach, mentor, or colleague. And it's also in your interest to re-energize and nurture this relationship.

Readers

Probably the most useful advice here is something that's pretty obvious but that people fairly often forget: Make sure this person knows you well and can speak specifically and authoritatively about your experience, character, and qualifications. Resist the temptation to try to impress prospective employers by using as a reference some prominent person you know only distantly.

Arguments

It can be very useful to let your referees know what arguments and evidence you're making in presenting yourself to prospective employers. It can also be useful to remind them of the things they know best and most directly about your qualifications and character. Every referee doesn't have to speak to every aspect of your qualifications. A letter of reference from a writer who knows you well—who speaks with direct authority and has firsthand evidence about your experience in a specific context—is more persuasive than a letter from a writer who's trying to cover all aspects of your experience, including those that he or she doesn't have direct knowledge about. Notice in Figure 9.11 that Rachel Woodhurst doesn't weaken her strong, informed recommendation for Jennifer Turnbull by trying to talk about aspects of Jennifer's life that don't relate to her work at the Student Aid Commission.

When you ask for a reference, it's absolutely legitimate to tell your referee what arguments you think would be most helpful to you, as Elizabeth Kuoppala does in her memo to Laurie Potter (see Figure 9.12). Most people find this information very useful in helping them write or talk about you to prospective employers.

Conventions

More often than not, you'll speak to your prospective referee before you write, either face to face or via telephone. You should follow up that initial conversation with a letter and most likely a resume. In this case, the initial letter then becomes a thank-you letter. But here again, you'll probably want to take the opportunity to tell your referees about your hopes and remind them of their most relevant knowledge about you.

Obviously, when you're writing to friends, as you are here, your letter isn't going to get as critical a reading as when you're writing to a prospective employer. At the same time, though, you don't want to discredit yourself (and perhaps offend your referee) with a letter that demonstrates thoughtless disregard for the social or formal conventions of a professional business letter. Our advice is not to get careless with these letters, even though they are to friends and supporters. And don't forget that even though these people are your friends, colleagues, former employers, or even current employers, they may not remember all the details about your work that you'd like them to. So, it's a conventional courtesy, as well as a good idea, to include a copy of your resume, as Michael McKenzie does with his letter of thanks in Figure 9.13.

FIGURE 9.11 Sample Letter of Recommendation

CALIFORNIA STUDENT AID COMMISSION
P.O. Box 622
Sacramento, CA 94245-0622

July 31, 1998

To Whom It May Concern:

I am pleased to have the opportunity to recommend Jennifer (Jenny) Turnbull to you for consideration for a position with your firm. Jenny has been employed as a Student Assistant working in our Human Resources Office for the past nine months while she completed graduate school. During that time, her work has been exemplary, and she has established excellent rapport with all levels of staff within the Student Aid Commission.

Jenny was hired as a Student Assistant to assist with telephone and counter inquiries, open and sort incoming mail, perform word processing and photocopying tasks, and generally help where she was needed. She performed these tasks easily and also assisted our two Personnel Specialists with backlogged work on their desks. She also took several word processing projects home (employee surveys, leave accounting records, and record retention schedules) and tabulated and formatted them on her Macintosh. In addition, on her own initiative, she has revamped, organized, and vastly improved our filing systems. Jenny works very independently with little need for direction and acts on her own initiative when she sees projects which need to be done.

Jenny has truly been an asset to our office, and we hate to see her leave. Her capabilities and education extend far beyond the work of a Student Assistant, but she has handled those duties as a professional. I know that she has chosen the field of Human Resources for her course of study and feel that she will be highly successful in that field. Again, it is a pleasure to recommend her to you.

Should you have any questions that you would like to ask me in regards to Jenny's employment, you can reach me at (916) 555-6155.

Sincerely,

Rachel Woodhurst

Rachel Woodhurst
Human Resources Manager

FIGURE 9.12 Sample Request for Letter of Recommendation

TO: Laurie Potter

FROM: Elizabeth Kuoppala EK

DATE: October 1, 1997

My application for graduate school requires letters of recommendation from "three professors with whom you have studied a science." I realize that "professor" isn't listed in your job description, but I believe that my experience in the QA Lab sets me ahead of my peers and would like the grad school people to know about it. I am most proud of our Contingency Plan and believe that my work with ICP standards, the FT-IR, the titrino study, and field dosimeter work are all very relevant to my graduate studies. I think also that my experience in the lab, as well as my previous years at Minntac, have taught me to work successfully with a great variety of people from diverse backgrounds. Furthermore, I believe that my MSHA training and safety record at Minntac demonstrate that I am cognizant of and careful with workplace hazards.

However, this letter is supposed to contain your opinions, not mine. If you'd like to include any reference to my days in the Rail Department, I would encourage you to talk to Joe Scipioni, my former supervisor.

I think that it is not important for you to be really familiar with the field of Medicinal Chemistry. In my mind, the perfect letter from you would say that I had a very positive summer intern experience; therefore, my decision to go to graduate school is an educated one. My personal essay will explain that although I loved my job at Minntac, and had challenging tasks, and good relations with my supervisors and co-workers, I still prefer to do the in-depth research that happens at graduate school.

I thank you very much for taking the time to help me with this application process. You can send your letter to:

Director of Graduate Studies
Department of Medicinal Chemistry
University at Buffalo
39 Cooke Hall
Box 601
Buffalo, NY 14260-1200

FIGURE 9.13 Sample Thank-You for a Job Lead

21432 Jacobs Avenue
Grand Junction, CO 81501
January 6, 1998

Ms. Katherine Winston
Valley View Vistas
254 Main Street
Boulder, CO 80344

Dear Ms. Winston:

Thank you for passing on the job announcement that you got from El Paso Environs. I'm very interested in residential and light commercial design—the areas specified in this job listing—and appreciate your thinking about me.

Right now I'm concentrating my job search in Arizona, where I'll spend spring break. Even so, I'll apply for the position in El Paso and let you know if my application lands me an interview.

The enclosed resume shows what I've done since I worked with you last summer. As you suggested (and as you can see on the resume), I've begun volunteering for the city and am learning a great deal about the process that project proposals must go through for approval as well as implementation by the city.

Thank you again for taking the time to send me this job listing. People like you make job hunting much easier.

Sincerely,

Michael McKenzie

Michael McKenzie

Enclosure: Resume

Expression

In a deep sense, expression is what these letters are all about. Your whole aim in requesting testimonials is to clarify for your referees your aspirations, values, and whole sense of who you are and why you want to make the career move you're planning. We've talked at length about how difficult it is to make arguments directly about your own character in a resume and employment letter to a prospective employer. It's much easier, though, to talk candidly about these things with a friend, and it's much easier for your friend, as a third-party witness, to make direct arguments to a prospective employer about your character. So, don't overlook the possible usefulness of giving a detailed expression of your sense of yourself and your goals when you request a reference.

Following up and Responding to Interviews, Offers, and Rejections

In these days of electronic communication, a lot of the dialogue between prospective employees and employers takes place over the telephone. This is especially true of good news, such as invitations to interviews and offers of jobs, to which your response should probably also be a telephone call. But taking the effort to write a follow-up letter—whether you accept or reject the interview invitation or the job offer—is a powerful and tangible demonstration of your conscientious regard for your reader and his or her institution. We would write that letter in *every case.* Not to follow up an interview with a letter would probably be looked upon as a significant breach of the conventional etiquette of the employment dance. So, all three of these occasions—interviews, offers, and rejections—are letter-writing prompts.

Goals

In all three cases, your goal is primarily to maintain and nurture the relationship you've established. This is obviously true if you're still in the running as a prospective employee and are writing a thank-you letter to follow up an interview or respond to a job offer. But it's also true of a letter where you are rejecting an offer or responding to a rejection.

Your goals in a follow-up letter of thanks for an interview are fairly complex. Your main goal is similar to that in the initial employment letter. Where your initial goal was to start a dialogue with this prospective employer, your goal now is to keep that conversation going. You may well have thought of more questions as you've reflected on the interview, and you may also have thought of things you would like your readers to know as prospective employers. So, one of your goals is to give and receive some more information. At the same time, you want to be—and to appear to be—a job candidate who is a critical thinker. Think about what you now know and what you still don't know about your prospective employer:

- What are the implications of what you do and don't know?
- What kinds of institutional values and goals did your readers express?
- How do you feel about those values?

- What implications do you see in their goals and plans?
- How do these mesh with your own goals and values?
- Without being cheeky or presumptuous, should you make observations about any of these issues?
- Did questions or suggestions your readers made in the interview suggest arguments about your qualifications? If so, you should probably make those arguments or reply to any arguments your readers implied in the interview.

Of all these letters, the easiest is the acceptance of a job offer. This letter is probably a follow-up to a telephone conversation where you've accepted the offer already, so you're really just giving your new employer a formal, tangible piece of evidence they can put in the file to confirm that you've accepted the job.

Your goals in a letter responding to an offer are more complex if your answer is anything but an acceptance. Because one of your goals is maintaining and nurturing the relationship, you don't want your response to be taken as a rejection of the relationship. You need to think carefully about what your other goals are. Do you need more time to think about the offer? Do you need a better offer? What, specifically, do you need? Can you reasonably ask for it?

In the case of responding to a rejection letter, ask yourself whether you'd like to invite your readers to reconsider their decision, either in the near term or some time in the future. This is especially true if the position you have sought is a sales position. We hear persistent reports that companies hiring for entry-level professional sales positions sometimes write rejection letters to *all* their job candidates—including those they hope to hire—as part of their screening process. Candidates pass the company's persistence test if they write back, expressing the hope that the rejection is not final.

If you're writing this letter (or most other letters) with the therapeutic goal of venting anger or frustration because you've gotten a response you didn't like, you'd do better to find another outlet for your emotion—perhaps put on your running gear and jog a few miles or go to some secluded place and scream. In Chapter 2, we talked about the danger and inappropriateness of "flaming," or venting your hostility in an e-mail message. The same caution also applies in paper communications.

Readers

In general, the possibilities for readers of follow-up letters are essentially the same as those for readers of your initial employment package. But because you've already passed through some initial screening as a candidate, it's likely that more people in the organization will see your material now. In addition, your dossier may be placed in a set of files that will continue to be actively searched and reviewed for a year or so, even if you aren't offered a job immediately. Your letter might be read six or nine months from now by someone else in the organization who hasn't met you and doesn't know anything about your earlier transaction with the person you're currently addressing as your reader. Given all this, you shouldn't make careless assumptions about your reader. You may not even know who your ultimate reader is.

Arguments

Unless you're rejecting an offer, the three broad "can do," "want to do," and "will do" employment arguments are places where you may want to look for brief themes for these letters. You should clearly tie these themes to the relationship that has developed since your initial contact.

Even if you're rejecting an offer, you may want to reprise one or more of these arguments, especially the "want to do" argument in expressing regret. You want to affirm that you have carried on your dialogue with this prospective employer in good faith and out of a real interest in working for this organization. This would be especially true if you're attempting to negotiate a better offer from your readers. Otherwise, your readers may suspect that, in asking for a better offer, you're not really interested. And if you're asking for a better offer, you will probably want to make, in some way that's not too self-congratulatory, the argument that you're worth it.

If you find you are in one of these rhetorically and ethically challenging situations, revisit Chapter 6, where we discussed strategies for dealing with situations involving conflict and delicate emotional and relational issues. In addition, you should seek specific advice from career counselors and other mentors if you find yourself in a negotiation like this. In principle, we believe you are better served by arguments that are candid and forthright. You will stand a better chance of reaching an employment agreement that serves both you and your employer well if you are realistic and truthful about your needs, timelines, and options, including any other offers and the deadlines for responding to them.

Conventions

We've already mentioned probably the two most important social conventions of follow-up letters: (1) that you should write these letters on these occasions and not let the opportunity pass and (2) that you should maintain a professional, mature, responsible expression of your self. Like other employment correspondence, these letters should conform to standard formal conventions. Brevity is once again essential out of consideration for your busy readers.

Expression

We've just mentioned expression. As with the other employment correspondence, expression of your goals, qualifications, and character is really the primary element in follow-up letters.

As we've suggested throughout this chapter, various sorts of situations and contexts during the employment search provide opportunities for you to continue the conversation you've initiated with prospective employers. In addition to the standard employment package, opportunities for written conversation range from letters requesting information interviews, to follow-ups after interviews or site visits, to thanks for references or career leads, to acceptance, rejection, or negotiations of job offers. All of these employment letters enable you to make and reinforce the argument that you have a strong, informed interest in the organization. They also allow you to assert and demonstrate the claims you make about yourself in a new context—perhaps developing new layers of your argument as you focus your communication on getting a job. It's important to remember, as well, that these employment letters are as much about nurturing and developing a professional network as they are about getting the job that's immediately in front of you.

WRITING CHECKLIST

You can use the following guidelines to build effective employment letters. For guidelines relevant to managing your career search or writing your resume, see the Writing Checklists for Chapters 7 and 8. For any of these guidelines, remember the superordinate guideline: Disregard *any* of this advice if it would cause you to do something that's inappropriate or silly for your situation.

Cover Letters

- Remember that the immediate goal of a cover letter is to get the reader to read the resume.
- Don't think of a cover letter and resume as a one-shot communication but as an invitation to a conversation that might go on for years.
- Network and do your homework to generate specific names of people in the organization who can serve as prospective readers and to learn data about the organization that will enable you to show that you have a strong, informed interest in it.
- Immediately let your reader know why you're writing—in terms that will speak to the reader's professional needs and responsibilities.
- Consider beginning with the "want to do" argument because it clarifies your interest in the position and organization and answers the reader's question about why you're writing. Include your claim and supporting data. To demonstrate your interest, document what you know about the organization.
- Don't assume that all letters should begin with the "want to do" argument. Don't use it, for instance, if your reader already knows you, if your interest is already established, or if simply knowing about the position demonstrates your interest.
- Don't tell readers what they already know.
- Be careful not to make claims that are the reader's responsibility instead of yours.
- Immediately establish the context in which you're writing: Tell your reader how you learned about the position and what position, exactly, you're applying for.
- Use relatively short, tightly developed paragraphs that make your claims and provide evidence to support them.

- In closing, direct the reader toward the specific action you seek and provide all necessary information the reader needs to take this action.
- Keep in mind that making the offer to call the reader to follow up gives you control over the subsequent exchange but has risks, too, because some readers find such calls distracting.
- Introduce your resume late in the body of your letter and type the word *resume* right after the word *Enclosure*, double-spaced below your typed name.
- Follow the conventions governing letter format.
- Embody your ethical stance—your "will do" argument—in a clear, vivid, specific style that shows you are interested in the reader's organization and that your interest is grounded in your background and knowledge.
- Express appropriate confidence in your abilities and pride in your accomplishments.
- At the same time, express a humble eagerness to learn more.
- Choose language that's clear, direct, and professional.
- Use active voice and show yourself as a doer.

☑ Requests

- Remember that if you're requesting a reference, you have both task and relationship goals: You're invoking the relationship you've had with this reader and encouraging the writing of a letter of support.
- Make sure the reader knows you well enough to speak authoritatively about your qualifications.
- Let your reader know what arguments you plan to use in your employment documents; perhaps also suggest arguments the readers could make that would be helpful to you.
- Thank the readers for helping.
- Write your letter carefully, even though your reader is a supporter.
- Include a copy of your resume with your request.

☑ Following up Interviews, Offers, and Rejections

- Making the effort to write a follow-up letter powerfully demonstrates your regard for your reader and the organization.
- Not following up an interview with a letter is a significant breach of etiquette.
- Remember that your goal is to maintain and nurture your relationship—to keep the conversation going and to provide and receive additional information.
- Follow up interview questions by making relevant arguments about your qualifications or by replying to your reader's arguments.
- Follow up a phone conversation with an acceptance letter when you've accepted a position.

- Respond to an offer when you're not directly accepting the position by reasonably asking for what you need.
- You might invite readers to reconsider their decision when responding to a rejection letter.
- Remember that writing to vent your hostility isn't appropriate.
- Keep in mind that your follow-up letter will certainly be read by those individuals who've already read earlier correspondence but may also be read by others reviewing files in the future.
- Tie your "can do," "want to do," and "will do" arguments to the relationship that you've developed with readers.
- Even if you reject an offer, affirm that you've communicated in good faith throughout your dialogue with the reader.
- Don't miss an opportunity to write a follow-up letter.
- Be sure to maintain professional, mature expression.

ACTIVITIES AND PROJECTS

1. Select one of the resumes in Chapter 8, and decide the specific claim you would make if you were writing a cover letter to accompany it. Also determine how you would support this claim. What specific data or evidence would you draw on in your letter, and in what order would you present this data or evidence? Why?

2. Find a job listing—on the World Wide Web, in your university's career services offices, or in a professional publication in your field—for a particular position that you might want to apply for in the near future. Look at the language and content of this advertisement, and determine how you might present your qualifications to match criteria established in the job listing.

3. A student applying for elementary education vacancies sent the letter shown in Figure 9.14, prospecting for jobs in his field. Using the GRACE benchmarks, analyze the effectiveness of this letter, paying particular attention to the reader and the argument. As you analyze, be sure to identify both the letter's strengths and weaknesses. Also suggest ways in which this letter might be strengthened.

4. Review again the six letters in Figures 9.4 through 9.9 for evidence of the "want to do," "can do," and "will do" arguments. Try to identify places in any of the letters where any of the three claims need to be made more directly. Do you feel that an important argument or evidence is missing? Why do you suppose it might have been left out? Do you feel that anyone is protesting too much at any place? In other words, do any of the letters seem too assertive at any point? Why might the writer have decided to be as direct/assertive as he or she was?

FIGURE 9.14 Sample Prospecting Job Application

I have a sincere interest in obtaining a teaching position within the Appleton School District. I am writing to inquire if any elementary education vacancies are anticipated for the 1997–1998 school year.

As stated on the enclosed resume, I am a graduate of the University of Illinois (U of I) with a major in Elementary Education. U of I also provided me with a broad liberal arts background. In addition to my course work at U of I, I had a successful and rewarding student teaching experience at Mound Elementary School. During this ten-week experience, I taught classes in kindergarten and the fourth grade. I developed units, bulletin boards, and lessons which encompassed all academic areas and involved active student participation. Some of these activities included students making their own nutritional snacks, a tour of a local bank, guest speakers, and a Mexican fiesta. These activities were extremely well received by the students and my supervising teachers.

I am confident that my knowledge of the teaching field would be a valuable asset to your teaching staff. If there are additional application procedures I should follow, please advise me. Thank you for your consideration.

5. Considering conventional ways in and out of the employment letter, assess the effectiveness of the two openings and closings that appear in Figure 9.15. What elements of these openings and closings work well? Why? What elements need improvement? And why? In addition to making a general assessment about the effectiveness of these paragraphs, look at their arguments. What claims are being made? And what sorts of evidence do you suspect might appear in the body paragraphs of these letters?

6. Essays used for graduate school applications share many of the features of job application letters. Read the application in Figure 9.16, and write or talk about the specific features of this essay that resemble those of cover letters. Also respond to the differences you notice. Look, too, at Elizabeth Kuoppala's letter to SUNY Buffalo (Figure 9.10) as yet another way of responding to the situation of a graduate school application. Finally, based upon your observations and the GRACE benchmarks, make suggestions about improvements the writers might make in these texts.

7. Write a cover letter to accompany the resume you've already written in response to Chapter 8. You can write a letter responding to an advertised position or

FIGURE 9.15 Sample Openings and Closings for Two Employment Letters

Letter 1

Opening

I seek a dispatcher position with your company. I learned of the position from Justin Stahnke, who informed me that interviews were in progress. I was also in attendance when you spoke about your company at St. Cloud State University.

Closing

Thank you for your consideration. I am excited about the possibility of working for a rapidly growing company such as yours.

Letter 2

Opening

I am writing about a possible position as a financial analyst with your firm. I heard about the junior financial analyst position with Bear Stearns through Career Services at St. Cloud State University. I recognize your firm as one of the industry leaders in terms of fund management and investment banking. The financial planning skills I have attained through continuing education and my ability to work in a team-based environment would be valuable assets to furthering your firm's excellence.

Closing

Thank you for your time and consideration of my qualifications and the needs of your firm. I would greatly appreciate your sending me a job application. I will be available for a job interview Mondays, Wednesdays, and Fridays from 8:00 A.M. to 5:00 P.M. I look forward to hearing from you in the near future.

prospecting for a job. In preparation for writing this cover letter, do an analysis of the letter-writing situation and determine the primary reader for your text. You'll need this reader's name and address and enough information about the organization and position to write a forceful argument, so complete any organizational reconnaissance you need to do to adapt your letter to the specific needs of the reader and organization.

FIGURE 9.16 Sample Graduate School Application Essay

Being intrigued by the natural world since childhood has made it easy for me to be a biologist. Through undergraduate classes and research, I have developed a strong background in wildlife biology. With increasing competition in the job market, a graduate degree is becoming a necessity for many wildlife positions. A Master of Science in Biology would complete the package I need to be successful in a wildlife-related career.

Growing up on a farm has had a positive influence on the person that I've become. Long hours, responsibility for specific chores and tasks, and hard work were all major components of my upbringing. These attributes will make the rigors of graduate school and thesis work easier to overcome.

Since I grew up in a heavily forested area of southwestern Wisconsin, I was provided with a great opportunity to observe the natural world on my own. I have always loved to just sit in the woods and watch and listen. Central to many types of research, observation is an acquired skill that I had a head start on. This background allowed me to excel in my plant and wildlife courses. It also helped prepare me for research projects, including a clear-cut tree study and my senior thesis on loggerhead shrikes, which I have been working on for the last year.

By the time I graduate with my BS in Biology this May, I will have done extensive research for several classes as well as for the U.S. Fish and Wildlife Service. Eight independent study credits at the BIOL 499 level involved two research projects. One dealt with a clear-cut oak woodland and the other with behavior of northern shrikes. I gained professional research experience through two projects with the U.S. Fish and Wildlife Service at the Sherburne National Wildlife Refuge. One project was a two-week long breeding bird census, the other a loggerhead shrike census and habitat suitability study.

These research projects, as well as my senior thesis research, are applications of what I've learned while pursuing my BS. Additional graduate-level coursework in biology would give me the additional experience and skills that I'll need to succeed in a career in wildlife biology.

8. Suppose Figure 9.17 is the body of a letter you've received from a prospective employer you've been communicating with. Read and analyze this letter carefully. What does it mean? The text itself is pretty straightforward, but what about the subtext? Maybe it's straightforward, too, but don't assume so immediately. Do a GRACEful analysis of your situation in light of this letter. You can imagine the specific details as they may be relevant to your own life and career goals.

FIGURE 9.17 Sample Letter from an Organization to a Job Applicant

Thank you for your interest in our position in ________. We received inquiries from many well-qualified candidates, many more than we could place at this time. This strong response from such a large pool of candidates has made our selection process very difficult and rather slow.

You were one of many well-qualified candidates to whom we decided we could not offer a position at this time. We will keep your dossier on file for one year in case our needs change.

We wish you success in your career search.

For example, you can decide whether you've had an interview with the organization. You can decide the specific kind of job that's involved here and the specific kind of organization that's sending you this letter. As you analyze this situation, ask the following questions, in particular, using GRACE as a frame for your analysis:

- Should you respond at this point?
- If you respond, how should you respond? Letter? Telephone? E-mail?
- If you respond, what should you say? Why?

9. The thank-you letter shown in Figure 9.13 was written in response to a job lead Katherine Winston sent to Michael McKenzie. Analyze the letter using the action/relationship matrix (Figure 5.1, p. 212). Cite specific evidence to support what you say about the letter's action and relationship arguments.

10. The letter shown in Figure 9.11 is a recommendation letter written by Rachel Woodhurst on Jenny Turnbull's behalf. Read the letter carefully, looking for the claims Rachel makes and the ways in which she supports them. What sort of argument is Rachel making, and how does she frame it? Based upon your analysis of this letter, write a set of principles or guidelines for writing letters of recommendations.

11. Write three letters to three different people about three different career-related goals you have. These letters should be to real people and speak to real career goals that you have over the relatively near term. In other words, they should be letters that would actually be useful to you in, say, the next six to nine months. They won't necessarily be letters in which you ask for an actual job interview. Rather, they may be letters you're using to get an internship, explore a possible summer job opening, or even seeking an informational interview or career ad-

vice or a chance to "shadow" somebody in their work for a few hours. You might write a letter in which you're laying the groundwork for what you hope will be an employment opportunity in a couple of years or longer.

12. Write a memo to your teacher, in which you talk briefly about what you did for Activity 11. Specifically, speak to the following:
    - Why you wrote to each of these three people: Why are you interested in their organization? What are your goals in writing to them? What do you think your chances are of achieving those goals?
    - What reconnaissance you did: What research steps did you take to find these people and their addresses (including library or Internet research and any other research such as telephone calls)? What prior contacts did you use (e.g., FOPs [friends of parents], POFs [parents of friends], previous interviews or conversations, people you know in common, etc.)?

Part IV

When a Letter or Memo Is Not Enough: Proposals, Business Plans, and Formal Reports

Chapter 10

Design Conventions for Long, Complex Documents

Graphic design refers to how type and other visual elements appear on the page. Good design means they appear harmonious to ensure efficient, enjoyable reading. . . .

The primary purpose of design is to make content accessible. Its secondary purpose, following at a great distance, is to represent personality or image. Style is not substance. Design can stimulate interest and make reading efficient, but design cannot camouflage thoughtless content or careless writing. . . .

Designing takes place mostly in your imagination and on your dummy, not on your pasteup board, light table, or computer. Those tools are for experimenting with your vision and carrying it out, not creating it.

—Mark Beach

Given the kinds of hectic, distraction-filled scenarios we've imagined for readers of most business documents, it's easy to see the importance of brevity. All other things being equal, shorter is better.

But, of course, all other things *aren't* always equal. Complex situations tend to call forth long, complex documents. As the situation becomes more complex, the stakes often are higher. The arguments become more complex, and the layers of the arguments deepen. A straightforward problem of the location of files and desks in a small department may be addressed in a one-page memo that recites the facts of the situation and proposes a new layout. But if the same organization proposes a multimillion dollar computer network, the claims it makes about that network need to be grounded in extensive data, and the data and claims need to be connected and warranted by an extensive discussion of underlying criteria, assumptions, and values.

In these complex situations, even busy readers who are pressed for time expect to receive long, complex documents. But they also expect to be able to comprehend these documents easily and quickly. Herein lies the creative challenge in planning, designing, and writing formal proposals, business plans, and reports: how to fulfill the competing demands for readability and thoroughness. The good news is that creative document design can serve both needs. Effective document design starts with thinking about how busy professionals, in general, tend to read long business documents.

How Busy Professionals Read Long Documents

Research on how people read professional discourse shows that it's extremely rare for anyone to read straight through a document, from the first word to the last. People don't often savor business documents the way they do a good novel. Instead, they tend to read opportunistically, with the kind of "bottom-line" perspective they would bring to the reading of a financial statement. The same kind of scenario we suggested that you imagine for the reader of a job search letter and resume—a reader who is pressed for time and looking for answers—is the scenario we see for readers of longer documents.

These readers are going to approach your document with two urgent, impatient concerns: content and organization. Readers will ask several different questions about content as they approach a document and as they move through it. The following list suggests a kind of rough order in which readers are likely to ask these generic questions:

- What's the essential issue here?
- Why should I care?
- What *can* be done?
- What *should* be done?
- What are the costs?
- What are the benefits?
- Why should I believe you?

You should view this order of questions with some caution, however. In fact, readers tend to be asking all these content-related questions almost simultaneously when they approach the document. And the other question they are asking at the same time speaks to organization:

- Where is the information I want to know?

Given the impatience of readers of business documents and the way they tend to ask these questions, it would be a major mistake in document design to answer each question in complete, exquisite detail before saying anything about the next question. Readers tend to want answers—short answers, obviously—to all these questions at once. This means that your long document will almost invariably need to have a carefully drafted summary at the front, where your readers will look first.

Furthermore, readers are not fully predictable or consistent. One reader, perhaps the chief financial officer, may be interested in looking at detailed financial information almost immediately. Another reader, perhaps a director of research and development, may be interested in detailed technical information. A third reader, perhaps a project manager, may be interested in information about personnel, logistics, and timelines. All these readers may read the same document at the same time with the same sense of urgency but with these different priorities, reflecting their respective interests and responsibilities.

If you think about these readers in terms of the egocentric solar system that we talked about in Chapter 1, you can see that each of them is drawn to your document and your concerns from a different angle and distance. Each is interested in different details and in different levels of detail. In one sense, each is asking the same organizational question: "Where is the detailed information I want to know?" But the same question means different things to each reader.

Helping Readers Navigate Long, Complex Documents

"Where is the information I want to know?" This question is on readers' minds as they approach the document, and it's on their minds repeatedly as they read or, more likely, skim and browse through your document. To help readers navigate your document, you can give them a lot of helpful "traffic signals"—some of them easy and obvious. Here's a list:

- **Make a table of contents.**
- **Number your pages, and use the page numbers in your table of contents.** Figure 10.1, a section of a proposal on disability awareness on a university campus, shows one conventional format for a table of contents. Other conventional formats for tables of contents appear in Chapter 4, Figure 4.17, and Chapter 13, Figure 13.2.
- **Use headings and subheadings often, and make them vividly descriptive of the contents of their sections.** Headings like *Background, Introduction,* and *Section 3,* aren't as useful as headings like *Contributing Factors in the Contamination of Bitter Springs* and *Consumers' Six Most Urgent Concerns about Reliability of Electrical Power Tools.* Even a heading like *Conclusions* might be replaced by one summarizing what the principal conclusion is (though this would be a judgment call, based on the specific circumstances).
- **Make headings and subheadings consistent in grammatical structure, format, and typeface.** Your company may have either an official style manual or an informal set of conventions for managing headings consistently in documents. If so, you'll want to follow those conventions. For templates of two generally used conventions for managing headings, see Figures 10.2 and 10.3. Notice how both templates use the principles of parallelism and placement. (For more information on using parallelism, see Part VI.)
    - **Parallelism:** Make all headings on the same level parallel to one another. In other words, if you use a noun or noun phrase for a main section heading, follow this grammatical structure for other main section headings, too.
    - **Placement:** Place same-level headings in the same positions so readers will know where to find them. Main section headings are often centered or printed in a larger type size, while subheadings tend to be flush left and printed in a size midway between the size of the body text and the main section headings. All headings and subheadings should appear in boldfaced type.

  The placement of headings in the proposal shown in Figure 10.1 is distinctly different from the placements in Figures 10.2 and 10.3. The use of side headings in a boldfaced, sans serif font—unlike the typeface of the body text of the proposal—is a distinctive format. Nevertheless, the headings are consistent and demonstrate the principle of parallelism.

FIGURE 10.1 Sample Excerpt from Research Proposal

i

DESCRIPTIVE ABSTRACT

Research has never been conducted to determine the attitudes and awareness levels of the campus community toward disability issues. Students seem ignorant and apathetic where disability issues are concerned. Research in the form of a survey must be done to gain a clearer understanding of disability issues on campus. This survey would point out specific areas on campus that need improvement. When problems are recognized, solutions become possible. Increased awareness toward disability issues would lead to the eventual improvement of accessibility and facilities on campus.

(continued)

FIGURE 10.1 Continued

ii

Table of Contents

FIGURE 10.1 Continued

1

Introduction

St. Cloud State University students with disabilities have long been filled with feelings of exasperation, frustration, and hopelessness when faced with the timeless issue of disability services. For years, the university's attitude and accessibility for students with disabilities have been far less than satisfactory. Unfortunately, the campus community has little understanding of the problem at hand.

Approximately 270 students at St. Cloud State University are considered legally disabled. The office for these students functions as a testing area, a storage room, and a meeting place where students can congregate. However, the office is hidden in a small corner of Atwood Memorial Center. With approximately 200 students constantly coming in and out of the small office, the situation could be described as pandemonium at best. While the small office is a large problem for students with disabilities, it is one of many problems that must be overcome each day on campus.

Before progress can be made to improve current conditions for students with disabilities on the St. Cloud State University campus, research must be conducted to determine the attitudes and awareness levels of the campus community concerning disability issues. Proposed research of this kind has never before been conducted on this campus. Determining campus attitudes and awareness levels would suggest specific areas that need increased understanding, attention, and accessibility. In this respect, increased awareness of disability issues would lead to the eventual improvement of the campus.

Determining and correcting attitudes and awareness levels regarding disability issues on campus would lead to an eventual improvement in tolerance and accessibility.

(continued)

FIGURE 10.1 Continued

2

Statement of Problem

Research has never been conducted at St. Cloud State University to determine the climate of the campus community concerning student disability issues. Many students are ignorant at best and blatantly apathetic at worst concerning disability issues on campus. Accessibility is poor: ramps are inconvenient, many automatic doors do not fully open, and the student disability office could easily be considered one of campus' least accessible offices. The awareness levels of students and faculty on the campus must be studied in order to pinpoint specific areas on campus that need improvement and increased understanding.

Purpose of Study

Research, perhaps in the form of a survey, must be done to determine the current attitudes, awareness, and tolerance toward disability issues in the campus community. Because this research has never before been conducted at St. Cloud State University, it is absolutely critical that a current measure of beliefs and awareness be attained. Information discovered through this kind of study could be used to determine specific areas on campus that need improvement. Only through the discovery and investigation of a problem can a solution to the problem be found.

Significance of Proposed Research

A proposal of this kind is significant for a number of reasons. Attention must inevitably be given to a subject as relevant as disability services on a campus as large as St. Cloud State. With roughly 270 students considered legally disabled, the research is unprecedented on campus. Determining the attitudes and tolerance levels of the campus community is a vital first step in the right direction. Researching the campus community and determining which specific areas need improvement will eventually enable St. Cloud State to become a disability-friendly university.

FIGURE 10.2 Template 1 for Headings and Subheadings

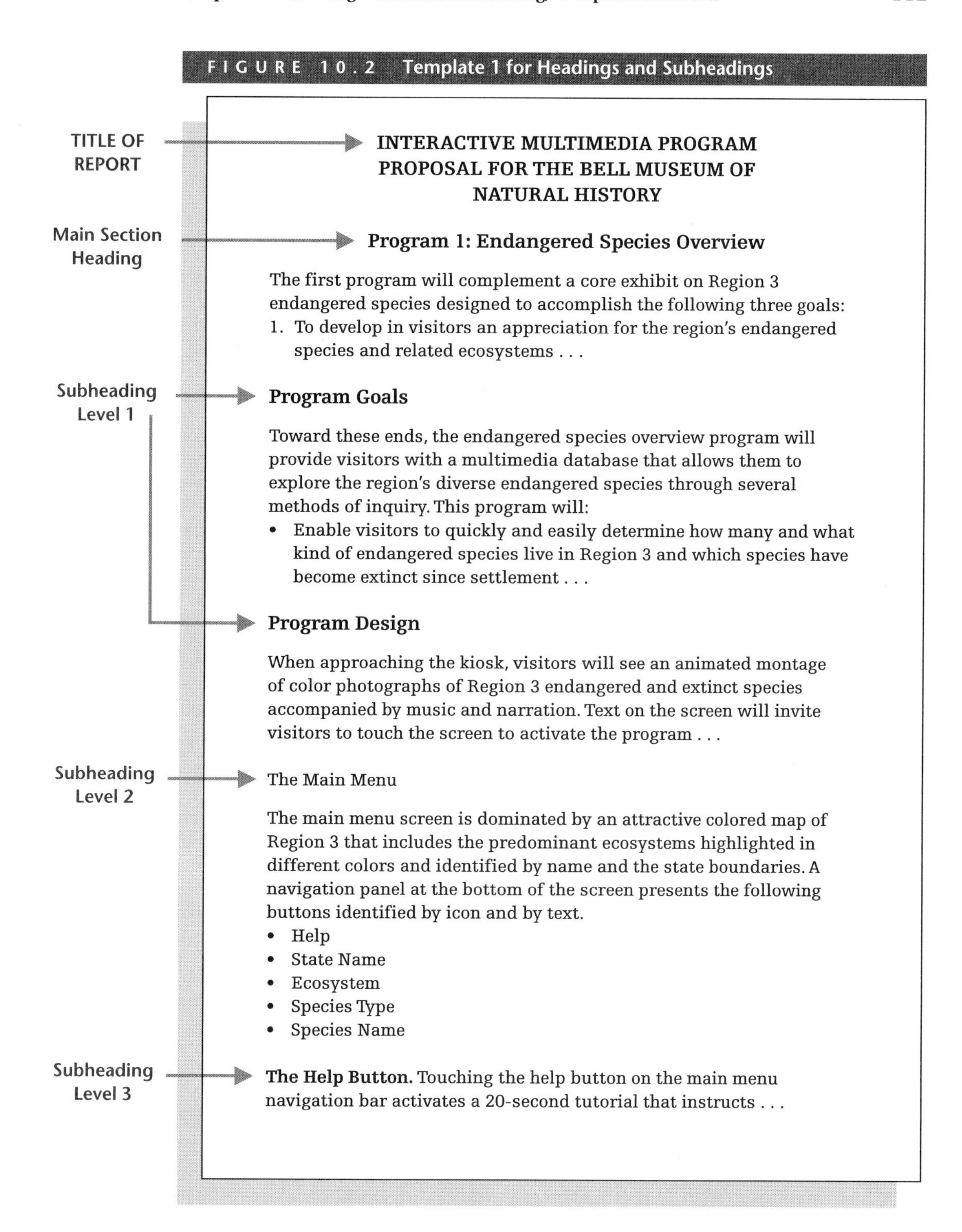

TITLE OF REPORT
Main Section Heading
Subheading Level 1
Subheading Level 2
Subheading Level 3
INTERACTIVE MULTIMEDIA PROGRAM PROPOSAL FOR THE BELL MUSEUM OF NATURAL HISTORY
Program 1: Endangered Species Overview
The first program will complement a core exhibit on Region 3 endangered species designed to accomplish the following three goals:
1. To develop in visitors an appreciation for the region's endangered species and related ecosystems . . .
Program Goals
Toward these ends, the endangered species overview program will provide visitors with a multimedia database that allows them to explore the region's diverse endangered species through several methods of inquiry. This program will:
• Enable visitors to quickly and easily determine how many and what kind of endangered species live in Region 3 and which species have become extinct since settlement . . .
Program Design
When approaching the kiosk, visitors will see an animated montage of color photographs of Region 3 endangered and extinct species accompanied by music and narration. Text on the screen will invite visitors to touch the screen to activate the program . . .
The Main Menu
The main menu screen is dominated by an attractive colored map of Region 3 that includes the predominant ecosystems highlighted in different colors and identified by name and the state boundaries. A navigation panel at the bottom of the screen presents the following buttons identified by icon and by text.
• Help
• State Name
• Ecosystem
• Species Type
• Species Name
The Help Button. Touching the help button on the main menu navigation bar activates a 20-second tutorial that instructs . . .

FIGURE 10.3 Template 2 for Headings and Subheadings

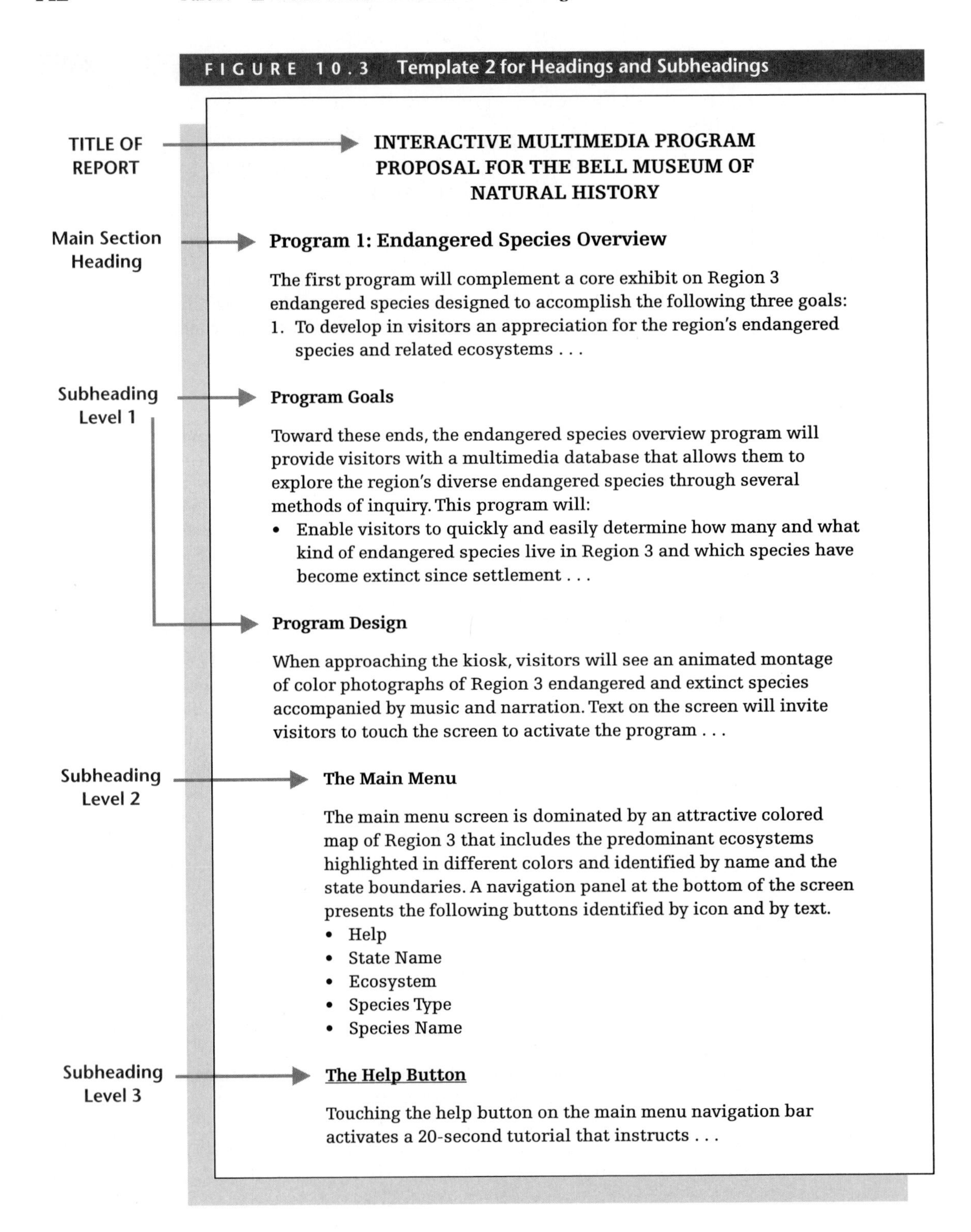
TITLE OF REPORT
INTERACTIVE MULTIMEDIA PROGRAM PROPOSAL FOR THE BELL MUSEUM OF NATURAL HISTORY
Main Section Heading
Program 1: Endangered Species Overview
The first program will complement a core exhibit on Region 3 endangered species designed to accomplish the following three goals:
1. To develop in visitors an appreciation for the region's endangered species and related ecosystems . . .
Subheading Level 1
Program Goals
Toward these ends, the endangered species overview program will provide visitors with a multimedia database that allows them to explore the region's diverse endangered species through several methods of inquiry. This program will:
• Enable visitors to quickly and easily determine how many and what kind of endangered species live in Region 3 and which species have become extinct since settlement . . .
Program Design
When approaching the kiosk, visitors will see an animated montage of color photographs of Region 3 endangered and extinct species accompanied by music and narration. Text on the screen will invite visitors to touch the screen to activate the program . . .
Subheading Level 2
The Main Menu
The main menu screen is dominated by an attractive colored map of Region 3 that includes the predominant ecosystems highlighted in different colors and identified by name and the state boundaries. A navigation panel at the bottom of the screen presents the following buttons identified by icon and by text.
• Help
• State Name
• Ecosystem
• Species Type
• Species Name
Subheading Level 3
The Help Button
Touching the help button on the main menu navigation bar activates a 20-second tutorial that instructs . . .

- **Include the headings in the table of contents** as well as in the text.
- **Use the headings in the summary** at the front of your document if possible. These redundant signals will help your readers move between the summary and those sections of the extended text that are of particular interest to them. For more information about summaries, see the next section of this chapter.
- **Begin each report section with an overview sentence or paragraph** that lets readers know what they can expect as they move into the particulars that follow. This overview will help readers to find information they need and to understand what's coming next.
- **Give your readers other redundant directional signals by providing cross-references throughout the document.** For example, our discussion of headings, just above, forecasts our discussion of summaries later in this chapter. And just before this section on helping readers navigate long documents, we refer you back to our introduction of the egocentric solar system in Chapter 1. We hope you've read Chapter 1, but in case you haven't, we want you to know where you can read more about the egocentric solar system.
- **Move large, complex, or difficult chunks of data out of the main body of your document and into an appendix** or into several appendices unless the information is vital to readers' understanding of the issues at this point. When you move this material to an appendix, don't forget to provide clear directional signals in the text and table of contents referring to the appended material.
- **Put things where your readers expect to find them in the document.** If your company or agency has a corporate style manual for internal documents, follow it. If you're writing the document for readers in another organization, follow any guidelines they have provided. You should generally try to meet your readers' conventional expectations, even if they are at odds with our other suggestions or with your own sense of effective ways of organizing the document.

Summaries: Answering Readers' Primary Questions Quickly

Summaries, often called *executive summaries* or *abstracts,* forecast what readers can expect to read in your document. A well-designed summary anticipates and answers readers' primary questions and provides a clear road map for readers moving into a long, complex report.

Summaries are important because they are the most extensively circulated and read part of proposals, business plans, and long reports. Some readers who simply want to keep abreast of what's going on in the organization may read *only* the summaries of reports, and executives may decide if proposals are approved or the recommendations in reports are enacted based simply upon what they see in the summary. Furthermore, in today's electronic information retrieval systems, titles and summaries are often filed electronically, and keywords are put in electronic storage. When people search for information, they enter keywords related to the subject, and the computer selects articles, papers, and reports containing those words. So, use keywords in your summary that accurately describe the essential contents of your document—keywords that someone looking for this kind of information is likely to use as search terms in a computer-based search.

Types of Summaries Typically Used

Two types of summaries are typically used:

1. **Descriptive summaries** are always very short (usually, under 100 words) and provide readers with an overview of the information the document contains. They introduce the subject of the document to readers, who must then read it to find out specific results, conclusions, or recommendations.
2. **Informative summaries** are also short—usually 10 percent or less of the length of the original piece. In addition to forecasting content, informative summaries provide readers with the key results, conclusions, and recommendations. Executive summaries of business documents typically are informative summaries, which are used by busy executives to make strategic decisions about urgent issues quickly and to delegate decisions about specific details to other staff.

Samples of descriptive and informative summaries appear in Figure 10.4. Another example of a descriptive summary—called an *abstract* in the text itself—is shown in Figure 10.1, where it precedes the table of contents in the proposal on disability awareness. In this instance, it would directly follow the title page of the proposal.

Steps for Writing an Effective Summary

Drafting a summary that includes just the right amount of information to answer readers' key questions and provide an effective road map for the report can sometimes be challenging. We encourage you to follow these steps:

1. Reread your document with the goal of summarizing in mind:
   - Look specifically for the main parts of the document, including goals, methods, results, conclusions, and recommendations.
   - Use the headings, subheadings, and table of contents as a guide to writing your summary.
   - Note the information that's likely to be most important to your readers.
2. After you've finished rereading your document, draft your summary *without* looking back at what you're summarizing:
   - Don't merely copy key sentences out of your report; you'll put in too much or too little information.

FIGURE 10.4 Samples of Descriptive and Informative Summaries

Descriptive Summary

An article in the October 1995 *Journal of Marketing* ("The Relationship between Cartoon Trade Character Recognition and Attitude toward Product Category in Young Children," pp. 58–70) examines and analyzes the effects of repeated exposure to the advertisements of certain products on young children. Included in the article are comparisons of the effects of such characters as Mickey Mouse, Ronald McDonald, and Joe Camel on the attitudes of young children toward the product categories these characters represent.

Informative Summary

It has often been argued that children can be strongly influenced by commercials originally produced for adults. Children's capacity to recognize and associate various trade characters to the products they represent grows steadily with age and exposure. In fact, age was found to be the outstanding determinant in influencing attitudes about specific advertisements and products. Though Joe Camel was recognized almost as easily by children as Mickey Mouse, the controversial Marlboro Man was most difficult to identify for each group tested and showed no obvious association with age. Advertisements have been proven to be far more effective with repeated exposure, causing a "mere exposure phenomenon" to surface. The phenomenon implies that attitude toward a specific product is improved dramatically simply through frequent and repeated promotions.

Mizerski, Richard. "The Relationship between Cartoon Trade Character Recognition and Attitude toward Product Category in Young Children." *Journal of Marketing* 59 (October 1995): 58–70.

- Don't rely on the way material was phrased in your document; summarize the information in a new way.
- However, do write your major headings in the summary so that they forecast the main points in the document.

3. Test and revise your rough draft to address the following:
   - Highlight your most important claims and their supporting evidence and rationales.
   - Make sure you answer your readers' most urgent questions about the document's contents.

- Make sure your directional signals in the summary forecast the directional signals in the body of the document—especially headings indicating major ideas or issues in the document—so that you also answer your readers' most urgent questions about organization.
- Correct weaknesses in organization.
- Improve logical connections (transitions) among pieces of information.
- Drop superfluous information and eliminate wordiness.
- Add important information you omitted.
- Fix errors in grammar, spelling, and punctuation.

Testing Your Summary

Once you've drafted and revised your summary, use the following checklist to test its effectiveness:

- Does your summary use one or more well-developed paragraphs that are unified, coherent, and able to stand on their own?
- Does your summary use an introduction/body/conclusion structure that presents the document's goal, results, conclusions, and recommendations?
- If the summary doesn't use an introduction/body/conclusion convention, does its organization mirror that of the document so that it still forecasts the organization of the document?
- Does your summary provide transitions between pieces of information?
- Does your summary contain information that's not in the main document? (It shouldn't!)
- Will your summary be understandable to all the various people who will read it?

With the summary, you have a chance to put your best foot (or arguments) forward, so the effort you invest in it should be some of your best writing.

Other Conventions of Long, Complex Documents

In addition to document design features that serve as "traffic signals" for long, complex pieces of writing, you'll need to make decisions about other conventional elements that readers expect in formal documents. Here's a checklist of elements:

- **Cover.** What kind of cover and binding should you use? A three-ring binder? A plastic comb binding? A perfect binding? An expensive stitched binding? A staple or a paper clip? A heavy card stock cover? A plastic cover? A book cover? Do you want a fancy, customized logo or design? Your answers will depend on what's customary practice in your and your readers' organizations, your budget, the formality of the occasion, and the readers' intended use of the document. For example, even if you have an unlimited budget, it wouldn't make sense to have the document bound and stitched if your readers will want to separate it into sections. Similarly, if the contents of the document are likely to change (for example, if the document is a policies or procedures manual), you'll want to be able to remove outdated pages and insert new ones when policies and procedures change.

- **Paper, ink, type size and font, other medium.** What quality, weight, color, and size of paper do you want? How do you want the document printed? Laser printer, ink-jet printer, FAX, xerographic copier, offset printer, typewriter? Here again, budget, anticipated use, and customary practice can probably guide you. Another issue is the number of copies you'll need. Offset printing would make no sense for ten copies, but it might be your most economical option for a thousand copies.

  You'll also want to decide what typestyle and size to use. Most experts in document design recommend that you select a 10- or 12-point type for body text and 12- to 18-point for headings and titles. You'll probably want to use a serif font, like Times Roman or Palatino, for your body type, since the feet at the bottoms of serif letters anchor the line of text and enhance readability. But sans serif fonts, like Geneva or Helvetica, are often used for headings because of the openness and crispness of the letters. Keep in mind, though, that you'll want to be consistent in your use of fonts, generally using at most two—one for body text and one for the headings—and varying type size only to distinguish levels of headings.

- **Cover letter.** Especially if the document is written for someone outside your own organization, it's common practice to write a cover letter that helps establish the context. The letter gives a very brief summary, highlighting only the most important point or two, especially any legal or technical conditions or limitations that define appropriate or inappropriate uses of the document. Often, the letter also speaks specifically about the professional relationship between you and your main reader. For examples of cover letters, see the Dick Cottrill cover letter (Figure 12.3, pp. 516–523) and the collaborative cover memo for the Student Organization Booklet Proposal (Figure 13.2, pp. 579–584).

- **Executive summary.** Do you need an executive summary specifically for the reader who's reading under tight time constraints and needs to see the whole picture in broad strokes quickly?

- **Appendix.** Do you want an appendix? Can some of the more detailed evidence go in it—your background material, for example, if it is extensive, or lengthy documentation of your investigative process or analytical or statistical procedures? Do you have extensive biographical information about a number of people, for example, that could go in an appendix?

- **Typographical features.** What typographical conventions are available for improving the readability of this document? Do the style guidelines of an RFP (request for proposal) or other instructions allow informative headers, boldfaced type for headings and subheadings, creative use of vertical and horizontal white space to clarify and emphasize chunks of text, markers such as bullets to highlight items in a list, callouts in margins to dramatize key points, and other graphic manipulations of the text? For instance, the proposal shown in Figure 10.1 uses white space creatively to emphasize section divisions and callouts to highlight key concepts for readers.

- **Graphics.** We'll talk more about graphics in the next section. But in order to use graphics strategically and appropriately, you first have to ask yourself whether the issues, information, and arguments lend themselves to graphic presentation. Namely, would tables, pie graphs, bar graphs, timelines, calendars, schematics, formulas, architectural drawings, blueprints, photographs, line drawings, or other graphics summarize the issues, information, and arguments vividly and effectively? What kinds of graphics are permitted—or required—by your own organization's guidelines or those of your readers? What kinds of graphics would *most* effectively communicate your arguments?

- **Sentence-level conventions.** See Part VI for detailed guidelines and tactics for testing and editing your text for sentence-level conventions that promote greater readability and efficiency. Here, we'll just quickly review some of the most important ways you can do so:
  - Remember that the most common sentence order in English is subject-verb-object. In the following example, cast in active voice, someone who is clearly identified performs a straightforward action upon some clearly identified thing:

    Ben threw the ball.

    If we cast the sentence in passive voice, we need more words to convey the same information, and the responsible actor is just a bit harder to identify:

    The ball was thrown by Ben.

    Or the responsible actor might disappear altogether:

    The ball was thrown.

  - Conventional practice in some professional disciplines, especially technical disciplines, has discouraged use of the pronoun *I*, partly on the grounds that it sounds unprofessionally egotistical. Fortunately, this convention is in retreat across the whole landscape of professional writing, but it remains strong in some disciplines and in quite a few organizations, so be sensitive to the local practice in your own writing. The problem with this convention is that it tends to produce sentences like the last example just above—that report something was done but don't report who did it. Instead of saying "I then correlated the frequency of assembly errors with the days of the week," you would say, "The frequency of assembly errors was then correlated with the days of the week." This kind of passive sentence structure, where the subject of the sentence receives the action, isn't always problematic. In fact, sometimes it's necessary. But unless you can see specific reasons to use the passive structure or to avoid the *I* pronoun, you should prefer the active voice.

DILBERT

Source: DILBERT reprinted by permission of United Feature Syndicate, Inc.

- Prefer active verbs to *nominalizations,* which are verbs turned into nouns, and *euphemisms,* which are high-sounding words substituted for clear, direct language. Here's an example of a nominalization. Notice how the verb *threw* got turned into the noun, *throwing*:

  Throwing the ball is what Ben did.

  And here's an example of both nominalization and euphemism:

  Levitation and projection of the ball is what Ben did.

  And if the sentence really runs amok, you can have nominalization, euphemism, passive voice, confusing nesting of prepositional phrases, and enough other sins against clarity that a reader can't tell what happened:

  The status of the ball, by means of a process of rapid rotation of the upper arm around the shoulder joint, combined with a snapping motion of the wrist with the elbow and the rapid contraction of the abdominal muscles, was converted to one of levitation and projection.

- **Diction.** The euphemism we just described really is an example of a problem with diction, or word choice. More generally, ask yourself what level of specialized technical language you need to communicate your information and arguments appropriately. Will this level of technical vocabulary match the needs and expertise of the various readers of your report? Will conventions allow you to provide intext explanation and definition of difficult technical terms? Are you sure your readers will understand your terms, or will you need to provide a glossary? Are you sure you understand these terms correctly yourself?

- **Correctness.** With proposals, business plans, and reports—as with resumes and employment letters—breaking conventions of grammar, spelling, and usage can seriously damage your readers' confidence in you and thus make it difficult to get a sympathetic reading. For this reason, make sure your document is mechanically clean and correct.

The Power and Importance of Graphics

We can't make too strong a case for the power and importance of graphics. Along with executive summaries, they are the parts of a document most likely to be studied by all readers. Often, readers will rely almost exclusively on your graphics. At their best, graphics organize large quantities of complex data and make the overall, global significance of your document almost instantly clear. At their worst, graphics confuse or mislead readers. So, as with summaries, you need to invest careful thought and work in your graphics.

Graphics can even be a powerful composing/thinking/discovering tool for you as a writer, helping you organize and explore your information and visualize and test the significance and credibility of your arguments while your writing is still in progress. So, don't think of graphics as accessories that you add at the last minute to dress up your document. Start thinking and doodling with graphics early in your writing cycle. Think of them as integral parts of your arguments—as ways of organizing your data so that both you and your readers can see how the data are significant and how they justify your claims.

Tables

Tables are effective for presenting detailed numerical information—and even text—in easily readable columns and rows. Because tables are the simplest graphics to make, they are the most frequently used. They are especially useful when readers are interested in specific amounts or numbers. For example, Table 1 (see Figure 10.5), which appeared in a real estate appraisal report, provides the specific acreage of industrial parks in a midsized midwestern city. Readers would find the table easy to read with its clearly labeled, boldfaced table title and boldfaced column titles.

Tables sometimes appear like lists, without borders, boxing, or shading. Often, however, especially with more complicated tables, borders, boxing, and shading enhance readability. This is particularly true for summary tables, sometimes known as *general purpose tables,* which contain large amounts of information—probably information from an entire report. And because they contain material that applies to an entire document, rather than a small part of it, summary tables usually appear in an appendix, rather than in the body of a report. Table 2 (see Figure 10.6, p. 452), which appeared in the appendix of a report, shows how complicated these tables can be; it also illustrates how borders, shading, and rules (or dividing lines) can make these tables easier to read.

Tables commonly appear, too, in documents that delineate the steps in a process. For instance, the text shown in Figure 10.7 (p. 453), taken from an affirmative action plan for a large government agency, indicates appropriate management responses to specific sorts of employee complaints using a simple table that predicates *if/then* scenarios.

A word of warning is appropriate here: Because tables are so easy to set up—especially with the Insert Table feature available on most word-processing software—it's tempting to use them when other sorts of graphics might be more compelling to

FIGURE 10.5 Sample Special Purpose Table

Table 1: ST. CLOUD AREA INDUSTRIAL PARKS

Industrial Park	Location	Available	Comments
Sauk Rapids Industrial	Sauk Rapids	60.00 acres	1.5 to 3 acre lots
Industries West	Waite Park	190.00 acres	2 to 5 acre plots for industrial or commercial
Industrial Center West	St. Cloud	60.00 acres	4 to 22 acre plots
Sartell Industrial	Sartell	44.25 acres	200 additional acres available
Sauk River	St. Cloud Township	46.00 acres	One-half acre to 20 acre sites
Southway	St. Cloud Township	7.00 acres	3 to 7 acre sites
Suncrest	St. Cloud Township	45.00 acres	0.75 to 7.5 acre sites; 40 acres unplatted
Sundial	Waite Park	36.00 acres	3 to 7 acre sites
Burlington Northern	Waite Park	23.50 acres	Tax increment financing

your readers. Consider, for example, Table 3 (see Figure 10.8, p. 454), which appeared in a proposal recommending that students be required to register with career services. As you can see, the table provides concrete numbers and percentages about how graduates found jobs. These concrete numbers and percentages, however, may not make your key claims and evidence as highly visible and comprehensible as you might like. As we'll demonstrate with this example later in this chapter, your claims and evidence might be better served by more dramatic graphics, which are usually considered under the general category of *figures*.

Figures

Figures include a wide variety of presentation modes, including bar and line graphs, flowcharts, pie charts, timelines, calendars, schematics, architectural drawings, blueprints, and photographs. We'll describe the most common sorts of graphics in the list that follows and discuss examples after that.

- **A bar graph** enables readers to compare information—quantities of the same items in the same timeframe, for example, or quantities of the same items in different timeframes, as Figure 10.9 (p. 454) illustrates.
- **A line graph** helps readers understand trends by showing changes—in prices, sales totals, production, and so on—over time. And if a line graph includes more than one line, it can illustrate comparative data—among prices for individual products, sales totals for various products, and production numbers for those

FIGURE 10.6 Sample General Purpose Table

Table 2: Life Expectancy at Birth by Race and Sex, United States: 1940, 1950, 1960, and 1970–1994

							All Other					
	All Races			White			Total			Black		
Year	Both Sexes	Male	Female	Both Sexes	Male	Female	Both Sexes	Male	Female	Both Sexes	Male	Female
1994	75.7	72.4	79.0	76.5	73.3	79.6	71.7	67.6	75.7	69.5	64.9	73.9
1993	75.5	72.2	78.8	76.3	73.1	79.5	71.5	67.3	75.5	69.2	64.6	73.7
1992	75.8	72.3	79.1	76.5	73.2	79.8	71.8	67.7	75.7	69.6	65.0	73.9
1991	75.5	72.0	78.9	76.3	72.9	79.6	71.5	67.3	75.5	69.3	64.6	73.8
1990	75.4	71.8	78.8	76.1	72.7	79.4	71.2	67.0	75.2	69.1	64.5	73.6
1989	75.1	71.7	78.5	75.9	72.5	79.2	70.9	66.7	74.9	68.8	64.3	73.3
1988	74.9	71.4	78.3	75.6	72.2	78.9	70.8	66.7	74.8	68.9	64.4	73.2
1987	74.9	71.4	78.3	75.6	72.1	78.9	71.0	66.9	75.0	69.1	64.7	73.4
1986	74.7	71.2	78.2	75.4	71.9	78.8	70.9	66.8	74.9	69.1	64.8	73.4
1985	74.7	71.1	78.2	75.3	71.8	78.7	71.0	67.0	74.8	69.3	65.0	73.4
1984	74.7	71.1	78.2	75.3	71.8	78.7	71.1	67.2	74.9	69.5	65.3	73.6
1983	74.6	71.0	78.1	75.2	71.6	78.7	70.9	67.0	74.7	69.4	65.2	73.5
1982	74.5	70.8	78.1	75.1	71.5	78.7	70.9	66.8	74.9	69.4	65.1	73.6
1981	74.1	70.4	77.8	74.8	71.1	78.4	70.3	66.2	74.4	68.9	64.5	73.2
1980	73.7	70.0	77.4	74.4	70.7	78.1	69.5	65.3	73.6	68.1	63.8	72.5
1979	73.9	70.0	77.8	74.6	70.8	78.4	69.8	65.4	74.1	68.5	64.0	72.9
1978	73.5	69.6	77.3	74.1	70.4	78.0	69.3	65.0	73.5	68.1	63.7	72.4
1977	73.3	69.5	77.2	74.0	70.2	77.9	68.9	64.7	73.2	67.7	63.4	72.0
1976	72.9	69.1	76.8	73.6	69.9	77.5	68.4	64.2	72.7	67.2	62.9	71.6
1975	72.6	68.8	76.6	73.4	69.5	77.3	68.0	63.7	72.4	66.8	62.4	71.3
1974	72.0	68.2	75.9	72.8	69.0	76.7	67.1	62.9	71.3	66.0	61.7	70.3
1973	71.4	67.6	75.3	72.2	68.5	76.1	66.1	62.0	70.3	65.0	60.9	69.3
1972	71.2	67.4	75.1	72.0	68.3	75.9	65.7	61.5	70.1	64.7	60.4	69.1
1971	71.1	67.4	75.0	72.0	68.3	75.8	65.6	61.6	69.8	64.6	60.5	68.9
1970	70.8	67.1	74.7	71.7	68.0	75.6	65.3	61.3	69.4	64.1	60.0	68.3
1960	69.7	66.6	73.1	70.6	67.4	74.1	63.6	61.1	66.3	—	—	—
1950	68.2	65.6	71.1	69.1	66.5	72.2	60.8	59.1	62.9	—	—	—
1940	62.9	60.8	65.2	64.2	62.1	66.6	53.1	51.5	54.9	—	—	—

—Data not available.

Note: Deaths based on a 50 percent sample.

Source: Singh GK, Kochanek KD, MacDorman MF. Advance report of final mortality statistics, 1994. *Monthly vital statistics report;* vol 45 no 3, supp, p 19. Hyattsville, Maryland: National Center for Health Statistics. 1996. www.cdc.gov/nchswww/datawh/statab/pubd/453st5h.htm, 11 June 1997.

FIGURE 10.7 Sample Table Showing Steps in a Process

MANAGEMENT RESPONSE TO COMPLAINT

Management initial response to employee: These are the responsibilities of the supervisor or other management representatives if contacted by an employee for assistance.

Step	If . . .	Then . . .
1	an employee complains of discrimination,	• ask the complainant to define his/her perception of the problem and the desired solution, • explain the rights involved, and • discuss potential solutions.
2	the employee desires primarily to discuss personal thoughts and feelings,	• listen to the employee, • advise of the availability of counseling through the County Employee Assistance Program, and • document the conversation with a memo to the file.
3	the employee desires to pursue the complaint further or discuss additional options regarding the incident,	• offer consultation and advice, or • refer the employee to the departmental discrimination counselor/investigator.
4	the employee gives permission,	• conduct a brief informal investigation, and • make every effort to resolve the problem on an informal basis as described on page 11.
5	the employee wishes to file a formal complaint,	• do not try to talk her/him out of it, • request she/he submit the complaint in writing, and • refer to "management responsibility for formal investigation" (page 12).
6	the employee does not prepare a written complaint,	• prepare your own written description of the allegation, • ask the employee to sign it to show agreement with its accuracy, and • investigate the complaint regardless of whether the employee signs the written description.
7	the alleged discrimination appears serious but the employee does not want an investigation,	• see below.

FIGURE 10.8 Sample Ineffective Use of Table

Table 3: How Graduates Found Jobs in 1997

Source of Job Information	Number of Students	Percent of Students
Newspaper	106	20.50
Networking	101	19.54
Company	63	12.19
University Career Services	61	11.809
Internship or Volunteer Experience	58	11.22
Previous Job	27	5.22
Job Service or Merit System	16	3.09
Temporary/Employment Agency	15	2.90
Military	3	.58
Other	5	.98
Did Not Indicate	62	11.99
TOTAL	517	100.00

FIGURE 10.9 Sample Bar Graph

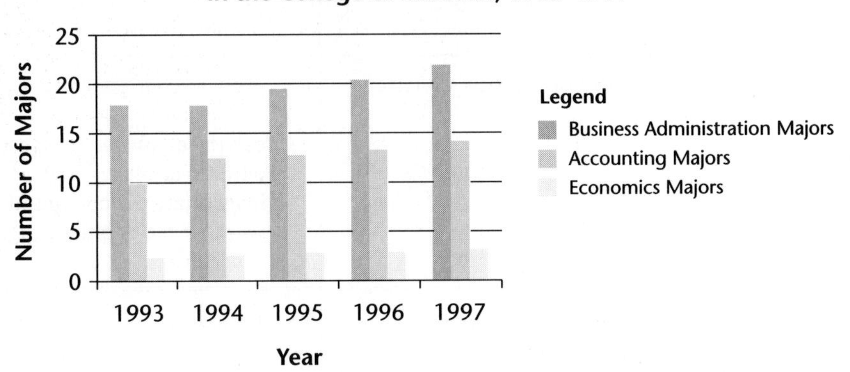

products, for instance. Figure 10.10, an illustration of a line chart, shows sales of four different cables over four different quarters in a year.

- **A flowchart** presents specific steps in a process or procedure in a schematic form, enabling readers to visualize the steps involved. For instance, Figure 10.11 illustrates the process that a student loan application goes through from the time the student completes the borrower section of the application until the time the borrower signs the loan check. And if readers are in the midst of a process or procedure, a flowchart will enable them to see at a glance where they are and what they need to do next. In this regard, a flowchart is much easier to follow than a narrative explanation of the same material. The flowchart in Figure 10.12 also provides a road map through a series of conditions and decisions, but it looks very different from the flowchart in Figure 10.11 (p. 456). Figure 10.12 (p. 457) was designed to help nonnative speakers of English determine whether they need to use *a, an,* or *the* in specific instances with nouns.
- **An organizational chart** shows the chain of command within an organization and illustrates how the various people or units within the organization are related to one another. Sometimes, such a chart includes only the names of the organizational components (functional units, departments, divisions, offices) within rectangles arranged in a hierarchy from the top to the bottom of the page, with those units with the most authority listed first. See Figure 10.13 (p. 458) for an example of the human resource division of an organization. Sometimes, organizational charts map out key people and their titles, as Figure 10.14 (p. 459) shows.
- **A pie chart,** which illustrates the component parts of a whole, is appropriate if you want readers to compare various parts within a whole or to compare a part to the whole.

FIGURE 10.10 Sample Line Graph

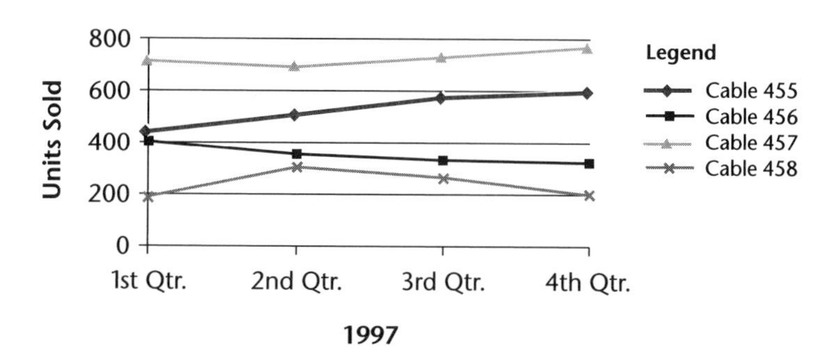

FIGURE 10.11 Sample Flowchart

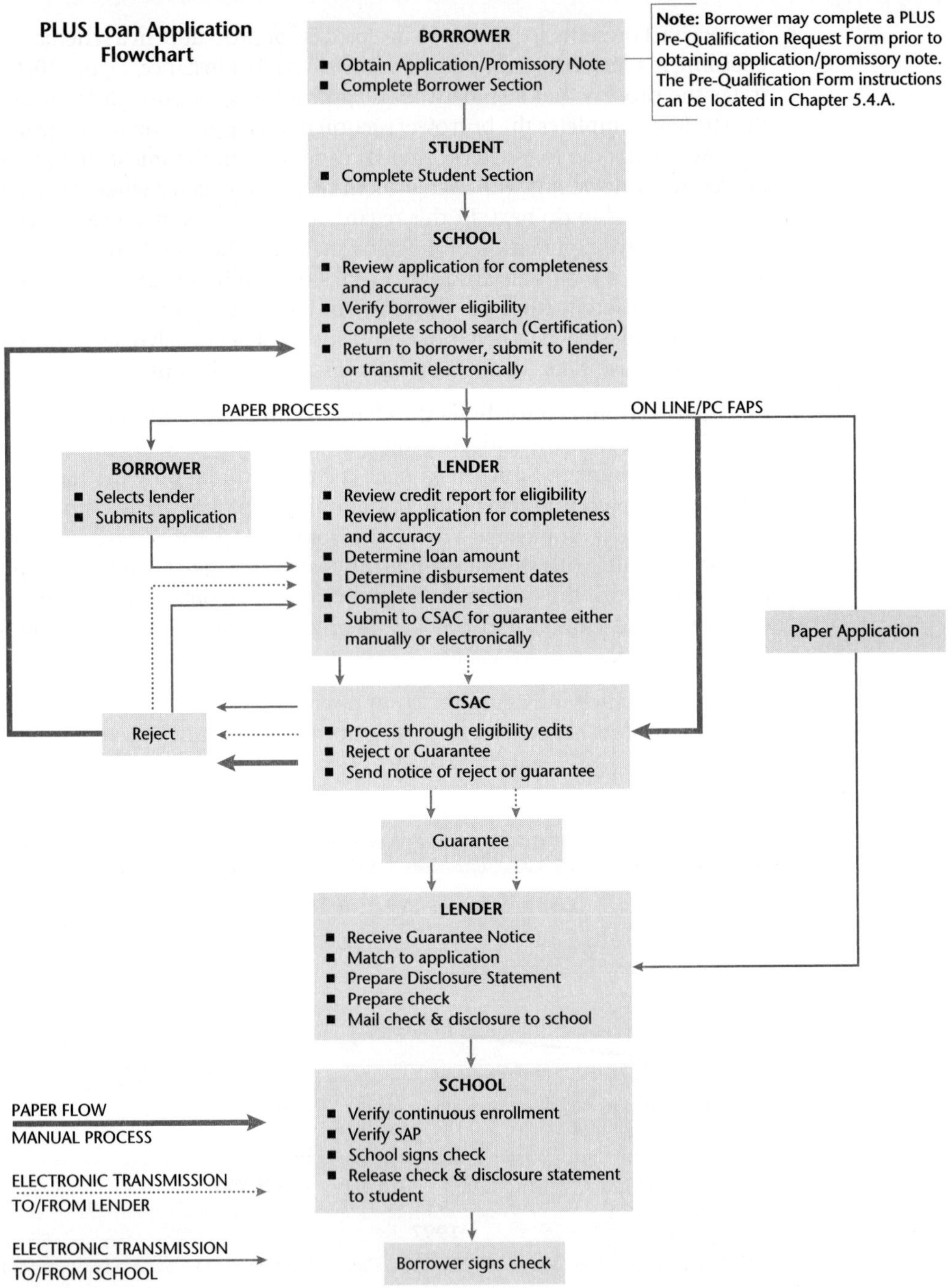

PLUS Loan Application Flowchart

BORROWER
- Obtain Application/Promissory Note
- Complete Borrower Section

Note: Borrower may complete a PLUS Pre-Qualification Request Form prior to obtaining application/promissory note. The Pre-Qualification Form instructions can be located in Chapter 5.4.A.

STUDENT
- Complete Student Section

SCHOOL
- Review application for completeness and accuracy
- Verify borrower eligibility
- Complete school search (Certification)
- Return to borrower, submit to lender, or transmit electronically

PAPER PROCESS

ON LINE/PC FAPS

BORROWER
- Selects lender
- Submits application

LENDER
- Review credit report for eligibility
- Review application for completeness and accuracy
- Determine loan amount
- Determine disbursement dates
- Complete lender section
- Submit to CSAC for guarantee either manually or electronically

Paper Application

CSAC
- Process through eligibility edits
- Reject or Guarantee
- Send notice of reject or guarantee

Reject

Guarantee

LENDER
- Receive Guarantee Notice
- Match to application
- Prepare Disclosure Statement
- Prepare check
- Mail check & disclosure to school

SCHOOL
- Verify continuous enrollment
- Verify SAP
- School signs check
- Release check & disclosure statement to student

Borrower signs check

PAPER FLOW / MANUAL PROCESS

ELECTRONIC TRANSMISSION TO/FROM LENDER

ELECTRONIC TRANSMISSION TO/FROM SCHOOL

FIGURE 10.12 Sample Flowchart

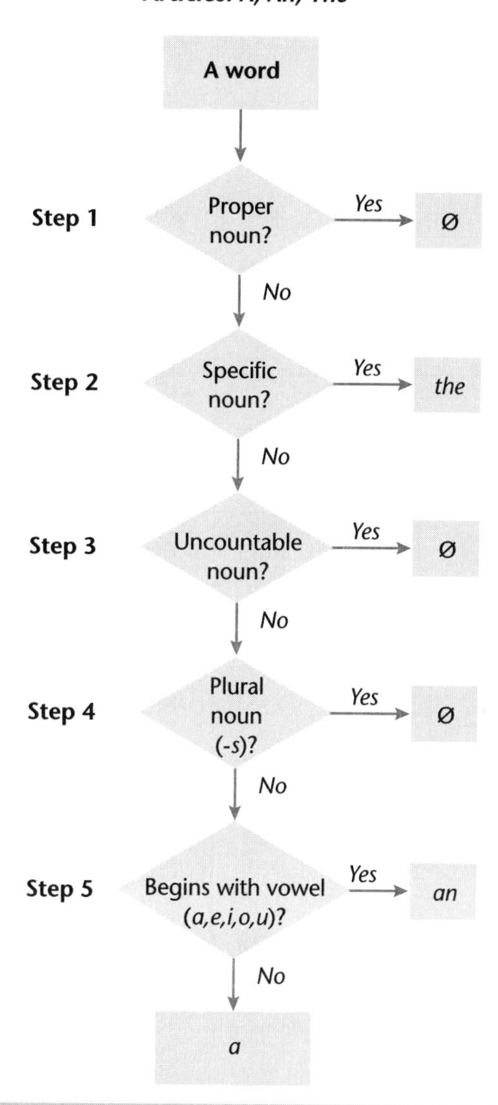

FIGURE 10.13 Sample General Organizational Chart

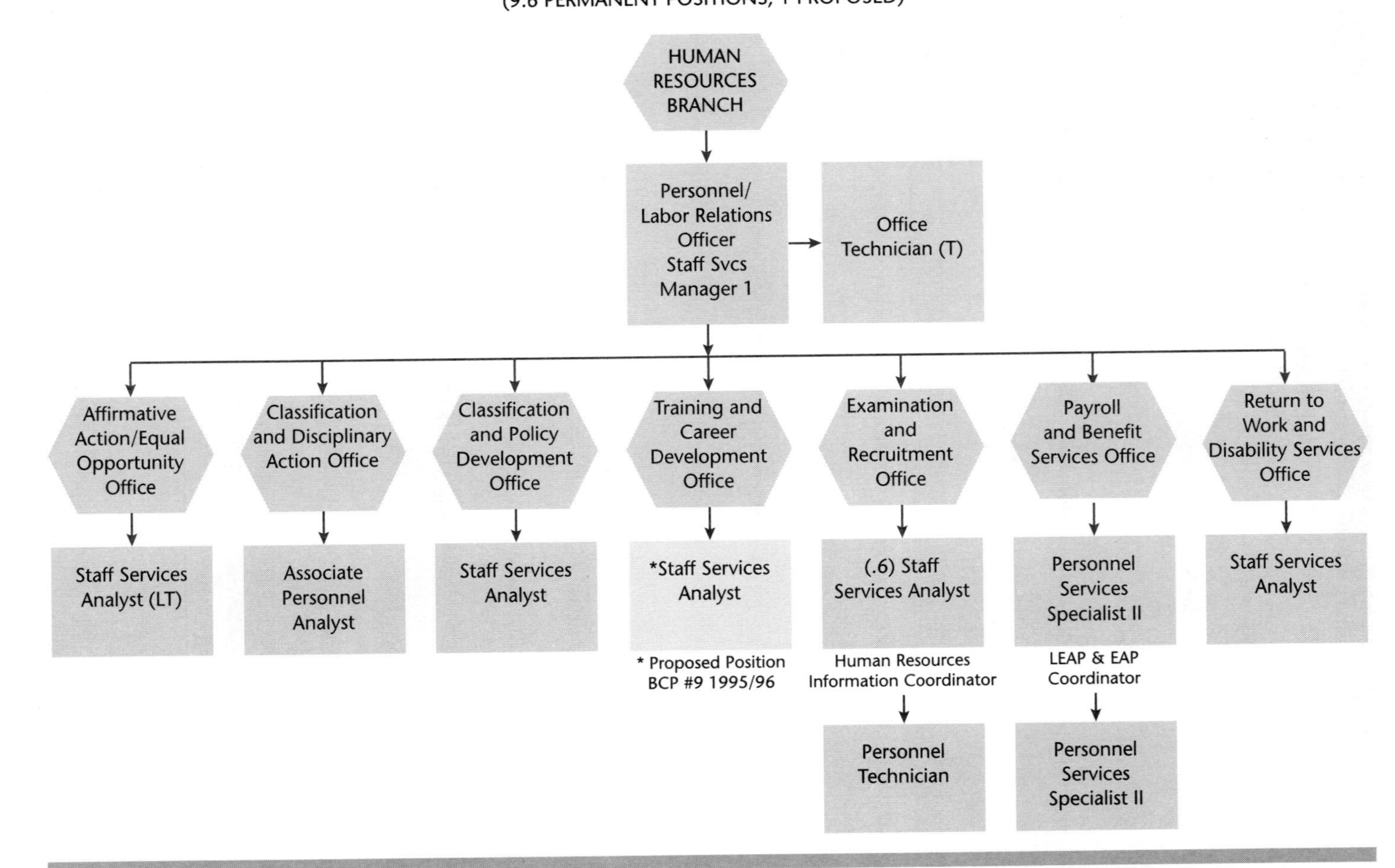

FIGURE 10.14 Sample Organizational Chart Listing Key People

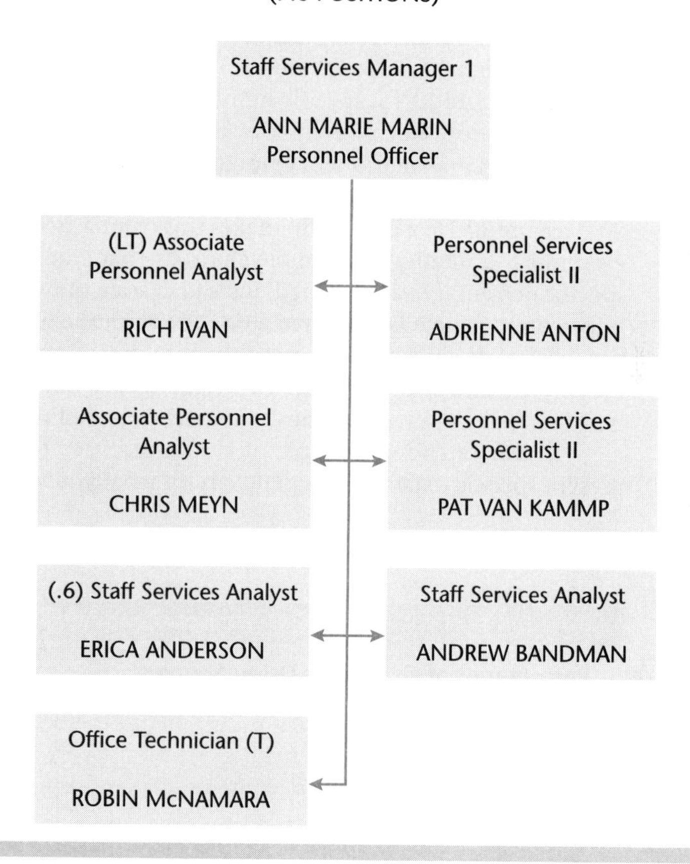

To illustrate the appropriate uses of these various graphics, let's consider the information presented in Table 3: How Graduates Found Jobs in 1997 (Figure 10.8, p. 454). The table presents both numbers and percentages of students who found jobs via various means. This tabular display would be appropriate for readers who were most interested in the exact numbers and percentages. But let's say, now, that you're trying to persuade readers that newspapers and networking are the most significant sources of job information. You probably want a more visual means of presenting your data—a means that emphasizes the large percentages of people who found jobs through newspapers and networking. In this case, using a pie chart would enable readers to compare the sizes of individual slices of the pie to the whole pie.

Figure 10.15 uses a pie chart to illustrate How Graduates Found Jobs in 1997. Notice that the largest slices of the pie, indicating the most often used sources of job information—20.5 percent for newspapers and 19.5 percent for networking—appear in the upper-righthand quadrant of the pie; other slices are arranged in decreasing order of importance or size, moving in a clockwise fashion. In addition, the data (percentages) are clearly labeled in the *legend*, or *key*, which identifies the elements used to distinguish the different pieces of the pie—different colors, shadings, and pattern. Such data might also appear within the slices of the pie or in both the slices and the legend. In Figure 10.15, specific numbers are omitted from the pie itself for purposes of simplification. But nonetheless, the pie chart speaks forcefully about the major sources of job information for graduates, allowing readers to compare sizes of the various slices of the pie—the means of finding jobs.

Figure 10.16, a bar graph, makes this comparison among means of finding jobs even more dramatic. Like the pie chart, the bar graph simplifies the data. Here, the specific percentages are omitted; instead, a scale of numbers of graduates using each information source is indicated along the vertical axis. The legend on the right clarifies what each bar signifies, and horizontal lines (optional) enable readers to interpret more readily the approximate length of each bar. However, the specific numbers here aren't as important as the comparative sizes of the bars.

As this extended example of How Graduates Found Jobs illustrates, how you present specific data really depends upon what you want to show. So, as you decide

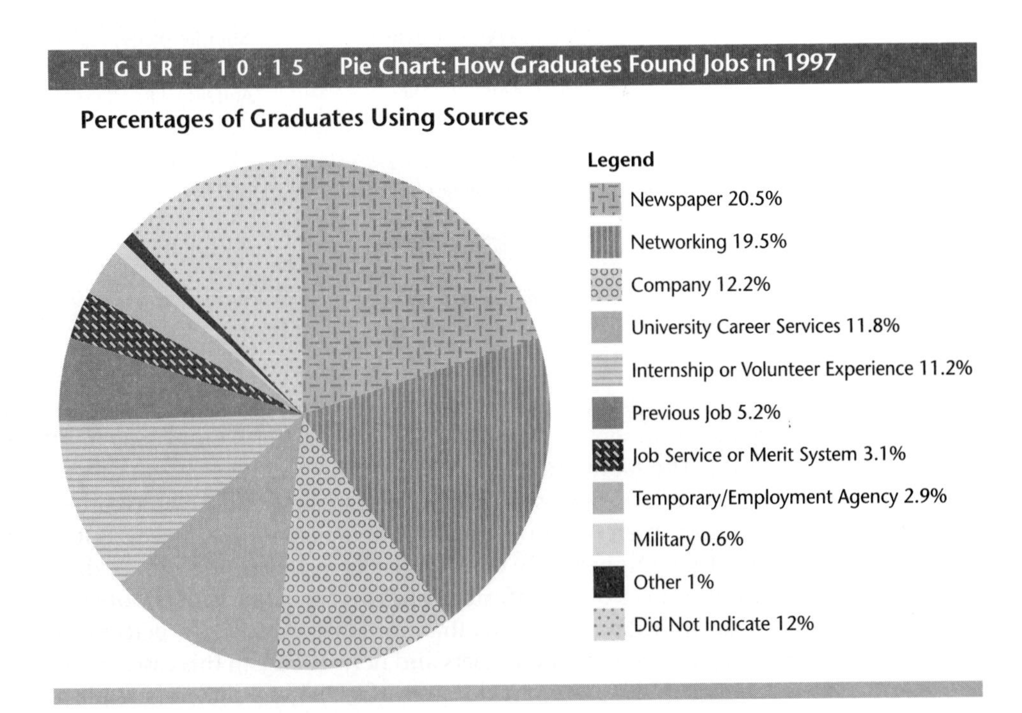

FIGURE 10.15 Pie Chart: How Graduates Found Jobs in 1997

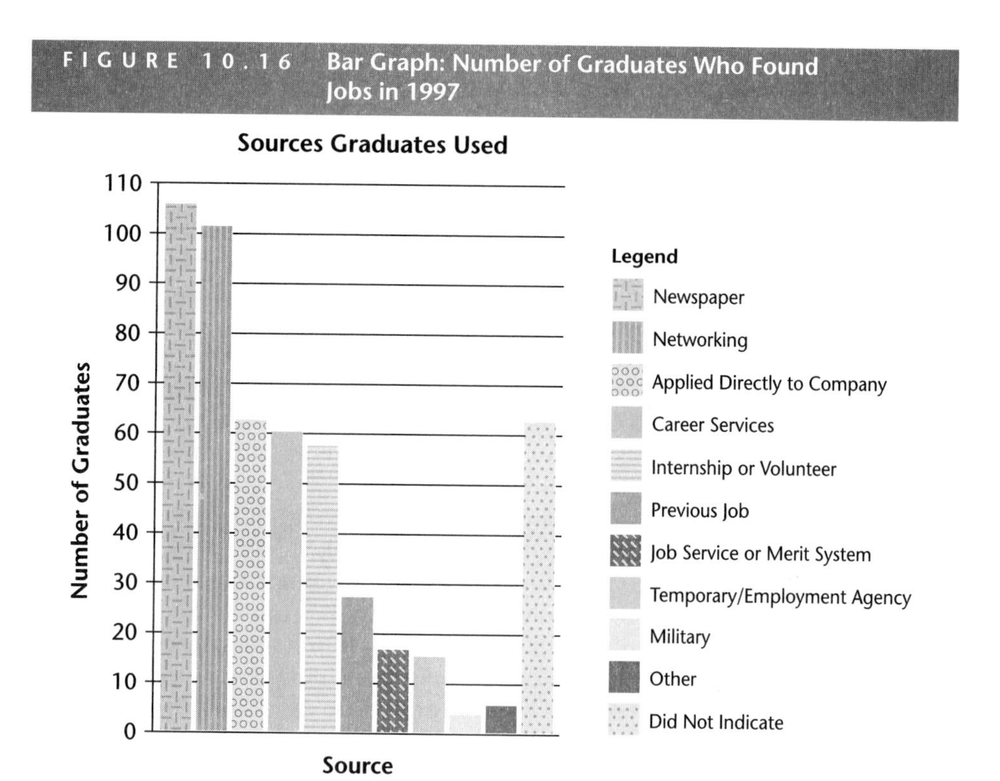

FIGURE 10.16 Bar Graph: Number of Graduates Who Found Jobs in 1997

on the sorts of visual displays you plan to use in a long, complex report, ask yourself the following questions:

- Why do you want to use graphics? To clarify and simplify your message for readers? To add dramatic impact and credibility? To emphasize particular points or relationships?
- Do you want to substantiate in graphic form points made in the text?
- Do you want to provide concrete numerical or textual information in a form that's easy to read?
- Do you want readers to see trends or changes over time?
- Do you want to compare quantities? Percentages? Parts of a whole?
- Do you want to provide information about the steps in a process? The overall structure of a business?
- Do you want to help readers visualize a process or product?

And once you've determined your purpose in using a graphic, follow these general conventions:

- Make sure all graphics are self-explanatory. Readers should be able to look at the visual and its title and legend and know exactly what they're looking at.
- Even though graphics should be self-explanatory, integrate them carefully into your text. This generally means that you should follow three steps:
  1. Introduce your graphic in the text of your document, pointing out key elements that readers should notice.
  2. Insert the graphic in your text, making sure to number and title the visual. Table titles and numbers conventionally appear *above* tables and figure titles and numbers usually appear *below.*
  3. Explain or analyze important information in the graphic so that readers have no chance to misinterpret it.

  This process of introducing, inserting, and analyzing graphics will ensure that your text and graphics are carefully designed and work together to make your argument. This process also accommodates two diverse groups of readers: those who are visually oriented as well as those who are textually oriented. Figure 10.17 illustrates this process of introducing, inserting, and analyzing graphics. The graphic and text work together in this case to show concretely the diversity of the area labor force. And the two are integrated carefully so that readers move seamlessly from text to graphic and back again.
- If you're using material from another source—as we did in Figures 10.6, 10.17, and 10.20—indicate this source, generally in a notation that appears below the graphic.
- If your graphic is small and applies to a specific part of the discussion, place the graphic within the document, right next to the text that explains it. However, if the graphic doesn't fit a particular part of your discussion but instead summarizes large amounts of information used in the report as a whole, as in Figure 10.6, place it in an appendix. Common appendix material includes detailed research results presented in summary or general purpose tables, structured interview forms or questionnaires used in research, complex schematics or computer printouts, and graphics that are too detailed or technical for the majority of readers—especially the busy decision makers—but are necessary for completeness.

In this chapter, we've introduced document design conventions you can use when writing long, complex documents. We've discussed how busy professionals tend to read long documents, and we've talked about conventional "traffic signals" that can help readers find information they expect to see in these documents. The major traffic signals we've talked about have been tables of contents, summaries, headings and subheadings, and some other obvious but often overlooked directional signals—like numbering pages and using white space to show breaks and transitions. We've also considered other conventional elements of long, complex documents—physical elements like covers, typefaces, paper, cover letters, and appendixes. And we've discussed,

FIGURE 10.17 Sample of Incorporating Graphics into Text

Employment

The following chart reflects changes in the labor force for the St. Cloud MSA between 1982 and 1993.

	1982	1987	1993	1987–1993 % Change
Manufacturing	10,650	11,636	15,495	33.2%
Non-manufacturing	42,360	59,860	75,525	26.2%
Total labor force	76,392	94,065	113,338	20.5%
Number in labor force available	7,130	5,845	6,156	5.32
Unemployment rate	9.3%	6.2%	5.4%	—

Source: Minnesota Department of Trade and Economic Development.

As shown in the previous chart, the labor force in St. Cloud increased by 19,273 persons or 20.5% over the last six years. The majority of this growth occurred in the non-manufacturing sector, which experienced growth of 15,665 jobs or 26.2%.

Manufacturing employment also increased at strong rates, adding 3,859 new jobs. Major manufacturing employers in the St. Cloud area follow:

Major Employers	Product/Service	Employees	Union	Union
Fingerhut Corporation	Consumer goods	4,315	ACWA	32%
Cold Spring Granite	Granite	1,000	—	—
Saint Cloud Hospital	Health care	2,300	—	—
Frigidaire Co.	Refrigerators/freezers	1,700	IAMAW623	90%
Jack Frost/Gold'N Plump	Broiler chickens	1,300	—	—
Bankers Systems	Financial forms	950	—	—
Champion International	Printing paper	700	IMAW/UPIU	65%
DeZurick	Industrial valves	656	IMAW/IAM	55%
Vision-Ease Corporation	Lens blanks, lenses	450	—	—
Quebecor Printing	Catalogs/magazines	400	—	—
Woodcraft Industries	Cabinet components	466	—	—
Stearns Manufacturing	Flotation products	375	—	—
Stone Container	Shipping containers	161	UPWI 1976	73%
Lantz Lenses	Optical lens blanks	140	—	

The 14 largest employers represent several different industries, with only lens manufacturing and printing represented more than once. The 14 companies represent 13% of the St. Cloud area work force. These factors indicate the diversity of the labor force. This diversity helps to stabilize the economy of the area.

in some detail, strategies for writing summaries that can answer readers' preliminary questions and conventions for using graphics strategically to make your key claims and evidence visible and comprehensible. The document design principles we've discussed in this current chapter are applicable to all sorts of reports. In Chapters 11 and 12, we will look more particularly at various types of long, complex documents and their situations: proposals and business plans, progress reports, researched position papers, and final project reports.

WRITING CHECKLIST

The following guidelines will help you design long, complex documents in ways that enhance readability and help people find what they need. For any of these guidelines, remember the superordinate guideline: Disregard *any* of this advice if it would cause you to do something that's inappropriate or silly for your situation.

☑ Formatting

- Use conventional formatting elements to help readers find what they need: a table of contents, page numbers, headings and subheadings, summaries and overview sentences, and cross-references.
- Word headings and subheadings so they describe precisely the contents of their sections.
- Make sure that headings are consistent in grammatical structure, format, and type treatment.
- Use summaries and overview sentences to preview information for readers.
- Use cross-references to point out related information in other parts of the document.
- Place in appendices any large, complex, difficult chunks of data that will distract readers from the line of your argument.
- Introduce all appendices in the body of your text.
- Include a cover and use good-quality paper and copying.
- Use graphics that enhance the document's readability.
- Establish in a cover letter the context of the proposal, business plan, or report, and summarize the contents of the document.

☑ Summaries

- Forecast what readers can expect to find in your document, and anticipate and answer reader's key questions in a summary.
- Remember that summaries are the most extensively circulated and read parts of proposals, business plans, and long reports; they keep busy executives apprised of what's going on in the organization.

- Use a descriptive summary if you want to provide an overview of a document but not specific results, conclusions, or recommendations.
- Use an informative summary if you want to forecast the document's content and provide key results, conclusions, and recommendations.
- To draft an effective summary, reread the document with the goal of summarizing in mind.
- Draft your summary without looking back at the document.
- Test your summary against the document being summarized, and revise accordingly.

☑ Graphics

- Use graphics to organize complex information and clarify its significance; remember that graphics should be integral parts of your arguments.
- Present detailed numerical information in tables with easily readable columns and rows.
- Use borders, boxes, and shading to enhance the readability of tables.
- Include a large amount of information from a whole report in a general purpose table in an appendix.
- Use bar graphs when you want readers to be able to compare information.
- Use line graphs to show changes over time and help readers understand trends.
- Use flowcharts to present steps in processes or procedures.
- Use organizational charts to show a chain of command and relationships among various people or units within organizations.
- Use pie charts to illustrate the component parts of a whole.
- Make sure that graphics really illustrate what you want to show and that they help you make your arguments.
- Ensure that graphics are self-explanatory.
- Carefully integrate graphics into the text so that the text and graphics work together to make your argument.
- Indicate material from other sources through source notations.

ACTIVITIES AND PROJECTS

1. The paragraphs in Figure 10.18 (p. 466) are from a report on the growth of nontraditional student enrollments at universities. Design graphics that highlight significant data and make the text more comprehensible. Revise these paragraphs, integrating the graphics into the text where they should appear.
2. The graphics in Figure 10.19 (p. 467) were taken from the report mentioned in Activity 1 on the growth of nontraditional student enrollments at universities

FIGURE 10.18 Paragraphs for Revision Activity

In fall 1987, 4.9 million students age 25 and older were enrolled in colleges. The number increased 25 percent to 6.1 million in 1995, and according to the National Center for Education Statistics in Washington, D.C., the projected figure for 2007 is 6.4 million, or an increase of 6 percent. Students age 25 and older represented 55.0 percent of all college enrollments in 1995; the proportion of students 25 and older is projected to be 58.2 percent by the year 2007.

Just as significant as this growth is its comparison to increases in the number of younger students. The number of undergraduate students ages 18 to 24 grew from 7.64 million in 1987 to an estimated 7.65 million in 1995, an increase of only 0.1 percent. This number is expected to increase to 9.4 million by 2007, an increase of 23 percent over 1995.

nationwide. They appeared in the report as you see them here. Describe the design problems in these graphics and the sorts of confusion they create. Then, explain how you would redesign the graphics so that they communicate clearly and persuasively. Finally, write a paragraph or two in which these redesigned graphics might occur, making sure to integrate text and graphics so that they are comprehensible and convincing.

3. Select a process or procedure that you perform frequently on your job. Design a flowchart that an employee-in-training might use to perform this task. First, determine the key parts of the process or procedure, and list them in chronological order. Then, place each step in a rectangle, placing the first step at the top of the page and then moving, step by step in sequence, to the bottom of the page. Indicate the movement of the process or procedure by connecting the rectangles with arrows. Test your graphic by having a colleague on the job or in your classroom actually perform the task, using only the flowchart for instructions.

4. Draw an organizational chart for your workplace—the entire organization, if it's small, or your department or unit, if the organization is large. For the purposes of this exercise, map out organizational units *or* key people.

5. Look through your document file for an example of a report with strong document design and one with weak document design. Bring the examples to a small group discussion, and be prepared to explain why you believe each document design is strong or weak.

6. Start combing newspapers and magazines for examples of well-done graphics. Save both the graphics and the text accompanying them. After you've found 10 or so effective examples, select your favorite three or four. Explain why you've selected each and why you believe it works so well.

FIGURE 10.19 Sample Graphic with Design Problems

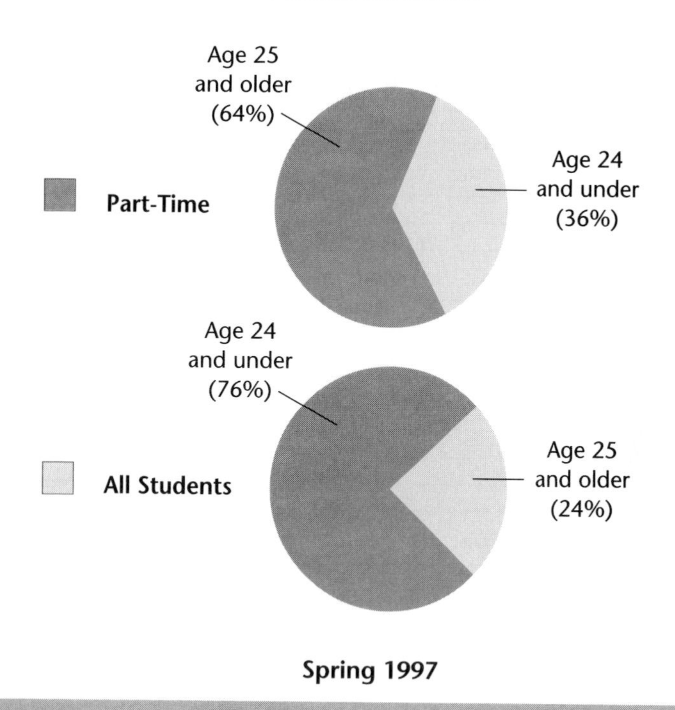

7. Review the data on civilian employment from the U.S. Bureau of Labor Statistics that appear in Figure 10.20 (p. 468). Consider what claims and what arguments you might make, based on data from this table. Then, construct several paragraphs using this data and one or two graphics that you design and integrate carefully within your text.

8. Select a recent report or published article in your field, and write an informative summary for this article using guidelines from this chapter. After you've drafted this summary, use Testing Your Summary (p. 446) to test its effectiveness. Assume that readers know nothing about this article. In addition, provide full bibliographic information at the bottom of your summary—or at the top, if your teacher advises you to—so that readers know where to find the article if they wish to read it themselves. Figure 10.4 provides an example of an informative summary and full bibliographic citation. Use the example as a model for your bibliographic citation, or follow a stylesheet in your field.

9. Write a descriptive summary of the same document as in Activity 8 or of a different document. Again, provide full bibliographic information at the bottom of your summary—or at the top, if your teacher advises you to do so. Figure 10.4 provides an example of a descriptive summary and full bibliographic citation.

FIGURE 10.20 Sample General Purpose Table

Civilian Employment in the Fastest-Growing Occupations

	Employment per Year (in thousands)				Percent Change		
	1992	1996	2000	2004	1992–1996	1996–2000	2000–2004
Total, all occupations*	127,015	140,261	144,708	150,212	10.4	13.9	18.3
Personal and home care aides	179	382	391	397	114.0	118.7	122.3
Home health aides	420	832	848	863	98.3	102.0	105.7
Systems analysts	483	893	928	972	84.9	92.1	101.3
Computer engineers	195	355	372	394	81.8	90.4	101.9
Physical and corrective therapy assistants and aides	78	141	142	143	82.3	83.1	84.5
Electronic pagination systems workers	18	32	33	34	77.2	82.8	88.2
Occupational therapy assistants and aides	16	28	29	29	80.0	82.1	86.5
Physical therapists	102	182	183	185	78.9	80.0	81.9
Residential counselors	165	284	290	295	72.7	76.5	79.5
Human services workers	168	284	293	303	68.8	74.5	80.0
Occupational therapists	54	91	93	95	68.7	72.2	77.3
Manicurists	38	63	64	64	68.7	69.5	69.9
Medical assistants	206	329	327	324	59.9	59.0	57.9
Paralegals	110	170	175	179	54.3	58.3	62.4
Medical records technicians	81	125	126	130	53.5	55.8	59.8
Teachers, special education	388	545	593	648	40.6	53.0	67.2
Amusement and recreation attendants	267	398	406	414	49.2	52.0	55.2
Correction officers	310	430	468	513	38.5	50.9	65.2
Operations research analysts	44	65	67	69	45.5	50.0	55.8
Guards	867	1,248	1,282	1,322	44.0	47.9	52.5
Speech-language pathologists and audiologists	85	120	125	130	40.3	46.0	52.8
Detectives, except public	55	77	79	80	41.7	44.3	47.2
Surgical technologists	46	64	65	68	39.3	42.5	48.6
Dental hygienists	127	182	180	178	43.3	42.1	40.1
Dental assistants	190	271	269	266	43.1	41.9	40.0
Adjustment clerks	373	505	521	540	35.1	39.6	44.6
Teacher aides and educational assistants	932	1,211	1,296	1,393	29.9	39.0	49.5
Data processing equipment repairers	75	100	104	108	33.3	38.2	44.1
Nursery and greenhouse managers	19	26	26	26	38.3	37.5	37.3
Securities and financial services sales workers	246	328	335	343	33.6	36.6	39.5
Bill and account collectors	250	334	342	351	33.3	36.5	40.1
Respiratory therapists	73	96	99	104	32.3	36.4	43.8
Pest controllers and assistants	56	75	76	78	33.2	35.6	38.6
Emergency medical technicians	138	178	187	197	29.0	35.6	42.6

*Includes other occupations, not shown separately.

Notes: Occupations are in order of employment percent change, 1992–2004 (moderate growth). Includes wage and salary jobs, self-employed, and unpaid family members. Estimates based on the Current Employment Statistics estimates and the Occupational Employment Statistics estimates. See Source for methodological assumptions. Minus sign (-) indicates decrease.

Source: U.S. Bureau of Labor Statistics, *Monthly Labor Review,* November 1995. http://www.census.gov:80/statab/freq/96S0639.txt, 12 June 1997.

Chapter 11

Beyond the Library: Information Resources and Research Strategies in the Contemporary Organization

The way to do research is to attack the facts at the point of greatest astonishment.

—Celia Green

Information is our lifeblood, both individually and institutionally. Without it, we're paralyzed—unable to act. And we almost never feel we have enough of it. In the uncertain world where we live and work, we almost never act in complete confidence that we know everything about our situation. We are almost always at risk of making a mistake because of something we don't know.

But we reduce this risk at a cost. Information is expensive. Sometimes, when we buy it in a straightforward transaction, we can put a precise dollar amount on its value. More often, though, its cost is represented largely in terms of the human investment we make in time and effort. And the human cost includes not only the hourly wages of those who gather and interpret the information but also opportunity costs. Our investment in our research has a point of diminishing returns, past which the financial, social, technical, and ethical risks and costs begin to outweigh the benefits. If we always wait for complete information and complete certainty before acting, then we will be caught in what is often called the *paralysis of analysis*. So, in all of the research that we do, we should try to find the ideal level of effort between investing too much in the research (in which case we may miss a crucial opportunity) and investing too little (in which case we may plunge into an inappropriate project and into bad decisions it embodies or proposes). Research, like all other writing activities, always entails risk, and research, like writing, is a process of risk management.

Deciding What You Need to Know and Where to Look for It

As the title of Chapter 2 says, managing your writing is managing your work. And managing your research effectively, as a part of your writing project, means that you need to know what organizational goal your research is serving. You need to ask the same kinds of questions we suggested in Chapter 2.

First, you need to decide what kind of information you need. Think of where your research need would fall along a scale of complexity, as illustrated by the continuum in Figure 11.1. At one extreme (far left), a writing project may entail just a single, well-defined issue, and all the relevant information may already be inside your head. As you move toward the other end of the continuum, the number and complexity of issues increase. At the far-right end, the issues become so complex that you need to do substantial preliminary research just to clarify the issues and figure out the questions you need to ask. These questions will then guide the later stages of your

FIGURE 11.1 The Research Continuum

Simpler ⟷ More Complex

Mnemonic Research	Minimal Research	Consultative Research	Creative/Collaborative Research
■ Limited to one or two well-defined issues. ■ Information is in your head, on your hard drive, or at your fingertips. ■ Primary activity is remembering and using the information.	■ Issues require reflection and sorting. ■ Information is in correspondence in files, contracts, reports, policies, precedents, and perhaps other corporate documents.	■ Issues affect others in or even outside your organization. ■ Understanding the issues and their implications requires consultation with others through informal interviewing—office or hallway conversations or e-mail chats. ■ You may encounter increasing demand for systematic documentary research in handbooks, indexes, directories, reports, studies, and other lengthy documents, both public and proprietary. ■ Electronic research, especially via the World Wide Web, may be a major source of your information.	■ Issues may demand systematic data collection, requiring you to work with others, either as teammates in the project or as sources of information. ■ Documentary research may need to be supplemented with extensive, systematic interviews, focus-group interviews, surveys, or other kinds of systematic observation. ■ Information may need to be coded, compiled, reduced, analyzed, and otherwise manipulated, perhaps using rigorous, sophisticated statistical procedures.

research. In this kind of complex, multistage research, your modes and methods of research are likely to shift from stage to stage. For example, informal interviews may identify initial questions that are then explored and refined in focus groups and subsequently distributed as a questionnaire, yielding responses that are subjected to rigorous statistical analysis.

As shown in Figure 11.1, four types of research can be identified along the continuum of complexity:

1. **Mnemonic research.** Just one or two well-defined issues are involved. The necessary information is already in your head, on your hard drive, or at your fingertips. Essentially, all you're doing here is remembering the information and using it.

2. **Minimal research.** The issues involved require you to pause, reflect, and sort. You may have to refer to correspondence in files—contracts, reports, policies, precedents, and perhaps other corporate documents.

3. **Consultative research.** You may find that the issues involved affect others in your organization or even outside your organization. Understanding the full implications of these issues—and even recognizing what all the issues are—may require consultation with others. Crucial information may be in their hands or files, which you may need to obtain through some informal interviewing (e.g., office or hallway conversations or telephone or e-mail chats). Toward the high range of this section of the continuum, you encounter increasing demands for systematic documentary research; you may invest substantial "seat time" consulting handbooks, indexes, directories, reports, studies, and other lengthy documents, both public and proprietary. Electronic research, especially via the World Wide Web, may be a major source of your information.

4. **Creative/collaborative research.** The issues demand systematic data collection that requires substantial work with others, either as teammates in the project or as sources of information. You may need to supplement your documentary research with extensive, systematic interviews, focus-group interviews, surveys, or other kinds of systematic observation.

   Triangulation—where one source of information or one research measure is tested by using another source or research measure—may become an important research strategy. For example, you may do a series of interviews or even a series of focus-group interviews, rather than rely on just a single interviewee or focus group. You may also use a survey to test whether the attitudes expressed in a focus-group session are representative of a larger population. Or you may use a focus-group interview to explore in greater depth some of the attitudes identified in a survey. As your information becomes more extensive and more complex, you and your readers will be increasingly challenged to manage and understand it. The risk of information overload will increase. To manage this risk, you will need to use systematic procedures, protocols, and even sophisticated statistical analysis for compiling, coding, organizing, reducing, analyzing, and interpreting information. Only when you have reduced the data to a coherent, meaningful pattern can you use it to make a claim or back a warrant.

Using Information Resources Creatively, Responsibly, and Effectively

The continuum pictured in Figure 11.1 gives you a scale for managing your research investment. Responsible management of your research means moving no further to the right on the continuum than is necessary to get the information and analysis you need. This scale also gives you a schedule for staging your research. It suggests that you should almost never take the plunge into full-scale systematic research as a first step. Rather, you should start at the left of the continuum, where the research investment is minimal. And as Figure 11.2 shows, you should keep checking your results with two questions in mind:

1. Do I have enough information to go forward?
2. Do I have enough information to know I should abandon the project?

If the answer to either question is "yes," you should consider your research project a success. You've gained the information necessary to make a rational decision. If the

FIGURE 11.2 Systematic Research Process

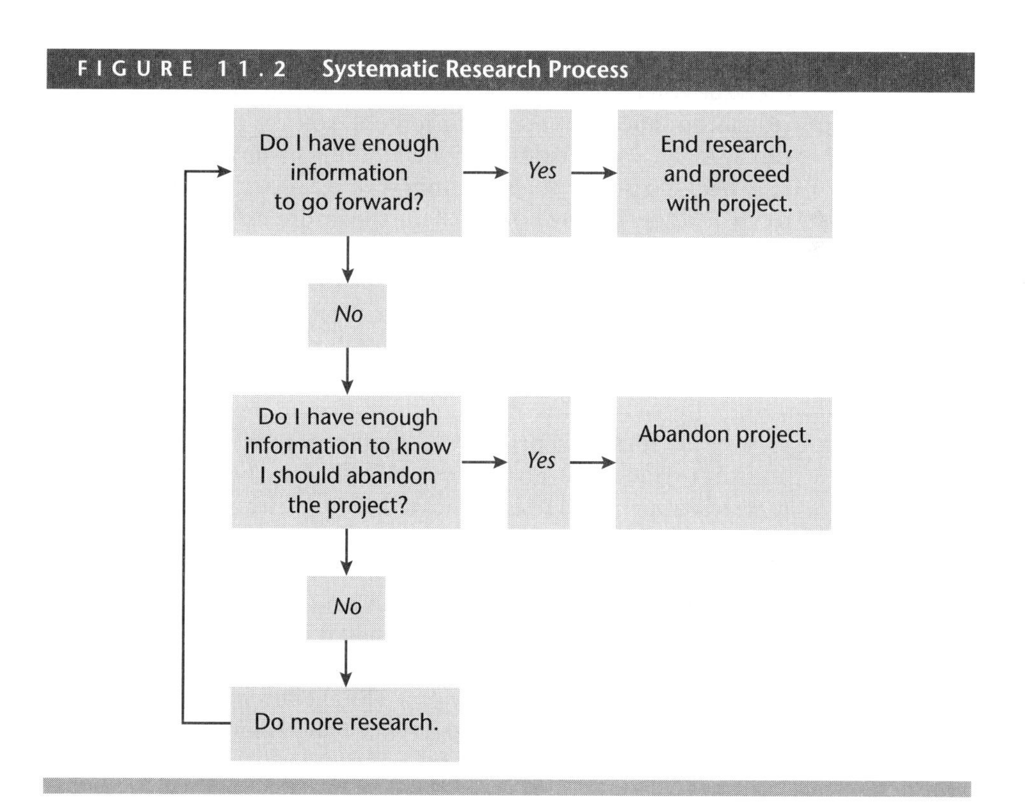

answer to both questions is "no," then you probably need to keep investigating, moving further to the right on the continuum to more elaborate, systematic research.

This whole strategy of starting at the left of the continuum and moving to the right only as needed can be summarized in this simple rule:

Try the simplest, easiest, cheapest research first.

In some ways, this is a bit like the advice "First, check to see if the computer is plugged in." It seems almost condescending even to say it! We're saying it, nevertheless, because this rule should guide your approach to every research project. Your starting with what's simplest, easiest, and cheapest is better than having some corporate vice president look at what you're doing and ask, "Why are you spending all this effort on this research? We investigated this five years ago, and the information is already in the file."

People as Resources

People are often your most accessible, efficient, and reliable information resource. Often, a colleague, supervisor, client, or others who are steeped in information about the issue you're investigating can jump-start your research by providing not only specific information but also leads to good sources of more information. Such people can also give you personal insights into the historical or organizational context that may help focus your goals, identify your readers, and clarify issues and arguments so that you know exactly how to shape the information as grounds for your claims and warrants.

But precisely *because* people can be so accessible, it's easy to abuse this resource. While people should be almost the first information resource you think of, you need to respect their needs and limits. One of the quickest ways to generate resentment and resistance in a personal source of information is to waste this person's time and attention by asking a lot of questions you could answer yourself with, say, a quick review of the files. This person will soon start to wonder about both your work ethic and your good sense. So, do your easy file-based research first. Another way to generate resentment and resistance is to be stingy in acknowledging the help you receive. Be generous in acknowledging personal help—both informally when you receive it and formally when you credit the individual in your document.

As you move along the research continuum toward a more systematic use of people as an information resource, you'll find that the formal structure of your query, the effort entailed for both you and your informants, and the number of people queried generally increase. The procedural conventions for this kind of query are detailed and rigorous enough that we'll talk about some of the commonly accepted procedures for formal interviews, focus group research, and survey research in separate sections later in this chapter.

Paper Resources

Normally, when we think of paper resources for research, we think of library materials. To be sure, they are often a crucial element in business and professional research, just as they are in academic research. Almost every office in every professional field in this country has at least a minimal professional library, consisting of standard trade handbooks, encyclopedias, dictionaries (both general and specialized), tables of frequently used formulas, codes of professional conduct, and the like. Larger firms often have full-fledged libraries, and some even have professional librarians.

Clearly, these materials are not required by research at the left of the continuum. So, before you make the substantial commitment to library research, test the adequacy of your most accessible paper resources and their electronic equivalents—your computer hard drives and other electronic storage. Here's a checklist of things to do or to ask yourself first:

- Check your files, both paper and electronic.
- Check any correspondence and other files that relate directly to this issue or client. Does a paper trail establish what you need to know and be able to demonstrate? Is there, perhaps, even text already written that you can simply incorporate as boilerplate?
- Check your files for reports on closely related or similar issues and clients. Do they provide information and language that answers your crucial questions?
- Consider your organization's policies and procedures statements; statements of corporate mission, philosophy, and values; and organizational brochures, proposals to clients, and other similar documents, including your own organization's website. Can you find the answers you need there or perhaps a lead to other sources for the answers?

Extending this minimal "fingertip" research, ask yourself what else is readily available, on your desk or in your office: dictionaries, handbooks, industry guidelines, and the like. Perhaps you keep copies of relevant regulatory and legal guidelines that relate to your work. Maybe other quick-reference information, including electronic sources, might be available on your own computer screen with a few minutes' effort. We'll focus especially on electronic resources at the end of this chapter, and we'll note some specific websites that may be of particular interest. We mention the electronic resources here, too, because if you have ready access to the information on your own computer, there's very little difference between reaching for your keyboard and reaching for a desktop reference book.

Conducting Interviews, Focus Groups, and Surveys

As your writing situations become increasingly novel, your arguments increasingly complex, and the stakes increasingly high, you'll find yourself moving ever further toward the right end of the research continuum. The complexity of the issues and the risks of being wrong will demand systematic data collection and rigorous documentation of the warrants linking your data to your claims. At some point, the following discussions of interview, focus-group, and survey methods (which we intend only as introductions) will not answer all the methodological questions you'll have, and you'll want to consult more specialized resources. With this need in mind, we'll mention some of the best-known and most respected works on these three techniques. These books, in turn, have their own extensive bibliographies of further resources.

As you think about your research, it's especially helpful to keep reminding yourself of your goal. You should focus on your key arguments and their counterarguments. Then you need to remember or figure out what evidence is needed to sustain these arguments. And, finally, you need to know what kinds of analysis and interpretation of the evidence will serve as strong warrants for reaching the conclusions you need to draw.

The literature about research and research methodologies tends to use different vocabularies—*dependent* and *independent variables, causation, control for confounding variables, rules of inference, confidence levels, replicability, generalizability*, and the like. The fact is, though, that these are simply different words for talking about *good arguments*. All research—whether it's classified as *prescriptive* (research that says things should be a certain way) or *descriptive* (research that says things are a certain way)—is making arguments. In each case, it is making claims based on evidence and warranting, or justifying, those claims based on its criteria of validity and methodologies of analysis. Research that talks about *independent* and *dependent variables* is arguing that the independent variable (A) caused the dependent variable (B). It may warrant this claim by replicating the conditions numerous times. It may defend its warrant against the claim that some other independent variable caused B by showing that it has controlled for confounding variables. It may qualify its warrant by specifying the level of confidence (usually in precise mathematical terms) it has in the likelihood that A really did cause B. It may specify exceptions to its claim by identifying limits to its generalizability. In all these cases, the process of effective researching and reporting of research is simply the process of building effective, responsible arguments.

Interviews

The same conventions and protocols governing the etiquette of information interviews that we talked about in Chapter 7 apply to setting up interviews generally. When you plan and compose an interview with a busy professional, visualize the world, in general, and yourself, in particular, from that person's perspective. You need to be especially sensitive to the risks your interviewee is taking by agreeing to this interview. For example, in Chapter 7, we talked about two risks: (1) that the interview will waste this person's time and (2) that you have a hidden agenda. There's a third risk, as well: that you will somehow use the information inappropriately.

So, your prospective interviewee will likely have a list of questions in mind, including some or all of these:

- Is this person qualified to be asking me about this topic?
- Is this person going to waste my time?

- Is this person going to misquote or misconstrue what I say?
- Is this person going to respect the limits of proprietary or confidential information?
- Is this person going to use this information for some purpose I won't like?

You can alleviate your prospective interviewee's anxiety about these risks by thinking carefully about the E of GRACE when you request the interview. That is, express clearly, specifically, and convincingly what your intentions are. Specifically, what do you need to know? Why do you need to know it? And how did you arrive at this point in your research? Notice that these are all contextual questions that establish your bona fide interest in the interviewee and the topic as well as your qualifications to be thinking about this topic at all. In addition, it's crucial that you express your intentions: What are you going to do with this information? And maybe even more important, what are you *not* going to do with it? Finally, what's a reasonable estimate of the time this interviewee will need to commit to the interview?

Next, you have to treat what you say or write to a prospective interviewee as an ironclad promise. If you say you'll take no more than half an hour, be prepared to offer to break off the interview at the end of half an hour. If you delimit the use of the information in your request for the interview, you need to honor those delimitations. You cannot use the information for additional purposes or disclose the information to additional readers that you did not identify in your request.

As you begin to think about the interview and your prospective interviewee, do something akin to a GRACEful analysis. What are your key goals in this interview, and who is the best interviewee? Stano and Reinsch, in *Communication in Interviews* (1982), discuss eight different types of interviews:

1. **The survey interview,** where you interview a series of many different people, doing orally what you might otherwise do with a paper survey
2. **The journalistic interview,** where you gather information from a single interviewee
3. **The performance appraisal interview,** where a supervisor and employee discuss and evaluate the employee's performance and make a plan for future performance goals
4. **The selection interview,** where a job seeker and prospective employer interview one another
5. **The nonprofessional counseling interview**
6. **The medical interview**
7. **The legal interview**
8. **The sales interview**

Thinking about the general kind of interview you're going to do and the kind of person you're going to interview will help you begin to think, in a broad sense, about what your goals are. Once you've clarified your goals, you can begin to think about more specific arguments, issues, and questions.

Stano and Reinsch (1982) insist that successful interviews require planning. You need to have a clear sense of what the key issues are and what questions to ask to elicit the information you need to understand these issues. And you need to think about not only the specific content of questions to ask but *how* to ask the questions, as well. Stano and Reinsch's taxonomy of kinds of questions gives you a framework for both planning the interview and composing new questions while the interview is in progress so that you improve your chances of getting the kind of information you need. Consider these six kinds of questions:

1. **Open versus closed questions.** Questions can range from completely open ended, at one extreme, to completely closed or defined, at the other extreme. A completely open-ended question would be "Tell me about yourself." You would close your interviewee's options slightly if you asked, instead, "Tell me about your career as a personnel consultant." You would close the options further if you asked, "What are the two or three most satisfying things about working in this organization?" And finally, you would be asking a completely closed question if you inquired, "On a scale of 1 to 5, with 1 being high and 5 being low, what number would you give to the quality of service at this bank?" Generally, open-ended questions concede more control to the interviewee and elicit longer, richer, more detailed responses, but they also require more effort from the interviewee. Often, these answers are more difficult to interpret, categorize, and analyze than the answers to more strictly controlled questions.
2. **Primary or secondary (follow-up) questions.** After the initial, primary question and response, you may sense a need to follow up. If you feel your interviewee hasn't understood the primary question, you may simply restate or rephrase it. If you want more information or detail, you may probe as a follow-up: for instance, "Tell me more about that." At key points in the interview, especially at the end, you may want to use some *reflective questions,* where you mirror back to your interviewee your understanding, summary, or interpretation of the response to a key question, a series of questions, or even the entire interview. Your purpose in doing so is to make sure you've correctly understood the responses. Again, at key points in the interview, especially at the end, you may want to ask *clearinghouse questions* to find out if there's other important information that your questions up to this point haven't given the interviewee a chance to talk about.
3. **Neutral or leading questions.** When opposing lawyers object to questions asked in a trial, they sometimes complain that their opponent is "leading the witness" by asking questions that indicate what response the lawyer expects or prefers. There are several kinds of leading questions—some more overtly leading than others. For example, you would be clearly trying to lead the interviewee with a question like "You wouldn't ever do that, would you?" Other leading questions may not be as obvious. For example, "Do you prefer A or B?" is not leading if A and B are the only possible options available, but if options C and D are also available, then this is a leading question. Generally, in an interview, you don't want to bias your interviewee's response by asking a leading question.

4. **Direct or indirect questions.** Normally, a direct question is the most efficient and effective. But sometimes, you may not want to probe directly, especially if you think your interviewee will be evasive to a direct question or even offended or hurt by one. You can approach an issue indirectly in one of several ways: Ask about one or more other issues that correlate in some way with the issue directly at hand. (For example, ask about a person's views about alcohol and try to correlate those responses with the person's likely views about tobacco.) Or ask your interviewee to speculate how someone else would answer a particular question.
5. **Simple versus complex questions.** In general, simple questions are more effective than complex ones. The more complex the question, of course, the higher the probability that you will confuse your interviewee or give him or her an opportunity to avoid providing the information you want. For example, if you ask a question that really contains more than one question, you may be unable to tell which question has been answered. Of course, a complex issue may require a complex question. And in an interview, you can provide follow-up clarification of your question and probe for clarification of the answer.
6. **Reproduction versus evaluation questions.** Thinking about your questions along a continuum of reproduction/evaluation can help clarify your goals at different points in the interview. At certain points, especially early in the interview, you may be looking primarily for factual information that the interviewee can simply recall from memory. At other points, you may be expecting your interviewee to interpret, translate, or analyze information. At still other points, often later in the interview—when you have established a foundation of factual recall and have built rapport with your interviewee—you may be seeking an evaluative, critical response.

The other important conventional elements of the interview have to do with achieving graceful and effective entries and exits. Stano and Reinsch (1982) point first to the conventional greeting rituals of our culture—eye contact, smile, verbal salutation, personal inquiry (e.g., "How are you?")—and perhaps a conversational gambit such as a comment about the weather. These kinds of comments merge naturally into more specific rapport-building comments (e.g., expressions of thanks) that orient (or perhaps re-orient if you've had a previous conversation or correspondence) the interviewee to the purpose and planned structure for the interview. Such comments also lead to further comments that provide incentives for the interviewee to participate in the interview (e.g., specifically how the interview will help you in your work, perhaps how the information you gain and analyze will help the interviewee, perhaps how what you learn may benefit a larger community or other interest you both share, etc.). Even though you may have already explained the purpose of the interview, make sure your interviewee understands it along with the procedure you will follow, including the use of tape recorders, notes, and so on.

There are also conventional leave-taking rituals, parallel to the greeting rituals at the beginning of the interview, that are appropriate at the end of the interview. And to a considerable degree, their purpose is the same: to continue to build and maintain rapport and motivation, reselling the interviewee on the interview and setting the stage for any possible follow-up interview that might be required. Probably the most obvious convention, then, is a sincere expression of your gratitude for the interview. Reflective questions and clearinghouse questions, discussed earlier, may be especially appropriate here as a means of confirming that you've understood your interviewee in key points and covered all the important issues, as seen by your interviewee. This kind of recapping of the interview also is a good signal of closure, although it's possible these questions could open a whole new line of inquiry. If the interview has been a particularly intense emotional experience for your interviewee—perhaps bringing up difficult or traumatic events—then you may need to give the interviewee the opportunity to talk himself or herself down from the heightened emotion. Finally, you should be sensitive to nonverbal cues, both your own and your interviewee's, that signal closure: leaning forward at the waist, standing up, offering a handshake, manipulating papers (e.g., closing your notebook), and so forth.

Focus Groups

Essentially all the same issues that you need to address in planning and conducting an individual interview are also present when you're doing focus-group research—plus the added dimensions of planning, managing, and facilitating the dynamics of a group discussion of your interview questions and analyzing and interpreting the complex give and take of the discussion that your questions generate. Instead of working out the logistics of meeting and interviewing one person, you have to schedule and organize a half dozen or more people to be interviewed. Instead of explaining to just one person the logical and ethical rationale for what you will and won't do, you have to explain yourself to a group of people and persuade them all that what you're doing is legitimate and worthwhile—specifically, that it's worth their time to help you by participating in your focus group. In fact, it's common to offer some kind of incentive to people for participating in a focus group, ranging from a snack during the session to an actual cash payment.

The complexity and difficulty of planning, conducting, and analyzing focus-group sessions can be well worth the effort, though, as is demonstrated especially by the popularity of focus groups in product design and marketing research. Focus-group research has also become a popular and powerful planning and evaluation tool in the sphere of public service and politics. Many educational and social services programs use focus groups routinely to understand more accurately how well they are serving their constituents and clients. In recent years, the use of focus groups has spread so aggressively to political campaigns that it's become common for candidates to be accused of building their campaigns not on principles but on the findings of focus-group research.

In effective focus-group interviews, the researcher takes a nondirective role, initiating discussion with carefully developed open-ended questions and letting the discussants enrich one another's recollections and responses. During the several decades that this technique has been used and refined, it has been shown to yield especially deep, rich, and authentic insights into the attitudes and beliefs of consumers, constituents, clients, and other groups with common interests in the program, service, product, or concept being marketed or evaluated.

Source: © 1997, Washington Post Writers Group. Reprinted with permission.

Two of the most useful resources on developing focus-group research projects are David L. Morgan's *Successful Focus Groups: Advancing the State of the Art* (1993) and Richard A. Krueger's *Focus Groups: A Practical Guide for Applied Research* (1994). Morgan's book is a wide-ranging discussion of effective uses of focus groups in different environments and cultures, including in series with each other and in combination with other research strategies. These multiple investigations—each confirming (or disconfirming) and enriching the insights of the other investigations—provide *triangulation,* which instills an increased sense of confidence over time that the data and your interpretation are accurate and valid.

Krueger's book is an excellent how-to reference of focus-group research. According to Krueger, a typical successful focus group has the following characteristics:

- Size may range from four to twelve people, but the ideal range is from seven to ten people. If the number is too small, there may not be enough interaction and discussion. If the number is too large, the group dynamic will be too unwieldy.
- The group should be homogeneous. The purpose of the research is to identify the state of mind of a particular, essentially similar, group of people. If there are important differences in characteristics among group members, you should conduct multiple focus-group sessions, each with people who are similar in terms of the crucial characteristics you have identified.
- If possible, the members of the group should not be acquainted with each other. People who are closely affiliated—especially people from the same organization where one has supervisory authority over another—should not be in the same focus group. The risk of distorting responses because of relationships outside the group is too high.
- The moderator who runs the focus-group interview (presumably you, but you can have someone else do this for you) should not be well known by members of the group. If they know the moderator well, their responses to the questions may be skewed by their sense of what they think the moderator would like them to say.

DILBERT

Source: DILBERT reprinted by permission of United Feature Syndicate, Inc.

The questions, of course, are crucial to the substance you hope to gain from the interview. Krueger (1994) offers specific advice about preparing, testing, and presenting the questions:

- You don't need very many questions—probably fewer than ten for a 90-minute interview, perhaps only five or six. The people in focus groups usually take a long time mulling over and elaborating their responses to your questions.
- Ask open-ended questions that will generate a richly textured, informative discussion. Effective question templates include the following:
    - What did you think about the plan to . . . ?
    - What do you like best about the new . . . ?
    - Where do you go when you need . . . ?
    - How did you feel about the announcement that . . . ?
- But avoid *why* questions by reframing them as *what* questions.
- If you need to focus the group's attention more narrowly and specifically as the interview proceeds, do so by narrowing and specifying the subject matter of your questions while still keeping the questions open ended (e.g., "What did you think of the specific part of the plan to . . . ?").
- Brainstorm to generate your questions ahead of time with people who are knowledgeable about the programs and issues you are studying. Pilot-test your questions with such individuals, as well.
- Memorize your questions and the order in which you want to ask them, but stay alert and flexible. Be prepared to formulate and ask new serendipitous questions near the end of the session if the discussion has suggested them as fruitful questions.

The setting and dynamics of the focus-group interview are crucial to its success:

- The most desirable setting is a conference room or similar location, where participants can sit comfortably, see and hear one another, and have access to snacks, bathroom facilities, and so on.
- Useful materials include nameplates made from notecards and a tape recorder for recording the discussion.
- If you're going to moderate the session, first make sure everyone is comfortable, both physically and emotionally. Krueger suggests holding a brief period of small talk that flows into your kicking off the session. Here, you should remind people of your purpose for the session, identify yourself and your assistant (if you have one to help with the logistics, run the recorder, etc.), thank them for participating, and tell them whatever else they need to know, including the following:
    - How you will respect and protect the privacy of their responses
    - How long the session will last (Krueger suggests about 90 minutes)
    - Other ground rules, such as the fact that there's no right or wrong answer, that everyone's opinion is valued and should be heard, that one person at a time should be allowed to speak, and the like
- Then, proceed to ask the first of your carefully prepared questions. Krueger strongly recommends memorizing your questions and the order you'll ask them. He also recommends that your first question be an "ice-breaker," where you go around the table and ask members of the group to introduce themselves and tell briefly about their interest in the topic.
- During the course of the interview, your primary role will be to ask the key questions you've planned; then just listen and encourage response. But don't make your encouragement so enthusiastic that it biases the response. Comments like "Uh-huh," "OK," "Yes," "I see," and similar verbal and nonverbal indications that you hear and understand are fine, but don't say things like "Excellent!" or "Right" and don't nod your head excessively.
- Even so, don't be afraid to pause and probe. As with an individual interview, you should resist the impulse to fill anxious moments of silence after you've asked a question. Give people time to ponder the question and formulate a response; also give them time to ponder and respond to each other's comments. And while your role is highly nondirective, you should still be ready to follow up people's initial responses with probes for further details and explanations—within reason, of course. (You don't want people to feel as if they're being cross examined.) Reasonable follow-up probes are simple, direct requests for more information (e.g., asking people to give examples, describe what they mean, explain further, say more, etc.) or perhaps, just a direct statement that you don't understand.
- Don't be afraid to assert some responsibility for the pace of the discussion. While you don't want to direct the content of people's responses, you have a

responsibility to cover the issues you've identified and ask the questions you've planned. You also have a responsibility to your participants to finish the session within the time you've planned. If someone tends to monopolize the conversation or to babble, be prepared to interrupt that person politely by asking your next question or redirecting the question you've asked to someone else.

- An effective closure to the focus-group interview certainly should include another expression of appreciation to the people who have participated. In addition, it's almost always helpful to both you and your participants in the group to close by summarizing the main points and themes you believe you've heard. This may trigger powerfully insightful comments from the group, and it will also give people an opportunity to correct you if you've misinterpreted some of their responses. Finally, give participants the chance to provide these kinds of additional interpretations, elaborations, or corrections by asking them a question that asks something specific, like "Is there anything else that you'd like to add or anything else that you think we should know about this?"

Sorting, coding, analyzing, and interpreting the results of a focus-group session should begin as soon as possible after the session is finished. If possible, meet immediately with your assistant moderator, while your memories are still fresh, and recap the session, comparing your impressions, memories, and written notes and even checking the taped record if you have time and energy. What key themes have the two of you identified in your written notes? What themes generated the most frequent or emphatic mention by the participants? What significant nonverbal messages did you notice during the session—posture, tone of voice, gestures, facial expressions, and so on? During this postsession debriefing, the two of you should flesh out your written notes from the session to create a complete, elaborated narrative of your immediate impressions.

Almost as soon as you start this postsession recap, you'll probably find that the richness of the information from a focus group can be a burden as well as a blessing. The task of managing the information may seem less daunting if you think of it as having three distinct modes or phases: The first phase is simply accounting for what happened—printing the transcript and coding and identifying the responses. The second phase builds on the first. Here, you summarize the most significant responses and the themes they represent. Finally, in the third phase, you infer what these themes mean. Your final written analysis typically includes this interpretation, a narrative summarizing the session, and, as concrete evidence supporting your interpretation, quotations of the most cogent, vivid, or otherwise significant comments.

Of course, the effectiveness and validity of this analysis and interpretation depends on all the processes that have preceded them, including the thoughtfulness with which you have designed your initial questions. Focus-group sessions are often conducted in series, with subsequent sessions and their questions building on what has been discovered in earlier sessions. And often focus-group research is used in combination with survey research, which we'll discuss next. Sometimes, a survey is used to get a rigorous statistical verification of attitudes that a focus group has identified. Other times, focus groups are used to get a more richly textured understanding of trends that are suggested by surveys.

Surveys

Survey research has achieved a level of sophistication and power of prediction that can be astonishing. Polling organizations like Gallup can predict, with very small margins of error, the voting behavior of the entire U.S. population based on a sample of only a thousand or so. But on the other hand, many surveys are done casually and informally, and too often the people reporting the results make erroneous and unreasonable claims for the power and validity of their techniques and results.

One of the most common mistakes is describing the group of people surveyed as a *random sample* when they are not. To the untrained ear, the term *random sample* sounds rather casual: survey somebody here, survey somebody there, survey somebody else, all at random. But to the professional statistician and survey researcher, a random sample is anything but casual. The randomness is carefully and rigorously controlled. Random number charts and computer-generated random selections are used to ensure a sample that is statistically equivalent to the larger population it represents. Aside from the strict random sample, probably the most common type of sample is the *convenience sample:* a surveying of people who are accessible to the people doing the survey. Generally, people conducting a convenience sample take some care to find respondents who seem representative of the larger population. Sometimes, in both rigorous random samples and convenience samples, researchers *stratify* the sample, or survey people who are representative of particular groups within the population.

An important point to remember at the outset, then, is that if you're new to survey research, you should think carefully about your goals in terms of the rigor with which you want to be able to manipulate your survey data. If you want to do sophisticated statistical procedures and make confident predictions based on these analyses, then begin by selecting a *statistically* random sample, which is truly representative of the population you're investigating. Then, subject your results to the appropriate statistical procedures. If what we've said in the last two or three sentences is new to you and you truly need statistically rigorous analysis, then this means you will also need to get help from an experienced survey researcher and statistician. However, if you're able to work effectively with the limitations of a less rigorous survey, then you can probably proceed on your own. In any case, you need to invest extensive and careful thought to the design of your survey questions and instructions. The pointers, guidelines, and checklists we offer in the following sections are derived mainly from Linda Bourque and Eve Fielder's *How to Conduct Self-Administered and Mail Surveys,* which is volume 3 of a 9-volume set published by Sage in 1995 as *The Survey Kit.* All 9 titles are listed in the chapter-ending References.

If you've never done a survey before, you'll probably be skeptical when we describe the difficulty of writing good survey questions and instructions. But if you have done a survey and seen the almost infinite ingenuity with which people can misread the questions and instructions, you'll appreciate our advice for revising, testing, rewriting, piloting, revising, and retesting your questionnaire as many times as possible.

Introducing the Survey Questionnaire

In an oral interview, you have what Stano and Reinsch (1982) call the "greeting rituals" that establish rapport, orient the interviewee to the purpose and structure of the interview, and nurture the interviewee's motivation to participate in the interview. A written survey also needs to fulfill this introducing, orienting, and motivating function. Bourque and Fielder (1995, p. 121) recommend using a cover letter for this function and offer these general points for explaining the survey and its value:

- Explain the purpose of the study.
- Describe who is sponsoring the study.
- Consider also sending an advance letter.
- Consider using other methods, such as newsletters or flyers, to publicize the study.
- Include a cover letter with the questionnaire:
  - Use letterhead.
  - Use a date consistent with the actual mailing.
  - Provide a name and phone number to call for more information.
  - Personalize the salutation if feasible.
- Explain how respondents were chosen and why their participation is important.
- Explain when and how to return the questionnaire.
- Describe incentives if you're using them. (These might range from offering to share the results to enclosing a gift with the questionnaire.)
- Provide a realistic estimate of the time required by the average respondent to complete the questionnaire.

Designing Survey Questions

Like a focus group, a survey is simply a means of extending the individual interview to a wider group of people—maybe thousands, potentially even millions, of people. The range of questions possible in a survey is basically the same as that in an interview. In *Mail and Telephone Surveys,* Don Dillman (1978, p. 80) notes four kinds of information can be discovered in a survey. We call these the A's and B's of survey information:

1. **Attributes:** What people are
2. **Attitudes:** What people say they want
3. **Beliefs:** What people think is true
4. **Behavior:** What people do

Dillman notes that you need to think carefully about which kind of information you need as you approach the design of your questions. All too frequently, people waste effort in trying to perfect the wording of a question, only to realize the question is asking for the wrong kind of information—perhaps information about a respondent's attitude when what's really wanted is information about the respondent's behavior.

Surveys impose conditions on both researchers and respondents that constrain the kinds of questions that are practical to ask. For example, open-ended questions on a survey can be problematic for several reasons:

1. In an interview, if you ask an open-ended question that your interviewee doesn't understand at first, you can still get good information by restating or explaining the question or asking a clarifying question as a follow-up. But if a question is misunderstood in a survey, you usually have no opportunity to follow up with that respondent.
2. The level of resistance to completing a survey is often significantly higher than the resistance to completing an interview, especially when your interviewee has already agreed to the interview.
3. Open-ended questions on a survey are more difficult to answer than closed questions; they require more thought and longer answers. The answers will also be more difficult for you to interpret and classify. If you receive 100 completed surveys, each with 10 open-ended questions answered, you will have a daunting task of reading and interpretation. So, while open-ended questions on a survey can generate valuable information that closed questions can't, you should use them judiciously and thoughtfully so you don't overtax both yourself and your respondents.

Because you typically can't follow up and clarify a question that's confused someone on your survey, you need to design a testing process that will give you this kind of feedback before you make a major investment in printing and mailing out questionnaires. First, you (and as many collaborators who are willing to help) need to read the questionnaire with a paradoxical combination of a critical eye and a naive eye, looking for language and visual design issues that may mislead a reader or bias a response. In addition, we suggest at least one formal pilot test, where you administer the questionnaire to a small group of people who aren't familiar with the document. Ask them to answer the questions, and then debrief them after they've completed the questionnaire. Find out how they interpreted the questions and listen particularly to their reports of how the wording or sequencing of questions or the layout of the questionnaire may have puzzled or confused them, perhaps even offended them, or otherwise made them resistant to giving you accurate answers.

Addressing Specific Problems in Question Design

Dillman's (1978) book, which we mentioned earlier, is widely regarded as a classic on questionnaire design. Most of the following suggestions for specific question design are from his chapter titled "Writing Questions: Some General Principles."

Difficult Words and Question Length. Avoid the use of confusing jargon and other language your respondents won't understand, yet make each question as brief and efficiently worded as possible. These two goals can conflict with one another sharply, as illustrated by these examples—both of which ask the same basic question:

Difficult words	Excessive length
Should ACS spec minimum RAM and CPU MHz for tyro users?	So nontechnical campus computer users can be assured of buying equipment that will enable them to operate the sophisticated new software programs and work efficiently on the World Wide Web, should Academic Computer Services (ACS) specify minimum requirements campuswide for operating memory (RAM) and processor speed (MHz) for all personal computers purchased on campus?

You need to find some happy medium, using language that you believe is appropriate for your particular respondents.

Excessive Vagueness and Excessive Specificity. Here again, you should make thoughtful judgments about the kind of information you need and what your respondents are able to supply. Look at these examples, which ask the same question but with different degrees of specificity:

Uses vague terms in the question	Revised for more specificity	Revised again for still greater specificity
What changes should the government make in its policies on disaster relief?	What changes, if any, do you think the federal government should make in its programs for flood relief?	What changes, if any, do you think the federal government should make in helping subsidize flood insurance for people living on the 500-year flood plain of the Red River?

Also consider the specificity of the answer categories your questions provide:

Provides vague answer categories

How often did you dine out during the past year?

1. NEVER
2. RARELY
3. OCCASIONALLY
4. REGULARLY

Revised for clearer answer categories

How often did you dine out during the past year?

1. NOT AT ALL
2. A FEW TIMES
3. ABOUT ONCE A MONTH
4. ABOUT TWO TO THREE TIMES A MONTH
5. ABOUT ONCE A WEEK
6. MORE THAN ONCE A WEEK

But don't ask questions demanding more precise answers than respondents can likely provide:

Requires overly precise answer	**Revised to provide manageable answer categories**
How many videotaped movies did you watch last year? ____ (NUMBER)	How many videotaped movies did you watch last year? 1. NONE 2. 1–5 3. 6–10 4. 11–20 5. MORE THAN 20

Other Varieties of Bias and Ambiguity in Questions. As we noted earlier in our discussion of types of interview questions, you should avoid phrasing questions in ways that lead respondents to give the answers you want. Consider these examples:

Suggests behavioral expectations	**Revised to eliminate bias**
Surveys show that Brand X is the treatment of choice for physicians treating patients complaining of sinusitis. Do you prescribe Brand X? 1. YES 2. NO	Do you prescribe Brand X for patients complaining of sinusitis? 1. YES 2. NO

The way you balance your answer categories can create bias in readers' responses. Compare these two questions:

Unbalanced answer categories create bias	**Revised to balance answer categories**
On average, state universities spend about $7,000 per student a year for educational services. This amount should be: 1. INCREASED SLIGHTLY 2. KEPT THE SAME 3. DECREASED A LITTLE 4. DECREASED SOMEWHAT 5. DECREASED A GREAT DEAL	On average, state universities spend about $7,000 per student a year for educational services. This amount should be: 1. INCREASED GREATLY 2. INCREASED SLIGHTLY 3. KEPT THE SAME 4. DECREASED SLIGHTLY 5. DECREASED GREATLY

Notice that in the left-hand example, the middle (and presumably neutral) response calls for a slight decrease in the funding of state university educational services. The revised question on the right is balanced so that the response in the middle of the list is, in fact, a neutral response between increasing and decreasing funding.

You should also avoid writing questions that actually ask more than one question. Look at these examples:

Contains more than one question

Should the costs of doctor-assisted suicide be covered by Medicare, or should doctor-assisted suicide remain illegal?

1. YES
2. NO

Revised to separate the double question into two questions

Should doctor-assisted suicide be illegal?

1. YES
2. NO

If doctor-assisted suicide is made legal, should a doctor be able to submit a bill to Medicare for payment of her or his services?

1. YES
2. NO

Revised to specify all four possible responses to the original double question

Which of the following best describes how you feel about doctor-assisted suicide?

1. IT SHOULD BE AGAINST THE LAW.
2. IT SHOULD BE LEGAL, BUT DOCTORS SHOULD NOT BE ALLOWED TO COLLECT MEDICARE PAYMENT FOR IT.
3. IT SHOULD BE LEGAL, AND DOCTORS SHOULD BE ALLOWED TO COLLECT MEDICARE PAYMENT FOR IT.

The problem in the left-hand example is that it asks two questions: How will you know which question or questions the respondent is answering with "yes" or "no"? The middle example breaks out the two questions, giving the respondent an opportunity to answer each. The right-hand example asks a single question but provides three options that cover the possible answers.

A closely related problem is writing questions with answer categories that overlap, like those in the following left-hand question:

Provides answer categories that are not mutually exclusive

How did you first hear about this product?

1. FROM A FRIEND OR RELATIVE
2. AT A MEETING OF AN ORGANIZATION I BELONG TO
3. AT WORK
4. FROM MY SPOUSE

Revised for coherence and completeness

Through what medium did you learn about this product?

1. ADVERTISEMENT:
   - _____ ON TELEVISION
   - _____ ON RADIO
   - _____ ON OUR WWW HOMEPAGE
   - _____ IN A NEWSPAPER

5. OVER TELEVISION OR RADIO
6. IN A NEWSPAPER
7. PRODUCT DEMONSTRATION
8. INTERNET

2. NEWS ITEM:
   _____ ON TELEVISION
   _____ ON THE RADIO
   _____ ON AN INTERNET LISTSERV
   _____ IN A NEWSPAPER
3. WORD-OF-MOUTH REPORT:
   _____ FROM ACQUAINTANCE
   _____ FROM MY SPOUSE
4. PRODUCT DEMONSTRATION
5. OTHER: __________

Where were you when you first heard about it?

1. AT WORK
2. AT HOME
3. AT A PROFESSIONAL MEETING OR TRADE SHOW
4. OTHER: __________

Notice how in the left-hand question, categories describing media, places, and sources of information could elicit multiple correct answers, yet the question doesn't ask for multiple responses. The revised question, on the right, eliminates the overlapping of categories and enables respondents to answer with more meaningful, useful information. Also notice in the right-hand example that it's possible the specific answer choices we've provided may not cover all the possible answers our respondents might need to give, so we've added a limited open-ended option, an "Other" category. When you provide this option, you should generally also provide a space for the respondent to specify what the "Other" choice is.

Answer categories that exclude conceptual ground between categories are the opposite problem of answer categories that overlap. Notice how in the following left-hand question, two values are actually excluded: organizations that have had either four interns or ten interns cannot accurately respond to the question:

Provides answer categories that exclude the middle answer

How many interns has your organization hosted from St. Cloud State University in the past year?

1. FEWER THAN FOUR
2. FIVE TO NINE
3. MORE THAN TEN

Provides answer categories that overlap one another

How many interns has your organization hosted from St. Cloud State University in the past year?

1. ZERO TO FOUR
2. FOUR TO TEN
3. TEN OR MORE

Revised to provide categories that are distinct and include all possible answers

How many interns has your organization hosted from St. Cloud State University in the past year?

1. ZERO TO FOUR
2. FIVE TO NINE
3. TEN OR MORE

And notice how the middle question above has hypercorrected for the gap and created another overlap: Now, organizations that have had four interns can respond by circling *either* answer 1 or 2, and organizations that have had ten interns can respond by circling *either* 2 or 3. The revision on the right corrects for *both* gaps and overlaps.

The final design flaw that we want to discuss here is drafting a question that assumes too much knowledge on the part of the respondent. Look at the question on the left below:

Assumes too much knowledge

Do you tend to agree or disagree with the governor's recent national television position statement on school vouchers?

1. AGREE
2. DISAGREE

Revised into two stages, first checking respondent's background knowledge

The governor recently made a statement on school vouchers on national television. Were you aware that he had taken a stand on that issue?

1. NO
2. YES ⟶ (If yes) Please describe in your own words what you consider his position to be:

____

____

____

Do you tend to agree or disagree with his stand?

1. AGREE
2. DISAGREE

The question that assumes too much knowledge is similar to the question that asks more than one question. Indeed, when you make this mistake, you have assumed you know the answer to the second, unarticulated question. The revision shown in the right-hand question demonstrates this. Here, the question first asks if the respondent knows the governor has taken a position, and then it asks the respondent to summarize that position. Only after it has asked the respondent to describe the governor's position does it ask if the respondent agrees with it. Notice how the respondent is directed by the arrow to the question that's contingent upon the "Yes" answer. Notice also Dillman's (1978) consistent use of the convention of distinguishing answers from questions by setting answer categories in all capital letters.

Using Electronic Resources

It seems safe to say that the Internet is the most revolutionary research and communication development since the printing press. And as the Internet has quickly evolved and grown more technically sophisticated, an interesting, paradoxical thing has happened: The technology, rather than making it more difficult to use, has actually made it more accessible and more easily usable (more "user friendly"). If you're a relative newcomer to the Internet—and even if you're not—we recommend a good general purpose reference, like *The Internet for Dummies* (Levine, Baroudi, & Young, 1995). But don't assume that you have to read a manual before you can actually venture into this rich new medium.

Listservs and Newsgroups

For several years now, electronic mailing lists (or listservs) and newsgroups have been increasing in popularity. More recently, with the explosive growth of the World Wide Web, these resources have been pushed from the center of the cyberspace stage. Even so, they remain an immensely important information resource—in fact, one that is often much more personal and direct than the web. This is especially true of electronic mailing lists. At the most modest end, a listserv may involve just a handful of people in an office who use it to broadcast messages to each other. At the most ambitious end, a listserv may involve thousands of people worldwide who share a common professional or avocational interest.

Many professional organizations now support listservs that enable their members to discuss problems and issues electronically. For example, a member might raise a question about a practical dilemma that has arisen in his or her office, asking if others on the list have experienced this problem and inquiring what they have done about it. Or a member might raise an ethical issue that affects professional practice in the field, in general, and invite responses. To join a mailing list, you must subscribe to it electronically by sending a message to the computer handling the list, asking that you be added. Typically, these requests are read and processed automatically by the computer, so you need to write the request in exactly the correct form.

In addition to mailing lists, many professional organizations and news services maintain newsgroups. A newsgroup is much like a mailing list, except that in order to read the postings, you must connect to the newsgroup site. If you are on a mailing list, the information will come to you without your requesting it.

The following two websites provide a starting place for locating listservs and newsgroups in your field and special interest areas:

List of Listservs
http://www.cuc.edu/cgi-bin/listservform.pl

The List of Listservs offers a list of interest groups/e-mail discussion groups on special topics.

biz.*newsgroups
http://www.lib.ox.ac.uk/internet/news/biz.html

This site lists newsgroups focusing on business topics. (Note that many of these groups are located in the United Kingdom.)

World Wide Web

If you've done any exploration of the World Wide Web, you know how apt the web metaphor is. Any particular site may have links to a dozen or more others. This linking, which is created by the makers of the web pages themselves, reflects the essentially infinite variety of interests and associations of these web authors. It also denotes both an immensely large source of information and a potential barrier to access. The range of possibilities behind that flat screen on your computer monitor may seem too random and too vast to lend itself to any effective exploration. But fortunately, convenient tools are available that let you systematize your search and focus the power of the web. As websites continue to evolve, many are actually incorporating links to these *search engines* into their homepages. It may well be that your own Internet service provider (ISP)—whether it's a commercial service, an educational institution, a government agency, or some other community Internet provider—will have links to these search engines on the homepage that appears when you log on with your web browser. In addition, you can set "bookmarks" for your favorite search engines and other websites that will take you directly to those web pages.

Search Engines and Search Terms

General purpose search engines include Lycos, WebCrawler, and InfoSeek. New search engines are created every day, but the list provided in Figure 11.3 of common search engines and their electronic addresses will give you a start.

These search engines are computer programs designed to search for keywords. Most search engines use some sort of Boolean operators (AND, OR, and NOT *or* + and –) that allow you to put together different sets of terms so that the "hits" produced provide the information you're seeking without a lot of extraneous material. For instance, let's say that you need to find out more information about *managed health care.* Using Alta Vista, you type in those terms, and the search engine produces 527,260 hits. These hits include web pages for clinics in the United States and abroad, research guides, requests for proposals (RFPs) for grants, and articles on legislative initiatives. To cut down on the number of hits, you add another term, + *costs,* but this only lowers the number of hits to 501,050. You notice, though, that some of the summaries of the sites located included the term *cost containment,* which is really what you're

FIGURE 11.3 World Wide Web Search Engines

Alta Vista	http://www.altavista.com
Electric Library	*Paid:* http://www.elibrary.com
Excite	http://www.excite.com
HotBot	http://www.hotbot.com
InfoSeek	*Paid:* http://www.infoseek.com
	Free: http://www2.infoseek.com
Lycos	http://www.lycos.com
WebCrawler	http://www.webcrawler.com

interested in. And you realize that you're really looking for research. When you try *managed health care + cost containment + research,* you limit the number of hits to 10,020, and when you add the year *1996,* you cut the number of hits to 3,970. Scanning the descriptions of the hits, you realize that you're not interested in the material on taxes or on mental health, so you can subtract items with those terms from your search. When you refine your search again to *managed health care + cost containment + research + 1996 – tax – mental,* you limit the number of hits to 2,960. Granted, this is still too many items to read, but in just a few moments, you've narrowed the focus of your search considerably. Limiting your search by adding and subtracting other key terms will probably provide a list of web pages that have the sorts of information you're seeking.

Keep in mind, too, that different search engines will lead to different search results. Alta Vista—the search engine we just used for a preliminary search on managed health care—is one of the most extensive Internet search tools and claims to index more than 30 million web pages and newsgroups. As our preliminary search illustrates, this search engine may often provide more information than you need. Using Lycos to perform the same search produced 15,898 hits for *managed health care,* 5,036 hits for *managed health care* AND *costs,* 341 hits for *managed health care* AND *cost containment* AND *research,* 164 hits for *managed health care* AND *cost containment* AND *research* AND *1996,* and 70 hits for *managed health care* AND *cost containment* AND *research* AND *1996* NOT *tax* NOT *mental.* In this particular search, then, Alta Vista produced approximately 42 times the number of hits that Lycos did. And if you were to actually review the search results, you would notice that in addition to producing a different number of hits from Alta Vista, Lycos found different sorts of sites, too.

You may find that you switch from one search engine to another, depending upon the search results you get, or that you use a combination of search engines to find the information that you need. You also may find that given your particular field, you tend to rely upon a particular search engine—perhaps one developed for your field that's not included in our list or maybe one that didn't even exist at the time we were writing this book.

As these two examples illustrate, every search engine works a bit differently, but essentially, you find information by stringing together key terms that are important to your research and excluding others that produce material you're not interested in. If you haven't used a particular search engine before, you'll find specific guidelines for doing so by clicking on a term like *hints, tips, help, options,* or *custom search* on the search engine's home page.

Specific Websites: Descriptions and URLs

Some of the very best electronic resources for business and professional information are federal government websites. Many state government sites are also evolving into powerful information resources. Two of the most noteworthy of the federal sites are those of the Securities and Exchange Commission (SEC) and the Federal Reserve Bank. Descriptions and URLs for these and some other business-related sites are listed in Figure 11.4.

FIGURE 11.4 Business Sources on the World Wide Web

Securities and Exchange Commission
http://www.sec.gov

The SEC database, EDGAR, provides access to all corporate documents required to be filed with the SEC as well as SEC rules, decisions, and the like. This information is also available on EDGAR Online, a commercial site at http://www.edgar-online.com as well as http://edgar.stern.nyu.edu/edgar.html

Federal Reserve Bank at St. Louis
http://www.stls.frb.org

This site has direct links to most U.S. government sites. Its FRED database includes most monetary and business indicators, both current and historical—for example, the Consumer Price Index monthly figures back to 1946 and the discount rate changes back to 1934.

Hoover's Online
http://www.hoovers.com

Published by the Hoovers of *Hoover's Handbook* fame, Hoover's Online contains essentially the same information—on about 2,500 companies—as the handbooks, but in electronic form. Like EDGAR Online, it is a commercial website. Some of the information is accessible for free, but full access requires paying a fee. The site includes lists of other useful websites and links to them.

Commerce Business Daily
Paid: **http://www.stat-usa.gov/BEN/Services/globus.html**
Free: **http://www.ld.com/cbd/today/index.htm**

These sites provide daily announcements of contract/procurement opportunities with the federal government. Some of the information is accessible for free, but full access requires paying a fee.

NETworth
http://www.networth.galt.com

This site lists the homepages of about 2,000 publicly held companies.

Business Yellow Pages
http://www.niyp.com

This site provides basic identifying information on nearly 17 million businesses nationwide.

Westergaard Online
http://www.westergaard.com

Westergaard Online specializes in information on small companies.

FIGURE 11.4 Continued

Small Business Administration
http://www.sbaonline.sba.gov

This Small Business Administration website offers information and advice commonly sought by small businesses and also describes its programs and services.

Open Market's Commercial Website
http://www.directory.net

This site provides an index of all businesses and corporations on the web.

Securities Exchange Websites

New York Stock Exchange
http://www.nyse.com

NASDAQ
http://www.nasdaq.com

Vancouver Stock Exchange
http://www.vse.com

Financial Information
http://www.finweb.com

This site is a depository of corporate financial reports.

Dun and Bradstreet Web Server
http://wwwdbisna.com

The Dun and Bradstreet Web Server provides some information free of charge—demographics, industry trends, reports—and additional information on a paid basis.

Best Market Reports
http://www.stat-usa.gov/ntdb/

This fee-based website provides industry overviews of 12 industries based on data collection in 62 countries. This site uses the U.S. Industrial Outlook format.

Country Commercial Guides
http://www.stat-usa.gov

These guides are available for a fee and provide annual comprehensive reviews of countries worldwide, including economic data, trends, trade statistics, marketing information, and industry sectors.

Internet Business Library
http://bschool.ukans.edu/intbuslib/'virtual.htm<EBT >

This site links to domestic and international business resources.

(continued)

FIGURE 11.4 Continued

Madalyn, a Business Research Tool
http://www.udel.edu/alex/mba/main/netdir2.html

This site provides resources for business administration.

Better Business Bureau (BBB)
http://www.bbb.org/bbb

This site provides links to business resources and a directory of the BBB's services.

Legal Information Institute
http://www.law.cornell.edu/topical.html

This Cornell University site provides a searchable index of law information.

REFLAW: The "Virtual" Law Library Reference Desk
http://lawlib.wuacc.edu/washlaw/reflaw/reflaw.html

REFLAW links to legal reference information available on the Internet.

The WWW Virtual Library—Law
http://www.law.indiana.edu:80/law/lawindex.html

This virtual library links by subtopic, type, or source; it includes law schools and firms as well as links to federal and state government servers.

U.S. Government Legislative Information
http://thomas.loc.gov

This site provides a searchable database of U.S. congressional legislation.

Statistical Abstracts of the United States
http://www.census.gov/stat_abstract

Statistical Abstracts provides national statistics on every subject for which the U.S. government collects statistics.

Online Newspapers

Wall Street News
http://Wall-Street-News.com

New York Times
http://www.nytimes.com

Los Angeles Times
http://latimes.com

Chicago Tribune
http://chicago.tribune.com

FIGURE 11.4 Continued

Scott Yanoff's Special Internet Connections
http://inet.services.txt

This site provides a list (updated yearly) of World Wide Web, Gopher, and Telnet sources, listed alphabetically by categories, with a brief description of what can be found at each site.

Business Sources on the Net
http://www.library.miami.edu/staff/sjl/bsn.html

Business Sources lists Internet addresses for more than 200 business-related sources: Gopher, Telnet, FTP, and World Wide Web sites.

In closing, information is essential: It's the basis for rational decisions and arguments, and research generates the data that enables us to support the claims we need to make—especially in long, complex reports. But the research we do should be appropriate for our goals, our readers, and our arguments. Sometimes, we may have the information we need in our memory, on our desks, or perhaps on the hard drive of our computer. At other times, we can find information that we need in our files (correspondence, contracts, policies) or in other documents immediately at hand. And sometimes, we need to consult others: colleagues, customers, others' files, e-mail chats, libraries, the World Wide Web, and so on. Finally, at times, we need to do systematic data collection through surveys, interviews, focus groups, or other types of hands-on research.

In general, you'll find that you can monitor and control your research investment by answering these questions: Do I have enough information to go forward with this project successfully? If not, do I have enough information to know that this project is not going to succeed and should be abandoned? And whether you consult paper, people, or electronic resources, always try the simplest, easiest, cheapest research first.

WRITING CHECKLIST

The following guidelines can help you design interviews, set up focus groups, and write surveys as you perform research beyond the library in the contemporary organization. For any of these guidelines, remember the superordinate guideline: Disregard *any* of this advice if it would cause you to do something that's inappropriate or silly for your situation.

☑ Interviews

- Don't abuse your people resources; do your easy, file-based research first, and be generous in acknowledging personal help you get.
- Consider as potential interview subjects colleagues, supervisors, clients, and others who are steeped in information about the issue you're investigating.
- Because interviews can be risky for interview subjects, answer their probable questions about your qualifications, your ethical treatment of what they say (including accurate representation and respect for the limits of propriety or confidential information), and appropriate use of the information shared.
- Honor the commitments you make to interviewees (e.g., about how long the interview will take).
- Think about whether interview questions should be open or closed.
- Design both primary and follow-up questions.
- Avoid leading questions.
- Decide how direct or indirect each question should be.
- Determine how simple or complex each question should be.
- Decide whether each questions should be a "just the facts" question or an interpretation/evaluation question.
- Prepare for the informal rituals of greeting and leave taking; use these times to lay out the plan of the interview, to recap the interview, and, especially, to assure your interviewee of your goodwill and competence.

☑ Focus Groups

- You will typically manage the data you collect in three stages: identifying and coding the responses, summarizing the significant responses and themes, and interpreting the themes.
- Plan for size ranges from 4 to 12 (most commonly 7 to 10).
- Choose group participants that are homogeneous.
- Yet don't choose participants from the same organization; preferably, they should not know each other or the moderator of the group.
- Select a setting that is comfortable but professional.
- To start, issue nametags, set ground rules, introduce participants, and provide an "ice-breaker" question.
- Plan ten questions at most; five or six are generally ideal for a 90-minute session.
- Ask open-ended questions. For more specific responses, narrow and specify the focus of your question while keeping it open ended.
- Avoid questions that start with "why."

- Get multiple perspectives in developing your questions; brainstorm and pilot-test to prepare.
- Memorize your questions and their order, but be prepared to improvise if necessity demands or opportunity arises during the session.
- Don't bias participants' responses or dominate the interview; instead, probe with follow-up requests for clarification or amplification when appropriate.
- Facilitate the focus-group interview, pausing to let people respond to questions and to each other, and, if necessary, redirecting the discussion.
- In closing, thank the participants, summarize the main themes and points, and invite final observations.
- Throughout the interview, pay careful attention to nonverbal cues as well as to what participants say.
- Immediately after the session, write detailed initial notes on the focus-group interview.

☑ Surveys

- If you need a scientifically valid survey and are not an experienced survey researcher and statistician, enlist people with this expertise to help you.
- If you want to conduct a relatively informal survey, you still need to design your survey instrument carefully—testing, revising, and rewriting the questions themselves, the instructions and cover letter, and other introductory material.
- The introductory material stands in the place of the greeting rituals and introductions that set up interviews, so it needs to establish your credibility, professionalism, and good intentions.
- The introductory material also needs to explain the survey's purpose and tell the readers how to complete it.
- Design your questions to gather the kind of information you need.
- Keep in mind that surveys can discover information about people's attributes, attitudes, beliefs, and behaviors.
- Remember, also, the two contrasts in question design: open-ended versus closed questions and difficult, technical language versus excessive explanation.
- Avoid excessive vagueness in your questions.
- Make sure that questions don't ask for overly specific answers.
- Check for questions that are biased because they suggest behavioral expectations.
- Avoid questions that are biased because they provide unbalanced answer categories.
- Revise complex questions that are biased or confusing.
- Ensure that answer categories are mutually exclusive.
- Make sure that answer categories don't exclude the middle.
- Check for questions that assume too much knowledge.

ACTIVITIES AND PROJECTS

1. Collect several examples of surveys, and bring them to a small-group discussion. In your group, determine the purpose and research subjects for the surveys. Then, determine if the surveys will accomplish this purpose with these research subjects, given the overall design of the survey and the wording of the questions. Be prepared to share your examples and the results of your group's analysis of these examples with others. In short, be ready to explain why you believe the surveys are good or bad examples of research instruments.
2. Interview someone who does research for a living or who teaches research design or methodology courses to find out more about interview, survey, or focus-group methodology. Share what you find out in an oral or written report.
3. Research print resources on interviews, surveys, or focus-group methodology, and design a procedures document for people in your field who need to use the methodology you've selected for your research.
4. Do some reconnaissance to discover Internet resources useful in your field of study or in your career. Generate a bibliography of these resources that can be used by others in your field; include the name and Internet address for each site as well as a summary of what is available and useful there.
5. Interview someone who is already doing the sort of job you hope to have to find out the specific sorts of research it requires. Find out how often this person does research, what sorts of information he or she is usually looking for, and what resources and methodology he or she uses to find, manipulate, and interpret the information and data needed on the job.
6. Find a proposal or report that effectively uses research methodology common to your field. Look at how the writer or writers describe their methodology and use their research results to make and support their claims and clarify their warrants. Then, bring the proposal or report to a small group. Talk about what you noticed, and show your colleagues examples of how methodology is described and how the writers use data to make an argument.
7. Design and develop a survey or set of interview questions you can use as a research tool for a proposal, report, or other project you're doing for school or for work. Use the GRACE benchmarks to plan, write, and revise your survey or interview questions, and test your research instrument out on a group of your colleagues.

REFERENCES

Bourque, L. B., & Fielder, E. P. (1995). *The survey kit: Vol. 3. How to conduct self-administered and mail-surveys.* Thousand Oaks, CA: Sage.

Dillman, D. A. (1978). *Mail and telephone surveys: The total design method.* New York: Wiley.

Krueger, R. A. (1994). *Focus groups: A practical guide for applied research* (2nd ed.). Thousand Oaks, CA: Sage.

Levine, J. R., Baroudi, C., & Young, M. L. (1997). *The Internet for dummies* (4th ed.). Indianapolis, IN: IDG Books.

Morgan, E. L. (Ed.). (1993). *Successful focus groups: Advancing the state of the art.* Newbury Park, CA: Sage.

Stano, M. E., & Reinsch, N. L., Jr. (1982). *Communication in interviews.* Englewood Cliffs, NJ: Prentice-Hall.

Survey Kit, The. (1995). 9 vols. Thousand Oaks, CA: Sage.
Vol. 1: A. Fink, *The survey handbook*
Vol. 2: A. Fink, *How to ask survey questions*
Vol. 3: L. B. Bourque & E. P. Fielder, *How to conduct self-administered and mail surveys*
Vol. 4: J. H. Frey & S. M. Oishi, *How to conduct interviews by telephone and in person*
Vol. 5: A. Fink, *How to design surveys*
Vol. 6: A. Fink, *How to sample in surveys*
Vol. 7: M. S. Litwin, *How to measure survey reliability and validity*
Vol. 8: A. Fink, *How to analyze survey data*
Vol. 9: A. Fink, *How to report on surveys*

Chapter 12

Proposals and Business Plans: Getting to "Yes"

What proposal writing is not:

1. *It's not gimmickry, "grantsmanship."*
2. *It's not slick formats or facile writing.*
3. *It's not writing by committee. One person must be responsible.*
4. *It's not a "quickie." It takes time.*
5. *It's not an off-the-top-of-the-head exercise. It takes planning.*

—From the Lecture Notes of E. G. Meyer

Writing proposals and business plans can be some of the most intense, challenging, and satisfying work in your professional career. Often, your goals entail high stakes—both in terms of your potential benefits and potential obligations—and require the analysis of processes and concepts that are technically complex and problematic. Generally, readers are considering your proposal with a highly critical eye—often, a skeptical eye. Sometimes, they are expert in your technical area, sometimes they aren't, and sometimes they are mixed, presenting a variety of levels of expertise that you have to speak to all at once. In most cases, readers' goals are not in perfect synch with your own, so you are challenged to formulate plans and arguments that serve this complex mixture of goals. The particular format conventions are often well defined by the readers, but other conventions—of both the writing and the communication and negotiating in the wider context—may be quite subtle and require careful observation as well as some trial and error. And proposals are by nature highly expressive documents. Their whole purpose is getting to "yes": to express your organizational and personal character, qualifications, expertise, and commitment to your goals in such a way that your readers will subscribe to these same goals and give you the resources (time, money, people, equipment, etc.) to achieve them. Finally, you are generally under a tight deadline when you are writing a proposal or business plan, so you are facing all these complex rhetorical and technical tasks with the distraction of the clock ticking loudly in your ear.

Writing Proposals with GRACE

Goals

A clear and sure sense of your goals—and especially the relationship of your immediate goals to your enduring organizational and personal goals and values—is crucial in proposal writing, just as it is in employment communication. In both situations, the pressure to compromise core elements of your organizational mission or even your own personal values and priorities can be immense. Part of what makes proposal writing such an intense and exciting project is the thrill of the chase, the prospect of "hitting pay dirt." But this thrill can also tempt you away from your core personal and organizational goals. Veteran proposal writers are unanimous in advising that you review very carefully the *RFP (request for proposals)* or other guidelines and descriptions disseminated by the client or granting agency in light of your own organizational mission and your institutional and personal priorities and values. They are also unanimous in advising that you should *not* write or submit the proposal if its requirements can't be reconciled with your priorities and mission—no matter how lucrative the promised sale, contract, grant, fellowship, or other award.

So, because the stakes are often so high in the case of proposal writing, the immediate goals you seek must be examined in light of your broader, long-term goals and values:

- What are these immediate goals? How do they serve to advance your long-term goals? Is the problem/project/goal that you're being asked to think about in this proposal one that interests you personally and institutionally? Do you have the appropriate background, expertise, people, equipment, financial resources, physical plant, transportation and communication infrastructure, vendor network, time, and other resources to achieve what you would be asked to propose? Would writing a winning proposal enable you to get the additional resources you would need? Would these resources be consistent with your long-range goals, and would they enable you to achieve other aspects of your mission? In other words, do this project and its goals offer the possibility of synergies with other projects and goals? Would getting these resources and committing to the goals required by this proposal require you to change other goals? Would this be a desirable change?

- What costs/risks are entailed in writing this proposal? How much time is needed? How many people? Are there hidden opportunity costs in pulling people off other projects in order to work on this proposal? Are you being asked to disclose proprietary technical, marketing, or financial information in making this proposal? Will there be adequate protection if you make these disclosures?

- What resources are readily available in preparing this proposal? Have you written proposals for similar projects previously? Could substantial pieces of text from these or from other documents be copied into this proposal as boilerplate, or could existing text be easily modified and revised to serve this proposal? Do people with the appropriate interest and expertise have some down time or slack time so they are available to work on the proposal? Do you yourself have the interest, expertise, and time?

- Is there some probability that even an unsuccessful proposal could advance some of your goals? What if you don't get the contract, grant, leave, fellowship, or equipment you argue for in this proposal? Will the effort and resources you invest in the proposal be a dead loss, or will the thinking, planning, and networking you do and the text you generate in preparing this document still pay dividends in the future? Will writing the proposal help clarify your goals and identify your resources? If the proposal is unsuccessful, will you have an opportunity to do a postmortem evaluation with the client or funding agency and learn why they chose not to accept this proposal at this time?

The questions in these last two paragraphs highlight two crucially important points: First, the proposal does not exist in a vacuum. It exists in a rich context of present, past, and future problems, projects, people, and goals. The proposal, then, is not a one-shot project that you think up, write up, and then forget about. Most of the time, the proposal by itself will not—*cannot*—achieve the particular goals you explicitly identify in the proposal. Most of the time, a history and a context support it: previous proposals you have written, similar proposals by other people, similar projects you have done, a network of colleagues, clients, vendors, and others—even, perhaps, previous conversations and professional relationships you have had with the readers of this proposal.

The second point is really a variation on the first: Veteran proposal writers often describe the proposal-writing process as *iterative.* That is, the ideas, processes, goals, and even language of a proposal tend to be reiterated or recycled in subsequent proposals and projects. The professional network you are building and using in developing a proposal tends to be the same one you already plug into in your professional life, and the two tend to reinforce one another. The goals, relationships, and resources that tend to resonate as a network in one proposal tend to resonate in the next proposal. These iterations are not just dull repetitions in the life of your organization and your career. Rather, they are occasions where you reaffirm your goals and articulate a consistent and coherent progression toward achieving them, both organizationally and personally.

Readers

Knowing as much as possible specifically about the prospective readers of your proposal is vital. There are many ways of doing this research. Often, the readers of your proposal have gone to considerable lengths to help you know what their goals are and how those goals will translate into criteria for their evaluation of your proposal. Your readers may have published guidelines, an announcement, or an RFP. They may have published a list of criteria or may even make available previously funded proposals as samples of the kinds of activities they support or services they expect. In both your own interest and that of your readers, you should study these formal guidelines and suggestions with great care. Given the high stakes in proposal writing, you owe it to yourself and to your readers to make every effort to submit a proposal that meets your goals and your readers' goals.

Do you have any indication, either from the written materials from the readers or from other sources, how receptive your readers would be to a telephone inquiry or even to an inperson interview? In some proposal-writing situations, prospective clients or funding agencies actively seek this kind of contact. Some even conduct workshops for people who are thinking of submitting proposals to them. Many others at least find it beneficial to have informal conversations with prospective proposal writers—on the theory that having this preliminary chat is ultimately a better use of their time and resources than would be reading a lot of inappropriate proposals they can't accept. They generally find it in their own best interests, then, to help a prospective grantee or vendor interpret their criteria and show him or her what kind of proposal they are interested in. Some granting agencies have lists of successful grantees who are available to discuss their proposals and the programs they developed with their resulting grants. Still others, however, may look upon this kind of contact with some degree of disfavor. (This is sometimes the case with federal agencies.) We suggest an initial inquiry about making further contact, unless you have a clear indication that such contact is unwelcome. But before you make that inquiry, do your homework—as much as you can possibly do with what information you have. You won't make a friend of a prospective proposal reader by calling and asking a question that's answered on the cover sheet of the RFP you have in your hand from this reader.

In addition to researching your specific readers for your specific proposal, keep in mind some important generic points about readers of proposals. For one thing, it's useful to remember that if your proposal has been solicited through an RFP or other announcement, your readers want to award the grant or contract. If there's a clear match between your goals and theirs, they probably don't have to be convinced that your cause is just. So, in terms of the layers of argument we talked about in Chapter 1, these readers share your values and assumptions that are the warrants for key parts of your argument. It would actually be counter-productive to make them spend a lot of time and energy reading these warrants. Rather, they're likely to be interested primarily in whether you can achieve what you are aiming for. Proposal readers are a lot like investors who are reading the prospectus for a new stock offering or mutual fund. They're asking if you are a good investment—if your proposal shows a favorable risk-to-payoff ratio, especially in comparison with competing proposals. In other words, while their goals and your goals may be highly idealistic, they are likely to be reading your proposal with a cold, practical eye, trying to decide whether you are, practically speaking, an organization or person that can get the job done. In this sense, *all* proposals are like business plans.

On the other hand, if your proposal is unsolicited, then you may have a heavy burden of proof in arguing the *virtues* of your idea as well as its practicality. That is, you may have to change your readers' perceptions of their own goals in this case. You don't have the same level of confidence that your readers share your underlying assumptions and values that warrant your claims, so you need to make those assumptions and values explicit. And then you still need to make the practical case that you're a wise investment. No matter how exciting your concept or how just your cause, you still need to have a feasible, credible plan.

While your readers are investors, they are nonetheless short of both time and money. Anything you can do to alleviate their stress as readers will serve both you and them. Unless you know for certain that the scenario is different, we think it's helpful to visualize a reader who is harried and distracted, busily reading a tall pile of proposals while trying quickly to make judgments about them—or perhaps trying to read your proposal while being distracted by other unrelated demands. Readers in this kind of situation behave in predictable ways, asking generally predictable questions—about the issue or problem, its costs and benefits, your credibility, and so on—and wanting a general, summative answer to all these questions immediately. If they are frustrated in finding the answers to these questions, they will likely be frustrated with your proposal and with you, so you need to try not to frustrate them. In Chapter 10, we described in detail the two common design strategies that can help your readers avoid this kind of frustration: providing a good summary of the proposal at the front of the document and designing the document itself so that it has redundant road maps and traffic signals. We'll mention these strategies again as conventions.

Finally, do your readers stipulate a submission deadline? If they do, be sure you meet it. If the deadline for submission is an October 1 postmark and yours is October 2, your proposal probably won't even be taken out of the envelope.

Arguments

Proposals make arguments that tend to take on the nature of promises, and they tend to move toward agreements that are contractual in nature. Typically, they are argued in the framework of a *quid pro quo:* something of benefit offered in exchange for something of benefit to be received. The skeleton argument for proposals also fits a problem/solution/offer/request template. The writer/proposer identifies and analyzes a problem, proposes a solution, offers to take action to become part of the solution, and asks for resources (time, money, people, equipment, etc.) to support this action:

Skeleton Argument for a Proposal

Here's a problem (or opportunity). Here are its features as we understand them. To solve the problem (or capitalize on the opportunity), we will do this if you will do that (the *quid pro quo*).

In Chapter 10, we talked about the general questions readers tend to have in mind when they approach long, complex documents, and we showed how these questions are helpful guides for thinking about document design. Now, we want to use them again as starting points for thinking about the general arguments you'll need to make in developing a proposal. Here are the questions again:

1. What's the essential issue here?
2. Why should I care?
3. What can be done (what are the alternatives)—and how?
4. What are the costs and risks?
5. What should be done?
6. What are the benefits?
7. Why should I believe you?

Answering these questions tends to generate three kinds of arguments. The first two questions generate what we call the *significance* argument: "Here are the crucial issues, and this is why they're important to you, the reader." The second two questions generate what we call the *feasibility* argument: "Here are the possible alternatives, and here's what it would take to achieve them." The fifth and sixth questions generate the *action* argument: "Here's what should be done, and here are the good things that would happen if we do it."

The seventh question challenges you at every step of framing every argument. First, it reminds you that you have to find a frame or window for your readers that will help them see this issue as you do. And as you lay out the scene for your readers, you have to keep asking, "Have I said enough? Have I said too much?" The following questions are credibility tests that you should run repeatedly as you write and rewrite:

- How should you frame the argument so it's persuasive to these readers?
- How deeply into the layers of the argument do you need to go?
- How directly and bluntly should you make your claims?
- How much evidence should you recite?
- Should you make your underlying assumptions and principles explicit, so your readers can see why you think this evidence warrants your claims of significance, feasibility, and the need for action?

Significance

It's absolutely crucial that your readers understand the issues and their significance the same way you do. Otherwise, the rest of your arguments will seem pointless to them. Significance authorizes you to make the rest of your arguments. Even so, this doesn't mean that you necessarily should spend a lot of your time and your readers' time making the significance argument directly. Handling the significance argument appropriately depends on getting an accurate reading of your readers. Here are a couple of contrasting examples.

Example One. Your readers already appreciate the significance of the issue. How might you know this? Suppose you're responding to an RFP that lays out in detail the issues and their significance. In three of the samples in this chapter, this, in fact, is the case:

- In Figure 12.1, the students describing themselves as the "Activity Fees Group" are responding to a detailed class assignment based on Activity 8 at the end of this chapter, which is actually an RFP.
- In Figure 12.2, Tom Barker's letter proposal identifies itself as being in response to a verbal RFP.
- In Figure 12.3, Dick Cottrill's proposal to Texas A&M International University (TAMIU) at Laredo is responding to a written RFP, which Cottrill identifies in the subject line of his cover letter and refers to several times in the course of both the letter and the proposal.

These are cases where your readers have already analyzed a situation that they see as constituting a problem or an opportunity that's significant enough for them to write requests for proposals. Your readers have already told *you* the issues and their significance. You know you're literally on the same page with these readers unless you decide they've somehow misunderstood the issues and their significance. In fact, for you to make the claim directly that this is an important issue and then set out all the layers of a significance argument would probably offend these readers because it would seem condescending. At the very least, you'd be wasting a lot of their time (and your own, as well), telling them something they already know.

FIGURE 12.1 Sample Proposal

Date: January 23, 1997

From: Paul Renslow
Carrie Jean Schroeder
Darrin Todd
Mark Peterson
Karen Blattner

To: Bob Inkster

Subject: "Activity Fees Group" Project Proposal

Our Project's Goal and Audience

We want to encourage SCSU to make information about activity fees and student organizations available to students in a yearly booklet. As the system is now, students have access to whatever financial information they need *if* they ask Student Government for it, but the students usually do not ask for the information and are simply angry about how much money they pay every quarter for activity fees. Information about student organizations is also vague or unavailable unless students actively seek out the information. Our proposal to SCSU Admissions, Student Government, the Student Representative Assembly (SRA), Academic Affairs, Housing and Student Development, and Career Services will request that the six offices work together to publish (in a yearly booklet) information about student organizations and how the organizations spend the money they are allotted by Student Government. We want the booklet to be distributed to all students to make them aware of where some of their activity fee money is going and to introduce them to what different student organizations offer them. We plan to present the booklet as a positive way of promoting student involvement and awareness.

Parts of the Project

- **Survey**—We will conduct a multidisciplinary survey of 150 SCSU students. We will ask questions about awareness of what student organizations exist, about how readily available information is concerning both the activities of student organizations and how activity fees are spent, and about the usefulness of a booklet such as we propose.
- **Samples**—We will gather information about how five student organizations use the money they are allotted by Student Government and what the organizations offer to students who participate in their activities or use their services. We will compile this information into five sample entries that might be found in the booklet to show the target audience what the booklet could include.
- **Proposal**—We will write a proposal to SCSU Admissions, Student Government, SRA, Academic Affairs, Housing and Student Development, and Career Services that reports our survey findings, requests the publication of a yearly booklet on student organizations, and includes five sample entries that could be included in the booklet.
- **Informational Interviews**—One group member will conduct an informational interview with SCSU Admissions in hopes of gaining an ally for the project. When gathering

FIGURE 12.1 Continued

information about student organizations, group members may conduct interviews with an organization's director or president. This information will help the group member to write his/her sample entry about what the organization offers SCSU students.
- **Thank you letters**—These letters will be written to those people group members interview or ask for information.

Individual's Responsibilities

- **Paul**—gathering information from Student Government about organizations' funding; first draft of survey; final draft of survey; distributing copied surveys to group members; researching one organization and writing one sample entry for the proposed booklet; conducting 30 surveys; thank you letters to those who provided information to him for his work; revision of project
- **Carrie Jean**—draft of memo proposal to Bob; drafting conclusion section of project's proposal; editing project; researching one organization and writing one sample entry for the proposed booklet; conducting 30 surveys; thank you letters to those who provided information to her for her work; revision of project
- **Darrin**—revision of/printing/turning in memo proposal to Bob; drafting introduction section of project's proposal; researching one organization and writing one sample entry for the proposed booklet; conducting 30 surveys; thank you letters to those who provided information to him for his work; revision of project
- **Mark**—informational interview with SCSU Admissions; drafting introduction section of project's proposal; researching one organization and writing one sample entry for the proposed booklet; conducting 30 surveys; thank you letters to those who provided information to him for his work; revision of project
- **Karen**—compiling survey information; preparing graphs or charts of survey information; researching one organization and writing one sample entry for the proposed booklet; conducting 30 surveys; thank you letters to those who provided information to her for her work; revision of project

Our Established Deadlines

Paul plans to have a draft of the survey for group discussion and your approval by Thursday (1/23) morning. Once the survey has been revised and edited, he will get it to the other group members ASAP so we can have people fill them out. The surveys will be given to Karen by 1/30 in class so she can have them compiled by 2/3. Each group member will have his/her sample entry drafted by 2/3. Darrin and Mark will have the project introduction drafted by 2/3, and Carrie Jean will have a draft of the conclusion by 2/3. The group will meet in class and on Monday evenings at 6:00 p.m..

Nitty Gritty Details

- All group documents will be done on Microsoft Word 6.0.
- We will share editing and revision responsibility for the final drafts; all group members will work on the table of contents, title page, and bibliography (if needed).
- All costs for copies, binding, etc. will be shared equally.

FIGURE 12.2 Sample Proposal

Professional
Consultants

LETTER PROPOSAL

February 27, 1997

Mainstreet Sheridan Association
3123 E. Brundage
Sheridan, WY 82801
ATTN: Edre Major, Executive Director

RE: Conceptual Design Services for the Brooks Street Enhancement Project

Dear Edre:

This proposal is in response to the verbal Request for Proposal CER received during a meeting early in February. We understand that the scope of work will include conceptual design services and cost estimates for street scape enhancements along Brooks Street, from Burkitt to First Street including intersecting streets east to the alley, and one block west on Brundage. A proposed scope of services and fee follow:

Item 1

CER will provide conceptual design services for street scape enhancements related to the Brooks Street Reconstruction Project. These concepts will include two options consisting of trees, decorative functional lighting, street corner neckdowns, and miscellaneous other amenities. Preliminary colored drawings will be prepared for each option, for review by USA. From this review and evaluation, the preferred alternative will be further developed with the City and USA prior to final preparation of presentation boards. Upon consensus by all parties of the final conceptual design, CER will prepare final display boards in 24 × 36 colored format.

Very preliminary cost estimates will be prepared for each of the two options. Following the selection of the preferred option, CER will prepare more accurate cost estimates in conjunction with the final presentation boards.

Architecture - Engineering
Materials Testing - Surveying

2237 North Main Street Sheridan, Wyoming 82801 (307)555-1711 Fax: (307)555-5014 cer@wave.net Offices in Gillette and Douglas Wyoming

FIGURE 12.2 Continued

Item 2

CER will be responsible for determining 90% complete ownership of properties encompassed by the project. This information will be obtained from the Sheridan County Assessor. A preliminary Special Improvement District (SID) map will be prepared, showing ownership.

Item 3

CER will provide a preliminary assessment roll for the selected conceptual design program, based on the same method of assessment that was used for the City's previous Gould project (assessment based on area owned within the SID).

Item 4

CER will attend two USA Board meetings and two public meetings with members of the City and USA and property owners within the proposed area of improvement.

Item 5

CER will provide technical assistance and cost estimates to Les Jayne, Sheridan County Grantsman, for the purpose of preparing and submitting grant applications associated with this project.

Item 6

CER will review information regarding current pavement thickness on streets within the project.

Item 7

CER anticipates that all work associated with this proposal will be complete by May 1, 1997.

Item 8

CER proposes to complete the work outlined within this proposal for a lump sum fee of $3,500. Monthly invoices will be prepared in conjunction with the description of services related to those fees.

Item 9

Should the scope of the project change during the process based on input from property owners, the city of Sheridan, USA, or other interested parties, CER reserves the right to renegotiate this fee.

Sincerely,

Tom Barker

Thomas L. Barker

TB/lm

FIGURE 12.3 Sample Proposal

June 26, 1997

Ms. Elizabeth Martinez
Director of Human Resources
% Purchasing Department
TAMIU
520 University Blvd.
Laredo, TX 78041

RFP: Job Evaluation and Compensation Plan

Dear Ms. Martinez:

Pursuant to the above noted RFP, Professional Management Group [PMG] is pleased to submit to TAMUI [University] the enclosed proposal for a job evaluation and compensation plan of its classified, professional and administrative positions [approximately 232 positions]. PMG's proposal for services meets the requirements of the University based upon information noted in the RFP.

Briefly stated, the PMG process and product offers the University the following:

- A results-oriented and cost-effective approach to establishing internal equity and pay for responsibilities among the positions and classifications.
- An on-going methodology for monitoring the internal equity of positions and classification relationships.
- A plan for reduction or elimination of employee discontent and/or lack of understanding and trust.
- The review of Position Analysis Questionnaires [PAQs] for the purpose of confirming or reallocating duties and responsibilities [based upon actual duties] including supervisory responsibilities.
- A review of compliance with the Fair Labor Standards Act [FLSA] via a determination of exemption status for each position.
- A review of compliance with the Americans With Disabilities Act [ADA].
- A determination of benchmark positions to improve the existing market comparability study and then a process to ensure an annual review of its competitive posture.
- A review of the staff compensation philosophy.
- A valid planning and budgeting process related to compensation which frees, or at least limits, the institution from "out-of-cycle" tilting or salary adjustments, playing catch-up, or other compensation difficulties.
- An appropriate and necessary supervisory training program and employee information sessions for the implementation and maintenance of the plan.

FIGURE 12.3 Continued

Via a consulting contract with PMG, the end product for the University will be a classification and compensation plan which clearly meets or exceeds the University's compensation philosophy as noted on page three of the RFP.

Professional Management Group offers the University the unique opportunity of leveraging decades of higher education human resources experience including many years of developing, implementing and maintaining classification/compensation systems. Given our extended experience in higher education, we are confident our company can clearly exceed all the University's stated qualifications noted on page four of the RFP.

With the full cooperation of all the persons involved and barring unforeseen difficulties, I am certain PMG could successfully complete this engagement in a timeframe mutually agreeable [PMG anticipates a 90–120 day project schedule]. You will note in the proposal that the PMG approach to development and implementation of a staff classification/compensation plan is one of interaction and participation. It is the best approach to have if the University desires adequate employee "buy-in" and supervisory acceptance. This approach coupled with the very nature of the project [one which needs time, reflection, analysis, discussion and debate] makes the timeframe of 90–120 days "doable." Because PMG **is a Texas domiciled, sole proprietor company, it can easily commit itself** to the University and will be readily available to respond to emergencies or necessary schedule changes.

I truly do look forward to assisting the University and you with this project and am convinced that the outstanding experience, expertise and knowledge of higher education classification/compensation systems offered by PMG will give the University a tremendous finished product.

Sincerely,

Dick Cottrill

Dick Cottrill, President
Professional Management Group

enc. proposal w/attachments

NOTE: PMG agrees to abide by conditions noted on page five of the RFP.

(continued)

FIGURE 12.3 Continued

ENGAGEMENT PROPOSAL

ON

A JOB EVALUATION & COMPENSATION PLAN
FOR CLASSIFIED, PROFESSIONAL AND ADMINISTRATIVE POSITIONS

FOR

ELIZABETH MARTINEZ
DIRECTOR OF HUMAN RESOURCES
TEXAS A & M INTERNATIONAL UNIVERSITY

BY

PROFESSIONAL MANAGEMENT GROUP
GEORGETOWN, TEXAS
DICK COTTRILL, PRESIDENT

JUNE 26, 1997

FIGURE 12.3 Continued

GENERAL OVERVIEW & PHILOSOPHY

Professional Management Group:
1410 Tamara Drive, Georgetown, TX 78628
Dick Cottrill, President
Phone: 1-512-555-8879 Fax: 1-512-555-8880

Professional Management Group [PMG], a sole-proprietor, full service management firm, **specializing in assisting colleges and universities** review and solve human resource concerns/problems, is pleased to submit this proposal to Texas A & M International University [University] in response to the RFP.

Dick Cottrill, PMG President, in addition to his full-time chief HR administrator positions (which included the successful implementation of five classification systems] at two large public universities, was a part-time consultant between 1982 and 1995. During that time period his consulting practice included successful classification/compensation projects for four public entities [two community colleges, a school district and a county library]. In 1995, PMG came into existence as a full-time, sole proprietor consulting firm specializing in the higher education arena.

PMG will assist the University in developing and implementing a job evaluation and compensation plan which includes the following important criteria:

- Internally equitable
- Externally competitive
- Easily updated
- Legal
- Personally motivating [to employees]
- Efficiently administered
- Technically sound
- Readily comprehended
- Financially responsible
- Within the College's Mission

PMG has a very straight forward concept regarding compensation in public higher education: the goal of the organization should be to pay each individual a competitive salary for the level of the work performed. This is to say that *both* external market *and* internal equity are the components to determine the "salary structure"; and then, the final component/s could be a "merit" factor, bonus pay, project pay, or other special compensation programs [if desired by the client/organization].

1

(continued)

FIGURE 12.3 Continued

PROJECT STAFFING

PMG is a sole proprietor business and has no paid employees. The thrust of the company is to provide the expertise via the effective utilization of additional independent contractors pursuant to the nature of the engagement. Dick Cottrill, PMG President does the work himself, but uses selected individuals of the following Engagement Study Team as necessary. The detailed resumes of the PMG study team are in Appendix 1. Ms. Houser has been with PMG since its formal inception in 1995; Mr. Kessler assisted Mr. Cottrill with projects during the 1980s; while Mr. Walker, Ms. Cacciola and Mr. Lookingbill are new to PMG. Mr. Curl, while new to PMG, is a former colleague of Dick Cottrill at the University of Wyoming and is a recognized leader in classification/compensation systems. Each study team member possesses excellent classification and compensation experience and is uniquely qualified to assist PMG/the University with this engagement. It is also important to note that all of these individuals are aware of this proposal and are committed to working on the engagement through its successful completion.

Dick Cottrill—Project Manager

Bruce Curl—Asst. Project Manager

Rhonda Houser—Senior Consultant

Jim Kessler **Larry Walker** **David Lookingbill** **Jeanette Cacciola**

PMG Support Staff as Required

2

FIGURE 12.3 Continued

EMPLOYER EXPERIENCE

In addition to the clients noted on the PMG brochure [Appendix 2], we have assisted the following organizations:

CLIENT	CONTACT	PROJECT	STATUS
City of Balcones Heights, TX	Roy Miller, City Admn PHONE: 210-555-9194	assisted with classification study	completed
County of Jefferson, TX	Cary Erickson, HR Dir. PHONE: 409-555-2391	assisted with classification study & performance evaluation system	completed
Mankato State University, MN	Dean Trauger, VP PHONE: 507-555-6622 NOTE: THE CLASS STUDY IS A REPEAT ENGAGEMENT	audit of HR function & HR Director Search and a major department classification study	completed will be done 7-23-97
Austin Community College	Penny Levisay, Emp. Man PHONE: 512-555-7564	wrote affirmative action plan	completed
Santa Fe Community College, NM	Alice Ortega, Dir/HR PHONE: 505-555-8200	review of employment practices	completed
Kalamazoo Valley C. College, MI	Sandy Bohnet, Dir/HR PHONE: 616-555-5409	staff class/comp plan	will be done 8-15-97

PMG has completed the following related projects during the past [3] years.

- E.T.A. Established the HR function which included a classification and compensation plan for approximately 125 employees.
- Southwestern University Served as the HR officer and advisor covering all aspects of the human resource function including but not limited to benefits, employment, employee relations and classification of staff positions. The initial engagement was five months, however, due to the University's need was extended twice for a total of eleven months.
- ROXELL INC. Researched and wrote the employee handbook including the classification and compensation policies.

Finally, with respect to prior experience, the PMG President and the key study team members for the University's project possess a wealth of directly applicable skill and knowledge [higher education background and expertise]. Please see Appendix 3—reference letters.

3

(continued)

FIGURE 12.3 Continued

JOB EVALUATION METHODOLOGIES [AND MORE]

INTRODUCTION

PMG will complete the engagement during the successful completion of a seven phase process which will satisfactorily and effectively address the essential components of the University's desired classification/compensation program. The seven phases are a very logical and rational approach to the development and implementation of an excellent classification and compensation program:

- One Start-up activities
- Two Develop basic position information
- Three Prepare job descriptions
- Four Conduct job evaluations
- Five Perform salary survey/market analysis
- Six Determine pay grades
- Seven Issue final report and recommend policies and procedures, etc.

A detailed description of each phase with results noted follows. This complies with Sections E and F of the RFP.

PHASE ONE: START-UP ACTIVITIES

- Interview University administrative leaders to familiarize PMG with the University organization and to identify any unique compensation problem/s.
- Review the University's current classification/compensation policies, rules, etc.
- Review compensation philosophy, engagement timeline, data needs, etc. with the Director of Human Resources [HR].
- Establish a Task Force [5–7 individuals] to assist with the engagement and provide guidance to PMG.
- Communicate the engagement effort to affected University employees via memo, letter, and/or other normal communication vehicles AND announce a series of open meetings. The purpose of this effort is to ensure that employees know the "whys and whats" of the engagement and that they are reassured no person will suffer a loss in pay as a result of the effort. The estimated engagement timeframe will also be communicated.
- Review PAQ format used by the University in gathering essential position information.
- The result of **Phase One** is a well organized approach to the engagement including effective employee communication, PMG understanding of the current staff classification/compensation situation, and a well-informed Task Force.

FIGURE 12.3 Continued

LEGAL ACTIONS

PMG does not have, nor has it ever had, any legal actions brought against it for any reason.

CLOSING COMMENTS

Rest assured, the proposal offered by PMG, if accepted by the University, will result in the development and implementation of an outstanding classification and compensation plan. It is a logical and rational approach to determining the relative worth of each job [internal equity] as well as the market competitiveness [external equity] for the University. It is a participative process offering the opportunity for input, review and appeal by some/all affected employees. The University will have, in the end . . .

• POSITION DESCRIPTIONS [PAQS]	Updated description of work for each position.
• JOB DESCRIPTIONS [JDS]	Accurate and meaningful descriptions which will be the foundation for many other personnel functions [e.g. recruitment, job evaluation, training, performance, etc.].
• JOB CLASSIFICATION SYSTEM	Consistent job titles and career paths.
• JOB EVALUATION SYSTEM	A systematic approach to internal pay equity.
• PAY GRADE STRUCTURE	The relationships between job classifications for pay determination and ongoing administration.
• MARKET ANALYSIS	External data used to price the pay grades and to ensure competitiveness.
• PAY RANGES	Specific pay grade minimums and maximums for each covered position/job classification.
• POLICIES & PROCEDURES	Guidelines for consistent treatment of recurring pay transactions.
• COMMUNICATION PLAN	A system for ensuring adequate employee and management information and communication about plan and plan changes/enhancements.
• TRAINED HR DEPARTMENT STAFF	A trained staff to successfully implement and maintain the plan.

If the University wishes to seek information regarding the competency of PMG, the consultant encourages the University to contact any of the provided references. PMG encourages the University to contact Sandy Bohnet, Director of Personnel Services, Kalamazoo Valley Community College, Kalamazoo, Michigan [616-555-5409] or Dean Trauger, Vice President for Fiscal Affairs, Mankato State University [507-555-6622].

5

Or suppose you're submitting a grant proposal to a funding agency that has a clearly stated mission of supporting projects like the one you propose and a history of funding these projects. Here, again, it would be condescending to argue to these readers that this kind of problem is significant or important. All you need to do is explain your particular issue or problem so that your readers can see it's one they find significant. Your readers have already built the box that has the label "Significant Issues" on it. All you need to do is convince them that your issue belongs in their box. What are the criteria your readers will use to measure your problem or issue to see if it fits in their box?

Example Two. Your readers don't appreciate the significance of the issue. You're most likely to encounter this situation when you're submitting an unsolicited proposal—although it's possible to encounter it when you're responding to a generic RFP that may be written to invite a wide range of different kinds of proposals. How do you know your readers don't understand the issue and its significance? In fact, you never really know exactly what is your readers' understanding of the issues. Instead, you have to make intelligent guesses, and your level of confidence in your guess will vary depending on what you're able to learn about your readers. If it appears you're having to write to readers who are utterly unappreciative of your situation, you should probably reconsider whether you should even be submitting a proposal to them.

You build your significance argument based on where you think your readers are on a scale of understanding of the critical issues and their significance. At the very least, make sure your readers know the facts of the situation. But this isn't a just-the-facts, random listing of data. You have to make the facts speak for themselves. To do this, you shape the facts so they tell a story, and you make sure that the heart of that story is the significance you see in those facts. For an example, look at the brief section from the Kilimanjaro proposal we've excerpted in Figure 12.4. (The complete proposal, downloaded from the World Wide Web, appears in Figure 12.5.)

Even if you're responding to a detailed RFP, where the readers have given you the facts, you will still probably want to give them back a concise synopsis to show that you understand the situation as they do, raising their confidence that your proposal will respond to the issues they find significant. Notice how Tom Barker and Dick Cottrill both take special care to echo back their understanding of what their readers have told or written to them (see Figures 12.2 and 12.3).

How do you decide which points of significance to emphasize? Of course, you should think about your readers and what you know about their goals, values, and assumptions that will shape their sense of the significant. But your own sense of significance should probably be your primary guide:

- What problems, concerns, issues, and opportunities prompted your interest in the first place?
- What makes them significant, especially for you?
- How do they relate to other issues and concerns?
- Who else is interested—or should be interested—in them?
- What's their history, and what are their implications for the future?
- What are the subproblems and subissues?

These are all probably good entry points for your proposal.

FIGURE 12.4 Example of the Significance Argument

ABSTRACT

The Catholic diocese of Same, Tanzania, currently operates a minor seminary (equivalent to a U.S. high school) for 200 students and the Appropriate Technology Center (ATC) for 150 students. These two educational centers are located in Chanjale village, which is comprised of 550 villagers. Presently, a water tank is needed to support both the school and community to continue the work done by Miserior in 1989. The villagers and students are requesting financial assistance to construct a bigger water tank that will cater to the high demand of the quickly increasing population.

Currently, the centers receive running water from a river seven miles away. A water project funded by Miserior in 1989 allowed water from the river to be used in Chanjale by supplying pipes and small reservoirs. At that time, the number of students, faculty, and villagers was half the present population.

The two small reservoirs, with a combined capacity of 384 gallons, can no longer fulfill the needs of the present community. Demands on the water supply have forced students to abandon growing vegetables and fruit, a substantial part of their diet and an important part of their educational experience. A student reforestation project, which is part of their training on environmental issues, is also threatened.

This project will provide enough water for domestic use by the entire community, enable students to get a balanced diet, and also prepare them to be champions of their own environment.

The total cost of this program is $15,000 (US). Of this, parents and local corporations have already committed $4,950 (US), which is equivalent to 20 yearly wages. This request is for the balance needed of $10,050.

Feasibility

The feasibility argument really breaks down into three subarguments, or phases of argument and analysis:

1. Alternatives
2. Costs/risks
3. Resources/constraints

The feasibility argument is the crucial center of the proposal. When proposals break down, the fault usually lies in the feasibility argument. In an effective proposal, the

FIGURE 12.5 Sample Online Proposal

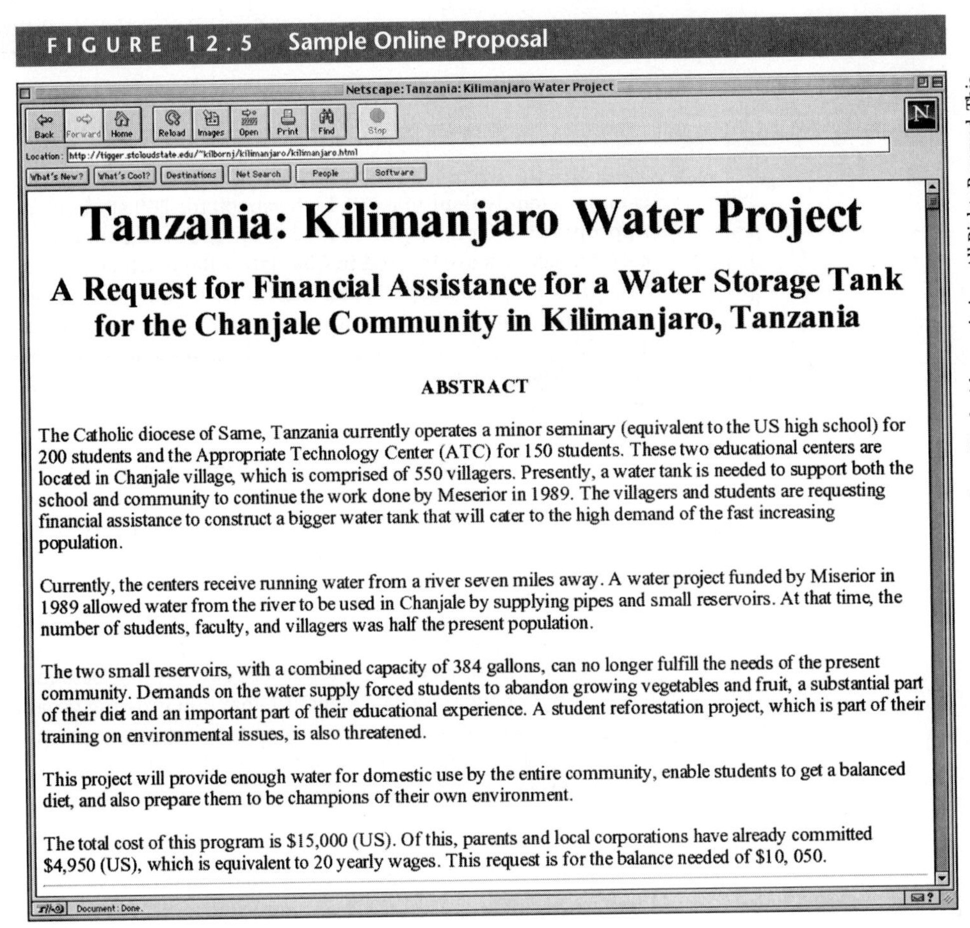

Tanzania: Kilimanjaro Water Project

A Request for Financial Assistance for a Water Storage Tank for the Chanjale Community in Kilimanjaro, Tanzania

ABSTRACT

The Catholic diocese of Same, Tanzania currently operates a minor seminary (equivalent to the US high school) for 200 students and the Appropriate Technology Center (ATC) for 150 students. These two educational centers are located in Chanjale village, which is comprised of 550 villagers. Presently, a water tank is needed to support both the school and community to continue the work done by Meserior in 1989. The villagers and students are requesting financial assistance to construct a bigger water tank that will cater to the high demand of the fast increasing population.

Currently, the centers receive running water from a river seven miles away. A water project funded by Miserior in 1989 allowed water from the river to be used in Chanjale by supplying pipes and small reservoirs. At that time, the number of students, faculty, and villagers was half the present population.

The two small reservoirs, with a combined capacity of 384 gallons, can no longer fulfill the needs of the present community. Demands on the water supply forced students to abandon growing vegetables and fruit, a substantial part of their diet and an important part of their educational experience. A student reforestation project, which is part of their training on environmental issues, is also threatened.

This project will provide enough water for domestic use by the entire community, enable students to get a balanced diet, and also prepare them to be champions of their own environment.

The total cost of this program is $15,000 (US). Of this, parents and local corporations have already committed $4,950 (US), which is equivalent to 20 yearly wages. This request is for the balance needed of $10, 050.

alternatives, costs/risks, and resources/constraints arguments converge to lay a foundation from which you step naturally into your third major argument, the action argument. Your feasibility analysis and argument identify a preferred course of action, and in the end, you will be able to argue convincingly that this course of action is most beneficial.

The more complex, costly, and novel the project that's proposed, the more difficult and detailed the feasibility argument must likely be. Compare the four proposals in this chapter, for example (Figures 12.1, 12.2, 12.3, and 12.5). The most complex feasibility argument is in Figure 12.3, the Cottrill proposal, which is also the longest of the proposals by far. We've cut 8 pages from the body of the proposal and left out the entire appendix of about 20 pages. Because the proposed project is labor intensive and crucially dependent on the expertise and character of the people who implement it, Cottrill spends a large part of the proposal identifying key personnel and documenting the experience both of the firm and of individual consultants. He then devotes the main body of the proposal to a detailed description of the timeline for the

FIGURE 12.5 Continued

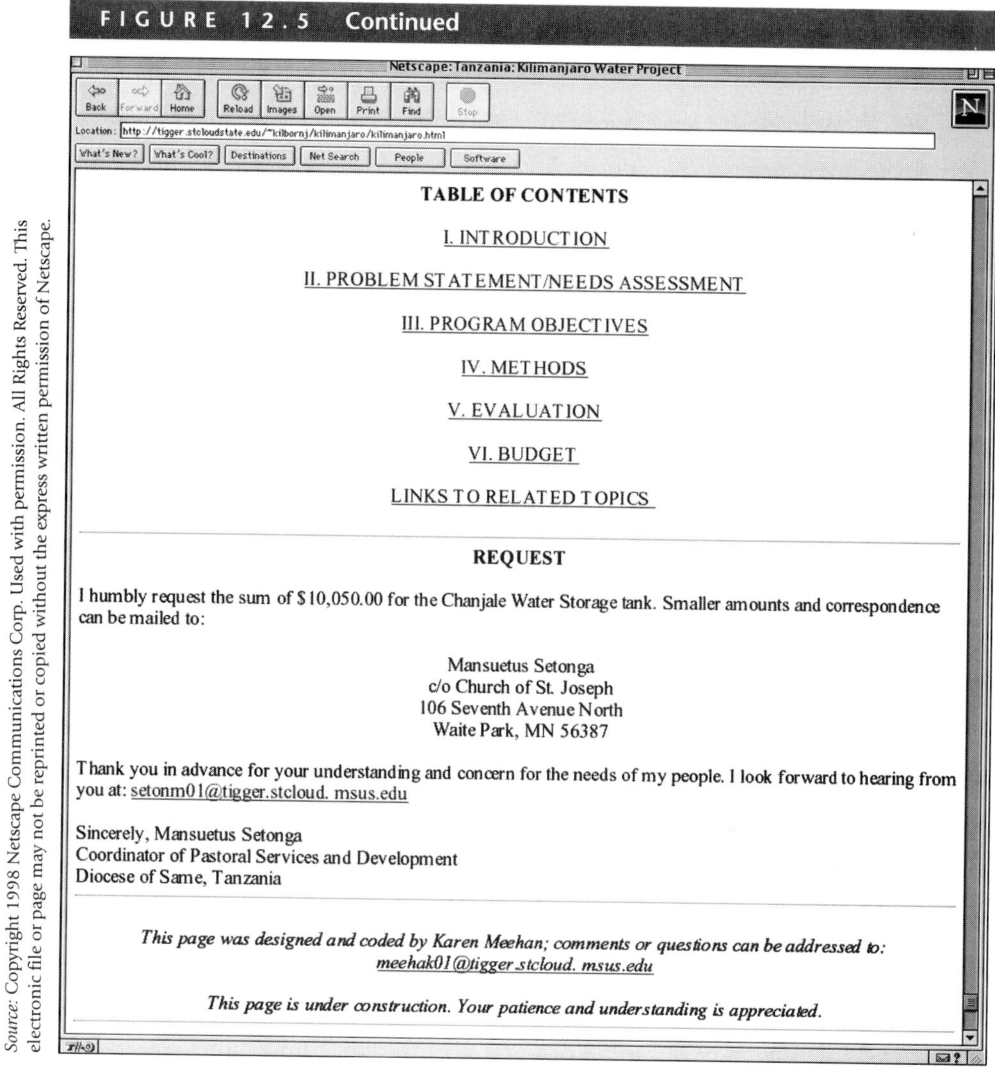

TABLE OF CONTENTS

REQUEST

I humbly request the sum of $10,050.00 for the Chanjale Water Storage tank. Smaller amounts and correspondence can be mailed to:

Mansuetus Setonga
c/o Church of St. Joseph
106 Seventh Avenue North
Waite Park, MN 56387

Thank you in advance for your understanding and concern for the needs of my people. I look forward to hearing from you at: setonm01@tigger.stcloud. msus.edu

Sincerely, Mansuetus Setonga
Coordinator of Pastoral Services and Development
Diocese of Same, Tanzania

This page was designed and coded by Karen Meehan; comments or questions can be addressed to: meehak01@tigger.stcloud. msus.edu

This page is under construction. Your patience and understanding is appreciated.

(continued)

seven phases of the project he proposes (most of which we have cut out for the sake of brevity). Finally, near the end of the proposal, he discusses in detail his estimated budget of time and expenses as well as his billing system and rationale. (Again, we've deleted this discussion, both in order to shorten the example and also to protect the proprietary information it includes.) In discussing the timing, scope, staffing, cost, and plan of payment for the project, Cottrill emphasizes the flexibility of his organization, demonstrating to his readers that, while he, in his expert opinion, sees some clearly preferable strategies, he's prepared to offer his readers a range of alternatives and the choice of deciding on a plan of action that's best for them.

FIGURE 12.5 Continued

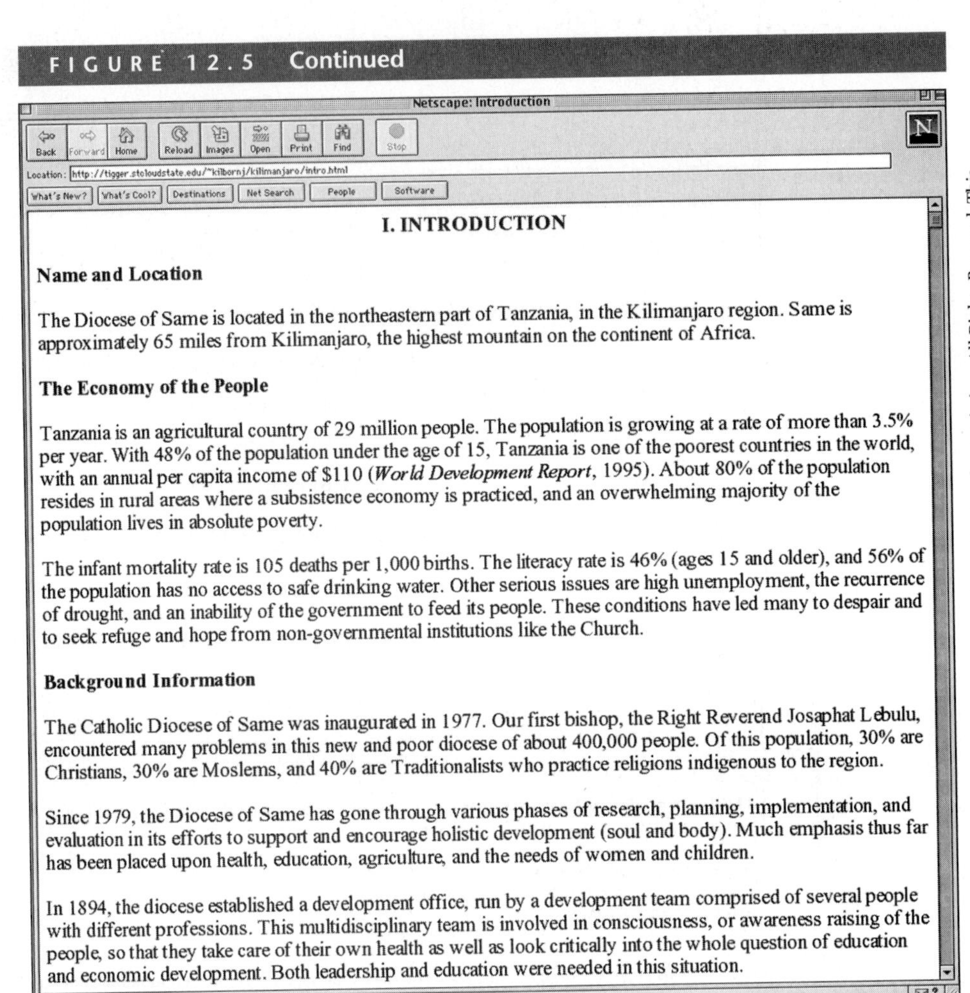

I. INTRODUCTION

Name and Location

The Diocese of Same is located in the northeastern part of Tanzania, in the Kilimanjaro region. Same is approximately 65 miles from Kilimanjaro, the highest mountain on the continent of Africa.

The Economy of the People

Tanzania is an agricultural country of 29 million people. The population is growing at a rate of more than 3.5% per year. With 48% of the population under the age of 15, Tanzania is one of the poorest countries in the world, with an annual per capita income of $110 (*World Development Report*, 1995). About 80% of the population resides in rural areas where a subsistence economy is practiced, and an overwhelming majority of the population lives in absolute poverty.

The infant mortality rate is 105 deaths per 1,000 births. The literacy rate is 46% (ages 15 and older), and 56% of the population has no access to safe drinking water. Other serious issues are high unemployment, the recurrence of drought, and an inability of the government to feed its people. These conditions have led many to despair and to seek refuge and hope from non-governmental institutions like the Church.

Background Information

The Catholic Diocese of Same was inaugurated in 1977. Our first bishop, the Right Reverend Josaphat Lebulu, encountered many problems in this new and poor diocese of about 400,000 people. Of this population, 30% are Christians, 30% are Moslems, and 40% are Traditionalists who practice religions indigenous to the region.

Since 1979, the Diocese of Same has gone through various phases of research, planning, implementation, and evaluation in its efforts to support and encourage holistic development (soul and body). Much emphasis thus far has been placed upon health, education, agriculture, and the needs of women and children.

In 1894, the diocese established a development office, run by a development team comprised of several people with different professions. This multidisciplinary team is involved in consciousness, or awareness raising of the people, so that they take care of their own health as well as look critically into the whole question of education and economic development. Both leadership and education were needed in this situation.

The resources of time, people, and money are also clearly important in Figure 12.2, the Barker letter proposal, but they aren't the crucial variable that they appear to be in the Cottrill proposal, probably because the project is less expensive and there is an already established working relationship between Barker's firm and the readers. Even so, notice that the engineering firm reserves the right to renegotiate the financial terms if the scope of the project changes.

The student proposal in Figure 12.1 does a good job of speaking to the feasibility issues germane to the activity fee research project: time available, definition of the project in such a way as to give it an appropriate scope for their time, and the personal commitment the students are willing to make in budgeting time to research the project adequately and share the workload equitably among themselves.

As you consider your feasibility argument, then, think as Barker, Cottrill, and the students did about the three subarguments: alternatives, costs/risks, and resources/

FIGURE 12.5 Continued

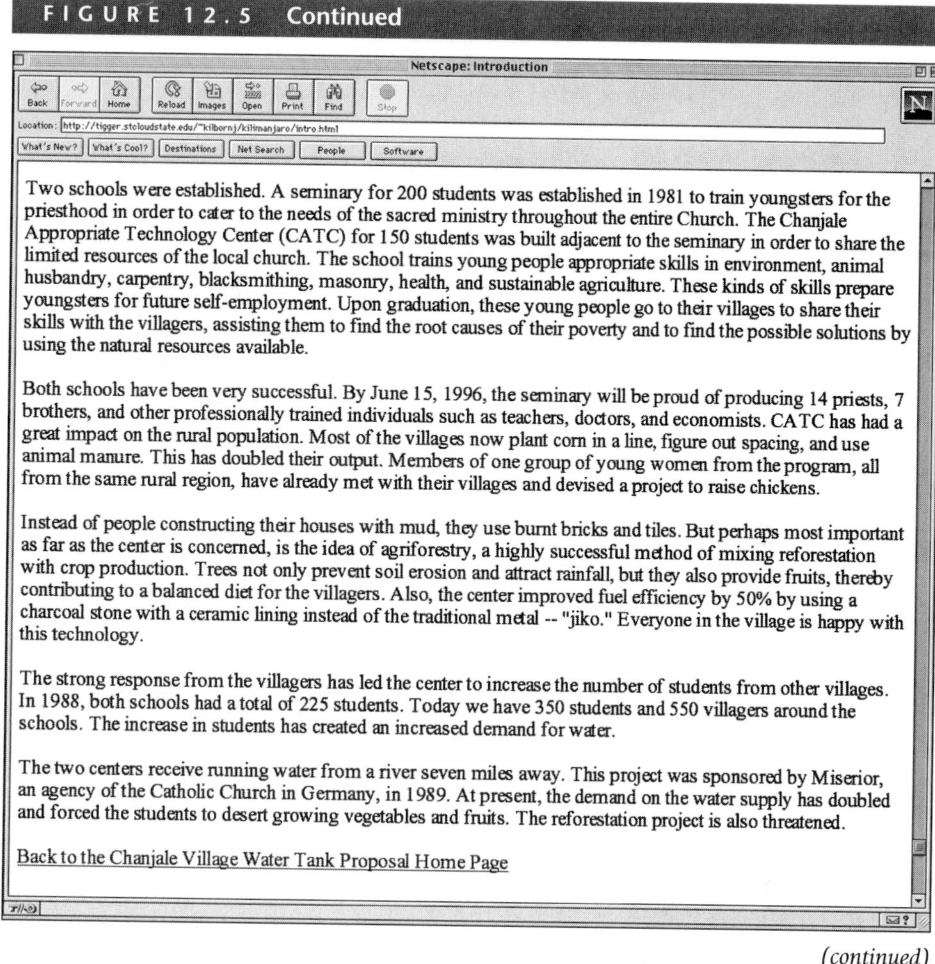

Two schools were established. A seminary for 200 students was established in 1981 to train youngsters for the priesthood in order to cater to the needs of the sacred ministry throughout the entire Church. The Chanjale Appropriate Technology Center (CATC) for 150 students was built adjacent to the seminary in order to share the limited resources of the local church. The school trains young people appropriate skills in environment, animal husbandry, carpentry, blacksmithing, masonry, health, and sustainable agriculture. These kinds of skills prepare youngsters for future self-employment. Upon graduation, these young people go to their villages to share their skills with the villagers, assisting them to find the root causes of their poverty and to find the possible solutions by using the natural resources available.

Both schools have been very successful. By June 15, 1996, the seminary will be proud of producing 14 priests, 7 brothers, and other professionally trained individuals such as teachers, doctors, and economists. CATC has had a great impact on the rural population. Most of the villages now plant corn in a line, figure out spacing, and use animal manure. This has doubled their output. Members of one group of young women from the program, all from the same rural region, have already met with their villages and devised a project to raise chickens.

Instead of people constructing their houses with mud, they use burnt bricks and tiles. But perhaps most important as far as the center is concerned, is the idea of agriforestry, a highly successful method of mixing reforestation with crop production. Trees not only prevent soil erosion and attract rainfall, but they also provide fruits, thereby contributing to a balanced diet for the villagers. Also, the center improved fuel efficiency by 50% by using a charcoal stone with a ceramic lining instead of the traditional metal -- "jiko." Everyone in the village is happy with this technology.

The strong response from the villagers has led the center to increase the number of students from other villages. In 1988, both schools had a total of 225 students. Today we have 350 students and 550 villagers around the schools. The increase in students has created an increased demand for water.

The two centers receive running water from a river seven miles away. This project was sponsored by Miserior, an agency of the Catholic Church in Germany, in 1989. At present, the demand on the water supply has doubled and forced the students to desert growing vegetables and fruits. The reforestation project is also threatened.

Back to the Chanjale Village Water Tank Proposal Home Page

(continued)

constraints. In the Kilimanjaro Water Project proposal (Figure 12.5), the combined scope, alternatives, and resources compared to the need make a persuasive feasiblity argument. The scope is small, but the needs and benefits are compellingly detailed. Almost one-third of the needed resources have already been raised ($4,950), and only $10,050 remains.

Alternatives. Is there more than one plausible way of solving the problem or seizing the opportunity you've described? If so, you should probably acknowledge, however briefly, all these alternatives. If your readers think of a plausible alternative that you haven't mentioned and analyzed, they may not trust that your analysis is as complete and thorough as it should be. This doesn't mean you're obliged to discuss every conceivable alternative, however—just those that seem reasonable and plausible.

FIGURE 12.5 Continued

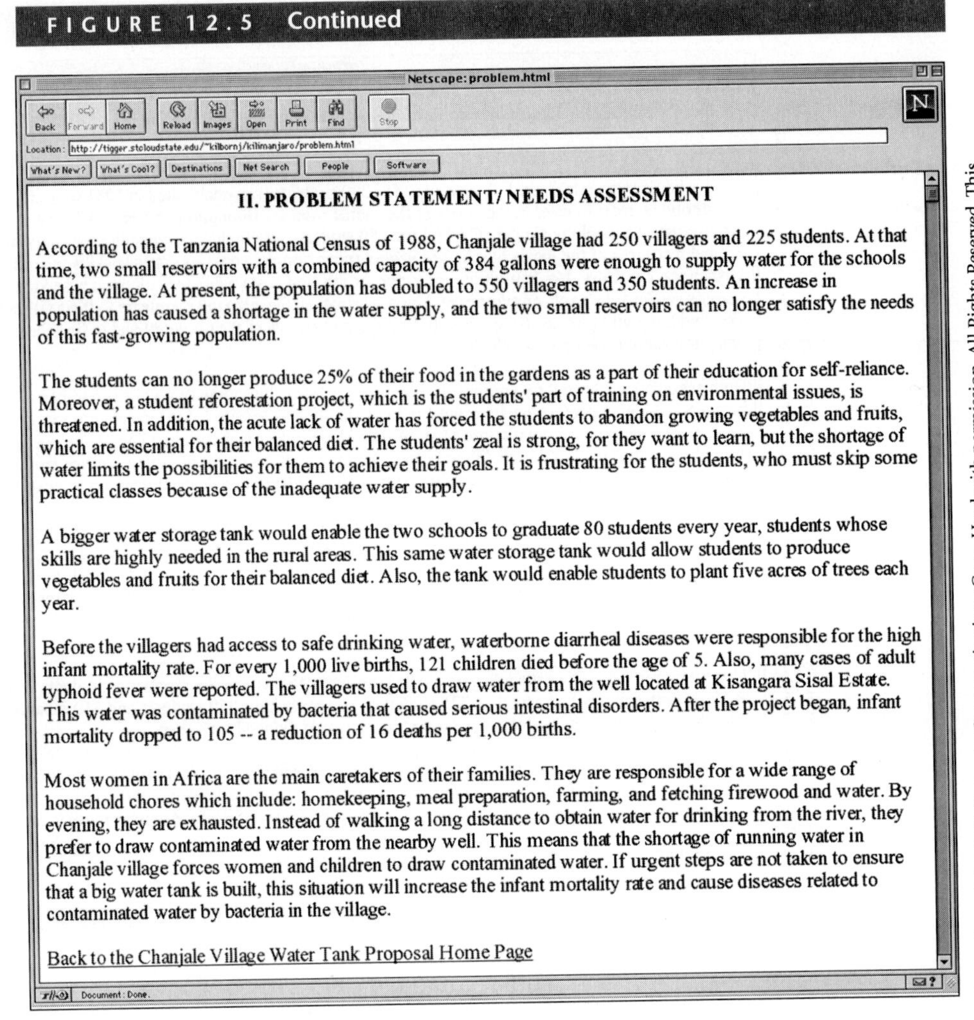

Netscape: problem.html

Location: http://tigger.stcloudstate.edu/~kilbornj/kilimanjaro/problem.html

II. PROBLEM STATEMENT/NEEDS ASSESSMENT

According to the Tanzania National Census of 1988, Chanjale village had 250 villagers and 225 students. At that time, two small reservoirs with a combined capacity of 384 gallons were enough to supply water for the schools and the village. At present, the population has doubled to 550 villagers and 350 students. An increase in population has caused a shortage in the water supply, and the two small reservoirs can no longer satisfy the needs of this fast-growing population.

The students can no longer produce 25% of their food in the gardens as a part of their education for self-reliance. Moreover, a student reforestation project, which is the students' part of training on environmental issues, is threatened. In addition, the acute lack of water has forced the students to abandon growing vegetables and fruits, which are essential for their balanced diet. The students' zeal is strong, for they want to learn, but the shortage of water limits the possibilities for them to achieve their goals. It is frustrating for the students, who must skip some practical classes because of the inadequate water supply.

A bigger water storage tank would enable the two schools to graduate 80 students every year, students whose skills are highly needed in the rural areas. This same water storage tank would allow students to produce vegetables and fruits for their balanced diet. Also, the tank would enable students to plant five acres of trees each year.

Before the villagers had access to safe drinking water, waterborne diarrheal diseases were responsible for the high infant mortality rate. For every 1,000 live births, 121 children died before the age of 5. Also, many cases of adult typhoid fever were reported. The villagers used to draw water from the well located at Kisangara Sisal Estate. This water was contaminated by bacteria that caused serious intestinal disorders. After the project began, infant mortality dropped to 105 -- a reduction of 16 deaths per 1,000 births.

Most women in Africa are the main caretakers of their families. They are responsible for a wide range of household chores which include: homekeeping, meal preparation, farming, and fetching firewood and water. By evening, they are exhausted. Instead of walking a long distance to obtain water for drinking from the river, they prefer to draw contaminated water from the nearby well. This means that the shortage of running water in Chanjale village forces women and children to draw contaminated water. If urgent steps are not taken to ensure that a big water tank is built, this situation will increase the infant mortality rate and cause diseases related to contaminated water by bacteria in the village.

Back to the Chanjale Village Water Tank Proposal Home Page

Document: Done.

Costs/Risks. Remember, your proposal readers are investors. They are vitally interested in what risks they are undertaking and in what your proposed project is going to cost them. It is absolutely vital to provide detailed, explicit financial information—grounded in the very best historical data you can discover and projected into the future with the most careful analysis you can perform. It's also important that you carefully define the areas of uncertainty in your analyses and projections:

- What kinds of economic or demographic assumptions are you making when you project these figures?
- What are the areas of uncertainty in these assumptions and projections?
- Within what ranges are you reasonably confident in your assumptions and projections?

FIGURE 12.5 Continued

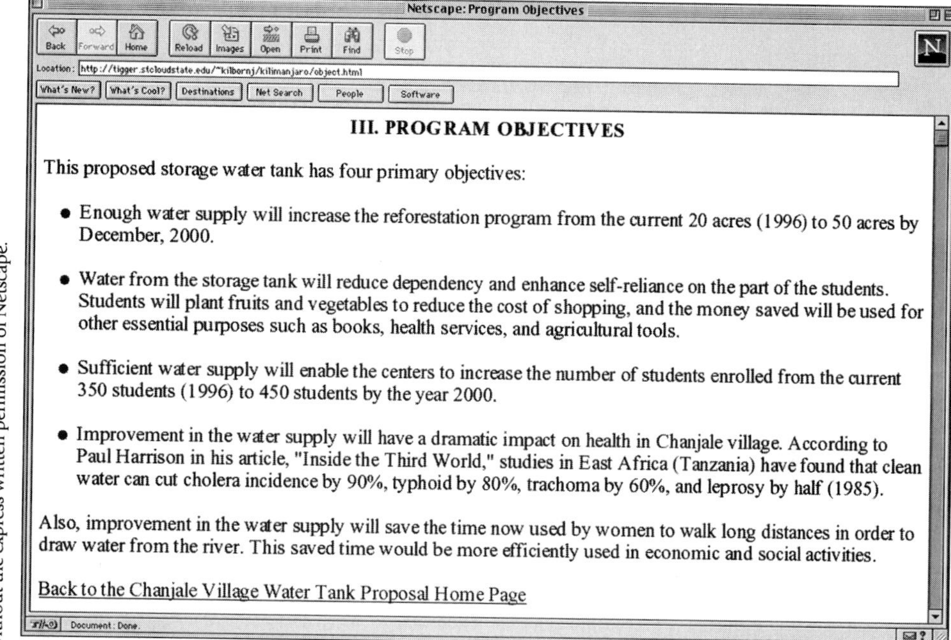

III. PROGRAM OBJECTIVES

This proposed storage water tank has four primary objectives:

- Enough water supply will increase the reforestation program from the current 20 acres (1996) to 50 acres by December, 2000.
- Water from the storage tank will reduce dependency and enhance self-reliance on the part of the students. Students will plant fruits and vegetables to reduce the cost of shopping, and the money saved will be used for other essential purposes such as books, health services, and agricultural tools.
- Sufficient water supply will enable the centers to increase the number of students enrolled from the current 350 students (1996) to 450 students by the year 2000.
- Improvement in the water supply will have a dramatic impact on health in Chanjale village. According to Paul Harrison in his article, "Inside the Third World," studies in East Africa (Tanzania) have found that clean water can cut cholera incidence by 90%, typhoid by 80%, trachoma by 60%, and leprosy by half (1985).

Also, improvement in the water supply will save the time now used by women to walk long distances in order to draw water from the river. This saved time would be more efficiently used in economic and social activities.

Back to the Chanjale Village Water Tank Proposal Home Page

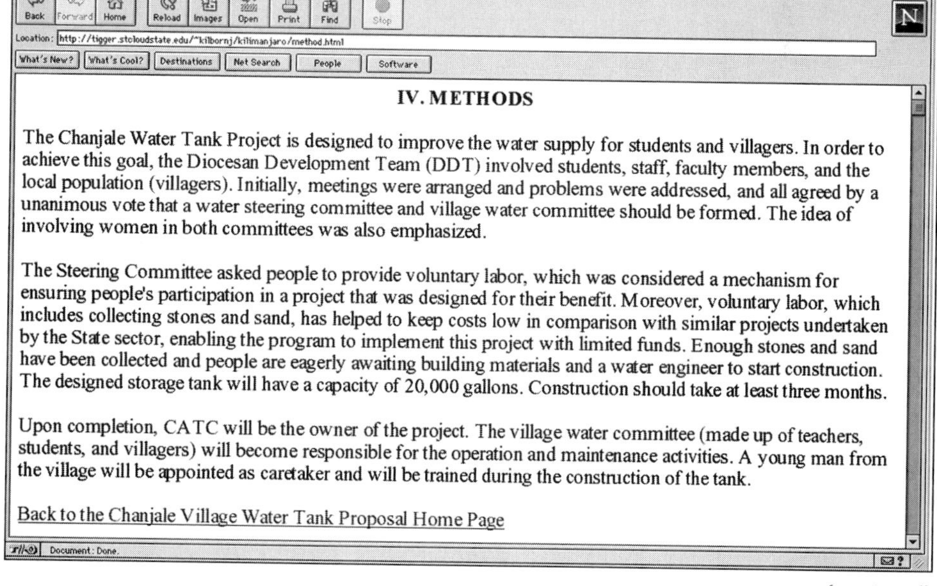

IV. METHODS

The Chanjale Water Tank Project is designed to improve the water supply for students and villagers. In order to achieve this goal, the Diocesan Development Team (DDT) involved students, staff, faculty members, and the local population (villagers). Initially, meetings were arranged and problems were addressed, and all agreed by a unanimous vote that a water steering committee and village water committee should be formed. The idea of involving women in both committees was also emphasized.

The Steering Committee asked people to provide voluntary labor, which was considered a mechanism for ensuring people's participation in a project that was designed for their benefit. Moreover, voluntary labor, which includes collecting stones and sand, has helped to keep costs low in comparison with similar projects undertaken by the State sector, enabling the program to implement this project with limited funds. Enough stones and sand have been collected and people are eagerly awaiting building materials and a water engineer to start construction. The designed storage tank will have a capacity of 20,000 gallons. Construction should take at least three months.

Upon completion, CATC will be the owner of the project. The village water committee (made up of teachers, students, and villagers) will become responsible for the operation and maintenance activities. A young man from the village will be appointed as caretaker and will be trained during the construction of the tank.

Back to the Chanjale Village Water Tank Proposal Home Page

(continued)

FIGURE 12.5 Continued

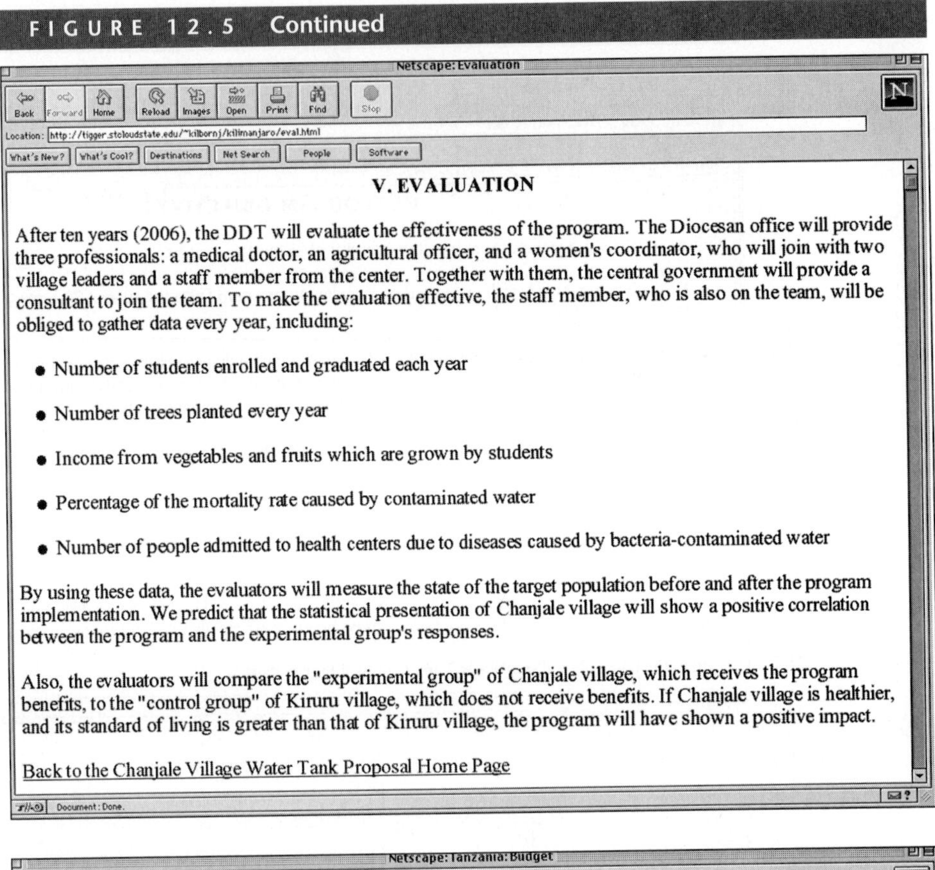

Netscape: Evaluation

Location: http://tigger.stcloudstate.edu/~kilbornj/kilimanjaro/eval.html

V. EVALUATION

After ten years (2006), the DDT will evaluate the effectiveness of the program. The Diocesan office will provide three professionals: a medical doctor, an agricultural officer, and a women's coordinator, who will join with two village leaders and a staff member from the center. Together with them, the central government will provide a consultant to join the team. To make the evaluation effective, the staff member, who is also on the team, will be obliged to gather data every year, including:

- Number of students enrolled and graduated each year
- Number of trees planted every year
- Income from vegetables and fruits which are grown by students
- Percentage of the mortality rate caused by contaminated water
- Number of people admitted to health centers due to diseases caused by bacteria-contaminated water

By using these data, the evaluators will measure the state of the target population before and after the program implementation. We predict that the statistical presentation of Chanjale village will show a positive correlation between the program and the experimental group's responses.

Also, the evaluators will compare the "experimental group" of Chanjale village, which receives the program benefits, to the "control group" of Kiruru village, which does not receive benefits. If Chanjale village is healthier, and its standard of living is greater than that of Kiruru village, the program will have shown a positive impact.

Back to the Chanjale Village Water Tank Proposal Home Page

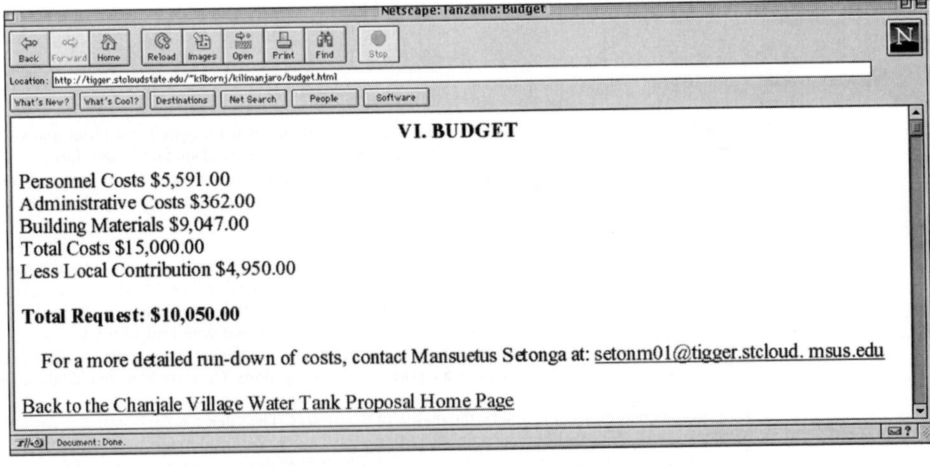

Netscape: Tanzania: Budget

Location: http://tigger.stcloudstate.edu/~kilbornj/kilimanjaro/budget.html

VI. BUDGET

Personnel Costs $5,591.00
Administrative Costs $362.00
Building Materials $9,047.00
Total Costs $15,000.00
Less Local Contribution $4,950.00

Total Request: $10,050.00

For a more detailed run-down of costs, contact Mansuetus Setonga at: setonm01@tigger.stcloud. msus.edu

Back to the Chanjale Village Water Tank Proposal Home Page

- What do you think are the best-case and worst-case scenarios?

Above all, you need to take special care to ensure that you're making honest, responsible projections.

FIGURE 12.5 Continued

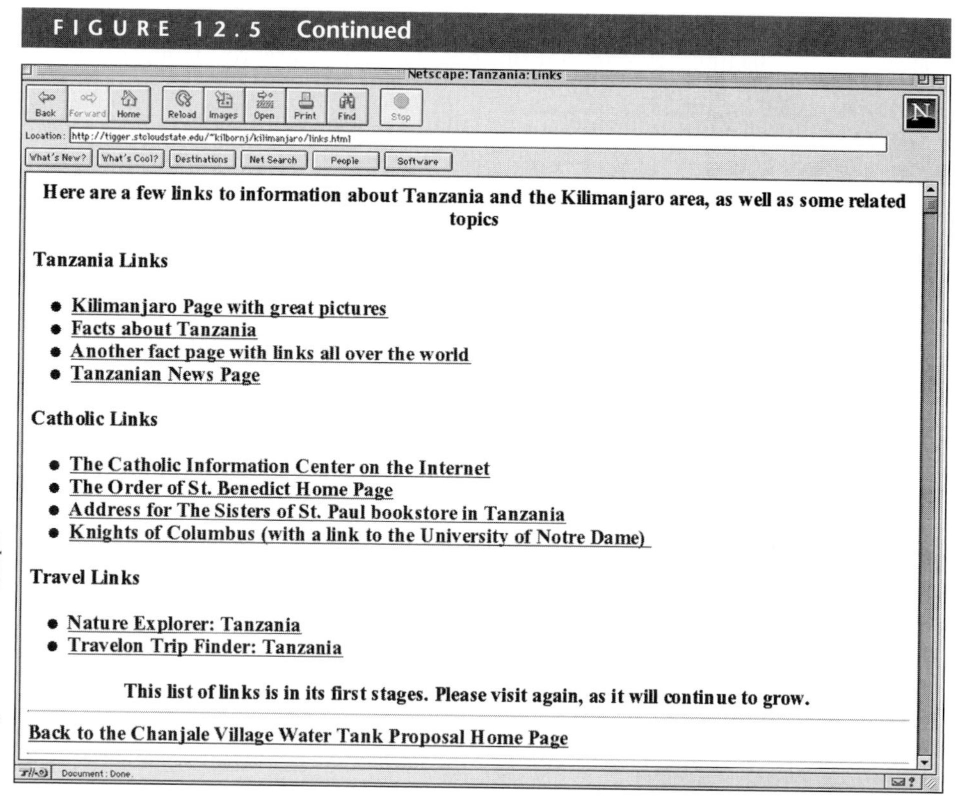
Netscape: Tanzania: Links

Back Forward Home Reload Images Open Print Find Stop

Location: http://tigger.stcloudstate.edu/~kilbornj/kilimanjaro/links.html

What's New? What's Cool? Destinations Net Search People Software

Here are a few links to information about Tanzania and the Kilimanjaro area, as well as some related topics

Tanzania Links

- Kilimanjaro Page with great pictures
- Facts about Tanzania
- Another fact page with links all over the world
- Tanzanian News Page

Catholic Links

- The Catholic Information Center on the Internet
- The Order of St. Benedict Home Page
- Address for The Sisters of St. Paul bookstore in Tanzania
- Knights of Columbus (with a link to the University of Notre Dame)

Travel Links

- Nature Explorer: Tanzania
- Travelon Trip Finder: Tanzania

This list of links is in its first stages. Please visit again, as it will continue to grow.

Back to the Chanjale Village Water Tank Proposal Home Page

Document: Done.

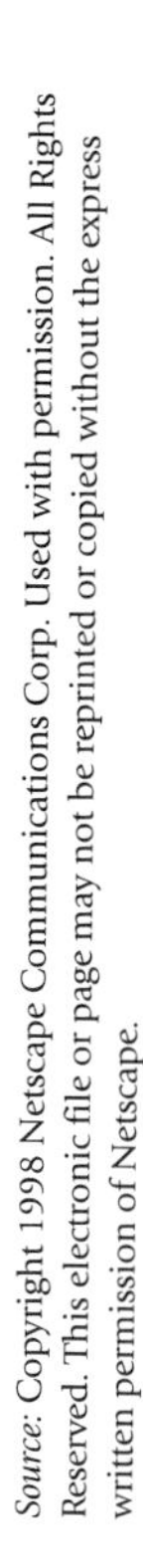

Risks are probably harder to account for and talk about. In fact, there are even risks in *talking* about risks explicitly and directly; it may be much more effective, in most cases, to talk about the factors and strategies in your plan that will help lead to success. Nonetheless, it is useful to think about risks, even if you decide not to focus sharply on them. What are the risks to your readers if they accept your proposal? What are the risks to you? Brainstorm all the worst-case scenarios you can imagine:

- What if you lose a key person in the project?
- What if key equipment fails?
- What if a key assumption is far too optimistic?
- What if the project fails?
- What if the project succeeds? What risky ramifications are possible then?

The idea here is not to scare your readers (and certainly, not yourself) out of this project you want to propose but to be prepared for problems—both during the proposing process and later, during the project itself. How can you control and mitigate the risks for both you and your readers? What can you say here that will give your readers a realistic sense of the risks and help them see your effective strategies for managing risk?

Resources/Constraints. Your resources—time, money, people, vision, ideas, and technology—are not unlimited. If they were, you wouldn't need to write any proposals. The whole energy behind writing the proposal comes from some sense of possibility for the way things could be and a contrasting sense of the way things are. Yet things can't appear hopeless either. You have to be able to demonstrate credibly to your readers that you have sufficient strengths and resources to be able to do what you propose to do. The resources/constraints argument, then, actually serves both the significance argument that lays out the problem and the feasibility argument that begins to lay out the solution. And there is an inevitable tension inherent in the resources/constraints argument. There is always the risk of forcing the argument too far in either direction in the proposal: namely, convincing your readers that your resources are so strong you don't need their contract or help *or* that your resources are so meager you are beyond help.

So, for both your own thinking and your readers' thinking, you need to take a careful inventory of your resources—and any constraints on them—in light of what you want to achieve:

- What is your vision of this state of affairs where you want to arrive?
- What resources will get you there?
- Which of these resources do you have now?
- Which do you need to get from your readers?
- Is it possible that you can get additional resources elsewhere?

Remember, grant proposal readers usually love to see this kind of synergy—a creative combining of their resources with other resources to initiate a program or project that's greater than what the separate resources could achieve alone. Occasionally, though, proposal readers respond unfavorably to this synergy argument. Sometimes, a granting agency, for example, wants to take full credit for a successful project, not having to share the credit with any other agency.

Action

We've already pointed out how vitally the action argument is rooted in the feasibility argument. It follows that when the feasibility argument is weak, the action argument suffers. Proposals often do a good job of helping readers visualize both the current state of affairs and the desired state of affairs, but they don't provide a road map of how the writers propose to get from one state to the other. The action argument, then, needs two elements: (1) a vision of the goal, the benefits you seek, and (2) a plausible argument of how you propose to achieve this goal and its benefits.

Both the vision of your goals and the map of how you propose to achieve them need to be data-rich arguments, as do the feasibility arguments that are their foundation. Proposal readers will not be persuaded if you simply *claim* you can achieve these benefits. Proposal readers are generally sophisticated and skeptical readers, and, as we pointed out earlier, they tend to read with an investor's eye. They want to see the benefits documented, not just asserted. And they want to see reassuring, plausible descriptions of plans for achieving those benefits.

The Vision of the Goals. Proposal readers need a concrete vision of your goals, the benefits that will result if the proposal is approved:

- What good things do you envision if your proposal is successful?
- How will you benefit personally?
- How will your community, company, agency, or other organization benefit?
- How will humanity, in general, benefit? Can you make this argument? Do you want to?
- How idealistic do you want to sound?
- Perhaps most important to your readers, how will they benefit?

In many grant-awarding situations, of course, the readers neither seek nor gain any personal benefit; rather, their mission is to bestow a benefit on some other worthy organization or person through their grant. But they still have a mission and vision and a goal-directed framework in which they read your proposal. In other situations, where you're submitting a business plan or proposing a business relationship, for example, your readers obviously are reading with a self-interested eye. The student proposal (Figure 12.1) and the Kilimanjaro proposal (Figure 12.5) are clearly written for readers who are expected to have the interests of the writers or the organization they represent primarily in mind, while the Barker and Cottrill proposals (Figures 12.2 and 12.3) are clearly written for readers who are reading with a self-interested perspective.

The Map of How You Propose to Achieve the Goals. This is the crucial argument that answers most directly—or fails to answer—your readers' concern as investors:

- How will they get their money's worth?
- How can you *show,* not just assert, that they'll get their money's worth?
- How will you get from where you are now to where you claim you (and your readers) will be afterward? What steps must be taken to get there?
- Can you cite any precedents as evidence? For example, can you show that you've already made progress on this issue? Have other agencies or clients already committed resources to you, and can you point to specific successful outcomes?

Here is where you need to make a convincing, even compelling case by showing who will do what, when, where, how, and with what and whom. You need to show that this plan is not only feasible but is the most desirable of the plausible alternatives, based on the criteria that you argue are the most important. You need to convince your readers that you know what you're talking about, step by step, as you move from before to after. And as you draw this map, you also have to present in vivid, realistic, honest detail the complementary arguments about costs/risks and resources.

Key Criteria in the Benefits Argument. Readers of proposals tend to be intrigued by *novelty* but not necessarily drawn to it. By itself, in fact, novelty may often make proposal readers uneasy. But novelty combined with efficiency and replicability can be a very powerful argument.

Efficiency by itself isn't necessarily a compelling argument, either. The preeminent criterion in most proposal readers' minds is *effectiveness.* Plan A might process a larger number of customers more efficiently than Plan B, but it might not give them the benefits and satisfactions of Plan B, so it's not necessarily the better plan, even though it's more efficient. On the other hand, if both plans yield the same customer satisfaction, Plan A is obviously preferable.

Combined with the other criteria in the benefits/products argument, the *replication* criterion can offer a powerful argument. If you achieve what you propose, can this become a model for other similar ventures? Can you learn or create something that can be exported or replicated and can benefit many others? If you can point to this kind of synergy or multiplier effect in your proposal, you may have a compelling argument.

In the context of risks, we just raised what may have seemed a strange question: What are the risks to you if your proposal is successful? In fact, this risk is real. You need to ask yourself—as an organization and as an individual—whether you have the resources, time, talent, and commitment to do what you promise to do if you get the proposal accepted. You have to be sure you're not promising more than you can deliver. *Be careful what you wish for—you may get it!*

Conventions

We've already mentioned that you should pay particular attention to your readers' expectations relative to conventions. The RFP, if there is one available, should give you a good sense of the conventions of organization, style, presentation of arguments and evidence, and self-expression that your readers are likely to expect. Remember that readers of proposals are likely to be busy readers, and they will likely look for key information in particular formats in particular places. If your readers have these expectations about formal conventions and you opt to express this information in your own creative variations of format and vocabulary, you run a risk that they will not even see your key information or arguments. On the other hand, if you know your readers have a much more laissez-faire attitude about these conventions, then you may decide that the risks of some creative variations on conventions are warranted.

Frequently Encountered Conventions

Depending on the situation, many elements of proposals are not only expected but, in fact, required. For example, you almost always need to buttress your resources part of your feasibility argument by attaching resumes of your key people and a financial statement, perhaps even audited by an independent certified public accountant (CPA), showing that your organization has the financial resources to complete your proposed project. If your proposal is a business plan, a variety of financial statements and projections will be required. If equipment and physical plant are crucial elements in the success of your project, you will be expected to attach inventories and perhaps even blueprints and photographs.

If you are submitting a proposal that entails research on human subjects or animals, you will almost certainly have to attach a certification of approval by an institutional review board (IRB), which evaluates proposals to assure that research projects do not endanger people or animals and that researchers fully disclose the possibilities of risk to their subjects and design the research to mitigate those risks. If you are submitting a proposal to undertake a substantial project for a government agency, you will likely be required to attach a performance bond that insures the agency against your failure to complete the project. If you are submitting a proposal for a project in your official capacity as a member of an organization, either public or private, you will probably be required to attach a letter from your chief executive officer, certifying that the organization knows about your proposal, approves it, and is committed as an institution to supporting your project if you receive the award or contract you're seeking. If your proposed project will require the support or collaboration of organizations or people outside your own or if it will have an effect on people outside your organization, you will be expected to attach letters certifying the support of these people and organizations. And if the expertise or financial resources of any of these people or organizations are relevant to the success of your project, you will be expected to attach resumes and financial statements—and perhaps even performance bonds—from these people, too.

Also consider what procedural conventions your organization has for a proposal-writing situation like this:

- Are you expected to collaborate or confer in the preparation of the proposal?
- If so, who is in this collaboration/consultation loop?
- What are people's respective roles?
- Who's in charge of what on this project?
- Who has editorial veto power over the project?
- Whose voice will be the voice of your organization?
- Are there conventions for the way you frame the problem and solution, lay out the arguments, organize the evidence, and express your personal and organizational character in this kind of report?
- For example, does your organization have a corporate style manual?
- Are there samples of past proposals available as models or even templates?
- Can someone with more experience give you advice?

In the absence of a specific proposal template—or even if a specific template is called for in an RFP—you may want to keep in mind the generic organizational convention of problem/solution/rationale, with the rationale being a discussion of alternatives, constraints, costs and resources (including your personnel) and an explanation of your plans, processes, and timeline (with mileposts) for achieving your proposed solution.

The template shown in Figure 12.6 is the general sequence of arguments usually followed in a proposal. But there may be good reasons for you to modify the sequence for a specific purpose. For instance, do you want to present your solution last? You might do so for a couple of reasons. Maybe you know your readers expect to find it there or will be skeptical of your solution if they don't see your rationale first. Do you want to present your solution first? You might if you know your readers are already familiar with the problem. Background/problem/solution/rationale? Problem/solution/rationale/background? Depending on the circumstances, any one of these variations might be the most appropriate organizational scheme.

Other Conventions

In Chapter 10, we discussed the conventions of document design at length, so this section is intended as just a quick checklist specifically for proposals. (For more information on conventions of document design, see Chapter 10.)

- **Cover.** The cover, of course, is the first thing your readers will see, so your proposal needs to "dress for success." This doesn't necessarily mean you should bind it in the fanciest, most expensive, most ostentatious way possible. In fact, depending on your situation and your readers, it could mean just the opposite. Some governmental agencies strongly prefer—and specify—no cover at all, other than a cover sheet with specific information identifying you, the RFP, and so on. Certainly, if the RFP or other suggestions from your readers provide any guidance, you should scrupulously follow those cues.

  The length of the document and the way your readers are likely to read it should help you decide, too. An inexpensive plastic comb binding is perhaps

FIGURE 12.6 Generic Organizational Convention for Proposals

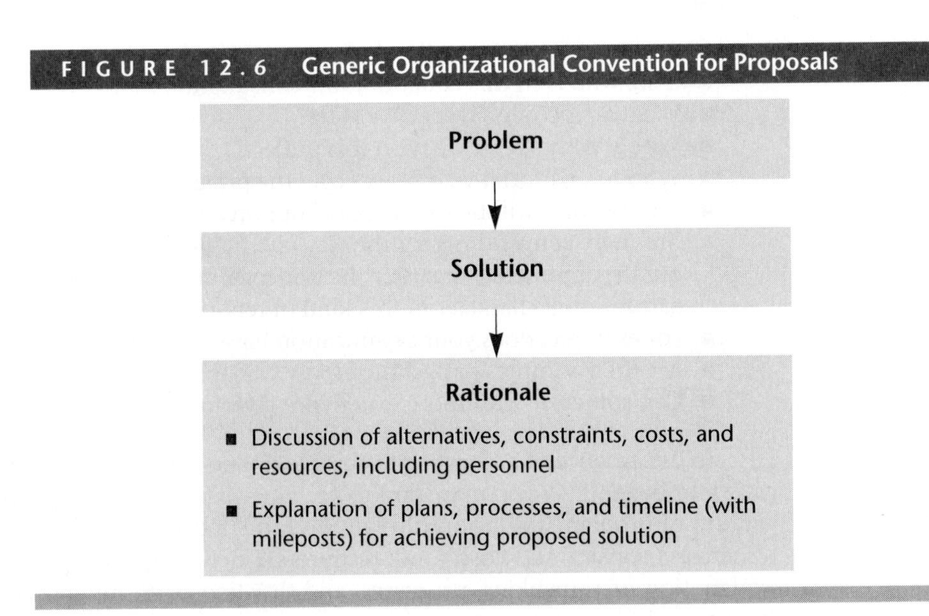

most popular for proposals. Comb bindings are available in a variety of sizes that can accommodate a variety of document lengths, are relatively easy to assemble, and are easy to handle. They also allow readers to lay the document flat while reading. If the proposal is a large document with extensive appendices and if both you and your readers will likely be adding notes and other items to the original proposal, then a large three-ring binder might be most appropriate. Additional possibilities range from a simple staple in the upper-left corner to a document stitched and bound at a print shop.

- **Paper versus other media.** In some cases, it is now possible to submit proposals via other media: FAX and e-mail, in particular. And we have already referred to the Kilimanjaro Water Project proposal (Figure 12.5), which was developed as a web page. As always, you should follow any instructions in an RFP or other guidelines from your readers. But your general goal here is readability and economy. For body text, a serif style font, such as Times Roman or Palatino, is more readable than a sans serif style, such as Helvetica, so in general, we recommend using a serif font. With modern word-processing and desktop-publishing software and with the high resolutions of most laser printers (and even many inkjet printers), you can produce highly readable, attractive proposal documents in your office or home. And with the availablility of fast, high-quality duplication equipment and services, you can also reproduce them yourself. (See Chapter 10 for more information.)
- **Cover letter.** Unless there is specific instruction to the contrary, you should include a cover letter that helps establish the context of your proposal and summarizes it, as well. If it's appropriate, your letter should also help clarify or affirm the grounds of your relationship with the main reader of the proposal or the relationship between your organizations. Your letter should almost certainly say something about your enthusiasm for and commitment to the project you're proposing and, if appropriate, about your goodwill toward your readers. Of course, if you're writing your proposal to a governmental agency that uses an impersonal, quantified process of blind review by anonymous readers (who don't know whose proposal they're reading and evaluating), then this friendly kind of style in the cover letter wouldn't be appropriate. (See Chapter 5 if you'd like to review general strategies of reader analysis and self-expression in letters.)
- **Executive summary.** Keep in mind the scenario of the harried reader who's looking for immediate answers, identifying the essential issues, their significance, the feasibility of your proposed solutions, and your overall credibility. Your executive summary should answer all these questions and also point the reader efficiently to the places in the proposal where the details are located.
- **Table of contents and numbered pages.** Even if your proposal is only two pages, we suggest numbering them. And when the length of your proposal reaches just eight pages or so, we suggest that you create a table of contents. (For more information, see Chapter 10.)

- **Appendix.** Much of the detailed evidence in your proposal can probably go in an appendix—your background material, for example, if it is extensive, or lengthy documentation of your investigative process or analytical or statistical procedures. Extensive biographical information about a number of people, for example, would also be appropriate material for an appendix, unless there's specific reason to move it to the body of the proposal.
- **Graphics.** First, check to see what typographic conventions are available to you for improving the readability of your document. Do the style guidelines of the RFP or other instructions allow informative headers, boldfaced type for headers and subheaders, and creative use of vertical and horizontal white space to clarify and emphasize chunks of text? Are you permitted to use markers such as bullets to highlight items in lists, callouts in margins to dramatize key points, and other graphic manipulations of the text? Do the issues, information, and arguments lend themselves to graphic presentation? Would tables, pie graphs, bar graphs, timelines, calendars, schematics, formulas, architectural drawings, blueprints, photographs, line drawings, or other graphics summarize the issues, information, and arguments vividly and effectively? (For good ideas on the effective use of graphics, see Chapter 10.)
- **Sentence-level conventions.** You should use conventional sentence structures that enhance clarity and directness. (For helpful guidelines for identifying and fixing problems at the sentence level, see Part VI, The Business Writer's Quick Reference.)
- **Diction.** What conventions govern the level of specialized or technical language in this situation? How do these conventions interact with your perception of the needs and expertise of the various readers of your report? Do conventions allow you to provide intext explanations and definitions of difficult or unusual terms? Are you sure your readers will understand your terms? Are you sure you're using the terms correctly?

With proposals, as with resumes and employment letters, breaking conventions of grammar, spelling, and usage can seriously damage your readers' confidence in you and make it difficult for you to get a sympathetic reading. So, make sure your proposal is mechanically clean and correct.

Expression

Expression of your own character—your interest in the problems and issues you've identified and your commitment to making progress toward a solution—is vital in a proposal. You modulate this expression depending on whether you read the proposing situation as *high ethos,* which calls for providing a vivid sense of your personal engagement in the proposed project, or *low ethos,* which calls for muting your personal engagement and concentrating instead on the technical details and, by implication, your technical competence. For an example of a high-ethos situation, see the RFP in

Activity 1, requesting proposals for a collaborative project among colleagues in a class. Here, the reader is clearly interested in the proposers' personal engagement and personal stake in the project. The writer of the RFP wants to know that the proposers see the significance and feasibility of the project and can foresee personal benefits that will motivate them to appropriate action. The student proposal in Figure 12.1 (pp. 512–513) that responds to this RFP responds in a relatively high-ethos mode that is appropriately consistent with the RFP. Note the strong sense of the presence of a writer or writers behind the Kilimanjaro Water Project proposal, as well (Figure 12.5, pp. 526–533). In other situations—especially in those where you may have made similar proposals to the same reader that have resulted in successful projects—the reader probably assumes your personal engagement in the project and is simply interested in its technical dimensions (e.g., time to completion, cost, risks and constraints, etc.).

Proposal Guidelines

The process of reviewing your goals in a proposal-writing situation is so important, we think, that we advise using the following guidelines or designing your own:

- What do you hope will happen as a result of your writing this proposal? What, specifically, do you want your readers or their organization to do for you or your organization? Who will do what when, where, and how?
- What will you be obligated to do if your readers accept this proposal? Who will do what when, where, and how? Are you sure you can do what you promise to? Can you afford this commitment of time, people, and other resources?
- Are these benefits and obligations consistent with your overall, long-term goals?
- In balance, is this a good mix of benefits and obligations?
- What if this proposal is not accepted? Is the negotiation and clarification of your organizational goals and mission worth the effort invested in the proposal? What other potential venues exist for arguing the case you want to make?

Keep in mind that your proposal should match your short- and long-term goals and help actualize the priorities, mission, and values of the organization. In fact, if the RFP is not a good match with your organization's goals and mission, you shouldn't write a proposal. Ideally, your proposal should enable you and others in your network to deal with issues of significance to the organization in a timely and efficient manner and with a reasonable commitment of human and physical resources. In sum, your proposal should complement other projects and the day-to-day work of your organization. It should be just one document in a rich context of other documents, projects, people, and goals, all of which are moving toward fulfillment of the organization's vision.

WRITING CHECKLIST

The following guidelines will help you design proposals that get you to "yes." For any of these guidelines, remember the superordinate guideline: Disregard *any* of this advice if it would cause you to do something that's inappropriate or silly for your situation.

☑ Proposals

- You need a clear sense of your goals so you don't compromise your organization's mission or your own values and priorities.
- Review the RFP carefully; *don't* submit the proposal if its requirements can't be reconciled with your priorities and mission.
- Make sure that your immediate goals are in synch with your long-term goals and values and that the project and its goals offer synergies with other projects and goals.
- Determine what costs/risks are involved in this proposal, including time as well as human and physical resources.
- Remember that proposals exist in a rich context of other projects, people, and goals; they are not isolated and cannot by themselves achieve their goals.
- Learn as much as you can about prospective readers through published guidelines, RFPs, examples of proposals previously funded, and direct consultation with readers.
- You need to convince readers that there is a match between your goals and theirs, and you need to provide evidence that you can achieve your stated goals, that your ideas are virtuous as well as practical, and that your project is a good investment.
- Simplify your document to make it easier reading for harried business readers by providing a proposal summary and by using redundant road maps and traffic signals.
- Answer the readers' likely questions about the essential issues: what can be done, the costs and risks involved, resulting benefits, and your ability to do what you propose.
- Show that you understand the situation as your readers do.
- Discuss only plausible alternatives.
- Provide detailed financial information, defining the areas of uncertainty in your analyses and projections.
- Discuss risks to help readers get a realistic sense of possible problems and your plans for managing them.
- Consider resources and constraints to show readers that you have the resources and strengths to do what you propose to do.

- Include a careful inventory of your resources and constraints on them in view of what you propose to accomplish; consider what resources might be available elsewhere as well as what your readers might provide.
- Clarify what should be done by whom and how.
- Provide a vision of the goals and benefits likely to result from the proposed action.
- Show that your plan is not only feasible but the most plausible of the alternatives.
- Provide any elements required by the RFP: resumes of key people, financial statements and projections, details about equipment or the physical plant, approvals for human subjects research, performance bonds, support letters, and the like.
- Consider using a conventional problem/solution/rationale organization, discussing alternatives, constraints, costs, and resources as well as explaining plans, processes, and a timeline for achieving your proposed solution.
- Include all of the conventional elements of proposals: a cover, binding, cover letter, executive summary, table of contents, appendix, formatting and typographical elements, and graphics, as appropriate.
- Be clear and direct, use any specialized or technical language appropriate for readers, and follow exactly the conventions of grammar, spelling, and usage.
- Express your interest in the problems and issues of the proposal and your commitment to solving them.
- Decide whether it's a high-ethos situation, calling for vivid presentation of your personal engagement in the project, or a low-ethos context, requiring that you mute personal engagement and stress technical details and competence.

ACTIVITIES AND PROJECTS

1. Find out what sorts of resources are available on the web for organizations wishing to develop business plans. Report your findings in an oral presentation to your colleagues.
2. Interview someone from the unit or office in your university that supports grant-writing activities. Ask about the sorts of organizations that provide funding for special projects in your field. What sorts of projects tend to be funded and why? Also talk about what characterizes an excellent grant application, and discuss strategies or processes for writing successful grants. Write an informal report to students in your field, informing them about what you have learned through your interview.
3. Interview someone who is currently in a job you would someday like to have to find out how proposals are used in his or her organization and how he or she is involved in producing or implementing these proposals.

4. The proposal for the Style Guide Development Project (see Figure 12.7) responds to a request to the writer, Kathy Sole, to coordinate development of a style manual that will establish document and publication standards for the California Student Aid Commission. Consider this report in terms of conventions—for framing the problem and solution, for laying out the arguments, for organizing the evidence, as well as conventions for document design. In addition, consider the needs and interests of the organization that this proposal considers and the ways in which the proposed project might help to actualize the priorities, mission, and values of the organization.

5. Find an example of a proposal or business plan, and bring it to class for small-group discussion. Be prepared to explain the things you like and dislike about the proposal or business plan and why you feel that way.

6. Find an RFP in your field. Review the requirements outlined, and talk with a small group of your colleagues about how this RFP would shape and otherwise affect how a proposal would be designed and developed. What sorts of goals does this RFP seem to encourage? What does the RFP tell you about readers' needs and interests? What sorts of arguments, data, and claims does this RFP encourage, and what sorts of arguments, data, and claims does it discourage and why? What conventional elements does the RFP require?

7. As an individual or a group, write a proposal responding to the RFP you located for Activity 5.

8. As an individual or a team, propose a research project or report that will be a major assignment for your class. Select a project or report that will enable you to learn something that will be useful in your career preparation or in your job right now.

9. With several colleagues, write a proposal that responds to a problem in an organization (e.g., on your campus, in your community, or on your job). Address the proposal to a reader or readers who are in a position to act upon the recommendations that you make, and do the research needed to produce appropriate data to bolster your argument.

10. With several colleagues, imagine the particulars of a business that you would someday like to own. Then, write a business plan to take to prospective lenders or venture capitalists for the purpose of getting start-up money.

FIGURE 12.7 Sample Proposal

California Student Aid Commission

and

EDFUND

A Service of The California Student Aid Commission

Proposal for:

Style Guide Development Project

Submitted to:

Chris Montoya
Deputy Director

Roland Byers
Deputy Director

Maria Paulsen
Chief

Pat Noland
Associate Governmental Program Analyst

By:

Kathy Sole
WriteSource

March 17, 1997

(continued)

FIGURE 12.7 Continued

Background

A primary component of the California Student Aid Commission's Communications Plan is the development of document and publication standards for the agency and its auxiliary corporation. These standards will be compiled into a style guide to be distributed to all Commission units. The style guide will serve as a foundation for all internal and external communications, will standardize communications within the Commission, and will enable the Commission to deliver consistent, professional messages to its external customers.

A considerable amount of preliminary work has already been accomplished with regard to the style guide's development:

- Deputies have evaluated Commission communications from an overall perspective.
- Outside consultants Dr. Roger Carlson and Susan Daniels, Inc., have provided input on the strengths, weaknesses, and purposes of various Commission materials and have made recommendations for improvement.
- The Financial Aid Services Division has revamped Commission Special Alerts, Policy Bulletins, and Operations Memos to utilize a standard format and consistent language.
- Editorial decisions made during the development of the Lender Procedural Manual the CalSOAP Manual, and the pending revision to the Cal Grant Manual have been documented.
- Alice Myers of the Communications Department has gathered examples of style guides from other organizations and document samples from throughout the agency.
- The Training Department has identified a number of writing reference materials and specific writing needs within the Commission.

On March 12, 1997, Chris Montoya, Pat Noland, Ann Nguyen, and Kathy Sole (technical writing and editing consultant) met to discuss the development and implementation of the style guide. At that meeting, Kathy Sole was asked to coordinate various aspects of the project and to propose a structure, methodology and time line for the style guide's development. This proposal follows.

FIGURE 12.7 Continued

Goals

The California Student Aid Commission's and EDFUND's objectives in developing this style guide are as follows:

- To improve the quality of Commission documents
- To develop a consistent, professional image in communications sent outside the Commission
- To develop standards for communication with one another within the Commission
- To provide answers to routine questions and to tailor document formats and English usage and grammar rules to the Commission's communication needs
- To determine and communicate the preferred style when more than one correct document or publication style exists
- To save Commission staff time spent repeatedly making decisions about document and publication format, grammar, punctuation, style, and language usage.

Rationale

Commission and EDFUND departments and units produce different types of documents for different audiences and different purposes. However, the Commission needs to speak with one voice to its lender, school and student customers and to present a consistent and professional image in all its publications. The number of different writers and subject matter experts throughout the organization necessitates documentation and publication standards to avoid confusion and to present a unified image to customers. These standards are also expected to assist Commission and EDFUND staff by resolving ambiguous style issues and allowing them to borrow information from other units' documents without having to make extensive style revisions.

It is envisioned that the style guide will be distributed in a three-ring binder for ease in revising specific pages. The guide is expected to be disseminated throughout all Commission and EDFUND units and formally adopted as the definitive source for document and publication guidelines.

(continued)

FIGURE 12.7 Continued

Approach

In the initial stages of developing the Commission style guide, three considerations are of paramount importance:

- The methodology for developing the guide
- The tone and degree of prescriptive language the guide employs
- The scope of the guide and the issues covered

Each of these considerations is briefly discussed below.

Methodology

To ensure that all relevant issues are considered and that the needs and concerns of all units within the Commission are addressed, it is imperative that the style guide be developed by a collaborative process. It is suggested the process begin by conducting focused interviews with various units to identify key issues and concerns. These interviews would be followed by designation of representatives from each unit (selected by unit managers) who would serve as members of a style guide task force and as liaisons for their units.

The goals and processes of the project must be clearly delineated to the task force, with an objective of achieving consensus and determining standards everyone can live with.

This task force would initially meet twice monthly and would have responsibility for identifying documents and publications within their unit, communicating to their units and to other task force members style guide issues and concerns, and achieving consensus on style guide standards. Kathy Sole will facilitate these task force meetings.

In addition, initial drafts of the style guide should be sent to individual units, giving them adequate time to revise and respond. The task force would then review this feedback for incorporation into the guide, and any conflicts will be discussed with groups affected by the decisions.

It is hoped this collaborative process will help develop teamwork among units as they work toward a common goal, assist in support for the guide among all units, and ensure that no units have equipment problems or other issues that would result in their inability to conform to the standards set forth in the guide.

This methodology is intended to help ensure that the style guide will be a dynamic document and not relegated to a shelf to gather dust.

FIGURE 12.7 Continued

Tone

It is suggested that particular attention be paid to the tone of the style guide and the degree to which it prescribes rules versus suggests preferences. As we know, the English language and usage guidelines are fluid. In some instances, hard and fast rules for usage and format will need to be adopted. In other instances, the style guide should suggest preferences and allow for employee discretion.

Project Scope

It is suggested the Commission's style guide incorporate the following key areas, which are detailed on the following page in the section entitled Overall Style Guide Components.

Communication Protocols
Document and Publication Design and Production Standards
Writing and Editing Standards

Once the style guide (or key sections) have been completed, a key component of the project would be to conduct sessions for staff in how to use the guide and any accompanying references.

(continued)

FIGURE 12.7 Continued

Style Guide Components

Below are suggested topics in the key areas identified under Project Scope above:

Communication Protocols

- Privacy, confidentiality, and libel issues
- Unit document and publication responsibilities
- Commission requirements for document approval and editorial review
- Document production process guidelines and time frames
- Form numbering and document control processes
- Protocols for use of memos, letters, and electronic communications for communicating information or reaching agreements among units
- Protocols and etiquette for use of GroupWise™, Internet, World Wide Web, and other electronic communications

Document and Publication Design and Production Standards

- Standards for consistency in appearance and format
- Templates for formatting memos, letters, reports, manuals, and other documents
- Document organization guidelines to ensure that publications serve users' needs
- Standards for document titles, headers, footers, and levels of headings to allow users to familiarize themselves quickly with the document and to simplify revisions
- Guidelines for proper display of Commission logos and corporate identity components to ensure consistent Commission identity and protection of copyrights and trademarks
- Standards for typographic display (e.g., font sizes, bold, italic, underline, bullets)
- Formats and labels for vertical lists, figures, and tables
- Use of color and preferred binding methods
- Checklists for document or publication preparation

FIGURE 12.7 Continued

Commission Writing and Editing Standards

It is suggested that a standard style guide or English grammar and punctuation guide be adopted and incorporated into the Commission's style guide, by reference. In addition, the Commission style guide would address the following specific issues:

- Basic guidelines for document preparation (professional responsibilities; basic writing and editing guidelines, and Commission writing style preferences)
- Uniform industry terminology and language
- Generally accepted English usage and the Commission's preference in ambiguous format, usage, grammar, and style situations
- Acronyms and jargon
- Abbreviations and standards for prefixes and suffixes
- Compounds and word division preferences
- Grammar guidelines and common errors
- Spelling, hyphenation, and capitalization preferences for selected words and phrases
- Punctuation preferences, if alternative acceptable methods exist
- Case sensitivity
- Gender-neutral language usage
- Spelling out numbers or use of numerals, decimals, fractions, and percentages
- Recording money, dates, department names, addresses, and telephone numbers
- Standard Proofreading Marks
- Models of well-written documents
    - In order not to "talk down" to employees or to clutter the guide with standard English grammar, punctuation, and usage rules, I suggest we assume staff members have basic writing and English skills and establish standards for situations that are debatable, ambiguous, or particularly troublesome. If these basic skills are not present, I recommend the training department conduct classes in specific areas, as needed.

(continued)

FIGURE 12.7 Continued

Task Force Issues
The following issues should be addressed at initial meetings of the Style Guide Task Force:

1. **Target Audience and Specific Objectives**
   a. Who is the target audience for the guide—managers, analysts, technical staff?
   b. What is the objective of the style guide—do we want a 2,000 page combination writing handbook, style guide, usage guide, abridged dictionary, production specifications handbook, word list for spelling, compounding, and abbreviations—or just a quick reference guide?
   c. Should the guide include proformas of all document types and other visual elements?

2. **Other References**
   a. Identify the types of reference works that will supplement the Commission style guide and be incorporated into the style guide, by reference. Possible references might include the following:
      - English language dictionary for spelling, compounding, and usage guidelines
      - Published style guide references for punctuation and grammar issues
      - Technical guides for engineering specifications or other technical document preparation
      - Guides to graphic arts, publishing conventions, and corporate identification

   b. Assess these reference works and determine where they meet the Commission's needs and where they do not
   c. Establish policies regarding how these other references will be used. Will they be regarded as authorities or suggested references? Will the style guide serve as a supplement to the body of literature available on writing and editing, or will it be the only authority for style that employees use?

FIGURE 12.7 Continued

Style Guide Development Project

3. Communication Types and Priorities

a. Memos

b. Letters

c. Reports

d. Manuals

e. Internal training materials

f. External workshop material

9. Commission policies and procedures

h. Newsletters

i. Electronic Communications (GroupWise™, E-mail, World Wide Web, FAPS documents, PCFAPS documents)

4. Style Guide Organization and Development

a. Consider ease of use regarding documentation (alphabetic or subject matter versus by document type or other organization scheme)

b. Edit carefully to make sure the style guide follows its own rules

c. Communicate the task force's decision-making process and how firm or flexible its decisions will be

d. Decide who will make the ultimate determination of appropriate style in the event of differences of opinion that cannot be resolved

e. Establish a process for submitting changes, acknowledging receipt, and filing them for the next style guide update

f. Determine a schedule for style guide updates

California Student Aid Commission 9 March 17, 1997

FIGURE 12.7 Continued

Style Guide Development Project

Schedule of Activities and Calendar

Obviously, a project of this magnitude will not be accomplished overnight. On the other hand, this type of project can grow beyond the original scope intended and consume an inordinate amount of time and resources. The Commission has a need to move this project forward and to achieve uniformity among its documents and publications, in some areas, as early as April 1, 1997. To balance the scope of the work with the need to achieve definitive results, it is proposed the project be rolled out in phases, as outlined below and on the attached Gantt chart.*

Phase One

- Establish corporate identity standards and identification of communication protocols and policies that can be determined without collaborative processes, e.g., EdFund and Commission logo usage guidelines, Commission communication policies, legal requirements)
- Communicate style guide project to management; outline the guide's purpose, rationale, and approach; and request project liaisons/task force members from each unit

Phase Two

- Develop Style Guide Task Force guidelines and style sheets (written summaries of style decisions that must be made and will apply to a particular document. The style sheets will ensure that the guide is consistent within itself.)
- Designate Task Force Members
- Convene Task Force and establish project timetables and tasks

Phase Three

- Determine style guide components and organization, prioritize these components, and implement the development process. This phase will include project schedules with deadlines for completion and milestone dates.

Summary

This proposal is an initial attempt to identify the various elements and considerations for development of a Commission style guide and to propose a plan to advance this project. Areas may have been omitted that should have been included and, perhaps, other areas have been identified that go beyond the scope envisioned for the guide. Your feedback on this proposal is sincerely welcomed.

Kathy Sole
WriteSource

California Student Aid Commission **10** **March 17, 1997**

*The chart is not included in this sample.

Chapter 13

Formal Reports

Developing Your Report with GRACE

A problem well stated is a problem half solved.

—Charles F. Kettering

When do you need to write a report? In some ways, this seems a silly question. But the fact is, it's not always clear when you need to write a report. And because writing a good report takes significant effort and resources (including your valuable time) that could be invested in other projects, it's worth asking whether you really need to write a report in a particular situation.

Sometimes, the need is obvious. Perhaps you have contracted with a client to write an environmental assessment of the client's worksite and have promised the report by the first of the month. Maybe your company is required by the Securities and Exchange Commission (SEC) to submit an annual financial report and narrative. Or perhaps your agency is required by law to submit an annual report to the governor. In these cases, a report is clearly not optional—it's mandatory. And the length and format may not be optional, either. Both may be clearly and specifically prescribed, right down to the details of how to word subheadings in the table of contents.

So, when do you know you should write a report even though you're not bound by contract or law to do so? As the title to this part (Part V) of the book suggests, one test for the need to write a report is to ask whether a letter or memo is enough in this situation. If it's not, then you probably need to write a full-dress report, complete with all the formatting conventions we talked about in Chapter 10.

Developing Your Report with GRACE

Goals

What is your primary goal, and how do you know?

You always put yourself and your colleagues at serious risk, even in a routine reporting situation, if you define your report-writing assignment as "just getting the thing done." It is vital to think about the historical and organizational context of this report. In a very real sense, you are creating a vision for your readers, your department, and your organization when you write this report. In some cases, this report may be the only vision its readers have of you and your colleagues. In other cases, it will stand alongside other reports and documents that have come before and after it, and it will constitute, along with these other documents, the historical reality of what your organization is and is becoming. So, you have a significant responsibility to represent yourself, your colleagues, your interests, and your work fully, fairly, accurately, and persuasively.

◣ MAXIM 1

Reports exist in organizations to solve problems, fulfill needs, and capitalize on opportunities.

Your goal in writing a report should be to solve a problem, to fulfill or find a new opportunity, to create a new concept or product, or to satisfy some other need. Your task is to identify this context of need/opportunity.

What is the function of your report?

Within this context of problems, needs, and opportunities, what is the function of your report? We're really talking here about a special application of the process we talked about in Chapter 2 under the heading What Is My Writing Task? Identifying the essential problem to be solved here is the key to defining your writing task. It's the key to answering the initial question of whether you should even be writing a report, and it's also the key to answering the question of what kind of report you should be writing: Should you be writing a progress report? A researched position paper? A final project report? The answer depends largely on how you understand your problem and its situation and context.

The Context and Goals of a Progress Report. The progress report can have the most complex situation and goals of all reports. It is looking in two directions at once: back on what has been done and forward to what is yet to be done. In the sense that it is forward looking, it shares the same goals as a proposal. In fact, it is a kind of second chapter to the proposal's first chapter. In the proposal, you made the following arguments: "Here's the problem, here's what we propose to do about it, and here's what we need from you, the reader, to help us do it." In the progress report, you first recapitulate the situation you began with: "Remember, this was the problem, this was what we said we'd do, and this is what you gave us to do it." Next, you tell what's happened since you started: "Here's what we did, here's what it cost, and here are the results." Then, you announce/propose further actions to move toward successfully completing the project. This process is fairly routine if you haven't encountered any unexpected obstacles or shortcuts along the way. (Note Maxim 3, on p. 559, about dynamic situations.) But even in a routine situation, you can't afford to get complacent. In recounting what you've done and what it's cost, you must give a convincing account of yourself and the organization you represent. You must give the specific details your readers need to be able to visualize, credibly, the progress you've made. This is, after all, a *progress* report.

If something unexpected has happened along the way, either good or bad, you need to report this development, analyze its significance, and make appropriate arguments on behalf of the changes you propose in light of the unexpected development. This is the *proposal* aspect of the progress report. It may well be that you need to propose a fundamental reconsideration of the project. At one extreme, you may want to argue that the project should be abandoned; at the other, you may want to argue that your readers should increase their investment in the project manyfold and give you many more resources. The changed circumstances present a new set of problems and opportunities different from when you began the project, and one of your crucial goals in the progress report is to begin an informed problem-solving, need-meeting, opportunity-seizing exchange with your readers.

The Context and Goals of a Final Project Report. If the progress report is, in effect, a second chapter following the proposal, the final project report is, then, the third chapter. The initial documents that began the project (e.g., proposals, contracts, bidding specifications, etc.) and the intervening documents (e.g., letters, memos, progress reports, etc.) provide the textual background for the final report, and the project work itself provides the rest of the context. Your goals in general are several: to make sure your reader recalls and understands the context and the requirements of the project and the report; to make clear that you also understand the context and the requirements; and to demonstrate that you have completed the project as you said you would do. It's possible that your final project report may have some proposal-like elements and goals, as well, and you should consider carefully whether you have this kind of goal. In other words, does this project, even though it is now completed, represent one stage in a larger project or series of related projects, and should you be involved in that larger picture?

The Context and Goals of a Researched Position Paper. Your goals in writing a researched position paper will most likely be primarily persuasive goals, and they are most likely to be aimed at a wide, heterogeneous group of readers. Unlike the progress report and the final project report, the researched position paper may not even be requested or expected by its readers. The position that you or your organization holds may even be in conflict with that of your primary readers. So, if your goal is to effect change in the minds of your readers and even persuade them to redefine their own best interests, the arguments you build in your position paper will have a heavy load to carry, and they will need to be able to withstand hostile scrutiny.

MAXIM 2

All problems are problems for *people*.

A problem really isn't a problem unless it's a problem *for somebody.* Problems, needs, and opportunities don't exist until some person feels a gap between what is and what ought to be or what might be. So, figure out as much as you can about who is touched or ought to be touched by this problem/need/opportunity. In other words, you can't think about your goals without thinking about your readers and others who are affected by them. Think about your own personal and organizational solar system.

Report Goals and Problems

Who else has a stake in this problem/need/opportunity?

Try to identify everyone else who has a stake in this problem/need/opportunity. How do their needs and their resources fit with your own, and how can they help you achieve your goals, both in producing this report and in making it more effective after it's produced? Who are potential fellow problem solvers, readers, opponents, and allies?

> **◣ MAXIM 3**
>
> **Because organizations and their people are dynamic, their problems also are dynamic.**

You need to remember that almost as soon as you finish analyzing your situation, your work will be out of date, at least in some minor detail, because the situation will have already changed. So, keep recycling these questions and the GRACE benchmarks, and stay alert to the need to adjust your goals as your understanding of your situation, your readers, your arguments, and the conventions of the situation deepens and matures.

What are your goals in this situation?

Now, once again considering your problem and its historical, organizational, and human context and reflecting on its implications and ramifications in this context, take another, closer look at your goals:

- What is this problem/need/opportunity? Why do you care about it? Why should you care about it? What's your relationship to the problem—are you taking it on voluntarily, or are you required to work on it? Can you opt out of continuing to work on the problem at some point, or are you mandated to stay on it all the way to the end?
- Where did the problem come from? Is it one you've discovered on your own, or does it originate with someone else inside or outside your organization? Did it get assigned to you as part of your regular duties? Did it get assigned to you on some ad hoc basis because of a special need? Is it part of a recurring process (e.g., a semiannual personnel review or a monthly project report), or does it appear to be a one-time project?
- Analyze the problem. How big is it? Can you divide it into some natural segments? Would having smaller segments to analyze make the problem more manageable? Do some of the elements appear to be more amenable to solutions than others? If so, would these be good entry points for you to engage the problem in

your report or to advise your readers to begin to engage the problem? Do some elements of the problem seem clearly unsolvable? Do these render the entire problem unsolvable, or does it appear possible to satisfice—to work around these unsolvable elements and achieve a partial solution of the problem?

- What else do you know about the history and background of this problem, need, or opportunity? What key events have contributed to the situation? Which of these events seem to have exacerbated the problem, and which seem to have ameliorated it? Who have been the key players in the past, and what have their contributions been—for good or for ill? How might you use this historical information and these key people to move toward a current understanding and satisfactory resolution of the problem?
- Have you seen this problem/opportunity before—or perhaps others similar to it? Have other people in your professional universe—colleagues, clients, or others—seen problems like this one? On the one hand, there's no point in reinventing the wheel; it's inefficient to re-solve a problem that's already been satisfactorily solved. But discovering a proven solution to a similar problem clarifies your goals and gives you powerful arguments by analogy on behalf of those goals. Nonetheless, it's vital that you analyze the possible differences just as carefully as you analyze the similarities. Case studies of failures in organizations are full of anecdotes about people who solved *last* year's problem when they thought they were solving *this* year's problem.
- How does this problem relate to other needs, issues, and people in and beyond your organization? As you think about potential solutions to this problem, how would these solutions affect these other needs, issues, and people? Could solving this problem create or exacerbate others? Could solving this problem also solve others? Or could there be solutions to other problems that would solve or mitigate this problem?
- What will a solution to this problem look like? How many possible solutions can you find? What is the range of acceptable solutions? How can what you write in this report serve as a part of the solution? Can it be the whole solution? If not, what part can it serve? (Think here, for example, of the limited function of the progress report, which, by definition, is not the final solution to the issues in the larger context.)
- What are the possible costs of the solutions you visualize? What are the potential adverse results? You don't want to establish a goal for this project and your report that you later realize is going to have the net effect of making matters worse. And if you discover costs in the form of new problems emerging from your solution to this problem, you need to assess those costs; then you need to make an intelligent judgment about whether the benefits are worth the costs and be prepared to argue on behalf of your best solution, notwithstanding the costs. Anticipating counter-arguments about costs and preparing to answer them is a good example of how you need to be aware of the layers in your ar-

gument and in opposing arguments. (We'll talk more about layering your argument under the A of GRACE.)

Readers

The three maxims we talked about earlier in this chapter are a good foundation for understanding the complexity of your readers when you are writing a report in an organizational context:

MAXIM 1

Reports exist in organizations to solve problems, fulfill needs, and capitalize on opportunities.

MAXIM 2

All problems are problems for *people*.

MAXIM 3

Because organizations and their people are dynamic, their problems also are dynamic.

Because the organization itself is complex—as are the relationships and communications among the people in it—any report written for even a single person in an organization is likely to have multiple readers. These readers will be approaching the report with different levels of understanding of the history of the problems, different perspectives and commitments both inside and outside the organization, different purposes in reading the report, and even different vocabularies for understanding and talking about issues in the report. If you aren't used to writing reports in an organizational context, you may underestimate the complexity of thinking about your readers. The following list, adapted from the work of J. C. Mathes and Dwight Stevenson (1976), identifies dangerous assumptions that even veteran writers in organizations sometimes make about their readers. You can avoid some of the major pitfalls by asking yourself whether you're making any of these assumptions and, then, if you're warranted in doing so. You can go on to ask yourself how your assumptions about your readers may be influencing further decisions you are making about your arguments (your claims, evidence, and warrants), the conventions you're using, the ways you are expressing your character, and even the goals you have set for this report.

It is dangerous to assume any of the following about your reader:

1. The person addressed—the *nominal* reader—is the only reader.
2. The readers are specialists in the field.
3. The report has a finite period of use; it won't be referred to again for months or even years.
4. You and the nominal reader will always be available for consultation and interpretation of the document.
5. The reader is familiar with the assignment.
6. The reader has been involved in daily discussions of the material and shares your contextual understanding and assumptions about it.
7. The reader awaits the report and has time to read it.

If you're in doubt about your assumptions, it's almost always smart to talk with the person who is the best available source of information about your readers of the report (e.g., your boss who gave you the writing assignment) and get a clearer and richer picture of them.

These seven assumptions create risks because they can lead you to oversimplify the nature and number of your readers. If you can't answer confidently that each one of these assumptions is true, then you should probably assume it is false and err on the side of explaining more of the context than is necessary. In the absence of more specific information about your readers—and sometimes even with more specific information about them—it's often useful to assume there will be three general levels of readers of your report, each with a different need for the level of detail.

Level 1 Reader

Your Level 1 reader may be an executive who has the authority to make the decision you would like made but doesn't really have time to do the background research to inform that decision or even time to read at length the research you have already done and written up in the report. This person needs a summary that gives the bottom line: the essence of the problem, the major details, the major alternatives, and a summary of your rationale for the best alternatives you see. This lets your Level 1 reader decide whether the problem deserves further attention and action.

Level 2 Reader

Your Level 1 reader may also be a Level 2 reader, or your Level 1 reader may pass the report on to another reader for detailed reading—say, a staff member who has responsibility for topics your report addresses. Or perhaps you may anticipate a Level 2 reader and deliver a copy of the report to one or more such readers. Your Level 2 reader will read the report critically, carefully, and in detail, probably studying carefully your analysis of the problem and its context, your alternative solutions, your arguments where you evaluate the alternatives, and your arguments where you project the implications of the alternatives. In other words, this person will study and evaluate your claims, your evidence for your claims, and your rationale that warrants your evidence as relevant and persuasive.

Level 3 Reader

If your report has passed a Level 2 reading, it will then go on to a Level 3 reader. This person will read the report in fine-grained detail, using it as a blueprint for specific action.

So now, having considered the list of dangerous assumptions about readers and having imagined three levels of readers using different levels of details in the report, let's turn again to the specific situation and try to visualize the actual readers, using the following questions to generate helpful information about them:

- Who in the organization has a stake in the issues your report addresses? What is their stake? Do they share the same stake you have in the issues, or is their stake adverse to yours?
- Who asked for the report? What is their particular stake in the report? What do they plan to do with it? Who do they plan to share it with?
- If nobody asked for the report, what will readers' attitudes be toward it when they get it? Will they be surprised? Should they be? If this might be an unpleasant surprise, should you prepare them for the report ahead of time?
- Who usually reads reports like this? Who do you think should read this report? Are they permitted to read it, or is the report confidential, for a few people's eyes only? Have these issues been addressed by reports in your organization before? Who has read those reports? Will these issues likely occur again? Who will likely read and write about these issues in the future?
- What will people probably need to do with this report? What will they need from the report in order to do it?

Arguments

Arguments are the primary reasons we write reports. That is, we write reports when the arguments we need to make are too long and complex to be contained in letters or memos. Often, multiple arguments are to be made, and almost without exception, the arguments in reports are multilayered, with extensive documentation. Figure 13.1, summarizing the final environmental impact statement (FEIS) of the Mexican wolf reintroduction in the Southwest United States, is a good example of an extremely data-rich document, reporting the results of a multiyear, multifaceted study.

Extensive data is provided in a report, and all this information means something. When you write a report, it's incumbent on you to interpret the data, to infer what it does mean. Chances are, you already had a pretty good idea of what the data mean before you wrote the report because you've already been thinking about your goals for the report. Chances are, as well, that a good deal of the data collection you've done has been framed by the problems, needs, and opportunities you saw when you started this project, and, of course, those problems, needs, and opportunities came into view because of the data you had to start with. So, reports exist primarily because of their arguments. And they are reports, rather than letters or memos, because the arguments need to be sustained by substantial data and perhaps extensive and sophisticated interpretation and analysis, including technical analyses of various kinds (e.g., statistical, chemical, physical, economic, psychological, rhetorical, ethical, etc.).

FIGURE 13.1 Sample Data-Rich Report

REINTRODUCTION OF THE MEXICAN WOLF WITHIN ITS HISTORIC RANGE IN THE SOUTHWESTERN UNITED STATES

Final
Enviromental
Impact
Statement

Fish and Wildlife Service
U.S. Department of the Interior

FIGURE 13.1 Continued

Reintroduction of the Mexican Wolf within its Historic Range in the Southwestern United States

Final
Environmental
Impact
Statement

Fish and Wildlife Service
U.S. Department of the Interior

November 1996

Prepared with the assistance of the
Center for Wildlife Law, Institute of
Public Law, University of New Mexico.

Cover illustration: Brian Cobble

(continued)

FIGURE 13.1 Continued

Final Environmental Impact Statement—Reintroduction of the Mexican Wolf within Its Historic Range in the Southwestern United States

Summary

Introduction

The United States Department of the Interior, Fish and Wildlife Service (FWS), proposes to reintroduce a nonessential experimental population of Mexican gray wolves (*Canis lupus baileyi*) within part of the subspecies' historic range in the southwestern United States. The endangered Mexican wolf currently is known to exist only in captivity. The FWS has prepared a final environmental impact statement (FEIS) on its reintroduction proposal and three alternative approaches to re-establishing the subspecies under the Endangered Species Act (ESA). This Summary outlines the full FEIS.

Cooperating Agencies in Preparation of the EIS

Arizona Game and Fish Dep't; New Mexico Dep't of Game and Fish; San Carlos Apache Tribe; U.S. Dep't of Agriculture, APHIS, Animal Damage Control; U.S. Dep't of Agriculture, Forest Service; U.S. Dep't of the Army, White Sands Missile Range.

States and Counties Where the Preferred Alternative is Located

Arizona: Apache and Greenlee Counties; New Mexico: Catron, *Doña Ana, Grant, *Lincoln, *Otero, Sierra, and *Socorro Counties.
(* indicates counties that are potentially affected by the Preferred Alternative only if the back-up White Sands Wolf Recovery Area is used.)

Scoping, Public Review, and Changes to the Draft EIS

This FEIS is based on a lengthy period of scoping, preparation, review, and revision of a draft EIS (DEIS). Four public scoping meetings were held in 1991 and 1992 to obtain public input regarding the FWS's general proposal to reintroduce Mexican wolves. A total of 838 people attended. In addition, public comment periods following the meetings resulted in 1,324 written comments, which the FWS compiled and analyzed. The seven main areas of public concern related to: 1) the FWS's planning of the Proposed Action and the alternatives to it; 2) impacts of wolf depredation on livestock; 3) economic impacts; 4) ecological and biological impacts of wolf recovery; 5) the viability of the captive Mexican wolf population; 6) impacts on wildlife management; and 7) philosophical and ethical concerns. The interagency Mexican Wolf EIS Interdisciplinary Team, which oversaw the writing of the EIS, considered these issues as well as additional issues.

The DEIS was prepared between 1993 and 1995; it was released in June 1995. The public comment period on the DEIS ended more than four months later, on October 31. Public review was extensive, with participation by almost 18,000 people or organizations, in a variety of ways. Fourteen public open house meetings were held throughout the potentially affected areas; total registered attendance was 1,186. Three formal public hearings were held in Austin, Texas; Phoenix, Arizona; and Socorro, New Mexico; total registered attendance was 951. Each written and transcribed oral comment has been reviewed and considered in the preparation of the FEIS. The public comments are on file and available for inspection at the FWS Regional Office in Albuquerque, New Mexico.

Notable changes from the DEIS to this FEIS are listed below; they largely are in response to comments received on the DEIS or to developments since the DEIS was written. Also, numerous minor corrections, revisions, and updates have been made.

ii

FIGURE 13.1 Continued

Alternatives

- Re-writing of the Proposed Action as the Preferred Alternative (Alt. A), now specifying use of the biologically preferable Blue Range Wolf Recovery Area (BRWRA) first, with the White Sands Wolf Recovery Area (WSWRA) as a back-up, only to be used if necessary and feasible and if additional information is available that the deer population can support a wolf population. The specific decision criteria in the DEIS regarding whether to use the BRWRA or WSWRA first have been deleted.
- Deletion of the provision for closing backcountry roads.
- Support for a Citizen Advisory Committee to advise on management.
- Alt. B now proposes reintroductions in both the BRWRA and WSWRA primary recovery zones at the same time.
- Alt. C now proposes full-endangered wolf reintroduction into the BRWRA only. The WSWRA is deleted as a potential reintroduction area under Alt. C, largely because the reintroduction objective could be met with releases to just the BRWRA with subsequent unlimited expansion of the reintroduced population. Related discussion of impacts to the WSWRA and the adjacent potential dispersal areas is deleted.
- Rewording of Alt. D to emphasize the "No Action" aspect and that natural recolonization is very speculative. Costs of this alternative are re-calculated. Less quantification is provided in the impact discussion due to greater emphasis on uncertainty.

Clarifications/Corrections

- More discussion of historic information about wolf depredation on livestock, in Chap. 1 under Reasons for Listing.
- New or more clear definitions of "problem wolves," "rendezvous sites," and "disturbance-causing land use activities" in the Glossary, Appendix G. The latter definition includes specific activities and types of public access that may not be allowed within a radius of one mile or less around active pens, dens, and rendezvous sites, as well as exemptions, i.e., activities specifically allowed.
- Deletion of the provision for removing wolves when they are "conflicting with a major land use"; addition of a provision for removing them if they endanger themselves by occurring when and where military or testing activities are scheduled.
- Clarification that modification of wolf habitat (outside the protection areas for pens, dens, and rendezvous sites) by land uses in the recovery areas would not be considered a "take" of nonessential experimental wolves under ESA sec. 9(a).
- Apportionment of potential impacts on deer, elk, hunting, and related economic impacts by whether they would occur in Arizona or New Mexico.
- Discussion of potential impacts on bighorn sheep in the BRWRA.
- More discussion of potential impacts on the San Carlos Apache Reservation.
- Revision and more detailed explanation of cost estimates for each alternative in Appendix B.

Updates

- Updated version of Appendix C, the Proposed Mexican Wolf Experimental Population Rule, as published in the Federal Register.
- Inclusion of the detailed Public Comment Summary and the Agency Comments on the DEIS, both as part of Chap. 5, and both with FWS responses to the comments.
- A summary of the DEIS review process, compilation of the numbers of various types of public comments received, and a listing of personnel involved in the public review process.
- New Mexico League of Women Voters wolf opinion survey results.
- Impacts from wolf reintroduction in Yellowstone and Central Idaho to date.

iii

(continued)

FIGURE 13.1 Continued

- Drought and management impacts on deer, oryx, and feral horse populations on White Sands Missile Range.
- Proposed reductions in permitted grazing to Apache National Forest allotments in BRWRA.
- Mexican spotted owl recovery in Cumulative Impacts section and discussion on impacts on National Forest management.
- Status of captive Mexican wolf population and genetics, and revision of taxonomy and historic range sections.
- More current information on investigations of whether any Mexican wolves remain in the wild in the U.S. or Mexico (none confirmed).

New Appendices

Appendix J - Update on Yellowstone and Central Idaho Gray Wolf Reintroductions and Economic Benefits of Wolf Recovery, and Appendix K - Response to Mr. Dennis Parker's Comment on the DEIS.

Future Decision Making

A Notice of Availability of this FEIS is being published in the Federal Register. The FEIS will be given to decision makers in the FWS and Department of Interior. A Record of Decision can be approved 30 days after publication of the Notice of Availability. Any decision on Mexican wolf recovery in the southwestern United States will be well publicized. Send information requests to: David R. Parsons, Mexican Wolf Recovery Program, U.S. Fish and Wildlife Service, P.O. Box 1306, Albuquerque, NM 87103.

Nancy M. Kaufman
(Signature)

November 6, 1996
(Date)

Nancy Kaufman
Regional Director, Region 2
U.S. Fish and Wildlife Service

Background

Mexican Gray Wolf Description

The Mexican wolf is the southernmost and one of the smallest subspecies of the North American gray wolf. Adults weigh 50 to 90 lbs., average 4'6" to 5'6" in total length, and reach 26" to 32" in height at the shoulder. Its pelt color varies. The "lobo"—its popular name—is genetically distinct from other wolves and no confirmed population exists outside captivity. It is one of the rarest land mammals in the world. International experts rate recovery of the Mexican wolf subspecies as the highest priority of all gray wolf recovery programs.

Reasons for Listing

Many factors contributed to the Mexican wolf's demise, but the concerted federal eradication effort in the early 1900s was predominant. Other factors were: commercial and recreational hunting and trapping; killing of wolves by game managers on the theory that more game animals would be available for hunters; habitat alteration; and safety concerns, although no documentation exists of Mexican wolf attacks on humans.

Reintroduction Procedures

All Mexican wolves to be released under Alternatives A, B, and C, below, would come from the certified U.S. captive population of 114 animals (as of March 1996) maintained in 24 zoos, wildlife parks, and other facilities located around the country. The wolves have exhibited no major genetics, physical, or behavioral problems affecting their fitness resulting from captivity. The FWS will move male/female pairs identified as candidates for possible release to its captive wolf management facility on the Sevilleta National Wildlife Refuge, north of Socorro, New Mexico. In the event of a decision to proceed with reintroduction, the FWS would select release animals

FIGURE 13.1 Continued

from among the candidate pairs based on reproductive performance, behavioral compatibility, response to the adaptation process, and other factors. Only wolves that are genetically well-represented in the remaining captive population would be used as release stock.

Alternatives

Alternative A (the Preferred Alternative): The U.S. Fish and Wildlife Service proposes to reintroduce Mexican wolves, classified as nonessential experimental, into the Blue Range Wolf Recovery Area. Wolves will be released into the primary recovery zone and allowed to disperse into the secondary recovery zone. If feasible and necessary to achieve the recovery objective of 100 wolves, a subsequent reintroduction of wolves into the White Sands Wolf Recovery Area will be conducted.

In 1997, the FWS will begin to reintroduce family groups of captive-raised Mexican wolves into the primary recovery zone of the BRWRA (Fig. 1). The FWS will gradually release up to 15 family groups into the BRWRA and later, if necessary and feasible, up to five family groups into the back-up WSWRA (Fig. 1). Reproduction in the wild would increase the populations to approximately the recovery objective. Wolves will be released into the primary recovery zone and allowed to disperse into the secondary recovery zone.

The recovery objective of the Preferred Alternative is to re-establish 100 wild wolves distributed over more than 5,000 mi^2 by about the year 2005, consistent with the 1982 Mexican Wolf Recovery Plan. The FWS projects that the population will eventually fluctuate near this level as a result of natural processes, such as intra-specific aggression and changes in prey abundance and vulnerability, and management actions, such as problem wolf control and translocation. The FWS and its cooperators will monitor, research, evaluate, and actively manage the wolves, including translocating or removing wolves that disperse outside the wolf recovery areas or that cause significant conflicts.

A federal regulation will designate the population to be released as experimental and nonessential to the continued existence of the subspecies. This Mexican Wolf Experimental Population Rule will delineate the precise geographic boundaries (see Box 1) and prescribe the protective measures and management authority that apply. No formal ESA Section 7 consultation would be required regarding potential impacts of land uses on nonessential experimental Mexican wolves, except on National Wildlife Refuges and National Park Service areas.

Reintroduction will occur under management plans that allow dispersal by the new wolf populations from the immediate release areas ("primary recovery zones") into designated adjacent areas ("secondary recovery zones") (Fig. 1). However, the FWS and cooperating agencies will not allow the wolves to establish territories outside these wolf recovery area boundaries unless this occurs on private or tribal lands and the land manager does not object. The FWS would attempt to enter into cooperative management agreements with such landowners regarding control of the wolves. If the land manager objects to the presence of wolves on private or tribal lands, field personnel would recapture and relocate the wolves.

The FWS and the cooperating agencies will use a flexible "adaptive management" approach based on careful monitoring, research, and evaluation throughout the release phase. This will include adjusting the numbers actually released according to the needs and circumstances at the time. Initially, to reduce the likelihood of wolf dispersal onto the White Mountain Apache and San Carlos Apache reservations to the west, the wolf releases will occur on the eastern side of the BRWRA primary recovery zone, close to the Arizona/New Mexico border. The FWS will encourage and support the formation of a Citizen Advisory Committee, or similar management oversight body, to assist the FWS and cooperating agencies in responding to citizen concerns.

(continued)

FIGURE 13.1 Continued

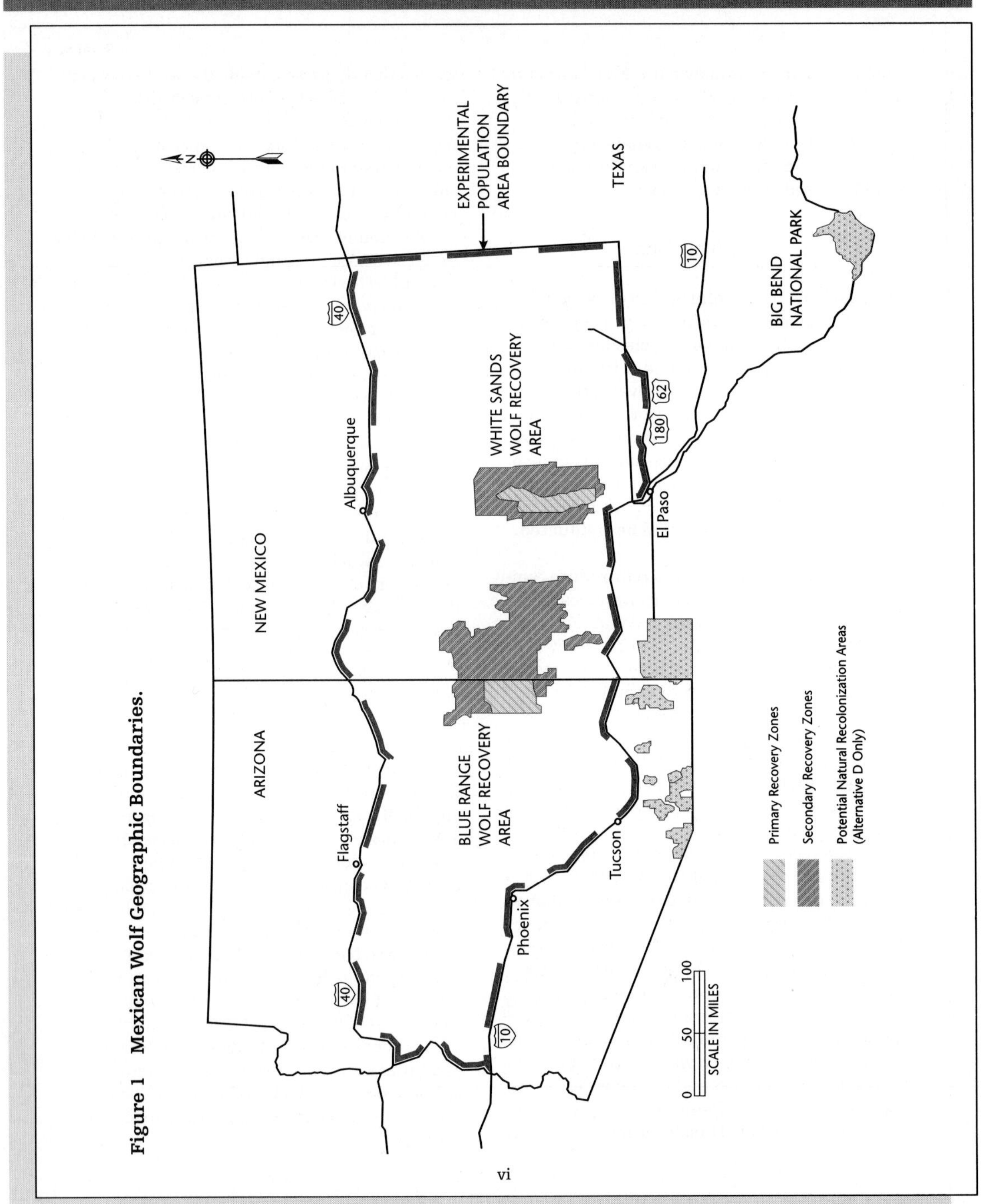

FIGURE 13.1 Continued

Summary

Box 1. Geographic boundaries for Mexican wolf reintroduction (see Fig. 1).

Blue Range Wolf Recovery Area: all of the Apache National Forest and all of the Gila National Forest.

BRWRA primary recovery zone: the area within the Apache National Forest bounded on the north by the Apache-Greenlee County line; on the east by the Arizona-New Mexico State line; on the south by the San Francisco River (eastern half) and the southern boundary of the Apache National Forest (western half); and on the west by the Greenlee-Graham County line (San Carlos Apache Reservation boundary).

BRWRA secondary recovery zone: the remainder of the BRWRA not in the primary recovery zone.

White Sands Wolf Recovery Area: all of the White Sands Missile Range, the White Sands National Monument, and the San Andres National Wildlife Refuge, and the area adjacent and to the west of the Missile Range bounded on the south by the southerly boundary of the U.S. Department of Agriculture Jornada Experimental Range and the northern boundary of the New Mexico State University Animal Science Ranch; on the west by the New Mexico Principal Meridian; on the north by the Pedro Armendaris Grant boundary and the Sierra-Socorro County line; and on the east by the western boundary of the Missile Range.

WSWRA primary recovery zone: the area within the White Sands Missile Range bounded on the north by the road from former Cain Ranch Headquarters to Range Road 16, Range Road 16 to its intersection with Range Road 13, Range Road 13 to its intersection with Range Road 7; on the east by Range Road 7; on the south by U.S. Highway 70; and on the west by the Missile Range boundary.

WSWRA secondary recovery zone: the remainder of the WSWRA not within the primary recovery zone.

Mexican wolf experimental population area: the portion of Arizona lying north of Interstate Highway 10 and south of Interstate Highway 40; the portion of New Mexico lying north of Interstate Highway 10 in the west, north of the New Mexico-Texas boundary in the east, and south of Interstate Highway 40; and that portion of Texas lying north of US Highway 62/180 and south of the Texas-New Mexico boundary.

The following future circumstances will be considered in decision-making about using the WSWRA subsequent to initial releases in the BRWRA:

- whether using the WSWRA, in combination with the BRWRA, is necessary to achieve the recovery objective of re-establishing 100 wolves; that is, it would be used if it appears that the initial introduction in the BRWRA will not achieve a total population of 100 wolves,
- whether, based on future research, it appears that the WSWRA deer herd could support a wolf population that would contribute to meeting the recovery objective, and
- other future circumstances that could affect the feasibility of using the WSWRA, such as the wolf program budget, management concerns, future military uses of the missile range, and so on.

The Proposed Mexican Wolf Experimental Population Rule was published in the Federal Register on May 1, 1996 (pp. 19237–19248). In summary, the Proposed Rule provides:

- No one will be in violation of the ESA for unavoidable and unintentional take of a wolf within the Mexican wolf experimental population area when the take is incidental to a legal activity, such as driving, trapping, and

vii

(continued)

FIGURE 13.1 Continued

military testing or training activities, and is promptly reported. Anyone may take a wolf in defense of human life.

- No private or tribal land use restrictions will be imposed for wolf recovery without the concurrence of the private owner or tribal government. On public lands, public access and disturbance-causing land use activities may be temporarily restricted within a one-mile radius around release pens, and around active dens between March 1 and June 30 and around active wolf rendezvous sites between June 1 and September 30.
- On *public lands* allotted for grazing, livestock owners and their designated agents: (1) may harass wolves for purposes of scaring them away from livestock provided the harassment is promptly reported, and (2) may be allowed to take wolves actually engaged in attacking livestock.
- Permission for private parties to take wolves on public grazing lands must meet all of these conditions: 1) six or more breeding wolf pairs occur in the BRWRA, or three or more breeding wolf pairs occur in the WSWRA (if used); 2) previous livestock loss or injury by wolves has been documented by an authorized FWS, ADC, or state employee and efforts to control the offending wolves have been undertaken but have not succeeded; 3) physical evidence exists that an attack occurred at the time of the take; and 4) the take is promptly reported.
- On *private or tribally-owned land,* regardless of location, property owners and livestock owners and their designated agents may harass wolves near livestock, people, buildings, facilities, pets, or other domestic animals at any time and may take wolves attacking livestock under more liberal conditions than those applicable to public grazing lands. That is, such take can occur regardless of the number of recovered wolf pairs in the area and no requirement exists for government agencies to have completed their efforts to take the depredating wolves. However, physical evidence that an attack occurred at the time of the take must be present and the take must be promptly reported.
- Any FWS-authorized person may capture and remove or translocate reintroduced wolves consistent with a FWS-approved management plan or special management measure. These may include wolves that: (1) prey on livestock, (2) attack domestic animals other than livestock on private land, (3) impact game populations in ways which may inhibit further wolf recovery, (4) prey on state-endangered desert bighorn sheep on the White Sands Missile Range (if used), (5) are considered problem wolves, are a nuisance, or endanger themselves by their presence in a military impact area, or (6) are necessary for research.
- The FWS does not intend to change the "nonessential experimental" designation to "essential experiment" or "endangered" and the FWS does not intend to designate critical habitat for the Mexican wolf.
- Any taking of a wolf contrary to the experimental population rule may be referred to the appropriate authorities for prosecution.

Post-release management will follow an interagency cooperative management plan. This will include working with the Arizona Game and Fish Department to meet the requirements of its Cooperative Reintroduction Plan and working with the New Mexico Department of Game and Fish. A wolf management team representing the FWS, the State Game and Fish departments, and other cooperating agencies will determine whether particular actions are necessary. The interagency management plan will cover issues such as release pen siting, veterinary management, depredation control, capture and relocation, research, radio tracking, aerial overflights, prey monitoring, and prey habitat management. Field staff will conduct monitoring and research, trapping, depredation investigation, mortality investigation, control, and other on-the-ground actions.

Alternative B: Reintroduction of Mexican wolves, classified as nonessential experimen-

FIGURE 13.1 Continued

Summary

tal, into both the Blue Range Wolf Recovery Area and the White Sands Wolf Recovery Area primary recovery zones. Wolves dispersing from the primary recovery zones will be captured and returned to the primary zones or captivity.

In 1997, the FWS will begin to reintroduce family groups of captive-raised Mexican wolves into both the BRWRA and the WSWRA primary recovery zones and actively prevent the populations from expanding beyond these zones (Fig. 1). In the BRWRA primary recovery zone the FWS will release about eight family groups over four years with the goal of reaching a population of 20 wild wolves by 2001. In the WSWRA primary recovery zone the FWS will release about four family groups over two years with the goal of reaching a population of 14 wild wolves by 1999. The total recovery objective will be 34 wolves.

The FWS will designate the population as nonessential experimental under the ESA. The FWS will adopt basically the same Mexican Wolf Experimental Population Rule as under Alt. A, but it would apply to the smaller areas. The FWS and its cooperators will follow the same release, monitoring, and management procedures as under Alt. A, but on a smaller scale due to the smaller areas involved. Control will be accomplished through a combination of aggressive monitoring and management methods to promptly recapture wolves that leave the primary recovery zones. Wolves could be translocated between the two areas as needed.

Alternative C: Reintroduction of Mexican wolves, classified as endangered, into the Blue Range Wolf Recovery Area only. Wolves will be released into the primary recovery zone and unlimited dispersal will be allowed. Wolves will receive full protection under the Endangered Species Act.

In 1997, the FWS will begin to reintroduce family groups of captive-raised Mexican wolves under their current full-endangered status into the primary recovery zone of the BRWRA in east-central Arizona, following the same release procedures as under Alt.s A and B. The FWS will gradually release up to 15 family groups into the BRWRA. No releases will occur in the WSWRA. The recovery objective of the alternative is to reestablish 100 wild wolves distributed over more than 5,000 mi^2 by about the year 2002, consistent with the Mexican Wolf Recovery Plan. The FWS and its cooperators will monitor and conduct research on the wolves, but they will not actively manage them.

The ESA allows unrestricted dispersal; that is, the FWS will not restrict the population to the designated wolf recovery areas, as under Alternative A, or to the smaller primary recovery zones, as under Alternative B. No attempts will be made to recapture or return wolves with the possible exception of individual depredators.

The wolves will have the full protection against "take" by humans provided by the ESA. Anyone who would "harass, harm, pursue, hunt, shoot, wound, kill, trap, capture, or collect, or attempt to engage in any such conduct" against a Mexican wolf will be violating the ESA. The only exceptions will be takings to protect human life or by special permit "for scientific purposes or to enhance the propagation or survival of the affected species," 16 USC sec. 1539(a)(1)(A).

Land use restrictions could be imposed under this alternative. Restrictions could include limiting the use of predator control methods that might kill or injure wolves, closing roads, modifying livestock grazing, and imposing other protections to limit any jeopardy resulting from human activities. Other federal agencies would be expected to pursue their responsibilities under the ESA to conserve, and not harm, a recolonizing population. This would include managing to maintain and create high quality ungulate and wolf habitat.

Alternative D: No Action

Under the No Action alternative, the FWS will take no action other than continuing its present course. It will neither release wolves nor take any other steps to directly ensure Mexican wolf

ix

(continued)

FIGURE 13.1 Continued

recovery. The FWS will neither adopt an experimental population rule nor designate any wolf recovery areas. The agency will continue to support the captive population objectives established in the SSP Master Plan, but the agency will not support breeding for maximum growth.

Based on its current ESA obligations, the FWS would still encourage protection and expansion of wild wolf populations under this alternative, if any were discovered. No evidence exists to indicate a likelihood of natural recolonization in U.S. portions of the historic Mexican wolf range, but the FWS will support continued research on this possibility. Natural recolonization is considered extremely speculative. Based on historical wolf abundance, recent sighting reports alleged to be wolves, proximity to Mexico, and other factors, the most suitable areas for potential natural recolonization by wild wolves probably would be the mountainous parts of southeastern Arizona and southwestern New Mexico, and Big Bend National Park in southern Texas. This alternative analyzes these three areas. No confirmed sighting reports have come from these areas or from Mexico in recent years.

Any wolves that did naturally recolonize would be fully protected as an endangered species in the United States. It would be illegal to harm or harass them except under very narrow circumstances authorized by an ESA permit.

Land use restrictions could be imposed under this alternative depending on if, and where, wolves occurred. Restrictions could include limiting the use of predator control methods that might kill or injure wolves, closing roads, modifying livestock grazing, and imposing other protections to limit any jeopardy resulting from human activities. Other federal agencies would be expected to pursue their responsibilities under the ESA to conserve, and not harm, a recolonizing population. This would include managing to maintain and create high quality ungulate and wolf habitat.

Impacts

Table 1 summarizes the features of the four alternatives. Table 2 outlines their projected environmental consequences. The FEIS provides detailed explanations of the impacts, descriptions of the methods of impact analysis, and supporting references.

So, where can you begin to look for effective arguments? Try these questions:

- What do you think should be done as a result of the report? What, to you, are the most compelling, cogent arguments relating to this report? Analyze these arguments to see why you find them persuasive. What are the essential claims you want to make here in support of your goals? What is the evidence that you find relevant and persuasive? Look at your claims, your data, and your analyses with a skeptical eye. Do they form a coherent argument? What underlying values and assumptions serve as warrants for these arguments?
- Do your readers share these assumptions and values and your understanding of the evidence? Do your readers share your stake in the problem and in the solutions you propose? If your stake is not the same as your readers', where is your common ground? Can you redefine the problem/issue/opportunity so that you and your readers share at least some common ground? Where do your interests converge? Where do they conflict?
- What are the most significant and persuasive opposing arguments? This is a terribly difficult question because it asks you, in effect, to lay down your defenses; step away from your own position; assume the mental, emotional, and ethical perspective of an opposing position; and understand that position sympathetically. Even so, this is also a terribly important question. If you don't ask it, you may end up in a wasteful and painful impasse that you could have prevented. As you study these opposing arguments, look as sympathetically and carefully as you can at the evidence that supports their claims and at the underlying values and assumptions that warrant connecting the evidence and claims.
- Based on your best efforts to give opposing arguments your sympathetic understanding, can you see boundaries past which your assumptions no longer hold true? What if you qualified your claim or claims based on those boundaries? If you delimited the area of validity of your claims yourself, rather than waiting for a rebuttal, would your remaining claim be stronger? Usually the answer is "yes." This tends to be true in all documents but especially in reports. Because of the document's length and complexity, there is an expectation that you've considered the issues and arguments in all their complexity. If you set reasonable delimitations on your claims, you enhance your credibility as a careful, thorough, ethical writer; strengthen your remaining claims; and may even gain the confidence of readers who have been inclined to oppose or distrust you.
- Again, based on your best efforts to give opposing arguments your sympathetic understanding, can you see areas of validity in these arguments? Would the Rogerian strategy (see Chapter 6) of pointing out these areas of validity likely increase the chances of achieving a mutually satisfactory understanding of the issues you discuss? If there are difficult, refractory disagreements, might this strategy break an impasse and enable you and your opponents to move toward an agreement?
- Aside from conflicting or converging interests, where else can you see points of resistance or potential affirmation for your report? Are there matters of personality

or character—either your own or somebody else's who is associated with your report as a reader or as some kind of stakeholder or collaborator—that are either a barrier or an avenue for acceptance? Are there emotional elements of resistance or acceptance? Where are these points located, either in your own arguments or in opposing arguments? How can you speak effectively and ethically to these elements? Would it be useful to acknowledge and clarify the underlying warrants of your own arguments? Would it be useful to try to acknowledge and clarify the underlying values and assumptions of the opposing arguments? Would a Rogerian approach be effective in handling these opposing arguments?

- As you consider all the arguments that are available to you and the counter-arguments they may raise, what potential risks as well as benefits are associated with using these respective arguments?

The arguments in the Summary of the final environmental impact statement by the Fish and Wildlife Service, *Reintroduction of the Mexican Wolf within Its Historic Range in the Southwestern United States* (Figure 13.1), are extremely complex and carefully balanced. The reintroduction of wolves to their traditional territories has been a highly controversial, conflicted issue since at least the mid 1980s. Wolves are extinct in most of their traditional territories precisely because there was, in the late nineteenth and early twentieth centuries, a virtually universal consensus that the proper management policy was one of extermination. In recent decades, the image of the wolf has undergone a transformation among many who now believe this animal serves an important function within its traditional niche in the ecology of the West.

However, many people in the West do not share this newly evolved benign view of the wolf. People who own livestock, for example, fear substantial financial losses from predation by wolves. Hunters fear loss of big-game hunting because of predation of wolves upon deer, elk, and other game animals. Representatives of the tourist industry fear financial losses because of reduced tourist income from hunters. People whose interests would be at risk if wolves were reintroduced note that many of the people who favor reintroduction do not have the same degree of interests—for example, their livelihoods will not be at risk if wolves are reintroduced. People with a lot at stake tend to see environmentalists and government agencies who favor reintroduction as acting irresponsibly and recklessly. This view is reinforced by a traditional suspicion of the big, distant federal bureaucracy. Even some environmentalists who would otherwise support reintroducing wolves to their traditional territories have misgivings because of their fear of wolves preying upon other endangered species.

Given this conflicted situation—with its opposing economic and political interests and theories—the people who conducted and wrote the study chose to solicit the widest possible participation in conducting it, and they chose to lay out a wide range of alternative strategies and scenarios in their recommendations. Notice how the detailed description of the history of the issue, the development of related studies and documents, and the methodology of the current study is itself an argument that meets any charge that the study has been conducted hastily or without giving an opportunity for full participation by interested parties.

Conventions

We have said that reports exist for their arguments and that the arguments tend to be long and extensively supported by data. Perhaps the most powerful conventions in reports generally, then, is that of thorough documentation with specific data. In professional reports, this thoroughness can be constrained by at least a couple of conditions, but the convention of thorough, specific documentation is very strong, nonetheless. If there are constraints on this thoroughness, they are likely to be either the limit on sharing proprietary information of methods of data analysis or the competing conventions of efficiency and concision in business and professional writing.

Don't make the mistake of confusing *concision* with *vagueness,* however. Except for the constraint on disclosing proprietary information, readers expect to see specific facts supporting your claims. If you present principles of interpretation as warrants for the conclusions you draw from your facts, your readers will expect to see the sources of these principles documented, unless they're universally accepted. If you employ particular methods of data analysis, readers will expect to see those methods explained and documented. Where you locate all this documentation in your report will vary, depending on the circumstances, including conventions of organization used by your firm or by your readers' firm. However, the overriding convention for reports is that the documentation—data, principles of interpretation, sources of data, methods of analysis, and justification and rationale for these methods—is included in the report somewhere. Our discussion in the rest of this section (and, especially, in Chapter 10) will give you some good general guidelines for conventional organization. Obviously, you should ignore these guidelines if your supervisor or your client prefers some other organizational scheme.

Consider these elements in your report:

- What are the procedural conventions for a report-writing situation like this in your organization? Are you expected to collaborate or confer in preparing the report? If so, who is in this collaboration/consultation loop? What are people's respective roles? Who's in charge of what on this project? Who has editorial veto power over it?
- Are there established conventions for how to frame the problem and solution, lay out the arguments, organize the evidence, and express your personal and organizational character in this kind of report? For example, does your organization have a corporate style manual? Or if this report is addressed to readers outside your organization, do your readers have established conventions guiding its design? In either case, are samples of past reports available to use as models or even templates? Can someone who is more experienced give you advice?
- Given your goals, readers, arguments, and the kind of personal and organizational presence you want to express in this report, what kinds of decisions do you need to make about the following conventional elements of reports?
    - **Cover.** What kind of cover and binding should you use? A three-ring binder? A plastic comb binding? A perfect binding? An expensive stitched binding? A

staple or a paper clip? A heavy card stock for a cover? A plastic cover? A book cover? Do you want a fancy, customized logo or design?

- **Paper versus other media.** What quality, weight, color, and size paper do you want? How do you want the document printed? Laser printer, inkjet printer, FAX, xerographic copier, offset printer, or typewriter? Or perhaps an electronic medium such as a computer screen, so that your report isn't even transmitted as a paper document? What size and style of type should you use?
- **Cover letter.** Should you use a cover letter that helps establish the context of the report, summarize it, and establish or affirm the grounds of your relationship with your main reader?
- **Executive summary.** Should you include an executive summary specifically for the Level 1 reader who's reading under tight time constraints and needs to see the whole picture in broad strokes quickly? (See Chapter 10.)
- **Table of contents and numbered pages.** For even a two-page report, we suggest numbering the pages, and for a report of just a few pages, we suggest creating a table of contents. For example, see Figure 13.2, which is a part of a student report urging the creation of a student organization booklet. The entire report is only 13 pages long, but it has a detailed table of contents. Including a detailed contents is a standard convention for reports because of the almost universal assumption that readers are busy yet want and need lots of redundant cues to help them grasp the organization of the report and find what they want within it.
- **Overall organization.** Do you want to present your conclusions last or first? Which organization is most appropriate: Background/problem/solution/rationale? Problem/solution/rationale/background? or Solution/problem/rationale?
- **Appendix.** Should you create an appendix? Can some of the detailed evidence go in an appendix—your background material, for example, if it is extensive, or lengthy documentation of your investigative process or analytical or statistical procedures? Do you have extensive biographical information about a number of people, for example, that could go in an appendix?
- **Graphics.** First, what typographic conventions are available to you for improving the readability of this document? Do the style guidelines of your organization allow informative headers, boldfaced type for headers and subheads, creative use of vertical and horizontal white space to clarify and emphasize chunks of text, markers such as bullets to highlight items in lists, callouts in margins to dramatize key points, and other graphic manipulations of the text itself? Do the issues, information, and arguments lend themselves to graphic presentation? Would tables, pie graphs, bar graphs, timelines, calendars, schematics, formulas, architectural drawings, blueprints, photographs, line drawings, maps (see the wolf study, for example), or other graphics summarize the issues, information, and arguments vividly and effectively? What conventions govern use of graphics for this kind of situation? Are you using graphic aids consistently with the standard conventions for their use (see Chapter 10) and with the specific conventions of your or your reader's organization? Again, are samples available for reference?

FIGURE 13.2 Section of Sample Student Report

MEMO

To: Barbara Grachek, Vice President of Academic Affairs
Rich Murray, Director of Career Services
Lee Bird, Vice President of Student Life and Development
Sherwood Reid, Director of Admissions
Will Littlejohn, President of Student Government
Jake Sedlacek, President of the Student Representative Assembly

From: Karen Blattner—blattk02@eeyore *Karen Blattner*
Mark Peterson—peterm06@tigger *Mark Peterson*
Paul Renslow—renslp01@eeyore *Paul Renslow*
Carrie Jean Schroeder—schroc01@condor *Carrie Jean Schroeder*
Darrin Todd—toddd01@condor *Darrin Todd*

Subject: Student Organization Booklet Proposal

Date: February 24, 1997

Are you feeling a bit haggard because potential and current SCSU students don't know what SCSU has to offer them? Many SCSU students are unaware of where their Student Activity Fees go and spend time complaining about losing money rather than making use of the services that SCSU can offer because of the fees. The attached proposal presents you with our solution to your awareness, recruitment, and promotion problems; we want SCSU to make information about Student Activity Fees and student organizations available in a yearly booklet.

As the system is currently, students have access to whatever financial information they need if they inquire to Student Government officials for it. The financial information they are given is typically vague unless students specifically request more details. In addition, advertisements pertaining to student organizations are lacking the information that students want to know.

In response to this lack of student awareness, we propose that your offices collectively publish a yearly booklet about student organizations and Student Activity Fees. This booklet would contain a brief description of each organization and the amount of money allotted to them by Student Government.

The booklet would serve many purposes. First, it would alleviate the mass confusion associated with Student Activity Fees. Second, it would serve as an outstanding recruiting tool for potential students. Lastly, it would present a positive way of promoting student involvement and awareness.

We ask that you consider this proposal and meet with our colleagues to discuss it. We hope you will find that our proposal offers a relatively simple solution to the awareness, recruiting, and promotion problems facing SCSU. Thank you for your time.

(continued)

FIGURE 13.2 Continued

Table of Contents

FIGURE 13.2 Continued

Executive Summary

St. Cloud State University should compile a booklet about student organizations and Student Activity Fees (SAFs) to be distributed to all students, both active and potential, to make them aware of what organizations and services are available to them as SCSU students.

The proposed booklet would explain what organizations receive funding, what they use the money for, and how to become involved in the organizations, among other pertinent details. The booklet could help solve some of SCSU's current problems with awareness, recruiting, and promotion by making relevant information readily available to students.

Currently, information about organizations and SAFs can only be obtained by actively and aggressively pursuing over one hundred direct sources. Though the amount of money paid in SAFs directly affects allocations to student organizations, students are uninformed when they look at their tuition statements and often become angry about the increasing SAF costs.

As seniors at SCSU, we also felt uninformed about SAFs to the point where it prompted us to investigate how our money was being spent. After obtaining information from Student Government about the 103 student organizations being supported by SAFs, we were still curious about many of the student organizations' activities and goals. We felt it necessary to improve awareness of student organizations because, as a group of five, we had only heard of fewer than half of the organizations.

With this goal in mind, we developed a survey (please see Appendix A) to be sure that other SCSU students would find more information about student organizations and SAFs useful. The survey was randomly distributed to 150 SCSU students of various majors and class ranking; 147 surveys were returned and evaluated.

The information we obtained from the surveys showed that most students are not aware of how much of their SAFs are spent on student organizations and that students do not know of all the different student organizations that exist at SCSU. Please refer to pages 2–6 for our findings about SCSU student awareness of organizations and SAFS.

From the survey results, it is clear that students have very little knowledge of and have no access to student organization information without actively pursuing it. This leads to a chicken and egg paradox: if students do not know what organizations exist, then how can they pursue something that they could be interested in?

It is clearly in the interests of the student community and St. Cloud State University that this information be more accessible to students. A booklet that would be distributed to all students could fulfill this need, as shown by student responses in Appendix B.

(continued)

FIGURE 13.2 Continued

The Results of Our Survey of Student Awareness: The Need for Better Information

Activity Fees Awareness

In our survey, we asked SCSU students to guess how much of their activity fees went to student organizations. The survey results showed that most students are not aware of how much of their SAFs are allocated to student organizations. Only 23 out of 147 SCSU students guessed in the $10–19 range (highlighted in black below), but not one student guessed the correct amount, which was $13.64.

Please note the section highlighted in white in the chart below. This segment shows that 7 out of 147 students guessed that over $110 in SAFs are given to student organizations quarterly; this is amazing, considering that students only pay a maximum of $109.20 per quarter. This shows that students are grossly unaware of how their SAFs are being used.

The booklet we propose would offer students information about how much money is collected, how it is allocated, and how the individual organizations make use of the money they receive. By making this information easily accessible, students will have no reason to complain about not knowing where their SAFs are being spent.

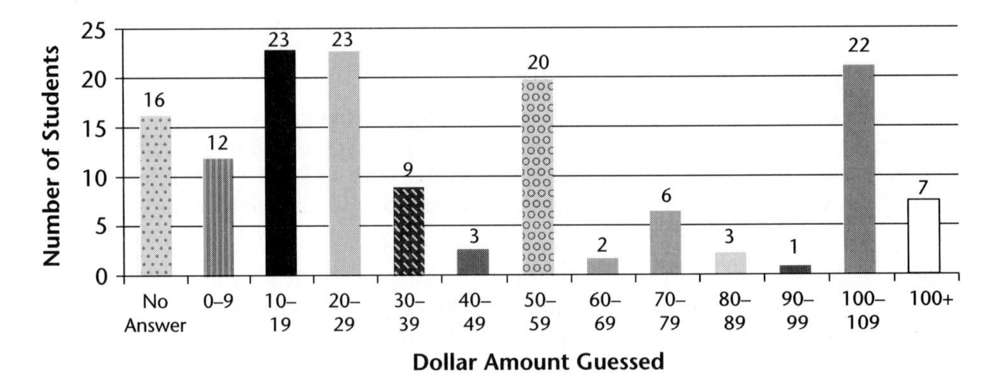

FIGURE 13.2 Continued

3

Student Organization Name Awareness

Our group randomly selected five organizations that use acronyms for identifying themselves and receive some the largest amounts of money from SAFs. We wanted to determine how many students could write out the organizations' full names, showing some kind of basic knowledge and awareness of the groups.

Out of 147 students, only 60 students knew what any one of the acronyms stood for. The acronym NOVA (Non-Violent Alternatives) was most widely known, having 27 people correctly write out the full name. However, we attribute this to the fact that NOVA's Week on Violence was taking place in the same week that we distributed the survey, and their promotional materials were plastered everywhere around campus.

This information is discouraging, but it greatly supports our argument: students need to be made more aware of the organizations that are available to them, and this could be done through our proposed booklet. The booklet would tell them not only the name of the organization, but also its activities, purpose, use of fees, and contact information.

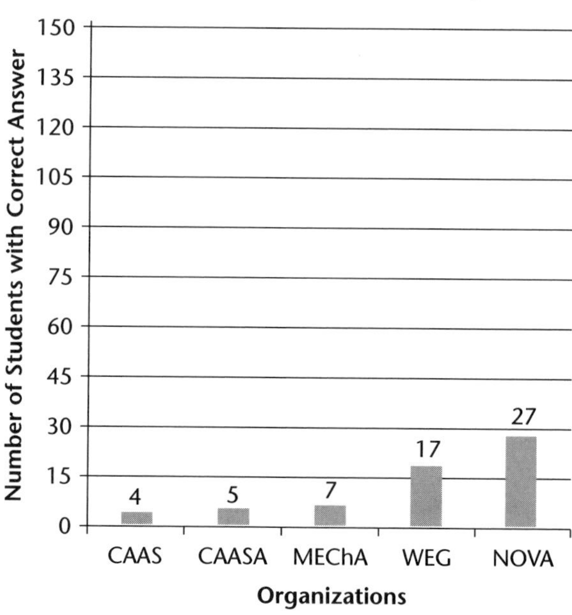

(continued)

FIGURE 13.2 Continued

Student Organization Awareness as Affected by Web Sites

Student organizations promote themselves using flyers, brochures, posters, booths at Mainstreet, and, most recently, web pages. To see how effective the web sites for organizations were, we asked students if they use the Internet to access information. 112 students out of 147 use the Internet for different purposes, and the graph below shows that only 47 SCSU students had searched through the available SCSU student organizations' web pages.

We expected that a larger percentage of students would be accessing organizational information through web sites, but it is clear that the web sites are not the answer to organizations' promotion problems.

We believe that our proposed booklet would fill in some of the promotional gaps for student organizations. The booklet would be useful to both students who are unaware that SCSU organizations have web pages and students who are not familiar with the Internet. The booklet's listings would include the web site address for each organization, and this would encourage students to access current information online.

Have You Searched through the Available SCSU Student Organizations' Web Pages?

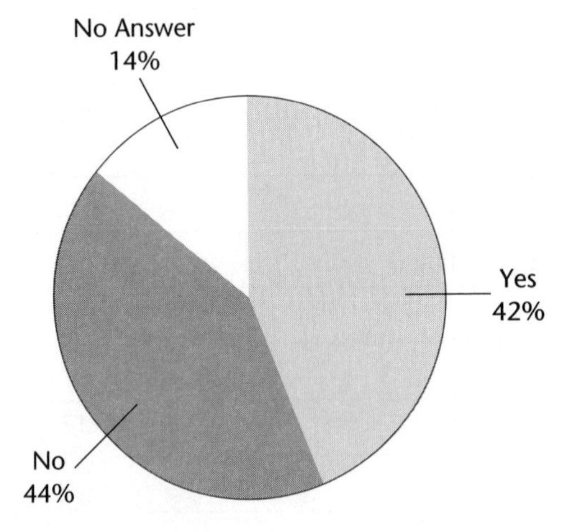

The power of a graphic presentation to reduce and summarize large quantities of complex data and analyses is dramatically demonstrated in the two tables from the Mexican wolf study (see Figure 13.3). Here, four alternative strategies and their projected ecological, economic, social, political, and legal ramifications—comprising about 400 pages in the full document—are summarized in three pages.

- **Sentence-level conventions.** Do the conventions of your organization permit or even require use of the conventional sentence structures that enhance clarity and directness (e.g., active voice, first-person pronouns when appropriate, nonperiodic sentences, active verbs in favor of nominalizations, and nestings of prepositional phrases)? (See Part VI for more information about such conventions.)
- **Diction.** What conventions govern the level of specialized or technical language in this situation? How do these conventions interact with your perception of the needs and expertise of your various readers? Will conventions allow you to provide intext explanations and definitions of difficult terms? Are you sure you're using these terms correctly yourself?

Source: © Tribune Media Services, Inc. All Rights Reserved. Reprinted with permission.

FIGURE 13.3 Sample Tables from Mexican Wolf Study (Figure 13.1)

Table 1. Summary of Mexican wolf re-establishment alternatives.
Key: BR = Blue Range Wolf Recovery Area; WS = White Sands Wolf Recovery Area.

Alternative	Description	Areas Analyzed	Definite Boundaries Around Recovery Areas?	Endangered Species Act Protection Status	Area Wolf Population Goal	Estimated Area to be Occupied by Wolves (square miles)
A (Preferred Alternative)	Nonessential experimental releases allowing dispersal into secondary recovery zones; BR first, WS back-up	BR and WS primary and secondary recovery zones	Yes	Per experimental population rule	BR and WS (if used): Total-100	BR and WS (if used): Total-5,000
B	Nonessential experimental releases preventing dispersal from primary zones	BR and WS primary recovery zones only	Yes	Per experimental population rule	WS-14 BR-20 Total-34	WS-720 BR-1,000 Total-1,720
C	Releases under full ESA protection	BR only plus likely dispersal areas	No	Endangered	BR-100+	BR->5,000
D	No releases; research and support possible natural recolonization	Southeastern Arizona, Southwestern New Mexico, and Big Bend National Park, Texas	No	Endangered (if wolves discovered)	(speculative) SE Ariz.-30 SW NM-20 Big Bend NP-5 Total–55	(speculative) SE Ariz.-1,500 SW NM-1,000 Big Bend NP-250 Total-2,750

(continued below)

Alternative	Meets 1982 Mexican Wolf Recovery Plan's Population Objective?	Estimated Years to Reach Area Population Goal	Estimated Annual Percentage of Established Population Lost to Control and Other Factors[1]	Major Land Use Restrictions	Intensity of Wolf Management and Control	Total Estimated Implementation Costs[2]
A (Preferred Alternative)	BR-Yes WS-No Together-Yes	BR-9 WS-3	B-35% WS-25%	None	Medium	$7,247,000 (over 14 years)
B	WS-No BR-No Together-No	WS-3 BR-5	WS-30% BR-40%	None	High	$5,890,000 (over 10 years)
C	BR-Yes	BR-6	BR-25%	Some possible	Low	$5,692,000 (over 10 years)
D	SE Ariz.-No SW NM-No Big Bend NP-No Together-No	Decades (speculative)	No estimates	Some possible (if wolves discovered)	Low	$150,000 to $217,000 per year (period indeterminate)

[1]In addition, about one-third of the captive-raised wolves that are released annually are expected to quickly die, disappear, disperse from the recovery area, or to require recapturing for a variety of reasons, and not to become part of the established population.

[2]See Appendix B for cost accounting.

FIGURE 13.3 Continued

Table 2. Summary of key projected impacts under each alternative.

Notes: Chap. 4 provides background for all information summarized here. All impacts in the back-up White Sands Recovery Area under Alt. A depend on whether the area is used. This table emphasizes quantifiable adverse impacts and is not a cost-benefit summary. Monetary losses are in 1994 dollars.

Key: BR = Blue Range Wolf Recovery Area; WS = White Sands Wolf Recovery Area.

Alternative	Net impact of wolf recovery on wild prey populations (low to high range)[1]	Impact on annual hunter take in area (low to high range)[1]	Annual lost value of hunting (low to high range)[2]	Annual lost hunter expenditures in region (low to high range)[2]	Number of cattle killed annually (low to high range)
A (Preferred Alt.)	BR: 4,800–10,000 fewer deer; 1,200–1,900 fewer elk	BR: 300–560 fewer deer; 120–200 fewer elk	BR: $716,800–$1,336,6000	BR: $579,100–$1,079,100	BR: 1–34
	WS: 1,200–3,000 fewer deer	WS: 10–24 fewer deer	WS: $3,000–$7,100	WS: $2,900–$7,000	WS: 0.01–0.3
B	BR: 970–1,900 fewer deer; 230–350 fewer elk	BR: 57–110 fewer deer; 24–33 fewer elk	BR: $123,100–$214,800	BR: $58,200–$101,500	BR: 0.03–1
	WS: 760–2,000 fewer deer	WS: 5–11 fewer deer	WS: $1,500–$3,300	WS: $1,500–$3,200	WS: 0
C	BR: 3,700–8,800 fewer deer; 870–1,700 fewer elk	BR: 240–480 fewer deer; 90–150 fewer elk	BR: $582,800–$1,119,200	BR: $470,700–$902,700	BR: 1–34
D[3]	not modelled	not modelled (none in Big Bend NP)	not modelled (none in Big Bend NP)	not modelled (none in Big Bend NP)	not estimated (none in Big Bend NP)

[1]Figures given compare prey populations under the wolf reintroduction scenario, at a point in time five years after the wolf population goal for the area is achieved, to what the prey populations are projected to be if wolves are not reintroduced.

[2]These figures likely overstate the actual losses. Hunters may not actually hunt less overall because of fewer deer and elk in the wolf recovery areas, but instead turn their attention to substitute areas or species. Further, deer and elk hunting in Arizona and New Mexico are dominated by resident hunters. Most of the money not spent by residents as hunter expenditures in the region probably will be spent in some other sector of the state economy.

[3]All projected impacts in the potential natural recolonization areas are speculative.

(continued on the next page)

(continued)

FIGURE 13.3 Continued

Table 2. Continued

Alternative	Value of cattle killed annually (low to high range)[4]	Economic benefits	Impacts on ADC activities	Impacts on government policies and plans	Impacts on land use and military activities	Impacts on recreation
A (Preferred Alt.)	BR: $640–$21,600	BR: increased recreational use and value expenditures	BR: M-44 and neck snare restrictions; limits on other tools	BR: conflict with local ordinances	BR: minor access restrictions near pens, dens, and rendezvous sites	BR: increased visitation
	WS: $10–$200	WS: little impact	WS: little impact	WS: limited conflict with local ordinances	WS: very limited access restrictions; inconvenience for security administration	WS: little impact
B	BR: $20–$600	BR: limited increased recreational use value and expenditures	BR: limited M-44 and neck snare restrictions; limits on other tools	BR: no conflict	BR: minor access restrictions near pens, dens, and rendezvous sites	BR: limited increased visitation
	WS: $0	WS: no impact	WS: no impact	WS: no conflict	WS: very limited access restrictions; inconvenience for security administration	WS: no impact
C	BR: $640–$21,600	BR: increased recreational use value and expenditures	BR: M-44 and neck snare restrictions; limits on other tools	BR: conflict with local ordinances; potential conflict with San Carlos and White Mountain Apaches' tribal sovereignty	BR: access restrictions near pens, dens, and rendezvous sites; restrictions on grazing and other activities	BR: increased visitation
D[3]	not estimated (none in Big Bend NP)	All 3 areas: increased recreational use value and expenditures	All 3 areas: M-44 and neck snare restrictions; limits on other tools	All 3 areas: no conflict	All 3 areas: access restrictions near pens, dens, and rendezvous sites; restrictions on grazing and other activities	All 3 areas: increased visitation

[4]Livestock losses may be compensated by a private depredation compensation fund.

Expression

Expression in your report may actually be determined. That is, you may be required by your own organization or another for whom you're writing the report to express yourself in a conventional way—perhaps in the bureaucratic, impersonal, faceless expression so common in more formal writing contexts. But since reports address such complex problems and diverse groups of readers, it makes sense to invest some time in thinking about the expression that's appropriate for your goals and readers:

- What character or ethos do you want to express, both personally and organizationally? Given the organizational context of the key issues, problems, and opportunities represented in this report; the prior relationships, conversations, and documents that have existed around them; and the style and tone of professional voices in which they have been expressed, what kind of expressions of your character are appropriate and useful here? What kind of voice, stance, or expression will your readers expect? Should you honor this expectation or break it?
- What ways of framing your arguments will be consistent with this kind of expression? For example, would a Rogerian style of argument (see Chapter 6) express the kind of character you want this report to embody? Or would it be at odds with the kind of voice, stance, or expression this situation seems to call for? Would your character be better represented by a low-key, just-the-facts style of argument that highlights the evidence and de-emphasizes your claims and warrants? Or would your ethos be better represented if you are more explicitly assertive in making your claims and setting forth your warrants?
- How can you use, modify, or even break the conventions of this kind of report-writing situation—at all levels, from conventions for organizing the global design of the report to specific microdecisions about such things as comma placement or word choice—to help you convey a voice, stance, or expression that indicates the aspects of your character you want to emphasize? What benefits and risks can you anticipate, especially if you decide to break a convention?

Reports solve problems, addressing the gaps between what is and what should be. So, as part of the report-writing process, writers should determine who is involved or affected by the problem and enlist their help in achieving report goals. Effective report writers also remember that organizations and their problems are dynamic and exist in historical, organizational, and human contexts amidst other written and electronic documents, projects, and daily activities. In fact, a report is usually one in a series of texts, including a proposal, progress reports, and other reports that are parts of the same project or series of projects.

While reports respond to complex problems and organizational contexts, they also speak to multiple readers with different perspectives, levels of knowledge, and purposes for reading. It's dangerous, then, to assume shared knowledge or assumptions or to take for granted reader interest, involvement, or familiarity with your assignment. Generally, you should assume that some readers will read only for the gist of your report, that others will read critically and analytically, and that still others will use your report as a specific guideline for implementing whatever you are recommending.

Reports also tend to be complex arguments that are sustained by extensive data and analysis; in fact, one of the strongest report-writing conventions is that readers expect to see claims and supporting documentation. Conventions also include ways of framing problems and solutions, laying out arguments, and formatting documents. Finally, reports conventionally express the organization's ethos, often (but certainly not always) in a formal or bureaucratic voice that mutes the presence of the writer.

WRITING CHECKLIST

The following guidelines will help you write formal reports, including progress reports, final project reports, and researched position papers. For any of these guidelines, remember the superordinate guideline: Disregard *any* of this advice if it would cause you to do something that's inappropriate or silly for your situation.

☑ Formal Reports

- Remember that identifying the essential problem to be solved is the key to defining your writing task, including deciding if you should even be writing a report and, if so, what sort of report it should be.
- In a progress report, you explicitly look back on what's been done and forward to what needs to be done.
- Since the progress report documents project work, it's like the second chapter of a proposal: You define the situation you began with, tell what's happened since you started the project, and announce what you plan to do to complete the project.
- In a progress report, you need to provide a convincing account of what you've done, even if the situation is routine; if something unexpected has occurred, you need to make appropriate arguments concerning changes you propose in view of what's happened.
- In a final project report, you make sure readers understand the project's context and requirements and demonstrate that you've completed the project as you said you would.
- In a researched position paper, your likely goal is to change the minds of a wide, heterogeneous group of readers.
- To prepare for writing a position paper, determine who has a stake in the problem, need, or opportunity. Then, figure out how their needs and resources complement your own and how they might help you achieve your goals.
- Remember that organizations and problems are dynamic; look closely at your goals in relation to the historical, organizational, and human context of the problems they address.

- Also keep in mind that reports are likely to have multiple readers with different levels of understanding, perspectives, and commitment as well as different purposes for reading the report.
- Generally, assume that there will be three levels of readers for your report: Level 1, those the report is addressed to (perhaps executives authorized to make decisions based on report content); Level 2, those who will read critically and carefully and study your analysis and argument thoroughly; and Level 3, those who will use the report as a blueprint for action.
- Provide the Level 1/decision-making reader with a summary of the problem, major details and alternatives, and a rationale for your recommendation.
- Because reports are written when arguments are too long and complex to be made in letters and memos, your arguments will likely be multilayered and need extensive supporting data and analysis.
- You should base your arguments on what you want to happen as a result of the report, what values and assumptions your readers hold, the significant opposing arguments inherent in the situation, and conflicting and converging interests among those with a stake in the problem.
- Consider all the available arguments and their likely risks and benefits.
- Remember that one of the strongest report conventions is thorough documentation with specific data; readers expect to see facts supporting your claims.
- Include your documentation—data, principles of interpretation, sources of data, methods of analysis, and justification and rationale for methods—in the report somewhere.
- Pay attention to procedural conventions for report writing in your organization: customary timelines for planning, drafting, and reviewing projects.
- Pay attention to conventional ways of framing the problem and solutions, laying out the arguments, organizing your evidence, and expressing your own and the organization's character.
- Make appropriate decisions about conventional elements of reports (e.g., the cover, paper, ink, type size and font, cover letter, executive summary, table of contents, overall organization, appendix, graphics, etc.) based on your situation and your goals.
- Decide what character or ethos you want to express as well as what style of argument will be consistent with this expression.

ACTIVITIES AND PROJECTS

1. Interview a professional about the sorts of reports typically done in your field. Some questions you might want to ask include the following:
   - What sorts of reports are written, how often, and why?
   - Who writes them?

- Are these reports written individually or collaboratively?
- What types of data are generally expected and why?
- What sorts of arguments tend to be made?
- And what questions and concerns do these reports often address?
- What kind of reservations or qualifications to their claims do they typically make in their reports?

Note that your interviewee may not know how you're using these terms (i.e., *reservations* and *qualifications*), so you may have to explain. They might be accustomed to using words like *delimitation* and *scope* instead.

2. Work in a small group to generate guidelines for writing collaboratively. Include strategies for working smoothly as a team, delegating responsibility, making various group members accountable, and encouraging group members to do their best work. Also include a list of "don'ts." Finally, describe various methods of doing the actual writing, selecting the method you feel is the best.

3. Write a progress report about the project you proposed in response to Activity 7, 8, or 9 in Chapter 12.

4. Write the report or complete the project you proposed in response to Activity 7, 8, or 9 in Chapter 12. Use appropriate research methodology (see Chapter 11) to generate data on which to build your argument and support your claims. Use GRACE to plan, write, and revise your report, and use guidelines on document design and graphics from Chapter 10. Finally, ask your colleagues to do a GRACEful review of your report draft and make constructive suggestions about how to improve it.

5. Individually or with several of your colleagues, write a researched position paper about a current controversy, a new procedure or technique, or a new technology or application of technology in your field. Your readers for this report might be students, professors, or other professionals in your field.

6. Investigate a problem in a local organization (e.g., on your campus, in your workplace, in your community), and write a report recommending a particular course of action.

7. Figure 13.2 is the cover memo, table of contents, executive summary, and first 3 pages of a 13-page report done by a group of university students in response to a class assignment based on Activities 4, 5, and 6 in this chapter. Have someone keep track of time for you (or keep track of time yourself using an egg timer, alarm on your wristwatch, etc.), and give yourself three minutes to scan the report. Then, ask yourself these questions:
   - Can you get a good idea of what this group's argument is?
   - Can you find their main claim?
   - Can you find their key evidence?
   - Do any features of the report help you find this information? If so, what are they?
   - Do any features of the report act as barriers to your quick understanding of the central argument and its significance? If so, what are they?

Now read the report taking as much time as you want. Ask yourself the same questions again. Also consider how persuasive the university students' argument is—first, to you as a reader and then, to the readers they address in their cover memo.

Incidentally, how would you justify using a cover memo here instead of a cover letter? How successfully would you say this report makes the leap from being just a class assignment to serving as a document that identifies and defines a problem that's significant to its writers, that discusses and analyzes the problem in a responsible way, and, finally, that makes a persuasive argument on behalf of a proposed solution?

Remember, of course, that you don't have the whole report here, so you have to decide these issues based on the pages you have. You could rate the report on each of these three criteria: (1) identifies and defines a significant problem/issue; (2) discusses and analyzes the issues effectively; (3) and makes effective arguments about the issue.

REFERENCE

Mathes, J. C., & Stevenson, D. (1976). *Designing technical reports: Writing for audiences in organizations.* Indianapolis, IN: Bobbs-Merrill.

Chapter 14

Presenting Reports Orally

It usually takes more than three weeks to prepare a good impromptu speech.

—Mark Twain

Often, when people write proposals, progress reports, business plans, and other sorts of reports, they're expected to give oral presentations, too. For instance, a project engineer might brief a client on the current status of a design project in addition to writing a progress report. A team leader might follow up a written proposal to upper management recommending a new inventory control system with an oral presentation that summarizes the details of the proposal and dramatizes the need for change. An entrepreneur seeking funding for a new company will probably make an oral presentation to potential lenders or investors in addition to submitting a written business plan. Or a marketing consultant who has researched marketing opportunities to help a company gain a competitive advantage might report those findings both orally and in writing.

Presenting Oral Reports with GRACE

Whatever your professional work, you are almost certain to be called upon to speak about the issues you write about. And a GRACEful analysis of your speaking situation can help you to frame a presentation that enhances the acceptance of your goals and arguments—both by listeners who have read your written text and by listeners who are relying completely on your oral presentation.

Goals

Oral presentations have many goals. Some presentations are intended to inform listeners—to brief them on the progress of a project, the development of a product or service, or the status of a new process or procedure. Other presentations provide listeners with information they need to understand the mission or vision of an organization, the steps in a process or procedure, or the nature of changes occurring in the worksite. Some presentations are meant to teach listeners how to do or use something—a specific piece of equipment, a new process, or a modified procedure. Finally, some presentations are intended to persuade listeners. In fact, in any presentation that you give, you'll want to convince your audience that you're credible—that you know what you're talking about, that you deserve your listeners' confidence, and that they should accept your ideas. And beyond instilling confidence and convincing listeners of your trustworthiness, you'll often want to convince them to take a specific action, to feel a particular way about what you're presenting, or to believe something regarding your topic.

In fact, many of the goals of your oral presentation may be the same as those of your written report. Nonetheless, it's important to keep the differences between your written text and your oral presentation firmly in mind. Think about the following:

- Why are you making this presentation? How are the goals of this presentation similar to those of your report, and how are they different?
- What specifically do you want to accomplish as a result of your presentation? Do you want listeners to sign off on a project? To authorize funds for hiring additional staff? To feel excited about the benefits of a new system?
- What do you want listeners to know, feel, believe, or do as a result of your presentation?
- What, specifically, do you want listeners to carry away from your presentation?

In addition to these action-centered goals, you might have other goals you hope your presentation will achieve. For instance, you'll undoubtedly want your presentation to be clear, complete, and effectively paced so that you're finished within the allotted timeframe. And you'll certainly want to appear confident and professional. In addition to these immediate goals, you'll have some long-term goals, too—to establish and maintain your own credibility or the credibility of your company, to make listeners responsive to your company's products or services, and to create ongoing awareness of your company's mission or vision and the listeners' part in that mission or vision. Finally, you might even want to entertain your audience, perhaps engaging their interest and participation in a somewhat playful way. To achieve your goals—whether to prompt listeners to take action or simply to enjoy your presentation and feel good about you and your organization—you'll need to know your listeners and their needs pretty well.

Readers

Obviously, the *readers* of your oral presentations are your *listeners*. Keep in mind, though, that they are "reading" your presentation with their ears. So, if they miss a word or phrase or forget a key point you've made, they can't skip back a few lines and reread it. They will hear your presentation only once and must formulate their response based upon your spoken text. This, of course, puts a great deal of pressure on listeners' memory. One of the real advantages of oral reports over written ones, however, is that listeners can give you immediate feedback through nonverbal responses like nodding, smiling, staring, or looking with eyes glazed over and sometimes more actively during formal question-and-answer periods, too.

We will talk more about these demands on listeners' memory and the opportunities for listener interaction in the following discussion. We also suggest some questions you can ask yourself about your listeners that will help target your presentation to meet their needs.

Listeners and Memory

Remember when we talked in Chapter 1 about George Miller's (1956) classic research on short-term memory, "The Magical Number Seven, Plus or Minus Two"? Miller established that most of us can hold about seven pieces of information at a time in our short-term memory, give or take a couple of pieces. This limit on short-term memory has special significance when you are preparing an oral presentation. When you write, the text fixes the information on the page so that it will hold still; readers can read the information and come back to it as often as they like. But when you present information orally, the text is transitory, and listeners will retain only a limited portion of it. That's why experts in oral communication recommend that speakers limit the information in their presentations to five main ideas if they wish listeners to remember them. Experts also recommend that you repeat any idea you want listeners to retain "*from three to ten times* during your presentation, either verbatim or expressed in different words with a slightly different slant" (Morrisey, Sechrest, & Warman, 1997, p. 57). In addition to using repetition thoughtfully, you can structure information to increase your listeners' recall and select strategies for delivering your talk that make it memorable. In fact, these structural and delivery strategies for enhancing your listeners' ability to remember are a firmly established part of oral presentations, which we will discuss in detail under Conventions.

Listeners and Their Questions

Unlike written reports, oral presentations offer listeners an opportunity to provide immediate feedback. Sometimes, in informal situations, presenters encourage listeners to ask questions any time during the course of the talk. More frequently, though, particularly in formal contexts, a question-and-answer period follows the presentation. A question-and-answer period offers a wonderful opportunity to involve your listeners actively in your topic and to gain valuable feedback; it also allows you to respond to any reservations or doubts listeners might have, to provide additional information, and to clarify or reinforce your message.

At the same time, a question-and-answer period also introduces risks—that you won't be able to answer listeners' questions or meet their objections, that you'll be so taken aback by a question that you'll bumble your response, that a loaded question may lead only to your embarrassed silence, or that irrelevant questions will detract listeners from the primary goals of your presentation. To minimize these risks, you'll want to spend some time preparing for the question-and-answer period, anticipating the sorts of questions and objections listeners might have and planning how you'll respond to them. You'll also want to consider how you might build upon likely listener needs and concerns to reinforce the goals of your presentation. We will talk later in this chapter about how to prepare for a question-and-answer period and exert some control over this final and therefore very memorable section of a presentation.

Questions about Listeners

Given the special demands that oral presentations place upon listeners' short-term memory and the opportunities for interaction they often provide, you should ask yourself questions like these as you prepare so that your presentation will be adapted to your listeners:

- What are the benefits to listeners of paying attention to your presentation?
- What do listeners expect from your presentation?
- What do your listeners already know about the topic of your presentation?
- What do your listeners need and want to know?
- In what specific ways is the topic relevant to your listeners' work environment, responsibilities, and interests? And what is going on in the work environment that they will expect you to consider in your presentation?
- What roles will these listeners play regarding what you're presenting? Do listeners have decision-making authority? Will they be in a position to influence those people who do?
- What skills and experience do your listeners have that are relevant to what you're presenting?
- What perspectives or opinions about your topic are listeners likely to bring to your presentation?
- What sorts of assumptions, beliefs, and values do your listeners hold regarding your topic? And what assumptions, beliefs, and values do they hold in general? How are they likely to use these assumptions, values, and beliefs to test your data and claims?
- What are listeners' needs and concerns related to your presentation topic? What are their priorities?
- What questions, concerns, and reservations are listeners likely to have? How receptive will they likely be to the ideas that you'll present?
- What activities regarding your topic will follow your presentation? How do you hope that listeners will participate in these activities?
- What reaction do you want from your listeners? Specifically, what do you want listeners to know, think, do, feel, or believe as a result of your presentation?
- What action must listeners take in order for your presentation to meet its goals?

Using these questions to analyze your listeners will help you frame and elaborate arguments appropriate for your specific audience and goals.

Of course, if you're presenting to listeners from another culture who speak another language, you'll want to ask additional questions to help meet the challenges of framing and presenting your arguments effectively. And you'll have additional concerns, too—about language differences and how you can adapt to the needs of listeners whose first language is not English, about cultural values and perspectives, about the use of humor, and about how to work effectively with a translator if you decide to use one. (For help with these issues, see Chapter 15, Opportunities and Risks in Cross-Cultural Communication.)

Arguments

The arguments you use for your oral presentation will rely heavily upon those you used for the written report on which it's based. So, much of what we've said about argument in Chapters 12 and 13 will be useful when you begin to think about the claims, data, and warrants you'll use in your talk. But you won't be able in your oral presentation to present the *exact* argument that you developed—in all of its rich complexity—in your written text. Time constraints and limitations on your listeners' short-term memory will force you to streamline your argument. Keeping in mind the guideline that listeners often retain only five key ideas, consider carefully the claims you want to make and the evidence you'll use to support them. What *are* your central claims, and what evidence is *crucial* to supporting them?

As you consider the claims you'll make and the evidence you'll use to back them, your knowledge of your listeners will be essential:

- What must your listeners understand or believe if your presentation is to be successful? And what data or evidence is likely to convince them to understand, believe, and do what you'd like them to?
- What kinds of information, techniques, and approaches are most likely to affect your listeners positively? Will your listeners want observable facts, statistics, citations from authorities, or examples? Will they want hard data or scientific explanations? Will they want personal stories that connect them emotionally to your topic?
- What sorts of presentational materials will listeners find compelling? High-tech? Low-tech? And what content do you want these materials to communicate? As we'll discuss in the section Conventions for Presentation Visuals, you have lots of options for displaying information that supports your arguments—ranging from simple, ad hoc sorts of tools, like flipcharts and chalkboards, to sophisticated multimedia presentational software represented by programs like Microsoft PowerPoint and Adobe Persuasion. So, what presentational tools will listeners expect you to use, and how will they expect you to use them? Also, what content will they want to see displayed in these materials?

As you plan your argument and the sorts of data and warrants you'll use to bolster your claims, remember that it's easy to overwhelm listeners with information. So in your presentation, you'll want to streamline your argument as much as possible, keeping in mind that you'll have the opportunity to provide additional data or extended examples during the question-and-answer period. In fact, it might be useful to think of an oral presentation in terms of its similarities to an executive summary, since the two share some features: both present a pared-down argument, including only key claims and crucial evidence and foregoing the rich elaboration characteristic of written reports. And, as with an executive summary, you'll also find it useful in your oral report to employ conventions for increasing listener retention, organizing your argument, and supporting your argument visually since these conventions make a streamlined yet compelling argument possible.

Conventions

To a large degree, what your listeners remember will determine whether your presentation is successful in meeting its goals, so it makes sense to structure your presentation to increase listeners' retention. And to do so, you must first improve their *attention.* The structure of your presentation should highlight your most important points and the vital links between them so listeners can follow your argument and see it as a reasonable, coherent network of data and claims. The use of visuals can also help illustrate the main ideas of your argument in concrete forms that will markedly increase your listeners' ability to understand and remember what you say and that will dramatically support your claims.

Structuring Presentations to Increase Listener Retention

As you design your presentation, remember that listeners will need repetition of content and guidance about how the parts of your talk fit together if they're going to make sense of what you say and retain your key ideas. To help them put everything together and keep the thrust of your argument, claims, and data in mind, use these conventional strategies:

- **In your opening,** provide a brief overview of your presentation, including the specific subject and purpose of your talk and a forecast of what you'll cover. Listeners need to have a feel for the shape of the presentation as an *advanced organizer,* which gives them a foundation for understanding the information that follows. This presentation overview is frequently supported by an outline of the talk, and it's common to announce the number of key ideas, steps, or stages that your talk will cover.
- **Throughout the body** of your presentation, provide your listeners with guideposts so they know where they are and where they're going. Garmston and Wellman (1992, pp. 46–47) suggest the following strategies for helping your listeners understand where they are in the presentation and how all the parts fit together.
  - **Foreshadowing** what's coming up not only lets listeners know where the presentation is going but also creates expectations about and interest in what's coming up.
  - **Bridging** links previous information with what's coming next and provides transitions between chunks of presentation content. For instance, you might say, "We've just considered strategies for enhancing listener comprehension in the opening of a talk and are moving into techniques you can use in the body of a presentation. Later, we will review methods you can use to enhance your listeners' recall as you close a speech." Sometimes, when a talk is long

or the issues are complicated, it helps at key transitions to summarize your main points and use visuals for support. This helps listeners connect your main ideas.

- **Backtracking** is the frequent review of what you've covered. Each backtracking helps listeners review where the presentation has taken them and refreshes their memory about the significant points you've made.

- **In the closing,** summarize the main points of your talk, and support this summary with a visual. Also, integrate your opening points back into your closing remarks to enhance understanding, provide listeners with a sense of coherence, and remind them of the purpose of your talk. Finally, keep in mind that the closing of a talk is a high-attention time, so what you say then is most likely to be remembered.

Conventions for Opening and Closing Presentations

Openings and closings of presentations are usually the times when listener interest is the highest, so it makes sense that conventions have emerged for taking advantage of this interest. The first few minutes of a talk are also essential in establishing your image and connecting with the audience since most listeners make judgments about speakers immediately. It's important, then, that you communicate respect and confidence, establish credibility, and show you're well prepared. You can do this by starting on time and by introducing yourself briefly, connecting what you're talking about with the listeners' work. Opening this way immediately answers three questions that listeners have:

1. Who are you? (assuming, of course, that they don't already know)
2. What is this talk all about?
3. What does this talk have to do with me?

In addition to answering these three key questions, openings can also motivate listeners to be attentive, often through one of these strategies:

- **A brief story** that's directly relevant to your topic often captures listeners' interest. And if the anecdote is workplace specific, it can show listeners the relevance of the talk to their own lives.

- **A startling statistic or fact** related to your topic can arouse interest and provoke questions in listeners' minds.

- **A vivid example of a problem in the workplace** that your presentation addresses can create audience concern and the need for answers.

- **Dissonance**—something that will trouble your listeners or encourage them to become involved in a problem-solving mode—can focus your session and energize your audience (Garmston & Wellman, 1992, p. 27).

- **A specific question** that's a key topic in your talk and is important to your listeners can focus your remarks and engage your listeners.

- **A quotation** that's meaningful to your listeners and relevant to your topic can help create an appropriate mood or window into the topic, engage the audience's emotions, or otherwise prepare them for your talk.

- **A direct statement** of what you plan to talk about and why the audience will find it important will be effective if the link between the presentation's content and listener needs or interests is firmly made.

Conventions for Developing the Body of the Presentation

Many conventional structures are available for developing the body of your argument. Of course, you'll want to select a framework that enables you to make your argument forcefully and that highlights your key claims and essential data. Here are some options to consider (although other arrangements also might be appropriate for your goals and listeners and the arguments you want to make):

- **A problem/reasons/solution approach** is useful if you want to identify a problem, isolate its causes, and show how to solve it. This sort of approach often opens with a startling statistic, a dramatic story, or some other opening tactic that creates dissonance for listeners.

- **A question/answer arrangement** poses key questions listeners are likely to have about the topic and immediately answers them, alternating questions and answers in the order that most effectively meets your presentation goals.

- **A cause/effect structure** is useful if you want to emphasize the causes that led to a particular effect or trace the results of a cause. This structure is particularly helpful if you need to explain research findings or clarify how something happened.

- **A chronological approach or time sequence** will enable you to explain the steps of a process, tell a story, or trace the history of something and perhaps project what might happen in the future.

- **Spatial organization** isn't used very often but is appropriate if you want to describe what a physical object or site looks like.

In addition to these conventional approaches to developing your presentation, you might find the *jigsaw puzzle approach* useful (First Books for Business, 1996, pp. 26–27). This approach—a variation of the problem/reasons/solution strategy—fits the following pieces together seamlessly in this order to create a high-impact presentation:

- **The introduction and background** set the stage for the rest of the presentation by providing a foundation of data or a perspective that helps listeners understand what follows.

- **A problem statement** makes listeners aware of the problem that needs to be solved, the issue that needs to be addressed, or the opportunity that should be embraced.

- **The data and analysis** section provides the facts, stories, and information that will enable listeners to make informed decisions.
- **The solution statement** provides your resolution of the problem and leads naturally to the benefits.
- **The benefits section** of your presentation explains why you're proposing this solution, shows how this solution will address listeners' interests and priorities, and clarifies advantages for the organization.
- **A summary with motivational elements** solidifies your main ideas by reviewing them. It also links your conclusions and specific requests for action to motivational statements like "to gain these advantages," "to improve quality indicators," or "if you would like to . . ."
- **An action statement** specifies what you'd like your listeners to do, think, or believe.

No matter what arrangement you use for the body of your oral presentation, you'll want to incorporate elements that will make your talk lively and maintain the interest of your listeners. Consider these approaches:

- **Use examples and illustrations** to connect your key ideas to your listeners' work and responsibilities.
- **Relate personal stories** to show your personal involvement in the topic or to connect your listeners emotionally to the information you're presenting.
- **Use humor** to relax your audience and make them receptive to your message. But make sure your humor is relevant to your message and appropriate to your audience. And avoid off-color jokes and those with racist or sexist messages.
- **Use an analogy**—a comparison that attempts to describe one thing in terms of something else—to explain technical information to a nontechnical audience. For instance, a student once explained *orthokeratology,* the process of reshaping the eye through use of corrective contact lenses, by comparing this technique to the use of braces for teeth.
- **Show visuals** that illustrate the key points of your argument (see the following section).

Conventions for Presentation Visuals

When you present a talk, bolster what you say with carefully crafted presentation visuals. You have a lot of options to consider, ranging from low-tech options, like handouts, whiteboards, and overheads to sophisticated, high-tech options, like multimedia software. *But caution!* Before you make irrevocable choices about what presentational aids to use, make sure the physical environment will permit you to use them. For example, make sure that lighting and room layout will enable your audience to see your visual aids. Make sure projection equipment and available electrical outlets are available and compatible with your equipment. (This is especially important if you're preparing for an overseas presentation, where standard voltages and configurations of outlets may not be compatible with American-made electrical devices and may require adapter plugs and voltage converters.) Also make sure both your audio equipment and your visual aids, whether high tech or low tech, are appropriate for the size of the room.

The following list reviews some conventional ways of presenting visuals, noting their respective advantages and disadvantages:

- **Handouts** are useful if you want to provide listeners with detailed technical information or hard copies of overheads you've used during your talk—particularly concrete data, drawings, charts, or other information you want listeners to review after your talk is over. The presentation software we'll discuss later allows you to reproduce high-quality copies of individual screens easily.

  When you provide handouts to listeners, though, carefully time when you distribute them. If you distribute them at the beginning of your talk, your listeners are likely to review them, rather than focus on what you're saying. So, unless you want your audience to use the handouts for taking notes, you're probably wiser to distribute them when your presentation is over and to mention that listeners will receive the handouts at an appropriate time during the talk. Also, if you have a lot of handouts, it's a good idea to bind them so that they look professional and are durable.

- **Whiteboards (dry-erase boards), chalkboards, and flipcharts (pads of paper mounted on easels)** allow you to write and draw simple illustrations or to map out ideas as you go. And all three tools allow spontaneity, providing lots of open space to record all sorts of things—say, outlines, lists of information, simple illustrations or graphics, or the results of group brainstorming. You can erase the whiteboard or chalkboard to provide more room for writing, and you can simply flip to a new page on the flipchart when you need more space.

  But these tools have disadvantages, too. Unless you have a reproducing whiteboard—a high-tech version that can capture what's written on it by producing hard copy—you'll lose information you've written using a whiteboard or chalkboard since it will be erased when you're done. You can, of course, save the sheets from a flipchart. It's difficult, too, to see flipcharts, whiteboards, or chalkboards if the room or the audience is large. And drawing complex visuals, like maps, for instance, is hard to do with any accuracy. Nonetheless, these support tools are very appropriate for smaller groups, less complex information, and less formal contexts.

- **Overheads**—like chalkboards, dry-erase boards, and flipcharts—give you the flexibility to map out your ideas as you go, generate text or illustrations as you talk, or write or draw information or illustrations you've planned ahead of time to give your presentation the feeling of spontaneity. You can also project visuals that you've prepared in advance. And if you want to emphasize particular data or parts of an image on a transparency, you can use a pointer (or your finger if the context is informal); you can even stand some distance away and use a laser pointer to shoot a beam of light to draw listeners' eyes to particular information.

But if you use an overhead projector, keep a few things in mind:

- It's best to pause briefly when you change transparencies since your pause will prompt your listeners to look at the new material you're placing on the overhead. And if you don't pause, listeners may not know where to look and may miss what you're saying.
- When you're not referring to material on a transparency, turn the overhead projector off so that the image from the last transparency you used or the light from the blank screen doesn't distract your listeners' attention.
- Be sure to address your remarks to your listeners, instead of turning around and looking at the image projected on the screen.
- If you're the one who's going to be changing the transparencies, be sure that you practice doing this while giving your talk so that the process will be automatic. If someone else is changing transparencies for you, make sure to let them know ahead of time when to put each transparency on the overhead.

■ **Slide projectors** allow you to project on a large screen colored visuals of products, equipment, or other still images you want listeners to see. If you have a remote control that enables you to change slides from anywhere in the room, you can control the amount of time the visuals are projected and easily adjust the pace of the presentation. Of course, high-quality slides can be expensive to produce and often require the help of media support people to take and develop, which requires advanced planning and coordination. However, slides are really useful if you have a lot of lead time and are making a formal presentation to a large audience.

■ **Video and motion picture projectors** enable you to provide action clips: for example, the testimony of a customer or expert, the demonstration of a complex procedure using specialized equipment, or a location shot or a tour of a new plant. Usually, you'll use videotape since the recording technology is easy and video players connected to large screens are readily available in many organizations. But like slides, video and film require advanced planning and often the support of media experts. Nonetheless, video and film are useful for formal presentations with adequate preparation time.

■ **Multimedia projectors and presentation software** can enable you to develop professional materials fairly easily using sound, motion, and color. A good presentation program—such as Microsoft PowerPoint, Aldus Persuasion, or Corel Presentation for Windows—provides templates or "wizards" that offer default colors, fonts, and basic layouts. And these programs often come with large clip-art collections and graphic capabilities, so you can design or alter visuals, as needed.

As with slides and videotape, presentation software is particularly useful if you're presenting in a formal context and the room and audience are large. Presentation software is also helpful if you want to present complex ideas simply, especially if you have a limited timeframe. And as we've already suggested,

"These gratifying figures show that our results have improved from total foul-up to half-baked."

Source: Reprinted with permission of Ted Goff.

you can easily reproduce the most significant slides from your presentation and distribute them to your listeners. A final advantage to using presentation software is that you can prepare your entire talk ahead of time and then read the slides, step by step, as you present to your listeners; in other words, using presentation software minimizes the need for memorizing your script. But this advantage is a disadvantage, too, since you need a reasonable amount of time to prepare the computer slides. A final disadvantage is that you may not always have access to the equipment needed to run the presentation software: a computer with the appropriate software, a liquid crystal display (LCD) or projector plugged into the computer so that the presentation can be projected, and a screen large enough for clear display to the audience.

As is clear from this discussion, there are lots of ways to add meaning and interest to your presentations through visual illustration. Yet, no matter what sorts of visuals you use, you should follow these principles:

- Design presentation visuals to support your presentation, not for their own sake.
- You'll find that some parts of presentations are natural spots for using visuals; for instance, presenters often open talks with striking images to get listeners'

attention. You'll often want to open with a summary visual to establish the goals or agenda of your talk. In the body of a presentation, use visuals to underscore your key ideas as you introduce them, and in the closing, review the central points of your talk on a visual so that listeners will retain them.

- Focus each presentation visual on one key idea—even if that visual provides a lot of information about that idea.
- When possible, use graphics or illustrations instead of text to support your argument. But limit yourself to one graphic element per page or screen, so it doesn't lose its impact.
- When you use text, try to fill up no more than one-half of the viewing area, so the visuals are easy to read and your points are emphatic. It's best to use no more than four words per line and six lines per visual. Key words and short phrases have more impact than full sentences (Morrisey et al., 1997, p. 94).
- Use type fonts and sizes that will be easy to see anywhere in the room you'll use for your presentation. Sans serif fonts are best for headlines, and serif fonts are best for body text.
- Use color to add interest and emphasize what you want listeners to notice.
- If you're using presentation software, be sure that the version of the program you'll be using is the same one you used to create your presentation. You might even want to take your own computer (easily done if you have a laptop) to ensure compatibility.
- In general, select the simplest method of presenting visuals that is appropriate for your listeners, your argument, and your goals. And if you decide that a high-tech presentation is the best way to go, be sure to take some sort of backup—additional disks, cables, or other equipment or a lower-tech set of presentation visuals—in case your high-tech equipment doesn't work.

Conventions of Question-and-Answer Sessions

As noted earlier, presentations are often followed by formal question-and-answer periods, which give listeners an opportunity to find out more about your topic, ask questions about things that concern them, and address issues your presentation didn't cover. And since the question-and-answer session is the last thing your listeners will hear, it's important that you leave them with a good impression. Here are some time-tested conventions for dealing effectively with listeners' questions:

- **Pause to think about what you're going to say.** Although there's real pressure to fill up the silence when you're standing in front of an audience, taking time to formulate your response will enable you to meet your listener's needs and answer the question that was asked. If you feel uncomfortable about delaying, remember that such silence is usually interpreted as thoughtfulness. And you can always acknowledge the delay by saying something like "You've raised a complicated and important question. Let me think about that for a minute."

- **Repeat the question, especially if the audience is large.** This will not only enable everyone to hear what was asked but will also enable you to check to make sure you've understood the question. Repeating the question will give you a few moments to think through your response, too.
- **Encourage your listeners' active involvement.** To invite questions, walk around and look at your entire audience, rather than just one section, so everyone feels included and encouraged to participate. And when people do ask questions, acknowledge their contributions by beginning your response with supportive statements like "That's a good question" or "That's an interesting point" (First Books, 1996, pp. 18–19).
- **Maintain openness.** If you're unable to answer a question, don't try to bluff your way through it. If someone is present in the room who *can* answer the question, refer it to him or her. In fact, if you make a presentation about something really technical—perhaps something produced by a team—you'll probably want to bring experts from the team with you, anticipating that you won't be able to answer every question. More often, though, you can simply admit that you don't know the answer but will find out and get back to the person who asked the question.
- **Stay focused.** If you're asked an irrelevant question, provide a brief answer and then tactfully offer to follow up on it in more detail after the presentation is over. Keep your answers to all questions short. The longer you talk, the more likely you are to lose focus and ramble. In general, you should try to tie every answer to the overall goal of your presentation.
- **Maintain tactfulness.** If someone asks a loaded question or one that is clearly intended to start a debate, the smartest thing you can do is to simply refuse to argue. Morrisey, Sechrest, and Warman (1997, pp. 138–139) suggest that when a person gets argumentative during a question-and-answer period, he or she is primarily looking for recognition and the opportunity to show off knowledge or expertise. It makes sense, then, to simply acknowledge him or her and move the debate outside the context of the presentation by saying something like "What you're saying is interesting and bears further discussion. Let's set up a time to go over this in more detail after the meeting." You can also answer the question briefly, defer more detailed discussion until later, and move on to the next question.
- **Remember your facts, data, and analysis.** If you've prepared thoroughly for your presentation, the questions listeners ask should enable you to tap into a wealth of information, to use facts for support, and to reiterate the key points of your presentation. In other words, the best strategy for dealing with questions takes place long before the presentation occurs: becoming so familiar with your material that you remain in full control, no matter what questions are asked.

Expression

When we first introduced GRACE in Chapter 1, we mentioned the challenge of trying to create in a written document something that's equivalent to the expression readers might see on your face if you spoke to them about what's represented in that document. Those written strategies of expression are also available when you make an oral presentation—namely, manipulating the level of formality in your word choice, adapting the formality and complexity of your sentence structure, using first-person and second-person pronouns for decreasing emotional distance between you and your readers or using third-person pronouns and other impersonal pronouns to increase the distance and level of formality, and the rest of your verbal repertoire.

But now, when your listeners can *see* the actual physical image of you in action, you also have an array of nonverbal means of expressing—enacting, even—the emotional and ethical essence that makes you and your organization who you are. Everything visible about you contributes to this expression: the clothes you wear, your facial expressions and hand gestures, your posture, and how well you control the nervousness that so many of us feel when we speak in front of a group of people. The exciting thing about all these nonverbal cues is that they present opportunities to powerfully reinforce your verbal argument by demonstrating your character, confidence, competence, and goodwill. And the unnerving thing about them is that they present opportunities to stub your toe, to send unintentional, even inaccurate, nonverbal messages that powerfully undercut your credibility.

Your Clothes

Unless you intend for your manner of dress to serve as a kind of costume or deliberate stage prop (as an extreme example, maybe dressing as Miss Piggy for a gag presentation), your clothing should not call attention to itself. Probably the best basic advice on dress is to pay attention to what your listeners will be wearing and then choose clothing that will match theirs in general style and level of formality. Conservative, classic clothes are always a good choice. If you're not sure what to wear, it's generally safest to err on the side of formality. In other words, dress as formally as (if not more formally than) you think your audience will.

Also be sure that your clothing—including shoes and other accessories—is immaculate. It's difficult to convince someone that you're careful with detail if your shoes are scuffed or your hem is hanging down. Instead, your clothing should match, in every respect, the image you wish to project. Finally, what you wear should fit well and be comfortable so that it doesn't hamper your movement during your presentation. You don't want your clothing to be a distraction, either to your listeners or to you.

Your Posture, Gestures, and Facial Expressions

Research shows that people rely heavily upon nonverbal cues to construct meaning. In fact, "nearly two-thirds of the meaning in any social situation is derived from nonverbal cues, leaving the remaining 35 percent to be accounted for by verbal information" (Garmston & Wellman, 1992, p. 57). In an oral presentation, this means that the way you present yourself—your facial expressions, eye contact, posture, hand and arm gestures, and other physical movements—will have a significant impact on the meaning you communicate and what your listeners feel about you and your message. The way you stand and move and the facial expressions you use can communicate a lot about your commitment to the topic of your presentation, your authority over the material, your confidence in general, and your opinions about your listeners. Generally, your credibility is established in the opening few minutes of your talk, primarily through body language, and if your listeners don't trust your body language, your credibility will be lost. "Simply put, if your audience doesn't like you—and, more importantly, doesn't trust you—they won't be receptive to what you say" (First Books, 1996, p. 66). With this is mind, be aware of the following:

- **Your posture** should be relaxed so that your muscles are loose, your movements are natural, and your appearance is confident. Maintaining a calm, upright stance will enable you to project your voice, too.
- **Your gestures** should be relaxed and natural and match the language you use as well as the size of your presentation space. That is, with a larger audience and presentation space, your motions should be larger and more dynamic so they're not lost; with a smaller space, your motions should be more subdued. In general, you should move slowly and deliberately and use gestures that underscore your message, rather than simply draw attention to themselves. Also watch out for distracting gestures: twisting or pulling on hair, beards, or rings; tapping pencils; bobbing your head; leaning back on your heels or forward on a podium; jingling change in your pocket; and pacing. Finally, avoid using gestures that might be interpreted as defensive, like crossing your arms in front of your body.
- **Your facial expressions** convey both feeling and meaning, so when you present a talk, your facial expressions should conform with your message and create a mood appropriate for your listeners and what you want to accomplish. For instance, smiling when it fits your message can make you appear both likable and credible. In fact, some experts on presentational speaking feel that although smiling is the most significant expression for presenters, people don't smile nearly as often as they should. And those who don't smile may be considered aloof. "Haughty, cold, or distant presenters are never well liked by their audiences. They also tend to be rated as less credible than down-to-earth, warm, and friendly presenters even though they exhibit the same general degree of expertise and knowledge" (First Books, 1996, p. 66). Of course, make sure that you don't overdo the smiling, or listeners won't believe you're sincere.
- **Eye contact,** like smiling, can communicate your openness, warmth, and confidence. It will also help you connect with your listeners, build the rapport so necessary for effective presentations, and hold people's attention. One common rule of thumb is that if you select several friendly faces from various sections of the room and regularly establish eye contact with those people, you'll assure yourself that you're not favoring one side of the room or the other. Maintaining regular eye contact can also supply you with immediate feedback about how individuals are responding to your ideas.

Your Voice

Much of your presentation's impact will rely upon your voice and how you use it—your volume, pace, and verbal mannerisms. Obviously, you'll want to project loudly enough so that all your listeners can hear what you have say. And to do so, you'll need to be relaxed and able to breathe deeply. Deep, relaxed breathing can also help you maintain a steady, measured pace and speak with the naturalness needed to vary tone, pitch, and emphasis. Speaking in a natural, conversational manner will ensure that you avoid the monotone that lessens listeners' attention. And you can draw attention to key ideas by emphasizing important language or pausing deliberately in strategic places so that listeners can absorb your ideas.

Of course, you'll want to avoid some verbal habits that distract listeners' attention away from *what* you're saying to *how* you're saying it:

- Take the time to look up the words you're unsure how to pronounce. Practice saying them so listeners don't have to try to figure out what you've said. It's especially important to check the pronunciations of proper names so that you don't offend people. Habitual mispronunciations can lead listeners to doubt your credibility and even your intelligence.
- Avoid the "ums," "uhs," "okays," and "you knows" that grate on listeners' ears. An occasional "um" or "uh," of course, shouldn't be a cause for concern, but if you find your presentations peppered with these filler words, practice eliminating them. For some people, consciously replacing these words with pauses can help. Others find it useful to tape-record and then listen to their presentations. Finally, being very familiar with your material and practicing your speech can help you relax and get rid of these nervous utterances.

Overcoming Nervousness

For many people preparing formal presentations, a major concern is the stress, anxiety, and nervousness that undercut confidence and make them feel less in control of their expression. And as the speaking context becomes more formal, the audience becomes larger, the number of important listeners in the audience increases, or risks in other ways intensify, this nervousness can be debilitating. However, there are many things you can do to manage your anxiety and channel your nervous energy so that it actually *improves* your performance.

Prepare Thoroughly. Most importantly, thorough preparation can enable you to achieve the calm and confidence to do your best. This preparation begins with having a good sense of your goals and listeners, including careful consideration of the questions listeners are likely to ask. You will lessen your sense of the unfamiliar and increase your confidence if you know your material well enough to answer listeners' questions and meet the objections of those who resist your ideas and if you know exactly what you want to accomplish and what your listeners' needs and concerns are likely to be. Your familiarity with your goals and listeners will also enable you to convince listeners that you have their needs firmly in mind and will make them receptive to your speech. And a receptive audience can go a long way in minimizing a speaker's apprehension.

Write Down Notes. After you know what you plan to say, write it down in concrete form on notecards. Don't write down every word you plan to say; instead, map out your talk in key words that will trigger the information you plan to present, section by section. And be sure to practice your talk using these memory prompts.

Practice, Practice, Practice! The value of practice for getting nerves under control cannot be emphasized too much. In fact, most experts in oral communication recommend overpreparation as the single most important method for reducing nervousness. One or more rehearsals can help improve your confidence level by confirming that you have the right amount of material for the time allotted and by getting you accustomed to speaking your text aloud—getting a feel for your language and the lengths of your sentences, establishing a comfortable pace, and figuring out points of emphasis.

When you rehearse, it's also important to practice with any technology you plan to use in your presentation—and we really mean *practice.* Actually place your transparencies onto the overhead projector and shut it on and off. Use your laser pointer to emphasize key data on visuals. Change your slides or click the mouse on your computer to move to the next screen. Turn the tape player or video machine on and off. Actually using the technology you'll incorporate into your presentation will accomplish two things: (1) It will assure you that the equipment actually works, and (2) it will enable you to move effortlessly through your talk, incorporating visuals seamlessly and smoothly, speaking with confidence.

You can also try out your presentation on colleagues, asking them to play the role of your listeners. Rehearsing in front of others will give you opportunities to test the clarity of your ideas, to practice maintaining effective eye contact while speaking, and to use technology in front of an audience so that you can make sure you're not, for instance, blocking your listeners' view of overheads. Your colleagues can ask questions afterward, as your audience might, and they can provide concrete feedback to help you improve your presentation. Some experts in oral communication recommend that you not only ask your colleagues to attend dry runs of your talk but that you also tape-record or videotape practice sessions—particularly for especially important presentations that you'll make in front of large audiences. Recording a presentation will allow you and your peers to view it several times and evaluate the way you sound or look, perhaps focusing on particular trouble spots.

Rehearse Mentally. Many experts recommend that, in addition to actual physical practice, you mentally rehearse for presentations. This technique requires that you visualize yourself giving a successful presentation; that you imagine what your talk will sound like, look like, and feel like; and that you picture how your listeners will react. Garmston and Wellman (1992) argue that such mental rehearsal relaxes nerves and muscles and makes the body react as if you've actually practiced your talk; they also contend that such envisioning "will alleviate 80 percent of most presenters' nervousness" (p. 39).

Finally, you can prepare mentally for your speech by arriving early enough to become comfortable with the physical layout for the presentation, check the equipment to make sure that it works, and chat informally with people as they arrive for your talk.

Use Physical Relaxation Techniques. In addition to thorough preparation and rehearsal, you can reduce prepresentation jitters by using a variety of physical relaxation techniques:

- **Breathe deeply.** Taking several slow deep breaths just before your presentation is a simple but very effective relaxation technique. Concentrate only on your breathing. Breathe in deeply, and imagine the air going into your lungs and filling them completely. Then visualize your lungs emptying as you breathe out. Pause for several seconds, and breathe in deeply again. Breathing deeply like this will help you focus your attention, center yourself, and relax.
- **Walk and stretch.** Athletes warm up their muscles before a game. This not only readies them physically for performance but psyches them up to do their best, too. Walking quickly and doing a few stretches can provide the same sort of physical and mental warm-up before speaking. Like breathing deeply, walking and stretching also provide the oxygen necessary for delivering an energetic performance.
- **Center yourself.** You'll be more relaxed and able to project your voice if you're physically centered before your presentation. If you stand with your back and shoulders straight and your feet spread so that your weight is evenly balanced, you'll be able to breathe more fully and naturally and speak more forcefully, too. And if you let your arms fall naturally so they dangle at your sides, and imagine that you're holding heavy weights, you'll ease the tension in your neck and shoulders so that your posture will appear relaxed and confident.

In this chapter, we've considered strategies for designing successful oral presentations. We've suggested the importance of distinguishing between the goals of written reports and those of oral presentations that often accompany such reports. We've also talked about the ephemerality of oral reports and the pressure this orality places on the short-term memory of listeners. And we've suggested some strategies to increase listener retention, build and maintain interest during presentation openings and closings (when listener attention is typically the strongest), and develop your argument and emphasize your key ideas.

In addition, we've described presentation visuals to use to support your argument and make your key claims and data memorable, and we've reviewed conventional methods for maintaining control during question-and-answer sessions. Finally, we've discussed how you can create a professional image through your nonverbal expression—your appearance, facial expressions and eye contact, posture, and gestures—and how you can control the nervousness that plagues many of us who give oral presentations. Using the conventions and strategies in this chapter can help you present yourself gracefully and professionally in situations where formal speaking accompanies written reports.

ORAL PRESENTATION CHECKLIST

The following guidelines will help you present effective oral reports. For any of these guidelines, remember the superordinate guideline: Disregard *any* of this advice if it would cause you to do something that's inappropriate or silly for your situation.

☑ Oral Reports

- Remember that although oral presentations share many goals with the written reports they accompany, there are firm distinctions between the two.
- Oral presentations may have long-term goals, such as establishing the credibility of the company or creating ongoing awareness of its mission, as well as short-term goals, such as engaging listeners' participation or interest in a project.
- In your opening, communicate confidence and respect and establish credibility by clarifying who you are, what your talk is about, and why it's relevant to listeners.
- Engage listeners' attention by opening with a brief story, a startling statistic or fact, a vivid example of a workplace problem, dissonance, a specific question, a quotation, or a direct statement of your intent.
- Adapt your message to the limitations of your listeners' short-term memory.
- Limit your information to five main ideas if you want listeners to remember them.
- Repeat any idea you want listeners to remember at least three times.
- Prepare to answer questions listeners will probably have.
- Analyze the needs and interests of your listeners so that you know how to frame your arguments for them and accomplish your goals.
- Although the argument for your oral presentation will rely heavily on the argument of your written report, you'll need to streamline that argument to meet the time constraints and limitations on your listeners' memory.
- Structure your presentation to aid listeners' retention by relying upon selective repetition: Provide a brief overview of what you'll cover in the introduction of your talk; foreshadow what's coming next; use bridging between chunks of the talk; use backtracking to review what's been covered; and close by summarizing your main points.
- Consider developing your oral presentation using one of these approaches: a problem/reasons/solution approach; a question/answer arrangement; a cause/effect structure; a chronological approach; spatial organization; or a jigsaw puzzle approach.

- Make your talk lively by using examples and illustrations, relating personal stories, using humor selectively, offering analogies, and showing visuals.
- Support what you say and emphasize your key ideas through carefully crafted visuals.
- Present detailed information in handouts your listeners can review after your presentation.
- Write and illustrate your ideas as you go, using whiteboards, chalkboards, or flipcharts.
- Use overheads to generate text or illustrations as you go or to show visuals you've prepared in advance.
- Project images you want listeners to see; slide projectors are particularly useful if you're presenting to a large audience and have reasonable lead time.
- Provide action video or motion picture clips—again, for formal presentations with adequate preparation time.
- Develop professional multimedia materials using sound, motion, and color to present complex ideas simply—especially if presentation time is sharply limited and preparation time allows development.
- Design visuals to support your presentation, not for their own sake.
- Use summary visuals to establish the goals or agenda for a talk, underscore key ideas as they're introduced, and review key points in the closing.
- Focus each visual on one idea.
- When possible, use graphics or illustrations, rather than text, to support your argument.
- Use no more than one-half the viewing area—or no more than four words per line and six lines per visual.
- Select type fonts and sizes that will be readable to anyone anywhere in the room.
- Use color to add interest and emphasize your key points.
- Make sure the presentation software you plan to use is compatible with the computer available for your presentation.
- Select the simplest method of presenting visuals that is appropriate for your listeners, your argument, and your goals.
- During a question-and-answer session, repeat the question and then pause to think before you answer it.
- Maintain openness and encourage your listeners' active involvement by acknowledging their contributions when they ask questions.
- Stay focused when people ask irrelevant questions.
- If people ask loaded questions, be tactful and avoid arguing.
- Prepare for question-and-answer sessions by reviewing and rehearsing your facts, data, and analysis.

- Match your clothing to that of your listeners in general style and formality so that it won't distract them or you.
- Transmit your confidence and credibility through relaxed, natural posture and gestures.
- Underscore your message through gestures and facial expressions.
- Use eye contact to connect with your listeners and maintain their attention.
- Speak in the natural style that enables you to vary tone, pitch, and emphasis.
- Use your voice to emphasize important language and ideas.
- Minimize verbal distractions, such as mispronunciations and filler sounds and words ("ums," "uhs," "okays," and "you knows"), by practicing.
- Practice and thorough preparation also lessen the anxiety and nervousness that come naturally when people make oral presentations.
- Use mental rehearsals and physical relaxation techniques to reduce your nervousness and increase your confidence.

ACTIVITIES AND PROJECTS

1. Interview a professional about the sorts or oral presentations typically done in your field. Find out information about the specific nature of these presentations by asking questions like these:
   - How large are the audiences? And what sorts of listeners populate these audiences?
   - How formal are the presentations?
   - What types of goals do they typically have, and what sorts of arguments are usually made?
   - Are the presentations high tech or low tech—or something in between?
   - What sorts of presentational aids tend to be used and why?

   Report what you discover through a memo to colleagues.

2. Interview one or more people who are experienced in giving presentations. Ask about the specific nature of the presentations they give and how they prepare for them. Ask questions like the following:
   - What processes or procedures do they follow to ensure the presentation's success and why?
   - What do they do to adapt what they say to the listeners?
   - What pointers do they have for meeting listeners' likely objections or for answering questions during question-and-answer sessions?
   - What presentational aids do they use, and how and why do they use them?
   - Do they tend to do high-tech or low-tech presentations or something in between? Why?

- What principles do they follow in determining or designing presentational media? And what pointers do they have about using particular presentational aids?
- What do they do to mentally prepare for the presentation and to ameliorate any nervousness they might be feeling?
- Do they ever present to an international audience? If so, what suggestions do they have for making such presentations successful?

Report what you discover orally or through a memo to colleagues.

3. Ask an expert in oral communication to talk to your class or group about presentational speaking. Be sure to have some interesting questions to ask this person in the question-and-answer session after the formal presentation.
4. Spend some time working with a presentation software program like Microsoft PowerPoint or Adobe Persuasion. Then write a memo to colleagues or develop an oral presentation that provides guidelines for using the software to design effective presentational aids.
5. Using the guidelines for oral presentations presented in this chapter, prepare and present your individual or collaborative report orally to colleagues.
6. Have a colleague videotape a presentation you give. Then view the tape with colleagues who can assess the strengths and weaknesses of your presentation and give you pointers for improving either that specific presentation or your presentation style in general.
7. As a member of an audience at a presentation your colleague/colleagues are giving, use the evaluation rubric in Figure 14.1 to give them constructive feedback.

REFERENCES

First Books for Business. (1996). *Business presentations and public speaking.* New York: McGraw-Hill.

Garmston, R. J., & Wellman, B. M. (1992). *How to make presentations that teach and transform.* Alexandria, VA: Association for Supervision and Curriculum Management.

Miller, G. (1956). The magical number seven, plus or minus two: Some limits on our capacity for processing information, *Psychological Review, 63,* 81–97.

Morrisey, G. L., Sechrest, T. L., & Warman, W. B. (1997). *Loud and clear: How to prepare and deliver effective business and technical presentations.* Reading, MA: Addison Wesley.

FIGURE 14.1 Evaluation Rubric for Oral Presentations

Oral Presentation Evaluation Sheet

Directions:

Rate presenters on the following aspects by placing an X at the appropriate place on the scale: 4 = Excellent, 3 = Good, 2 = Fair, and 1 = Poor. Write comments when appropriate.

Organization:

The presentation is structured to aid listeners' retention: It provides a brief overview of what will be covered in the introduction of the talk; foreshadows what's coming next; uses bridging between chunks of the talk; uses backtracking to review what's been covered; and closes by summarizing the main points.

4	3	2	1
Excellent	**Good**	**Fair**	**Poor**

Comments:

Content:

The body of the presentation is complete: It includes all information needed to persuade listeners of the validity of the argument, and the claims are well supported by the appropriate data and warrants.

4	3	2	1
Excellent	**Good**	**Fair**	**Poor**

Comments:

Clarity of Presentation:

The language is appropriate to the audience. Technical aspects are adequately explained.

4	3	2	1
Excellent	**Good**	**Fair**	**Poor**

Comments:

Oral Delivery:

The presenters speak clearly, loudly, and at an effective pace and with the naturalness that enables them to vary tone, pitch, and emphasis and to use their voices to emphasize important language and ideas. Verbal distractions—mispronunciations, filler sounds and words ("ums," "uhs," "okays," and "you knows")—are minimal or nonexistent.

4	3	2	1
Excellent	**Good**	**Fair**	**Poor**

(continued)

FIGURE 14.1 Continued

Comments:

Appearance:

Good eye contact enables presenters to connect with the audience. Gestures are natural, appropriate, and confident and underscore the presenters' message.

4	3	2	1
Excellent	**Good**	**Fair**	**Poor**

Comments:

Visual Aids:

The presenters use presentational software, transparencies, posters, flipcharts, handouts, and the like to effectively clarify points. These aids are simple, few in number, and large enough to be seen. Moreover, visuals are designed to support the presentation, not for their own sake.

4	3	2	1
Excellent	**Good**	**Fair**	**Poor**

Comments:

Timing:

Presenters kept to the time limit and spent appropriate amounts of time on individual topics.

4	3	2	1
Excellent	**Good**	**Fair**	**Poor**

Comments:

Overall Evaluation:

4	3	2	1
Excellent	**Good**	**Fair**	**Poor**

Overall Comments:

Part V

Special Risks and Challenges: Writing for the Global Marketplace

Chapter 15

Opportunities and Risks in Cross-Cultural Communication

We need a certain amount of humility and a sense of humor to discover cultures other than our own; a readiness to enter a room in the dark and stumble over unfamiliar furniture until the pain in our shins reminds us of where things are.

—Fons Trompenaars

In today's global economy, organizations need people who can work as members of multicultural teams and communicate across cultures. They need employees who are open to new experiences and new people, who are culturally self-aware and tolerant of differences, who are sensitive in interpersonal interchanges, and who have the patience, empathy, and sense of humor to work through ambiguous or conflicted situations successfully.

It's very possible that your company will expect you to interact internationally, and it's quite probable, too, that you'll be placed in new cultural and work environments without preparation. According to Stephen Rhinesmith (1996, p. 126), 70 percent of Americans sent abroad to do business currently don't receive any training or predeparture orientation before going. You can begin to prepare yourself for cross-cultural communication, however, by becoming more self-aware about your own culture and the values, assumptions, and beliefs underlying it. Having this awareness will, in turn, make you more conscious of the lens through which you see the world and enable you to become more attentive and sensitive to the values, assumptions, and beliefs of cultures different from your own. In other words, this attentiveness and sensitivity form the base upon which bridges to other cultures can be built.

Cultural Signposts Underlying Cross-Cultural Communication

Remember the egocentric solar system we introduced in Chapter 1? We used it there and in several later chapters as a way of locating yourself and your writing situation in the context of other people, documents, relationships, and transactions. If you use the egocentric solar system thoughtfully, it can help you visualize other people's egocentric solar systems. It can help you make the kind of imaginative leap Copernicus made almost 500 years ago when he imagined a heliocentric system, where the earth and other planets orbit the sun, rather than the geocentric system everyone had assumed must be the case since everything they saw from their perspective, including the sun, seemed to be flying around the earth.

In this chapter, we've adapted the egocentric solar system (see Figure 15.1), so it's now a way for visualizing the concentric spheres of ideas, goals, values, and assumptions that you rely on when you make sense of the world—moving from your

FIGURE 15.1 Cross-Cultural Communication and the Egocentric Solar System

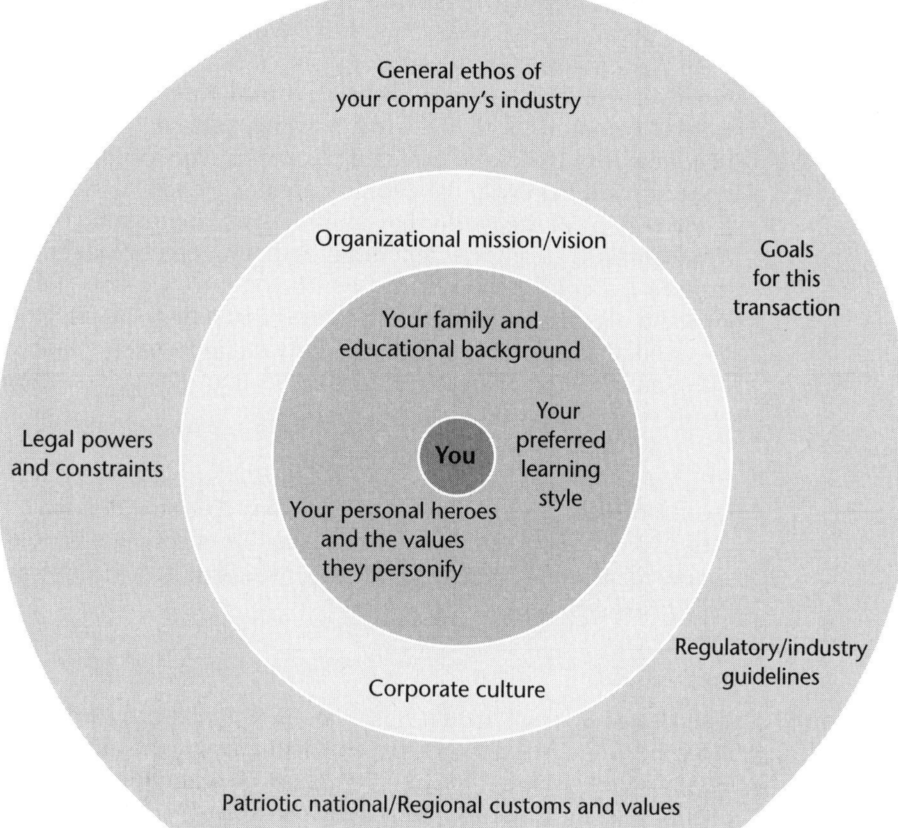

Cultural Signposts:

- Individualistic or collectivist tendencies
- Attitudes about hierarchy and status
- Low- or high-context culture
- Perception of time
- **Preferred style of argument:**
  —Assumptions for validating evidence
  —Ways of presenting evidence, assumptions, and claims: Quasilogical, presentational, analogical

most immediate, personal cognitive, emotional, and ethical resources to the most general cultural resources. And because we're talking here about *cross-cultural communication,* we're pushing the main focus of the egocentric solar system to the outer orbits—regions you generally don't look at in routine writing situations with your colleagues and clients who share your cultural background.

We're going to focus especially on "cultural signposts" (James, 1995), the very broad, general characteristics of how people living in the same general area tend to think in common about the world, how they process their experience, and, in particular, how they build and evaluate arguments. The following discussion of cultural signposts will help you make some informed guesses about the ways readers in different regions of the world may interpret and respond to your arguments. But you should make these guesses tentatively and cautiously because the inner orbits of each reader's egocentric solar system—which you can't see from a distance—will also be crucial tools for their understanding and evaluating you and your communication. Using our discussion of cultural signposts will more likely guide you to ask intelligent questions about your cross-cultural readers than give you conclusive answers.

Individualistic and Collectivist Cultures

Geert Hofstede (1980) describes cultures based upon individuals' relationships to society as a whole, focusing on whether a culture encourages people to be independent or interdependent. Hofstede refers to this aspect of culture as the *individualism/ collectivism dimension.*

Individualistic Cultures

The United States, Canada, Australia, New Zealand, and much of Western Europe have individualistic cultures. In general, they value the individual as the center of society, cherish personal freedom, emphasize competition and personal accomplishments, and stress independent decision making. In fact, decisions are based upon benefits to the individual. In the United States, the belief in individualism is so strong that many consider it our distinguishing cultural trait. And given the strength of society's emphasis on the individual, the importance of such words as *independence, privacy, self,* and *I* comes as no surprise. It's interesting to note, as Lustig and Koester (1993) do, that "English is the only language that capitalizes the pronoun *I* in writing. English does not, however, capitalize the written form of the pronoun *you*" (p. 144).

Collectivist Cultures

In collectivist cultures—those of Asia, Africa, Eastern Europe, and Latin America—the individual is subordinated to the group, and interdependence and group solidarity are valued. The family and the place of employment replace the individual as the basic social unit, and being connected to others and fitting in are very important. Collectivist cultures, therefore, stress harmony, politeness, and modesty (James, 1995, p. 13). Finally, decisions are based on what is best for the group, and members are expected to be loyal to that group.

Consequence of These Cultural Preferences

What are the consequences of these cultural preferences in the context of business? One consequence is that people from collectivist cultures—like that of Japan, for instance—generally see development of personal, long-term relationships as part of doing business and want to work on establishing a personal relationship before making any sort of official agreement. So, small talk in correspondence or face-to-face communication is very common. In contrast, people from individualistic cultures are usually known for cutting small talk to a minimum and getting right down to business. As James (1995, p. 14) points out, "Asians, for example, pay more attention to relationships than to contracts, while Westerners pay more attention to schedules than to social protocol."

A second consequence of these cultural preferences is that although people in individualist cultures have a lot of personal autonomy in decision making, decisions in collectivist cultures are generally made collaboratively after all people concerned in the group have been consulted. Therefore, decisions tend to take longer, particularly if the organization is large or the issues are complex and have wide-ranging effects. When discussion is occurring in meetings, it's not unusual for people from collectivist cultures to consult with others in the workplace before making decisions—either during or after the meeting. And when written decisions are required of people from collectivist cultures, these written decisions, too, will probably take longer than members of individualistic cultures would prefer. James suggests that although people from individualistic cultures might find this long decision-making process frustrating, it does result in decisions that are fully considered and easy to implement since they have been arrived at through discussions among all of the stakeholders (p. 18).

Hierarchy and Status

Attitudes toward hierarchy and status differ significantly between individualist and collectivist cultures. In general, people from collectivist cultures tend to respect authority and status more than people from individualistic cultures. Collectivist cultures also give more weight to hierarchy than individualistic cultures do and recognize elders and authorities more. Collectivistic cultures tend to place more weight on the value of experience, too.

A logical outcome of this emphasis on hierarchy and status is that people from collectivist cultures often want to know the titles and positions others hold in their organizations before they begin to do business. And when they work with someone from another organization for the first time, they may want a formal letter of introduction to establish their new business associate's status and to formally begin a relationship. This emphasis on hierarchy and status also means that people from collectivist cultures defer to their superiors and carry out instructions loyally (James, 1995, pp. 16–17). Finally, this emphasis on hierarchy and status means that business communications—whether oral presentations or written correspondence—tend to be more formal. (We'll discuss the conventional elements of formality later in this chapter.)

Low- and High-Context Cultures

Edward T. Hall (1977) describes cultures according to the amount of information implied by the context of their messages. Messages in *low-context cultures* tend to be overt and explicit, while messages in *high-context cultures* tend to be more covert and nonverbal.

Low-Context Cultures

In low-context cultures—primarily the European, British, and United States mainstream cultures—information is presented explicitly and leaves nothing to the imagination. In writing, this means precision, directness, and clear-cut relationships among ideas. Helen Fox (1994) describes the writing preferences of low-context cultures this way:

> In cultures that value directness, it is assumed that the reader needs to be shown exactly how any background information is tied to the ideas that the author wants to get across. Not only do we require transitional words and phrases and a careful, logical ordering of information, but we expect reminders of our previous points from one paragraph to the next, as well as careful emphasis on words that show precise and explicit relationships between ideas. (p. 12)

In other words, in low-context cultures, communication is intended to "convey exact meaning" (Lustig & Koester, 1993, p. 134).

High-Context Cultures

In high-context cultures—primarily those of Asia, Africa, and Latin America—much of the meaning of a message isn't stated at all but is implied by the physical setting or nonverbal cues or internalized in the individual's beliefs, values, and cultural knowledge. A high-context culture relies, in fact, "on a good deal of a previous history of shared understanding and assumes that very little information is required, or even desired, for the audience to get the message" (Fox, 1994, p. 21). In other words, more information is taken for granted, or assumed to be shared.

Given the assumption of shared knowledge in high-context cultures, it should come as no surprise that indirect communication is preferred. Helen Fox (1994) provides examples of this indirection:

> In many Asian and African languages and cultures, metaphor, euphemism, innuendo, hints, insinuation, and all sorts of subtle nonverbal strategies—even silence—are used both to spare the listeners possible embarrassment or rejection and to convey meanings that they are expected to grasp. In Japanese, for example, there are sixteen ways to avoid saying, "no"; in Arabic, a host of euphemisms designate the touchy subjects that no one wants to speak of directly; in Sinhalese, indirection takes the form of metaphors or universal symbols to which can be added prefixes or suffixes to create

> poetic mood or feeling. In Korean, verbs may be passive where we might expect them to be active. (p. 22)

This indirection lends itself well to one of the primary goals of communication in high-context cultures: "to promote and sustain harmony" among those interacting (Lustig & Koester, 1993, p. 134).

This goal of promoting and maintaining harmony is in direct opposition to the primary goal of communication in low-context cultures: to get a message across. And this opposition characterizes a crucial difference in perspective. In fact, as Lustig and Koester (1993) point out, it's a difference that can cause confusion and conflict:

> The Euroamerican* preference for "Putting your cards on the table" and "telling it like it is" presupposes a world in which it is desirable to be explicit, direct, and specific about personal reactions and ideas, even at the expense of social discomfort on the part of the person with whom one is interacting. For Euroamericans, good interpersonal communications include stating directly one's personal needs and reactions to the behaviors of others. Thus if Euroamericans hear that others complained about them, they would probably wonder, "Why didn't they tell me directly if they have a problem with something that I have done?"
>
> Contrast this approach to that of Asian cultures such as Japan, Korea, Thailand, and China, where saving face and maintaining interpersonal harmony are so highly valued that it would be catastrophic to confront another person directly and verbally express one's anger. (p. 123)

Lustig and Koester point out that when a message must convey a "no," it frequently is not spoken or written at all but, rather, implied through action. And when conflict and anger occur, communication frequently takes place through intermediaries, who "soften and interpret the messages of both sides, thereby shielding the parties from direct, and therefore risky and potentially embarrassing, transactions with each other" (p. 124). This indirect handling of negatives and use of intermediaries has a significant impact on written communication.

Perception of Time

High-context and low-context cultures also differ in their perceptions of time. High-context cultures, which stress the importance of the group, tend to see time as unstructured and responsive to the group's needs; in contrast, low-context cultures view time as highly structured and very valuable (Lustig & Koester, 1993, p. 135). The value of time in low-context cultures is perhaps best illustrated by the American maxim that "Time is money."

***Euroamerican* is the term that Lustig and Koester (1993) use when referring to people in the United States whose ancestors came from Europe. Lustig and Koester argue that Euroamerican culture is only one of many cultures in the United States although it is the mainstream culture.

It should be noted that high-context cultures don't share this perspective and, in fact, are bothered by "America's obsession with deadlines and need always to be moving in the direction of a deadline or a decision" (Stamps, 1996, p. 30). In fact, people from high-context cultures tend to follow agendas loosely. A representative example of this flexibility and the emphasis on people's needs taking priority over the constraints of time is the Mexican concept of *mañana*. In Mexico, time seems fluid, people do many things at one time, interruptions are common, and business is slower than in the United States. Essentially, time is not as important as the development and maintenance of relationships among people (Kenna & Lacy, 1994, p. 24).

One effect of these differences in perception of time can be seen in expectations about the relationship between meetings and decisions. Stamps (1996, p. 30) points out that Americans consider meetings the places to make decisions. But this perspective is not shared by the French, for instance, who consider meetings forums for finding out what others think. Decisions are made *after* meetings when decision makers gather and review information just presented. This view is common in many collectivist cultures, who value collaboration and place a higher priority on the *process* of making a decision than the time it takes to arrive at one. Decisions made in response to written texts take time, too.

Edward Hall (1988) describes the contrast in the length of time it takes individualist and collectivist cultures to make decisions in this way:

> The time that it takes to reach an agreement or for someone to make up his mind operates within culturally defined limits. In the U.S. one has about four minutes in the business world to sell an idea. In Japan the well-known process of "nemawashi"—consensus building, without which nothing can happen—can take weeks or months. None of this four-minute sell. (p. 151)

A second result of differences in the perception of time is that in low-context cultures, people tend to get right down to business, while in high-context cultures, people spend time getting to know one another before they do business. As we will discuss later in this chapter, this practice affects the shape of oral presentations and written texts, too.

Another way of thinking about a culture's perception of time, according to Lustig and Koester (1993, p. 202), is considering whether the culture is past oriented, present oriented, or future oriented. *Past-oriented cultures,* like those of China and Great Britain, value "tradition and the wisdom passed down from the older generation." Therefore, they respect elders, who are the sources of information about their history, and look to the past for solutions to present problems. *Present-oriented cultures* emphasize "spontaneity and immediacy" and are more interested in experiencing the pleasures of the present than achieving future gain. Cultures that are present oriented—including many of those in Central and South American countries and the Philippines—appreciate present activities for their own sake, not for possible future benefits. In contrast, *future-oriented cultures,* like that in the United States, believe that today's work is done to achieve results in the future, and these future benefits are what are important. A culture's orientation to time significantly affects the sorts of arguments and the data its members find viable and compelling.

Culture and Argument

When you consider the sorts of arguments you'd like to make in any given cross-cultural situation, keep in mind that the nature of argument is culturally bound. Lustig and Koester (1993, p. 222), for instance, point out that cultures vary in what they consider to be "acceptable evidence, who is regarded as an authority, how evidence is used to create persuasive arguments, and what ideas are reasonable." In fact, they use the term *alternative logics* because they believe that what is regarded as logical varies from culture to culture.

Stephen Toulmin (1972), the philosopher we've used as the basis for our discussion of argument throughout this text, is a good resource for thinking about alternative logics because his approach is "culturally neutral." He points out that what is considered rational varies from culture to culture and from timeframe to timeframe: "Within different cultures and epochs, reasoning may operate according to different methods and principles, so that different milieus represent the parallel jurisdictions of rationality" (p. 95). Toulmin believes that there are no universally accepted standards for what constitutes evidence. For instance, in the mainstream U.S. culture, people tend to prefer physical evidence and eyewitness testimony and "see 'facts' as the supreme kind of evidence." But in some Chinese cultures, "physical evidence is discounted because no connection between those pieces of the physical world and human actions is seen." And among devout Muslim cultures, parables or stories from the Koran are seen as powerful evidence (Lustig & Koester, 1993, p. 225).

So, the assumptions we take for granted as validating evidence—especially the high value we place on empirical evidence—may not be persuasive at all to our cross-cultural readers or listeners. If you find yourself frustrated in a written or spoken cross-cultural dialogue, here's a good test: Do your counterparts in this exchange seem unable to see obvious connections in your arguments? At the same time, do they seem to be making illogical connections in their arguments and leaping to unreasonable conclusions? These are good signs that your respective arguments are relying on deeply internalized, unspoken cultural assumptions and values. You need to open up the layers of your argument—as we described in Chapters 1 and 6—this time highlighting the assumptions you make about what's valid evidence and what are reasonable grounds for drawing conclusions from evidence. And you need to ask your cross-cultural counterparts to do the same thing for you: open up their arguments so you can see their underlying assumptions. You may even be able to head off this kind of frustration before it occurs if you can correctly anticipate a conflict in underlying warrants. You can then take the time to unfold your own argument systematically so that your cross-cultural readers can see and understand those assumptions. Expressing this kind of good faith in laying out the values and assumptions that inform your own arguments should, in turn, help encourage your readers to do the same to help you understand underlying assumptions that inform their arguments.

There are clearly differences, too, in the ways in which various cultures prefer to arrange their evidence, warrants, and claims. Barbara Johnstone (1989, pp. 139–156) describes these differences as three different strategies of persuasion: the quasilogical, the presentational, and the analogical. The *quasilogical style,* which is preferred by people in low-context cultures, is used by those who believe that truth can be objectively established and verified. It favors statistics and expert testimony and uses formal logic to convince readers to accept the evidence and the conclusions that follow from it. The quasilogical is clearly the style of argument preferred in the United States.

The *presentational style* is used in cultures in which truth is seen as relative. Since people are perceived as more important than ideas, the speaker or writer uses sensory language to appeal emotionally to listeners or readers. A presentational style is common in the Mexican culture, for instance, where people pay as much attention to verbal word play and expressiveness as they do to the content of the message.

Finally, in the *analogical style,* the writer or speaker tells a story to capture the gist of what he or she wants to communicate:

> The analogical style seeks to establish an idea (a claim) and to persuade the listener by providing an analogy, a story, or a parable in which there is either an implicit or explicit lesson to be learned. . . . An assumption underlying the analogical style is that it is the collective experience of groups of people—the culture—that is persuasive rather than the ideas themselves or the characteristics of a dynamic individual. Historical precedent takes on great importance because what convinces is a persuader's ability to choose the right historical story to demonstrate the point. (Lustig & Koester, 1993, pp. 228–229)

The analogical style is favored in many high-context cultures that are past oriented, including some African and Chinese cultures.

If you're unsure about the sorts of argument that are appropriate to your goals and the readers or listeners you're addressing, a little bit of digging is probably in order. We recommend that you check with others in your organization who are experienced in writing and making presentations to these readers and listeners, especially those who've lived in this culture for a while or visit it frequently. You can also connect with other members of your network: those who've introduced you to these readers or listeners or who know both of you through social or business contacts. And you can investigate general overseas resources to discover the area's conventional preferences: trade or economic organizations, chambers of commerce, embassies, and even tourist or travel bureaus. Finally, print resources are increasingly available to help with cross-cultural orientation for business.

We've considered several key cultural signposts underlying cross-cultural communication: the values and assumptions held within individualist and collectivist cultures; perspectives toward hierarchy and status; perceptions of time; the features of low- and high-context cultures and their preferences for direct and indirect argument, respectively; and the ways in which culture affects the style of argument preferred. Let's consider, now, some strategies for making oral presentations to listeners from other cultures. Then, we'll look more specifically at guidelines for cross-cultural writing.

Making Cross-Cultural Oral Presentations

Much of what we said about oral presentations in Chapter 13 will be useful when you present to listeners from other cultures. Certainly, guidelines for easing nervousness and preparing visuals will be applicable to presentations you give anywhere to anybody. But when you present to listeners from other countries, cultural norms may affect the goals of your presentation and the sorts of arguments you should use. You'll certainly want to analyze carefully your listeners' needs and accommodate these needs as you determine the expression appropriate for the occasion.

Of the most important factors to keep in mind when you prepare a cross-cultural oral presentation, we'll talk about the following:

- Preferred level of formality
- Cultural priority given to relationship building
- Assumptions about valid arguments
- Preferred decision-making processes
- Attitudes about humor

We'll also talk about navigating language barriers and working effectively with translators.

Preferred Level of Formality

People from collectivist cultures, which emphasize hierarchy and status, expect fairly formal presentations, including an introduction, in which you, the presenter, name your title and establish your credibility or area of expertise. This level of formality stands in contrast to the casualness so common in presentations given in the United States, characterized by such behaviors as speaking conversationally or writing on transparencies during the presentation, for instance.

Cultural Priority Given to Relationship Building

People from collectivist cultures also expect you to spend some time in the opening of your talk building your relationship with them. Sometimes, this comes through a formal introduction by someone who knows you and the listeners and can help make a personal connection. And sometimes, this relationship building comes through information about your credentials, a story about your individual involvement with the topic of your presentation, or details about the company's activities relative to the topic—in other words, "getting to know you" sorts of information. Finally, this relationship building often comes through making small talk and formally acknowledging your appreciation to your hosts.

Assumptions about Valid Arguments

The central argument of your presentation should, of course, be appropriate to your listeners. For instance, if you're talking to a group from a collectivist culture, it would be wise to emphasize benefits to the group and to solidarity, rather than stress advantages to individuals. You also should take advantage of cultural preferences for directness and indirectness, using direct arguments that are overt and explicit for listeners in low-context cultures and indirect arguments reliant upon analogy, metaphor, euphemism, innuendo, hints, insinuation, and all sorts of subtle nonverbal strategies to convey your message to listeners from high-context cultures.

Rowland (1985) points out, for instance, that the Japanese prefer a presenter to give a long explanation before coming to the main point or actual proposal. And she suggests that although the Japanese love raw data, they "dislike having others draw conclusions for them. To us this is a natural part of a . . . presentation. The Japanese, however, find it inappropriate and patronizing" (p. 105). To avoid cultural missteps like this, use the style of argument your listeners will prefer. It makes sense, for example, to share stories with listeners from cultures who tend to use an analogical style to persuade. And it's reasonable to use hard data, statistics, and well-crafted arguments for listeners preferring a quasilogical style. Finally, appealing to emotions and using sensory language is appropriate for listeners who are convinced by presentational style, rather than the rationality of ideas.

Preferred Decision-Making Processes

As we discussed earlier in this chapter, decision-making in collectivist cultures is a shared process that takes time. Therefore, if you're making a presentation to members of a collectivist culture, obviously, you shouldn't expect that presentation to result in an on-the-spot decision. Instead, you should plan to wait for listeners to engage others in the process after your presentation is over and to return with their decision at some later time.

Attitudes about Humor

Humor should be used infrequently and with caution in presentations to people from other cultures for several reasons. First, humor often relies upon verbal word play and cultural knowledge and generally doesn't translate well. Second, humor often depends upon stereotypes of some sort; this sort of humor should, of course, be avoided. If you'd like to lighten up your presentation with jokes or verbal witticisms, it's probably best to run them past someone who knows the local language and culture to make sure that your humor will translate successfully and not offend anyone. Checking with someone familiar with the local culture can also enable you to find out if humor of any sort would be perceived as inappropriate for the situation. For instance, according to Rowland, presentations in Japan are quite formal, and jokes simply aren't suitable for such occasions (p. 105).

Language Background

Differences in language raise particular issues for individuals presenting to listeners whose first language is not English. Many experts in cross-cultural communication recommend that speakers study a language—any language—so that they're empathetic about the difficulties people experience when listening to a presentation in another language. We don't recommend that you present in the local language, however, unless you have achieved fluency in it. If you feel comfortable, you might try a simple introduction in the local language. In general, though, present your talks in English (perhaps, as we discuss later, with the help of a translator).

When you present in English to people whose first language is not English, here are some ways you can enhance communication:

- Keep your language simple. Choose commonly used words—*use,* for instance, rather than *utilize*—and avoid slang, colloquial expressions, and idiomatic language that doesn't translate easily and is too informal.
- Use direct sentence structure—subject, verb, object—and relatively short sentences.
- Maintain a moderate pace and insert short pauses of several seconds in strategic places in your presentation, so listeners can absorb your key ideas. Slow down a bit during question-and-answer periods, too, since the conversational give and take of these sessions makes it easy for speakers to pick up the pace without thinking about it.
- Use written words, graphics, visuals, and pictures whenever possible to reinforce your message, and emphasize your central ideas by presenting them in a variety of forms.

Using Translators

When you're presenting to listeners whose first language is not English, you'll sometimes want to enlist the help of a translator. If you do use a translator, keep in mind that translation is not rote transcription from language to language; for a translation to be effective, the translator must understand and reformulate the message appropriately, given the target language and culture. In view of this fact, here are some things you can do to enhance the success of the translation, both before and during your presentation.

Before the Presentation

1. **Select your translator carefully.** Keep several things in mind as you select your translator. Hopefully, you'll be able to use local contacts to find someone who will represent what you say as accurately as possible. Embassies and overseas chambers of commerce may be able to recommend people, too. Ideally, you should use an interpreter who is familiar with your field, so he or she will already be well versed in any specialized vocabulary. This person should also be experienced in both your culture and the target culture. Weiss (1995, p. 415) points out "the more experience one has living in source and target cultures, the more adept one can become at resolving certain difficulties of translation." And if you're presenting your talk in a country that reveres status and authority, you'll probably want to engage an older translator to contribute to your credibility. Finally, if you hire a translator yourself, rather than rely upon someone that an overseas' company has on staff, your translator can give you advice before your presentation as well as help you analyze and evaluate your effectiveness afterward.
2. **Think about your work with the translator as collaborative.** When a translator presents your speech to listeners, the listeners don't hear what you say; they listen to the translator who is, in effect, giving your presentation. It makes sense,

then, to do all you can to help the translator do an excellent job. You can do so in these ways:

- Meet with the translator ahead of time so that he or she can hear your voice and get used to your speech patterns and idiosyncratic voice features. This will also enable you to identify how comfortable the translator is with English idioms so that you will know if you can use American slang or figures of speech in your presentation. In addition, if you need to let the translator know something—for example, that you're going to try to do a brief introduction in the local language or that you ordinarily speak quickly but plan to make a serious effort to slow down—this brief meeting will enable you to do so. Finally, you'll be able to get to know the person as an individual and begin to establish a sense of partnership.
- If your presentation is written out, give the translator a copy so he or she will have a chance to read through it ahead of time and figure out how to translate the more difficult parts of the text. The translator should also review handouts, visual aids, and other supporting material beforehand in order to ask questions about technical terms or unfamiliar expressions. This will enable the translator to arrive at precise translations ahead of time.
- Use the translator as a "local informant." That is, ask your translator to serve as an interpreter of language and culture, to explain things to you so that they make sense from your own cultural perspective (Rhinesmith, 1996, p. 134). As local informant, your translator can review your presentation and anything you plan to distribute to your audience and provide feedback about any sections that might be misunderstood based on cultural assumptions listeners will bring to your presentation. You can also clear any jokes or stories you'd like to use ahead of time and know for certain that they will be appropriate and understood.

3. **Find out the method of translation your translator plans to use.** Your translator might plan to translate simultaneously or consecutively. If the translator uses *simultaneous translation,* he or she will essentially present your message a few sentences behind you. You can expect, then, for the audience's reaction to what you say to be somewhat out of sync. *Consecutive translation,* often used in smaller meetings, avoids this problem of delayed reactions but presents other challenges. Essentially, if consecutive translation is used, you'll need to "chunk" your presentation into sections of several sentences each and then present a chunk, wait while your translator speaks, present the next chunk, and so on. This method of translation provides natural spots for listener reaction; listeners can react right after the chunk is translated and before the next chunk is presented, so they won't be reacting to information you've already presented while you're in the midst of presenting something else. But you'll need to plan ahead—to chunk your talk into logical, meaningful bits that emphasize your ideas appropriately. Also, as Albrecht (1996, p. 70) points out, consecutive translation means you can cover only half (if that) of what you can cover in a presentation that is not being translated, so you'll need to cut down the length of your presentation to allow sufficient time for the translation.

During the Presentation

1. **Acknowledge your translator.** Introduce the translator to your listeners by name, and acknowledge your appreciation for his or her services.

2. **Be aware of your pace and language.**
   - Maintain a moderate rate of speech. Keep in mind that not all languages take the same amount of time to develop an idea. Albrecht (1996, pp. 68–69), for instance, points out Spanish typically uses 20 percent more words than English. So, if you talk at your normal pace, your translator will have a hard time keeping up with you and probably won't do justice to your message. But if you slow down and purposely insert pauses, say, of five seconds or more, your translator can use the pauses to keep up or even catch up, should he or she get a bit behind.
   - Use simple sentences to ease translation. If you use a simple subject/verb/object pattern, your presentation will be easier to translate. But if you use long-winded sentences and complicated or inverted sentence structures, your translator will have to wait until each sentence is complete to begin translating it.
   - As much as possible, avoid idioms and aim for textual clarity. Weiss (1995, p. 421) points out that writers often don't "think of their audience as a potentially international one, nor do they recognize that American English can be highly idiomatic and therefore potentially confusing in a wider, international context." Speakers share the same limitation and need to concentrate on making their messages clear.
   - Remain observant and ready to adjust your pace and your language, as appropriate.

Many of the language practices that are ideal for oral presentations also contribute to effective written communications: use of common vocabulary and simple sentence structure, emphasis on textual clarity, and avoidance of idiomatic language, colloquial expressions, and slang. And, of course, you'll be dealing with many of the same cultural preferences when you write and when you make presentations. We'll address additional concerns of writing to readers from other cultures in the next section.

Writing to Readers from Other Cultures

As businesses increasingly work with others overseas, written correspondence will, of course, comprise a substantial part of building and nurturing business relationships. And much of that correspondence will be written in English. Kilpatrick (1984, p. 36) found in a survey that English was used for business correspondence in 95 of 100 businesses. (It should be noted, though, that English includes the various forms of the language used not only by those in the United States but by others too, including the British, Australians, Indians, and Nigerians [Boiarsky, 1995, p. 255].) Occasionally, you'll want to have your writing translated. James (1995, p. 237), for instance, says that it's common with extremely important communications—formal proposals, contracts, and minutes of meetings as well as anything of a legal nature—to send a translation with the English version. But for everyday business writing, you'll probably be writing in English and sending the message without a translation.

When you sit down to write, you'll certainly want to do a GRACEful analysis of the business writing situation, taking into careful consideration the readers' culture and how it affects written communication. In fact, your analysis should begin with the question of whether you should write at all. And once you've determined that a written document is appropriate, you should consider cultural expectations about content and format, too, which we address later in this chapter in Strategies for Cross-Cultural Communication.

When Should You Write?

When you're communicating with people from another culture, a key question you should ask yourself is whether you should write at all. James (1995) points out, for instance, the Asian preference for face-to-face meetings:

> Asians tend to be uncomfortable with communications that are not face to face. They value personal relations so highly that they often consider it disrespectful not to communicate in person. In the ranking of communications media, the face-to-face meeting is best, then comes a formal letter after an introduction, next comes a fax, and finally—in last place—comes an electronic message or a telephone call. Moreover, Asians rely heavily on subtlety in communications. They consider it highly important, if possible, to be able to read another person's full meaning by observing his or her expressions and body language. Accordingly, they have set up a preference for face-to-face communications. (p. 233)

Certainly, when a business relationship with an Asian organization is new, you'll want to focus on face-to-face meetings, which you can then follow up with letters documenting decisions and providing additional information and reports recounting the status of projects—making sure, of course, that you include something personal to continue building the relationship.

Form letters—used so frequently in the United States—are probably not a good idea when you're communicating with an organization from a high-context culture. James points out that alert readers can tell when a communication is a form letter, even if you've attempted to personalize it, and will be offended. When an executive receives a form letter, James says, "The purpose of the communication is irretrievably undermined, for the executive will feel slighted that you do not regard him or her as worthy of truly personal correspondence" (p. 40).

You'll also want to think carefully about whether you should write when your message is negative or you're angry or have a problem with something the reader or the reader's organization has done. We talked earlier about the use in high-context cultures of intermediaries, who negotiate when conflict or anger arises and soften and interpret the messages of both sides, shielding both parties from direct and embarrassing interactions. If you're involved, then, in a conflicted situation with an organization from a high-context culture, you'd be wise to follow the local custom of negotiating through a third party, rather than put your arguments and emotions on paper.

There are, however, plenty of times when you should write. When you'd like to meet with someone for the first time, you'll probably want to initiate this meeting through a letter. And if the culture is a more formal one, a letter of introduction from a third party who knows both you and the reader is common at the beginning of a business relationship. Boiarsky (1995, p. 247) explains that in China, when "a company has not done business with a firm previously, then it needs to know that another Chinese company has done so and has been satisfied with the work. In China this is known as 'kwan shi' connections." In Japan, these connections, or *kuchikomi,* are also expressed in introduction letters. And as the relationship continues, you should be sure to send thank-you letters for gifts, favors, and meetings. In short, James points out that you should "never miss an opportunity to build a relationship" (p. 39). He explains the need for ongoing relationship building in this way:

> In international business there is more to be gained from communicating a lot than from communicating a little. This is because differences in cultural and national backgrounds sow seeds of suspicion that can normally be dispelled with frequent communication. Accordingly, you should work hard at staying in frequent touch with an international counterpart. . . . Advise the counterpart of industry developments that are relevant to your activities. Even after a project with the counterpart is concluded, maintain an active correspondence. (pp. 36–37)

If one of the central purposes for writing to those from other cultures is to nurture a relationship, what sorts of strategies should you use when you write?

Strategies for Cross-Cultural Communication

To nurture your business relationship, James (1995, p. 39) recommends that you inject something personal into everything you write. He also suggests the use of *you* or the collective *we* more often than *I*. The collective *we*—meaning you and the reader, not you and your organization—is particularly important if you're writing to readers from a culture that emphasizes the group, not the individual. In addition, we recommend that you use these strategies:

- Most salutations use the standard *Dear* followed by the reader's name. Always personalize your letter by including the name of the reader in the salutation, rather than using the generic *To Whom It May Concern, Dear Sir or Madam,* or the like. In German letters, the salutation is commonly followed by an exclamation mark, not a colon or comma, to convey "special sincerity or emphasis" (Bell, Dillon, & Becker, 1995, p. 224).

- In cultures where status and hierarchy are emphasized, titles such as *Dr.* and *Professor* should be used when pertinent because education is considered very important (James, 1995, p. 148).

- Be more formal when you write to readers from collectivist cultures. And when the readers' culture emphasizes status and hierarchy, use titles and family (or last) names in salutations. James points out that in collectivist traditions, the last name is the most important part of a person's identity (pp. 33, 166). And in many cultures—including German, Mexican, and many Asian cultures—the last name is used even when people know each other well to indicate respect and establish appropriate boundaries between business and social interaction.

- Keep in mind that names are not always written as American names are, with the given name first and the family name last. In many Asian countries—including China, Japan, and Taiwan—family names appear first. And in some countries, China included, married women do not take their husbands' names. Finally, in some countries, such as Mexico, for instance, many people use hyphenated names. The first name is the father's name, and the second is the mother's name; it's common to refer to a person by both names (Kenna & Lacy, 1994, p. 41).

- If you're writing to someone from a culture that emphasizes status and hierarchy and that person's rank in the organization is higher than yours, either have someone of equivalent rank in your organization sign your letter or send that person's greetings and indicate that you are writing on his or her behalf. Letters to people of higher status also tend to be shorter (James, 1995, p. 34).

- In cultures where written communication is more formal, the way a letter looks is very important. Although letter format may be either full block or semiblock, the appearance should be neat and the letterhead on good-quality paper.

- For all readers except Americans and Canadians, dates are written with the day first and then the month: *2 April 1998*. In many European countries, Germany included, the date is given as numerals separated by periods. And if the letter is formal, the writer's city appears before the date: *Frankfurt, 2.4.1998* (Bell et al., 1995, p. 224).

- When writing to readers from collectivist cultures, include as one of your goals developing or maintaining a personal relationship. In some countries, personal talk is conventional. For instance, in Asian countries, the emphasis on personal relationships is translated into the letter conventions of beginning with something personal: an inquiry into the health of the reader, the well-being of his or her family, business prosperity, or another topic concerning the reader's interests (Boiarsky, 1995, p. 247). James (1995, p. 39) suggests "saying something pleasant about the last contact you had—a productive meeting or an enjoyable social event, or a suggestion by the . . . [reader] that proved useful to you."

- In some countries—Germany, for instance—a letter typically opens with a reference statement or specific note of appreciation for a previous letter or contact, even if that letter or contact isn't relevant to the topic of the current letter. Such openings show the writer's interest in a long-term relationship and his or her regard for the reader (Bell et al., 1995, p. 225).

- Letters addressed to readers who are Asian sometimes begin with apologies. As Rowland (1985, p. 51) points out, "Apologies are common in Japan. They show one's desire to atone for not meeting another's expectations. When fault is not an issue, they show one's sense of empathy and responsibility." So although apologies are not common in American correspondence, when it is appropriate, begin your letter with one.
- If you're writing to readers from a culture that is indirect in its communication and you're asking for information, phrase your question so that the reader isn't being asked to answer "yes" or "no." This will enable readers to provide specific information and to imply a negative, thereby saving face when their answer must be "no" (Boiarsky, 1995, p. 251). And keep in mind that if you do ask a question that requires a "yes" or "no" answer of someone from an indirect culture, you're unlikely to receive a response if the answer is "no."
- Remember the basic communication guidelines we've already presented: Use short sentences with subject/verb/object structure. Avoid colloquial language, slang, and idioms, and don't use humor unless you know the reader well enough to know that it will be appropriate. In other words, aim for clarity and simplicity when you write, and use formal language.
- Keep in mind the cultural signposts relevant to your readers' background as well as the style of argument preferred, and adapt your communications accordingly. For instance, in a high-context culture, favoring more indirect arguments, a persuasive appeal should probably be muted. Rowland points out that in Japanese communication, "when making an appeal in written form, demands are made in a 'softer' manner and persuasion is more subtle than is common in the West" (p. 80).
- Use FAXes, particularly if you're writing to readers from Asian countries. According to James (1995, pp. 189–190), in a survey of Asia Pacific executives, 68 percent said that one-half or more of their communication is sent by FAX. James believes the use of FAX is popular because of globally expanding communications technology and because the speed of delivery enhances productivity considerably. When people are doing business globally, FAXes cut across the barriers of time and space.

In closing, writers are increasingly being asked to communicate in an international marketplace where there are many opportunities for building bridges among cultures as well as many possibilities for making communication missteps. It's important to remember that people are, in general, *ethnocentric:* They believe that others share their values, beliefs, and assumptions. They presume that others see and reason about the world the same way they do. In other words, people see the world—and the more narrowly circumscribed world in which they do business—from their own perspective at the center of their own egocentric solar systems.

But if people are to be open to the opportunities of the global marketplace, they must become effective intercultural communicators. They must interact with people who populate other egocentric solar systems; who have alternate values, assumptions, and beliefs; and alternate logics and perspectives about the nature of the world and the ways things work. And as they listen to those from other cultures, they must allow themselves to learn about those cultures, to develop respect for the varied perspectives they encounter, and to understand the needs and preferences of others. In short, international communicators allow themselves to learn to communicate appropriately and effectively with people from a variety of cultures.

Part of learning to communicate effectively with people from other cultures is recognizing that cultural conventions affect how business is conducted, presentations are given, and documents are written. This chapter has provided a brief introduction to these cultural conventions and their effects on formal presentations and written texts. We recommend that you find out more about the communication preferences in the specific cultures where you do business. You can do so through your network of colleagues in both the United States and overseas, through organizations who serve as resources for businesses and travelers abroad, and through print resources. More importantly, we advise you to listen closely to your readers' (or listeners') written, spoken, and nonverbal communication since they will let you know much about what you need to know. A GRACEful analysis of your readers and listeners can enable you to adapt to their needs and conventions and help you to nurture long-term business relationships. This is the writing of business.

PRESENTATION AND WRITING CHECKLIST

The following guidelines will help you deal with opportunities and risks in cross-cultural communication. For any of these guidelines, remember the superordinate guideline: Disregard *any* of this advice if it would cause you to do something that's inappropriate or silly for your situation.

☑ Cross-Cultural Oral Presentations

- Avoid informality (which may be interpreted as rudeness) in establishing your credibility with people from collectivist cultures.
- Begin with relationship-building small talk and introductions.
- Emphasize benefits to the group and to solidarity.
- Structure your presentation indirectly, too.
- Base your argument on the cultural preference of your listeners.
- Allow time after your presentation is over for members of collectivist cultures to come to a decision.
- Use humor with care in cross-cultural presentations since it generally doesn't translate well.
- Use direct sentence structure and commonly used words when speaking to people whose first language is not English, and maintain a moderate pace to allow listeners to absorb your ideas.

- Use visual reinforcements of your spoken message.
- If you use a translator, select someone who is familiar with your field, and treat him or her as a collaborator.
- Meet with the translator ahead of time so that he or she can get used to your voice, read your presentation, and help you interpret the local culture.
- Find out if your translator plans to translate simultaneously or consecutively, and adjust your presentation accordingly.
- Whenever you plan to do business with people from another culture, find out what you can about their culture and communication preferences through networks both in the United States and overseas, through organizations that serve as resources for businesses abroad, and through print information.
- Listen closely to what your readers (or listeners) tell you about their needs, too.

☑ Cross-Cultural Correspondence

- Although much of your correspondence to readers in other countries will be written in English, you may want to send translations along with extremely important communications, like proposals and legal documents.
- Consider if writing is actually the preferred means of communication; for instance, many Asians prefer face-to-face meetings.
- When a relationship is new, focus on face-to-face meetings, followed by writing.
- Don't use form letters for people in cultures that stress relationships.
- Consider communicating negative messages through intermediaries.
- Use a letter of introduction at the beginning of a business relationship with an organization from a formal culture that stresses relationships.
- To nurture a relationship when corresponding with people from collectivist cultures, inject something personal into everything you write, and use *you* more than *I* or *we*.
- In general, you should be more formal—in salutations, with readers' names and titles, and with document design.
- If you need information, ask questions that don't ask readers to answer with *"yes"* or *"no"* since you're unlikely to receive a response if the answer is *"no."*
- Use FAXes to break the bounds of time and space; e-mail is much less frequently used.

ACTIVITIES AND PROJECTS

1. Research the conventions for oral and written communication in a specific country. In particular, consider such things as cultural characteristics that affect oral and written communication, guidelines for communicating effectively, and any sort of business etiquette that might be useful to know. Also, find out what sorts of letters are usually written, what they typically look like, what

conventions are generally followed, and what sorts of arguments people often make. Find out when letters are written, too. Finally, determine if any conventions govern the relationship between the writer and the reader and affect how the reader is addressed. Present this research in a formal report and in an oral presentation.

2. Interview an international student, colleague, or faculty member to learn about his or her cultural background and find out what you might experience if you were to visit or work in his or her country. In addition, gather suggestions for working effectively in that person's country: about business etiquette, about communicating effectively when writing and speaking, and about nonverbal communication. Write a memo or make a presentation to your colleagues about what you discover.

3. Do an informal case study of the challenges of learning to communicate effectively within another culture by interviewing an international student, colleague, or faculty member:
   - Ask this person to describe what he or she has learned about the American language and culture that would be useful for people from his or her home country to know upon arriving in the United States.
   - Find out about the similarities and differences in oral and written communication between the two cultures. Ask what steps are productive and unproductive when writing for American readers.
   - Find out what aspects of the language present particular problems for writing or speaking.
   - Finally, ascertain what about American business and/or education surprises or interests him or her.

   Report your findings orally or in writing to your colleagues.

4. Research the effects of language and culture on marketing and sales writing in another country, and report what you discover in an oral or written report.

5. Select a large, publicly held U.S. company, and find out what sorts of international connections it has:
   - Does it have overseas offices or manufacturing?
   - Does it market products or services in other countries?
   - Does it invest in companies overseas or have partnerships with companies in other parts of the world?
   - Does it send employees overseas? If so, what sorts of international employment opportunities are available, and what kinds of skills, educational background, and experience does the company require?
   - Does the organization train people for their overseas experience, and if so, through what sorts of programs?
   - What other sort of overseas connections does this organization have, if any?

   Describe the international connections that this organization has in a written or oral report.

REFERENCES

Albrecht, K. (June, 1996). Lost in the translation. *Training*, 66–70.

Bell, A. H., Dillon, W. T., & Becker, H. (1995, April). German memo and letter style. *Journal of Business and Technical Communication, 9*(2), 219–227.

Boiarsky, C. (Summer, 1995). The relationship between cultural and rhetorical conventions: Engaging in international communications. *Technical Communication Quarterly, 4*(3), 245–257.

Fox, H. (1994). *Listening to the world: Cultural issues in academic writing.* Urbana, IL: National Council of Teachers of English.

Hall, E. T. (1977). *Beyond culture.* Garden City, NY: Anchor.

Hall, E. T. (1988). The hidden dimensions of time and space in today's world. In F. Poyato (Ed.), *Cross-cultural perspectives in nonverbal communication.* Toronto, Canada: C. J. Hogrefe.

Hofstede, G. (1980). *Culture's consequences: International differences in work-related values.* Beverly Hills, CA: Sage.

James, D. L. (1995). *The executive guide to Asia-Pacific communications: Doing business across the Pacific.* New York: Kodansha International.

Johnstone, B. (1989). Linguistic strategies for persuasive discourse. In S. Ting-Toomey & F. Korzenny (Ed.), *Language, communication and culture: Current directions.* Newbury Park, CA: Sage.

Kenna, P., & Lacy, S. (1994). *Business Mexico: A practical guide to understanding Mexican business culture.* Lincolnwood, IL: Passport Books.

Kilpatrick, R. (1984). Business communication practices. *Journal of Business Communication, 21*, 33–44.

Lustig, M. W., & Koester, J. (1993). *Intercultural competence: Interpersonal communication across cultures.* New York: HarperCollins.

Rhinesmith, S. R. (1996). Training for global operations. In R. L. Craig (Ed.), *The ASTD training and development handbook: A guide to human resource development* (4th ed.). New York: McGraw-Hill.

Rowland, D. (1985). *Japanese business etiquette: A practical guide to success with the Japanese.* New York: Warner Books.

Stamps, D. (November, 1996). Welcome to America: Watch out for culture shock. *Training*, 22–30.

Toulmin, S. (1972). *Human understanding, Volume I: The collective use and evolution of concepts.* Princeton, NJ: Princeton University Press.

Weiss, T. (Fall, 1995). Translation in a borderless world. *Technical Communication Quarterly, 4*(4), 407–425.

Part VI

The Business Writer's Quick Reference

- General Strategies for Revising, Editing, and Proofreading
- Strategies for Increasing Reader Comprehension
- Editing Strategies for Specific Sentence-Level Errors
- Grammar Problems
- Other Conventions in Written Professional Discourse
- Beyond the Spell-Checker: Commonly Misused Words and Expressions

Overview

General Strategies for Revising, Editing, and Proofreading

Strategies for Increasing Reader Comprehension

- *trans* — Using Transition Cues to Guide Readers
- *coh* — Increasing Cohesion
- *w* 7 ± 2 — Avoiding Information Overload
- *w* — Reducing Wordiness
- *pass* — Using Active versus Passive Verbs
- *w* — Avoiding Nominalizations

Editing Strategies for Specific Sentence-Level Errors

- *ro cs* — Comma Errors
- *frag //* — Sentence Structure Problems
- *sp* — Spelling and Typographical Errors

Grammar Problems

- *agr s/v agr s/v* — Subject/Verb Agreement
- *pro ref pro agr* — Pronoun Reference or Agreement
- *cs fs ro* — Problems with Sentence Boundaries: Comma Splices, Fused Sentences, and Run-On Sentences

Other Conventions in Written Professional Discourse

- *//* — Maintaining Parallelism
- *ap* — Using Apostrophes Correctly
- *num* — Using Numbers: Words or Figures?
- *sxt* — Avoiding Gender Bias in Pronouns

Beyond the Spell-Checker: Commonly Misused Words and Expressions

- *ww*

In the beginning was the word. But by the time the second word was added to it, there was trouble. For with it came syntax.

—John Simon

General Strategies for Revising, Editing, and Proofreading

When you set aside time to fine-tune your letters, memos, and other documents, you make sure that your ideas are clear and fully developed and that they are presented free from the sorts of mistakes that can confuse readers or undercut your credibility with them. You also ensure that you've projected a professional image that both you and your organization can be proud of.

The following are general strategies for revising and editing your writing; specific guidelines for catching particular sorts of errors appear later in this Business Writer's Quick Reference (see p. 665).

- Plan a break between the time you finish writing something and when you begin editing it. Go for coffee or lunch, attend a meeting, or work on another project for a while; then come back to fine-tune your text. This break will enable you to rest your eyes, and it will provide a bit of distance so that you can actually see what's on the page, instead of what you *think* is there.
- Good writers may not know all the rules of writing or how to spell every word, but they do know when and where to look things up. And they keep the resources that they need—dictionaries or spell-checking programs, thesauruses, handbooks, and style guides—at their fingertips when they write so that they're not tempted to make guesses about what's correct.
- If you're trying to edit and find yourself concentrating more on the meaning of what you're saying than on the words and punctuation on the page, read your text backward—one sentence or one word at a time. This will enable you to focus on grammar and mechanics, instead of meaning.
- Slow yourself down by using two pieces of blank white paper or a straight-edge of some sort to cover all but one sentence at a time. This will keep you from reading ahead and will reduce visual distractions, as well.
- Because we often *hear* errors that we cannot *see,* read your text aloud. This will also slow you down and help you find sentences that don't sound smooth.
- Keep a list of errors you make often, and use the editing strategies reviewed in Editing Strategies for Specific Sentence-Level Errors (pp. 665–669) to look for particular sorts of mistakes you know you tend to make.

Strategies for Increasing Reader Comprehension

Using Transition Cues to Guide Readers*

trans

Transitions help readers connect the ideas in a piece of writing; these connective words and phrases show how pieces of text fit together. Often, all you'll need is a word or phrase to lead readers through your text from information they've already read to new information.

Cues That Lead Readers Forward from Old to New Information

- **To move readers into additional information or further development of your ideas**

Old Information ➡ **TRANSITION: Addition** ➡ **New Information**

Actually,
Additionally,
Again,
Also,
And
Besides
Equally important,
Finally,
First, Second, Third, etc.
Further,
Furthermore,
Incidentally,
Indeed,
In fact,
Lastly,
Moreover,
Not only this, but also this as well
What's more,

- **To move readers into specific examples**

Generalization ➡ **TRANSITION: Examples** ➡ **Examples**

As an illustration,
Especially,
For example,
For instance,
Including
In particular,
Namely,
Notably,
Particularly,
Specifically,
To demonstrate,
To illustrate,

*The strategies for using transitions as cues for the reader are based upon Linda Flower's *Problem-Solving Strategies for Writing* (1981, p. 200). We also wish to acknowledge the contributions of Kathleen Cahill to the development of these guidelines and examples.

- **To move readers from one timeframe to another**

One Time ➡ **TRANSITION: Time** ➡ **Another Time**

After a few hours,
Afterward,
At last,
At the same time,
Before
Before this,
Currently,
During
Eventually,
Finally,
First, Second, Third, etc.
First of all,
Formerly,
Immediately before,
Immediately following,
Initially,
In the end,
In the future,
In the meantime,
In the meanwhile,
Last, Last but not least, Lastly,
Later,
Meanwhile,
Next, Soon after,
Previously,
Simultaneously,
Subsequently,
Then,

- **To draw readers' attention to a particular location or place**

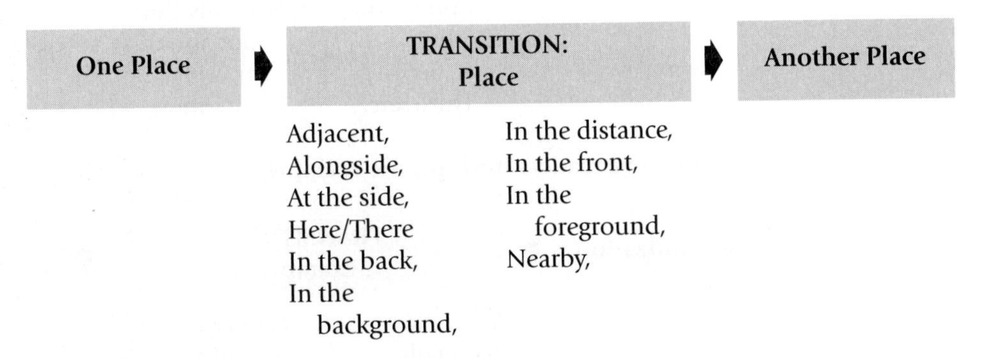

One Place
TRANSITION: Place
Another Place
Adjacent,
Alongside,
At the side,
Here/There
In the back,
In the background,
In the distance,
In the front,
In the foreground,
Nearby,

- **To let readers know that a digression is about to begin or end**

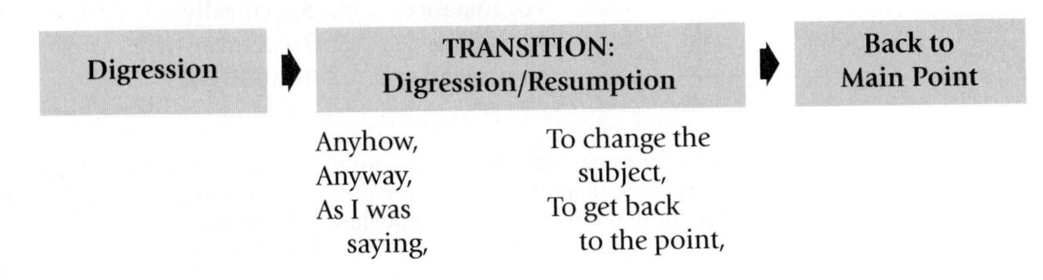

At any rate,
By the way,
Incidentally,
To return to the subject,
To resume,

Cues That Draw Readers' Attention to Cause-and-Effect Relationships

- **To emphasize a cause or reason**

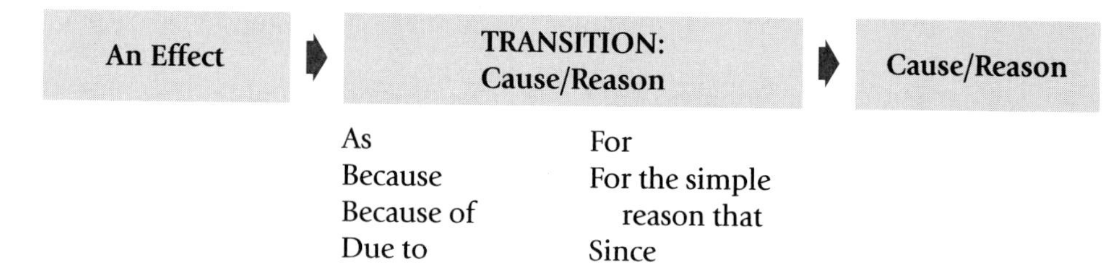

- **To stress a result or effect**

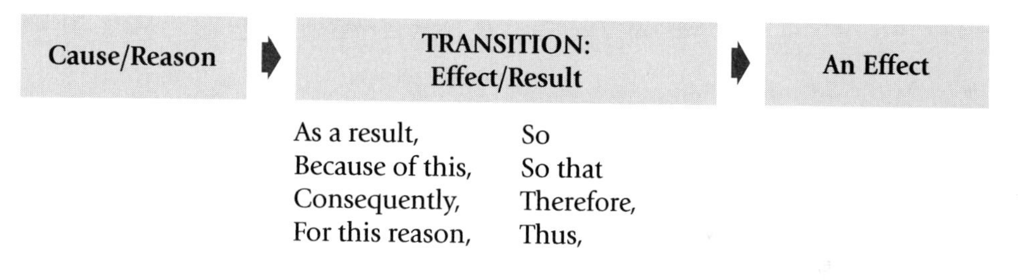

- **To clarify the purpose of something**

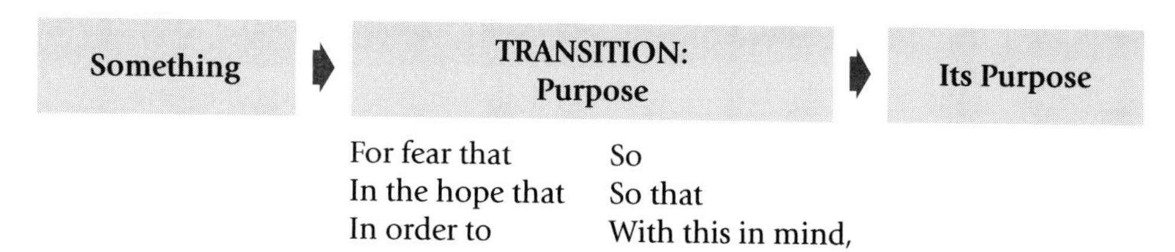

Cues That Make Readers Stop and Compare What They've Just Read to What They're about to Read

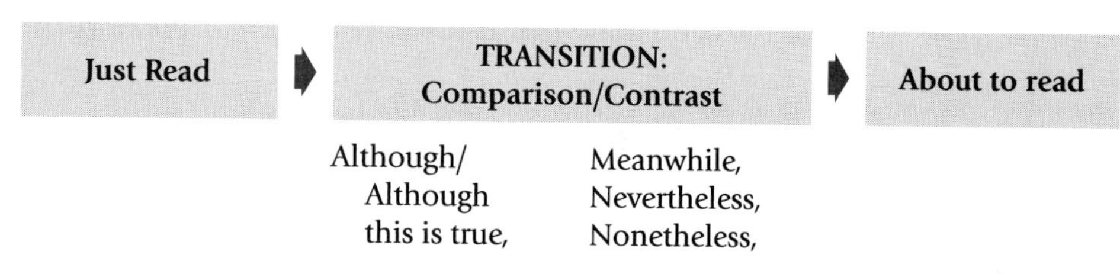

(continued)

And yet
At the same time,
But
Conversely,
For all that,
In comparison,
In contrast,
In the same manner/way,
However,
Likewise,
Notwithstanding,
On the contrary,
On the other hand,
Similarly,
Still,
While this is true,
When in fact
Whereas

Cues That Lead Readers into Statements That Clarify or Emphasize

- **To clarify a point that readers have just read**

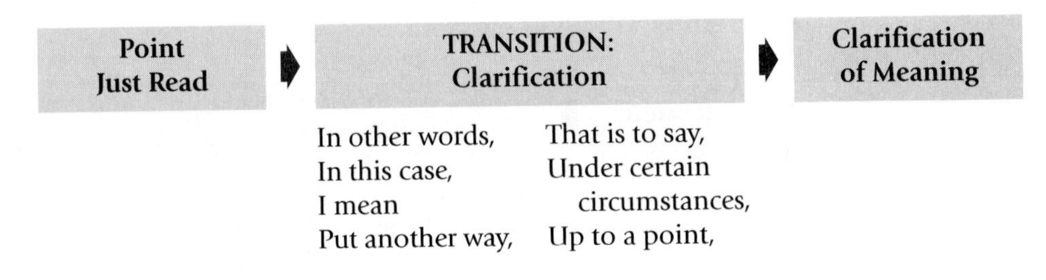

In other words,
In this case,
I mean
Put another way,
That is to say,
Under certain circumstances,
Up to a point,

- **To emphasize a point that readers are about to read**

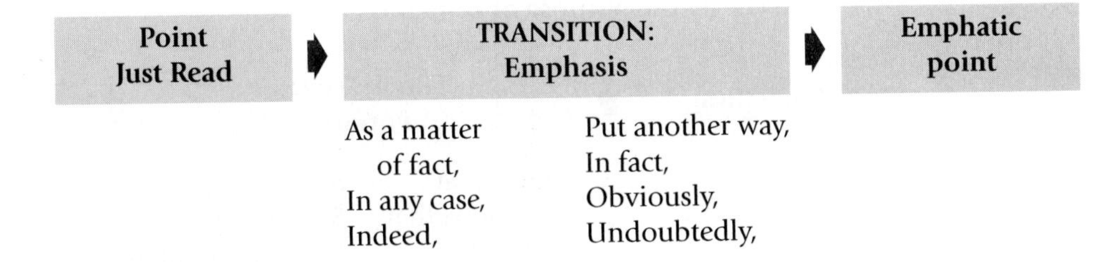

As a matter of fact,
In any case,
Indeed,
Put another way,
In fact,
Obviously,
Undoubtedly,

Cues That Lead Readers into Concessions, Reservations, Dismissals, or Conditions

- **To concede a point that readers are likely to think of**

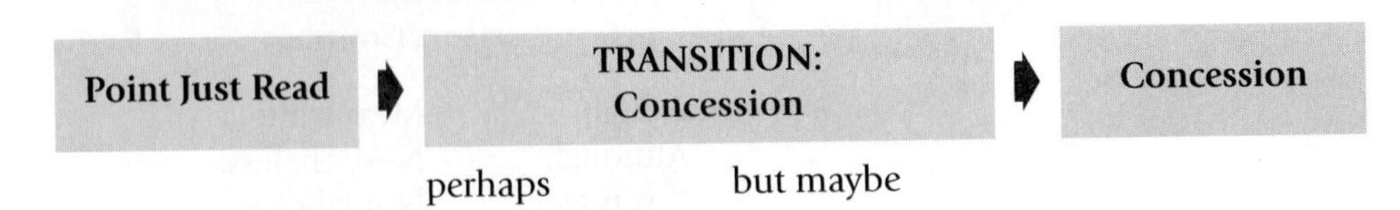

perhaps
but maybe

- **To clarify for readers the writer's reservations**

Point Just Read ➧ **TRANSITION: Reservation** ➧ **Reservation**

Admittedly,	Despite this
As a result,	Indeed,
As a matter of fact,	In summary,
Even so,	Nevertheless,
Even though	Notwithstanding,
	Regardless

- **To dismiss a point that readers are likely to think of**

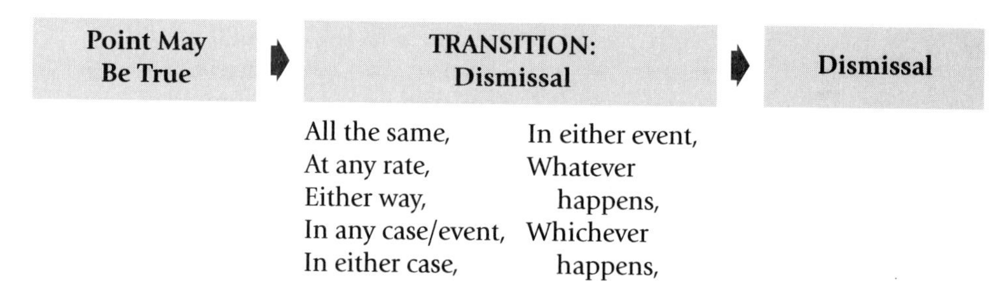

- **To establish a condition or conditions affecting the subject**

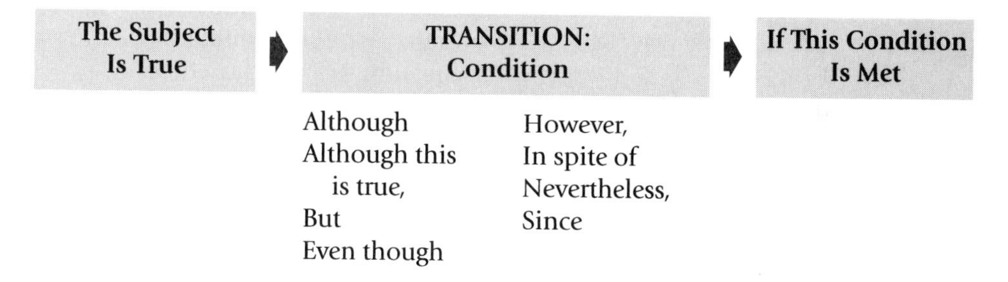

Cues That Lead Readers into a Summary or Conclusion

- **To repeat a point you've already made**

A Point ➧ **TRANSITION: Repetition** ➧ **The Point Stated Differently**

As I have noted,	As noted earlier,
As indicated above/earlier,	In brief,
As I stated,	In short,
As mentioned,	In summary,
	On the whole,

- **To summarize what you've already said**

Points Made Earlier	➧	TRANSITION: Summary	➧	Nutshell Summary

All in all,	In summary,
As indicated above/earlier,	On the whole,
All together,	Overall,
As I mentioned,	Since
As I stated,	So
Briefly,	Summing up,
By and large,	Then,
Finally,	Therefore,
Given these facts,	To conclude,
In brief,	To put it briefly,
In conclusion,	To review,
In short,	To summarize,

- **To introduce readers to a conclusion or conclusions**

Points Made Earlier	➧	TRANSITION: Conclusion	➧	Conclusion

Accordingly,	In short,
As a result,	In summary,
Consequently,	On the whole,
Finally,	So
Hence,	Therefore,
In brief,	Thus,
In conclusion,	To conclude,

For additional information on strategies that enable readers to connect the ideas in a piece of writing, see the next section: Increasing Cohesion.

Increasing Cohesion

coh

Cohesion is the cognitive glue that holds a piece of writing together—that connects sentence to sentence and paragraph to paragraph. You can establish cohesion in your writing through using transitional words and phrases—*therefore, furthermore, for instance,* and other transitions listed in the previous discussion—that clarify for readers the relationships among ideas in a text. But transitions alone aren't enough to make writing cohesive. You need to repeat keywords and use reference words, too.

Repeat Keywords

You can tie sentences and paragraphs together by repeating keywords. This repetition also helps to emphasize your main idea. For example, in the following paragraph, notice how many times the words *reconciled, reconciling, reconciliation,* and *vouchers* are repeated:

> In its response to the fiscal year 1995–1996 management letter, dated May 27, 1997, the department stated that the way in which food *vouchers* are *reconciled* had been modified, and as a result, the *reconciliations* are now being performed within 150 days. In our audit, we discovered that while the department is still not *reconciling* all the *vouchers* issued with *vouchers* paid within 150 days, we did note significant improvement during the last nine months of fiscal year 1996–1997. Specifically, during this period, the department was late in *reconciling* only 0.24 percent of the food *vouchers* issued with the food *vouchers* redeemed.

By repeating the words *reconciled, reconciling, reconciliation,* and *vouchers,* the writer has tied sentences together and clearly indicated what the main idea of the paragraph is. In this case, the main idea is *reconciling* something. And what exactly is being (or not being) *reconciled?* By repeating the word *voucher,* the writer shows us that the main idea is about *reconciliation* of *vouchers.*

Use Reference Words

Another way you can tie together sentences and paragraphs is by using reference words that point back to an idea you've already stated. Reference words—such as *this, these, those, that,* and *such*—shouldn't be used by themselves. Instead, you should use them in combination with the important words and phrases from previous sentences or paragraphs. For example, you can see in the following paragraph how reference words are combined with keywords so that they emphasize the main idea and tie sentences and the paragraph together:

> Touching an area of the map activates a brief, narrated sequence of photographs, video segments, and animated illustrations. *This* sequence illustrates the selected logging practice. Once *this* sequence is completed, the viewer can touch the gauges and drag the magnifying glass over the river to see how *this* logging practice has affected water conditions. Touching each gauge a second time allows the viewer to compare *these* water conditions to *those* of an undisturbed wooded environment.

Many words are repeated from one sentence to the next and from one paragraph to the next, as well. Can you identify the main ideas of each paragraph based on repeated words?

Avoiding Information Overload

w ⊤ 7±2

Remember "The Magical Number Seven, Plus or Minus Two"? That's the rule of thumb that says most of us can hold only about seven pieces of distinct information in our short-term working memory. As we argued back in Chapter 1, it's one of the reasons writing is such a powerful tool for working with the complexities of our professional work. But it's possible to structure sentences such that the writing itself overburdens readers' short-term memory.

The Midbranching Sentence

For example, the following sentence, sometimes called a *midbranching sentence*, creates this kind of cognitive overload:

> The marketing department, having identified a potential new niche that could be served by modifying the electronic circuitry in a way that was analogous to the process the research and development group tried with the prototype last year, proposed developing a scaled-down probe for microsurgery.

A midbranching sentence separates the subject of the sentence from the predicate by loading additional information into the sentence after the subject. By the time the reader reaches the closure on the idea that a new probe has been proposed, the fact that the marketing department proposed the idea may have gotten lost in all the intervening information.

The sentence would be much easier to understand without the complicating elaboration:

> The marketing department proposed developing a scaled-down probe for microsurgery.

Does this mean the additional information should be eliminated? Probably not. Presumably, the information about the earlier prototype is relevant and useful. In any case, you'd want to think about relevance and usefulness as the basis of whether to use the information. Assuming you decide you need the information, you should move it to another sentence so that the chunks of information represented by the sentences are manageable. Here are two possibilities.

1. Locate the elaborating information before the core sentence, using it as a preface:

   Last year, the research and development group modified the electronic circuitry of the prototype in a way that made it possible to scale down the device. Subsequently, the marketing department proposed exploiting a new marketing niche by developing a scaled-down probe for microsurgery using an analogous process.

2. Here's an example where the elaborating information is located after the core sentence as a way of elaborating upon the central idea:

 The marketing department proposed developing a scaled-down probe for microsurgery that uses technology analogous to what the research and development group tried last year with the prototype. Marketing sees a potential new market niche in this area.

The Left-Branching Sentence

Loaded with the elaborating information at the front end of the sentence, the following sentence is sometimes called a *left-branching sentence.* (Notice that the preceding sentence is itself a left-branching sentence.) Like the midbranching sentence, the left-branching sentence may overload the reader's short-term memory if the front loading is too complex, as in this case:

> Having identified a potential new niche that could be served by modifying the electronic circuitry in a way that was analogous to the process the research and development group tried with the prototype last year, the marketing department proposed developing a scaled-down probe for microsurgery.

The Right-Branching Sentence

The *right-branching sentence* below follows the normal subject/verb (or agent/act) pattern that is most common in English. Because it achieves closure on chunks of information as it goes along, this type of sentence is less likely to overload readers' short-term memory than either a left-branching or midbranching sentence. On the other hand, a document made up entirely of right-branching sentences, even a brief memo, quickly begins to read like a monotonous list and fails to take advantage of the opportunity to give important ideas emphatic placement within sentences. Consider, for instance, the following sentence:

> The marketing department identified a potential new marketing niche and proposed serving it by developing a scaled-down probe for microsurgery that would use electronic circuitry that was modified in a way that was analogous to the process the research and development group tried with the prototype last year.

Reducing Wordiness

w

Wordiness results from many sources. Two of the most common are padding to reach minimum length requirements or to sound more impressive and generating false starts when struggling to clarify your ideas. Regardless of the reason for padded writing, you can achieve conciseness if you use specific strategies for eliminating wordiness and are aware of the wordiness patterns typical of your own writing.

Strategies to Eliminate Wordiness

- **Mark sections of your writing you struggled to produce.** If you've had a hard time getting your ideas down on paper, chances are you've included some false starts or filler phrases in your writing—something like the *ahems, uhs,* and *okays* that occur when we're speaking and formulating our ideas at the same time. This is natural. Don't worry about fillers when you're writing. Simply mark the sections you've struggled to produce; then, after you're done with your draft, focus on trimming out unnecessary language. As you edit, pay particular attention to sections you've marked.
- **Give yourself a breather before editing.** Even if you just get yourself a cup of coffee or work on something else for a while, getting away from your text will give you the distance you need to see what language is needed and what's not.
- **Learn your wordiness patterns.** Most people fall into two or three wordiness patterns when they write. Learn what your patterns are, and look for them when you edit. In fact, editing your text *once for each wordiness pattern* will, with practice, enable you to tighten your writing more quickly and effectively than will a scatter-gun editing process.

The following section describes particular wordiness patterns. As you read, mark patterns typical of your writing.

Patterns of Wordiness

- **Omit the filler phrases *it is, there is,* and *there are* at the beginnings of sentences;** these often delay a sentence's true subject and verb.

  WORDY
  It is expensive to upgrade computer systems.

  CONCISE
  Upgrading computer systems is expensive.

- **Omit *this* from the beginning of a sentence, modify what's left, and join it to the preceding sentence with a comma.**

  WORDY
  Chlorofluorocarbons have been banned from aerosols. This has lessened the ozone layer's depletion.

  CONCISE
  Chlorofluorocarbons have been banned from aerosols, lessening the ozone layer's depletion.

- **Change *which* or *that* constructions to an *-ing* word.**

  WORDY
  The committee, which meets monthly, oversees accounting procedures and audits.

  CONCISE
  The committee, meeting monthly, oversees accounting procedures and audits.

- **Omit *which* or *that* altogether when possible.**

  WORDY
  Because the fluid, which was brown and poisonous, was dumped into the river, the company that was negligent had to shut down.

  CONCISE
  Because the brown, poisonous fluid was dumped into the river, the negligent company had to shut down.

- **Replace passive verbs with active verbs.** In a passive construction, the subject of the sentence is being acted upon; in an active construction, the subject is the actor. (You will find a fuller description of passive voice in the next section, Using Active versus Passive Verbs, pp. 662–664.)

  WORDY
  Rain forests are being destroyed by uncontrolled logging.

  CONCISE
  Uncontrolled logging is destroying rain forests.

- **Change *is* or *was* when it occurs alone to a strong verb.**

  WORDY
  A new fire curtain is necessary for the stage.

  CONCISE
  The stage needs a new fire curtain.

- **Replace *is, are, was, were, has, had,* or *have* + an *-ing* word with a simple present- or past-tense verb.**

  WORDY
  The South African government was undergoing significant changes.

  CONCISE
  The South African government underwent significant changes.

- **Replace *should, would,* or *could* with a simple past- or present-tense verb.**

  WORDY
  The environmental council could see several solutions.

  CONCISE
  The environmental council saw several solutions.

- **Substitute strong verbs for *-tion* and *-sion* words whenever possible.** (For more information about this wordiness pattern, see Avoiding Nominalizations, p. 664.)

  WORDY
  I submitted an application for the job.

  CONCISE
  I applied for the job.

- **Replace prepositional phrases with one-word modifiers when possible.** Prepositions—those little relationship words like *of, from,* and *after*—tend to bring in a lot of *-tion* and *-sion* words, too.

  WORDY
  The President of the Student Senate was in charge of the lobbying against the merger at the Minnesota Congress.

  CONCISE
  The Student Senate President oversaw lobbying the Minnesota Congress against the merger.

- **Use a colon after a statement preceding a sentence of explanation, and leave out the beginning of the next sentence.**

  WORDY
  The theater has three main technical areas. These areas are costumes, scenery, and lighting.

  CONCISE
  The theater has three main technical areas: costumes, scenery, and lighting.

- **Combine two closely related short sentences by omitting part of one.**

  WORDY
  The director is concerned about problems. Typical problems may occur with lighting, sound, and props.

  CONCISE
  The director is concerned about typical problems with lighting, sound, and props.

Using Active versus Passive Verbs

pass

Active voice is more direct, more emphatic, and more concise than *passive voice.* But what are other differences between the two verb forms?

Active Voice

If the subject of a sentence *does* the verb (the action), then the verb is in the active voice. In the samples below, each subject is underlined once and each verb is underlined twice. Notice that the subjects are *doing* the action of the verb.

The credit committee approved the loan.

State funding paid for the new public library near the downtown square.

The project team completed the needs assessment in record time.

Passive Voice

If the subject *receives* the action of the verb, the verb is in the passive voice. If we rewrite the preceding examples in passive voice, we have the following:

The loan was approved by the credit committee.

The new public library near the downtown square was paid for by state funding.

The needs assessment was completed by the project team in record time.

As you can see in these examples, passive voice downplays the agent's role by relegating it to a less emphatic position in the sentence. Using passive voice also adds words—helping verbs like *is, am, are, were, was, has,* and *have been*—so passive verbs are less concise than active verbs. Consider these examples:

He was told by the manager that his performance review would take place on October 15.

The computer was fixed after months of problems.

Both of these examples include a helping verb: *was.* And both of these sentences are more indirect than they need to be.

Notice, too, that in each of these sentences the subject is not doing the action but is being acted on by another agent. In the first sentence, for instance, *He* is being acted upon by another noun in the sentence: *manager.* But sometimes in passive voice, the actor doesn't even appear in the sentence. The second example above is a good illustration of this missing agent. In this instance, we don't know who fixed the computer and whom to thank for resolving the problems. However, when the agent of the sentence *does* appear, it will often be accompanied by the word *by,* as in the first example above. Sometimes, then, you can figure out if a verb is passive or not by checking for the word *by.* If you find it, you're probably looking at a passive verb.

Although in most instances you'll want to use active voice in your writing, you may actually prefer passive voice when you don't know the *doer* of the verb, when the *doer* of the verb is not important, or when there are too many *doers* of the same verb. Consider these examples:

Rastinen Corporation was founded in 1994 by Martin Rastinen.

The company's home offices were built in Maple Grove in 1962.

The proposal was approved and work begun in August 1997.

In the first example, the founding of the company is more important than who founded it, so the passive voice is appropriate; the founder's name does not take the emphatic subject slot but is delayed until the end of the sentence. In the second example, the people who built the home offices aren't even mentioned because they're unimportant; the fact that the offices were built takes the emphatic subject and verb slots. In fact, in all three instances, the sentences are in the passive voice for good reasons.

Keep in mind that passive voice is generally used when the actor isn't known or isn't important. In most cases, though, you'll know who the actor is, and it will be significant to your message; therefore, you'll want to emphasize that actor's importance by making it the subject of your sentence. Making the *doers* of the actions the subjects of your sentences makes your sentences direct, concise, and forceful.

Avoiding Nominalizations

Simply put, a *nominalization* is a noun derived from a verb, often through the use of *-tion*, *-ment*, or *-ance* endings:

Verb	Nominalization
evaluate →	evaluation
affirm →	affirmation
acknowledge →	acknowledgment
dominate →	domination
→	dominance

Nominalizations should be avoided because they tend to gum up language: The words themselves are longer than their verb counterparts, and they bring in extra language, too. Consider the following examples:

A Nominalization	Its Verb Counterpart
We made an *evaluation* of the new system.	We *evaluated* the new system.
The board's recommendation brought *affirmation* to the committee's decision.	The board *affirmed* the committee's decision.
The award was *acknowledgment* of the research team's groundbreaking discovery.	The award *acknowledged* the research team's groundbreaking discovery.
Ineffective CEOs use *domination* to control their subordinates.	Ineffective CEOs *dominate* their subordinates.

Effective writing, then, replaces these wordy nominalizations with their more direct verb counterparts.

Editing Strategies for Specific Sentence-Level Errors

Writers can rarely check a piece of writing for every glitch in one pass without overlooking *something*. Effective editors know the types of errors they typically make and search for them methodically. Your first step in becoming an effective editor, then, is to make a list of errors typical of your writing—starting with the most serious or most frequent errors and moving to the less serious or less frequent errors. (You can ask an instructor or someone else you trust for help with this.) Then, make several passes through your text, looking for one type of error during each pass.

In the following sections, we'll review errors writers frequently make and provide some "tricks of the trade" for catching each type. In particular, we'll cover these errors:

Comma Errors

- Omitted commas after introductory words, phrases, or clauses ^
- Omitted commas in compound sentences (run-ons) *ro*
- Extra commas (comma splices) *cs*

Sentence Structure Problems

- Sentence fragments

- Problems with parallel structure

Spelling and Typographical Errors *sp*

Comma Errors

Searching for Omitted Commas after Introductory Words, Phrases, or Clauses

^

Commas should appear after emphatic opening words as well as after introductory phrases and clauses that come before main sentences. To catch commas omitted after introductions, try these strategies:

- Check the first two words of each sentence to figure out if the sentence has an introductory element. Note that introductory elements (words, phrases, or clauses) always establish either time or condition. As a result, the first words of a sentence will help you to figure out whether you'll need an introductory comma.
- If the first words indicate that you're being teased and the main idea is being withheld until the time and/or condition is established, a break point will occur

where you should insert a comma to let readers know that the main sentence is coming up. The comma should appear at this break point.

- Until you get a feel for the types of words that establish time or condition, refer to the following list of words that commonly begin introductory phrases or clauses. (Keep in mind that this list is incomplete; other words signal dependence, too.)

Words That Establish Time or Condition

after	if	till
although	in	unless
as	in case	until
as if	in order that	when
as soon as	once	whenever
because	on condition that	where
before	provided that	wherever
even if	since	whether
even though	so that	while
for	though	whoever

Searching for Omitted Commas in Compound Sentences (Run-Ons)

ro

To connect two complete sentences (or *independent clauses*), you must use both a comma and a connecting word (or *coordinating conjunction*). If the comma is missing, the error is called a *run-on*. To check for run-on sentences, use the following two-step process:

1. Skim the paper, looking only for the seven coordinating conjunctions, which you can remember using the acronym *fanboys:*

   for
   and
   nor
   but
   or
   yet
   so

2. When you find one of the seven fanboys, cover it with your finger or a piece of paper; determine if the word groups on either side of it can stand alone. If there is a complete sentence on each side of the fanboy, then you should show the coordination or balance by placing a comma in front of the conjunction.

(For more information about finding and fixing run-on sentences, see Problems with Sentence Boundaries, pp. 671–673.)

Searching for Comma Splices

cs

If two complete sentences are connected by only a comma, the error is called a *comma splice.* To find comma splices, follow these steps:

- Skim the paper, stopping at every comma to check whether a complete sentence appears on each side of it.
- If a complete sentence *does* appear on each side of the comma, you'll need to decide whether to separate the ideas more and give each of them more emphasis or stress their relationship.
- If you'd like to separate and emphasize the ideas more, use a more emphatic punctuation mark—a period—which will signal to your reader that you are moving from one completed thought to another.
- If you'd like the ideas to remain in the same sentence because their relationship is important, fix the comma splice by linking the sentences with a comma and a coordinating conjunction (*fanboy*) or with a semicolon.

(Additional information about comma splices is available in Problems with Sentence Boundaries, pp. 671–673.)

Sentence Structure Problems

Searching for Sentence Fragments

frag

A *sentence fragment* is a group of words that's punctuated as if it's a sentence but is missing a subject or a verb—or has a subject and verb but includes a word that makes it dependent on another sentence. To find sentence fragments in your writing, try the following strategies:

- Check every sentence to ensure that it has a main subject and verb.
- Pay special attention to any sentence beginning with a word that signals clarification. Since most fragments are actually *pieces* of sentences, pay special attention to sentences that begin with *and, because, such as, for example, for instance*—or any other word or group of words indicating that it's going to explain something. Check the group of words carefully to make sure that it has a main subject and verb following such introductory elements.
- Also check for groups of words beginning with words showing dependence, or *dependent markers: after, although, because, before,* and so on. Even though a dependent marker may be followed by a subject and verb, this group of words (dependent marker + subject + verb) *can't* stand alone; it depends upon another subject and verb for its meaning. For example, *Because I followed the presidential debates carefully* is a fragment; although it has a subject and verb (*I followed*), the word *Because* makes the whole group of words dependent—probably on the sentence before or the one after.

Note that fragments aren't always a problem in a business document. A short fragment, even as short as a single word, can be powerfully emphatic in the right circumstances. Here's an example:

> What were the results of two years' planning and restructuring? Lower productivity. Lower morale.

But inadvertent fragments are almost always a problem because they confuse readers. If people who review your drafts—colleagues, supervisors, instructors, and others—are pointing out frequent, inadvertent fragments, you should analyze them, using the typology we've used here, to make your own search for fragments more efficient.

Searching for Problems with Parallel Structure

//

Items in lists and items being compared must appear in the same grammatical form; that is, if one list item includes a word with an *-ing* ending, all must.

> NOT PARALLEL
> Jesse Manzel will coordinate the team's efforts in planning, implementing, and project assessment.
>
> PARALLEL
> Jesse Manzel will coordinate the team's efforts in planning, implementing, and assessing the project.

As the previous example shows, sentences that aren't parallel feel awkward. To check for problems with parallelism, try the following strategies:

- Read your paper, pausing for sentences that trip you up. Check them for parallelism.
- Look in particular for words or word groups in a series; also check words or word groups joined by *and* and *or.*
  - Make sure that these items match in grammatical form—that is, in parts of speech and word order.
  - If the elements don't match, either revise them so they do or restructure your idea altogether to avoid the need for parallelism.

(For more information on parallelism, see the section Maintaining Parallelism, p. 674.)

Spelling and Typographical Errors

Searching for Spelling and Typographical Errors

sp

Most strategies for catching spelling and typographical errors involve either increasing your awareness of the types of errors you tend to make or slowing down so that you see what's actually on the page. As you read the following suggestions, consider which would be most useful for you. One or more of these strategies are usually appropriate:

- **Increase your awareness of the types of errors you tend to make.** Although spelling problems often seem overwhelming, most writers find that their errors typically fall into one or more patterns; therefore, the first step in addressing your spelling problems is to keep a chart of the words you often misspell. Use this list as a reference sheet when you write and as a diagnostic sheet to identify error patterns in your papers.
- **Slow down so that you see what's actually on the page.** In addition to learning error patterns typical of your writing, you can use specific strategies for checking your texts for spelling errors and typos:
  - Slow down and read for spelling and typos alone, rather than for content:
    - Isolate each line with a straight-edge—a piece of blank paper, a note card, the edge of a book—and point to each word with a pencil or pen.
    - Read from the end, rather than the beginning of a line, so that you don't get caught up in what you're saying. Using this strategy, you'll be able to separate the individual words from the meaning, you'll be able to proof quickly but systematically, and, of course, you'll be much more likely to catch extra letters, omitted letters, transposed letters, and so on. *Caution:* Reading backward won't allow you to identify errors with sound-alike words (such as *to/too/two, there/their,* or *its/it's*); therefore, you should skim your paper, looking specifically for them. If you're using a computer with a search and replace feature, you can use it to systematically look for words you consistently mistake for others. (For more information about these frequently confused words, see Beyond the Spell-Checker: Commonly Misused Words and Expressions, pp. 680–690.)
  - Find a good spell-checker, and learn how to use it. Note that this method doesn't catch sound-alike words, either, so skimming or searching systematically with the search and replace feature should supplement the spell-checker.

Searching for Omitted Words

Searching for omitted words is a bit different from searching for spelling or typographical errors, but some of the same strategies are useful:

- Read your paper backward—that is, read the last sentence, then go to the second to the last, and so on.
- If you prefer to read straight through your text, use some strategy to slow yourself down. Reading aloud often helps. In fact, any strategy that will cause you to be a careful reader, rather than a speed reader, will be useful:
  - Place your pencil or pen on each word as you read it.
  - Isolate each line with a straight-edge; even a piece of paper will work.

Grammar Problems

Subject/Verb Agreement

agr s/v agr s/v

Subject/verb agreement errors frequently happen when a phrase or clause separates the subject and verb. This sort of error is illustrated in the following examples, where each subject is underlined once and each erroneous verb is underlined twice:

SENTENCES WITH SUBJECT/VERB AGREEMENT ERRORS

The complexity of the processes baffle many new employees.

Managers who supervise by written directive finds that they know little about the employees in their charge.

If you were to look specifically for the subject and verb of each sentence, the error would probably be obvious and the correction easy:

SENTENCES WITH SUBJECT/VERB AGREEMENT ERRORS CORRECTED

The complexity of the processes baffles many new employees.

Managers who supervise by written directive find that they know little about the employees in their charge.

So, to find and fix subject/verb agreement errors, you need to systematically look for subjects and verbs:

- Isolate the main verb in each sentence. (Verbs are words that show action or state of being; however, it's sometimes easier if you think of them as words that indicate time through their tenses.)
- Then, match that verb to its subject, and make sure that they agree in number. (The trick is to make the numbers agree, and the simplest way to do that is to count them out [i.e., one thing is/two things are]).

Pronoun Reference or Agreement

pro ref pro agr

Searching for errors in pronoun reference or agreement requires that you look for pronouns and the nouns they point to:

- Skim the paper and find each pronoun.
- Once you find a pronoun, skim backward until you find the noun it's replacing.
- Make sure that each pronoun agrees in number with its corresponding noun. Once again, the simplest way to check agreement is to count.

- If you can't find the noun a pronoun refers to, you should either insert a noun to serve as a *referent* or change the pronoun to a noun. Note that when there is an article (*a, an*) in front of a noun, the article makes the noun singular:

  Parents have *a* tough job.

  A parent should recognize how tough *his or her* job is.

- Be particularly careful in checking for agreement with the singular pronouns *each, everybody,* and *everyone.*
  - Although people frequently say *Everyone/their* to avoid gender bias, writing requires that singular pronouns be matched with singular pronouns: *everyone/his or her, each/he or she,* and so on.
  - If you feel uncomfortable using either of these constructions, make all pronouns plural or omit the second pronoun altogether:

    All doctors have their reports.

    Each doctor has a report.

(For more information about making pronouns and verbs agree without using biased language, see Avoiding Gender Bias in Writing, pp. 679–680.)

Problems with Sentence Boundaries: Comma Splices, Fused Sentences, and Run-On Sentences*

When sentences are not joined correctly, their boundaries blur and shift. Errors in punctuation generally cause readers to join ideas in ways the writer didn't intend, to misunderstand the writer's ideas or how they fit together, or to stumble and then reread in an attempt to create the intended meaning. In any case, problems with sentence boundaries undercut the writer's credibility. Three different types of sentence boundary errors can occur when joining independent clauses: comma splices, fused sentences, and run-ons. (An *independent clause* is a group of words that contains a subject and verb, expresses a complete thought, and can be a sentence.)

Specific Sentence Boundary Errors Defined

cs

- **A comma splice,** or *comma fault,* is an error caused when two independent clauses are joined with only a comma. Often, the subject of the second sentence is *this, that, these,* or *those.*

  COMMA SPLICE

  Many income tax forms provide a space for indicating contributions to the wildlife fund, this generates revenue for preserving our natural resources.

*We wish to acknowledge Carrie Jean Schroeder's contributions to the development of this material on errors in connecting sentences.

CORRECTED
Many income tax forms provide a space for indicating contributions to the wildlife fund. This generates revenue for preserving our natural resources.

fs

- **A fused sentence** is an error caused by running two independent clauses together with no separating word or punctuation.

FUSED SENTENCE
The construction of the new library will be finished by June 29 then the downtown renovation will be complete.

CORRECTED
The construction of the new library will be finished by June 29; then the downtown renovation will be complete.

ro

- **A run-on sentence** is an error caused by joining two or more independent clauses with only a coordinating conjunction (*and, but, or, nor, for, so, yet*).

RUN-ON
Support groups have been organized in almost all of the major cities and research efforts to isolate the AIDS virus have been given substantial funding.

CORRECTED
Support groups have been organized in almost all of the major cities, and research efforts to isolate the AIDS virus have been given substantial funding.

Strategies for Correcting Sentence Boundary Problems

You can correct comma splices, fused sentences, and run-ons in several ways:

- **Separate the independent clauses with a period, forming two sentences.**

SENTENCE	.	SENTENCE	.
Honest dealings are the foundation of successful professional relationships	.	Ethical communication is the foundation of honest dealings	.

- **Join the independent clauses with a semicolon.**

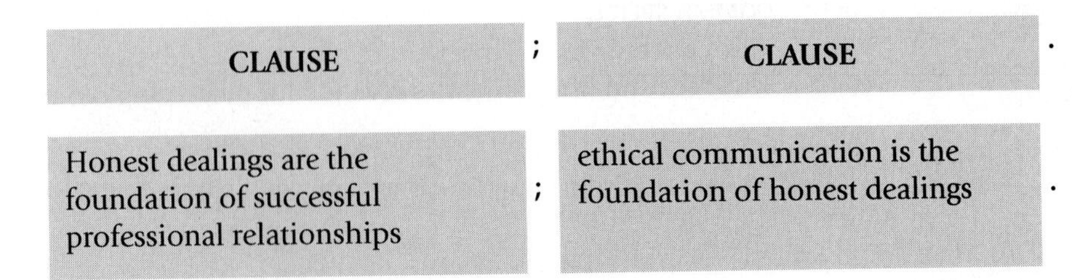
CLAUSE
;
CLAUSE
.
Honest dealings are the foundation of successful professional relationships
;
ethical communication is the foundation of honest dealings
.

- **Connect the independent clauses with a semicolon and a conjunctive adverb followed by a comma.** (A *conjunctive adverb,* like a *coordinating conjunction,* joins two independent clauses; however, it more strongly expresses the relationship [or a transition] between the two clauses.)

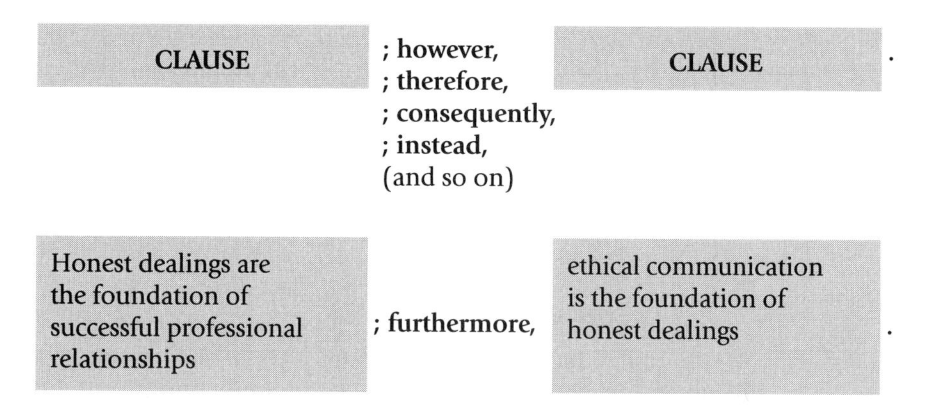

- **Connect the independent clauses with a comma and a coordinating conjunction.**

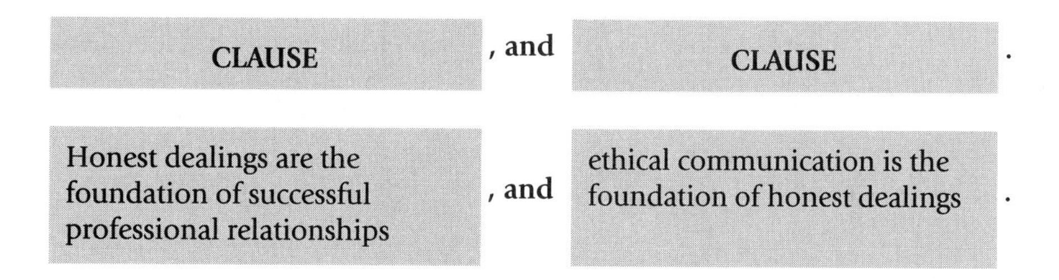

- **Use a subordinator to make one independent clause dependent upon another.**

Although CLAUSE , CLAUSE .

Since
Because
(and so on)

While honest dealings are the foundation of successful professional relationships , ethical communication is the foundation of honest dealings .

Other Conventions in Written Professional Discourse

Maintaining Parallelism

//

Parallel structure, or *parallelism,* occurs when elements alike in function are alike in grammatical form, too. In particular, a sentence element is balanced by one or more equivalent sentence elements: nouns with nouns, verbs with verbs, prepositions with prepositions, and so on. In other words, parallelism involves the repetition of equivalent sentence elements. Consider, for instance, the following effective use of parallelism:

> The workshop on writing for the World Wide Web includes segments on *conceptualizing* your website, *writing* HTML codes, *using* an HTML editor, and *establishing* links to other files.

Each item in the series begins with an *-ing* verbal, and each *-ing* word is followed by a modifier and its noun. The pattern established, then, is *-ing* verbal + modifier + noun—a pattern that is followed consistently throughout the list.

Whenever you list or compare two or more elements, they need to be parallel. In fact, in business writing, you'll need to maintain parallelism any time you use a list—within sentences, in bulleted or numbered lists, and in tables of contents. You'll also want to make sure that your headings and subheadings are parallel. And you'll want to use parallelism whenever you compare two or more elements. The following pairs of terms establish comparative structures and require parallelism:

either/or	*Either* we will complete the project on time, *or* we will pay for cost overruns.
neither/nor	*Neither* the Affirmative Action Office *nor* the Disciplinary Action Office is sure of the impact of the new laws on hiring and firing practices.
not only/ but also	The new performance review process is *not only* easy to follow *but also* simple to document.
whether/or	The project team had to determine *whether* to purchase a generic inventory program *or* to design customized software.

Often, when you proofread, you'll find that you can *hear* problems with parallelism. When you are listing or comparing two or more elements, check to see if you can hear the balance—the pattern or repetition of similar sounds. You can also *see* problems with parallelism: If you look at the beginning of each item in a list, or look at each item in a comparative structure, you should see that each element begins in the same way.

The pattern or repetition of similar sounds that occurs in parallel structure makes writing smooth. Parallelism can also be used to emphasize items that are being compared and to clarify the relationship between ideas. Finally, parallelism contributes to conciseness.

Using Apostrophes Correctly

ap √

Apostrophes are primarily used to indicate that words are possessive or that letters have been omitted. Apostrophes are also used in special cases with plurals, but in general, apostrophes are *not* used to make nouns plural.

Apostrophes Show Possession

One of the primary functions of apostrophes is to show ownership or possession. To make nouns possessive, follow these rules:

	Rule	Example
Singular noun	Add an -*'s* to make a singular noun possessive.	*customer* + -*'s* = *customer's*
Plural noun ending in -*s*	Add an apostrophe to make a plural noun ending in -*s* possessive.	*clients* + -*'* = *clients'*
Plural noun not ending in -*s*	Add an -*'s* to make a plural noun that doesn't end with -*s* possessive.	*media* + -*'s* = *media's*

But what do you do when you have more than one noun and want to show possession? In this case, you should add the apostrophe to the last noun only:

> *Meyer and Isolde's* book on New Age music has been reprinted.

Making pronouns possessive, though, is a bit more complicated. Indefinite pronouns—*everybody, everyone, no one, someone,* and so on—are like singular nouns: To make an indefinite pronoun possessive, you simply add an -*'s:*

> *Everyone's* paycheck must be picked up by 3 P.M. on Friday.
>
> We will solicit *everybody's* opinion in the survey.

Possessive Pronouns Don't Use Apostrophes

But some other pronouns—called *possessive pronouns*—are already in possessive form and do not take apostrophes:

his	ours	whose
hers	theirs	yours
its		

If you add apostrophes to these words—*it's* or *who's,* for instance—they are no longer possessives; they're *contractions.* (See the next section.)

Apostrophes Mark Contractions

In addition to using apostrophes to form possessive nouns or pronouns, apostrophes can also indicate that letters have been omitted. Consider, for instance, the words we've just mentioned:

> *It's* stands for *it is;* therefore, it's a contraction, not a possessive.
>
> *Who's* stands for *who is,* so it's a contraction, too.

Here are some additional contractions:

aren't = are not	hadn't = had not	isn't = is not
can't = cannot	hasn't = has not	let's = let us
couldn't = could not	haven't = have not	shouldn't = should not
don't = do not	I've = I have	they're = they are

You should keep in mind, by the way, that when you use these contractions, you're using informal language; ask yourself whether the informality is appropriate, given your goals, readers, and the context in which you're writing.

Finally, contractions are sometimes used informally to mark the omitted numbers in dates—'98, for instance—but most business writing contexts require that you write out dates.

Apostrophes Sometimes Indicate Plurals

Apostrophes are used in special instances to indicate plurals: In particular, you should use an apostrophe to form the plural of a lowercase letter or an abbreviation with periods:

Required Apostrophes	
Lowercase Letters	**Abbreviations with Periods**
a's	Ph.D.'s
b's	Dr.'s

An apostrophe is optional, though, when you pluralize a capital letter, an abbreviation without periods, and a number:

Optional Apostrophes	
Either With	**Or Without**
A's	As
CEO's	CEOs
1990's	1990s

Plural or Possessive? A Way to Test

Except for the special cases we've just reviewed, you should use apostrophes only to show possession or ownership and to mark contractions. But what can you do if you're just not sure if you need an apostrophe? The easiest way to test for a possessive is to see if your text still makes sense if you flip your words around a bit and add the phrase *belonging to* or *belonging to the.* Consider these examples:

the week's schedule	the schedule *belonging to the* week
the CEO's program	the program *belonging to the* CEO
Dr. James' lecture	the lecture *belonging to* Dr. James

If your text still makes sense, then you need to include the apostrophe. If the text doesn't make sense with one of these phrases added, then the word isn't possessive. Next, you need to ask yourself if the word is a contraction of two words. If the word isn't possessive and isn't a contraction, then no apostrophe should be used because the *-s* marks the plural.

Using Numbers: Words or Figures?

num

The treatment of numbers and figures will vary, depending upon the field you're in and the stylesheet you follow. Generally, though, the following rules will be in effect.

- **Write out as words all whole numbers from zero to ten, and use figures for those above ten.**

  The company can gain *four* benefits from implementing the new quality control system.

  Human resources hired *27* people last week.

- **Don't begin a sentence with a figure.** Even with a number over 10, write out the number as a word if you'd like to start the sentence that way, or recast the sentence so the number appears later in the sentence.

  Eighty-two privately held companies were established in the city last year.

  Last year, *82* privately held companies were established in the city.

- **Use figures for exact sums of money (and don't use the dollar sign and the word *dollar* at the same time).**

  The marketing department recommended that we price the new unit at *$69.95* to maintain a competitive edge.

- **Use figures for dates, times, and addresses.**

  We will meet on *Friday, August 15, 1997,* in Board Room B.

  The workshop will run from *9:00 A.M. to 4:30 P.M.*

Address your concerns to the following person:
Chris Runyon, Customer Service Representative
ABC Manufacturing
1127 Monroe Avenue
Chicago, IL 60197

- **Use figures for decimals, percents, and measurements.**

Sales decreased *7.25* percent in 1997.

The laptop weighed *6* pounds and was the size of a sheet of paper: *8½ × 11* inches.

- **Fractions that accompany whole numbers should appear as figures; fractions alone should be expressed in words.**

They discovered discolorations in *12½* percent of the production run.

Only *one-fourth* of the employees chose to take personal days last year although this option was considered a significant benefit during last year's contract negotiations.

- **Write out large, rounded-off numbers.**

Sales of the new software exceeded *five million* last year.

- **Be consistent in your use of numbers when you're including more than one number in a sentence.**

The program was implemented in *seven* factories in Chicago, *five* in Detroit, and *eleven* in Los Angeles.

In the last fiscal year alone, Airwave spent *$256,000* more on newspaper advertising and *$562,000* more on television advertising than it had during the previous year, or increases of *12.5* and *16.3* percent, respectively.

- **Combine figures and words if doing so will clarify your meaning.**

On the first night it was in effect, the new law resulted in the arrest of *twenty-one 16-* and *17-year-olds* who were out after curfew.

- **Fractions written out in words and numbers from 21 to 99 should be hyphenated.**

Four-fifths of all systems users indicated that they were very satisfied with the functionality the extension added.

The procedure enabled *sixty-eight* patients to recover fully in the first year alone.

Avoiding Gender Bias in Pronouns

sxt

> Biased language can cause your reader to focus on how you say something rather than what you say. If your language is free of bias, it should offend no one; ideally, no one should even notice that you have made an effort to reduce sexually biased words and phrases. (Jameson, 1979, pp. 170–178)

Achieving unbiased language—so that readers will concentrate on what you have to say rather than how you say it—is an admirable goal. It's also a necessity. For example, businesses and individuals have been sued because job descriptions used *he* and thus seemed to exclude women, regardless of whether the exclusion was intended. Therefore, gender-free language is a requirement in the workplace.

It may be easy to avoid gender-biased nouns by replacing sexist nouns with more neutral ones: *chairman* with *chair, mailman* with *mail carrier,* and *congressman* with *senator* or *representative.* But how can you avoid the pronouns *he, him,* and *his* when you refer to nouns meant to include both genders?

The following five options will enable you to revise your writing so that your pronouns are both gender free and correct. As you review this list, compare the biased language of the original sentences with the gender-free phrasing of the revisions. And keep in mind that your goal should ultimately be to change language in a way that doesn't draw attention to itself so that no one notices you've tried to reduce gender bias in your writing.

1. **Use the plural form for both nouns and pronouns.**

   BIASED LANGUAGE
   Studying the techniques by which a celebrated writer achieved *his* success can stimulate any writer faced with similar problems.

   GENDER-FREE LANGUAGE
   Studying the techniques by which celebrated writers achieved *their* success can stimulate any writer faced with similar problems.

2. **Omit the pronoun altogether.**

   BIASED LANGUAGE
   Each doctor should send one of *his* nurses to the workshop.

   GENDER-FREE LANGUAGE
   Each doctor should send *a* nurse to the workshop.

3. **Use *his* or *her, he/she,* or *s/he* when you occasionally need to stress the action of an individual.** Such references won't be awkward unless they're frequent.

   BIASED LANGUAGE
   If you must use a technical term *he* may not understand, explain it.

   GENDER-FREE LANGUAGE
   If you must use a technical term *he or she* may not understand, explain it.

4. **Vary pronoun choice when you want to give examples emphasizing the action of an individual.** Ideally, choose pronouns that work counter to prevailing stereotypes. *Growing Child Newsletter* decided to use this strategy throughout its publication, which focused on children's developmental levels. Here are a few examples from this publication:

   STEREOTYPE-ENFORCING LANGUAGE
   Gradually, Toddler will see the resemblance between block creations and objects in *his* world, and *he* will begin to name some structures, like *house, choo choo,* and *chimney.*

   STEREOTYPE-BREAKING LANGUAGE
   Gradually, Toddler will see the resemblance between block creations and objects in *her* world, and *she* will begin to name some structures, like *house, choo choo,* and *chimney.*

   STEREOTYPE-ENFORCING LANGUAGE
   The kitchen can serve as a center for new experiences, an interesting place where important things happen, and where *she* has a chance to learn about the way big-people things are done.

   STEREOTYPE-BREAKING LANGUAGE
   The kitchen can serve as a center for new experiences, an interesting place where important things happen, and where *he* has a chance to learn about the way big-people things are done.

5. **Switch from the third person (*he, she,* or *it*) to the second person (*you*) when this shift is appropriate for what you're writing.**

   BIASED LANGUAGE
   Each manager should report *his* progress to the undersigned by May 1.

   GENDER-FREE LANGUAGE
   You should report your progress to me by May 1.

   Report your progress to me by May 1.

In this last example, the *you* is understood.

▶ Beyond the Spell-Checker: Commonly Misused Words and Expressions

ww

You can use the spell-checker on your computer to find errors in spelling, but similar sounding words with different meanings are more difficult to detect. In some cases, commonly confused words require repeated checking. The following words or phrases are commonly cited troublemakers:

accept (verb): to receive; to agree to; to admit willingly
except (preposition): excluding; other than

affect (almost always used as a verb): (verb) to change; to influence; (noun, pronounced áf-fect) emotion
effect (almost always used as a noun): (noun) result; (verb) to bring about or cause

advice (noun): counsel; suggestion
advise (verb): to give advice

aisle: a passage between two rows or sides
isle: an island

allowed: to permit (past tense)
aloud: to speak in a voice that can be heard

allude: to refer indirectly
elude: to evade or escape
refer: to mention directly

allusion: an indirect reference to a specific source
illusion: an unreal image

already: by now; previously
all ready: completely prepared

allot: to dole out in portions
alot: word does not exist
a lot: a great deal; many

all together: gathered in one place
altogether: entirely

altar: a table or raised, level surface
alter: to change

among: a relationship involving more than two people or things
between: a relationship or comparison of two people or things

amount: uncountable quantity (as in grains of sand)
number: countable quantity (as in buckets of sand)

ante-: before
anti-: against

anybody: any person; anyone (singular)
any body: any human form or group

are (verb): to exist
our (possessive pronoun): yours and mine

aspire: to seek
expire: to die

assure: to set someone's mind at rest
ensure: to make sure or certain
insure: to guarantee the value of property or life against risk

a while (noun): a short time
awhile (adverb): for a short time; as an adverb, *awhile* modifies adjectives and other adverbs and cannot be used as the object of a preposition

B

bad: refers to a person, place, or thing
badly: describes how action is done

beside (preposition): next to
besides (adverb): in addition to

best: used when three or more things are compared
better: used when two things are compared

between: a relationship or comparison of two people or things
among: a relationship involving more than two people or things

between you and me: the correct usage because *me* is the object of the preposition *between*
between you and I: the incorrect usage because *I* is the subjective, rather than the objective case, and cannot be used as the object of the preposition *between*

biannual: twice a year (but we recommend using *semiannual* to reduce confusion)
biennial: every two years
semiannual: twice a year

bimonthly: once every two months
semimonthly: twice a month

bring: to move something *toward*
take: to move something *away*

can: is capable of; has the capability
may: is possible; is allowed to

cannot: cannot is *one word*
can not: cannot is *not two words*

capital: financial assets, money; a town or city that is the center of government; the death penalty (as in *capital punishment*)
capitol: the state or federal building in which the legislature meets

cite (verb): to refer to a source of information by name and content
sight (noun): what you see; (verb) to be able to see
site (noun): a location or place

coarse: rough textured or of inferior quality; vulgar or obscene
course: path of continuous movement; class in school

complement (noun): something that completes or makes perfect; (verb) to complete or make perfect
compliment (verb): to express praise, admiration, or respect

continual: frequently repeating; happening over and over again
continuous: occurring without interruption

core: the central part of fruits, planets, arguments
corps: a trained military group with special duties
corpse: a cadaver, dead body

council: a group elected or appointed to make or enforce laws
counsel (verb): to advise; (noun) a lawyer

credible: believable
creditable: worthy of praise

differ from: suggests that two things are not alike
differ with: suggests disagreement between people

different from: preferred to *different than* in professional discourse (see below)
different than: not often used in formal writing; acceptable when followed by a clause (subject + verb); still generally considered incorrect in formal usage because *than* expresses a degree of intensity (e.g., *bigger than, smaller than, quicker than,* etc.)

discreet: characterized by acting with care, confidentiality, and politeness
discrete: separate sections; parts; elements

disinterested: interested, but with an objective, impartial, unbiased point of view
uninterested: not interested

do: to act
due: to owe; date of payment

e.g. *(exemplar gratia):* for example; what follows *e.g.* should be just *part* of the concept that's being described
i.e. *(id est):* that is; in other words; what follows *i.e.* should be the same as the *complete* concept that's being described

elude: to evade or escape
allude: to refer indirectly
refer: to mention directly

emigrate: to leave one country or region to settle in another (*ex + migrate*)
immigrate: to enter and settle in another country or region (*in + migrate*)
migrate: to move from one place to another

eminent: famous; distinguished
imminent: about to happen

ensure: to make sure or certain
assure: to set someone's mind at rest
insure: to guarantee the value of property or life against risk

envelops (verb): to wrap or cover up completely
envelopes (noun): the paper cover of a letter

especially: particularly; exceptionally
specially: for a specific reason

et al.: and others (research sources)
etc.: and so forth; and other things (informal lists)

every day: every single day
everyday: ordinarily; ordinary; casual

evoke: to call up; to call out; to inspire a response
invoke: to appeal; to petition

except: excluding; other than
accept: to receive; to agree to

expire: to die
aspire: to seek

explicit: directly stated
implicit: implied rather than directly stated

extinct: dead species
instinct: inborn knowledge

farther: describes something that is more distant
further: describes a greater time or more of an abstract quality

fewer: refers to items that can be counted
less: refers to mass quantities that cannot be counted (e.g., water)

first: as in first, second, third
firstly: *not* firstly, secondly, thirdly

for: meant to be given to
fore: to have the lead position; in the front of
four: the number

foreword (noun): the introductory section of a book
forward (adjective or adverb): at or toward the front

formally: in a formal, structured manner
formerly: in the past

forth: forward (e.g., *The marketing campaign went forth.*)
fourth: to be the item that is number *four*

further: describes a greater time or more of an abstract quality
farther: describes something that is more distant

G

good (adjective): a word that describes the quality of a thing (e.g., *They did a good job.*)
well (adverb): indicates manner or degree of quality of an act (e.g., *They performed the task well.*)

H

hear: to receive sound through the ears
here: at, in, or to this location

I

i.e. *(id est):* that is; in other words; what follows *i.e.* should be the same as the *complete* concept that's being described
e.g. *(exemplar gratia):* for example; what follows *e.g.* should be just *part* of the concept that's being described

illusion: an unreal image
allusion: an indirect reference to a specific source

immigrate: to enter and settle in another country or region
emigrate: to leave one country or region to settle in another
migrate: to move from one place to another; less permanent

implicit: implied rather than directly stated
explicit: directly stated

imply: to hint or suggest something
infer: to reach a conclusion on the basis of evidence

indiscreet: lacking in prudence or sound judgment
indiscrete: not divided or divisible into parts

insoluble: incapable of being dissolved
unsolvable: incapable of being solved

instinct: inborn knowledge
extinct: dead species

insure: to guarantee the value of property or life against risk
ensure: to make sure or certain
assure: to set someone's mind at rest

invoke: to appeal; to petition
evoke: to call up; to recall

irregardless: nonstandard for *regardless*
irrespective: no matter what; regardless
regardless: no matter what

its: a possessive: it owns *something*
it's: a contraction of *it is* or *it has*

K

kindly: with compassion; substituting *kindly* for *please* is starting to sound old fashioned and stilted
please: the preferred qualifier for a polite request

know: to understand; to have the information
no: negative; opposite of *yes*

kind of: informal phrase for *type of;* do not use for *somewhat*
sort of: informal phrase for *type of;* do not use for *somewhat*

L

lay: to put *something;* present tense of *laid*
lie: to recline; present tense of *to lie;* past tense of *lay*

lead (noun): a metal
led (verb): past tense of *lead;* to go first; to precede

less: refers to mass quantities that cannot be counted (e.g., water)
fewer: refers to items that can be counted

liable: legally subject to; responsible for
libel: something in writing or pictures that injures someone's reputation
likely: probable

loose (adjective): not fastened; unrestrained
lose (verb): fail to win

M

may: is possible; is allowed to
can: is capable of; has the capability

may be: permission; possibility
maybe: perhaps

migrate: to move from one place to another
emigrate: to leave one country or region to settle in another (*ex + migrate*)
immigrate: to enter and settle in another country or region (*in + migrate*)

no: negative; opposite of *yes*
know: to understand; to have the information

notable: worthy of notice
noticeable: readily observed

number: countable quantity (e.g., buckets of sand)
amount: uncountable quantity (e.g., grains of sand)

O

ok, o.k., and okay: informal forms of *all right*

oral: what is spoken
verbal: what is in words, whether spoken or written

our (possessive pronoun): yours and mine
are (verb): to exist

P

passed (verb): an action: moving from behind something to in front of something and then beyond something
past (noun or adjective): an earlier time; before now; beyond the deadline

percent: replaces the % sign
percentage: indicates a portion or share of something
percentile: the ranking of a score in terms of the percentage of scores below it

piece: a section of a whole
peace: no conflict; quiet; serenity

please: the preferred qualifier for a polite request
kindly: with compassion; substituting *kindly* for *please* is starting to sound old fashioned and stilted

poor (adjective): of inferior quality; lacking money
pore (verb): to study hard; (noun) a small opening in the skin
pour (verb): to move liquid into something or over something

precede: to come before
proceed: to go forward

principal: most important; chief; head; a capital sum (as distinguished from interest or *profit*)
principle: a basic truth, value, rule, or belief

Q

quiet: gentle; silent
quite: very; completely; really

R

raise: to move to a higher position: *raise* is a transitive verb and *always* takes an object (e.g., *raise* pay)
rise: to move to a higher position; *rise* is an intransitive verb and *never* takes an object (e.g., stock prices *rise*)

reason is because: a colloquial expression not to be used in writing
reason is that: the appropriate replacement for *reason is because;* establishes the notion of cause

refer: to mention directly
allude: to refer indirectly
elude: to evade or escape

regardless: no matter what
irregardless: nonstandard for *regardless*
irrespective: no matter what; regardless

respectfully: with high regard
respectively: in the order designated

right (adjective): correct according to standard practice; (noun) an entitlement
rite (noun): ritual
write (verb): construct words into meaningful prose

S

semimonthly: once every two weeks
bimonthly: once every two months

should of: do not use *of* in place of *have*
should've: the correct contraction for *should* + *have;* this contraction is common in speech, but using it in *written* professional discourse would be risky because of its informality

sight (noun): what you see; (verb) to be able to see
site (noun): a location or place
cite (verb): to refer to a source of information by name and content

sort of: informal phrase for *type of;* do not use for *somewhat*
kind of: informal phrase for *type of;* do not use for *somewhat*

specially: for a specific reason
especially: particularly; exceptionally

stationary (adjective): standing still
stationery (noun): paper for writing

T

take: to move something *away*
bring: to move something *toward*

than: a comparative word
then: a word indicating time sequence

that: a relative pronoun that limits (or tells which one) and adds necessary information about the word it refers to; refers to things or animals
which: a relative pronoun that adds helpful but unnecessary information about the word it refers to; refers to things or animals
who: a relative pronoun that refers to people

their: a possessive: they own it
there: a location that is not *here*
they're: a contraction of *they are*

to: in the direction of
too: also; in addition
two: the number

toward: a variant spelling of *towards* used commonly in the United States
towards: a variant spelling of *toward* used commonly in Great Britain

uninterested: not interested
disinterested: interested, but with an objective, impartial, unbiased point of view

unsolvable: incapable of being solved
insoluble: incapable of being dissolved

ware (noun): article for sale
wear (verb): have on your body; damage from use
where (adverb): location

weather: refers to atmosphere or conditions
whether: refers to alternatives

well (adverb): indicates manner or degree of quality of an act (e.g., *They performed the task well.*)
good (adjective): a word that describes the quality of a thing (e.g., *They did a good job.*)

were: plural form of the past tense verb *was*
we're: contraction of *we are*

wet (adjective): damp or drenched with liquid
whet (verb): to sharpen (e.g., a *knife* or an *appetite*)

whether: refers to alternatives
weather: refers to atmosphere or conditions

which: a relative pronoun that adds helpful but unnecessary information about the word it refers to; refers to things or animals
that: a relative pronoun that limits (or tells which one) and adds necessary information about the word it refers to; refers to things or animals
who: a relative pronoun that refers to people

who's: a contraction of *who + is*
whose: a possessive: who owns it

your: a possessive: you own it
you're: a contraction of *you + are*

REFERENCES

Flower, L. (1981). *Problem-solving strategies for writing.* New York: Harcourt Brace Jovanovich.

Jameson, D. A. (1979). Reducing sexually biased language in business communication. In R. D. Gieselman, *Readings in business communication.* Champaign, IL: Stipes.

Bibliography

E-Mail and Other Electronic Discourse

Bacard, A. (1995, February 25). Frequently asked questions about e-mail privacy. In *The computer privacy handbook* [Online]. Available: Oxford University Libraries Automation Service World Wide Web Server, www.well.com/user/abacard/email.html (1996, June 1).

Blanton, T. (Ed.). (1995, November 22). *White House e-mail: The top secret messages the Reagan/Bush White House tried to destroy.* Washington, DC: National Security Archive.

Moylan, M. J. (1995, December 11). E-mail mania. *Saint Paul Pioneer Press,* p. 1E.

Smith, J. (n.d.). Frequently asked questions: Basic information about MUDS and MUDding [Online]. Available: www.math.okstate.edu/~jds/mudfaq_p1.html (1996, June 30).

Sproul, L., & Kiesler, S. (1991). *Connections: New ways of working in the networked organization.* Cambridge, MA: MIT Press.

Vitanza, V. (1996). *CyberReader.* Boston: Allyn and Bacon.

Dealing with Conflict and Emotion

Bramson, R. M. (1981). *Coping with difficult people.* Garden City, NY: Anchor/Doubleday.

Elgin, S. H. (1980). *The gentle art of verbal self defense.* New York: Wiley.

Elgin, S. H. (1993). *Gentle art of written self defense letter book: Letters in response to triple-f situations.* Englewood Cliffs, NJ: Prentice-Hall.

Fisher, R., & Ury, W. (with B. Patton, Ed.). (1991). *Getting to yes: Negotiating agreement without giving in* (2nd ed.). New York: Penguin.

Rapoport, A. (1960). *Fights, games, and debates.* Ann Arbor: University of Michigan Press.

Rogers, C. R. (1952). Communication: Its blocking and its facilitation. *ETC., A Review of General Semantics, 9,* 83–88.

Ury, W. (1991). *Getting past no: Negotiating with difficult people.* New York: Bantam.

Agendas and Minutes

Thomsett, M. C. (1989). *The little black book of business meetings.* New York: American Management Association.

Webber, R. A. (1991). *Becoming a courageous manager: Overcoming career problems of new managers.* Englewood Cliffs, NJ: Prentice-Hall.

Humor about Business Practices

Adams, S. (1995). *Bring me the head of Willy the Mailboy!* Kansas City, MO: Andrews and McMeel.

Adams, S. (1995). *The Dilbert principle.* New York: HarperCollins.

Adams, S. (1996). *Still pumped from using the mouse.* Kansas City, MO: Andrews and McMeel.

The Career Search

Bolles, R. (1998). *The 1998 what color is your parachute? A practical manual for job-hunters & career-changers.* Berkeley, CA: Ten Speed Press.

Breen, P. (1982). *76 career-related liberal arts skills.* San Francisco: The Learning Center.

Learning and Communication Styles

Hersey, P., & Blanchard, K. H. (1969). *Management of organizational behavior: Utilizing human resources.* Englewood Cliffs, NJ: Prentice-Hall.
Kolb, D. A. (1984). *Experiential learning: Experience as the source of learning and development.* Englewood Cliffs, NJ: Prentice-Hall.
Myers, I. B. (1976). *Myers-Briggs type indicator.* Palo Alto, CA: Consulting Psychologists Press.
Truell, R. (1976). *Comm-style.* Williamsville, NY: George Truell Associates.

Performance Appraisals

Barrett, G. V., & Kernan, M. C. (1987, Autumn). Performance appraisal and terminations: A review of court decisions since *Brito v. Zia* with implications for personnel practices. *Personnel Psychology, 40,* 489–503.
Field, H. S., & Holley, W. H. (1982, June). The relationship of performance appraisal system characteristics to verdicts in selected employment discrimination cases. *Academy of Management Journal,* 25, 392–406.
Lee, C. (1996, May). Performance appraisal: Can we "manage" away the curse? *Training,* 44–59.
Swan, W. S., & Margulies, P. (1991). *How to do a superior performance appraisal.* New York: Wiley.

Business and Strategic Plans

Gumpert, D. E. (1996). *Inc. Magazine presents how to really create a successful business plan: Featuring the business plans of Pizza Hut, Software Publishing Corp., Celestial Seasonings, People Express, Ben & Jerry's.* Boston: Inc.
Kahrs, K., & Koek, K. K. (Eds.). (1996). *Business plans handbook: A compilation of actual business plans developed by small businesses throughout North America.* New York: Gale Research.
Mancuso, J. (1992). *How to prepare and present a business plan.* New York: Simon & Schuster.
Mintzberg, H. (1994). *The rise and fall of strategic planning.* New York: Free Press.
Rich, S. R., & Gumpert, D. E. (1987). *Business plans that win $$$.* New York: Harper & Row.
Tiffany, P., & Peterson, S. D. (1997). *Business plans for dummies.* Foster City, CA: IDG Books.

Reports

Mathes, J. C., & Stevenson, D. (1976). *Designing technical reports: Writing for audiences in organizations.* Indianapolis, IN: Bobbs-Merrill.

Culture and Communication

Albrecht, K. (1996, June). Lost in the translation. *Training,* 66–70.
Bell, A. H., Dillon, W. T., & Becker, H. (1995, April). German memo and letter style. *Journal of Business and Technical Communication,* 9(2), 219–227.
Boiarsky, C. (1995, Summer). The relationship between cultural and rhetorical conventions: Engaging in international communications. *Technical Communication Quarterly,* 4(3), 245–259.
Copeland, M. J. (1987). International training. In R. L. Craig (Ed.), *Training and development handbook* (3rd ed., pp. 717–725). New York: McGraw-Hill.
Fox, H. (1994). *Listening to the world: Cultural issues in academic writing.* Urbana, IL: National Council of Teachers of English.

Hall, E. T. (1977). *Beyond culture.* Garden City, NY: Anchor.

Hall, E. T. (1988). The hidden dimensions of time and space in today's world. In F. Poyatos (Ed.), *Cross-cultural perspectives in nonverbal communication* (p. 151). Toronto, Canada: Hogrefe.

Hofstede, G. (1980). *Culture's consequences: International differences in work-related values.* Beverly Hills, CA: Sage.

James, D. L. (1995). *The executive guide to Asia-Pacific communications: Doing business across the Pacific.* New York: Kodansha International.

Johnstone, B. (1989). Linguistic strategies for persuasive discourse. In S. Ting-Toomey & F. Korzenny (Eds.), *Language, communication and culture: Current directions* (pp. 139–156). Newbury Park, CA: Sage.

Kenna, P., & Lacy, S. (1994). *Business Mexico: A practical guide to understanding Mexican business culture.* Lincolnwood, IL: Passport Books.

Lustig, M. W., & Koester, J. (1993). *Intercultural competence: Interpersonal communication across cultures.* New York: HarperCollins.

Rhinesmith, S. H. (1996). Training for global operations. In R. L. Craig (Ed.), *The ASTD training and development handbook: A guide to human resource development* (4th ed.). New York: McGraw-Hill.

Rowland, D. (1985). *Japanese business etiquette: A practical guide to success with the Japanese* (2nd ed.). New York: Warner Books.

Stamps, D. (1996, November). Welcome to America: Watch out for culture shock. *Training,* 22–30.

Toulmin, S. (1972). *Human understanding, Volume I: The collective use and evolution of concepts.* Princeton, NJ: Princeton University Press.

Trompenaars, F. (1994). *Riding the waves of culture: Understanding diversity in global business* (Rev. ed.). Burr Ridge, IL: Irwing Professional.

Weiss, T. (1995, Fall). Translation in a borderless world. *Technical Communication Quarterly, 4*(4), 407–423.

General Business Resources

Blanchard, K., & Johnson, S. (1982). *The one-minute manager.* New York: Morrow.

Deal, T. E., & Kennedy, A. A. (1982). *Corporate cultures: The rites and rituals of corporate life.* Reading, MA: Addison-Wesley.

Deming, W. E. (1982). *Quality, productivity, and competitive position.* Cambridge, MA: MIT Press.

Kreitner, R. (1995). *Management* (6th ed.). Boston: Houghton Mifflin.

Norman, D. A. (1990). *The design of everyday things.* New York: Doubleday.

Peters, T. (1994). *The pursuit of WOW!* New York: Vintage Books.

Peters, T., & Waterman, R. H., Jr. (1982). *In search of excellence: Lessons from America's best-run companies.* New York: Harper & Row.

Senge, P. M., Roberts, C., Ross, R. B., Smith, B. J., & Kleiner, A. (1994). *The fifth discipline fieldbook: Strategies and tools for building a learning organization.* New York: Doubleday.

Sperry, R. (1974). Messages from the laboratory. *Engineering and Science,* 29–32.

Research Methods and Sources

Dillman, D. A. (1978). *Mail and telephone surveys: The total design method.* New York: Wiley.

Glesne, C., & Peshkin, A. (1992). *Becoming qualitative researchers: An introduction.* White Plains, NY: Longman.

Herndon, S. L., & Kreps, G. L. (1995). *Qualitative research: Applications in organizational communication.* Speech Communication Association Applied Communication Publication Program. Annandale, VA: Hampton Press.

Kehoe, B. P. (1992). *Zen and the art of the Internet—Anonymous FTP: A beginner's guide to the Internet* [Online]. Available: IUCS DocProject, http://www.cs.indiana.edu/docproject/zen/zen-1.0_5.html#sec17.11 (1997, September).

Krol, E. (1994). *The whole Internet user's guide & catalog* (2nd ed.). Cambridge, MA: O'Reilly & Associates.

Krueger, R. A. (1994). *Focus groups: A practical guide for applied research* (2nd ed.). Thousand Oaks, CA: Sage.

Levine, J. R., Baroudi, C., & Young, M. L. (1997). *The Internet for dummies* (4th ed.). Indianapolis, IN: IDG Books.

Merriam, S. B. (1988). *Case study research in education: A qualitative approach.* San Francisco: Jossey-Bass.

Morgan, D. L. (Ed.). (1993). *Successful focus groups.* Newbury Park, CA: Sage.

Stano, M. E., & Reinsch, N. L., Jr. (1982). *Communication in interviews.* Englewood Cliffs, NJ: Prentice-Hall.

Survey kit, The. (1995). 9 vols. Thousand Oaks, CA: Sage.

Vol. 1: A. Fink, *The survey handbook*

Vol. 2: A. Fink, *How to ask survey questions*

Vol. 3: L. B. Bourque & E. P. Fielder, *How to conduct self-administered and mail surveys*

Vol. 4: J. H. Frey & S. M. Oishi, *How to conduct interviews by telephone and in person*

Vol. 5: A. Fink, *How to design surveys*

Vol. 6: A. Fink, *How to sample in surveys*

Vol. 7: M. S. Litwin, *How to measure survey reliability and validity*

Vol. 8: A. Fink, *How to analyze survey data*

Vol. 9: A. Fink, *How to report on surveys*

Yanoff, S. (1997). *Special Internet connections* [Online]. Available: ftp://ftp.csd.uwm.edu/pub/inet.services.txt.11 (1997, September).

Other Resources

Bruner, J. (1962). *On knowing: Essays for the left hand.* Cambridge, MA: Harvard.

Flower, L. (1989). *Problem solving strategies for writing* (3rd ed.). San Diego: Harcourt Brace.

Ong, W. (1967). The writer's audience is always a fiction. In *The presence of the word: Some prolegomena for cultural and religious history.* New Haven, CT: Yale University Press.

Ornstein, R. E. (1972). *The psychology of consciousness.* New York: Viking.

Young, R. E., Becker, A., & Pike, K. (1970). *Rhetoric: Discovery and change.* New York: Harcourt Brace Jovanovich.

Index